Ryan McGinness Works.

Paintings, Sculptures, Sketches, Drawings, Installations, Editions, and Other Stuff

RIZZOLI
NEW YORK

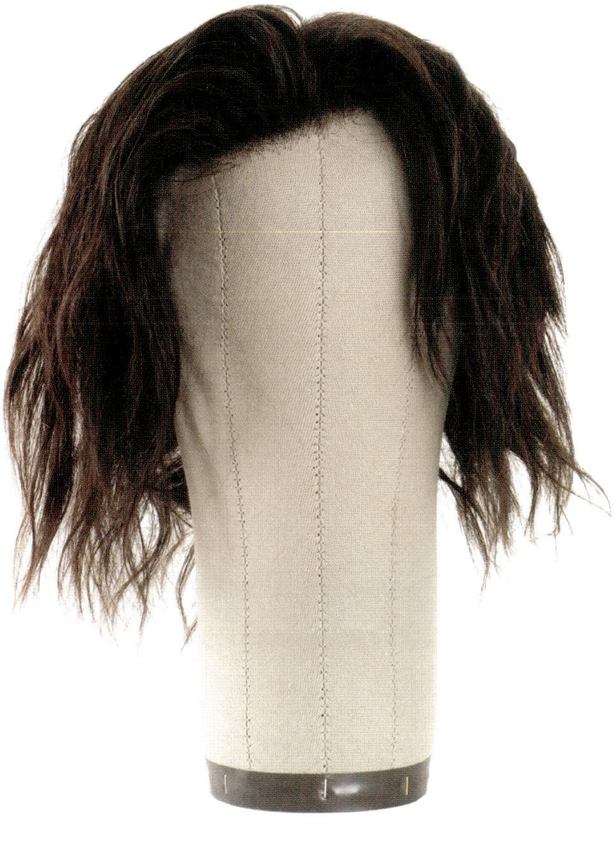

First published in the
United States in 2009 by
Rizzoli International Publications, Inc.
300 Park Avenue South
New York, NY 10010
rizzoliusa.com

Printed and bound in
The People's Republic of China

ISBN-13: 978-0-8478-3196-8

Editor: Julie Schumacher
Production: Kaija Markoe
Designer: Thumb
Writer: Amoreen Armetta

Library of Congress Control Number:
2008934770

2009 2010 2011 2012 / 10 9 8 7 6 5 4 3 2 1

Cover: *The Need to Know*, 2008, acrylic on canvas, 72 x 72 in. (Printed here as a 7 ½ x 7 ½ in. 5-color reproduction in cyan, magenta, yellow, black, and fluorescent pink.)

Endpapers front: *Untitled*, 2008, inverted photograph of squeegees in studio converted to coarse halftone line art and printed in fluorescent pink ink on paper, 8 ½ x 17 in.

Endpapers back: *Untitled*, 2008, inverted photograph of silkscreens in studio converted to coarse halftone line art and printed in fluorescent pink ink on paper, 8 ½ x 17 in.

Frontispiece: *Untitled (RM Wig)*, 2008, artist's hair with stretch lace cap (hand-tied construction) on form, 13 ½ x 8 ½ x 7 ½ in.

(1) Just be cool.

Contents (2)

(2) Dear Gentle Reader, Footnotes appear throughout this book. They are by Ryan McGinness and appear in 100% cyan.

(3) Some footnotes appear only online, so throughout the book you'll see URL's that look like this: .com/example. To access them, you'll need to type "ryanmcginness" before the dot, like this: ryanmcginness.com/example.

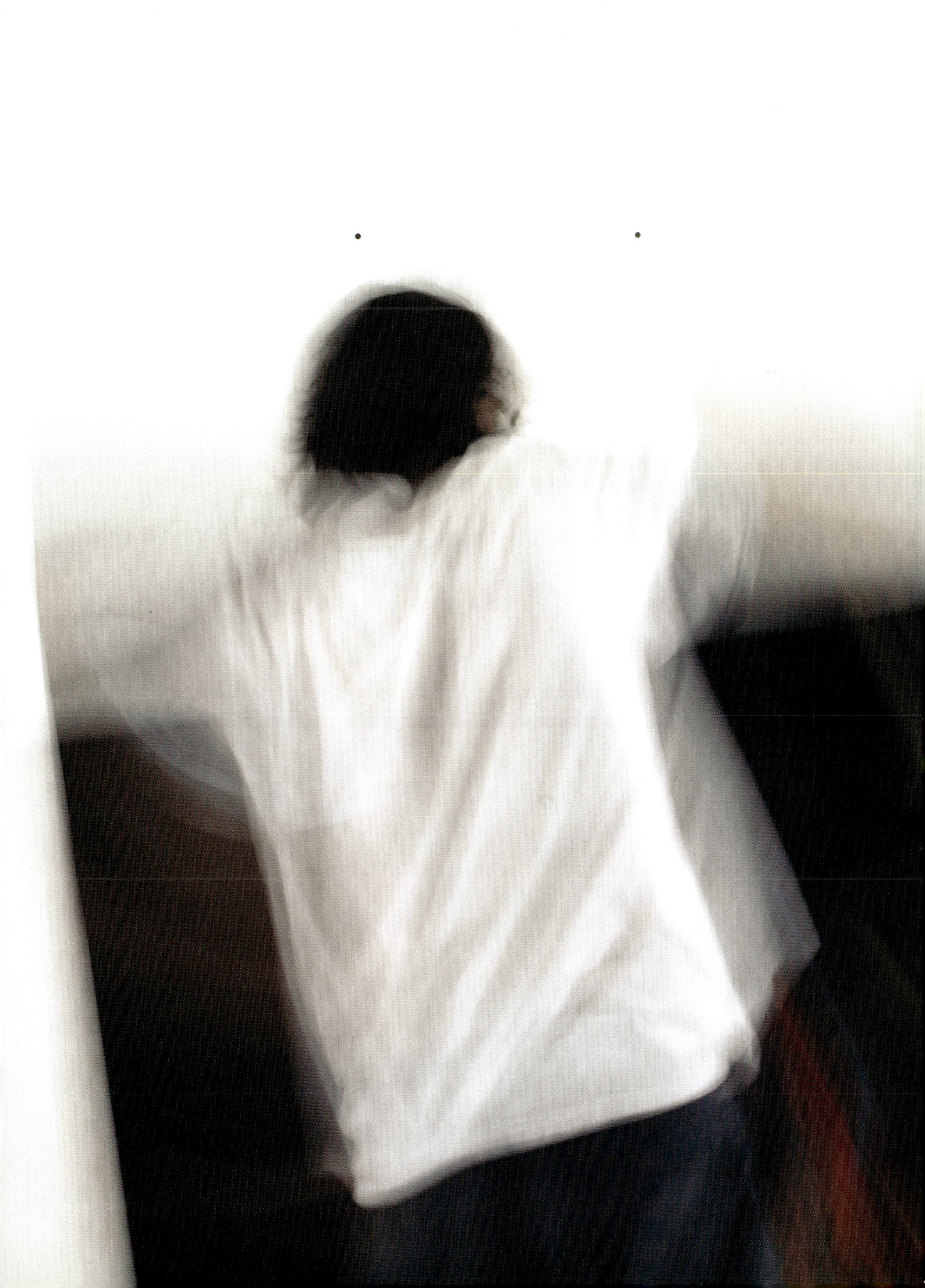

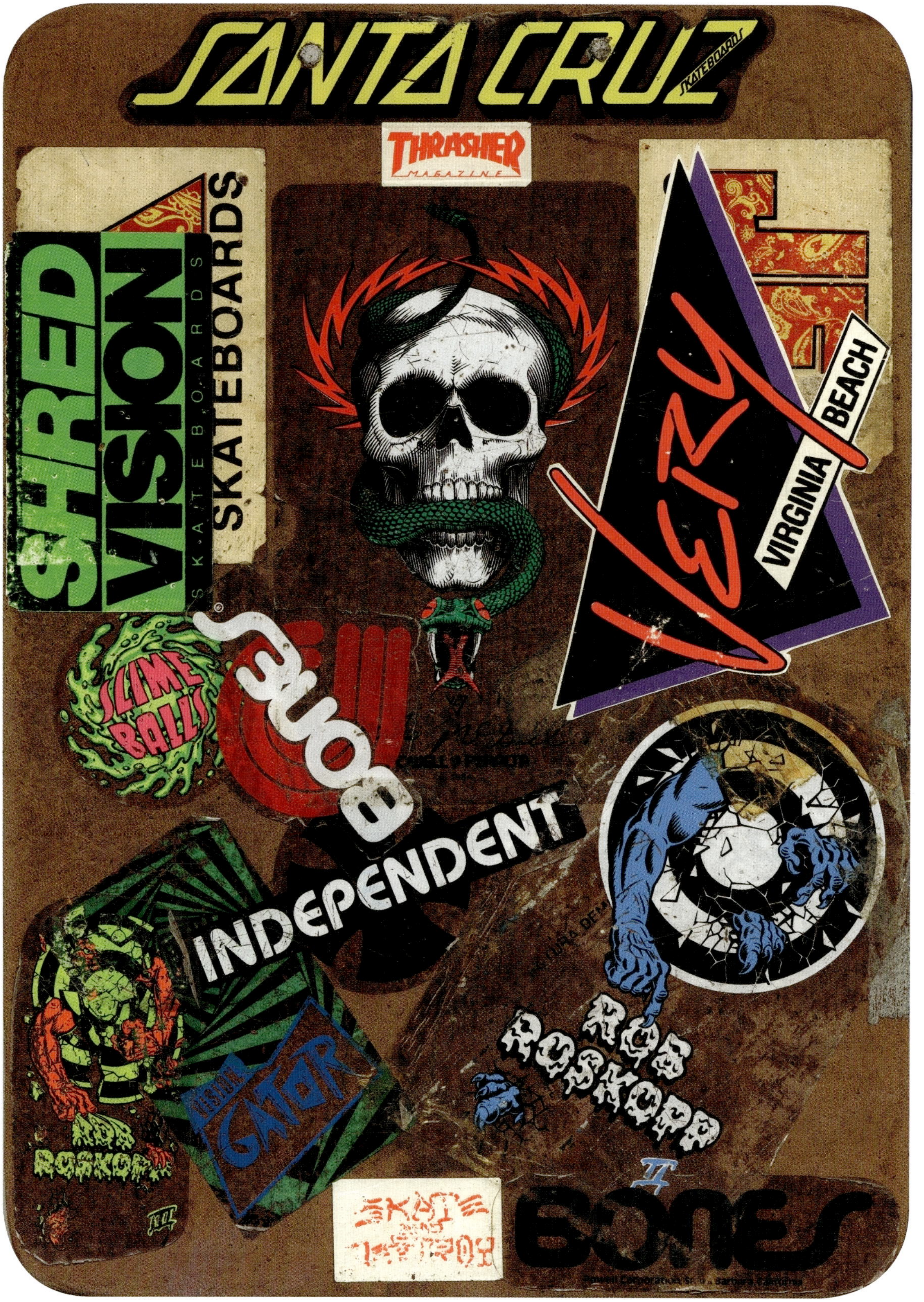

Untitled (Ryan McGinness Clipboard), 1986, metal, Masonite, and various adhesive stickers, 12 ½ x 9 in.

Interview

Peter Halley and Ryan McGinness

PH: In order to not be too predictable, I thought we could start off by talking about where your vocabulary for making the signs that compose the parts of your work comes from.

RM: This is simply how I learned to draw. I went through a rigorous graphic design program, where I learned a sketch process to develop these iconic forms in order to create images that could be read quickly, and be legible from different distances, and have the same level of visual information, and operate in the same way that logos operate.

PH: Well, all the other people who studied graphic design don't do what you do. So what is your relationship with this particular... do you call it a language of logos?

RM: Yeah, or an iconic language, or graphic language.

PH: This language has a kind of mainstream role in our culture as well.

RM: Sure. That's its primary role, and what I want to do is turn that around. I think my interest in it comes from growing up in Virginia Beach, which has a surf and skate culture obsessed with branding and saturated with a cult of cool. (4) At an early age I recognized that the power of a logo—the right kind of logo, the cool logo—can change the value of an otherwise ordinary object like a surfboard or a t-shirt or a skateboard.

PH: How so?

RM: Well, just by the fact that it's cool. It doesn't change the inherent value, of course; it changes, more accurately, the perceived value. So because I couldn't really afford cool brands, from an early age I was making my own brands, so to speak, or stenciling and screening my own shirts and decorating my own skateboards. Then my peers wanted those things, and that was very empowering. And then I recognized that what I was doing was called design.

PH: The effect of the logo on the object is to create a kind of thought process by which you experience the object?

RM: In general, yes, insomuch as that thought process brings one to a place of feeling cool or superficially empowered. Or, like I said, the logo kind of creates the object's perceived value in addition to the cool factor, which is a separate variable. But that's not how I'm using this language now.

PH: Before we move forward though, your early experience of it was a kind of DIY application? (5)

RM: Right.

PH: And at the same time your icon-making has a kind of clarity that can be associated more with the mainstream—I always think of the iconic wayfinding signs in the airport; you can't go wrong with them. And it seems to me that you're sort of wending your way between two uses of the iconic images, one subcultural and one mainstream. Is that how you think of it, or... ?

RM: You know, I think you're right, but I don't know where those positions meet—in the mainstream or in the underground, or if that is even an issue for me in the paintings.

PH: When I think of the application of logos to, say, skateboards, it strikes me that that mainstream language has been appropriated to make it more subcultural.

RM: Sure, but I also think that the co-opting of a visual style goes both ways—by subcultures, and especially when I was growing up, by the smaller skateboard companies—the adoption of a corporate-looking logo was a way to create an image that looked mainstream and mocked the mainstream at the same time. An official-looking logo legitimized their business endeavor, and again, created a kind of perceived value.

PH: Is that what was going on when you were a kid?

RM: Well, I think it was because I couldn't have the premium brands from the mainstream, so I wanted to create something for myself. I didn't even look at it as a simulation of the mainstream; I was just trying to make something that could equal it.

PH: You know, it's so funny. I talked to Tom Sachs for *index* [*index magazine*, Issue 29, June 2001] when he started making sculptures of various kinds of consumer objects. He said the exact same thing. He couldn't have what he wanted so he made it. (6)

RM: Yeah, and for me it also comes out of the fact that when I was a child my mom made most of my toys.

PH: Oh, really?

RM: She had numerous jigsaws and band saws in the garage and was always making crafts. I also grew up very thrifty. I didn't have the Star Wars store-bought At-At toy. I had a homemade wood version of it. (7)

PH: Was your mother just thrifty, or was it a kind of counterculture attitude?

RM: Maybe it was a little bit of both. She certainly sold the things that she made, too.

PH: So that's a precedent for your work.

(4) I was born in V.B., moved away, and moved back again for K–12.

(5) Do It Yourself—in this case I am spelling it out for you.

(6) See Q 363 on p. 288.

(7) .com/craftworks

RM: I guess so, yeah. She had a bit of a factory, an assembly line setup.

PH: What did she make?

RM: All sorts of wooden crafts—iconic imagery cut out of wood—angels, cats, hearts…

PH: Was it nature or nurture? [Laughs]

RM: Certainly I think being surrounded by her crafts was an influence. But just as with Tom, I assume, making things for myself was very empowering, especially when I realized, "Hey, other people want the things that I make."

PH: Uh-huh. The fact that your mom was making things that were aesthetic and attractive to people but wouldn't be classified as—the old-fashioned term is fine art, like a painting that's sold in a gallery—is interesting. And my perception of your work has always been that you're—like a variety of artists from Japan—operating between things that we used to call applied art, like making a sign to be consumed outside an art gallery, and the art gallery paintings and things that are considered fine art.

RM: For me the difference isn't necessarily one of form or even commerce; it's more of a conceptual difference that has to do with authorship. So I'm very careful about whatever I make, making it on my own terms and making sure I'm accountable for it, as opposed to making a t-shirt on behalf of a corporation or someone else's label. And also I want to present an alternative to all the other brands out there. I never understand it when I see people walking around with other people's names or company names on their shirts. I just don't get it. What does "Abercrombie & Fitch" or "Old Navy" mean, you know?

PH: What are the differences between making a painting that's going to be shown in a gallery or museum and making a t-shirt? Do you always make t-shirts?

RM: There is no conceptual difference as long as the approach is the same and as long as the production framework variables are the same. I mean, both can be an expression of the human spirit. Form is almost incidental in that regard. I've always made shirts, but right now I'm making them less frequently and only in editions of 100 so I have control of where they go. I mostly just give them away. They come free with a painting. [Laughter] (8)

PH: And is that perhaps the particular attraction of the fine art setting, that you have that control?

RM: Yes—nothing is more satisfying for me than making a painting—production and distribution-wise. Those variables are in my complete control.

PH: That's just what you said about the t-shirts.

RM: Exactly. So my challenge now is, because I have so much control, I don't have the kind of distribution I'd have with a distributor, for example. So how do I broaden my reach with the more accessible objects while still maintaining control?

PH: I'm wondering if you're working in the direction of consciously trying to integrate other ways of distributing with fine art.

RM: I think it just happens. (9)

PH: I think what you're saying is you want to reach as many people as possible as long as you can maintain your integrity.

RM: Yes, definitely. And, you know, maintain what I think is the right context for the work to be understood, perceived, and appreciated. (10)

PH: So it's not only what you make but where it is.

RM: Of course. Like when my shirts ended up in Urban Outfitters without me knowing about it; I had to shut that down immediately.

PH: It sounds like you also have a kind of anti-corporate outlook; seems like you might have gotten that from your mom?

RM: Yeah, perhaps. I don't know exactly what that's a result of, and I don't know if it's anti-corporate in a general sense, because my studio is set up as a corporation.

PH: Creative people seem to have a more flexible attitude nowadays, but traditionally, both within the art world and without, somebody who embraces the kind of populism that you do would be anti-gallery, uncomfortable with the art world mainstream. I don't hold this view. But, in an art gallery things are being sold for tremendous amounts of money to very wealthy people and it's a very, in one way or another, elitist system.

RM: But you also have to remember that art galleries are free to the public and welcome anyone and everyone.

PH: But why do you embrace the galleries' commodification of the work?

RM: Because I recognize the inherent value of artwork. You go through the process of making a painting, which takes a certain amount of time, and there is only one of those things in the entire universe. There's an inherent value to that—or at least there's a market value to that.

PH: Somebody once said that the art world doesn't matter, the gallery doesn't matter, that art making is like a laboratory. You're creating a prototype, something that really has no justification to exist as a thousand copies, either because it's too strange or because it's so labor intensive or thought intensive. It's like something right out of a lab, except it has a higher value.

RM: That makes a lot of sense, yeah.

PH: [Looking at an image in one of Ryan's paintings.] Here I see a kind of cartoonlike skull with floppy antlers embellished with stylized flowers.

RM: That's exactly what that is. Now what does that mean and where does that image come from? It's a hybrid; it's not a reproduction of something you would ever find.

(8) There was no laughter here during our conversation. This note was added later.

(9) .com/sometshirts

(10) I am aware that I am in a position to favor my position.

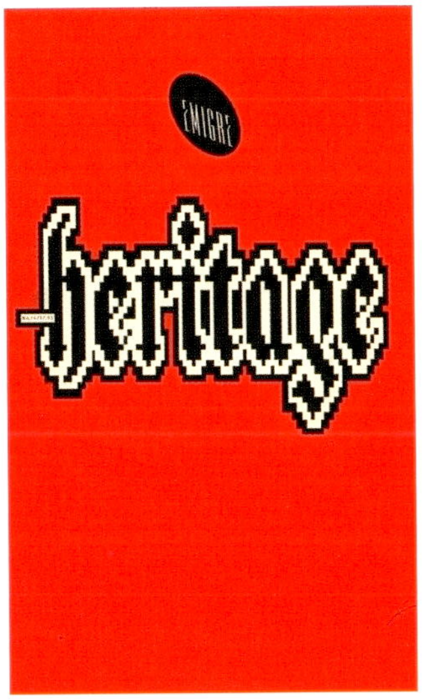

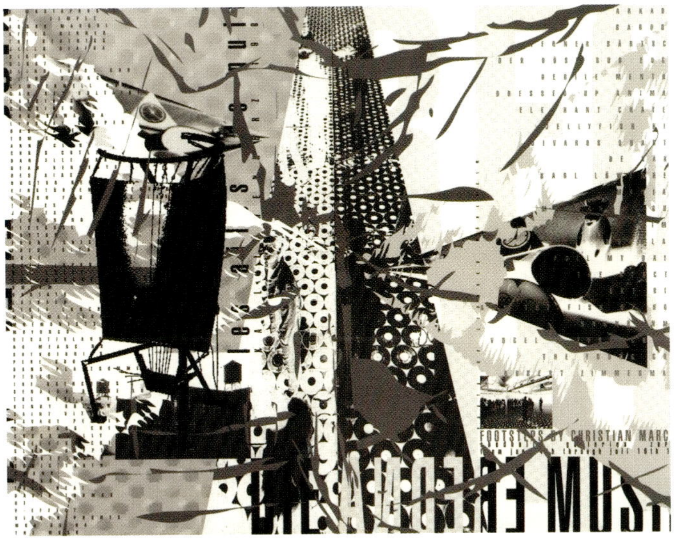

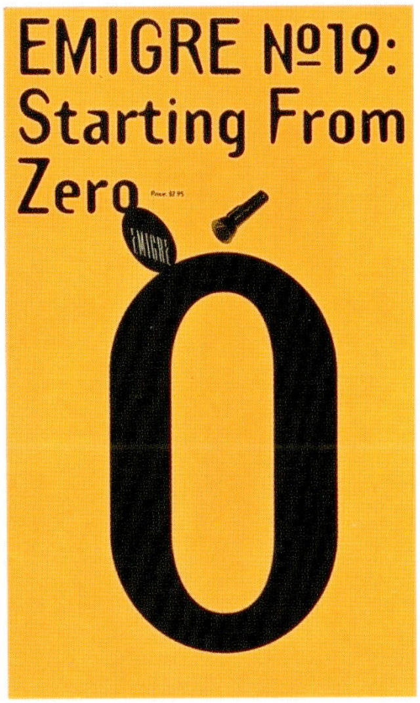

There's a kind of traditional romantic imagery that is certainly found in art, skull and flowers—it's a still life of sorts. Then again, it's its own thing. It's not trying to signal or sign that that thing really exists.

PH: This is from a historical perspective, but in a lot of ways, your approach of combining things in order to make signs and associations strikes me as having something to do with surrealism.

RM: It's definitely a big influence. I think surrealism, theater of the absurd, and those kinds of alternative, more poetic ways of communicating, ironically communicate with more volume than literal language does—that's why I've always steered clear of even using text in my work. So the buttons [*Island Universes* (2007)] are actually something new because they're text-driven. I've studied typography, I love typography, but I've never used it in my work, because I never wanted to use text.[11]

PH: When you went to school you were studying graphic design?

RM: I decided I wanted to study design after I discovered *Émigré* magazine. Do you remember that?[12]

PH: I've never seen it.

RM: *Émigré* was a great design magazine out of Berkeley, California, and it helped me recognize that the thing I was doing in high school—decorating skateboards, making cassette covers and posters for a band I was in—that this activity was called design. So everything kind of clicked. At Carnegie Mellon I was also studying fine art but more in lecture and theory classes. I studied postmodernism and of course art history and language and criticism. But my studio classes were all in design. When I got out of school, I soon realized the design industry has nothing to do with all the things that I loved in design school—how to actually communicate visually, how to use semantics, and how to build a picture plane—color theory and tension and dot problems and line studies and things like that.[13]

PH: You're right. They teach us in design school better than in art school. If you go back to the Renaissance, people like Leonardo were called upon to design fortifications, design a party, make a sculpture or a painting, to maybe make costumes for the theater.... But your paintings are a distinctive enterprise. Of course they relate to the other work, but my simple question is are they about—

RM: —What are the paintings about?

PH: Yeah.

RM: The paintings, by default, are about me. They are a reflection of how I see, understand, and organize the world around me.[14]

PH: For the most part, you only use silkscreen painting.

RM: Absolutely, as opposed to hand-painted images.

PH: I'm assuming you quote/unquote "draw" your paintings on the computer.

RM: I don't.

PH: You don't?

RM: No. They all grow intuitively. I've tried to pre-plan, to compose on a computer. Can't do it. It doesn't feel right, and it doesn't allow for the process of making a painting to inform the outcome of the painting, which is important to me.

PH: As a teacher, I always tell students that there are two ways of putting a painting together. One is that you kind of know what it's going to look like beforehand, and a lot of people do that, including myself. And other artists grow the painting without knowing what it's going to look like at the end, for example, Jackson Pollock. It's two distinct approaches.

Top left and top right: *Émigré* magazine, issues 14 and 19, 1990 and 1991.
Top center: Spread from issue 14.

(11) I've also wanted to avoid making English-centric work.

(12) I actually did a project for *Émigré* issue number 52 titled *Selfsameness*.

(13) .com/schoolstudies

(14) Is all art self-portraits?

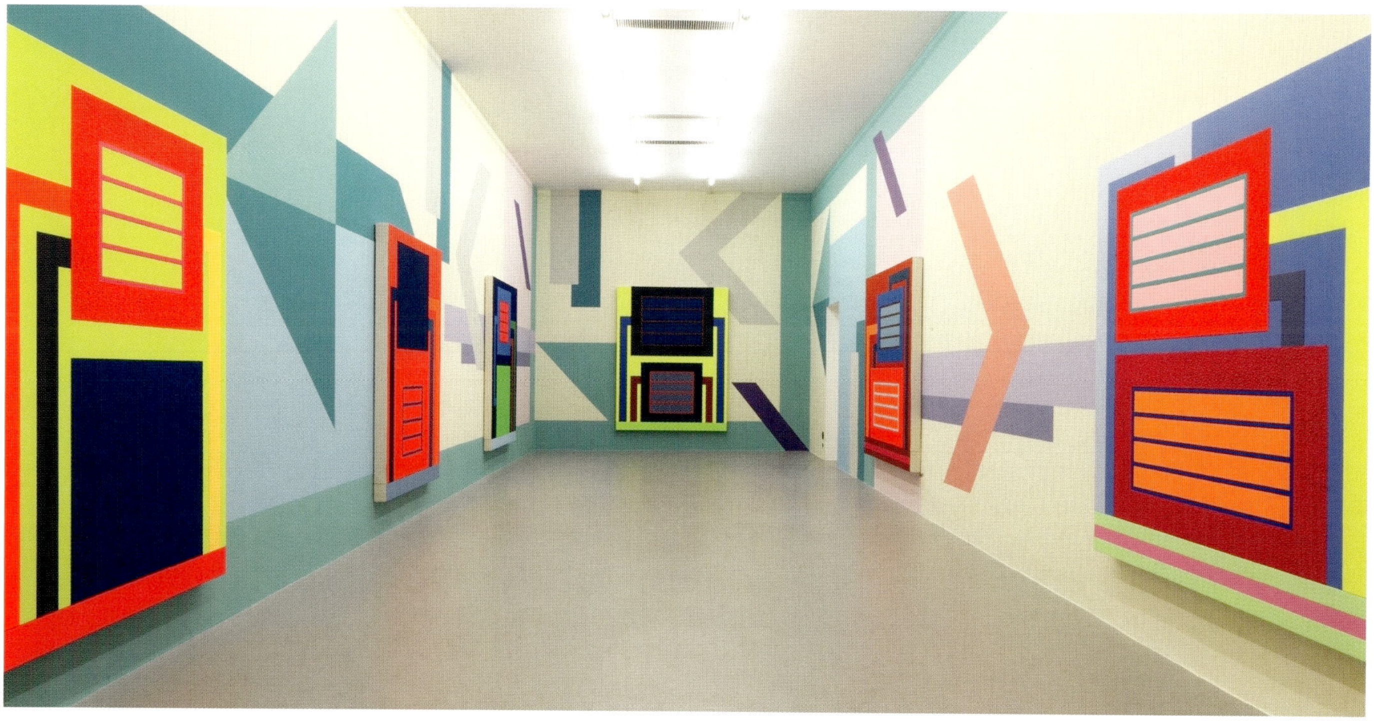

RM: It's surprising, because I work so much on the computer perfecting the forms, so yeah, I think you would assume that I plan these out, but I simply can't. Like I said, I've tried. (15)

PH: Now if I recall correctly, when we were talking one time, you said you were moving away from doing installations and wanted everything to be in the paintings.

RM: I want to go bigger with the paintings. You're right. I want the paintings to be the environment. (16)

PH: Is there anything you miss about the paintings you were doing around 2000?

RM: No.

PH: Or are you still able to do things like that?

RM: I guess now that my ability has been stretched, that there are different kinds of picture planes that I can build, there's a range there so I can apply an appropriate composition.

PH: So you don't quite see it as going from simplicity to complexity.

RM: Yeah, you know, in a kind of larger, overarching way, yes. But I'll still do very simple pieces and pieces that don't have so many overlapping images.

PH: If I were to try an analysis: as the paintings have become more complex, they seem to become more involved in the process of making them.

RM: Yeah, exactly—

PH: —or even intoxicated with the process of making them.

RM: It's the process of making the paintings that's informing the paintings. And more specifically, it's the process of pushing paint with a squeegee through a screen in all the different ways you can do that and all the different ways that you can reproduce an image. You know, you can almost create an under painting with different colors; you can create the impression that images weave through each other, which is one of my inside jokes—only someone who knows silkscreening is going to recognize what happened there—same with the silkscreen drip marks. I have screens that look like drips, and those drips become signifiers and symbols.

PH: I'm looking at this painting from 2005 [*Under Five Chairs Psychiatrists Wink*]. (17) Throughout your work I sense a kind of interest in a global language and older artistic languages, and this red and brown painting strikes me as almost having an affinity to an image from India or from Asia. It's like a Hindu profusion of shapes. The *Black Holes* kind of look like they're influenced by those cultures, as well. (18)

RM: Yeah. You know—and I'm not looking at Indian or Asian forms directly, but maybe the fact that I'm not means that there truly is some kind of universal language there that is independently surfacing.

PH: When I started off as a young artist there was a kind of general belief in self-expression, an expression of what you might call an individual

Peter Halley and Alessandro Mendini, collaboration with architect Alessandro Mendini, 2008. Galleria Massimo Minini, Brescia, Italy.

(15) Work should develop in its own space and time as dictated by its inherent material properties.

(16) See p. 178.

(17) A mnemonic device for remembering part of the Greek alphabet.

(18) See pp. 185–195.

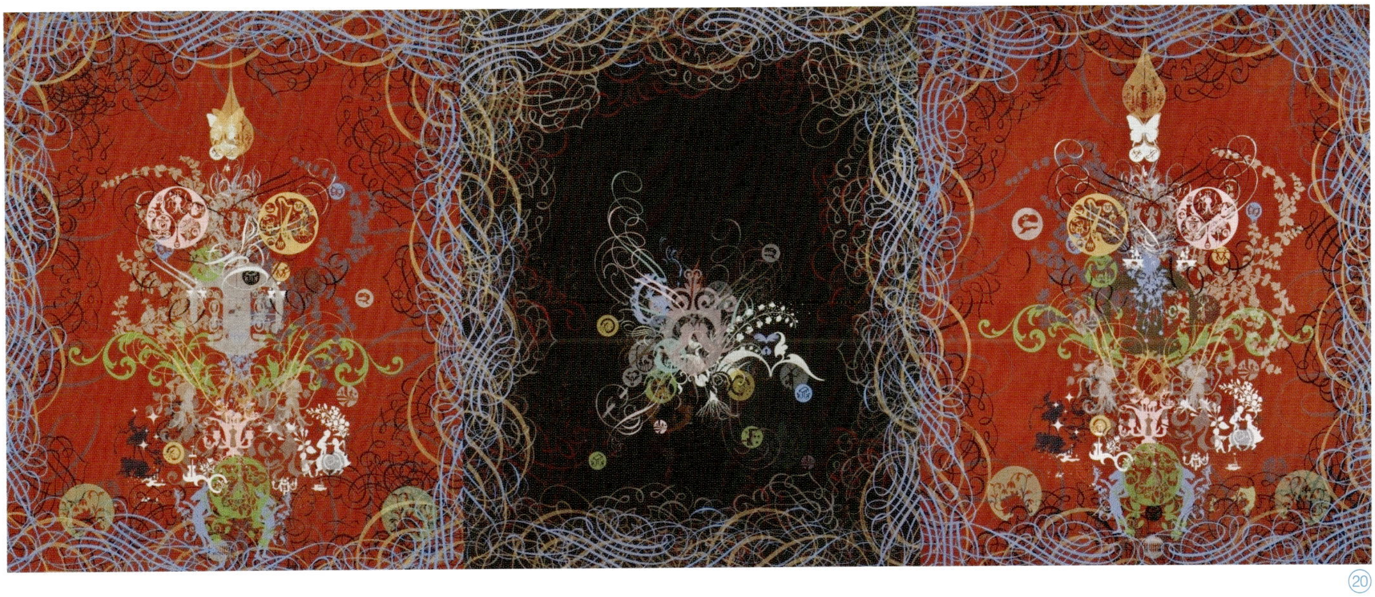

(20)

emotional state, which is what van Gogh—and perhaps de Kooning, as well—were doing. And now I see a real shift in art-making in which artists don't seem to be talking about the self quite so much; art isn't about emotional expression but something else. Does that make any sense to you in terms of where your art comes from?

RM: The personal expressions in my work can be found in the individual iconic drawings. When I bring those together it's purely about composition and color, and any narratives that result from the random juxtapositions are incidental. I also recognize the fact that I'm not so unique, that I'm actually, at the end of the day, just like everybody else. And so if I'm expressing something very personal, it's going to resonate in a universal way, hopefully, if I'm being true and honest with that self-expression.

PH: I share that belief with you. And I think there has been a kind of shift that has entered art where we're saying, "if I'm saying something about me, it could be you, too."

RM: Yeah, that should be the case, if it's truly about you at your core, because we all come from the same place.

PH: And some of your recent paintings have attained a kind of intensity and have employed forms that are characteristic of a spiritual experience, like the *Black Holes* are, in a sense, mandalas.

RM: Yeah, but, the *Black Holes* came out of an interest in the fleur de lis and flourishes which, to me, are just symbols like any other symbol. Over time, they evolved into symbols of fanciness or wealth. But actually, they originally came from nature; they're derived from leaves, vines, and ivy. So I really looked at these and thought, "let's repeat the symbol for wealth over and over and over and come up with something super fancy but also in a radiating composition like an asshole." And then—it kind of, just like you said, almost takes on this religious symbology, ironically. (19)

PH: Well Roland Barthes said that the nature of the modern work is that it's open and it lets the viewer or the reader do the work of finishing the story rather than the artist telling the reader what the story was.

RM: Which is a dictatorship.

PH: Yeah, and so that alone might explain its appeal.

Under Five Chairs Psychiatrists Wink
2005, acrylic on canvas, 72 x 180 in.

(19) .com/eventhorizons

(20) .com/underfivechairsdetail

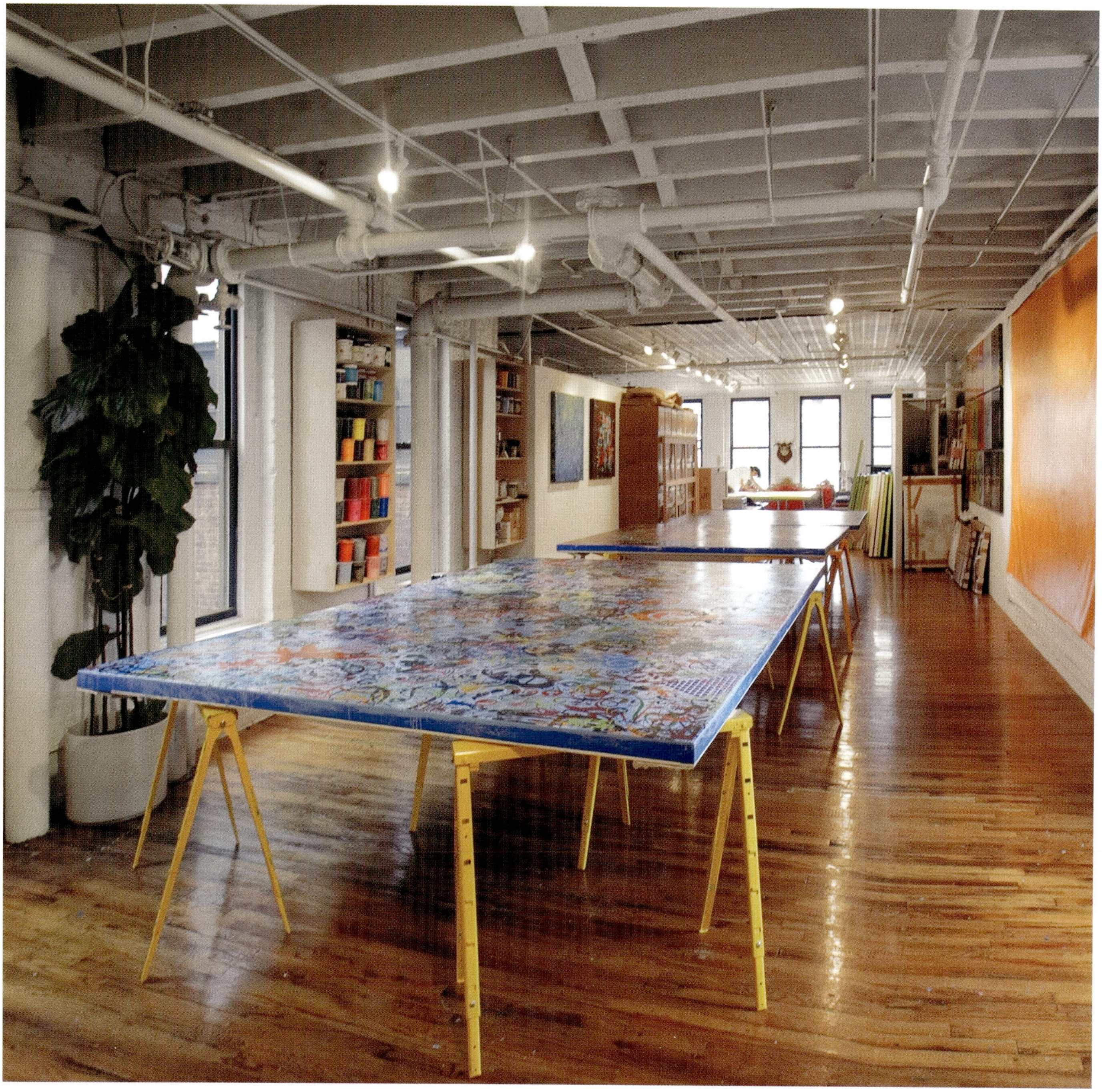

Studio view, 2007.

Inside the Studio: Notes from a Former Assistant

Greg Lindquist

Paintings lead to paintings; words never do.
—Henry Geldzahler, *Making It New*

Introduction

The idea for this essay arose from a conversation Ryan McGinness and I had about a review[1] I wrote of one of his recent exhibitions. One of the reasons I wrote the review was to formally gather my thoughts on Ryan's painting practice after working in his studio for two years. Because many insights are discovered through an active process of writing, one can go into a review with a certain opinion and finish with a radically different one. I was frustrated and somewhat distraught to finish the review on a highly critical tone. Still, I felt the exhibition was too even in its overall polished and glossy appearance. I ultimately acknowledged that this was probably the point of an exhibition presenting varied editions and multiples (which it was), but missing was the intuitive, painterly process that Ryan has consistently brought to the silkscreen technique. (21)

I hesitated to submit the review and almost didn't. After it was published, I worried that it had upset Ryan. I called him a couple months later to discover he hadn't even read it. When we finally discussed the review, I was relieved to hear that he thought it was good and wanted to talk about doing something even more critical at some point. Perhaps this incident is an example in itself of why people like to work with Ryan: he is receptive to criticism and continually thinking about how to better solve problems and improve processes.

This essay, which has proven just as difficult as the critical review, has become a further opportunity to appraise Ryan's processes, although in a different way. Rather than being overly critical, I fear being excessively complimentary, risking sentimentality and exaggerated praise. While discussing ideas for the essay, Ryan suggested interviewing past and present assistants to construct a broader timeline of experiences in the studio. I created a questionnaire[2] that developed into conversations and interviews aimed at forming a snapshot of each assistant's duties and how each was influenced by working with Ryan. The results helped confirm the surprising consistency of my observations. The aim of this essay is first to provide a transparent view of Ryan's studio practices and then, through specific accounts from both my and other assistants' experiences, a transparent portrait of his work habits through explanations of his organization, process, and business practices. Finally, one may see how these individual aspects relate to his personality as a whole.

A Glimpse of the Studio

While in graduate school, I worked with organizations that connected my MFA program to the outside New York art world. A classmate, who ran the Visiting Artist Lecture Series, asked me one day to recommend artists to invite. I suggested she invite Ryan, after having a conversation with my studiomate about his work. At the time, Ryan was installing his 2005 exhibition "Installationview." This semester, before my thesis exhibition, was a formative time to connect with the art world at large, outside of the academic environment. When I asked Ryan if he needed any help, I was surprised to hear him reply, "As much as I can get!"

I assembled a crew of enthusiastic friends, and we painted human-size symbols and logos from scaffolding at Deitch's space on Grand Street in SoHo. (22) We were immediately placed in various stages of the process. First, the symbols were enlarged from a digital projection of a vector-based Illustrator file. Using permanent marker and painter's tape, we created stencils that were then sealed and painted with matched colors. What seemed like straightforward tasks took twice as long as the specifics of these processes became more carefully considered in execution. According to my academic planner, we worked one day from 4 pm until 3 am and then another from 7 pm until 1 am. During this week before the opening, I imagine Ryan was there almost all day and night.[3]

Ryan's creative process immediately fascinated me. I had never considered how many people an exhibition's installation often involves. In the creative process, something always inevitably and unexpectedly goes wrong. In this case, it involved double-sided, fiberglass discs (resembling large lollipops) that extended from the gallery walls inbetween the symbols and logos. They were so massive that the walls could not support their weight. I remember overhearing a conversation between Ryan and Jeffrey Deitch during which Jeffrey sighed matter-of-factly, "This is certainly going to be a challenge for our collectors." Ryan, however, determined to make it work, eventually consulted a structural engineer, who

(21) Yes, that was the point.

(22) I really like that phrase, "human-sized symbols," to describe the wall paintings. It gives a logical sense of scale to those drawings.

added circular plywood plates (painted white to blend into the wall) to help distribute the weight of the sculptures.

Ryan worked alongside us the entire time. He was personable and even, at times, shy about giving instructions. One night he provided beer and pizza, ate with us, and entertained our, at best, overly flattering questions.(23) (Now that I am out of school, I understand how valuable my own time is and appreciate how generous Ryan was with his.) Later that night, we helped him with some paintings in his studio, a 2,500-square-foot commercial loft in Chinatown. After seeing Ryan's studio space, I was determined to work for him in order to understand how he made his work and organized his studio, two concerns in my own career.

For an artist in New York, openings can be a tiring ritual. Many are quickly forgotten. However, the opening reception for "Installationview" felt undeniably personal. All of us who worked on the installation spent a lot of time admiring the result and pointing it out to our friends. We felt connected to the installation, and we enthusiastically greeted Ryan as he wandered around in a daze after what must have been a string of sleepless nights. A friend and former roommate heard about an after-party, and after the opening, a large group of us piled into the building's elevator, which let us off directly into Ryan's studio, overflowing with revelers.

As my friends mingled and drank, I wondered about how Ryan ran his studio. The walls were covered with finished paintings, silkscreens bearing the symbols in the paintings, and process sketches and notes. It occurred to me that everything on view was intentional, almost as if he had installed a second exhibition in his studio, which revealed glimpses of his process.(24) This approach also suggested a strategic presentation and a keen attention to detail. When I finally made my way to the rear of the studio, I shyly asked Ryan if he needed any help. I left the party satisfied, with a scrap of paper bearing his distinctive handwriting[4] indicating his address and the time I was to report to work.

During one of the first sessions,[5] I proposed a trade where my hours would be used towards earning one of his works on paper. I thought that a trade was better than the actual cash; in hindsight it was a wise decision.(25) The work's value would appreciate as Ryan's career progressed. And, I have also been long obsessed by documenting experiences in my life, having mementos and reminders of things past. Having one of Ryan's works seemed like an appropriate form of payment for my work and gave me an inspiring object with which to live.

My artist assistant duties began with helping Ryan make paintings, which basically meant that I kept the screen-printing process in order. With several paintings on flat surfaces across the studio, Ryan selected one color and screen image and used a squeegee to print the image on usually more than one painting. I recognized that there was a certain economy to this way of working,[6] especially with all the possible variations in proportions of the painting support, color of the background, and structure of the overall image.[7] I was responsible for washing and drying these screens after their use and cleaning squeegees and paint spoons. At times, I would also hold larger screens for Ryan while he painted. We seldom talked during this time since he was usually deep in concentration. Because it was an intuitive process of which screen Ryan chose and where it was used, the resultant color combinations were often unpredictable. I became fascinated with how color relationships formed and was reminded that colors could often only be perceived in their proximity to other colors.[8] In particular, this was true in the layering of warm and cool combinations in his paintings, where, for example, a cool brown would appear differently next to a cool blue and warm blue, and so on. Most likely, these observations had an influence on the warm and cool, muted colors in the paintings that composed my MFA thesis exhibition.

After Ryan became more familiar with my work around the studio and with my own painting, he asked me to mix colors. Given a laser-jet-printed swatch, I would match the colors with paint. Because there is no right way of mixing a color, I used this as an opportunity to experiment with color mixing.(26) Often, the required primary color wasn't available so I had to improvise, or change the color slightly. But because my color sensibility is based on subtle variations of a subdued gray palette, I think Ryan and I both began to realize that his colors were beginning to look a little muted, which is the opposite of what he was going for—he often talked about a color in terms of how much it "popped" next to another one.

Inside the Studio: A Laboratory for Ideas, A Model for an Evolving Process

Ryan actually used to wear a lab coat in the studio at times while painting, and a laboratory is an apt metaphor for Ryan's artistic practice. The studio is a place of experimentation, trial and error, and active discovery. This is reflected in three major characteristics in Ryan's methodology: organization, process, and business practice.

Organization of the Environment

The space in Ryan's studio is arranged based on his ever-evolving needs. When I first began work, the front of the studio contained an office area, the middle was a spray booth, and the back, a kitchen. A few months later, Ryan had the spray booth and kitchen wall removed and a closet built in place of the office area. The spray booth was no longer necessary since Ryan had stopped using airbrushed metallic car paints, while the office was moved to the rear of the studio, which was once his bedroom. This configuration made the center of the studio open work space, allowing Ryan to make larger paintings. During the construction, I helped Ryan with such reorganization as rewiring stereo speakers, rerouting printer cables, and painting walls. Like Ryan's painting process, the organization of his studio encourages efficiency. As his process grows, so does the way he orders his space.[9]

(23) The cost of beer and pizza during installation is a business expense, so no big deal.

(24) Absolutely everything that can be considered is considered.

(25) Trade is culture.

(26) Assistants are discouraged from conducting experiments on my dime.

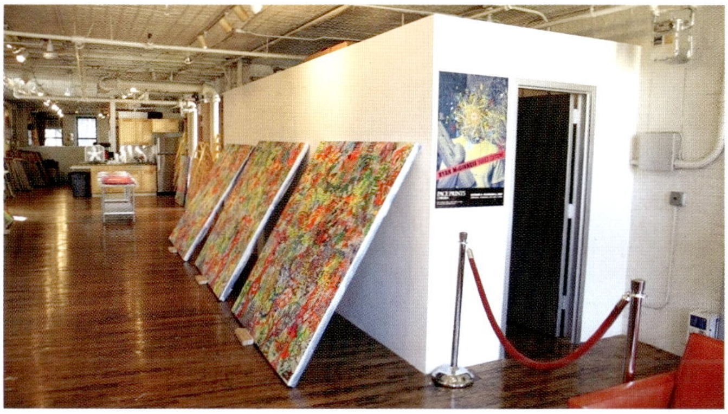

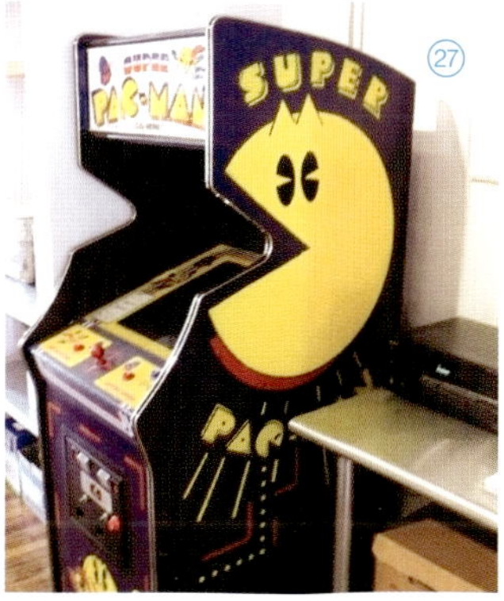

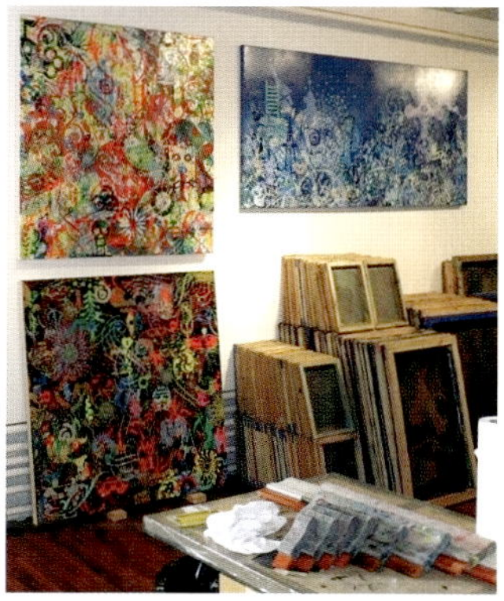

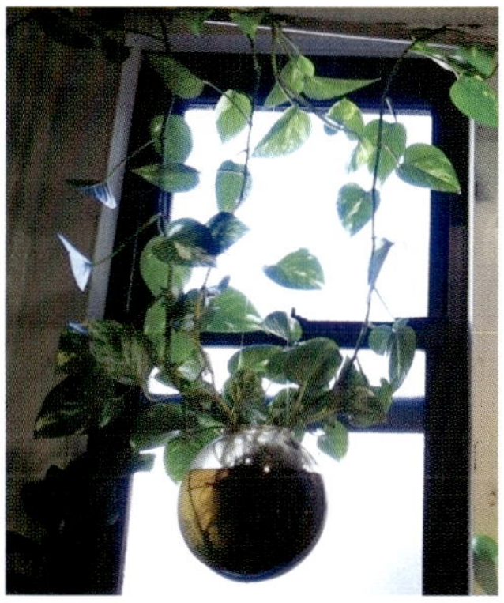

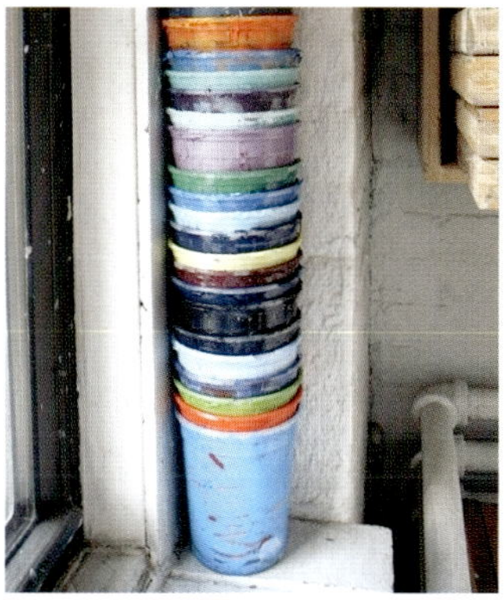

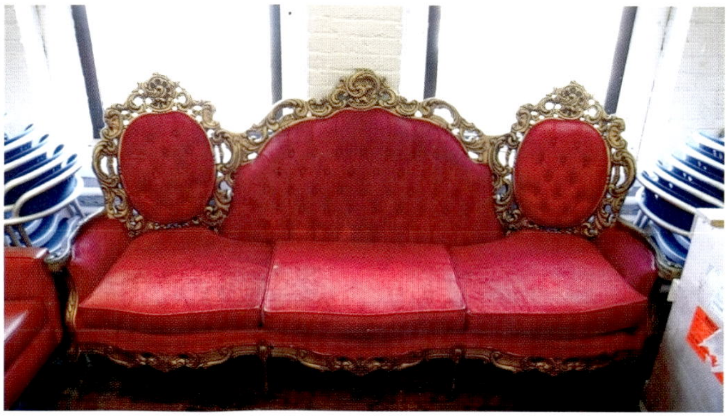

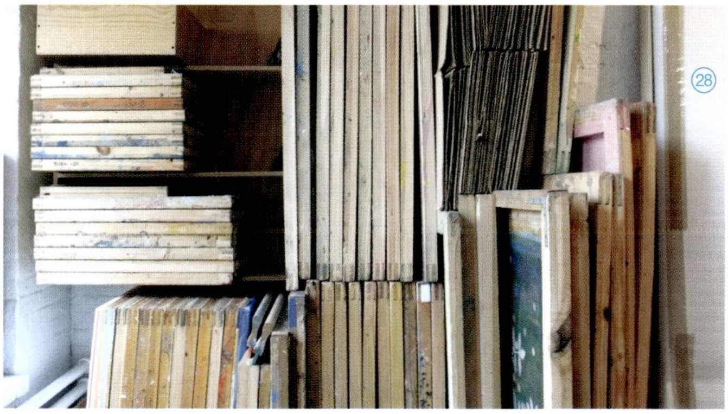

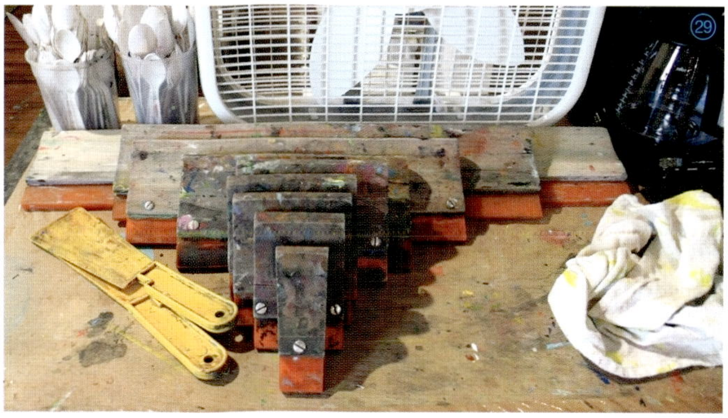

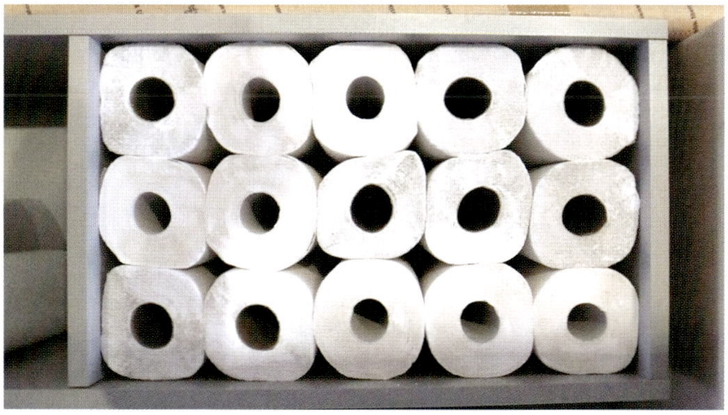

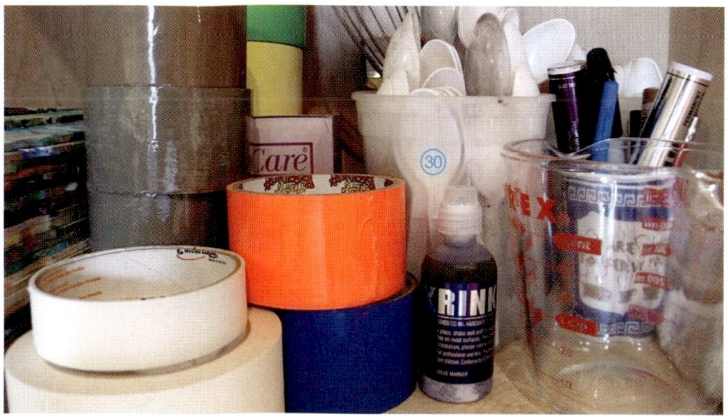

Systems of organization and various studio views, 2008.

(27) See Q 058 on p. 282.

(28) Old screens are retired to an area in the studio and saved for a future project.

(29) The coffee maker is perhaps the most important tool in the studio.

(30) KRINK.

(31)

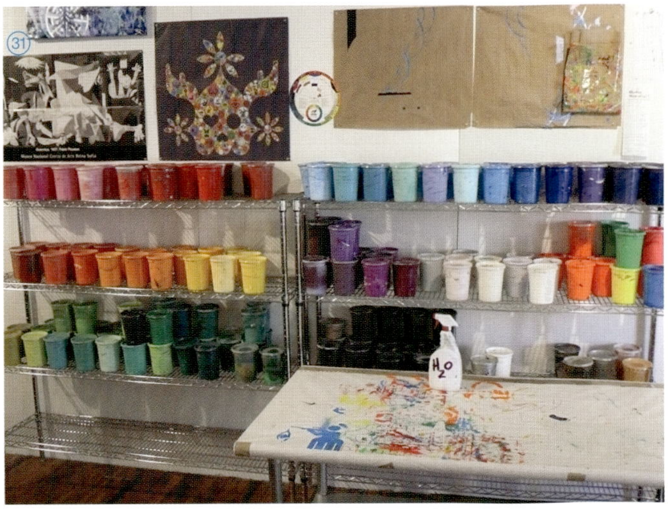

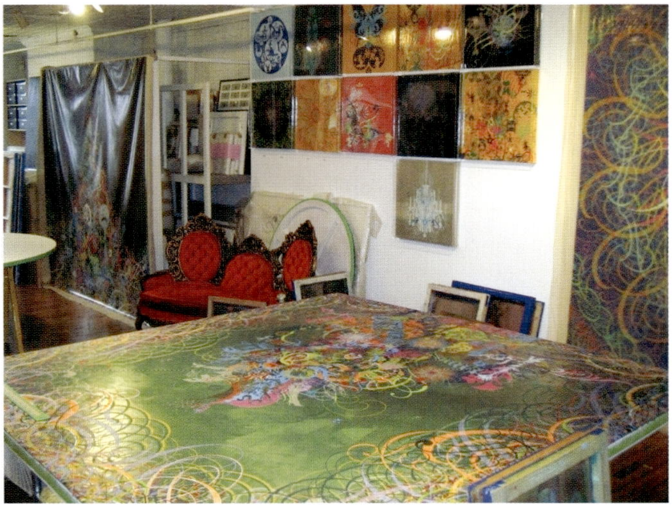

Ryan is continually developing systems for organization. As he once said, "I'm constantly trying to bring order to my environment." Lists of upcoming projects and exhibitions fill several white boards. Bookshelves hold binders—some archive all work, past and present, sold and available; others hold menus, labeled "Places to get food."[10] A computer devoted solely to music is connected to a stereo receiver and wired to speakers across the entire studio.[11] Tools are consolidated on a cart, various supplies stored in labeled boxes in his closet, and paints arranged in an orderly "RedOrangeYellowGreenBlueIndigoViolet" configuration on several shelves across a section of a wall.[12]

The more time I spent with Ryan's vocabulary of symbols and icons, the more I recognized items in his studio that inspired this vocabulary. A Pac-Man machine, plants in his bathroom, a candelabra, an ornate Baroque-style couch, a velvet rope, and shields are all items that appear in his studio and as silhouetted symbols in his paintings.

A Process for Problem Solving

An interesting aspect of Ryan's formal education is that he studied graphic design rather than studio art. While he has described his experience in design as learning how to "communicate visually," I wonder if Ryan was also exposed to a design process for problem solving. The book *The Universal Traveler* describes such an ideation process as a "problem solving journey."[13] The main premise is that a logical and orderly systematic process applied to creative problems leads to more efficient and effective solutions.[14] Fitting for Ryan's interest in mass production of multiples, this way of thinking is commonly applied in new product and concept development and market research.

Most recently, Ryan has been developing a manual for standardized tasks in the studio, such as preparing canvases. This manual involves flow-chart diagrams detailing step-by-step instructions from start to finish. Although he had already developed preferred procedures while I worked for him, these tasks have become more specific and specialized over time, evolving in efficiency like the space of his studio.

Such increased specialization also applies to the duties of Ryan's more recent studio assistants. While his earlier assistants (myself included) had a wider range of duties—including help with painting, work in Illustrator, errands, packing, and administrative tasks—his recent assistants' responsibilities appear much more specific. For example, former assistant Maria Wan described her duties as "mainly on the computer, making the illustrations that get used in the paintings and sculptures." She also did floor plans and elevations for proposed installations, mock-ups for products, security badges, and miscellaneous research. Other assistants still help Ryan only with the painting process. The association between Ryan's specialized processes and those used in the development and marketing of commercial products also relates to his business practices.

Business Practice

Ryan's entrepreneurial spirit and business practices, which he may have learned from his experience as a graphic designer, are great assets to his artistic practice. Wherever and whenever possible, Ryan presents himself as a professional. His interest in business was first apparent when he asked me to invoice him and fill out a W-9 form in order to be paid after I had completed our trade. I then learned that he has an accountant manage his books each month, has established Ryan McGinness Studios as an S-Corporation, and has a federal tax identification number and a resale certificate to receive sales tax exemption for art supplies.(32) In addition, he has Ryan McGinness Studios, Inc. letterhead, envelopes, and business cards that are branded with his signature crown logo and typeface. These formalities reflect the detailed professionalism he devotes to his career and also demonstrate the extent to which he is financially and logistically committed.

Studio views, 2007–2008.

(31) A four-color reproduction of *Guernica*—quite possibly the best painting in the world.

(32) All of this, of course, is standard practice.

(33) Pierre saved all the notes I wrote him and based his typeface on these. Of particular interest is Pierre's successful integration of my ligatures.

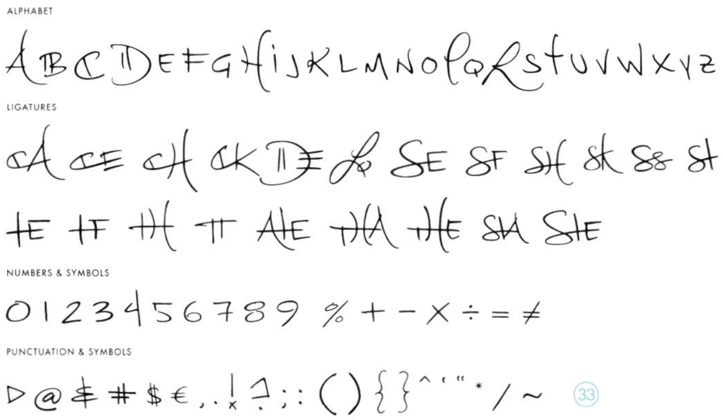

(33)

Additionally, Ryan's understanding of advertising and marketing has enriched the scope of his work. Because his style lends itself to many forms, blurring the boundaries of commercial product and work of art, he is able to offer more price points to establish a wider audience. Producing wrapping paper, soccer balls, calendars, buttons, and books, and print multiples, original works on paper, and paintings allows Ryan to build an economically diverse collector base. A variety of papers, from butcher's paper and exhibition posters to printmaking paper, generates various pricing differences within the category of works on paper. The paintings' prices vary by support (linen, canvas, or panel), size, and shape.

Although his studio is structured like a company, Ryan has a specific vision for his work that rejects corporate sponsorship, or any alliance that places his work in the service of another entity or idea. For him, authorship and control are key components in making art—he is not interested in co-branding or coopting the work.[15] In maintaining this artistic integrity, Ryan has rejected offers to use his work in advertising campaigns for Nike, Coca-Cola, and major car, cell phone, and record companies. In addition, Ryan has filed lawsuits against companies who have blatantly marketed copies of his work without his knowledge or licensing. For example, I arrived one day at the studio entrance to find piles of boxes filled with t-shirts that featured Ryan's drawings, studio logo, and hang tags. A friend of Ryan's had noticed that Urban Outfitters had been selling "Ryan McGinness" shirts. Ryan was astounded; he had approved no such deal. When I asked him what he had done next, he replied, "I sued them!" (34)

The settlement apparently involved acquiring the merchandise, so that Ryan had all the shirts in his possession, cluttering the studio. Former assistant Pierre Tardif asked Ryan what he was going to do with them, to which Ryan responded, "Sell 'em in Japan?" We were never sure if he was completely serious or what happened to the t-shirts. It became part of our job to fold the shirts, removing the defective ones. Ryan, of course, had a specific way for the shirts to be folded. Embarrassingly, I remember realizing that I never quite learned how to fold shirts in any consistent way until that moment. Pierre recalls, "I still don't know where all the tees ended up, but Ryan ran a great hustle. He confiscated the bootlegs, did a quick quality control check, and thought to release them as official gear. It was a clever table-turning strategy. All that time near Canal Street must have rubbed off on him."

The Influence of Ryan McGinness, the Person
While compiling the questionnaires from assistants, I noticed some consistent remarks about Ryan's personality: Ryan is hardworking.[16] He is great with people.[17] He is very clear about his instructions and patient. In these responses, a deep respect for Ryan as a person is clear. An assistant told me recently, "despite his fame and talent, he is empathetic and retains human decency... which I believe contributes to his success since people are eager to work for him.... During many experiences working for him, I have left feeling insecure and frustrated with my performance.... However, he was usually sensitive to this, did not lose his temper, and was always willing to give me a second chance. He once even called me to assure me that he was not upset with me... "

One particular situation reveals Ryan's empathic and understanding nature: assistants Pilita Garcia and Ben Callaway rolled a painting in order to move it, but it had a varnish layer that was not fully cured. Pilita recalls, "I can't remember why we rolled it... Ryan was definitely not in the studio. All I remember is when we started to unroll it. I was ready to faint. I... grabbed a sponge, pouring a bucket of soapy water and began scrubbing the millions of gesso marks that had stuck to the uncured varnish. We kept scrubbing; still Ryan did not show up. When he did, he reacted like a prince, saying, 'Oh, it's okay. It's just a painting.'"

Assistants also discussed the influence Ryan had on their professional lives. While many recognized and learned from his commitment to a daily practice of work, Pierre Tardif, while studying graphic design, found particular inspiration in Ryan's distinctive handwriting. In the fall of 2005, Pierre designed a working typeface called "Ryan McGinness," based on Ryan's handwriting. "When Ryan writes, he combines certain letters with a shared stroke, creating two- or three-letter ligatures," Pierre explained. "He also reserves certain letter styles for single words. For example, Ryan always draws the letter 'L' as a short, blocky uppercase letter except when he writes the word 'Love,' in which case he draws a cursive capital 'L,'" Pierre continued. These scrawls became interesting subjects for digital translation when used with open typeface font files (.otf), which automatically swap ligatures for certain letter combinations. (35)

It took Pierre four months to finish the font. Pierre admitted, "When I finally showed it to him, he seemed sort of uninterested. I guess it's hard to impress someone by showing them a font that they can pen themselves." He added, "Because the font is based

Typeface based on Ryan's handwriting, designed by Pierre Tardif, 2005.

(34) A company called UARM made bootleg shirts with my drawings and sold them to Urban Outfitters.

(35) For the record, I don't ever remember writing the word "love" to Pierre, unless I wrote him a note that said, "Please buy more beer, which I love."

on his calligraphy (and because of his kindly worded request), I felt I should not publish it lest it turn up in a ubiquitous ad campaign and end up branding Ryan's handwriting."

Despite Ryan's conflicted feelings about other people's demands on his time,[18] he is an extremely generous person. Even though I earned the work on paper five months into working, Ryan allowed me to take it home three months earlier in December 2005. On the day I received the piece, we stopped work early and spent the last hour sitting at a diner booth[19] in the kitchen area. Because I was growing anxious about my approaching MFA thesis exhibition, I asked for Ryan's advice and general guidance.

He told me that being an artist is a calling, much like that of a teacher, and advised not to let relationships get in the way of your work. At the time, a Brooklyn gallery had approached me about having a solo exhibition. I was hesitant about whether it was a good fit, and I was hopeful about a contact I had made with a Chelsea gallery. Should I commit at the risk of something else happening? Ryan told me that I don't want a show in June or July, but not to worry about losing my slot and to hold out for the best fit.

Ryan is extremely careful about the galleries with which he chooses to work. One reason he respects Jeffrey Deitch is that, in Ryan's experience, he is one of the few dealers who actually looks at the work when he comes to the studio. He takes a lot of time investigating what is happening with the work and makes himself available to Ryan to call for his opinion. Ryan told me that the most important thing to remember is context (of show, artist, location, collectors) and to focus on my work. "This might sound cheesy," he said, "but if you're focusing on the work and where it's going, everything will fall into place." Looking at my business card, Ryan made some suggestions: Get my e-mail address through my Web site (gmail and AOL look amateur). Don't list my phone number and street address. Don't have an image on the card—you don't want to apologize for it not reproducing accurately. I left the studio that day in a daze. As I said goodbye, Ryan casually encouraged, "Be productive."

As an aspiring artist, working for an established artist is a necessary stage in a career path. What I learned from working for Ryan could not be taught in graduate school. My experience in Ryan's studio motivated me to find my own commercial space when I finished my MFA. I also made my own stationery, envelopes, business cards, and Web site. Having discussions with Ryan about his S-Corp inspired me to form Greg Lindquist Studios LLC, acquire a federal tax identification number, set up a business checking account and credit card, and acquire a resale certificate. I even wired a stereo with speakers throughout my studio, after Ryan's model, using zip ties as I had learned while helping him organize his studio.(36) I have hired assistants—one who, ironically, worked for me when I was still working for Ryan—and even used the money Ryan paid me to pay my assistant. For my first solo exhibition, I organized an after-dinner and after-party, loosely modeled on Ryan's after-parties. Ryan inspired me to invest in my career, to be dedicated and committed to making work. I'll still call him or stop by his studio to ask for advice, see his most recent work, and observe his ever-evolving studio practice.

Of course, there are more challenging aspects to Ryan's personality. Several assistants discussed his obsessive-compulsive tendencies. These comments remind me of a time he asked me to scrub a label off a clear soap dispenser, so that it would be more attractive and he didn't have to look at the logo on the label. Another assistant commented that lids of boxes had to be placed in a certain direction, and during studio cleaning days, "sometimes he would run his finger through nooks and crannies to find dust and be completely grossed out, but it would probably be five specks of dust."(37) Another assistant was disappointed to find, "when he wrote inscriptions in the books he published, seven out of eight of them say, 'Thanks for all your help!'"

Although many assistants commented on the low pay, former assistant Pierre Tardif explains, "The pay was decent for a student, but that's not the reason that I worked for him." At times I, too, had similar reservations about pay and overall value of the experience. Sometimes it just felt like I had learned all that I could. During difficult days, I felt an inherent monotony and imminent lack of glamour in the work. I realized at one point that I had found myself in essentially the same job I had in high school—a screen-printing production job—but rather than doing the actual printing (which were mostly t-shirts), I was often cleaning up after Ryan. Also, at times, I was frustrated to realize that I had worked 80 hours for a work on paper that took Ryan five, at the most, to produce. But, I was the assistant and my time was valued as such. To be early in a career in New York means almost working for free in many situations in order to gain experience. In contrast, I've heard horrific accounts from friends who, as assistants, have endured extensive abuses from difficult, disorganized, and unstable artists.

Ryan's studio practice goes against a misconception we have as a culture that making art is magical and mysterious.[20] The assumption that work materializes from the artist's imagination and flows directly to its form is troubling because it overlooks a process present in creativity. Contrary to popular stereotype, it's not madness, fits of manic inspiration, bipolar mood swings, or suicidal predispositions that make good art. Rather, a singular vision, ambition, organization, business aptitude, and entrepreneurial spirit have become defining characteristics of a work ethic like Ryan's.(38)

Notes

1. To read the review, visit: http://artcritical.com/lindquist/GLMcGinness.htm
2. The questions included:
    1. When did you work for Ryan? (month/year) If presently working: since when have you worked for Ryan? (month/year)
    2. How did you get to work for him? Did he find you or vice versa?

(36) I cannot stress enough the importance of a decent sound system in a studio.

(37) All of this makes perfect sense to me.

(38) There are parts of this essay that were edited out in order to fit in this book. Those missing parts can be found here: .com/missinglindquisttext

3. What were/are your responsibilities? Did/do you work primarily in the studio or on any exhibitions?
4. What have you learned from the experience? Did anything have a lasting impact on your own creative endeavors?
5. Are you an artist? Designer? Where else do you work?
6. What did you learn about Ryan's process by working for him?
7. Was there anything that you didn't like about working for him or the studio environment? Please be specific and honest.

3. This work ethic extended beyond the time crunches of installations. Former assistant Pierre Tardif confirms this experience in the studio: "Some days went on into the night. When I was finally excused for the evening Ryan would stay on longer still. His stamina is hard to keep up with." Tardif, interview by the author, e-mail June 4, 2008.

4. See Pierre Tardif's Ryan McGinness typeface and discussion of Ryan's handwriting script on p. 19.

5. Soon after beginning work, Ryan commented on my work, which initiated a growing rapport: "Hey Greg, I... think your work is refreshing. I was pleasantly surprised to see it wasn't all wild-styled out and doesn't aspire to be anything like mine. That's really good." Ryan McGinness, e-mail correspondence, October 10, 2005.

6. Former assistant Pilita Garcia explains, "Ryan likes to work on many pieces at the same time in a way of transgressing the boundaries of the format. In order to do that, an assistant is needed to deal with all the gear involved, so that he can focus on looking and painting." Garcia, interview with the author, e-mail June 12, 2008.

7. Ryan had sketchbooks with these different structures, some based on symmetrical decorative patterns, others on cosmic patterns, such as black holes.

8. Former assistant Dustin Schuetz (39) elaborates on Ryan's method of working: "While working on sometimes 10 different paintings at once, he would use the same image and bounce back and forth from one painting to the next, screening layer after layer in a rapid fashion while not dwelling on the decision he had just made for more than a few seconds before moving on—each move determined by the previous one." Schuetz, interview with the author, e-mail May 27, 2008.

9. Regarding the continual problem solving that occurs in Ryan's organization, I am reminded of when painter Will Cotton once told me, quoting his father who is a pilot: "Every safety system on an airplane is there because something has previously gone wrong."

10. Joe Fig, an artist who builds miniature models of artists' studios and has made two models of Ryan's studio, told me he took an interest in the bookshelves in the back of the studio, whose binders and CD cases are neatly arranged in a grid format, which, for Fig, recalls a minimalist Donald Judd sculpture. Fig, interview with the author, telephone, June 16, 2008. (40)

11. Music was a popular topic of conversation in interviews with assistants. Ryan was open to others' musical taste and would allow assistants to play music. He introduced me to Podcasts and former assistant Pierre Tardif to NPR radio shows, such as *This American Life*. I still listen to Podcasts while working in my studio.

12. Assistant Maria Wan commented that "his organization: a spot, box, or place for EVERYTHING, and his ability to regularly keep everything organized" was a valuable thing she learned while working for Ryan. Wan, interview with the author, e-mail June 3, 2008.

13. During the editing stages of this essay, I asked Ryan if he encountered the ideation process in his undergraduate studies. He replied, "Totally—it was the bulk of the theory I studied."

14. The steps detailed in *The Universal Traveler* are: Accept Situation, Analyze, Define, Ideate, Select, Implement, and Evaluate. Former assistant Pierre Tardif added, "I learned the best way to get a lot done is to systematize the process using lists, routines, tests/measurements, and attention to details to the point where I would later find paint on the tip of my nose." Tardif, interview with author, e-mail June 4, 2008.

15. During the editing of the book, Ryan commented, "However, I am interested in making the kinds of things on my own terms that compete directly against corporations. Furthermore, the best way to fuck 'the man' is to create that which he can never make for himself and never allow him to coopt for his own agenda—art."

16. Former assistant Nina Stojkovic said, "I learned that if you want to make it, you have to work hard, very hard."

17. During editing this essay, Ryan asked, "Is it worth noting that I am actually not great with people? I cannot manage people, I hate people around me when I am trying to work, and consequently, I often spend all night in the studio alone trying to get the work done that I cannot get done during the day—like now at three in the morning." Maybe it's a matter of perspective, how one defines or evaluates management, or just having expectations of oneself that are nearly impossible to meet. Probably a bit of each in Ryan's case.

18. A button fastened on a painting in a recent exhibition expresses this best: "Most people just steal your time." This sentiment is also echoed in a post-it note that has resided on his computer monitor for the past few years, stating, "SAY NO." (41)

19. When Ryan did renovations, he gave me the diner booth, above which hung his framed work on paper, in a sense, a kind of reminder of this conversation. Today, the booth is a permanent fixture in my studio.

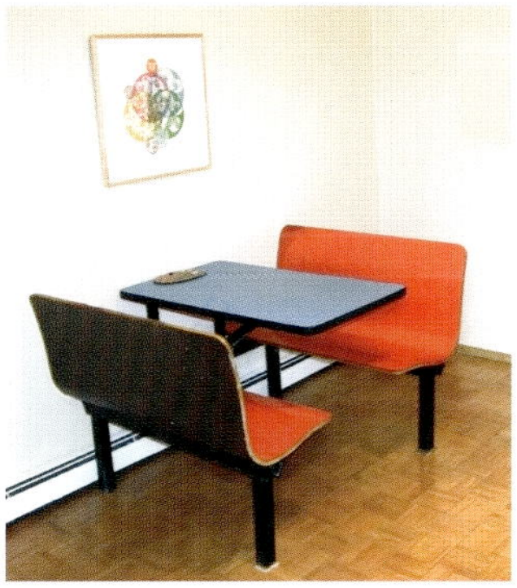

20. Former assistant Maria Wan adds, "The experience has been really insightful to how an established art studio runs, even though it probably varies from artist to artist. For me, there has always been this glamour to how art was made from only seeing the finished result beautifully exhibited in shows. Working in the studio and getting to see how pieces are made, the process, from start to finish made it more believable and more realistic. In some ways, it took the magic out of the artwork but has also shown me the ease and difficulties of making art on a large scale." Wan, interview with author, e-mail June 3, 2008.

Greg Lindquist's apartment with diner booth acquired from Ryan, 2005.

(39) See p. 84.

(40) See p. 61.

(41) .com/sayno

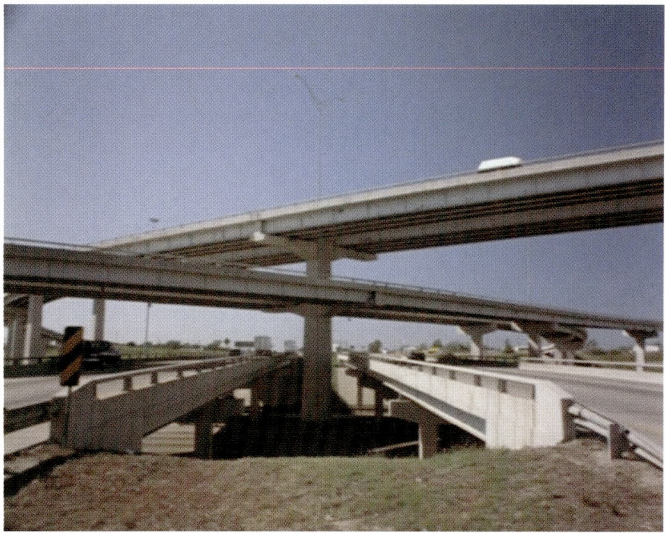

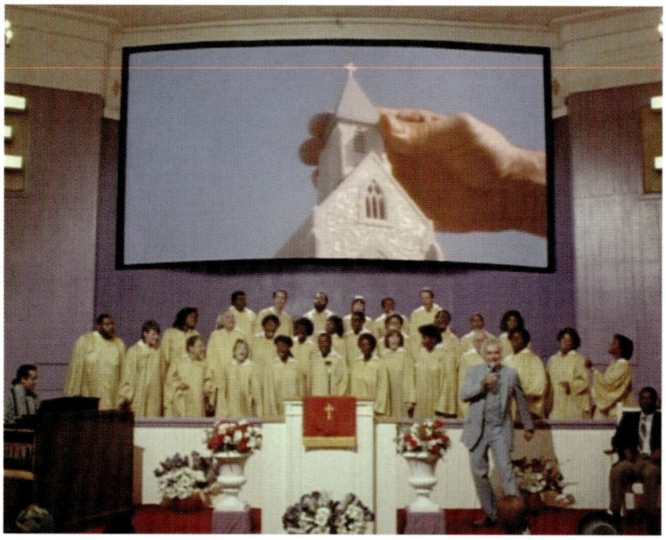

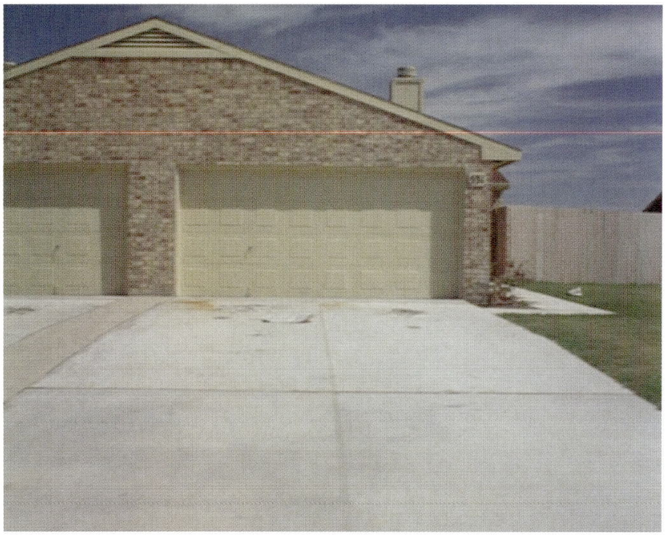

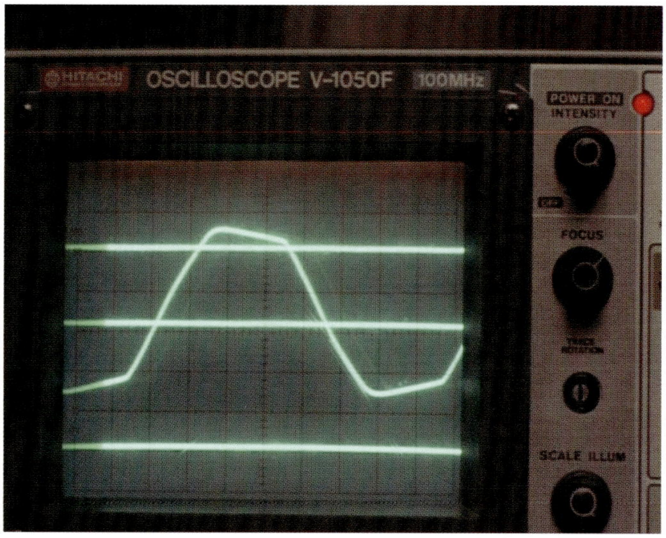

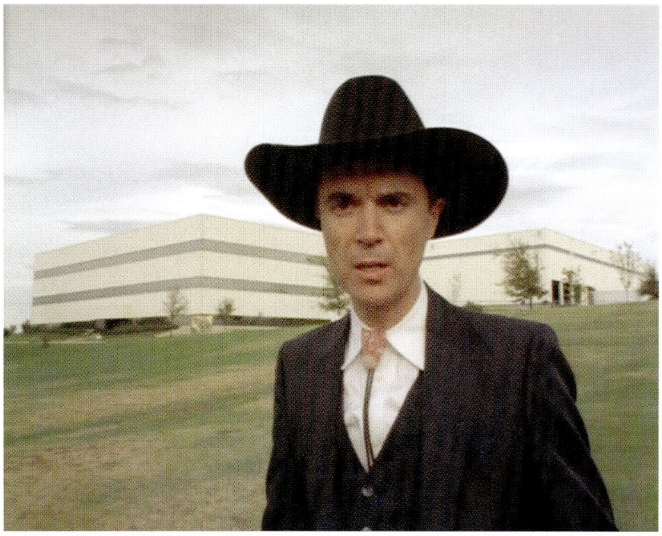

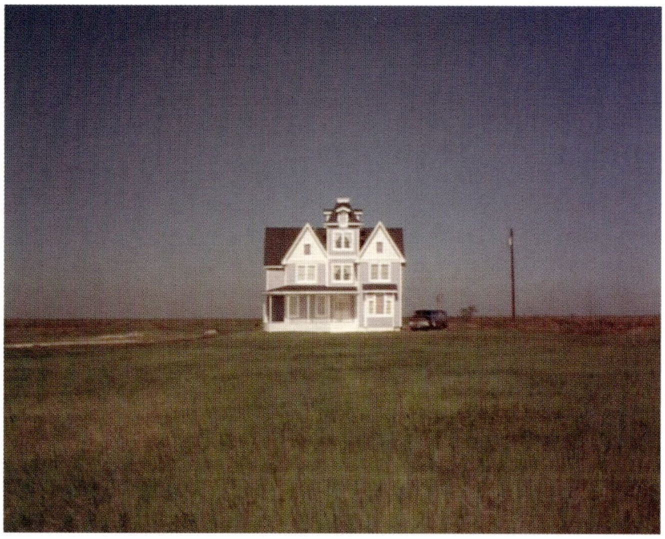

David Byrne, *True Stories*, 1986, color film stills.

Conversation
David Byrne and Ryan McGinness

I. Uncommon Sense

RM: *True Stories* (1986) was the most influential film for me during my formative years; the deadpan absurdity resonated. I had recently discovered Dada, my favorite art movement, and I drew parallels between the two. That film is so close to my heart that throughout the years it has served as a litmus test for evaluating new friends—you either get it or you don't. You probably don't want to talk about your old work, but would you mind telling me about your interest in the absurd and the surreal?

DB: I'm flattered that you like the film. The key, I guess, is that it mixes stagy, artificial scenes and settings with documentary stuff that often appears equally artificial. For me, much of the world is pretty surreal—in the sense that its veneer can be seen through or peeled away fairly easily. Often what appears normal is pretty odd if you take two steps to the side and view it from a slightly different angle—it just gives me more to love. The script, though, might have the strongest Dada connection: The jumps from scene to scene are what some folks say are like collages or found text.

RM: So, the film was a precursor to reality-infused fiction—I like that mix. And yes, the collage-style cuts, especially in the "Puzzling Evidence" scene, are like Craig Baldwin's *Tribulation 99* [1991], at times.

DB: I don't know that film—I'll look it up... okay, just added it to my Netflix queue!

RM: It's of the J. R. "Bob" Dobbs's Church of the SubGenius school. That clip-art-driven work was a big influence on me at one point. And talk about copyright—they were really pushing it with *The Sacred Teachings of J. R. "Bob" Dobbs* [1987].(42)

DB: Yeah, there seemed to be a little window before everyone got all crazy about copyright. I was in touch with the SubGenius people, as they were a big influence—obviously—on the "Puzzling Evidence" scene. It was a moment when a lot of stuff flew under the radar; we could clip, sample, and appropriate and no one cared. Maybe that was pre-the-great-wide-Internet.

RM: I was thinking, though, the film parallels Dada more in its anti-capitalist stance, in its reflection of the surreality of capitalism—the way many of the Dadaists reflected the senselessness of war with seemingly senseless art, rejecting logic and ignoring aesthetics (which in turn gave rise to a new kind of aesthetic). I love how the main character takes a very neutral, almost objective view of everything ("from the side," as you say) by pointing out the obvious as if an alien in a strange land—"It's a multipurpose shape... a box."(43)

DB: There is a little bit of an anti-official attitude towards art in the film—shiny metal buildings are presented as if they were minimal sculpture—or at least equally valid and interesting. Do you see the play of icons in your work as related to Dada? I can see a connection in your emphasis on the creative process as repetitive, almost assembly-line like—though your decisions are intuitive, your process is quasi-mechanical.

RM: There's a connection between my work and Dada formally, but not conceptually. My work is certainly not political in content—however, the act of taking a formal iconic language used by an anonymous authoritative power, assuming that power for myself, and giving authorship and accountability to these kinds of forms can be considered a political gesture. There is something Dada-inspired, Tzara-esque, in creating my own ingredients, which are then cut up and reassembled. I use a form of normalcy (signage) as a tool against itself—which raises another topic concerning the inherent paradox of making art that is anti-art: If you are opposed to a system, what is the best strategy for changing that system—subvert it, ignore it, create an alternative? How can you make an anti-anything in the context of that thing?

DB: Can you change the system from within? Pretty damn hard to do, if you ask me. I'll stick with Gandhi: "We need to be the change we wish to see in the world."

Can you talk about that great *Sponsorship [Sponsorship: The Fine Art of Corporate Sponsorship, The Corporate Sponsorship of Fine Art* (2003)] book you organized?

RM: *Sponsorship* accompanied an exhibition I did in L.A. at Shepard Fairey's gallery.(44) I solicited as many corporations as I could to sponsor the exhibition, for which there was no content. Instead, the gallery was filled with the enlarged logos of the sponsors, and at the opening we gave away all the swag they had given us. The sponsorship was the exhibition, of course. I think it was a hotter topic when I conducted all the interviews in 2002. It was a time when a lot of corporations were trying to get down with the cool kid artists coming from the subcultures of graffiti and skateboarding. After I concluded the book, I resolved my own position on the matter: I decided that I needed to protect

(42) .com/jrbobdobbs

(43) Here I do the dorkiest thing anyone can do with one of his heroes—quote his work back to him.

(44) .com/sponsorshipexhibition

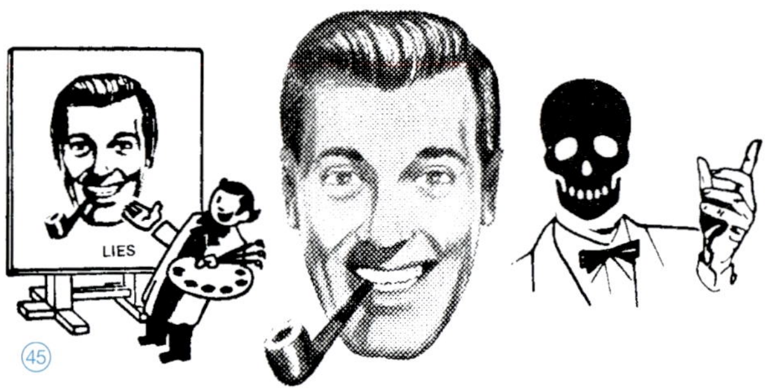

Characteristic depiction of J.R. "Bob" Dobbs, head of the Church of the SubGenius.

my work, which wants to stand on its own, independent of any agenda that tries to attach itself. It's key for me to preserve authorship and accountability. So, if a company wants to work with me (and galleries and museums are companies, too), they have to be willing to step into and support my world, not vice versa.

DB: Yeah, that particular group of artists may have been extremely cool for the culture vultures then—I can't imagine that some of you aren't still attractive to them. Now, though, there are more established artists working with fashion designers, etc., where the sponsorship is superblatant.[46]

II. Form Follows Feeling

DB: Do you run into any negative attitudes because your art is made with screens instead of being painted by hand? Do people assume that the partial involvement of software is a bad thing?

RM: No, I think people are more baffled by my process than anything else. The production is just as layered as the imagery—there is a lot of behind-the-scenes work—especially when I'm layering the same image on top of itself several times in different colors, with different degrees of legibility and fragmentation. It's like a secret code sent out to those who know about silkscreening—only those who are intimately familiar with the process can begin to understand how the images were made.

Your art-making practice flows from form to form—I see it as a solutions-driven approach to materializing concepts. You have an idea, and your problem is how to best express that idea—or, you have a feeling, and your problem becomes how to express that feeling. How do you decide what to make, and at what point do you decide to explore many forms versus investigating one form deeply?

DB: My brief time at art school must have indoctrinated me with the idea that there is an almost ideal material expression for each idea. Some ideas should be materialized as video and not graphic work, some should be songs instead of dances. The most obvious example is politics. I agree with Sam Goldwyn, who said, "Pictures are for entertainment; messages should be delivered by Western Union."

RM: Yes, I agree that sending a message is different than sending a feeling, or a mood, or a concept—which is more what we hope to do when we make art, I think. Stickers, buttons, and t-shirts are better vehicles for sharing messages.[47] These are things I like to make, but I haven't positioned them on the same end of the spectrum as paintings and sculptures, until recently with something like the button pieces [*Island Universes* (2007)].[48] I never really thought about this differentiation between messages and whatever we think the content of art is—this is assuming art strives to communicate something more than just a message. Otherwise, you—and Sam—are right: Let's just send telegrams (or bumper stickers).

However, my original point was that you seem rather fearless in tackling many different forms. I remember when you were on the cover of *Time* magazine [October 27, 1986] and declared a Renaissance man. That actually gave me permission and made me realize, "Oh, I really can do many different things."

DB: The "Renaissance man" tag was flattering, but I got a lot of, "Who does he think he is?" as a result—as if I had tagged myself with the label. When art separated itself from craft, way back in the—well, it might have been the Renaissance—we were given permission to use mediums in new ways and to use whatever medium seemed appropriate to an idea, feeling, or subject. An artist can make a movie, and sometimes a filmmaker can be considered an artist. Photography, needlepoint, taxidermy, software programming... all became valid mediums.

I know you've been diving deeper into 3-D pieces and some video as well. Do you begin to conceptualize something and then realize it wants to be a 3-D piece rather than a silkscreen?

RM: I'm trying to work toward creating total environments. When I close my eyes, I feel like I'm swimming in my own world, and I want to create that same kind of total immersion for others (how can I invite people into my head?).[49] So yes, when I'm conceptualizing an exhibition, I'm trying to figure out how I can control the entire experience—how I can extend the world in my head to the real world, and those extensions are always morphing into different forms depending on what each part wants to be. As a result, the environment/work includes everything down to the bottles of water. I always assumed that this desire to share one's world with others is at the core of all artists' work. Is it the same for you?

DB: Tentatively. I assume if something moves me that I have enough in common with others that maybe the experience will translate. It often does, but just as often something gets lost or skewed in the translation. I then ask myself how I can fix that. I realize there, in that gap, is where the skill lies these days—not in traditional artisanship, but in achieving a successful transmission.

RM: Which is to say that in this age of information, artists need communication and transmission skills more than anything.

(45) Artwork from the Church of the SubGenius respectfully and purposefully reproduced without permission.

(46) Artists are the free R&D departments for advertising agencies.

(47) .com/messages

(48) See p. 116.

(49) This world is not enough.

Many of your works on paper are sketches, plans, or ideas for what I imagine could be more finished or realized works, but perhaps you don't find it necessary to further formalize those ideas. At what point is an expression expressed or most fully expressed?

DB: I could ask you the exact same question. I was in school when a lot of the conceptual artists were doing work that was in the form of a text or series of instructions. Art was thought of as mainly an idea, and eventually we saw a whole group of artists who felt they didn't have to realize or manifest the idea physically—the dealers probably were tearing their hair out. For me, there's something immediate in your preliminary sketches for the icons—most people would assume they were all computer generated, and yet, here they are as drawings! I sense that, for you, part of the content of those lines and shapes is that they approach the cool look of mass-produced signage and logos—that because flatness and slickness are part of the content, leaving them as sketches wouldn't work.

RM: You're absolutely right; that is the idea. Furthermore, I find myself standing in opposition to what appears to be lazy or effortless work.(50) I have to go through this process of sketching, resketching, tweaking, developing, and reworking my drawings. I also take a sort of blue-collar pride in working hard to make something presentable and as perfect as I can. Still, I know what you mean about those sketches, and I agree. There is something immediate about them... I have been enlarging them onto the gallery wall to create a place in which to locate my paintings in an exhibition, and even using them as the ingredients for some prints.(51) Just last week someone was in the studio and made the same observation as you—he liked the sketches and was curious about what would happen if the work stopped there. The sketches, for me, are only part of the process, a means to an end. But still, if the means were the end...

DB: Yeah, I like seeing your sketches, but I sense that since the subject and content are bound up in the reference to signage and slick logos then the sketches can only be a part of the process.

Lately I've fabricated some of my chair drawings and drawings of imaginary bike racks. Sometimes, I can picture the finished thing just by looking at the original sketchy drawings—and so making a large physical object seems like it's being done more for other people... The anxiety-producing part is that, knowing what the work wants to be, I can only ruin it from there if I'm not lucky or careful. Have you ever had stuff start off right and then you ruin it?

RM: All the time—from artwork to relationships. I tend to be self-destructive on all fronts, perhaps as a way to challenge myself. I actually enjoy ruining a painting by pushing it too far, and then having to figure out how to save it. That struggle is often reflected in the finished piece—there's a trace left of an imperfect, organic path from beginning to end. For me, the process of making a work should inform the work.

DB: But then there's the part of music and visual art that is referencing, sampling, quoting. Your icons are like tweaked logos and refer to signage. To some, they might seem like sampling even though they're not. Do some people assume you've simply lifted the shapes and symbols from somewhere else?

RM: Yes, some people do assume that I've lifted the shapes and symbols and repurposed them. This is the inherent irony in making drawings that are designed to look anonymous—they are designed to look like they come from somewhere else, so I can't really complain if people make that assumption.

III. Piles

RM: This may seem boring, since it has to do with a very pragmatic/practical concern. However, it's of interest to me as I struggle on a daily basis to stay on top of everything that is going on in my studio. You also work on a variety of projects at the same time. How do you, literally, stay organized?

For example, I have to make a pile on my desk for each active project. This way I create a constant visual reminder of what is currently on my plate. I must physically get through each looming to-do pile in order to remove it from my life. I also make lots of lists—which are flatter versions of the same concept. I think people's working process reveals how one brings order to an inherently chaotic universe.

DB: I think that way, to some extent. I can compartmentalize various projects and keep a few balls in the air at the same time—some projects naturally evolve more slowly and incrementally than others—so it's nice to not have to rush those. (In the past, I suspect that ability might have been applied to my personal relationships as well, which is not always such a good thing.)

I also came to realize that the creativity and organizational skills of the folks who work in my studio or who I work with on music contribute a lot to my being able to keep multiple projects going.(52) Over the years, I've learned to delegate a little bit—I can trust that they'll keep on top of stuff and I don't have to keep it all in my head—what a relief!

RM: So, delegation and collaboration are key for you—that means a fair amount of people-management skills (which I lack). But what specific tools or strategies do you use? Scraps of paper, writing on your hands, paper or virtual calendars?

DB: All of the above. I had a diary/appointment book, then a few years ago I got a PDA that links to my computer calendar and addresses. I got pretty used to carrying it everywhere to put in appointments and reminders—it's not good for ideas and sketches though. For that I still carry a pencil and notebook. This past month, my office/studio (of three people) figured out how to have a calendar that automatically updates whenever anyone adds an appointment. I guess I'm pretty nerdy in that I can

(50) Who gave rise to the lazy aesthetic?

(51) See pp. 218–223.

(52) Multiple projects. Parallel projects. Parallel dimensions. Multiple universes. Parallel universes. Keeping many balls in the air.

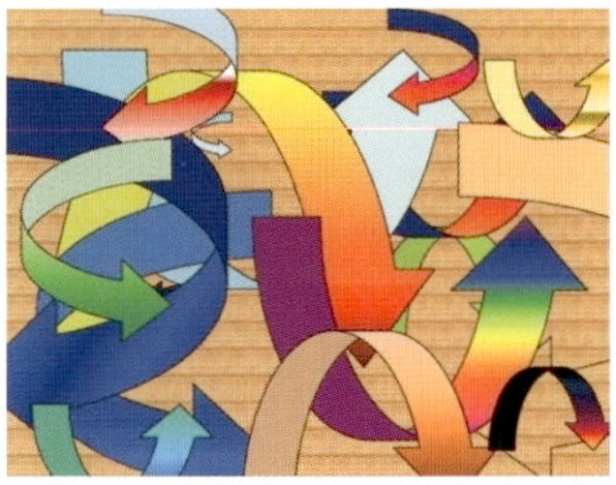

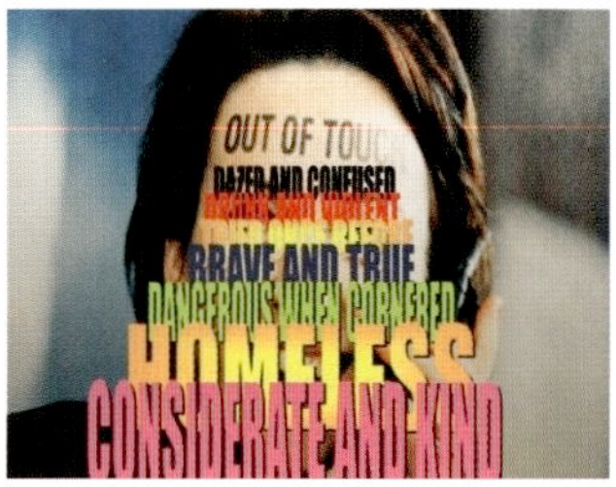

write an appointment down and then forget about it until the PDA or my calendar reminds me, and I can keep projects separate yet going simultaneously.

RM: I'm interested because I am constantly trying to develop a systematic framework for myself in which I hope to eventually find a fluid solution for staying on top of everything. I use exactly and only five kinds of pens.[53] I use an online calendar I can share with others in the studio, and I'm currently creating a calendar/to-do-list pad designed specifically for an end-user of one (me), but which will actually be published and available to the public. (Am I revealing how obsessive-compulsive I am?)[54]

DB: So what's the problem? It sounds like you're completely on top of this stuff. And yeah, I get a bit OCD at some stages, too. When I'm writing lyrics I use a number five mechanical pencil on metric graph paper—how's that! It's a system I've fallen into for keeping the ideas, verses, and choruses all separate and organized. Guess we all have our little systems.

IV. Failed Projects

RM: One topic I'd like to address—both because I find it interesting and also because it is often a topic that no one wants to publicly reveal—is failed projects. We learn from our mistakes—I have not failed to learn, and I have made many. What are some of your failed projects?

DB: A big one is a film based on *The Forest* [1988], the collaboration I did with Robert Wilson. It was to have been shot in Germany and would have had the same starting point as his stage interpretation, but it would have diverged from there. When we had a draft of the script and a budget, it turned out it would have been way too expensive for an art movie. There was another project—a mafia version of *Snow White* that never got realized. I may have chickened out, because I couldn't see how to solve some of the creative problems—so it's more unrealized than a failure.... And some of my recordings didn't have the lightness and sense of play that may have existed when I first wrote them—I overproduced some, I think. As much as I've learned from all of that, thinking about failed or unrealized projects is still a little painful and embarrassing—is it the same for you?

RM: That Snow White project sounds amazing! It's absolutely embarrassing—especially when failing publicly. I choose to show and share my work whenever and however possible from early on as opposed to developing in private and then waiting until I felt ready to debut—I don't think I'll ever feel ready for my flawless close-up. I hope to be continually embarrassed by my past work—not really embarrassed, but work that comes before a breakthrough or evolutionary development always seems not as good as the new stuff—I hope that will always be the case. Do you cringe when you look at any of your past work?

DB: Absolutely. There's some artwork that I prefer not to see and some songs that I hope never to hear again. Luckily, we keep going—and luckier still, we're sometimes forgiven for that crap work—or at least it seems that way. I read that someone did a study and found that people who succeed are those people who are willing to fail. When I'm asked if I miss the days at CBGB, I usually say I don't—which is true, but I do miss the possibility of failing in front of a relatively small number of people. That absolute passion and don't-give-a-shit attitude are a great combination.

V. Liquid Imagery

RM: Some of your work exists solely as digital information. This is most obviously true of recorded music (making a clear distinction from performed music), but the same idea applies to your ongoing PowerPoint project, *E.E.E.I.* [*Envisioning Emotional Epistemological Information*]. I don't know if you edition any of your PowerPoint pieces, but it would seem most logical, to me at least, to treat the commodification and distribution of digital artwork the same as recorded music. What do you think?[55]

DB: Good question—completely unresolved, too. The PowerPoint pieces I did played differently on every computer, depending on the speed of the CPU. So, I recorded them and made them into a DVD—sort of one digital form acting as a recorder of another digital form. Then—though in the past I'd tried to make my books as cheaply as possible and in limitless editions—for this project I thought, "What happens in the middle ground? What if this edition is not as limited (and expensive) as an artwork, but more expensive than a simple DVD or book?" Besides, I realized that, like any digital artwork, there was a good chance that the DVD would get ripped and that content would eventually be available free for anyone who was interested. So, we made an incredibly fancy DVD package in a limited edition of 3,000 [*Envisioning Emotional Epistemological Information* (2003)]. People who love, and can afford, the sensual and wacky visual experience of the lush book/package can have it. Others can get a copy of the DVD from their friends.

RM: Objects are mysterious vehicles that have personality and even mystical powers. Have you heard of the Serial Killer Sweater Experiment? (That's just what I call it, so perhaps not.)

Above left and right: David Byrne, *E.E.E.I.: Envisioning Emotional Epistemological Information*, 2003, stills from a PowerPoint lecture transferred to DVD. Left: *The Sea of Possibilities*. Right: *The End of Reason*.

[53] Pilot Precise V7 Rolling Ball Fine, black ink; Uniball Deluxe Fine, black ink; Sharpie Permanent Marker Fine Point, black ink; Pilot Precise V5 Rolling Ball Extra Fine, red ink; and Sharpie Permanent Marker Fine Point, red ink.

[54] .com/calendartodolistpadexample

[55] You can either create a lot for a little or a little for a lot. Depends on how much is in you and how much you want to share.

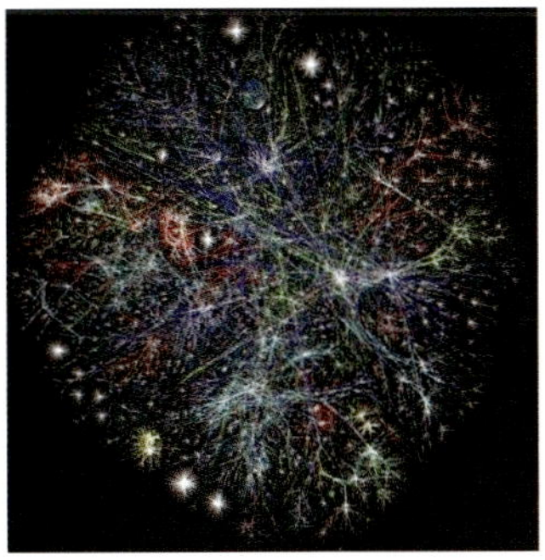

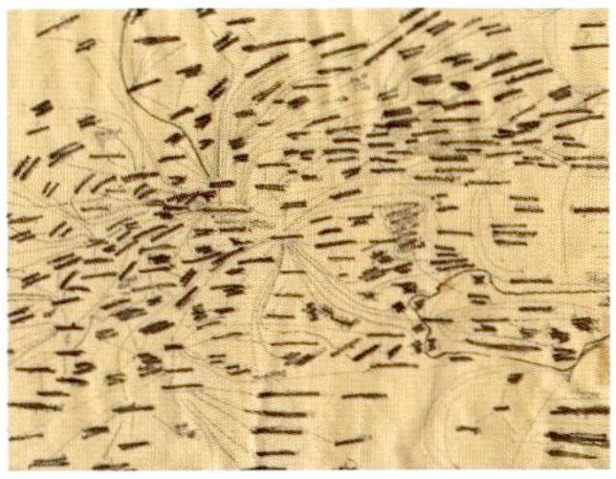

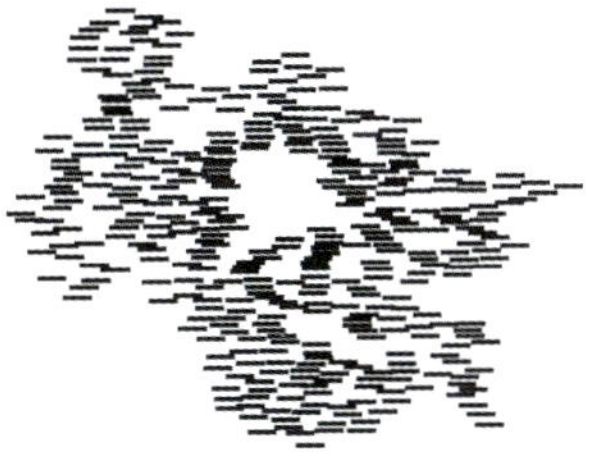

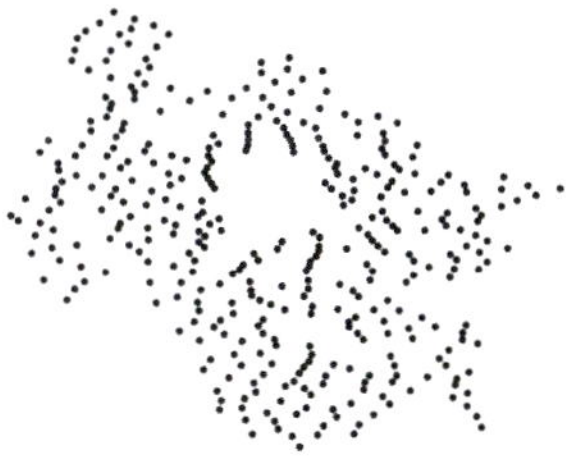

Essentially, people were offered money to put on a perfectly clean, new-looking sweater and most of them agreed. But then when they were told that the sweater had been worn by a serial killer, most could not bring themselves to wear it. A similar experiment was done when people were given a pen that they were told was used by Einstein, and then when they were told later that it was not, most were disappointed.

DB: Wow, those are great stories. You don't hear of people getting those kinds of attachments or superstitions about digital files.

A whole lot of what I do is digitized at one point or another. The music is recorded digitally these days, the photos I take are now all digital, DVDs, the PowerPoint pieces, the HD videos I've begun playing—even the bicycle diaries I've been turning into a book are written on a laptop. Only the drawings and sculptures—of which there are more and more—are truly physical. The books I think of as objects, but they are written and designed digitally—oh, I forgot—live performances are not digital.

RM: And do you try to edition those digital projects or do you assume they just leak out eventually?

DB: I assume that eventually someone, somehow, will access everything digitally—not just what I do, but everything in the world. Don't you think that eventually every movie, book, photo, piece of music will all be available online and/or digitally? It seems inevitable, and a little sad, because part of the information one gets in a book, for example, is how it feels and what it's made of, not just the words. At the same time I can't complain too loudly about all the cool stuff I can find online. This will mean that digitized information (images, books, movies, music) is all essentially worthless—in the sense that anyone can have it for free. You can edition and artificially limit signed objects, but I guess you have to also make the edition an object that is somehow different from what someone can print out on their home computer, burn on a DVD or CD burner, or listen to/watch online. The object, in that sense, is back.

Your paintings are unique, but with videos it becomes an issue—I don't know of anyone who's fetishized a videocassette. I just read an interview with Warhol where he said he didn't care if people made copies of his work as long as they didn't sign it. [56]

RM: I had made some videos, because they were the best medium for the expression of some simple ideas I had. They were eventually compiled on a DVD by a company in Japan and sold together for about $30 in an open edition. I liked the idea of packaging the videos together and making it the same price as any other DVD. [57] They are no more special because they're art. I would have no problem if they were copied and distributed. I actually don't make final pieces in digital form, even though the creation of digital files is a step in the process of making my work. I can't feel files and therefore I can't put much faith in them. And for the most part, art operates under a faith-based system. My mother told me that when I first encountered TV, I sat in front of the screen and outstretched my arms while grasping at the air complaining that I could not feel it while asking, "Where is it?"

DB: Some of your paintings with their deep layers of silkscreened images remind me of images from science or the Internet and digital technologies. It's pretty nice to imagine there might be a shape or pattern there—sort of a pattern without content.

RM: *Networking Is a Skill* [1998] is a piece that I did that specifically relates to brain network images. The information patterns are based on mapping everyone I know and my network of relationships to them—but that was ten years ago. Now I feel like I'm trying to make a twenty-first-century *Broadway Boogie Woogie*. [58]

DB: Funny that Mondrian's New York work seems almost African—like African textiles—Mr. Anal Retentive ended up making art that is almost funky. Wikipedia describes them as cartographic, and says that he worked on these paintings "until his hands blistered, he cried, and he became sick."

Above left: Orbital Teapot Blog, "How the Universe Looks Like a Brain," Thursday, October 25, 2007, http://orbitalteapot.blogspot.com/2007/10/how-universe-looks-like-brain.html. Above center: Ryan McGinness, *Networking Is a Skill (Study)*, 1998, ink on kraft paper, 20 x 33 in.

Above right: *Networking Is a Skill*, 1998, digital files, dimensions variable. Information patterns based on a mapping of everyone Ryan knows and the network of his relationship to them.

[56] .com/andywarholerasershield

[57] *Video Happiness*. The rights to publish this DVD expired long ago, but there is a company in Japan that is still making these.

[58] .com/broadwayboogiewoogie

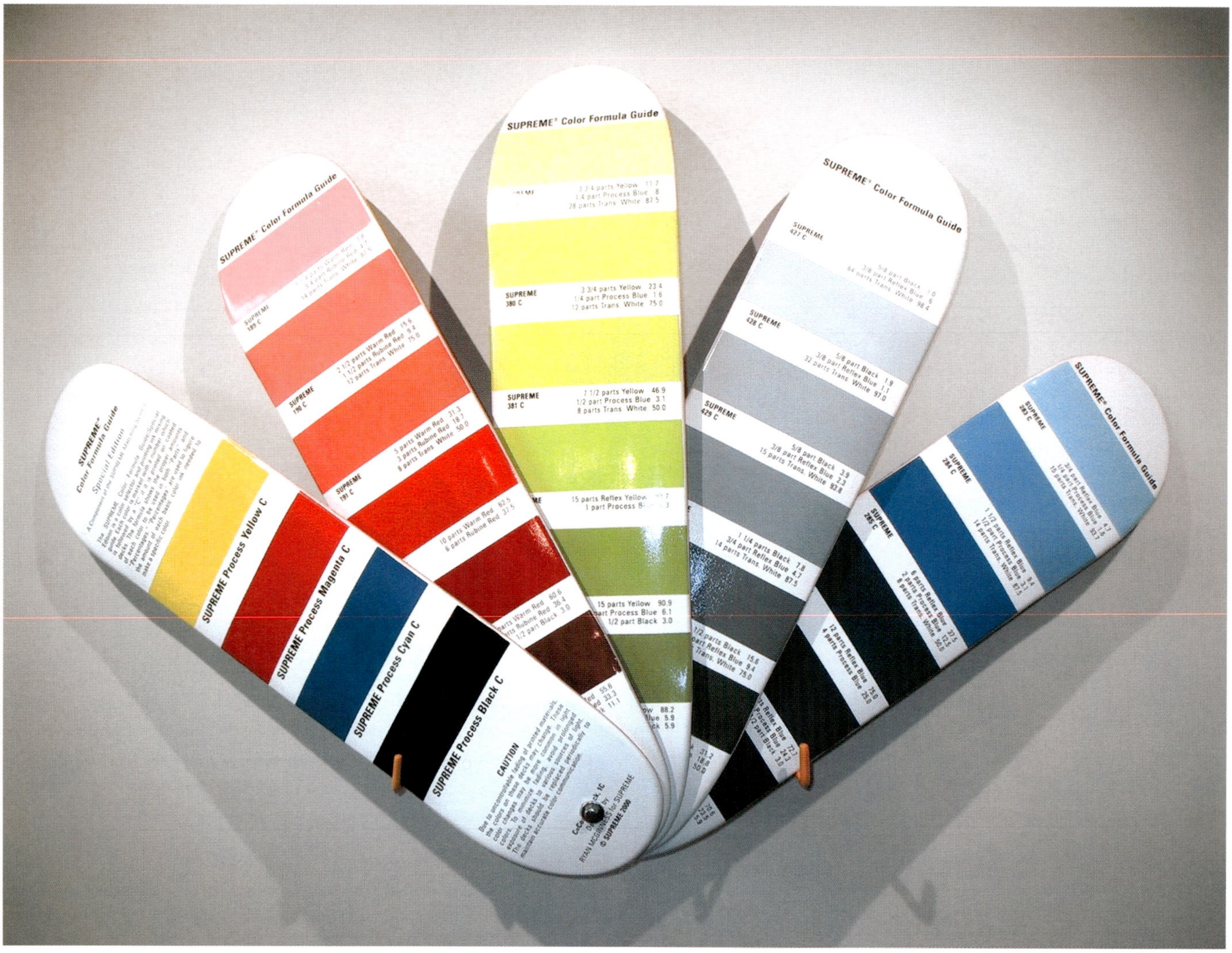

Supreme Color Formula Guide, 2000, oil on wood skateboards with steel hardware, 32 x 8 in. each, edition of 500. Published by Supreme, New York.

The Look of Looks, or, Ryan McGinness's Ontology of Color

Jonathan T. D. Neil

Those attending to the arc of Ryan McGinness's career will no doubt note that something striking happened in 2003 with an installation the artist titled *Worlds Within Worlds*. There, at Deitch Project's Grand Street gallery, McGinness transformed the back room into a rudimentary maze of mirrored walls. The mirrors added several layers of visual complexity to the audience's otherwise easily navigable path through the maze, whose literally self-reflective infinite regress was punctuated by white vinyl discs punched with designs familiar from McGinness's graphic vocabulary. Once inside the maze, the audience, quite simply, got a load of itself, and the experience could be quite disorienting. At the gallery's perimeter, large black wall drawings rose above the maze's roughly eight-foot-high dimension and so offered the tease of orientation, but only a tease. As the photographic documentation of the show demonstrates, even these putative landmarks began to fragment and dissolve in the upper regions of the maze's mise-en-abîme. (59)

What was striking about *Worlds Within Worlds*, however, was not this profusion of reflectance and the audience's immersion within its proliferating environment of graphic patternings. What was striking was what wasn't there, what was, in one sense, wholly absent from the scene, and that was color.

This is striking because *Worlds Within Worlds* is perhaps the first moment that McGinness evacuates color from the audience's experience of one of his installations, and does so in a purposeful manner. (There remains a series of signature color works as part of *Worlds Within Worlds*, but these serve more as appetizers to the main course of the maze.) It should be all the more striking to the historically attentive viewer, because in the year 2000, arguably the moment of McGinness's advancement to his current artistic idiom,[1] the artist practically announced his unique interest in color with his *Supreme Color Formula Guide* (2000), a series of skateboard decks arranged and painted to mimic a fan book of color print swatches like those that litter the desks of graphic and interior designers.

Prior to 2000, though obviously in a thrall to the visual lexicon of pattern and design, McGinness worked with two conventions that he quickly dropped from his visual vocabulary after that year: the photograph and the outline. Pieces such as *Interior View* (1999) and *Tug of War* (1999) exhibit McGinness's adherence to the use of drawing as a means to describe the contours of figures within an otherwise undifferentiated field of color (this is particularly the case with the "figures" of furniture against the undifferentiated yellow of *Interior View*),(60) or to the appropriation of photographic imagery, especially when human bodies and visages were involved, as a way to achieve similar effects when compositions grew more complex. But in 2000, photographic imagery all but disappears from the finished work, and the drawing convention of outlining—actually more like modeling through contour—undergoes a transformation, whereby the outline grows into the object or figure itself by hypostatizing contour while eschewing any kind of modeling. It is from this point forward that, as McGinness so aptly puts it in the title of his earliest catalogue (not coincidentally dating from 1999), "flatness is god."[2] (61)

If it is important that this sacrifice of photographic imagery and the negation of any kind of modeling is roughly coincident with McGinness's production of the *Supreme Color Formula Guide*, then it would seem logical to ask, what role might the *Guide* play in this transition from the "modeled" work (which I take to include both the photographic and drawing conventions) to the "flat" work? Pushing further we could ask, what is it about *color* in general that changed—or changed in—McGinness's enterprise? In conversation, McGinness admits that he does not necessarily think too hard about color, or at least he does not think about it in any systematic way, as if working with a *theory* of color in hand. From a practical standpoint, McGinness's approach to color is intuitive, in the sense that working over a long period of time with Golden-brand acrylic paints and Pantone color books, he has come to internalize something of this readymade color system. Nevertheless, this intuitive way of working does not preclude his usage of color from being theoretical. For one of the things that the *Supreme Color Formula Guide* points to is McGinness's readiness to let color stand or fall on its own, which is to say that here color is freed from mimesis or locality, from the necessity of "coloring" objects or imagery as they would appear in the world at large.

Let's take a moment with the *Guide*. The decks, an edition of 500, were commissioned by James Jebbia of Supreme, a skateboard shop with stores in New York, Los Angeles, and across Japan. Of the five decks, the top one shows the standard CMYK or process colors: cyan, magenta, yellow, and black. Within a standard color printing process, nearly any other color can be produced out of

(59) .com/worldswithinworlds
.com/miseenabime

(60) .com/interiorview

(61) Incidentally, the title for my book *Flatnessisgod* came from a passage in a Tom Wolfe book, *The Painted Word*.

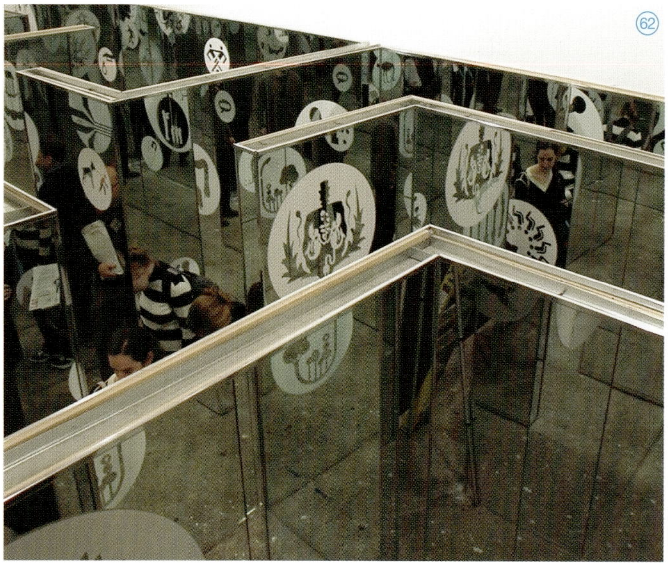

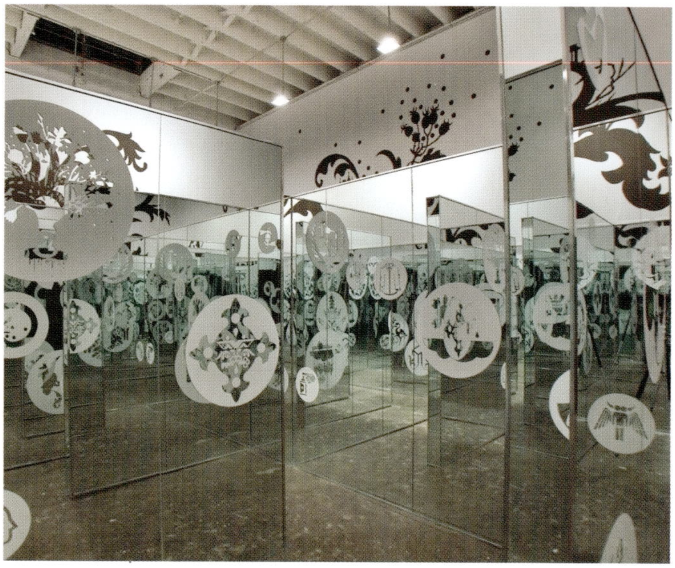

a proportioned combination of these four and their derivatives, as the remaining decks demonstrate with their respective color "families." Regarding each deck's design, McGinness explains that "[I] originally thought to make them Benjamin Moore paint chip samples like you get at Janovic [a local New York paint store], but I thought that Pantone was closer to my heart,"[3] which is to say, closer to McGinness's training as a graphic designer, and further away from the language of classical painting or, more generally, conventional artistic practice.

The ease with which McGinness moves back and forth across the increasingly thin boundary between fine art and graphic or commercial design is a commonplace observation in writing on his work, with the standard take being that McGinness adopts the language of graphic design, which is consistently in service to advertising and branding of one sort or another, and elevates, translates, or transposes it into the field or locale of fine art and aesthetics.[4] Whereas McGinness's work easily stands to the fine-art side of the art/design divide, McGinness's *Supreme Color Formula Guide* seems to straddle that boundary as something of a curious hybrid. McGinness's "design" for the Supreme decks is essentially an appropriation, an adoption of a design matrix that is the Pantone "look"—the formula breakdowns, reference keys, and even font and graphic layouts that the Pantone corporation uses for its own formula guides. Thus the *Guide* layers together fine art (a limited-editioned work produced by a recognized artist); a consumer product (a skateboard deck sold under the auspices of a respected skate shop); and a design matrix (a proprietary color matching system targeted for the printing and graphic design industries).

We have seen this strategy before, most saliently in the work of Jasper Johns, whose flags, targets, and number series slowed the conceptual trajectory of the readymade paradigm and turned it into an option by which to appropriate pictorial structures of a more resolutely graphic character. But, of course, none of this activity would be conceivable without Marcel Duchamp, who, we should note, had something very interesting to say about "art making" and color just around the time that Johns's work began to reverberate throughout the art world:

> *Now what is making? Making something is choosing a tube of blue, a tube of red, putting some of it on the palette, and always choosing the quality of the blue, the quality of the red, and always choosing the place to put it on the canvas, it's always choosing. So in order to choose, you can use tubes of paint, you can use brushes, but you can also use a ready-made thing, made either mechanically or by the hand of another man, even, if you want, and appropriate it, since it's you who chose it.*[5]

Duchamp is right of course, but contemporaneous developments within the history of what we might as well call the production of industrialized color would render his comment a bit reductive.

Nineteen sixty-two, after all, marked the incorporation of Pantone Inc., and the following year saw the introduction of the first printer's edition of the Pantone matching system, with subsequent editions, formulas, and systems following rapidly thereafter.[6] It is tempting to claim that Duchamp's identification of the tube of paint with the readymade (and thus, by extension, all painting as a simple act of nomination) takes into account something like the emergence of the Pantone system. What is the latter if not an entire industry designed to distill color down to a simple act of choosing? (63) But the appearance of the "palette" in Duchamp's statement, and his recognition that every painter must choose the "quality of the blue" or the "quality of the red," opens a space in which one may make some distinctions as to color's total subsumption under the weight of the readymade. For example, in noting how the color palette is inherently tied to color mixture, and that

Worlds Within Worlds, mirror maze installation, mixed media, dimensions variable. Installation views, 2003, Deitch Projects, New York.

(62) When I was seven years old, I chipped my front tooth in a fun house mirror maze at an amusement park. I still have a cap on that tooth.

(63) Or to tame and classify the wild. To turn the subjective into the objective so that there can be no dissent.

mixture to color theory's articulation and manifestation in the color circle, David Batchelor explains how such an understanding of color is "based on a geometry of triangulation and a grammar of complementarity" that underwrites color's traditional subservience to the world of representation and mimesis.[7] But, Batchelor continues, the color *system* that is Pantone, "divorces color from conventional color theory and turns *every* color into a readymade. It promises autonomy for color… that of each color from every other color, that of color from the dictates of color theory, and that of color from the register of representation."[8] This difference between a color *theory* and a color *system*, then, would seem to accord members of the latter the status of *things* out in the world, whereas the former is more concerned with how we see those things to begin with. If color theory is a theory of *vision*, then a color system, by rights, is a system of *objects*. (64)

This is an important distinction, one which I want to turn in two directions: the first turn takes us back to the role the *Guide* plays in McGinness's drop of both modeling and the photographic image from his visual vocabulary; the second turn takes us forward to the question of color's *ontology*—that is, to what color actually is—and how one way of posing this question bears upon McGinness's evacuation of color from the installation of *Worlds Within Worlds*.

As with most intersections of autonomy and aesthetics, the autonomy of color remains a high modernist idea. Ever since Kandinsky likened seeing colors oozing from their tubes to an encounter with "strange beings" who could teach him the new language of pure painting, color—freed from imitation and, in Kandinsky's case, in the service of a "spiritual" abstraction—has seemingly had a life all its own.[9] But the way to that high modernist liberation of color had been prepared by the divisionism of Georges Seurat, itself at once a positivist renovation of how a painting may be "seen" and a mechanization of the very act of painting, a kind of surrender of the artist to the logic of the assembly line, where all that is required is the application of "dots" of color, straight from the tube as it were. Furthermore, the possibility of divisionism itself was secured by a different moment of mechanization, that of oil paint manufacture and its distribution through the vehicle of tin tubes, which began earlier, in the 1830s, at roughly the same moment that Talbot, Daguerre, and Niépce were finding ways to "fix" images of the world using only chemistry and light.[10]

Though the early industrialization of artists' oil paints and the invention of photography may be entirely coincidental, their effect upon artistic practice, and modernist artistic strategies, in particular, were not. "What is called modernism in painting," writes Thierry de Duve, "is perhaps nothing but the history of the obstinate… resistance that painters opposed to the division of labor with which industrialization was threatening them. Competition with photography was the most obvious threat; competition with the pigment industry was a more insidious but no less crucial one and, by the way, linked to the first."[11] We can see this linkage in the way that early photography made a quick claim to the documentation of landscapes, to which the practitioners of *plein-air* painting and impressionism also directed their eyes, but only once premixed and easily portable tubes of paint freed them from the confines of the studio and the alchemy of pigments that took place therein.

On the impressionists' canvases, color came to displace the mimesis enacted by photography. Like photography, painting would become a means of recording light, but it would lay bare the process of that recording. Vision itself, rather than what vision held in its sights, became painting's charge. With divisionism, that process became equally mechanized. The brushstroke itself, the means of making lines, of establishing limits and contour, was similarly displaced, now by the single daub of color transferred directly to the canvas from the tube. And at the root of these two displacements lay the industrialization of color manufacture—the sole hue in a single tube of paint.

Though Pantone's entrance into this history of color manufacture comes 40 years prior to McGinness's own displacement of photography and modeling, we can now see how the *Supreme Color Formula Guide* serves as something of a symbolic marker that announces the replay of these historical shifts within the trajectory of McGinness's own artistic development. (65) I am not claiming here that the *Guide* is responsible for such displacements, that there is some sort of cause and effect relationship between the *Guide*'s appearance and the concomitant disappearance of photographic imagery and modeling from McGinness's subsequent work. But I do think that the *Guide*, and what it has to show about color, offers a way of thinking through, or conceiving, McGinness's breakthrough to the "flat" work of the last eight years.

What do the *Supreme Color Formula Guide* and, by extension, the Pantone system have to say about the ontology of color? This is a philosophical problem and one with a history too long to detail here.[12] Nevertheless, we can trace its basic contours by asking a series of albeit overly simplified questions: Are colors properties of objects in the world, or do they arise from our perception? In other words, are colors objective or subjective, real or illusory? If there were no human beings around, would the world still "have" color? Or do the colors we see—the reds and the blues, the vermilions and the ultramarines—belong only to us? (66)

From a certain perspective, the color "Supreme 190C," for example, just is that color for everyone because it is the color that is constituted by certain percentages of "Warm Red," "Rubine Red," and "Trans. White," which themselves must be constituted by certain percentages of the original CMYK pigments. In other words, these colors are reducible to the formula used to produce them. This is different than discussing how any particular color appears, or how we might experience color, or attempting to describe color in any other set of color terms. What that particular Supreme Color *is*, is just the formula that produced it.[13]

(64) See p. 66.

(65) .com/photographicimageryexamples

(66) See Q 205 on p. 285.

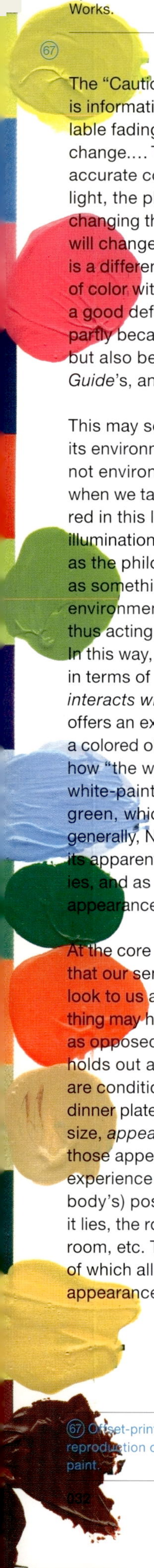

(67)

The "Caution" note included at the bottom of the *Guide*'s top deck is informative in this respect as well. It reads, "Due to uncontrollable fading of printed materials, the colors on these decks may change.... The decks should be replaced periodically to maintain accurate color communication." Due to the decks' exposure to light, the physical makeup of the pigments will change, thereby changing the colors' appearances. Just how the color pigments will change, how much they will fade, "yellow," or what have you, is a different question altogether. But when considering the place of color with respect to the *Guide*, the fact of the change itself is a good defense for its presentation of a *realist* ontology of color, partly because it is the effect or outcome of a physical process, but also because the change occurs within and as part of the *Guide*'s, and thus our own, external environment.

This may sound paradoxical at first. If color is dependent upon its environment, doesn't this effect how it appears to us? Are not environmental conditions exactly the things that we invoke when we talk about having certain experiences of color—i.e. this red in this light, or that yellow under those specific conditions of illumination? The way out of this paradox is to conceive of color as the philosopher Alva Noë does, as *enactive*, which is to say, as something that is affected by and at the same time affects its environment: "To perceive something as red is to perceive it as thus acting on and capable of acting on its visible environment. In this way, the enactive view is an account of what it is to be red in terms of the *phenomenally salient ways* in which the object *interacts with* its environment."[14] None other than Josef Albers offers an example of such a "phenomenally salient" way in which a colored object interacts with its environment when he describes how "the white ceilings of houses surrounded by lawns or the white-painted eaves of a roof on a sunny day appear in bright green, which is reflected from the grass on the ground."[15] More generally, Noë explains that "the color a thing appears to have, like its apparent shape and size, varies as our relation to the thing varies, and as its relation to its environment changes. Colors, like all appearances, are genuine features of the environment."[16]

At the core of Noë's enactive approach to perception is the notion that our sensorimotor skills and awareness inform the way things look to us and enable us to reconcile the myriad appearances a thing may have with what that thing actually is. Those appearances, as opposed to simply qualifying as subjective experiences, Noë holds out as *real*, as "things" themselves, which belong to, and are conditioned by, their environment. For example, just as a dinner plate, which I know is circular and of a specific, measurable size, *appears* elliptical, and smaller, from certain perspectives, those appearances are not reducible to some subjective interior experience of my own, but are rather a function of my (and my body's) position with respect to the plate, the table upon which it lies, the room in which we are situated, the lighting within that room, etc. These are real, physical conditions of the environment, of which all the attending "appearances" are a part, even the appearance of color. (68)

The mirror maze of McGinness's *Worlds Within Worlds* would seem to offer us a demonstration of just this kind of "reality of appearances" through an amplification of those appearances' number and kind. It is an unorthodox environment to be sure, but what we see inside the maze is a profusion of spaces punctuated, or interrupted, by the white vinyl discs, which, combined with the mirrors, produce a kind of instantaneous juxtaposition of multiple different "looks." Standing in one place and looking straight forward at a single disc offers a standard, verifiable view: this disc is circular, of such and such a size, with this particular figure punched through it serving as a device by which to distinguish it from the "look" of other discs. Looking just past this disc to one side or another, then, we see an infinite profusion of other discs, and as we move about the space, these "looks" are multiplied again and again.

All of this is captured in a short video that McGinness shot as a means of documenting the installation. In it we see a sequence when McGinness zooms in just to the right of his own reflection and finds ever more discs "in the distance." The infinite regress forges an artificial extension of space into which the discs recede, and though this recession is illusory, the various "appearances" of the discs (the slivers, the ellipses, the circles; in other words, the "looks") are not—they are real features of this specific environment.

Now, according to the enactive approach to perception, color does not occupy a position analogous to shape and size. "If colors, in contrast with shapes, are ways things look, then it is not possible to explain our experience of the actual color of a thing in terms of looks, in the way that we are able to explain the experience of the actual shape of a thing in terms of our experience of how it looks," which is to say, "colors, unlike shapes, it would seem, are themselves looks. This would seem to make apparent colors *the looks of looks*."[17] Noë admits that understanding colors as the "looks of looks" is probably "incoherent," but it is not all that far off from his conclusion that "we experience [colors] as imbued with possibilities of variation, as possessing degrees of freedom in a space of phenomenal possibilities."[18] Though, for example, the specific red that I see in my glass of wine will change as the conditions of its environment change, which includes my position with respect to it and a number of other variables, I understand all of these "reds" to belong to a single regime of color possibilities. From my experience, which is to say, from my sensorimotor confrontations with glasses of red wine in the past, I understand how the red of the wine should look in innumerable numbers of configurations, including those which I have yet to actually experience. Thus within my understanding of the red of the wine there exists a horizon of expectations and discernments that form a tacit field in which I am able to navigate all the possibilities of this particular red.

From a certain perspective, is this not the experience we are offered in the mirrored maze of *Worlds Within Worlds*? For while the maze evacuates any and all color from the viewer's experience, its

(67) Offset-printed four-color (CMYK) ink reproduction of digital scans of acrylic paint.

(68) .com/theappearanceofcolor

infinite regress would seem to produce that particular structure of color experience we can now conceive of as the "look of looks," as an experience "imbued with the possibilities of variation," and one which secures those looks as members of a reality quite independent of our own subjective impressions. Of course, within McGinness's installation these variations are played out upon the size and shape of the white vinyl discs, but the proliferation of those "looks" within the maze's fun-house environment offers the viewer that necessary multiplication of looks, the "looks of looks," which simulates the realist ontology of color, even when color of any kind is nowhere to be seen.

Notes

1. One hesitates to apply the more familiar and pedantic "mature style" here given that it is inevitable that McGinness will advance through many more and different stages before he is through, none of which may be any more or less "mature" than the next.
2. See Ryan McGinness, *Flatnessisgod* (New York: RSUB, 1999).
3. Ryan McGinness, interview with Takashi Murakami on Japanese radio, 2001, (http://ryanmcginness.com/mp3/murakami&mcginness.mp3).
4. Most recently see A. A. Bronson's "From Low to High and Back Again: Zen and the Art of Being in Consumer Culture," in Ryan McGinness, *Installationview* (New York: Rizzoli, 2005). But the basis for this argument has been given its most articulate and robust form by Arthur Danto; see his *The Transfiguration of the Commonplace* (Cambridge: Harvard University Press, 1981).
5. Marcel Duchamp, interview by Georges Charbonnier, radio interviews, RTF, 1961, quoted in Thierry de Duve, *Kant after Duchamp* (Cambridge and New York: The MIT Press, 1996), 162.
6. *International Directory of Company Histories* (New York: St. James Press, 2003), vol. 53.
7. David Batchelor, *Chromophobia* (London: Reaktion Books, 2000), 105.
8. Ibid. Italics added.
9. See Wassily Kandinsky, "Reminiscences," in *Kandinsky, Complete Writings on Art*, ed. Kenneth C. Lindsay and Peter Vergo (Boston: G. K. Hall & Co., 1982), 1:371–2, and *On the Spiritual in Art* in the same volume.
10. Joseph Nicéphore Niépce is widely regarded as having made the first photograph in 1826 and so may be named as its first true "inventor," but William Henry Fox Talbot and Louis-Jacques Mandé Daguerre turned the taking of photographs into *photography* by developing the process and the market for the new invention. See *Classic Essays on Photography*, ed. Alan Trachtenberg (New Haven: Leete's Island Books, 1980) and Abigail Solomon-Godeau, *Photography at the Dock* (Minneapolis: Minnesota University Press, 1991). There is however new research that claims the earliest photographic processes—photogenic drawing, a type of photogram—date to the 1790s. See Randy Kennedy, "An Image Is a Mystery for Photo Detectives," *New York Times*, April 17, 2008.
11. Thierry de Duve, *Kant after Duchamp*, 176.
12. See *Readings on Color, Vol. 1: The Philosophy of Color*, ed. Alex Byrne and David Hilbert (Cambridge and New York: The MIT Press, 1997).
13. This is an albeit very specific and perhaps idiosyncratic application of the modal-realist approach developed by Hilary Putnam and Saul Kripke, an approach that is meant to "fix" references for certain "natural-kind" terms, such as "water" or "gold." Christopher Norris describes the situation thus: the modal-realist approach "aims to re-establish fixity of reference for natural-kind terms like 'water' and 'gold' by supposing that those items were first picked out by a designative act of naming… despite various—sometimes radical—shifts in our range of scientifically informed identifying criteria. Thus *water* went from something like 'transparent, odourless, (normally) liquid substance that freezes or boils at certain temperatures, falls as rain, fills up lakes, possesses certain cleansing properties', etc. to substance 'with the distinctive molecular structure $H_2$0'." See Christopher Norris, *Philosophy of Language and the Challenge to Scientific Realism* (London and New York: Routledge, 2004), 20. See also Saul Kripke, *Naming and Necessity* (Oxford: Basil Blackwell, 1980), and Hilary Putnam, *Mind, Language and Reality* (Cambridge and New York: Cambridge University Press, 1975).
14. Alva Noë, *Action in Perception* (Cambridge and New York: The MIT Press, 2004), 143.
15. Josef Albers, *Interaction of Color* (New Haven and London: Yale University Press, 1963), 45.
16. Noë, *Action in Perception*, 144.
17. Ibid, 133. Italics added.
18. Ibid, 137.

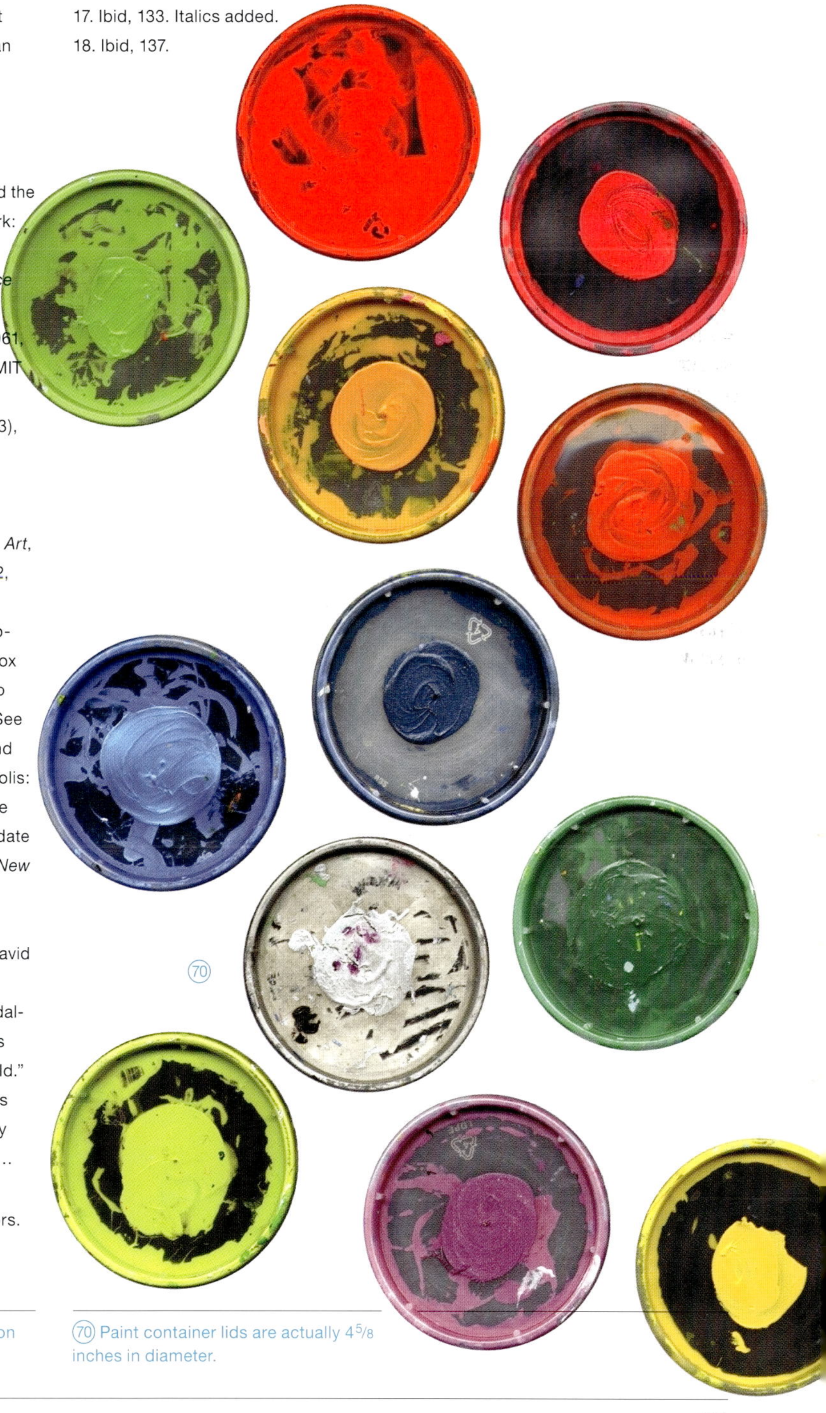

(70)

Following pages: A few of the hundreds of plastic containers of acrylic paint kept around the studio for many reasons, one of which is that they are used as guides to re-create specific colors. (Lids pictured on this page). (69)

(69) In this way, there is no color system in the studio. There are no labels, numbers, or naming systems for colors. The colors themselves are the description of the colors.

(70) Paint container lids are actually 4 5/8 inches in diameter.

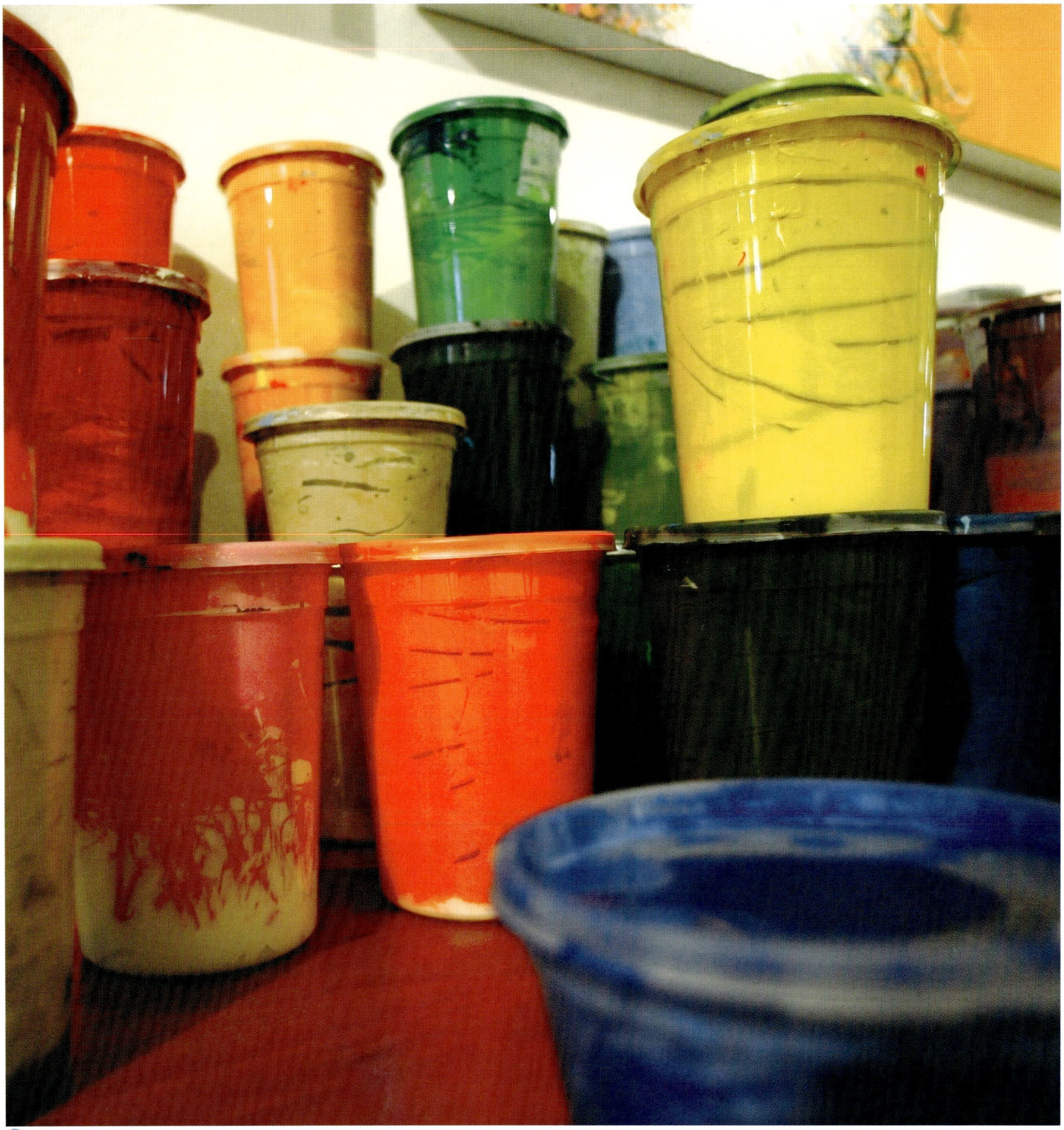

(71)

(71) The dried paint under the lids should always be cleaned in order to create a tighter seal.

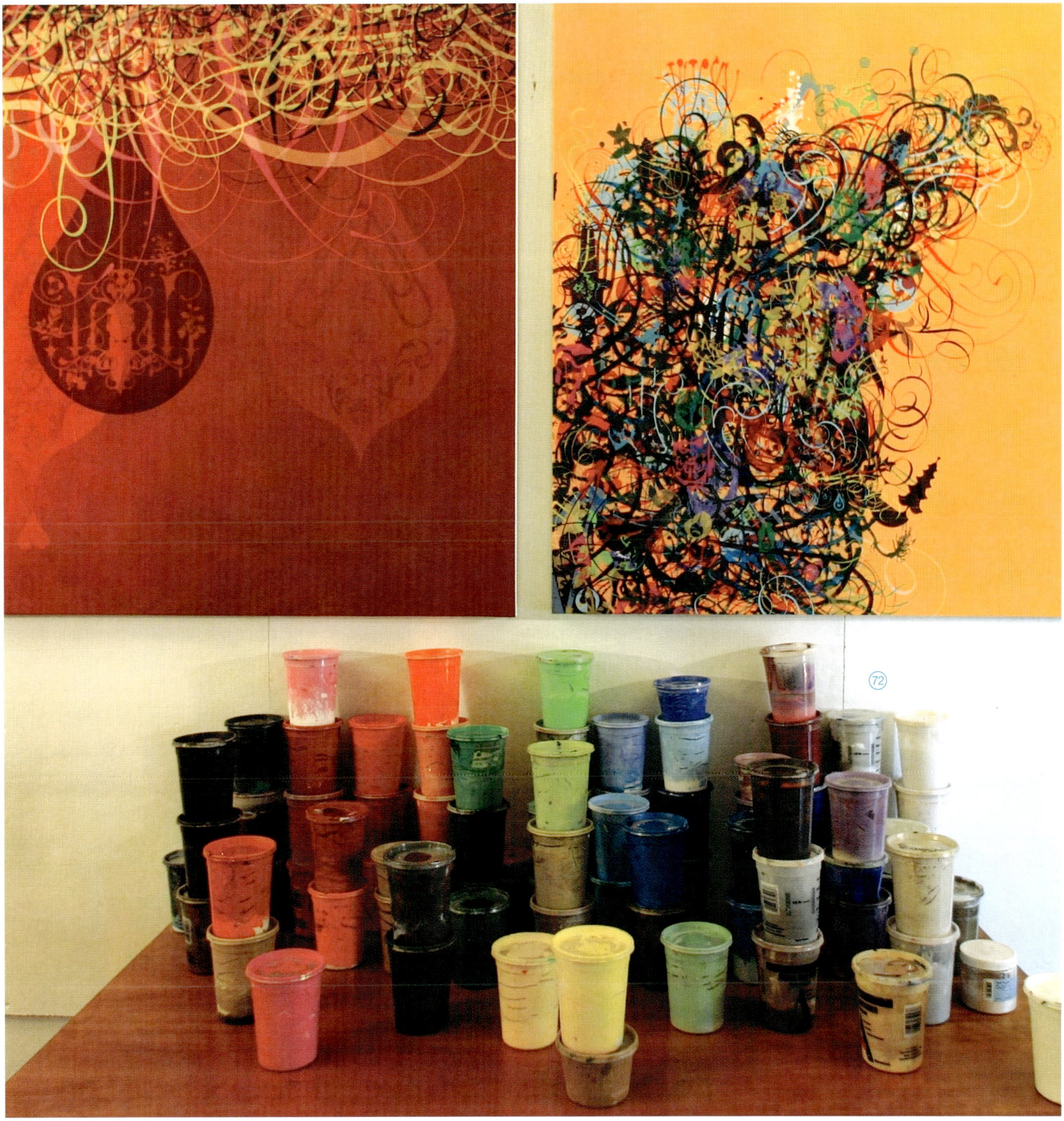

72

Studio view, 2006. Paintings on wall, from left: *Three Cheers for the Haute Couture Hippy* (detail), 2006, acrylic on wood panel, 48 x 48 in., *Richard of York Gave Battle in Vain* (detail), 2006, acrylic on wood panel, 48 x 48 in. 73 74

72 These paints have been set aside to create a palette for a specific painting.

73 R.O.Y.G.B.I.V.

74 The paintings shown in this photo are not so much details as they are cropped.

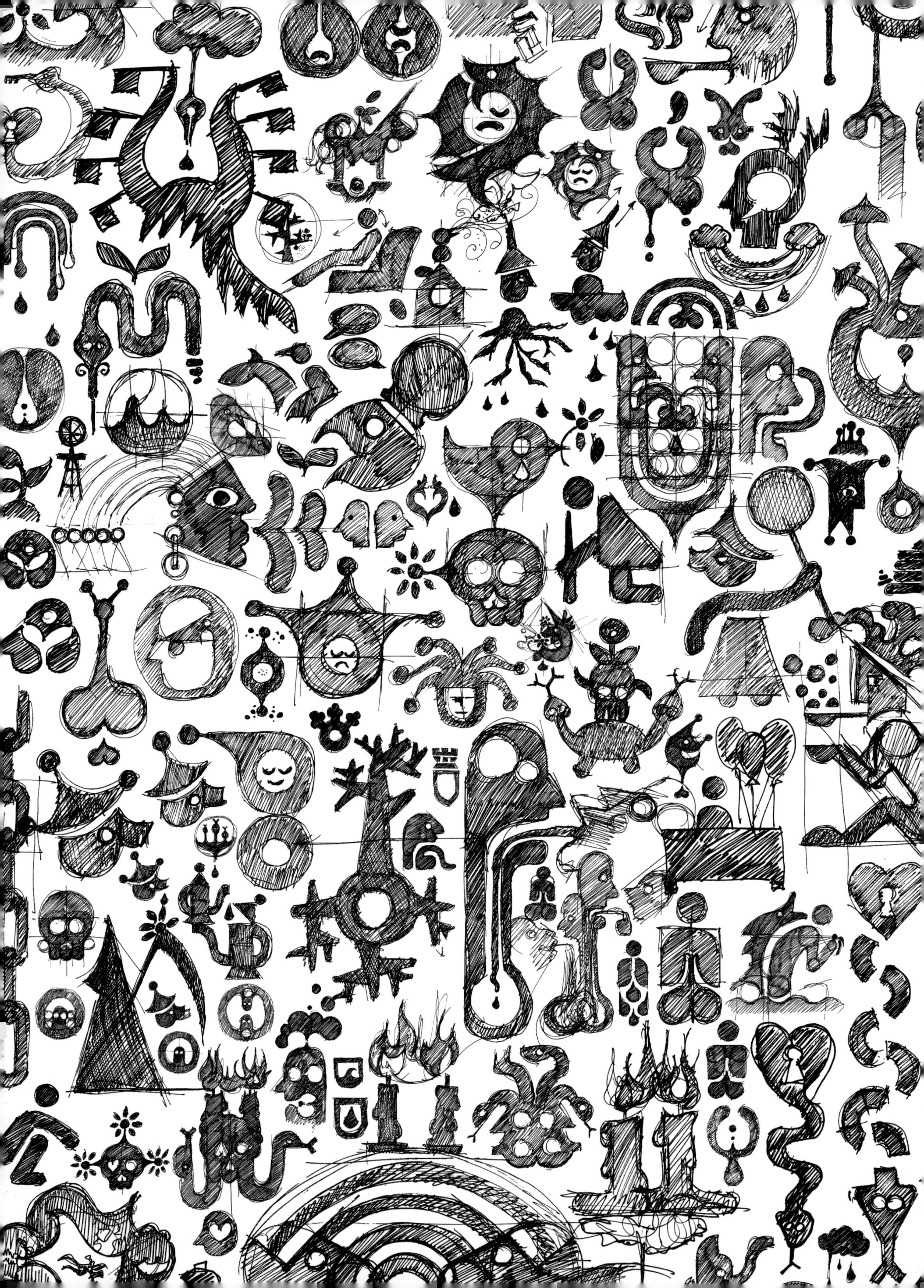

All of Ryan's works begin as drawings, which are made with a fine-tip Pilot Precise V7 Rolling Ball pen in a Mead composition notebook; these sketchbooks are kept neatly on a shelf in the studio. Each is filled with process sketches—iconographic images, usually one to a page, permutations of which cover the next dozen pages or so until the idea is clear. The resulting process sketch is scanned into Photoshop as a black-and-white bitmap, which is then saved as a tiff file. It is not a literal version of the scanned process sketch that finds its way into the slick imagery populating Ryan's prints, installations, editions, sculptures, and paintings. After this scanned sketch is placed into Illustrator, tinted gray, and locked as a background, it is used as a sort of template—a guide—so a new vector drawing can be created on top of it. Bézier curves, which were originally used in 60s automobile design, give these final vector drawings a perfect, smooth line in a digital format that is infinitely modifiable and reusable.

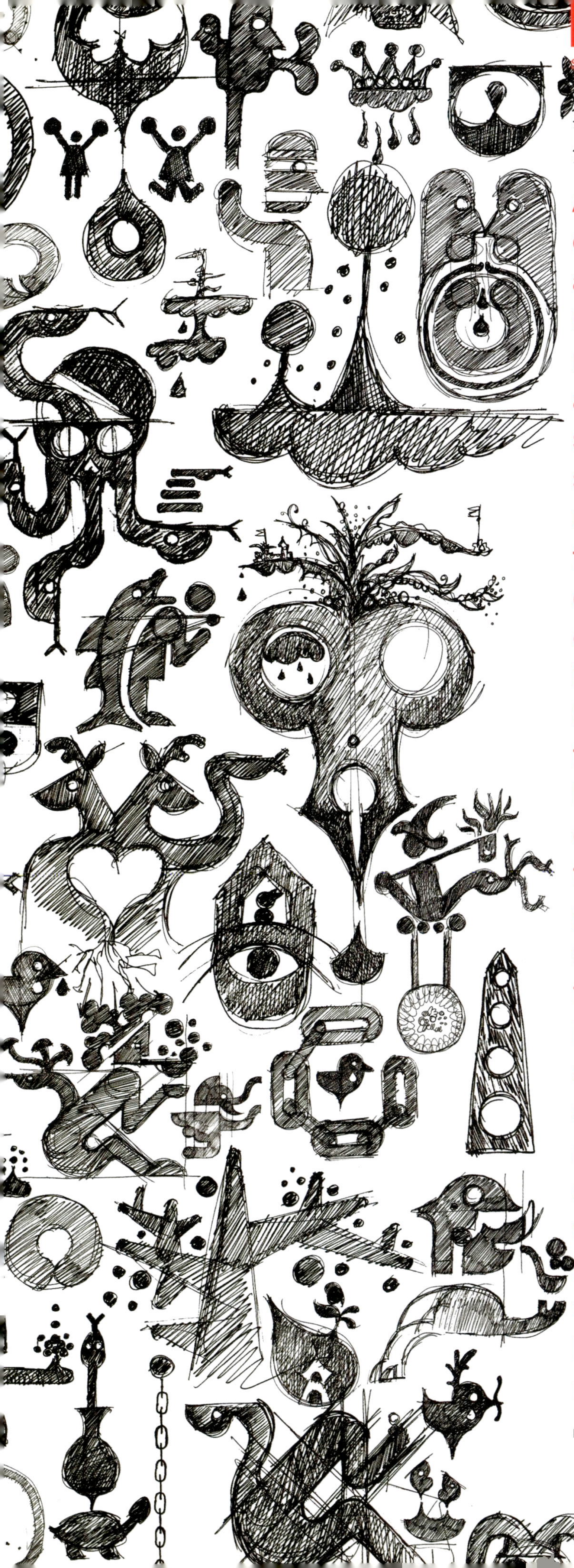

Miscellaneous process sketches, 2002–2007, ink on paper, dimensions vary.

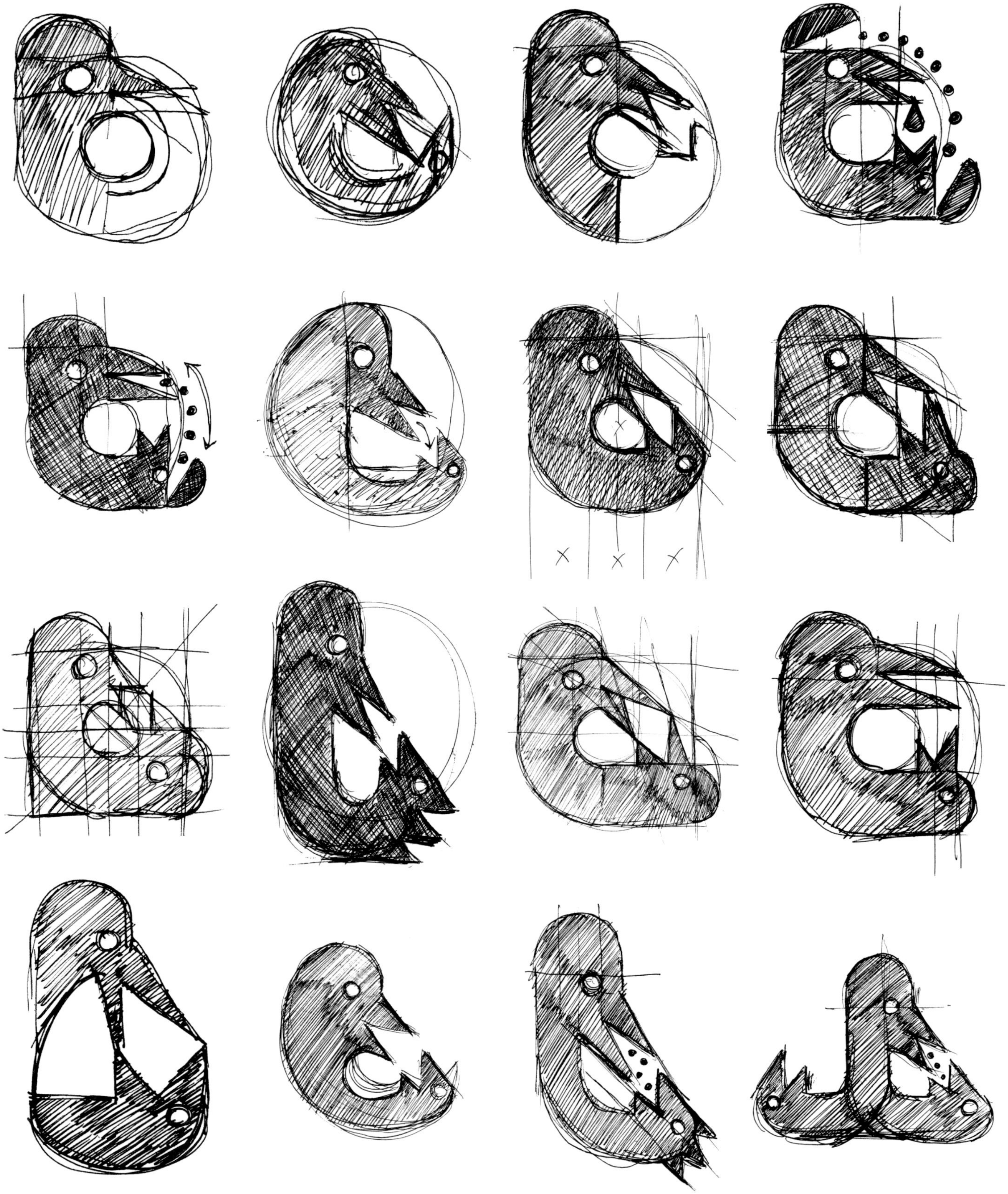

Above and opposite page: *Untitled (Feeding)*, 2005.

Above: Process sketches, ink on paper, dimensions vary. Development upper left to bottom right. Opposite page: Final vector drawings, digital files.

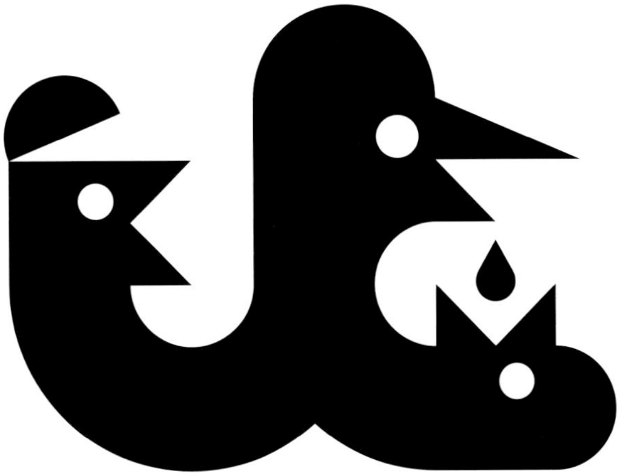

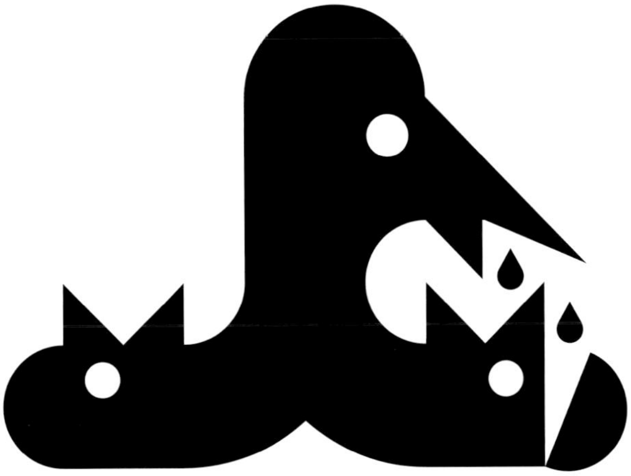

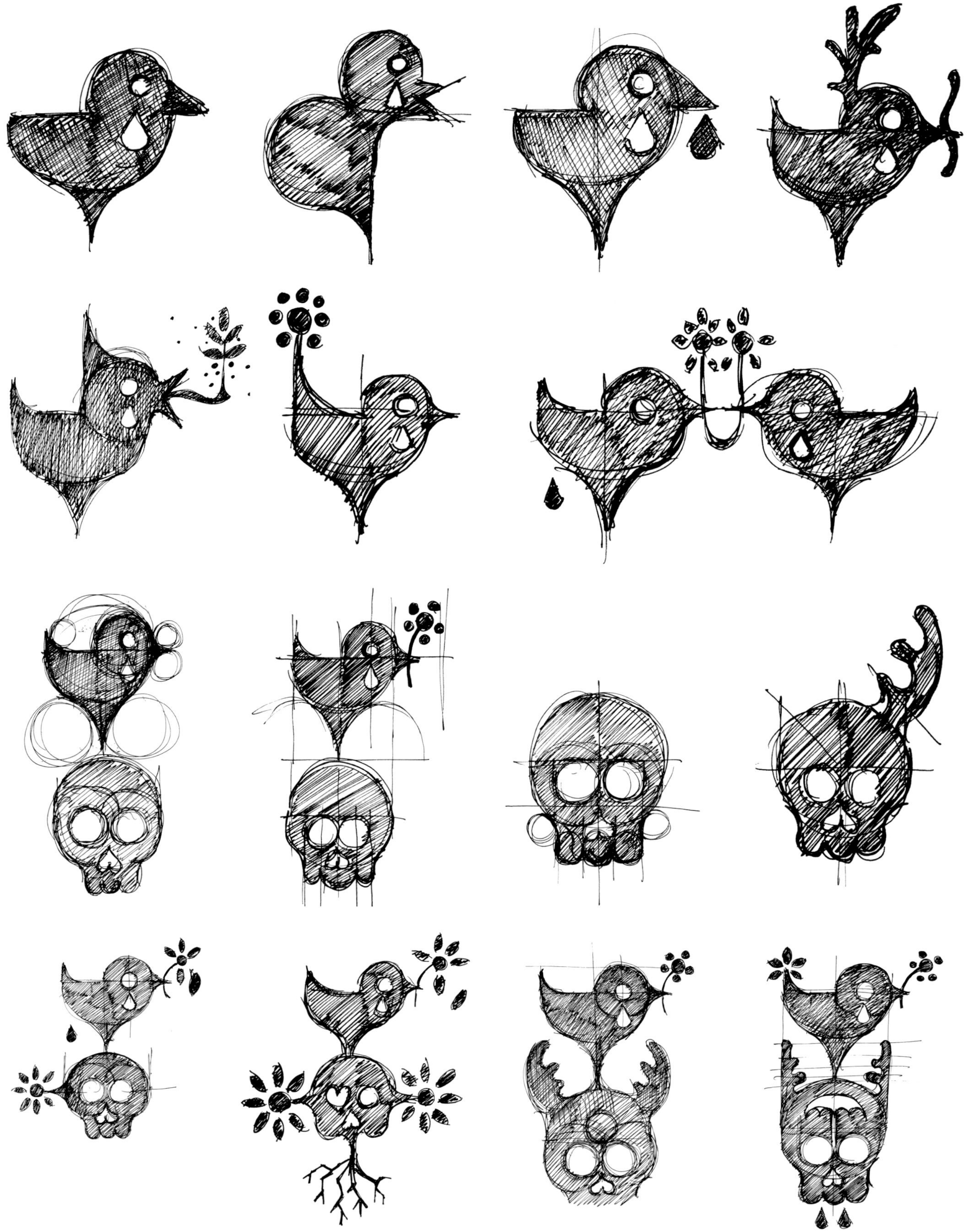

Above and opposite page: *Untitled (Birds & Skull)*, 2005.

Above: Process sketches, ink on paper, dimensions vary. Development upper left to bottom right. Opposite page: Final vector drawings, digital files.

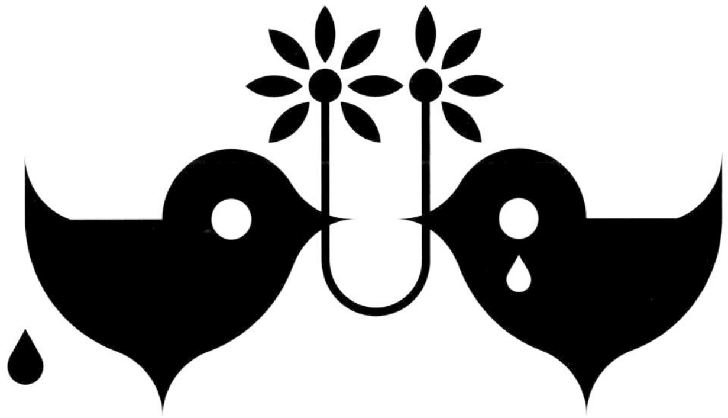

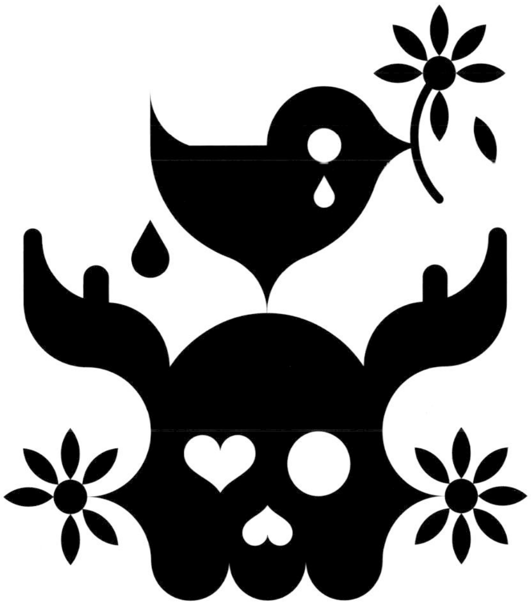

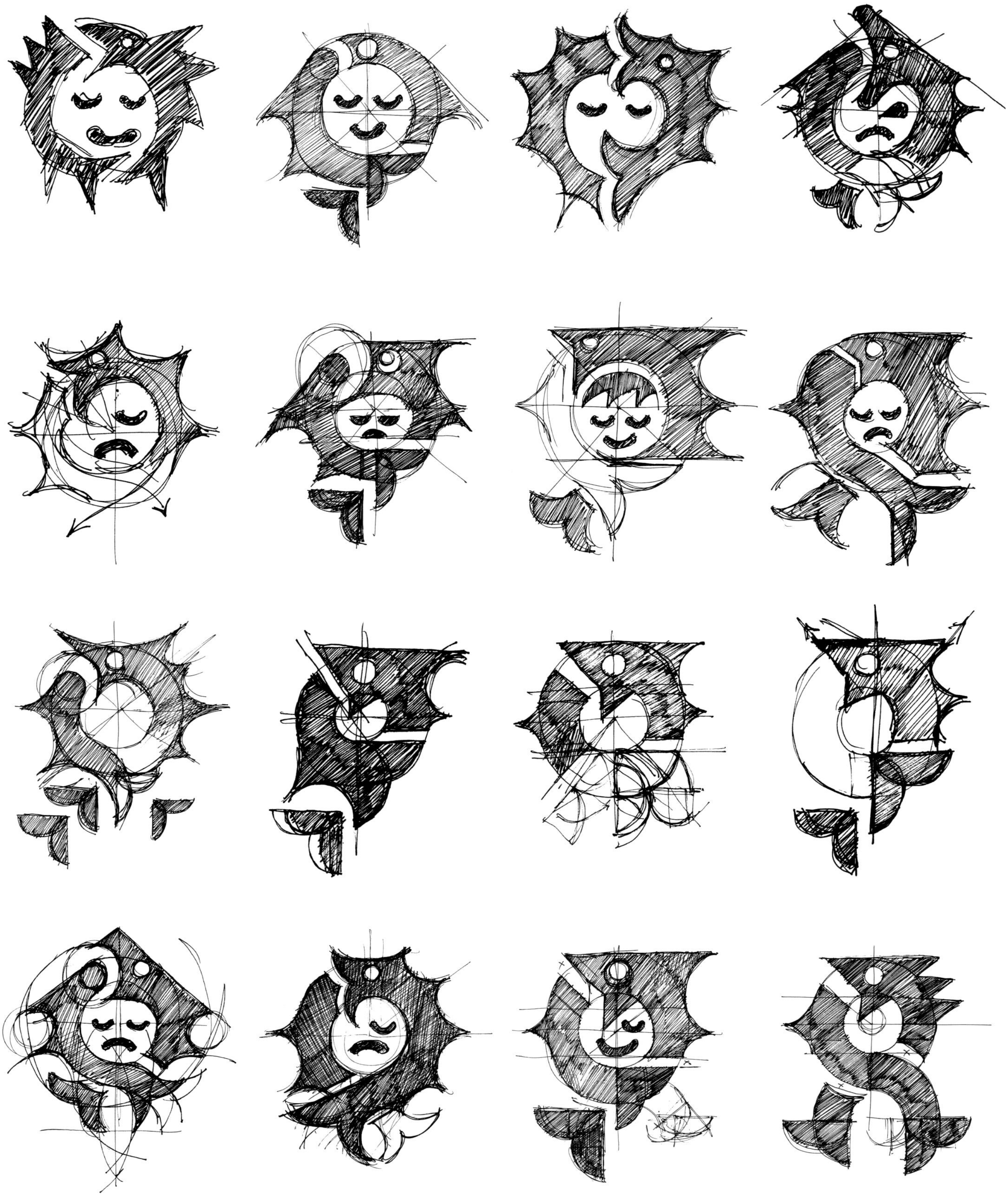

Above and opposite page: *Untitled (Fishwrap)*, 2005.

Above: Process sketches, ink on paper, dimensions vary. Development upper left to bottom right. Opposite page: Final vector drawings, digital files.

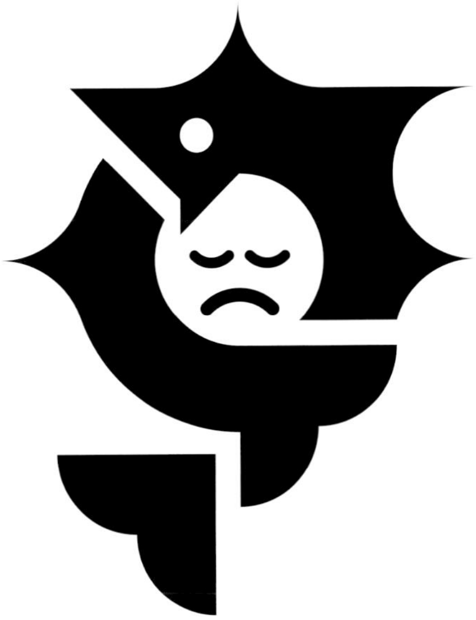

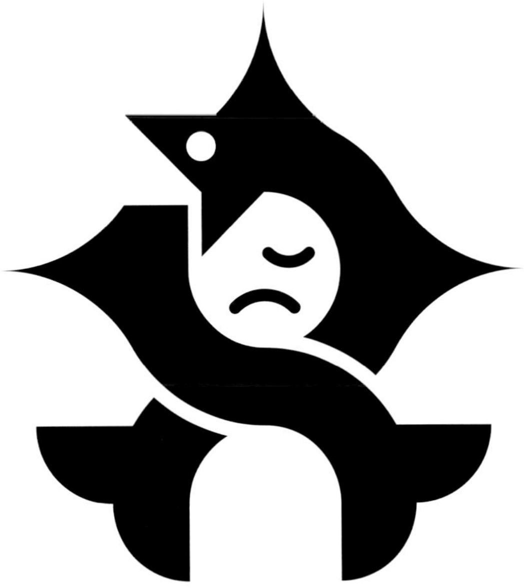

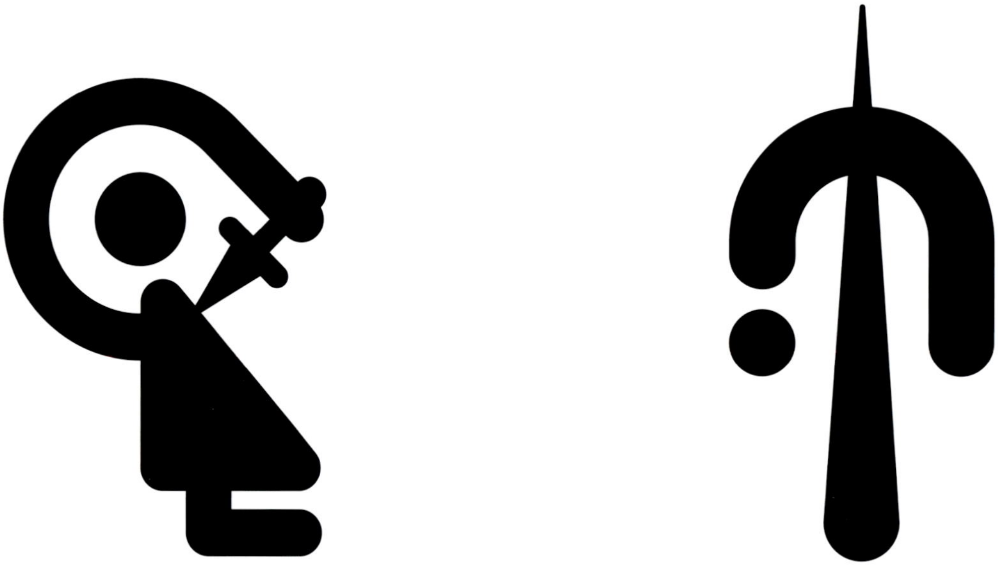

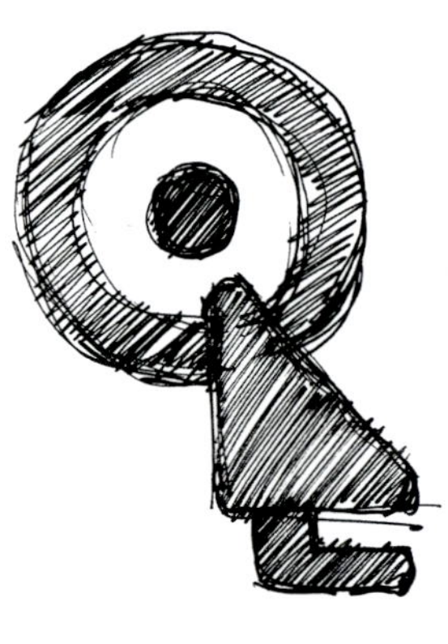

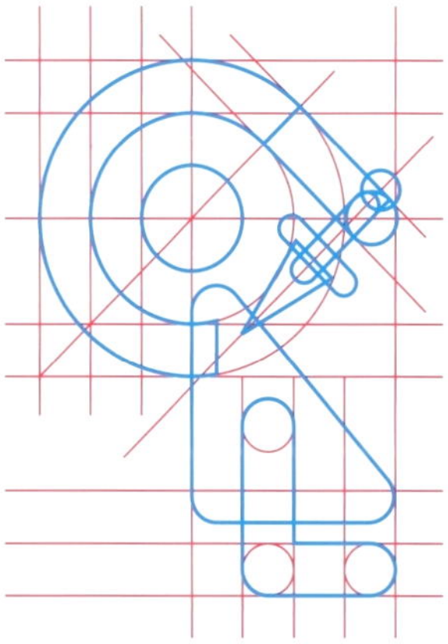

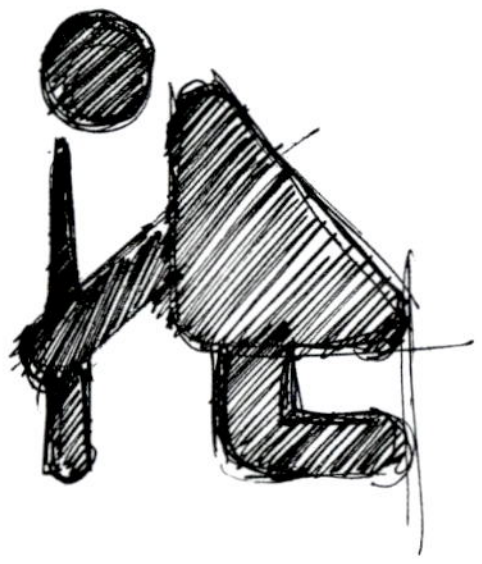

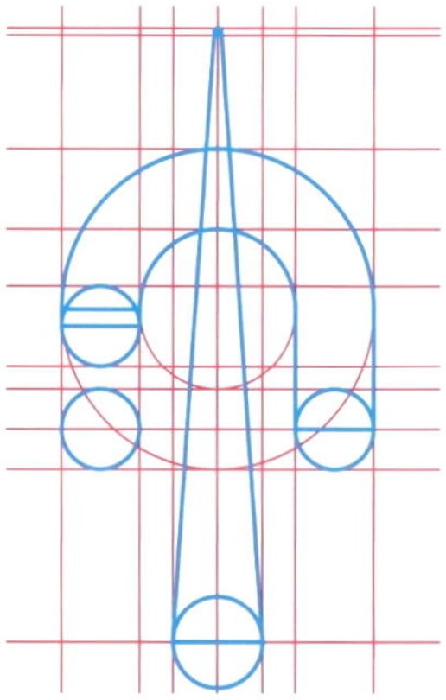

Untitled (Back Stabber & Suicide), 2007.
The process sketch, (lower left), is scanned and used as a template for the vector process drawing, (lower right), which reveals the underlying geometry for the final vector drawing, (top).

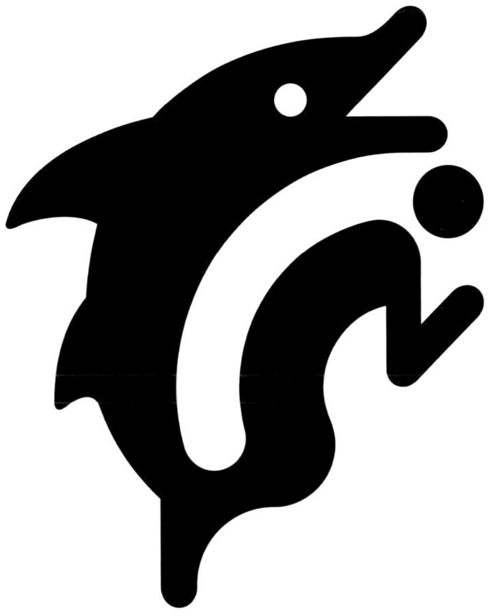

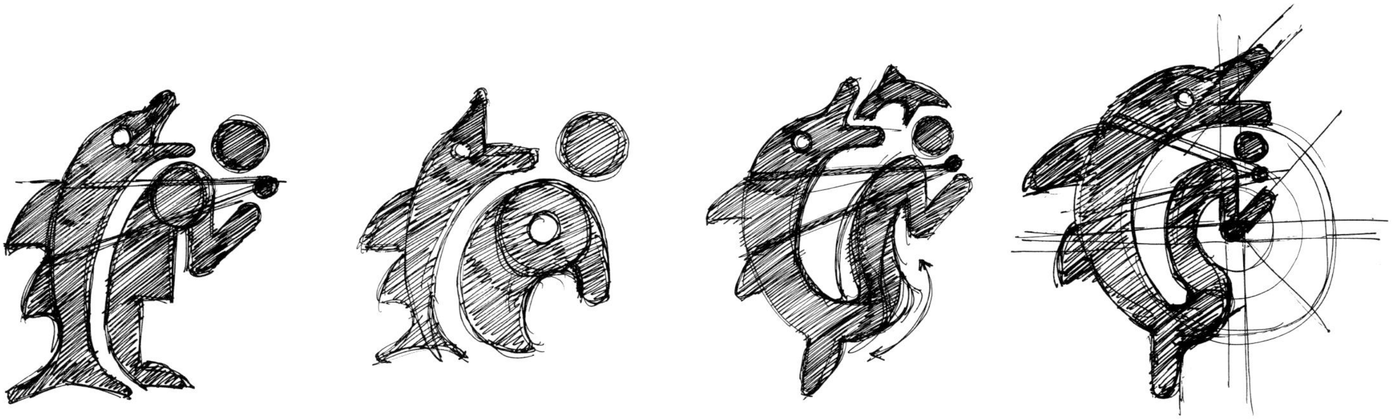

Untitled (Fish on Back), 2007.

Top: Final vector drawing, digital file. Above: Process sketches, ink on paper, dimensions vary. Development left to right.

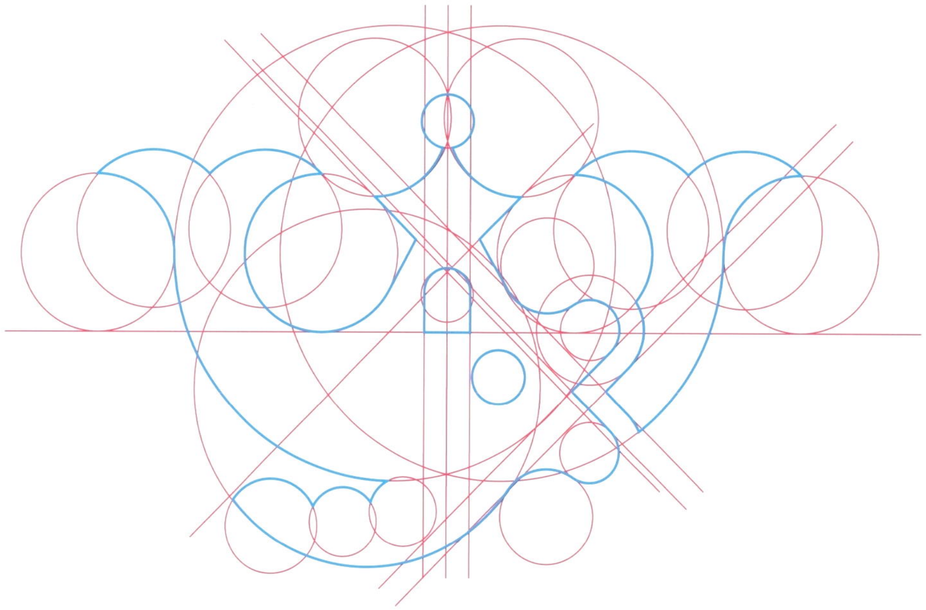

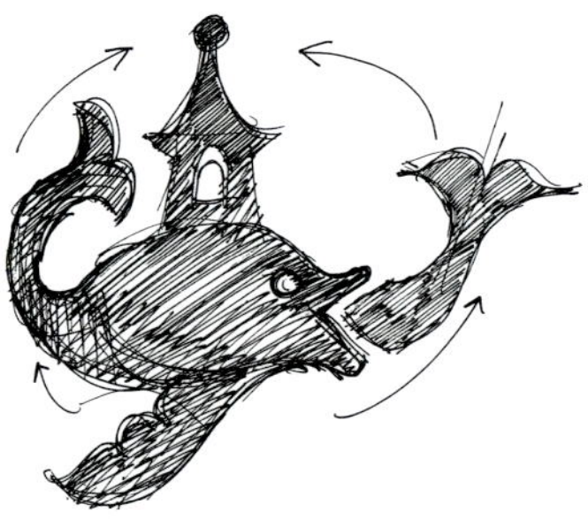

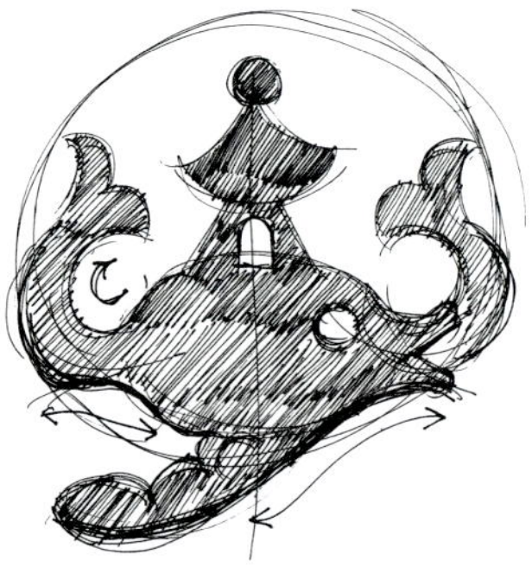

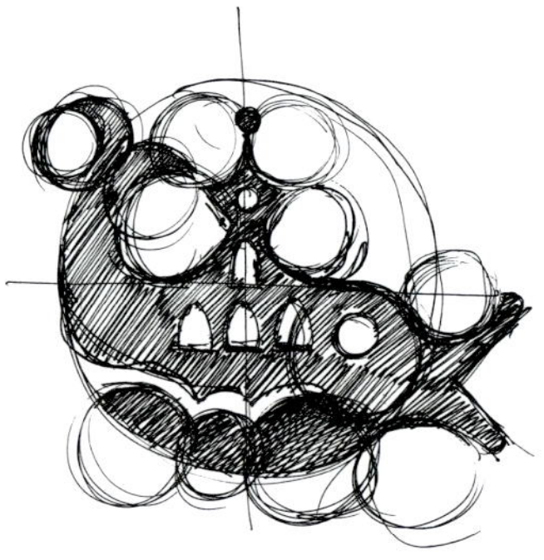

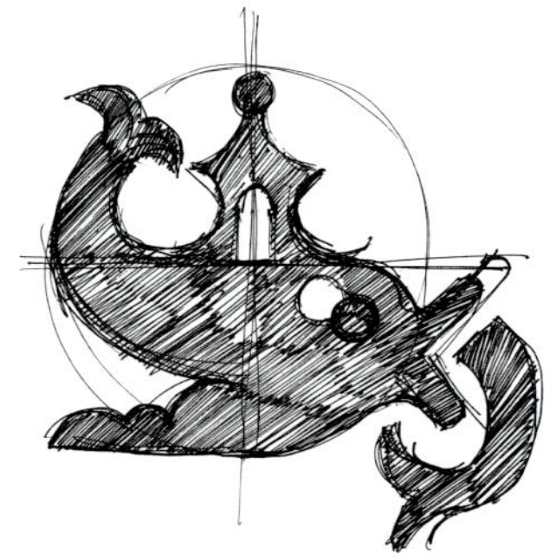

Above and opposite page: *Untitled (Fish Eat Fish)*, 2005.

Top: Vector process drawing, digital file. Above and opposite page: Process sketches, ink on paper, dimensions vary. Development left to right.

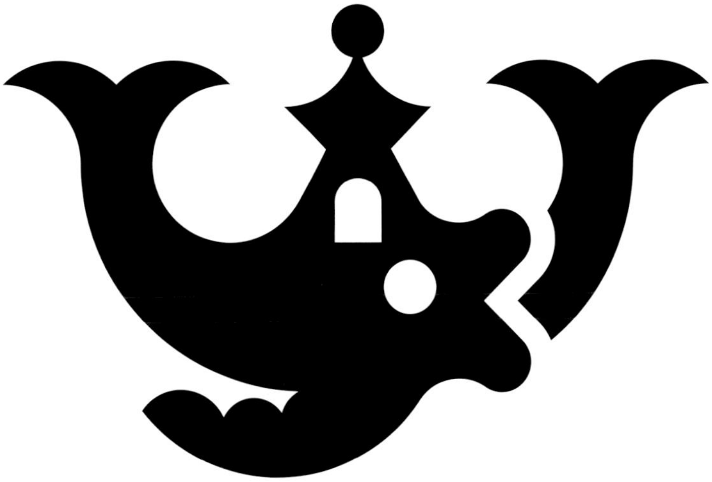

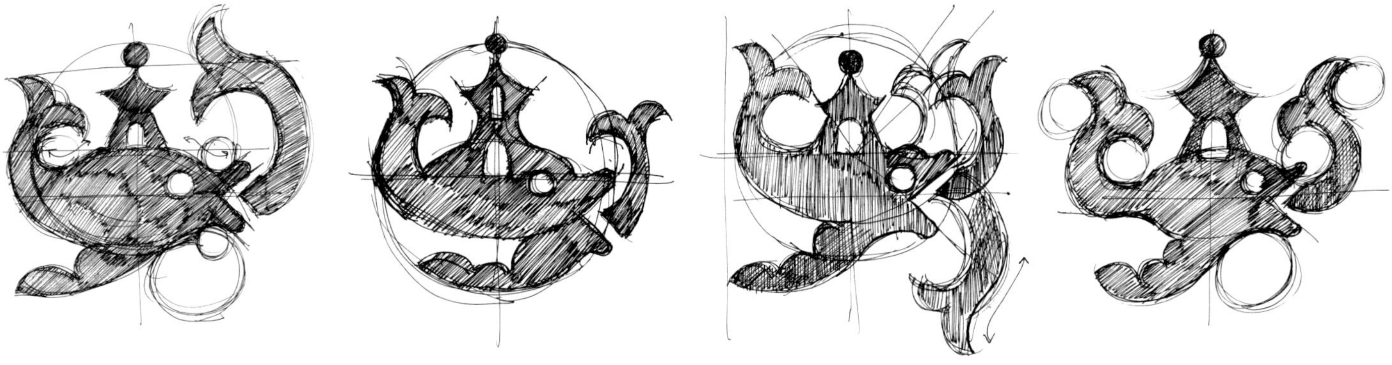

Top: Final vector drawing, digital file.

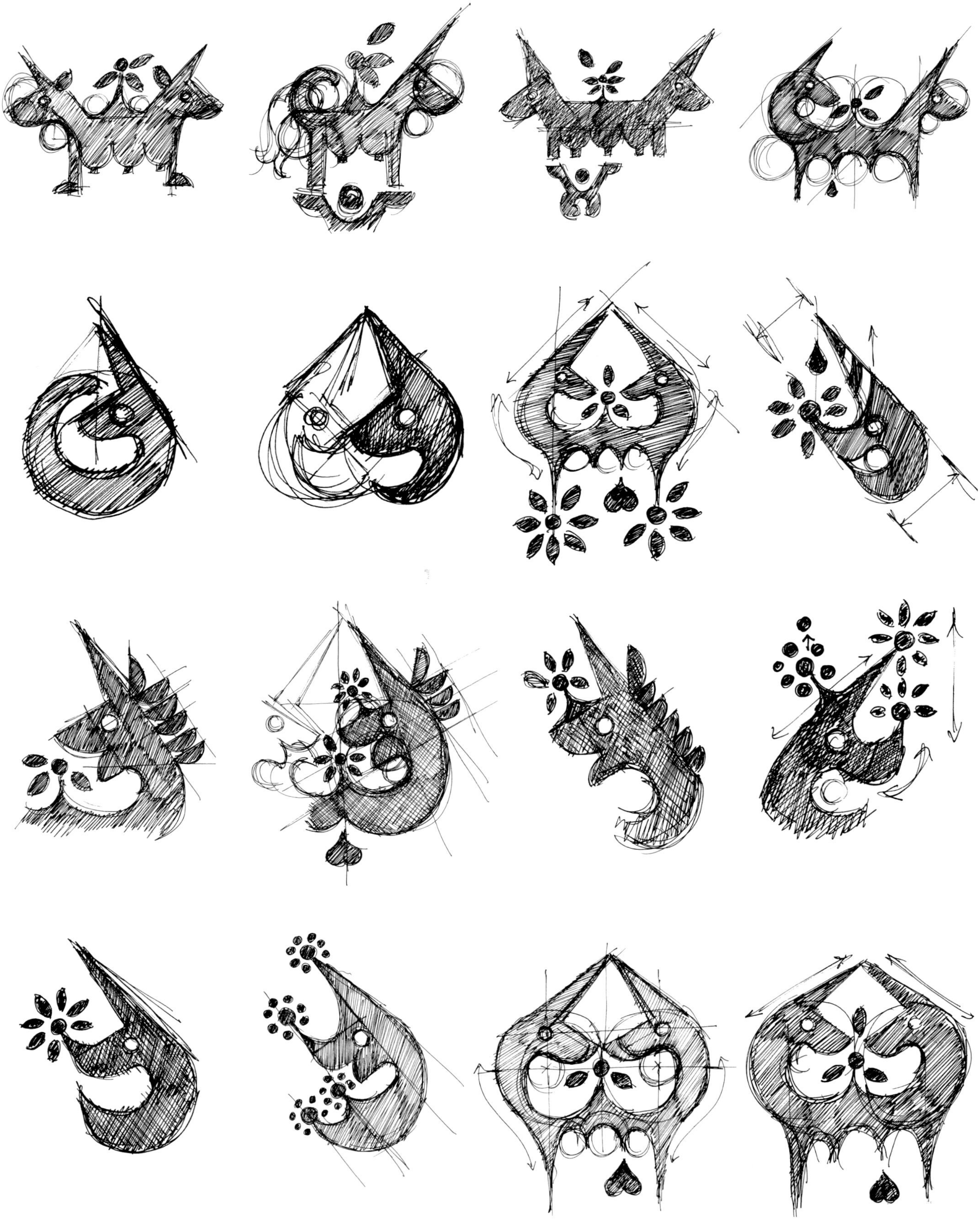

Above and opposite page: *Untitled (Siamese Unicorns)*, 2005.

Above: Process sketches, ink on paper, dimensions vary. Development upper left to bottom right.

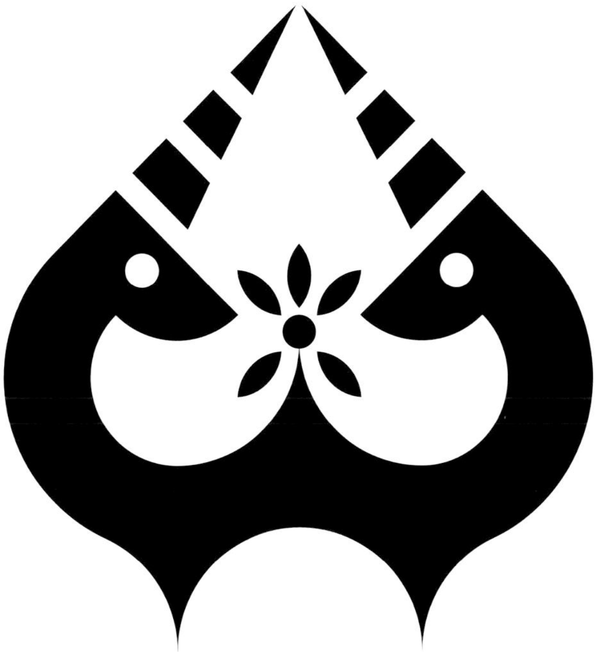

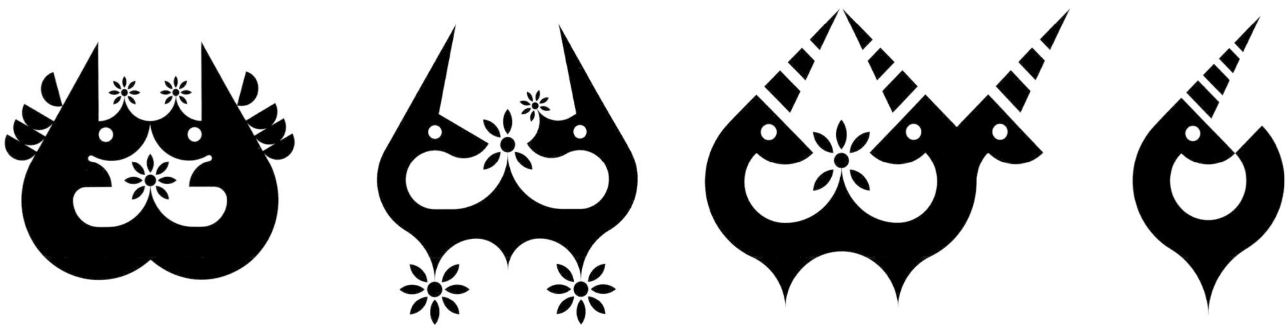

Top: Final vector drawing, digital file. Above: Vector drawings, digital files.
Development left to right.

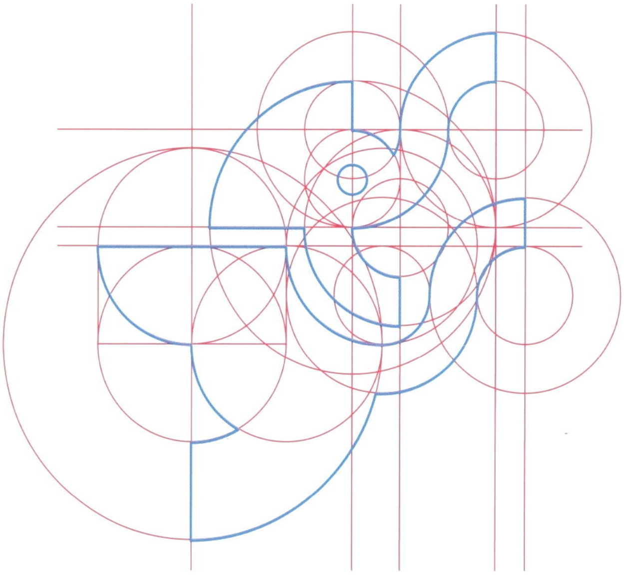

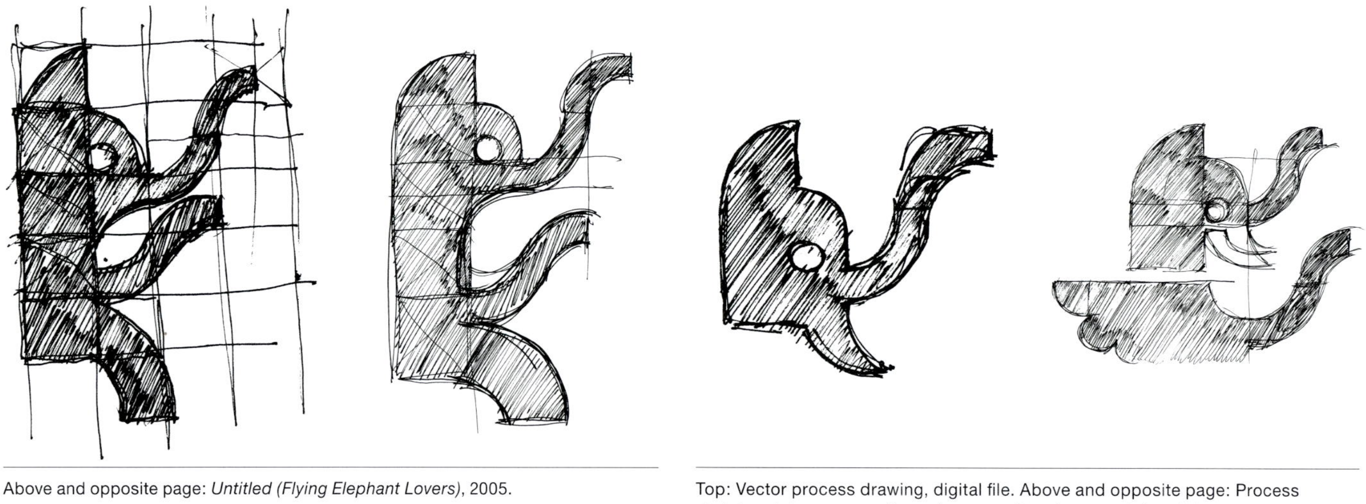

Above and opposite page: *Untitled (Flying Elephant Lovers)*, 2005.

Top: Vector process drawing, digital file. Above and opposite page: Process sketches, ink on paper, dimensions vary. Development left to right.

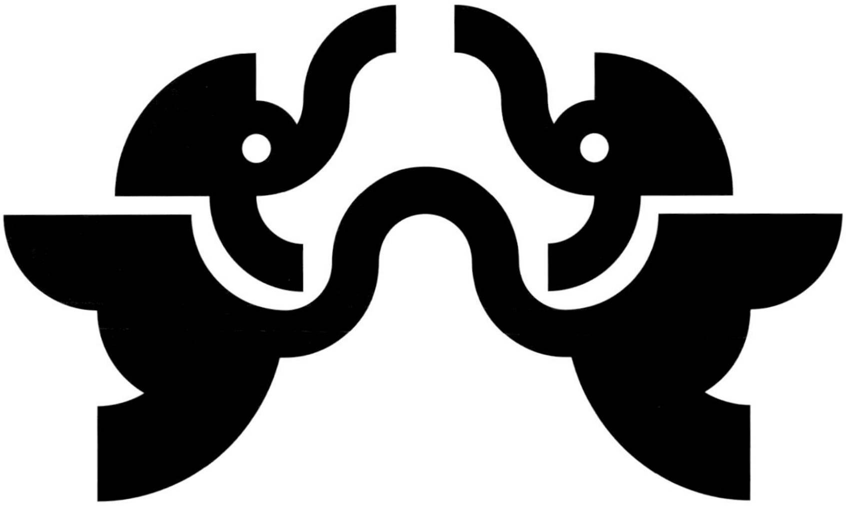

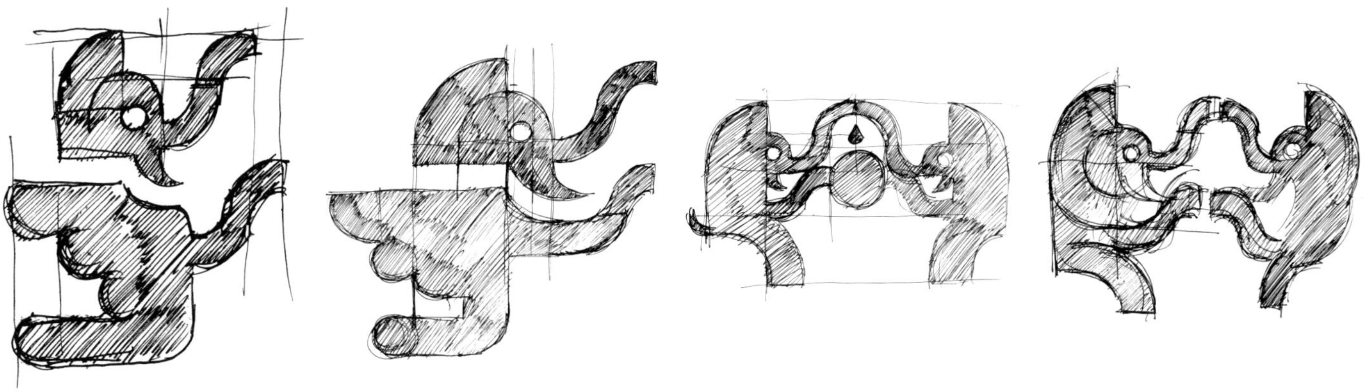

Top: Final vector drawing, digital file.

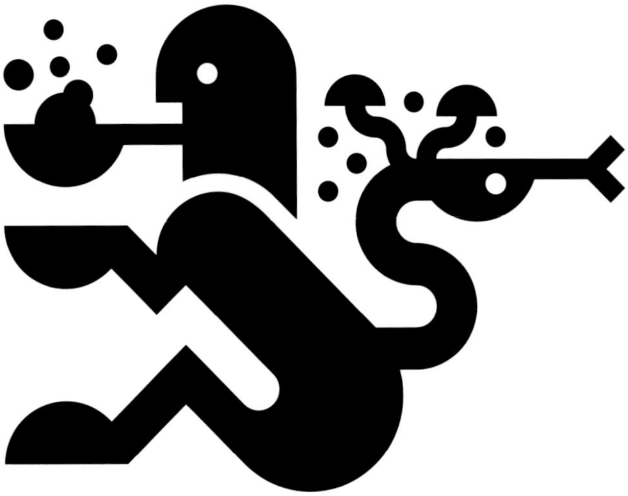

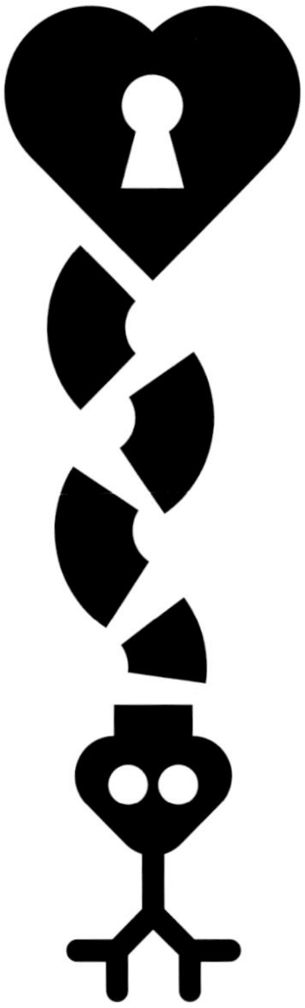

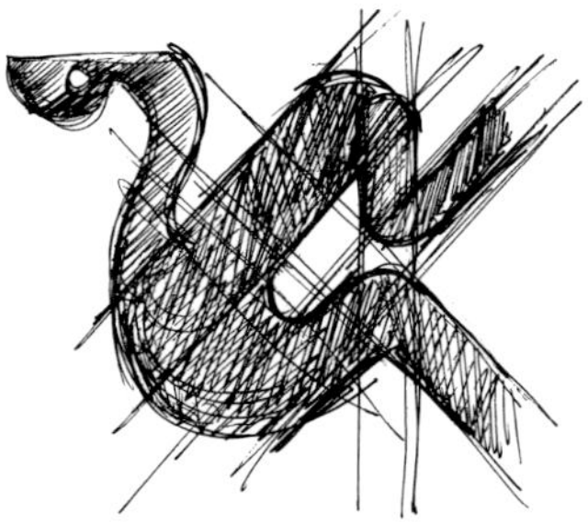

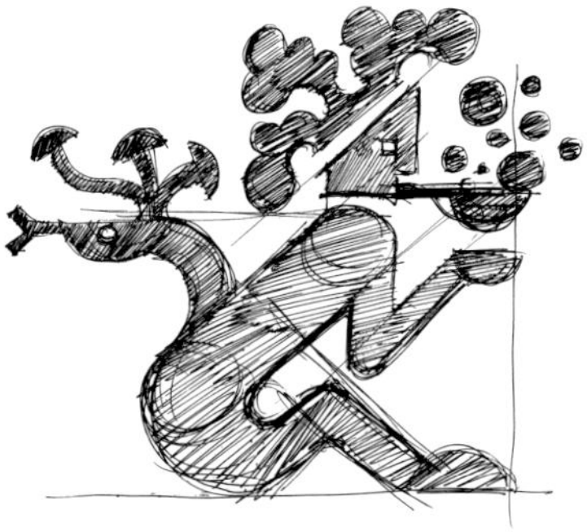

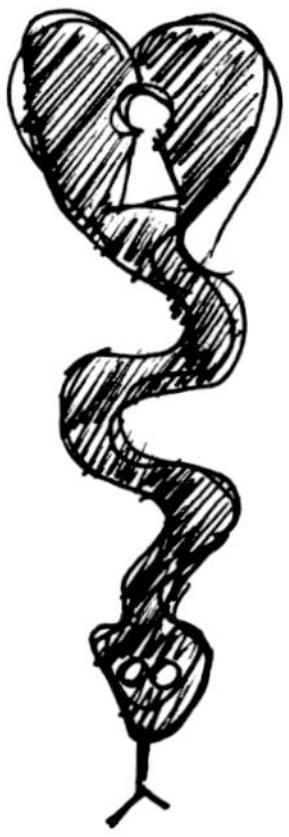

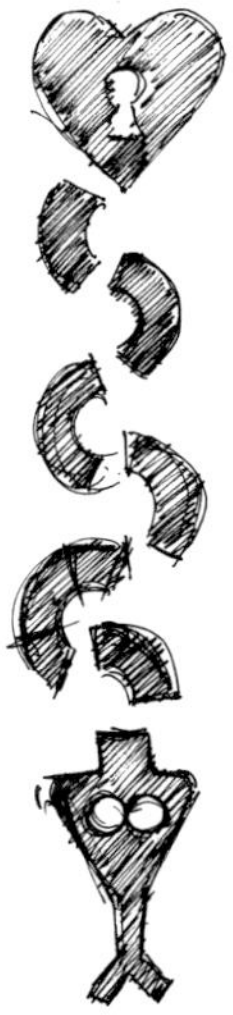

Untitled (Shaman & Heart Lock Snake), 2006.

Top: Final vector drawing, digital file. Above: Process sketches, ink on paper, dimensions vary.

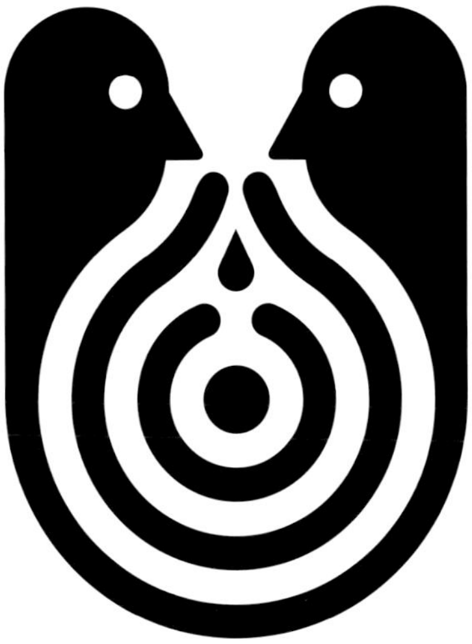

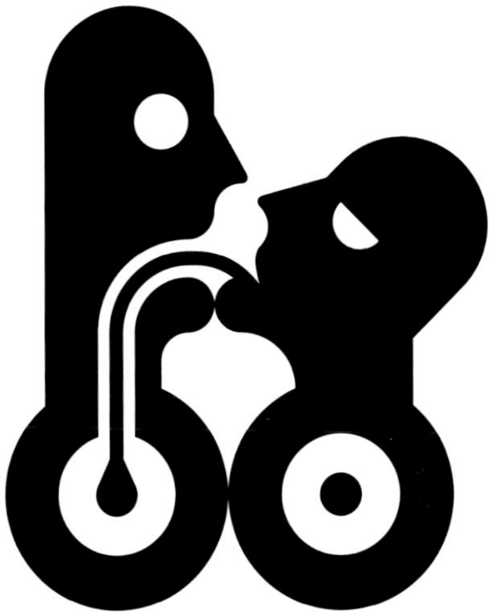

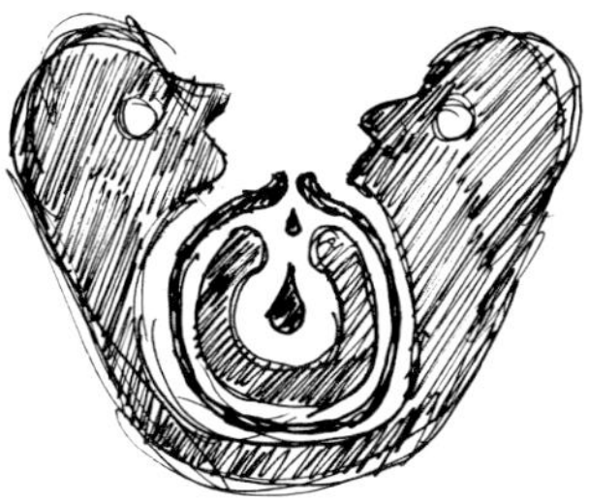

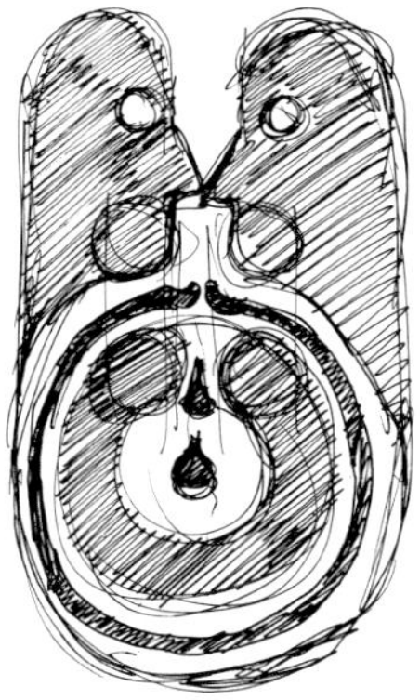

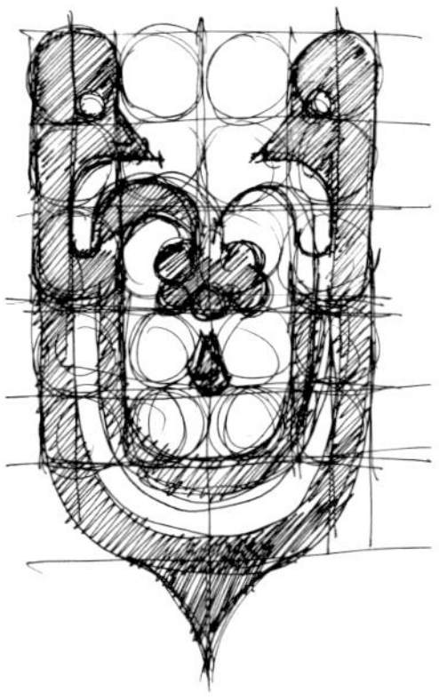

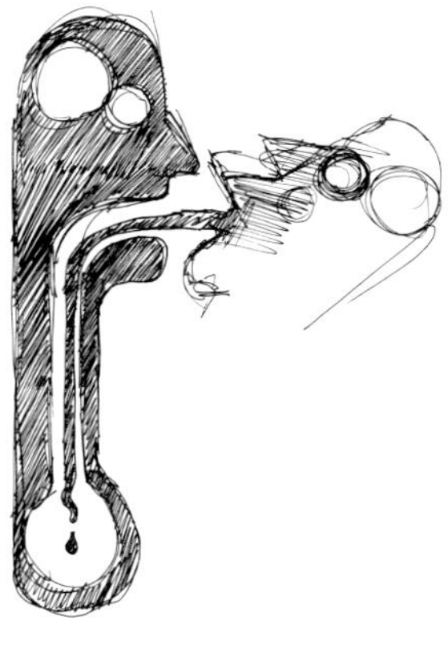

Untitled (French Kissing), 2007.

Top: Final vector drawings, digital files. Above: Process sketches, ink on paper, dimensions vary.

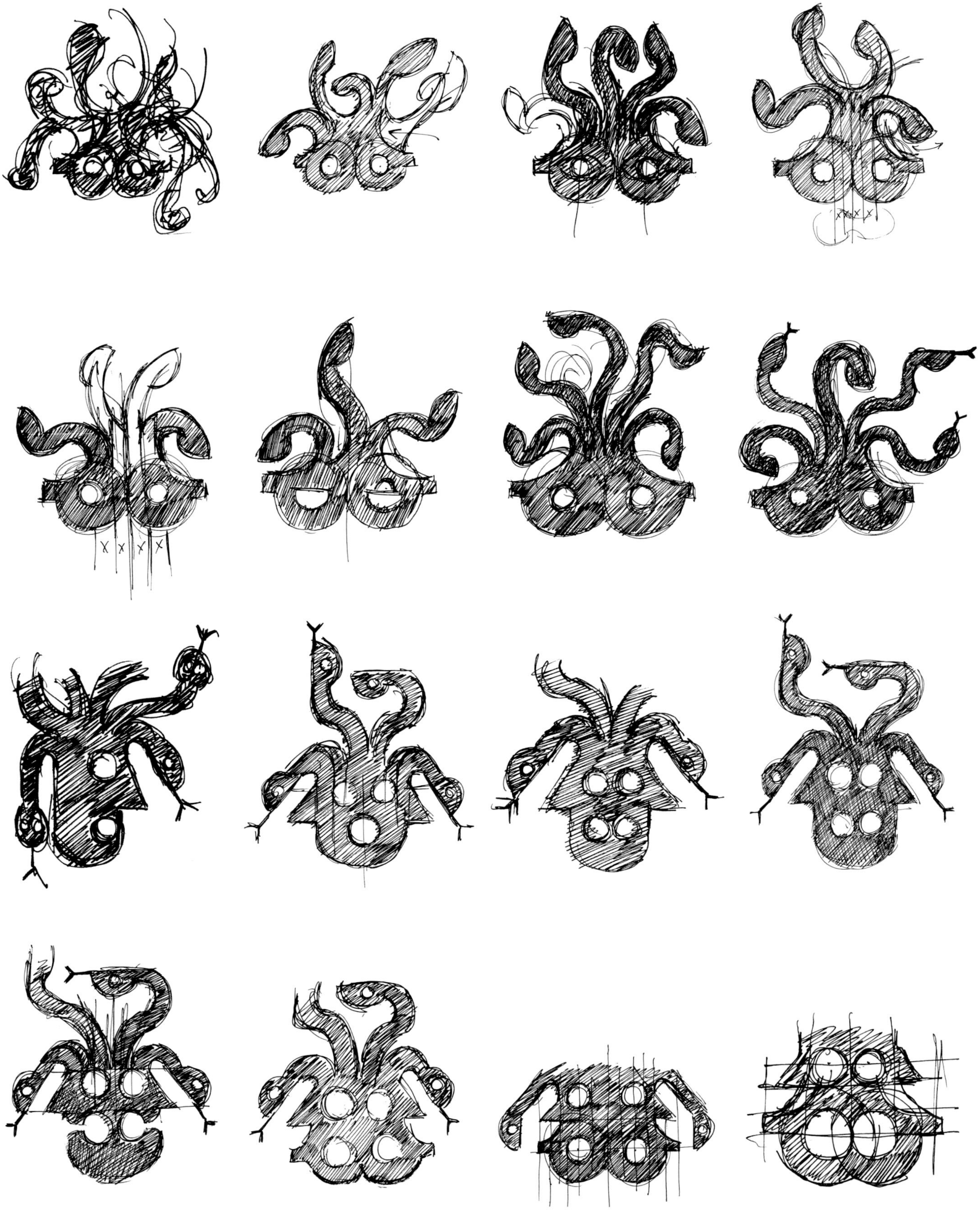

Above and opposite page: *Untitled (Medusa Naughty Parts)*, 2005.

Above: Process sketches, ink on paper, dimensions vary. Development upper left to bottom right.

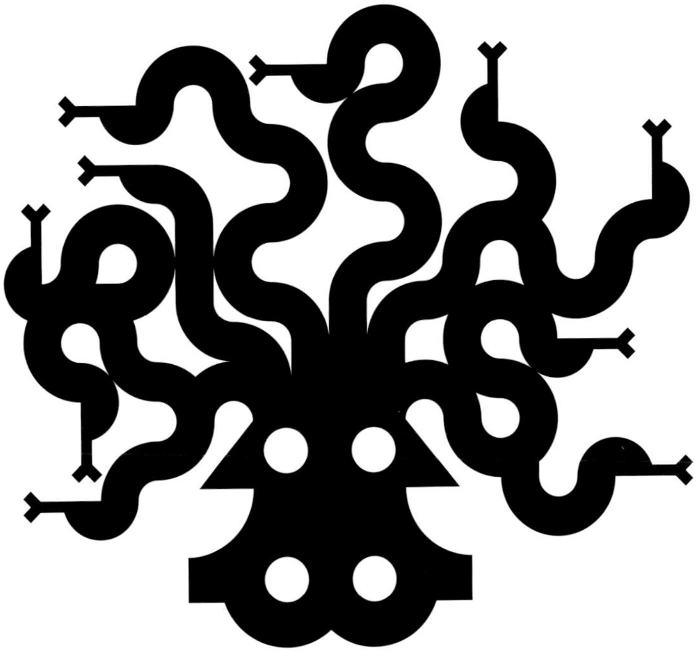

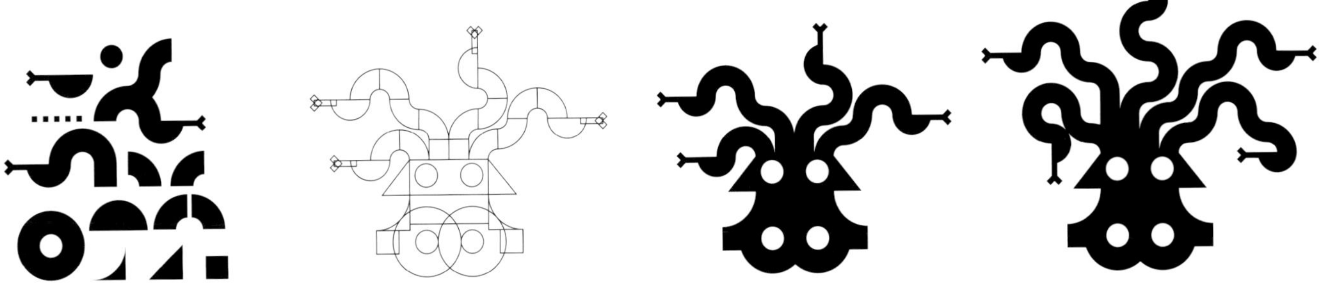

Top: Final vector drawing, digital file. Above: Vector drawings, digital files.
Development left to right.

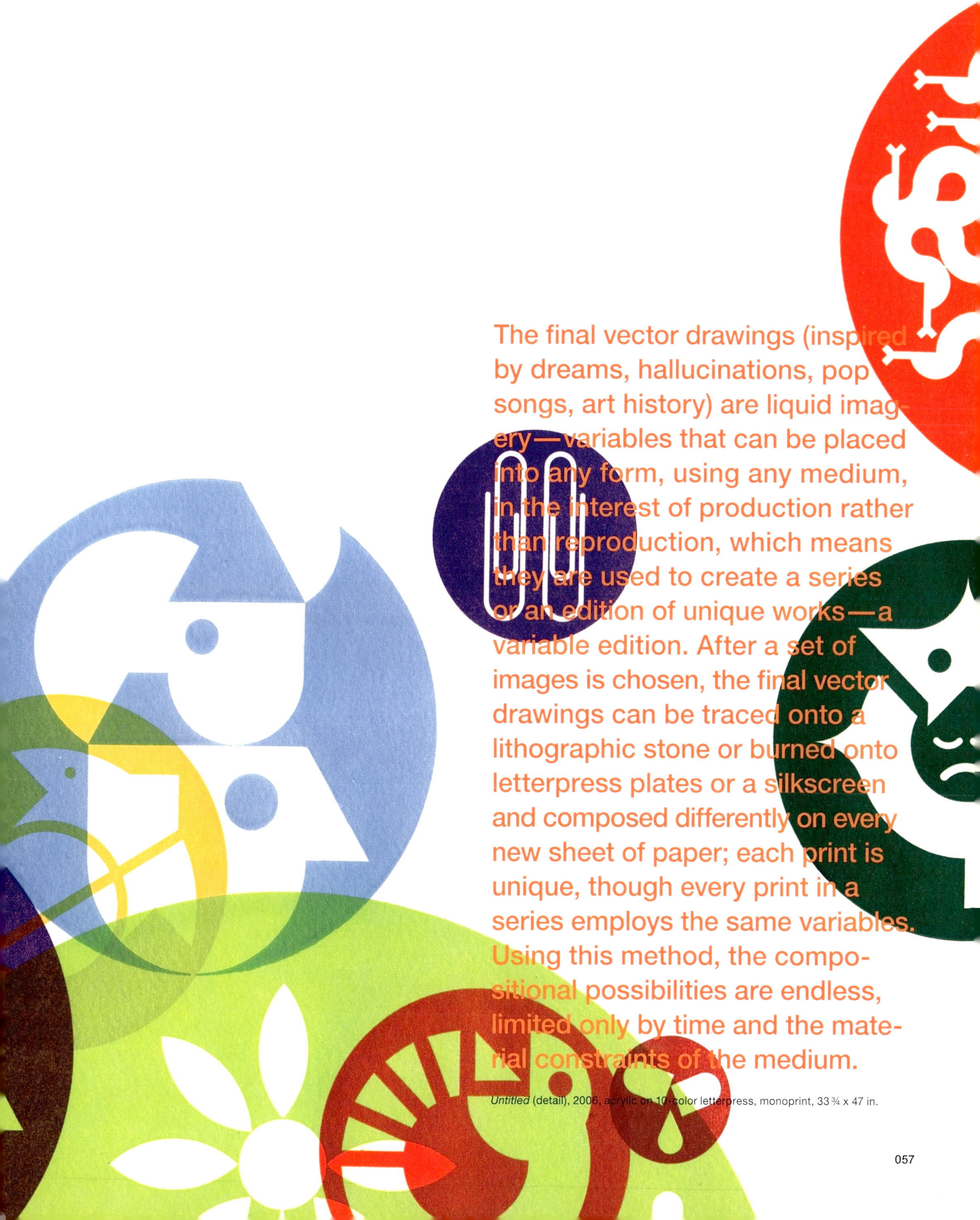

The final vector drawings (inspired by dreams, hallucinations, pop songs, art history) are liquid imagery—variables that can be placed into any form, using any medium, in the interest of production rather than reproduction, which means they are used to create a series or an edition of unique works—a variable edition. After a set of images is chosen, the final vector drawings can be traced onto a lithographic stone or burned onto letterpress plates or a silkscreen and composed differently on every new sheet of paper; each print is unique, though every print in a series employs the same variables. Using this method, the compositional possibilities are endless, limited only by time and the material constraints of the medium.

Untitled (detail), 2006, acrylic on 10-color letterpress, monoprint, 33 ¾ x 47 in.

Silkscreen constitutes Ryan's main studio practice; he used the process as a teenager to make t-shirts and posters, exploiting an easy and relatively cheap method of production.

His main objective has been to anticipate the next logical progression of Andy Warhol's silkscreen production. (75) Without a preconceived plan, Ryan puts the screen directly on the canvas or paper, intuitively placing each image, creating his own effective and idiosyncratic method of using the medium.

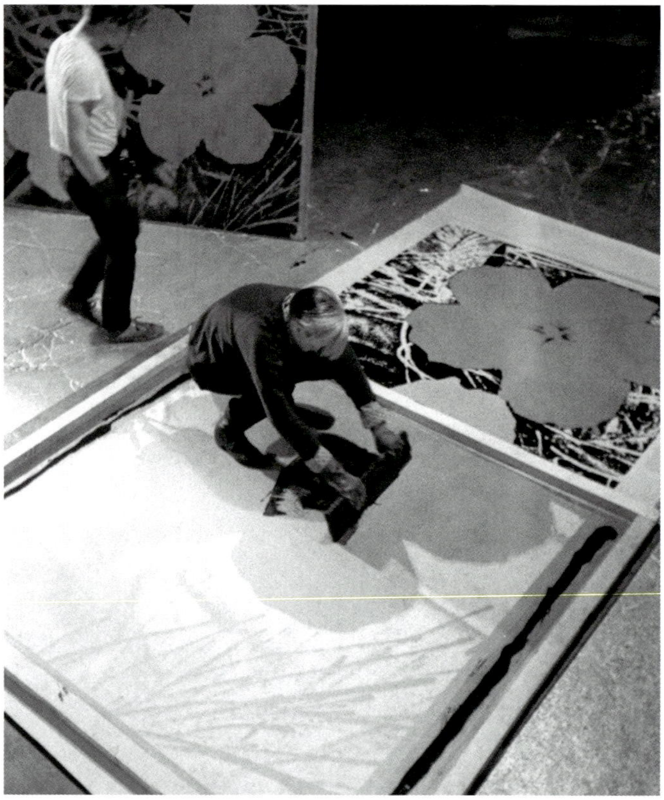

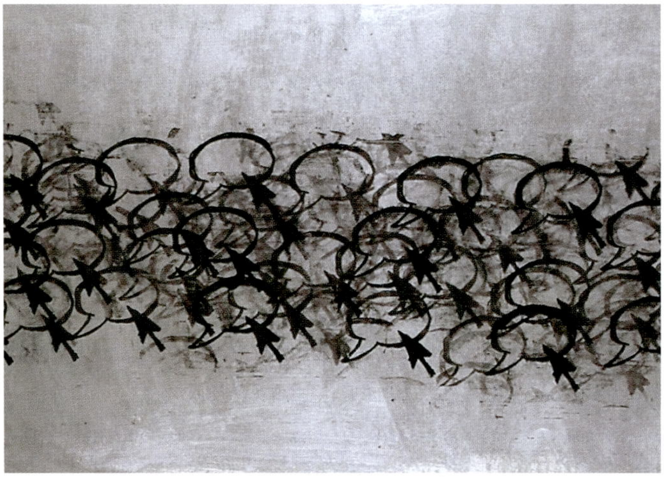

Untitled (Pointer Speak Bubble) (detail), 1998, oil and silkscreen ink on paper, 26 x 40 in.

Top: Andy Warhol and Gerard Malanga creating flower paintings at The Factory, East 47th Street, New York, March 1965. Photograph by David McCabe. (76)

(77)

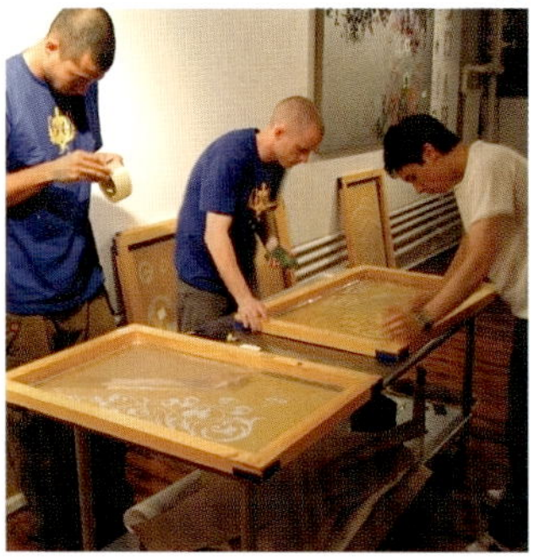

Assistants working in studio, 2004.

(78)

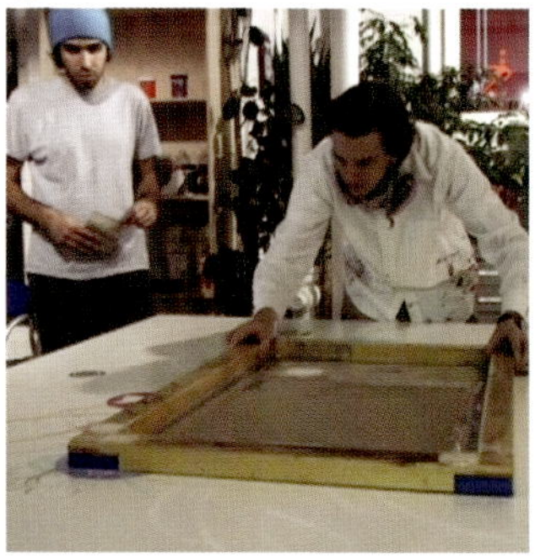

Joey Garfield, *The Run Up*, 2006. Color video still depicting Ryan and assistants working in studio.

(75) Single variable within a picture plane to multiple variables within multiple picture planes.

(76) We had to pay David McCabe $500 for the rights to reproduce this photograph.

(77) Carl Rauschenbach, Bobby Houlihan, Pierre Tardif.

(78) Joe Ferriso.

That's My Name (Don't Wear It Out) (detail), 1998, oil and silkscreen ink on canvas, 48 x 48 in.

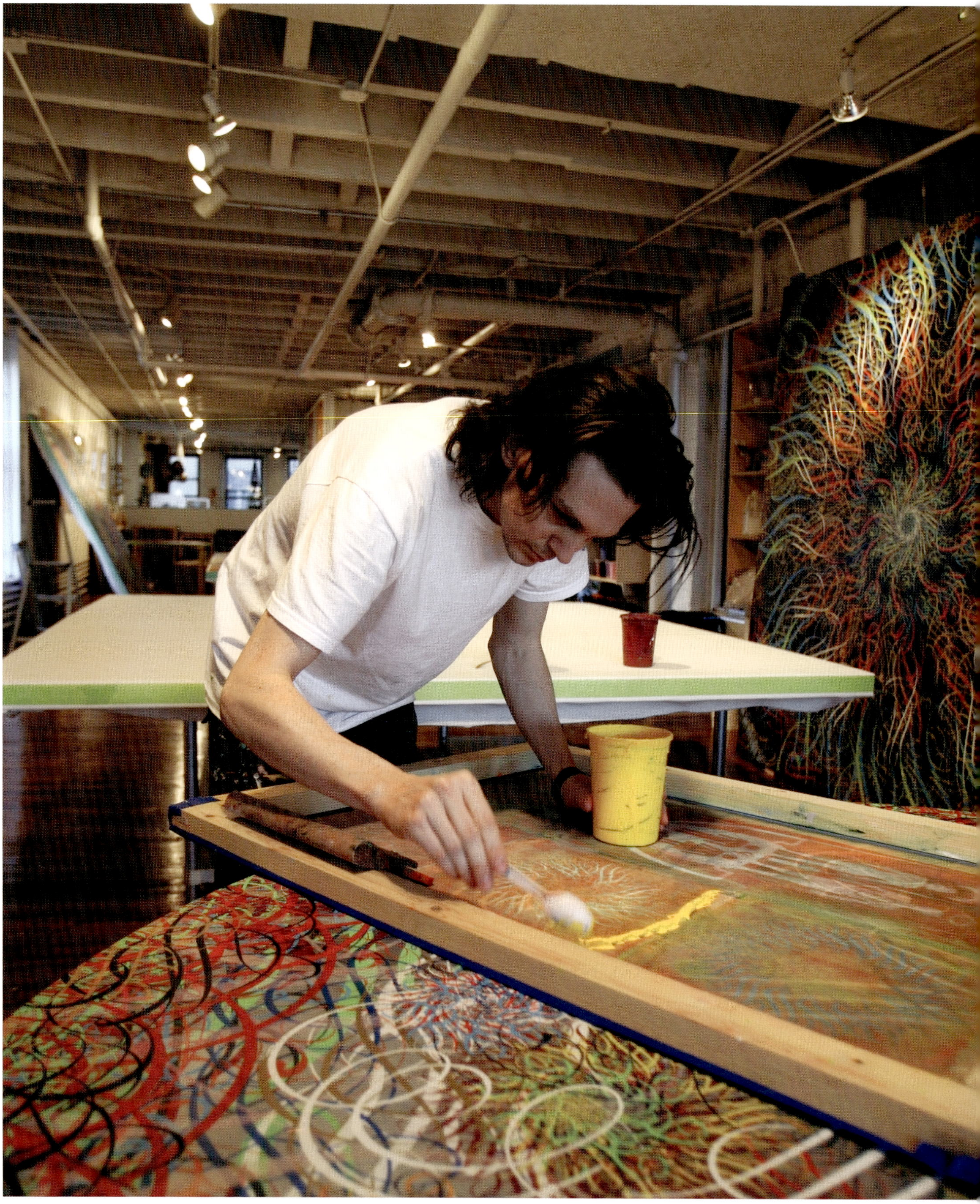

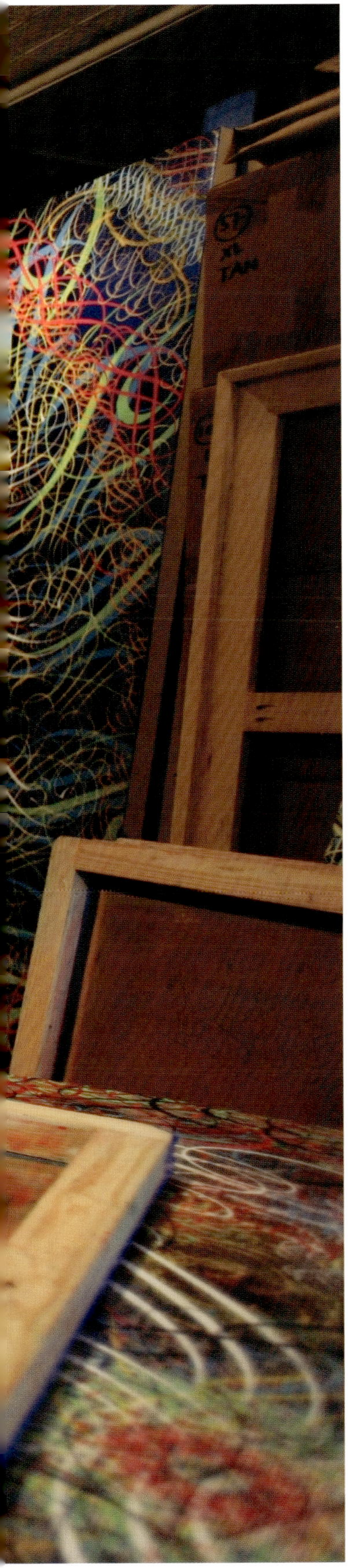

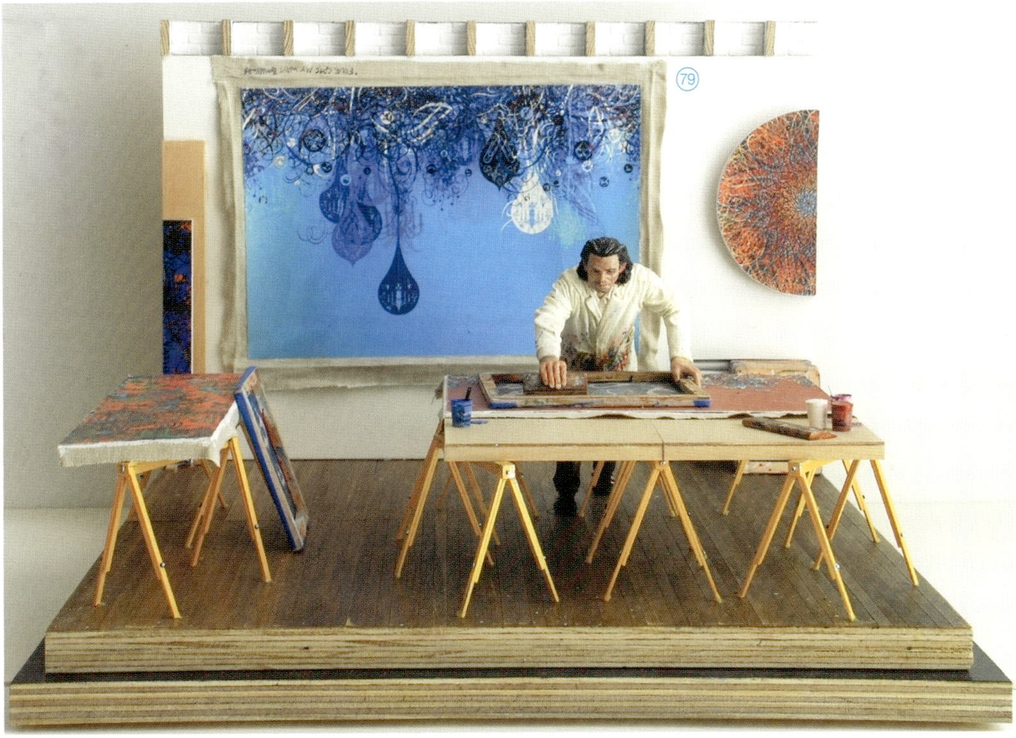

A few years ago, I made a sculpture of Andy Warhol from a 1965 photograph where he was on the floor, squeegee in hand, actually pulling a screen—you almost never see him working like that. Watching Ryan pull a screen made me think about that photograph—especially since Ryan is silkscreening paintings, too.

—Joe Fig
Artist

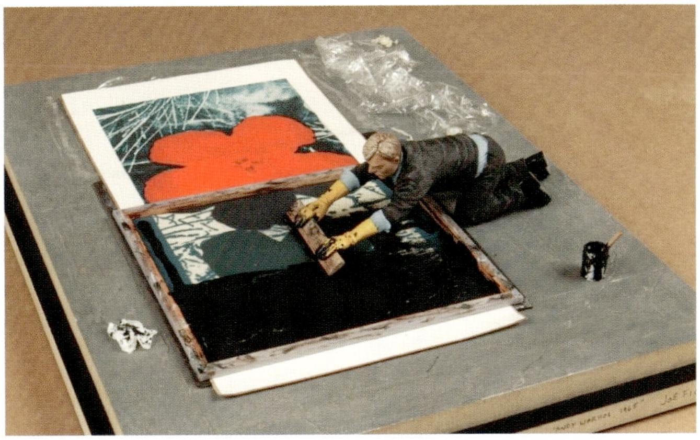

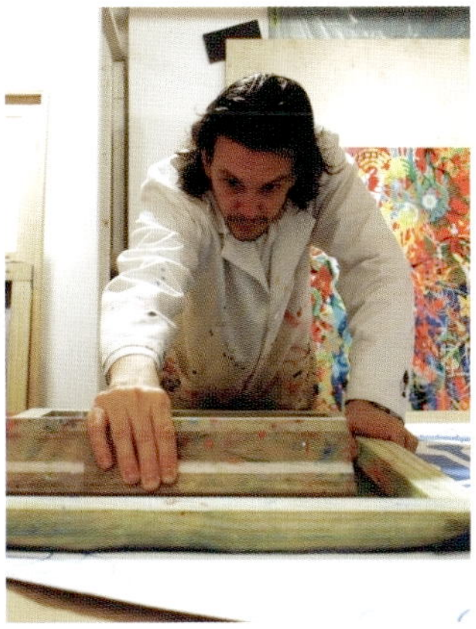

Opposite page: Ryan painting in studio, 2007. Top: Joe Fig, *Ryan McGinness*, 2008, mixed media, 12 ½ x 17 ½ x 17 in.

Above: Joe Fig, *Andy Warhol, 1965*, 2004, mixed media, 4 x 20 x 15 in.

Process photo of Ryan working in studio by Joe Fig, 2008. (80)

(79) See p. 270–271.

(80) This is Joe's model for his model of me: A one-of-a-kind reproduction of someone making one-of-a-kind works using a means of reproduction.

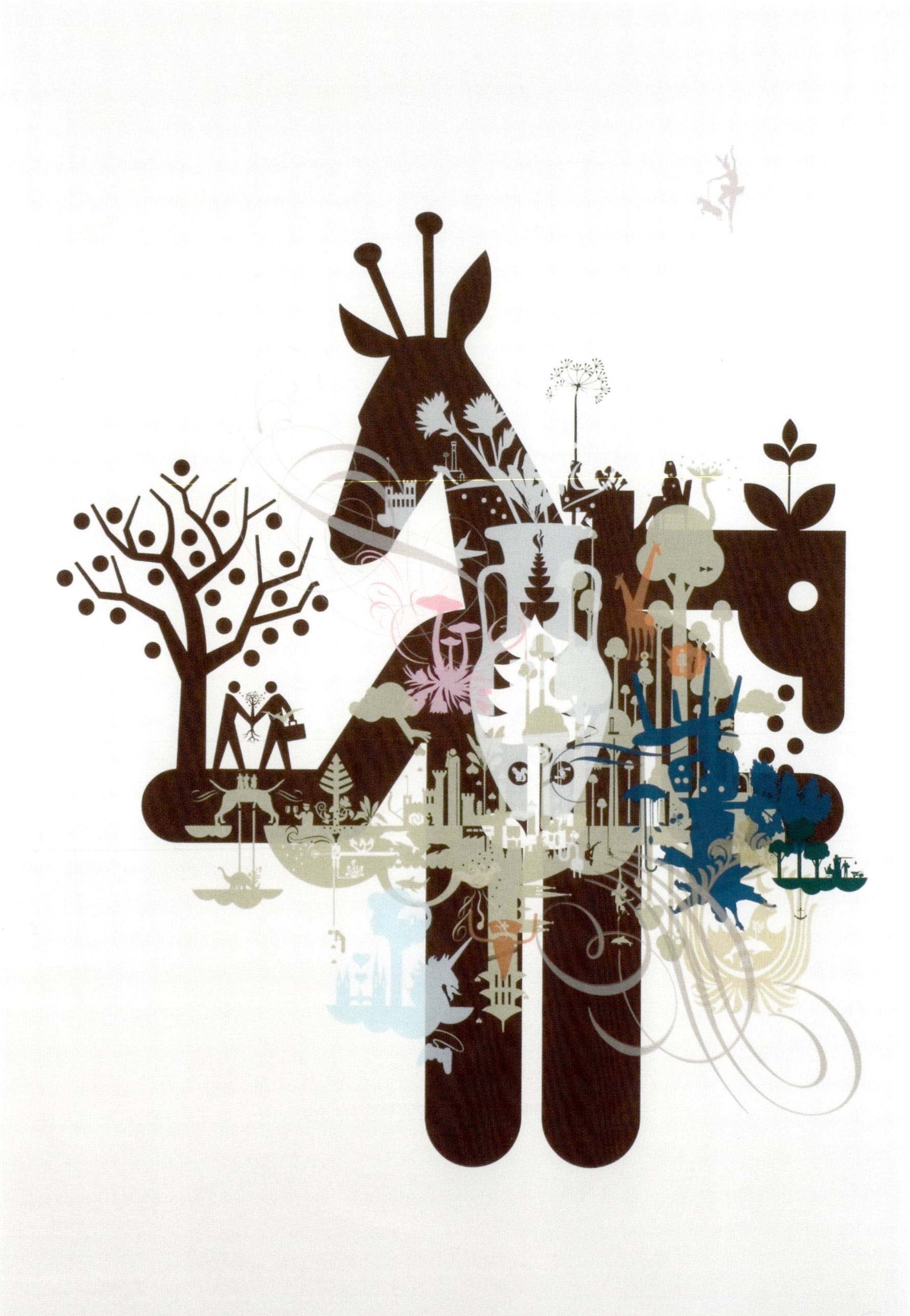

Untitled, 2002, silkscreen ink on paper, 39 x 27 in.

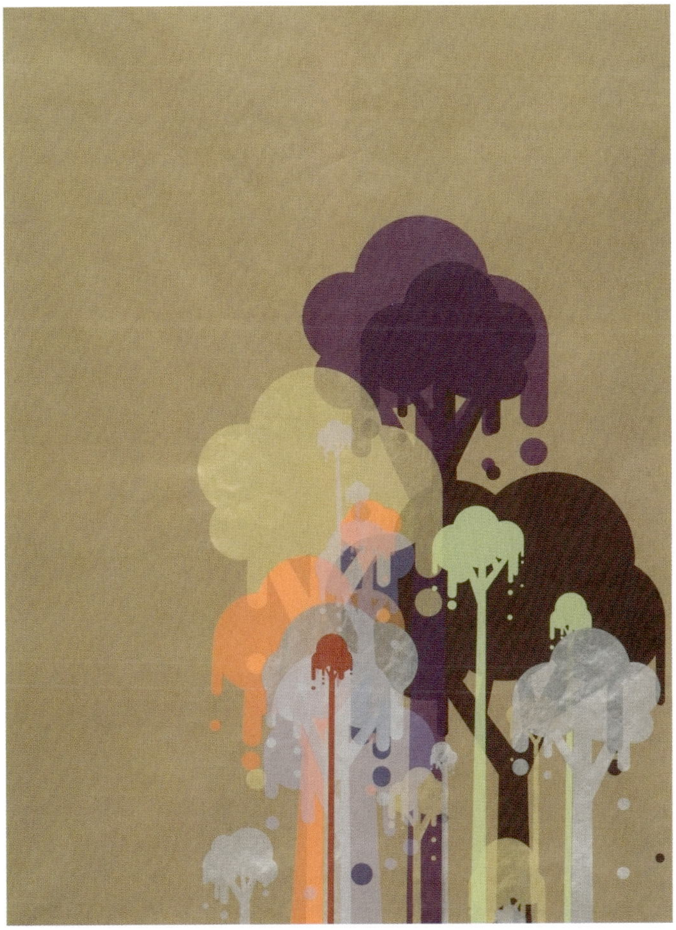

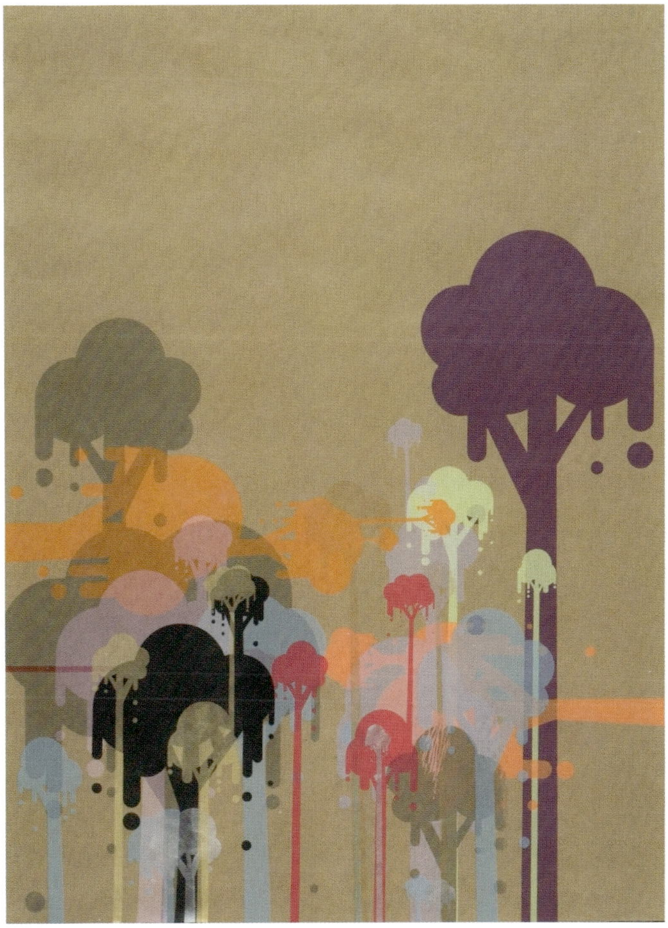

Ryan has a lot of curiosity, so it's hard for him to commit to just one composition and one edition. I bet in his mind there's always the thought, 'But what would happen if I printed it this way?' And that curiosity, that variety, I think, is the essence of his work.
—Dusica Kirjakovic
Executive Director, Lower East Side Printshop

(81)

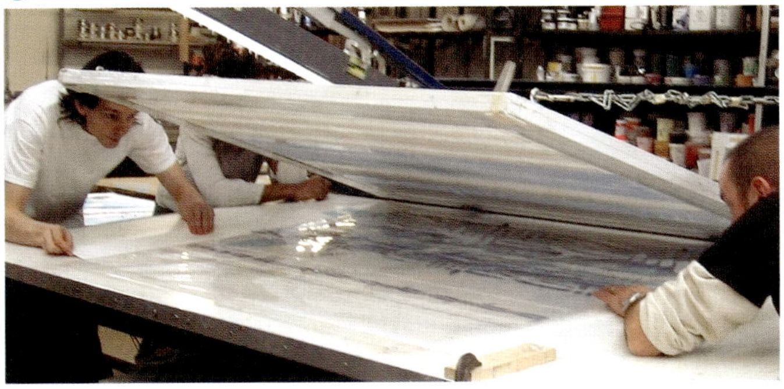

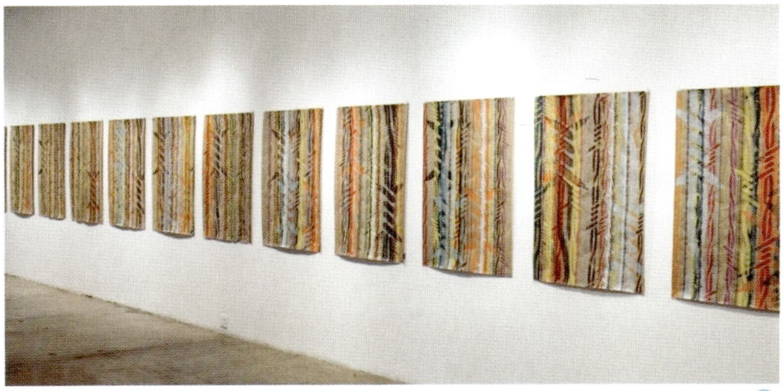

(82)

Top left and right: *Untitled (Ice Cream Trees)*, 2007, silkscreen ink on kraft paper, monoprints, 46 x 34 in. Published by Lower East Side Printshop, New York.

Printing at Lower East Side Printshop with Master Printer James Miller, 2007.

Untitled (Multi-colored Barbed Wire on Kraft Paper). Installation view, "Monumental Drawings," 2007, Blue Star Contemporary Art Center, San Antonio.

(81) At the Lower East Side Printshop everybody stops to eat lunch at the same time every day. I always thought this was a neat idea.

(82) I wanted to create beautiful things using symbols that refer to things usually associated with ugliness. See p. 73.

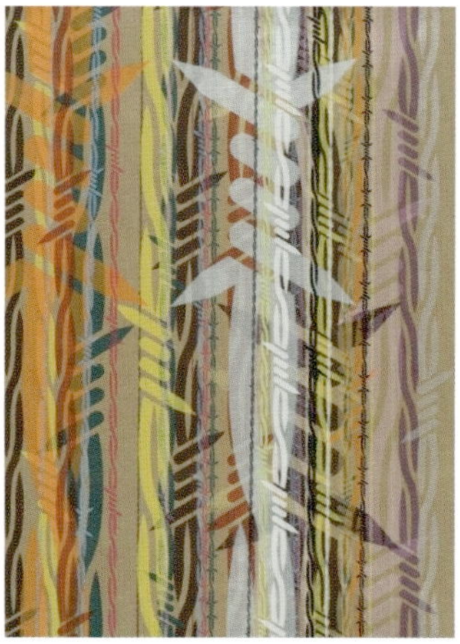
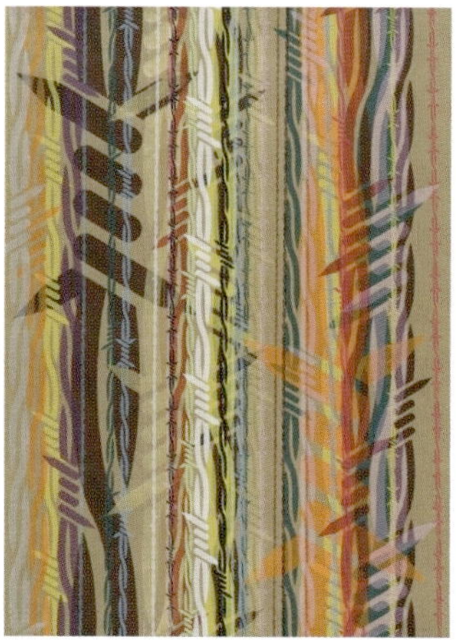
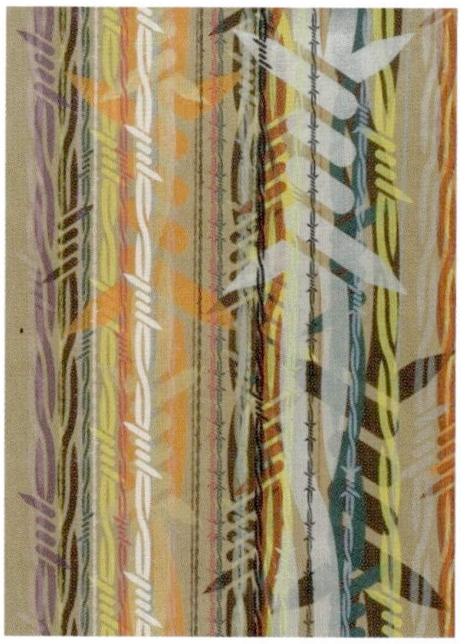
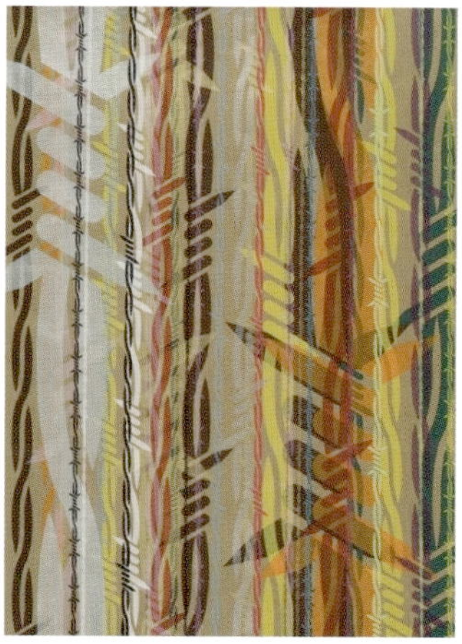
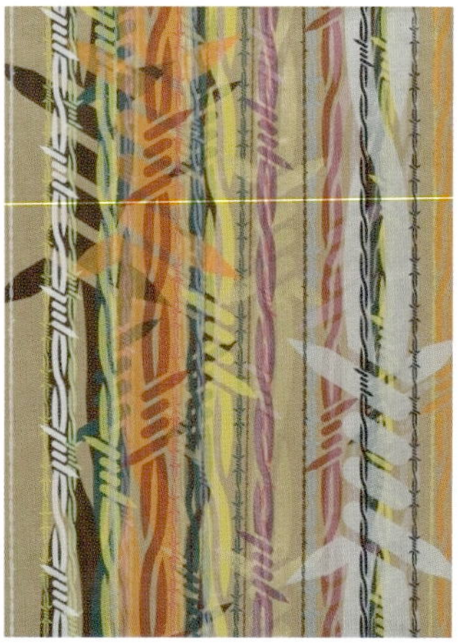
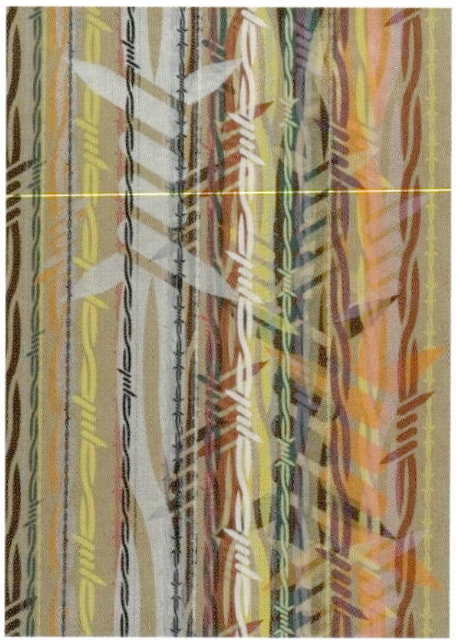
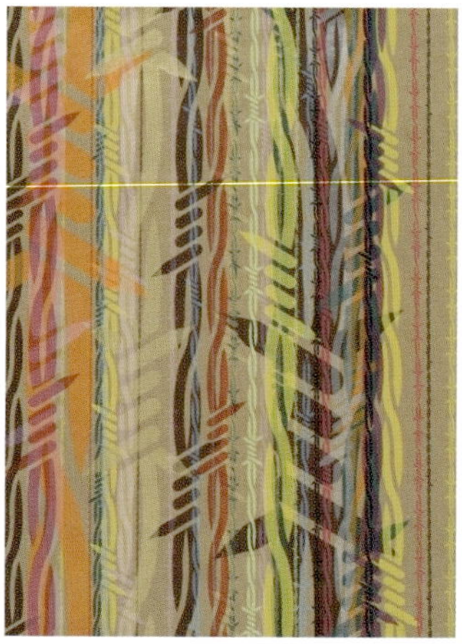
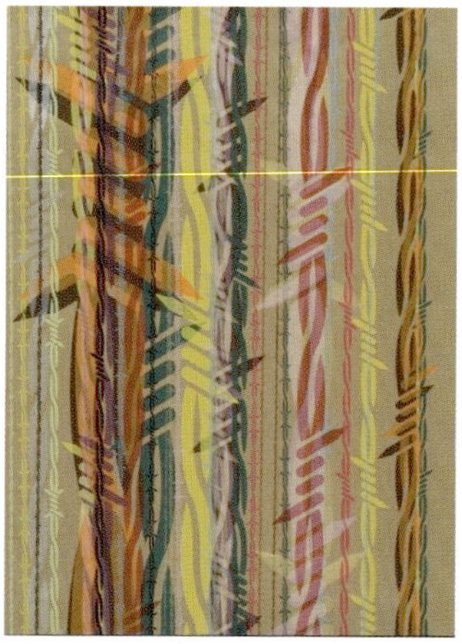
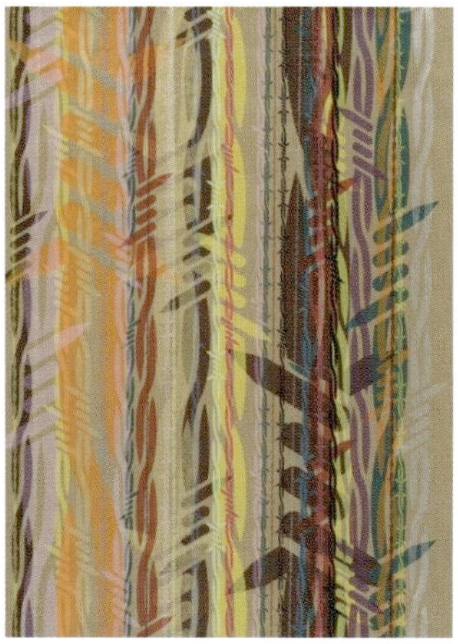
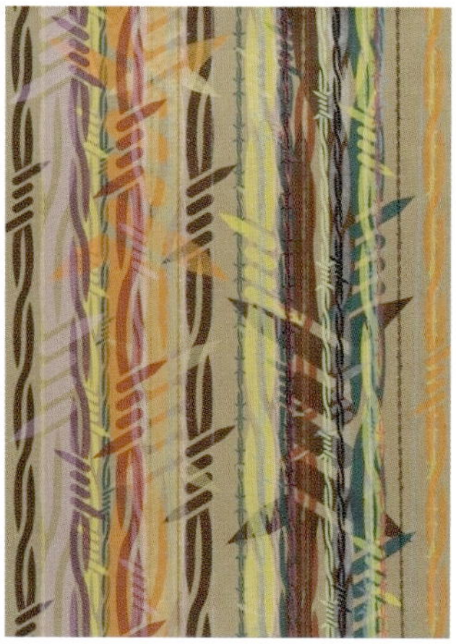
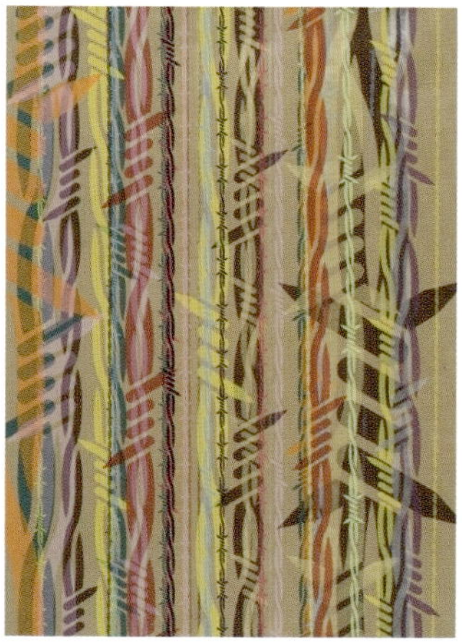
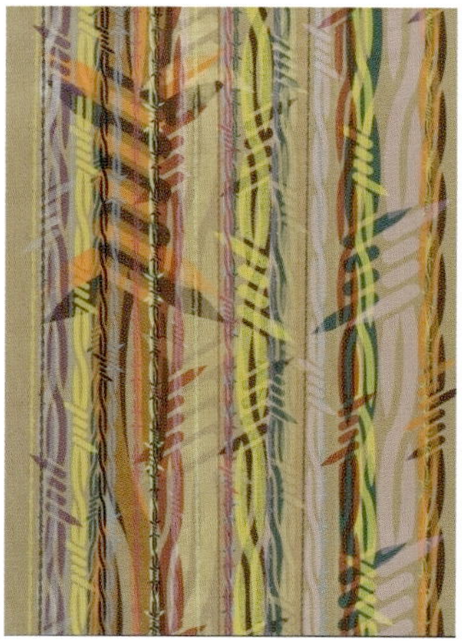

Above and opposite page: *Untitled (Multi-colored Barbed Wire on Kraft Paper)*, 2007, silkscreen ink on kraft paper, 46 x 34 in. each, 13 shown here from a series of 16 monoprints. Published by Lower East Side Printshop, New York.

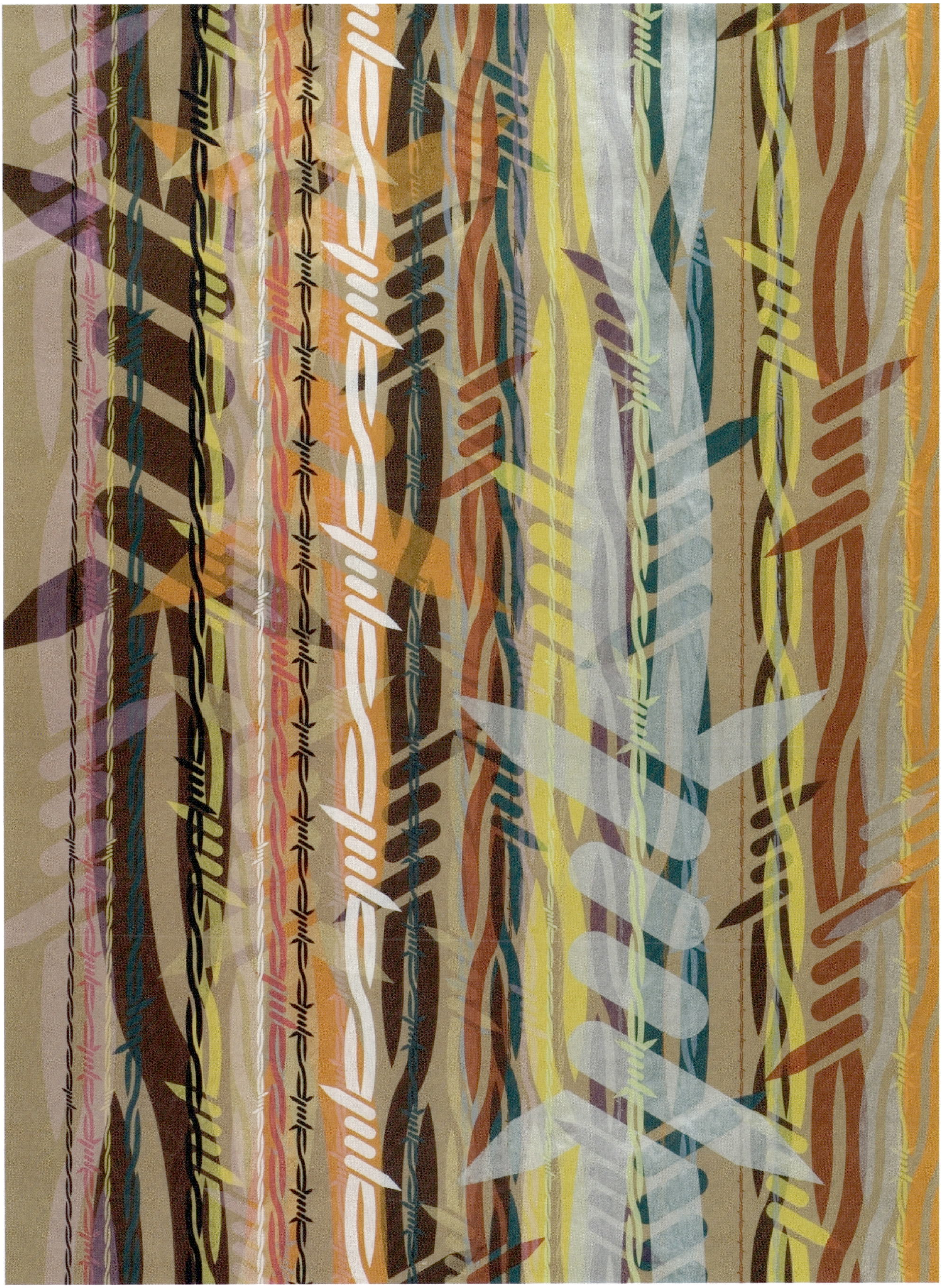

Letterpress is a relief form of printing in which the paper is embossed, lending texture and a sense of dimension to the finished print.

In 2005, Ryan worked with Coeur Noir Letterpress in Brooklyn to create a variable edition of 10 monoprints, each composed of different groupings of 72 variously sized drawings in 10 colors. The printers started with 80 pieces of paper, which were larger than the press bed—one of only a few large-format letterpresses in the world—and ended up with 10 finished prints due to misprints, mistakes, and editing.

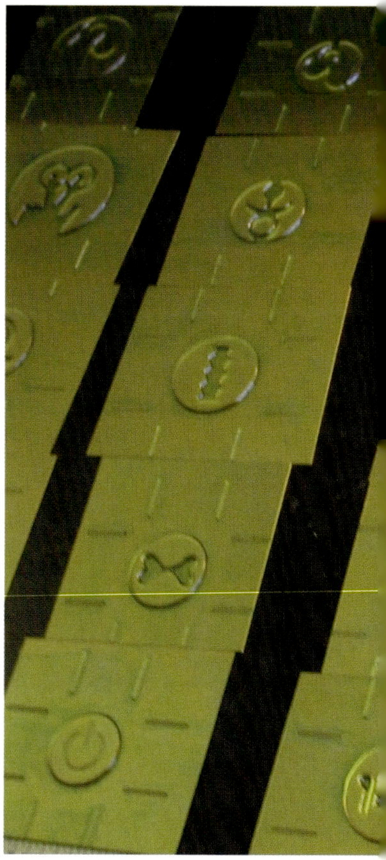

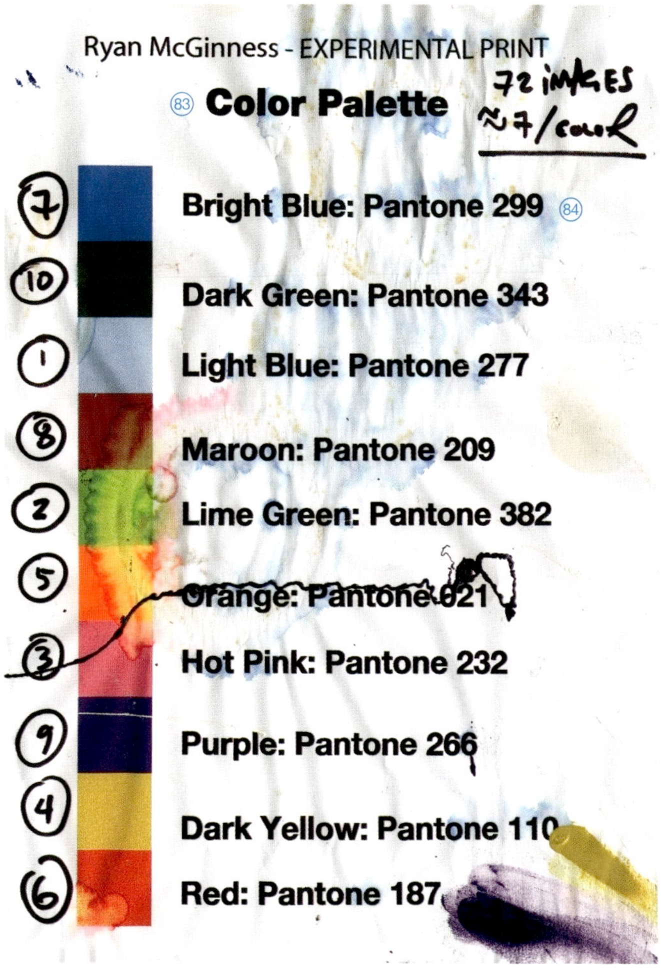

Color palette for Coeur Noir letterpress series. Numbers on the left delineate a printing order from light to dark.

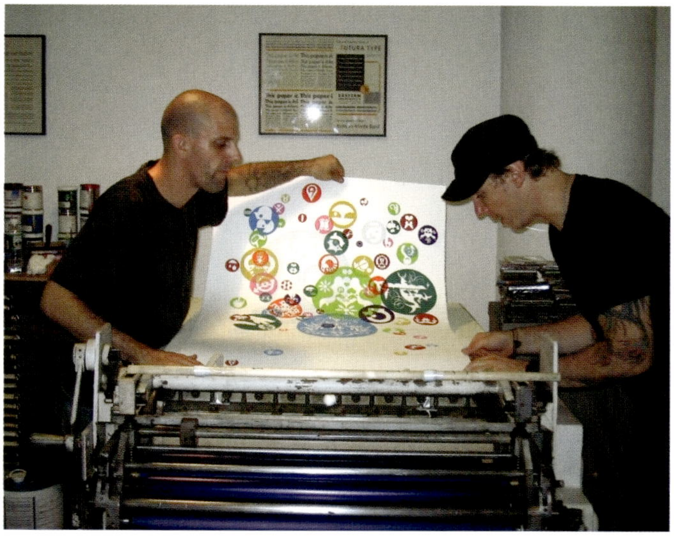

Positioning paper into the guides to feed it into the press. (All images this page and opposite page at Coeur Noir, Brooklyn, 2005).

Top center, and opposite page: Photo emulsion plates burned from digital files were arranged multiple times in variable orders on the press bed.

(83) Letterpress inks were mixed to match Pantone colors, but the Pantone ink system was not used. We just needed to use a common language.

(84) See p. 28.

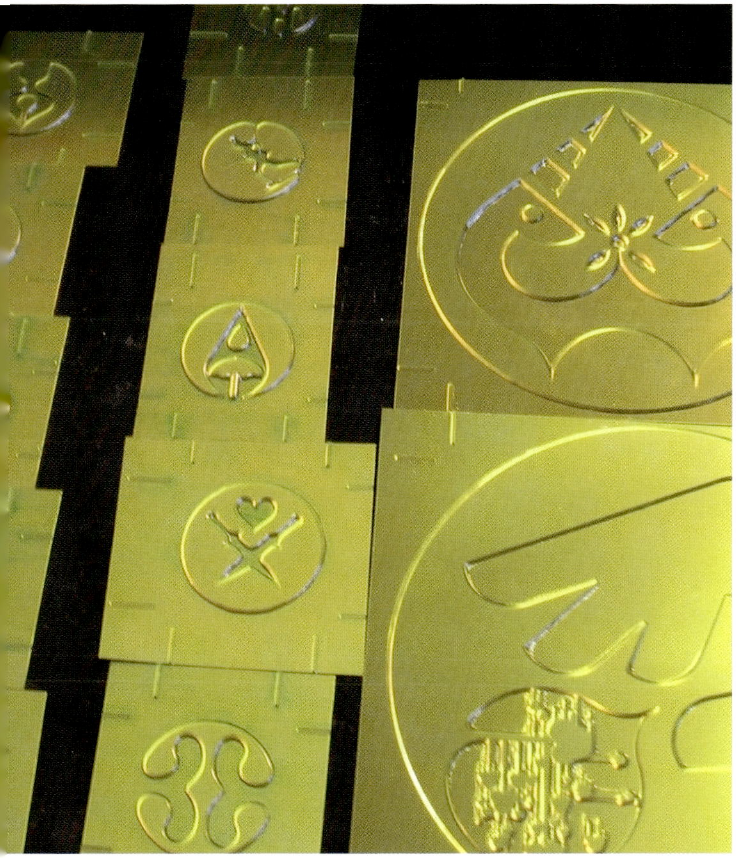

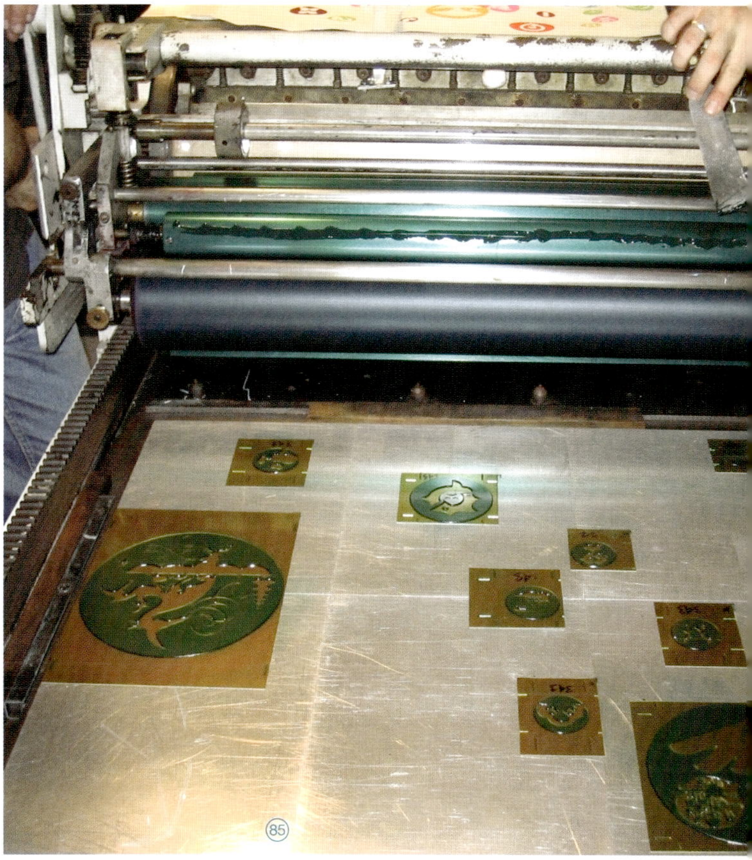

(85)

We had to specially treat the paper to get the best ink transfer and impression out of it, so we couldn't run the air conditioner because the paper would have dried out. It was the middle of summer and we were working 'til four in the morning—a marathon.
—Konstantin Grab
Printer, Coeur Noir Letterpress

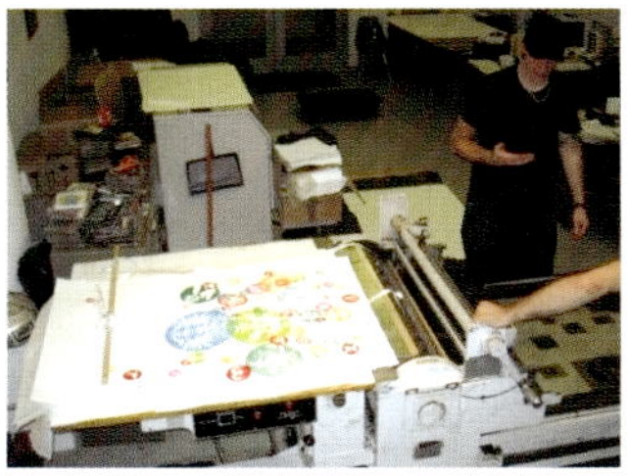

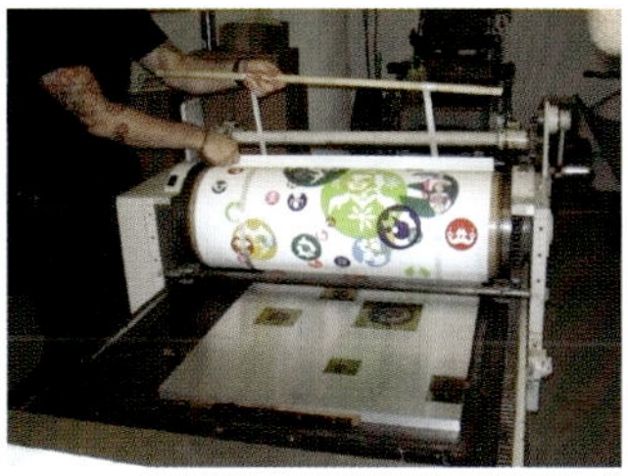

(86)

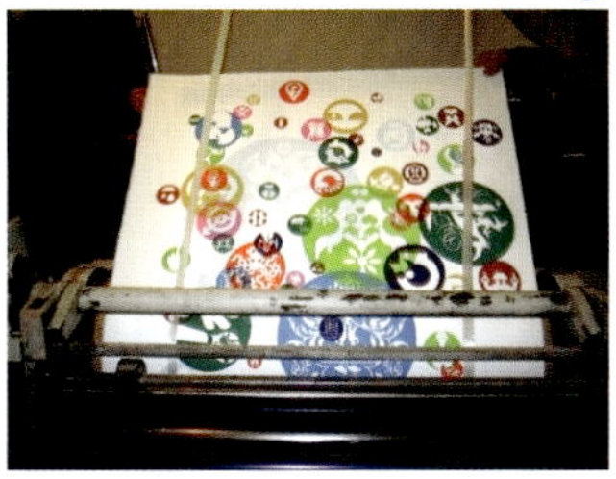

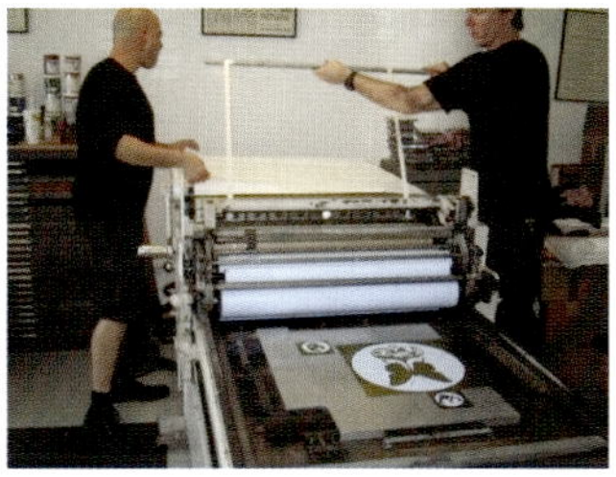

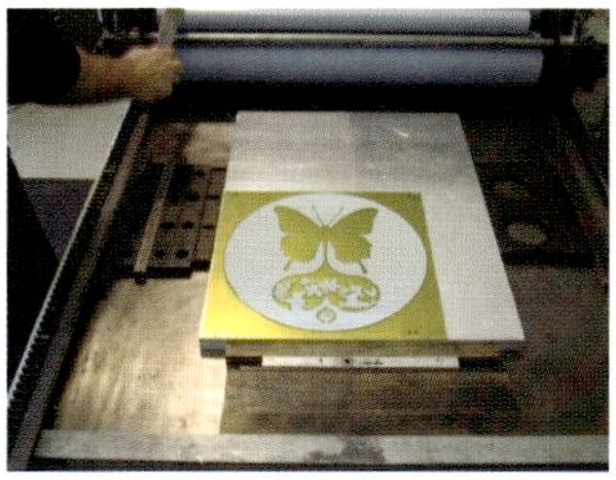

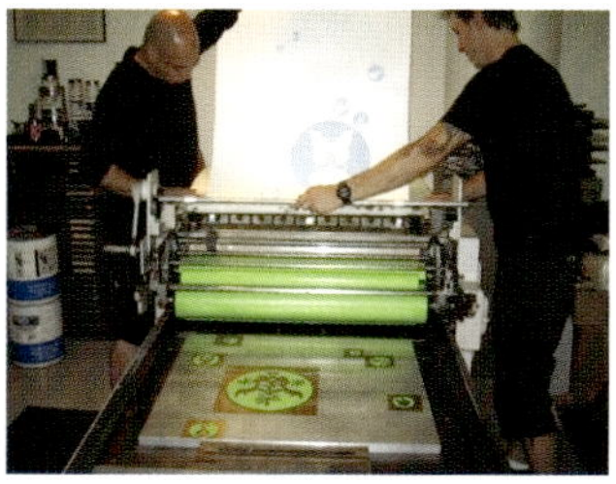

Rigging the press to accommodate paper that is larger than the large-format press bed.

Above and above right: Inking the plates.

(85) Different plates in different colors in different positions at different times. Multiple overlapping dot studies.

(86) These works on paper represent colliding worlds within worlds. Bubbling universes with intersecting membranes that give rise to new worlds.

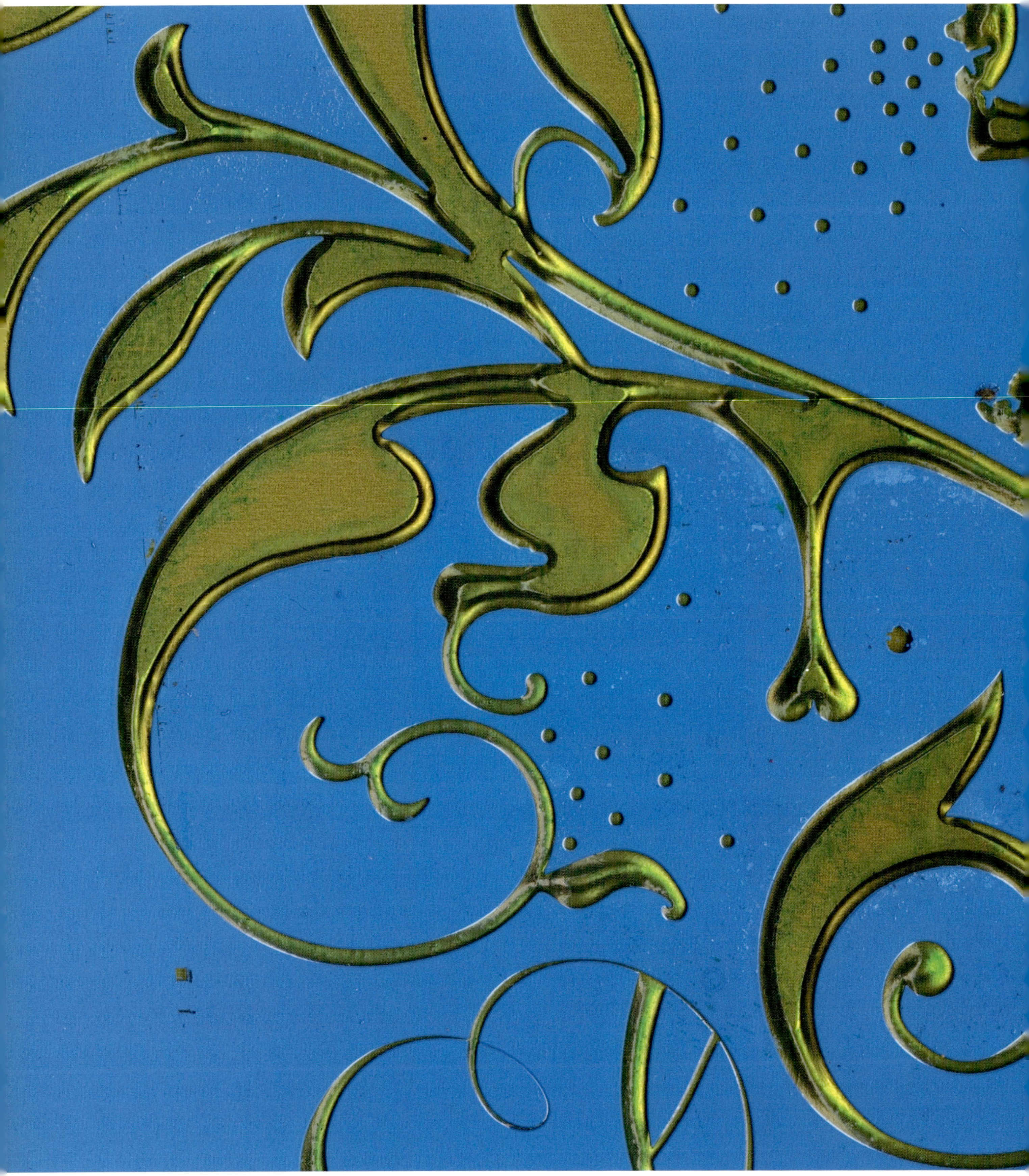

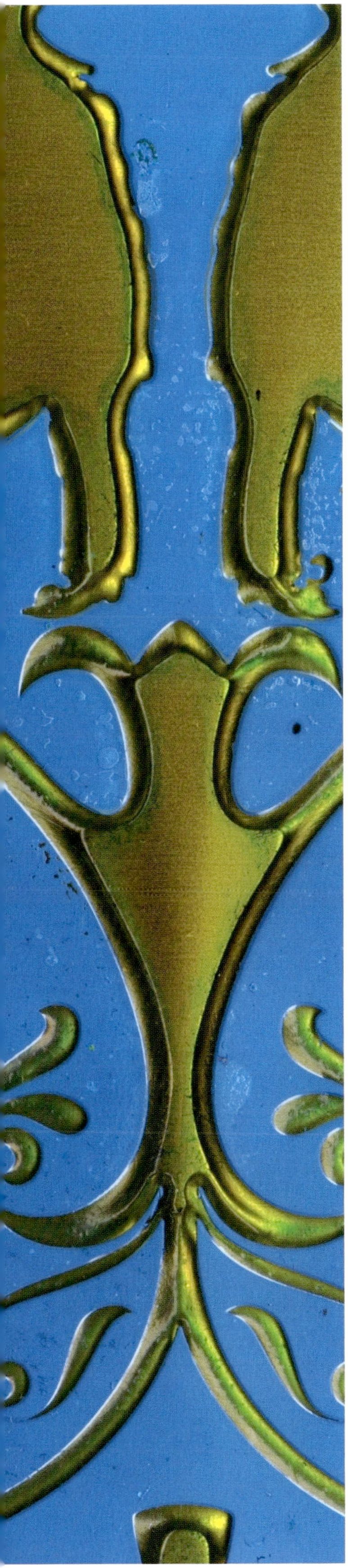

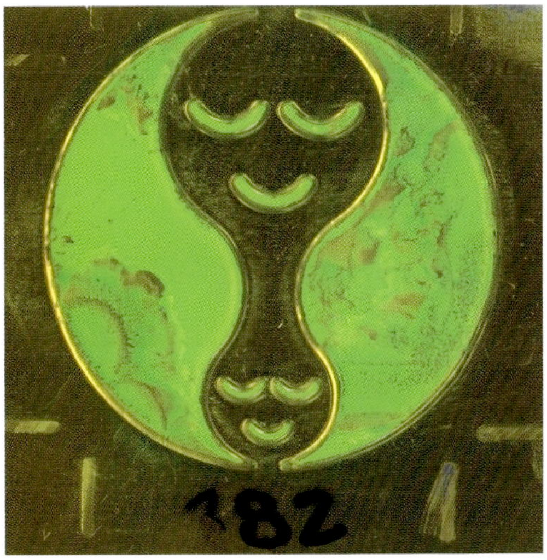

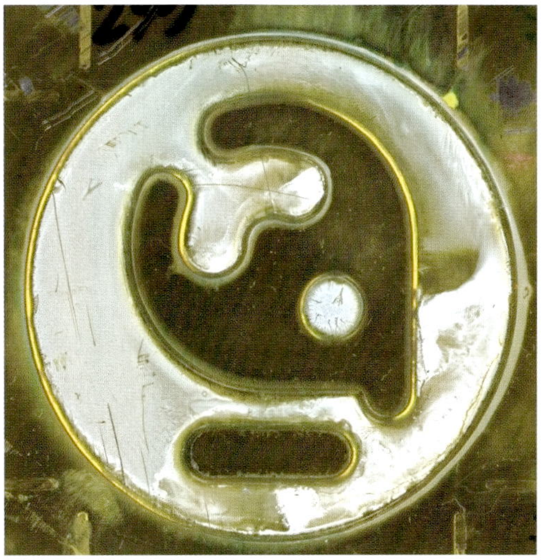

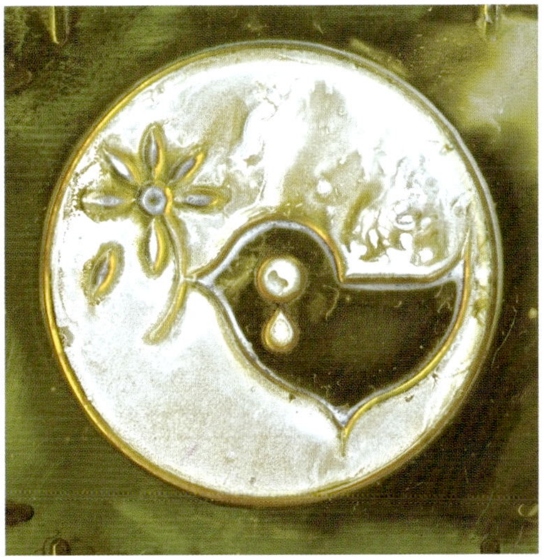

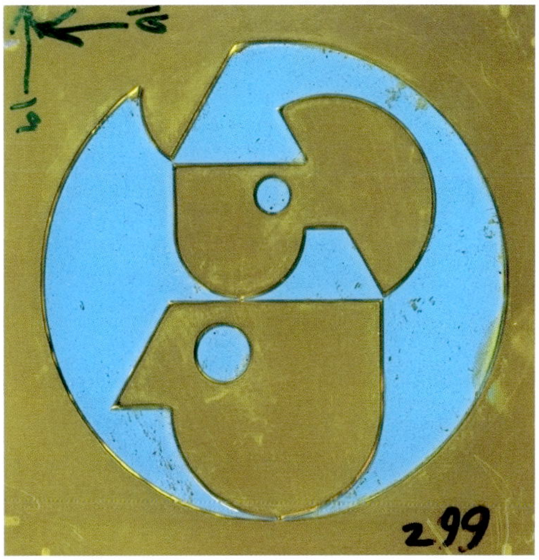

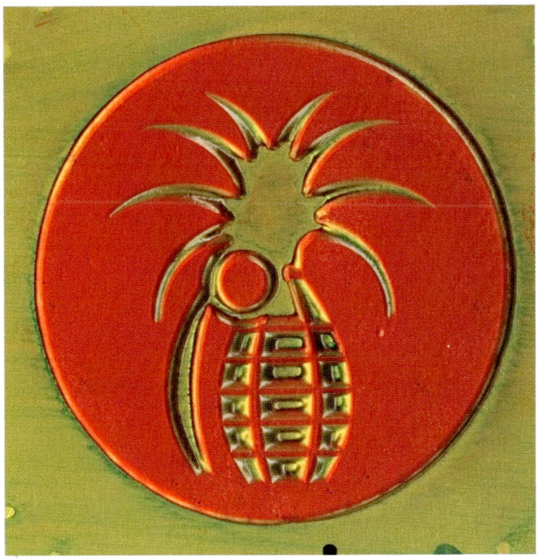

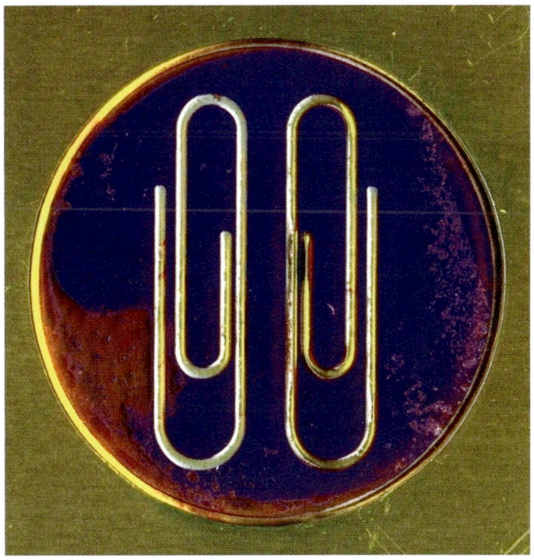

Details of inked UV reactive photopolymer letterpress plates. (87)

(87) Some people are against photopolymer plates the same way some people love vinyl and are against CDs and MP3s, but that's OK.

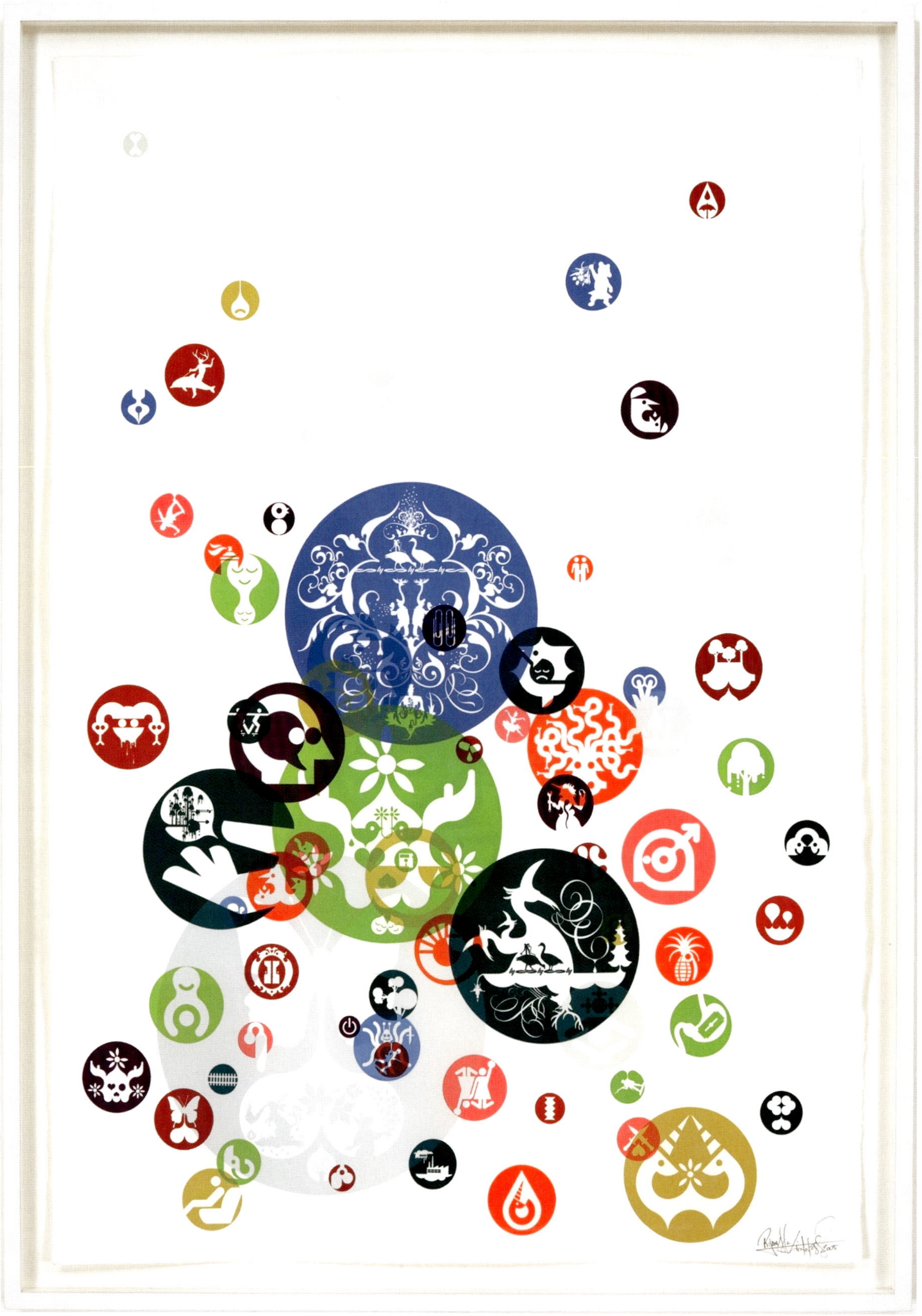

Above and opposite page: *Untitled*, 2005, 10-color letterpress, monoprints, 33 3/4 x 47 in. Printed by Coeur Noir, Brooklyn.

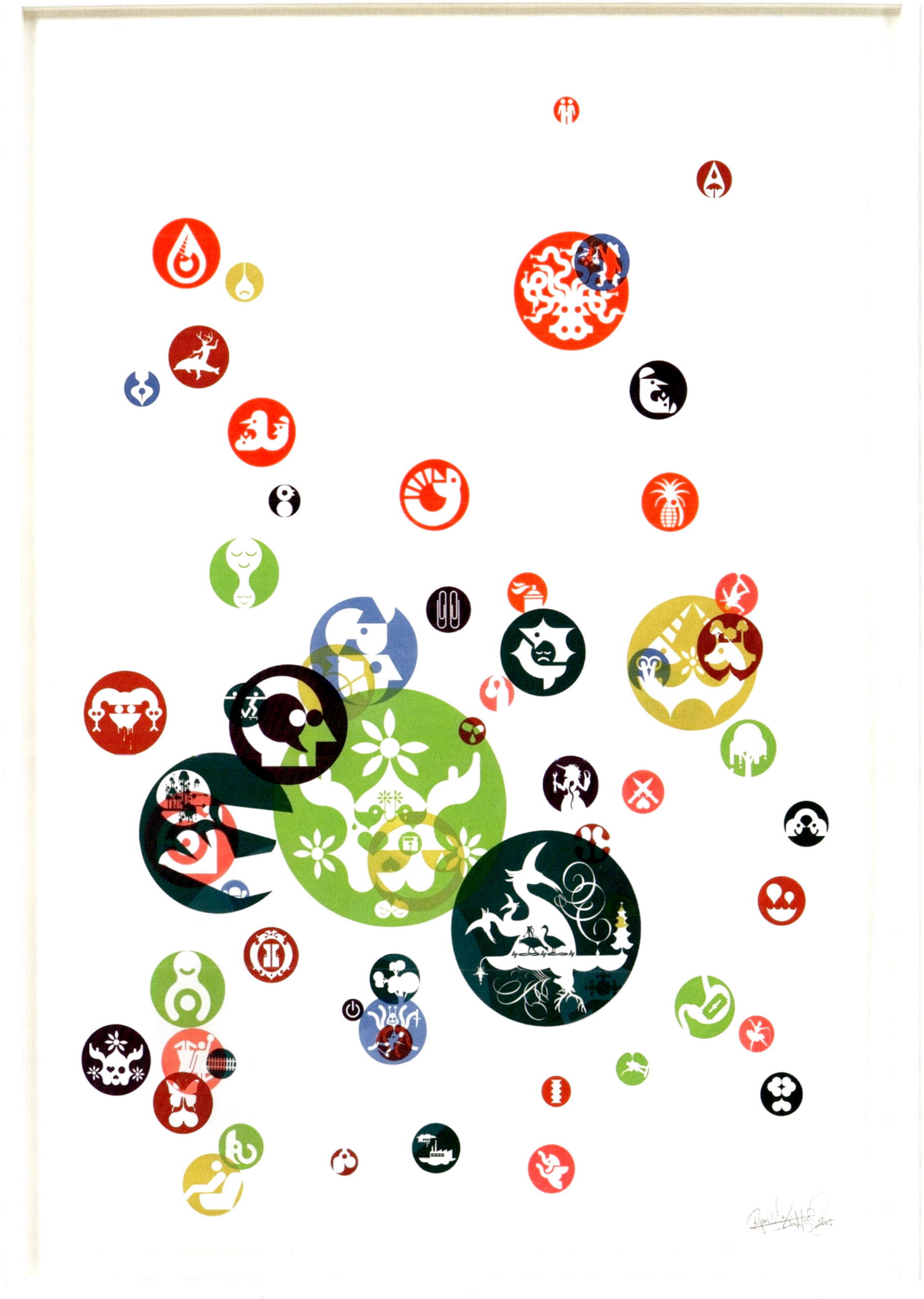

The lithographic stone allows for a more translucent ink application than other printing processes, though, as opposed to silkscreen or letterpress, once the stone is sanded down for reuse, the image is no longer reproducible.

In 2006, Ryan produced *Chain Reactions*, a portfolio of three lithographs in an edition of 33 and one monoprint at Edition Copenhagen in Denmark—and published in conjunction with World House Editions, New York. The portfolio was made in just one week, using several 42-by-37-inch stones on a large-format press. Each print consists of 10–15 different colored chains, making use of lithography's inherent translucency.

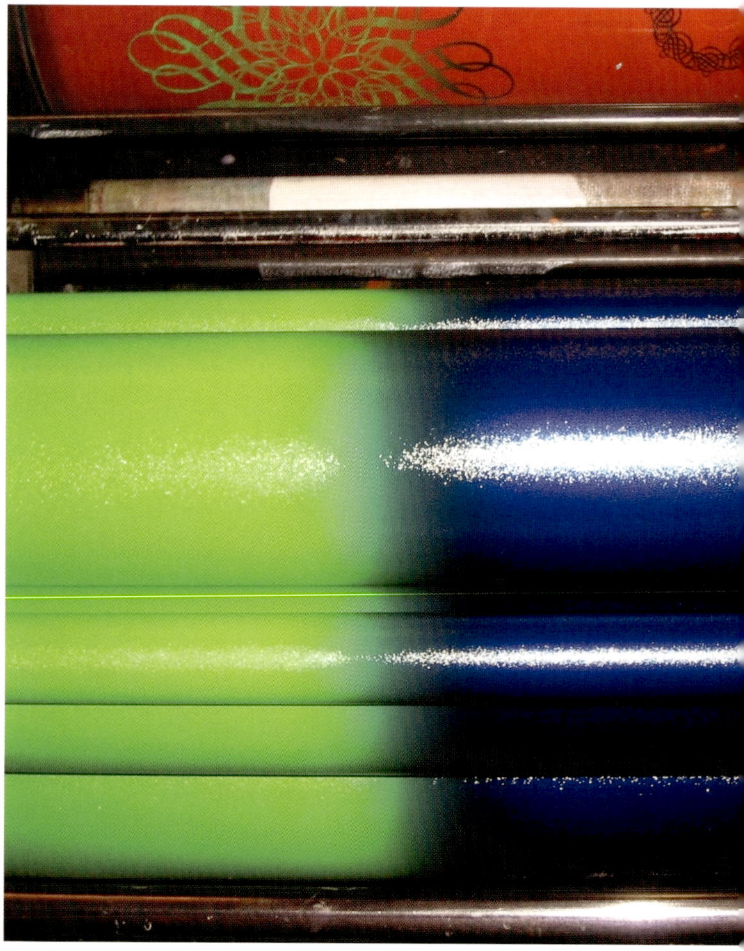

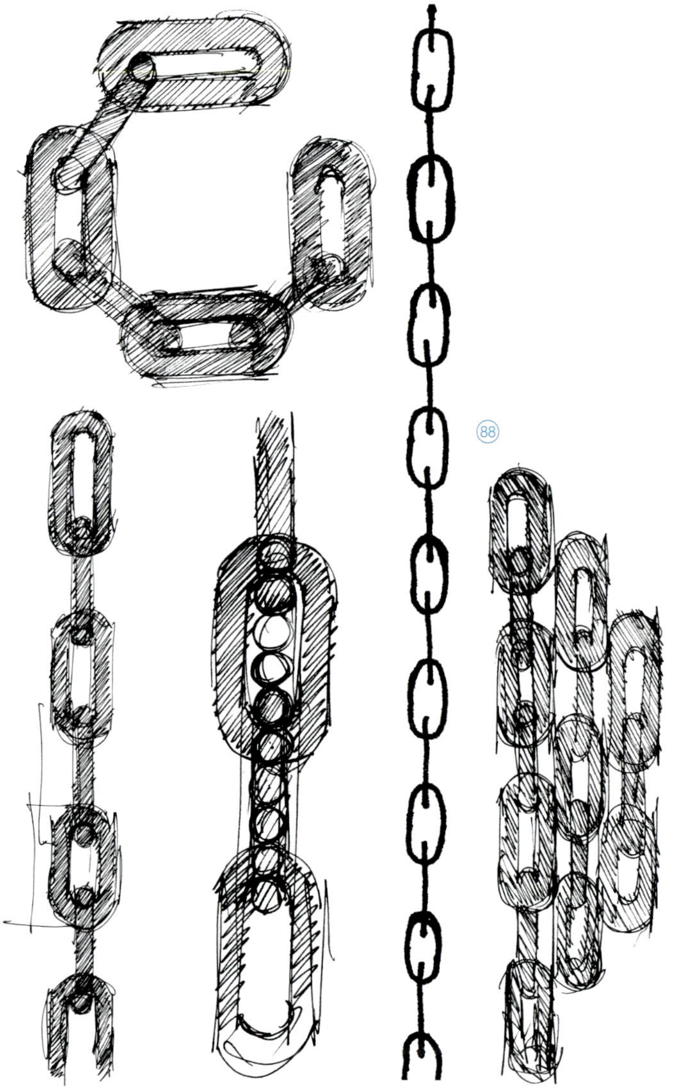

(88)

Process sketches for *Chain Reactions*, 2006. (All images this page and opposite page at Edition Copenhagen, and published by Edition Copenhagen and World House Editions, New York, 2006).

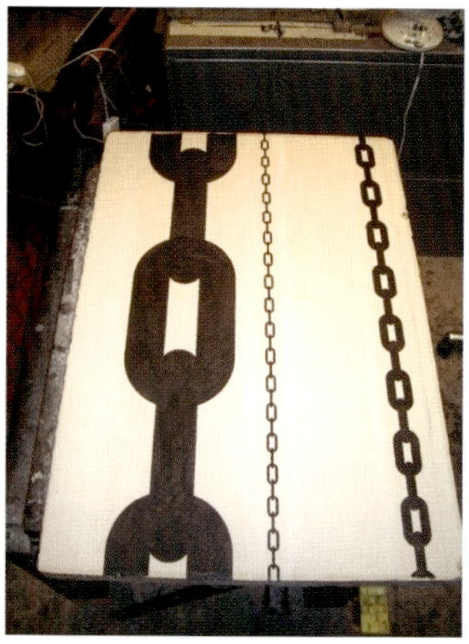

(89)

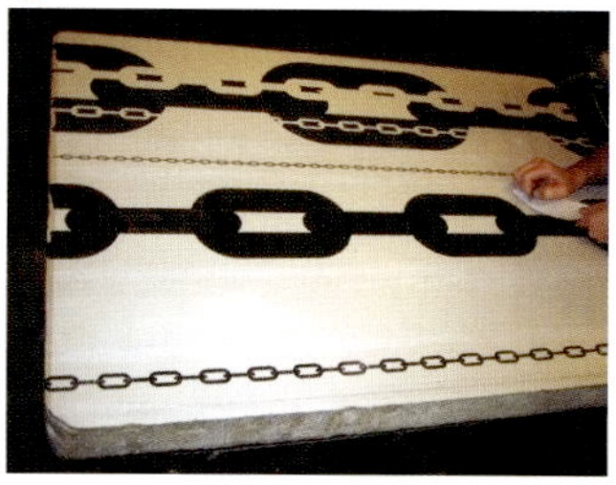

Top center: Detail of rollers inked with multiple colors at the same time in preparation for printing *Black Holes*, 2006, portfolio of 4 lithographs, 30 x 21 in. each, edition of 33.
Above: Inking the lithographic stone.

(88) Edition Copenhagen was nice enough to ship a 50-pound box of chains overnight from my studio because I wasn't sure they would have the right kind of chains in Copenhagen.

(89) The vertical chain links had to be drawn on the stones with precision. A razor blade was used to clean up the edges after the initial inking.

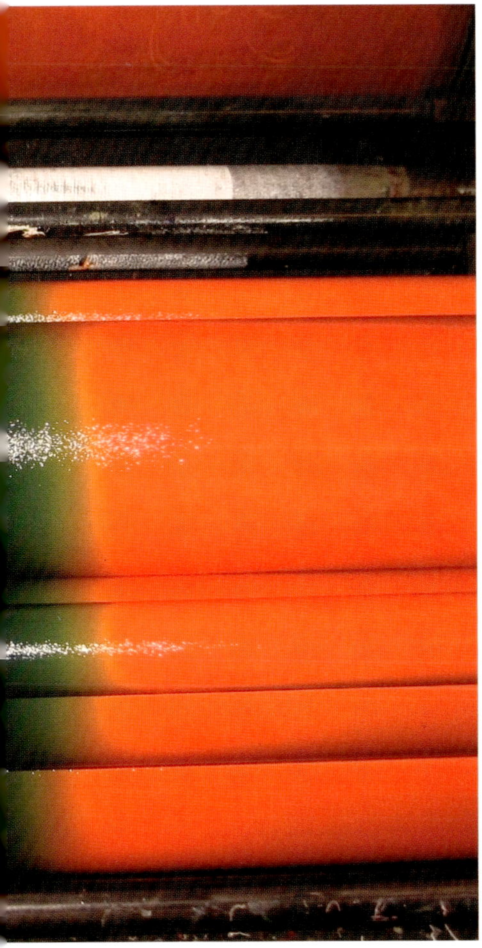

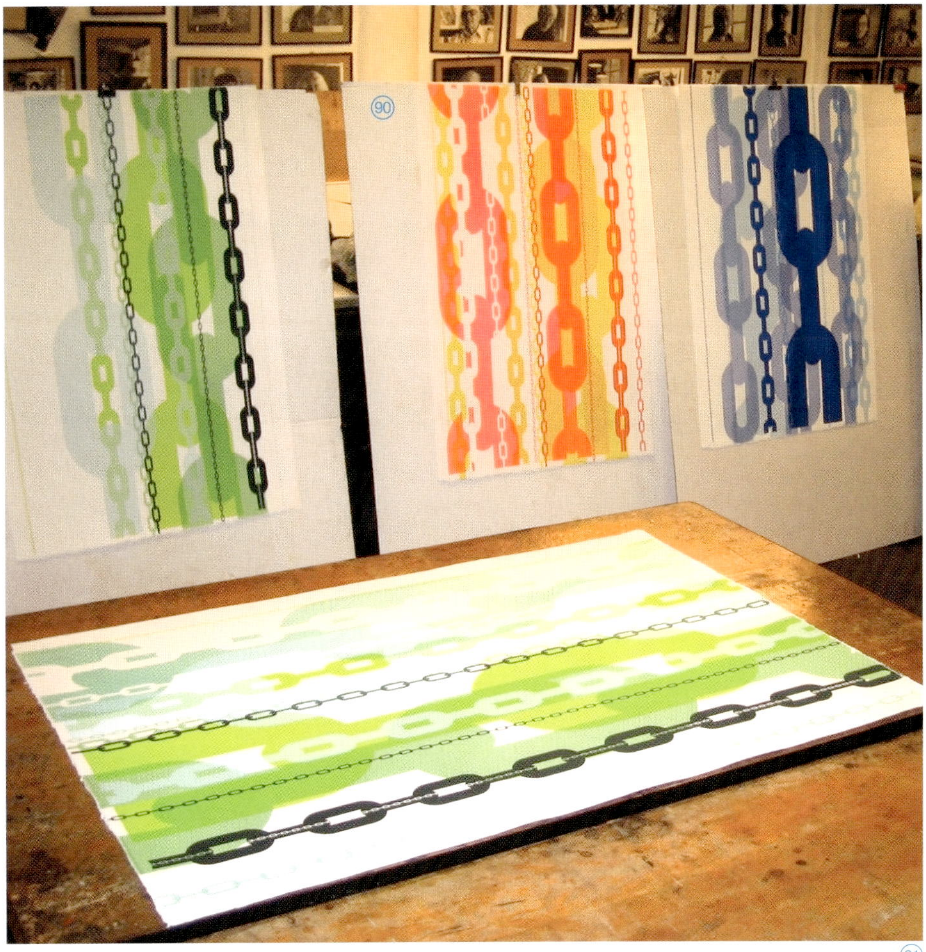

(91)

This was the first time Ryan had worked with lithography, so he was hesitant at first. I needed him to have a little faith in us that working with the stone would enable him to do things he'd never been able to do with a silkscreen.
—Donald Taglialatella
Publisher, World House Editions

(92)

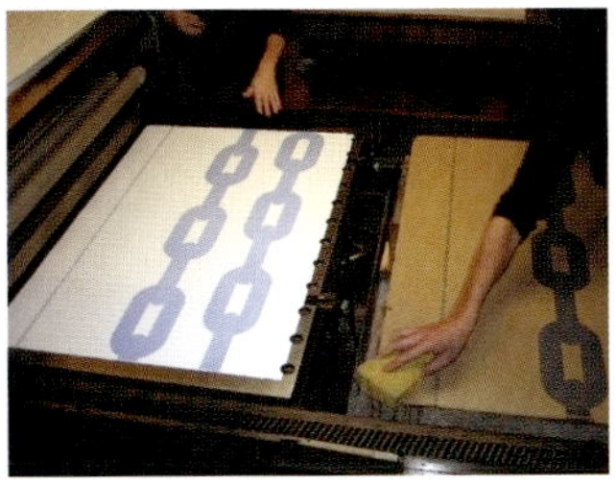

Wetting the stone.

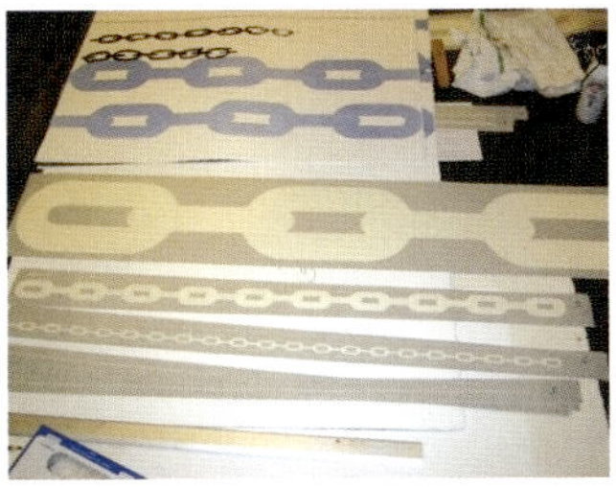

Detail of plotter-cut vinyl used for stenciling imagery onto the lithographic stone.

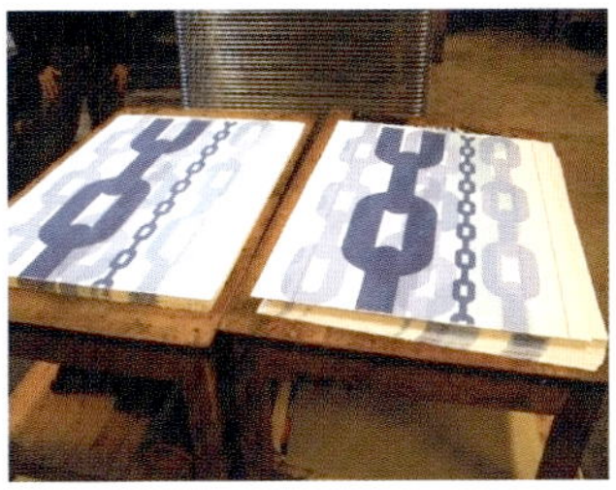

Top and above: *Chain Reactions* in process.

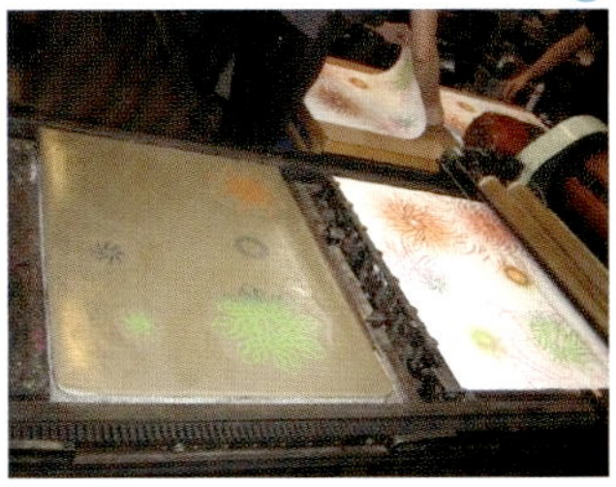

Printing *Black Holes*.

(90) The *Chain Reactions* brought me back to student line study assignments. Everything comes back to those foundation studies.

(91) I wanted to create beautiful things using symbols that refer to things usually associated with ugliness. See p. 63.

(92) I also made a series of *Black Hole* prints and a series of prints based on my sketches: .com/sketchprints.

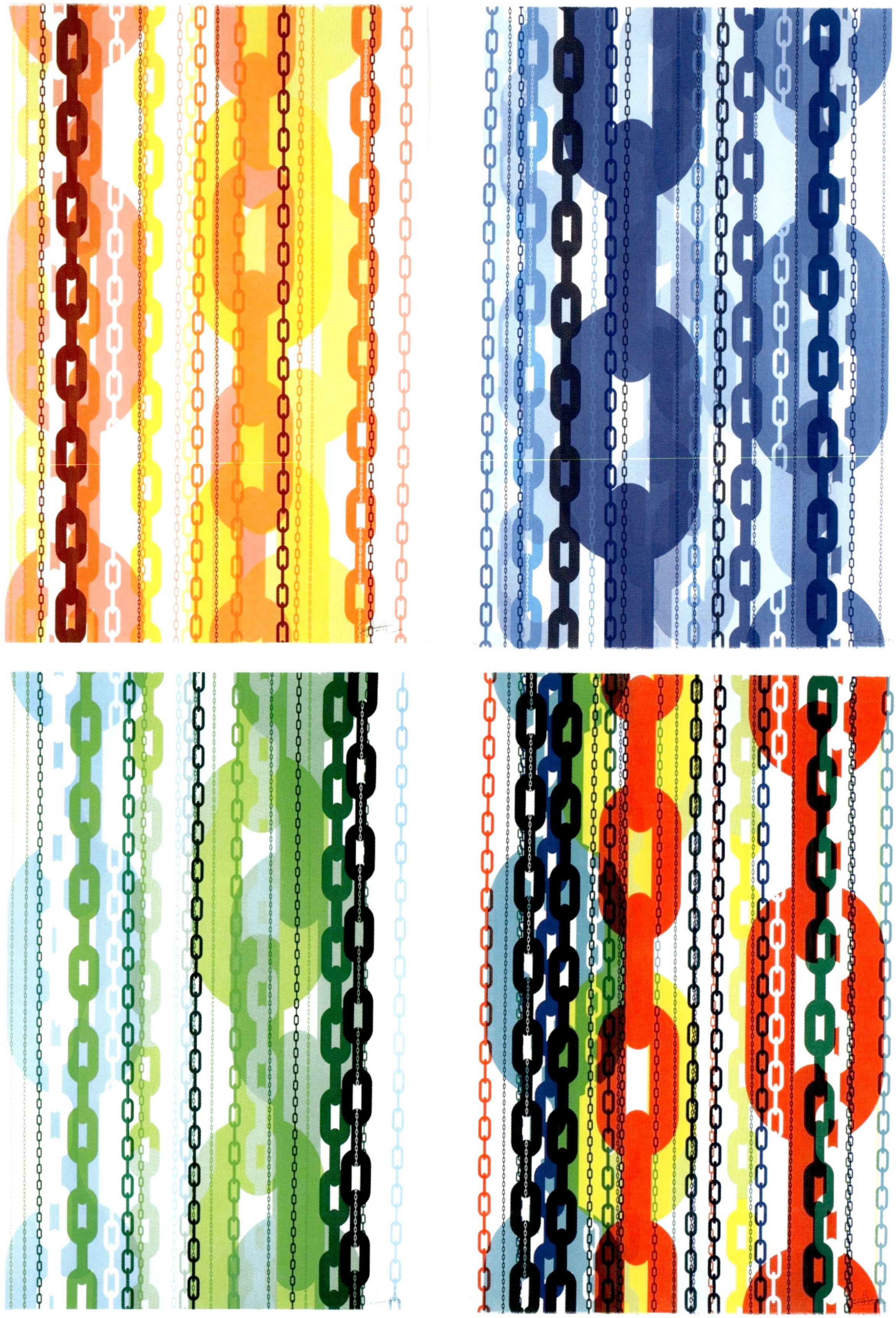

Chain Reactions, 2006, portfolio of 3 editioned lithographs and 1 monoprint, 38 x 27 in. each, edition of 33. Published by Edition Copenhagen, Copenhagen, and World House Editions, New York. Printed by Edition Copenhagen, Copenhagen (detail opposite page).

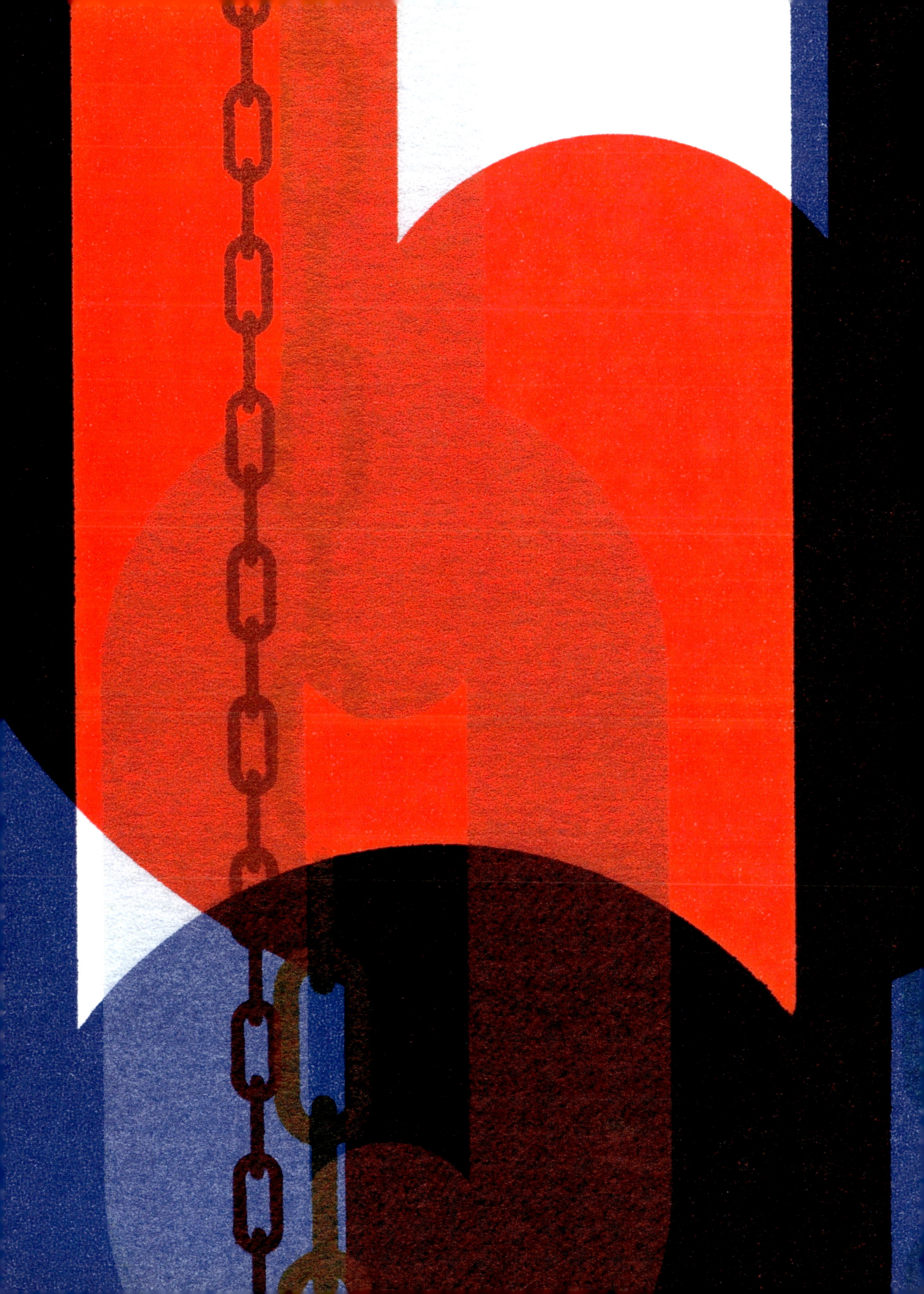

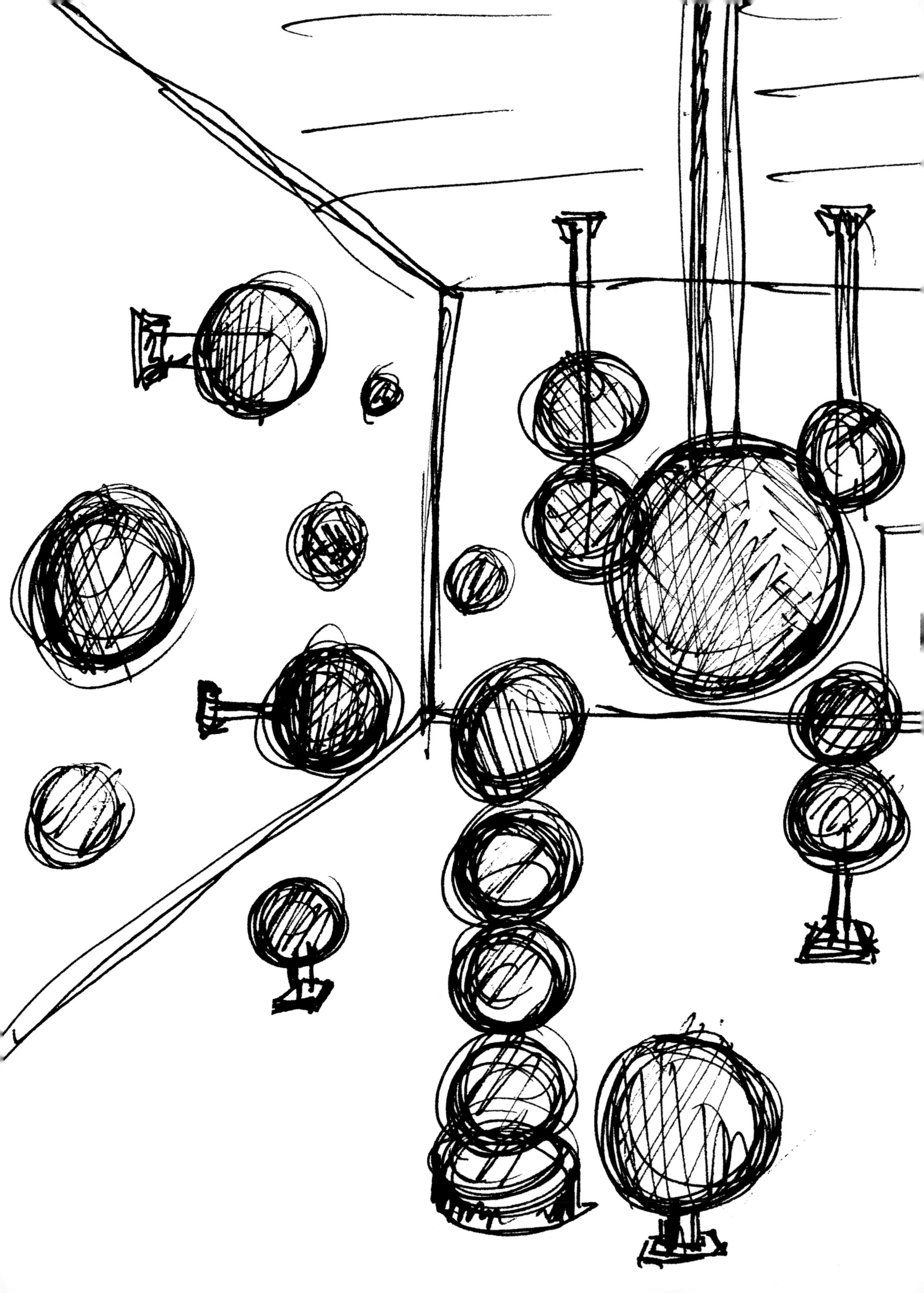

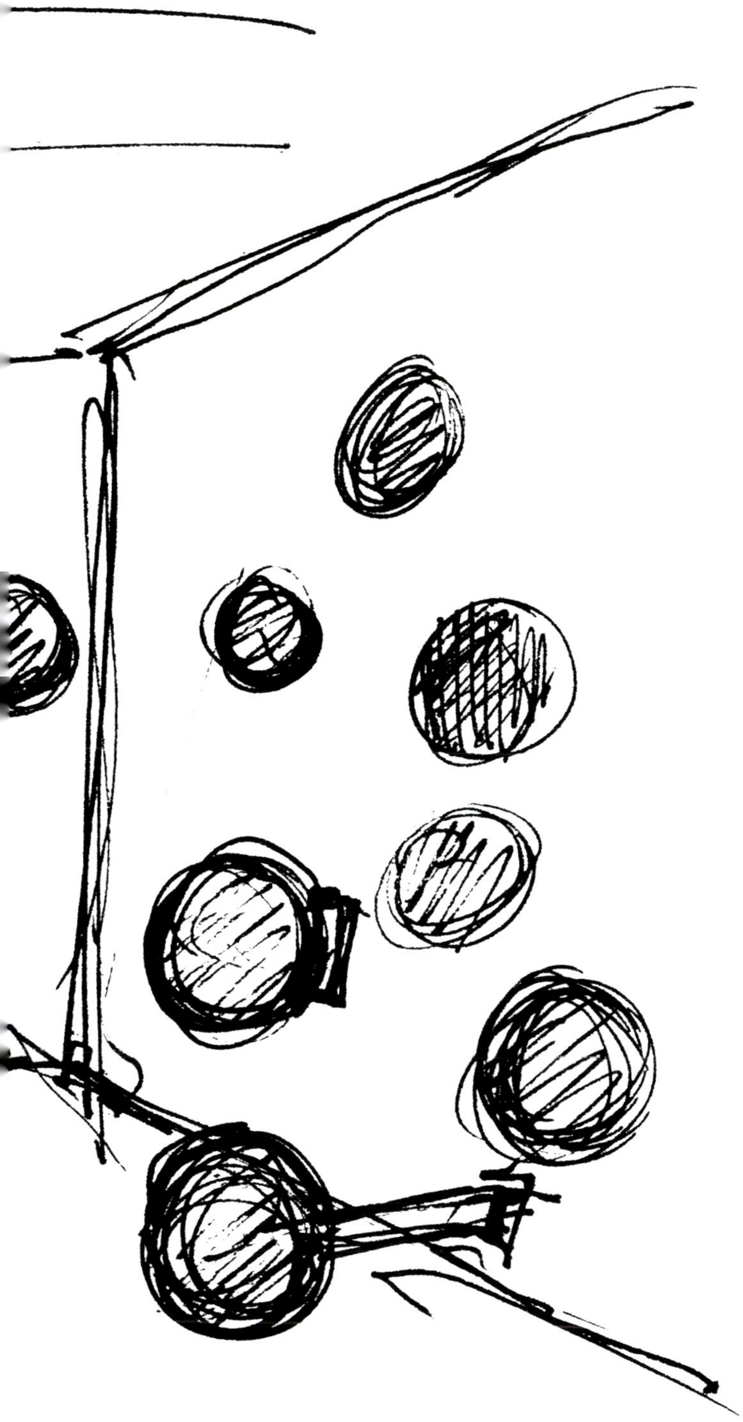

Installationview, an immersive environment, was on view at Deitch Projects in New York in 2005. The gallery was transformed with wall-sized paintings and *Universals*—two-sided fiberglass paintings of various sizes that cantilevered from the walls and ceiling, punctuating the space around them. Circular forms that represent distinct worlds, the *Universals* collided against each other visually within the installation to create a multiverse—a term borrowed from quantum physics that describes how universes are created by collisions in eleven-dimensional space.

Preliminary sketch for *Installationview*, 2005, ink on paper.

Fabrication of the *Universals* used in *Installationview* took about 10 weeks and was completed by Amaral Custom Fabrication in Seekonk, Massachusetts, where Keith Haring's and Roy Lichtenstein's sculptures were crafted.

Fiberglass was used to make two halves, which were then molded together and sanded in order to create a seamless surface. The forms were painted with AwlGrip, an industrial acrylic, and silk-screened with icons using a mixture of the industrial paint and a solvent, which had to be blasted out of the screens with a spray gun filled with turpentine immediately after application.

In addition to string theory, the *Universals* derived formally from the stone rings used in Tlachtli,(93) a 3,000-year-old Mesoamerican ball game, as well as from urban signage. After visiting Tlachtli courts in Mexico, Ryan created a series of one-sided, circular "doughnut paintings," but the form soon lost its hole and became the two-sided *Universals*, which are a precursor to later sculptures that use the forms in various stacked configurations. The *Universals* endeavor to marry the form, imagery, and materials of signage, to capture an anonymous, graphic look that demands attention with its authoritative presence. Unlike urban signage, however, the *Universals* remain intentionally open to interpretation.

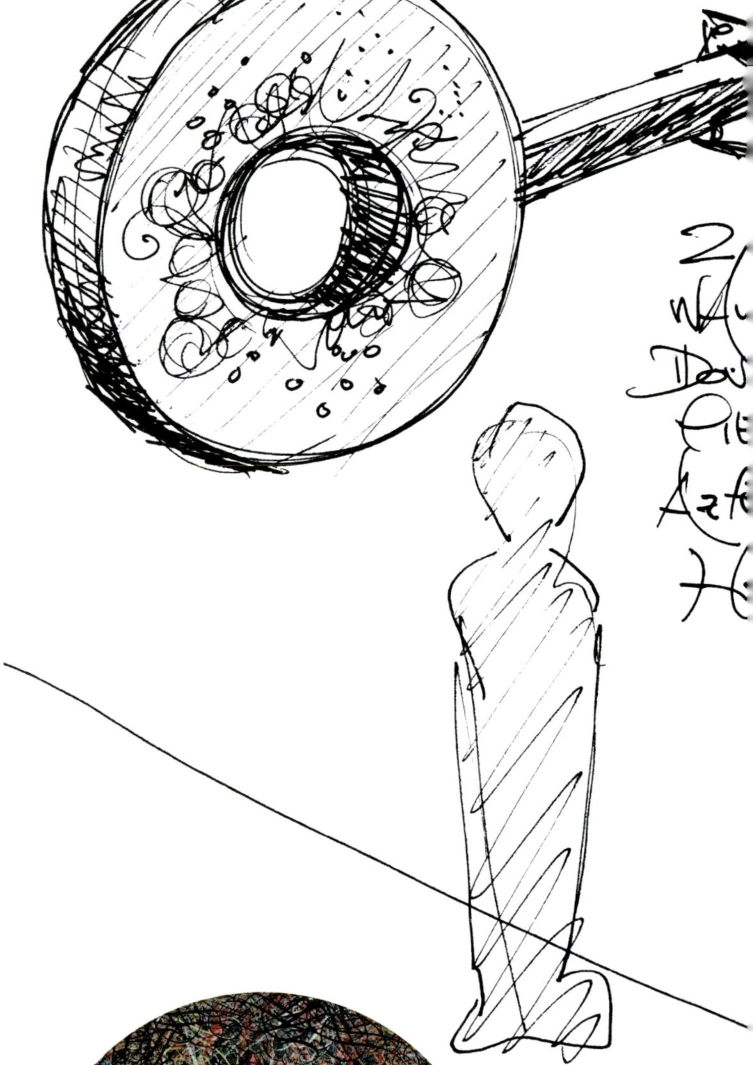

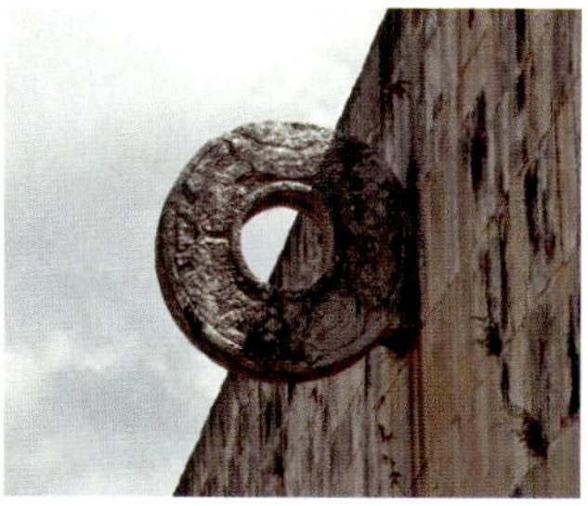

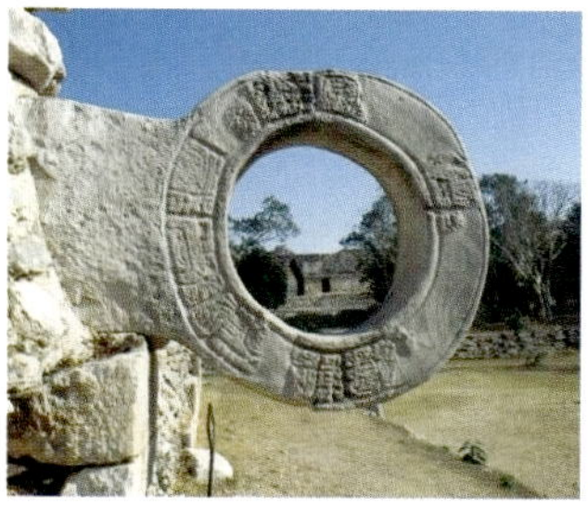

Tlachtli, a 3,000-year-old Mesoamerican ball game using stone rings, was an early influence for the *Universals*.

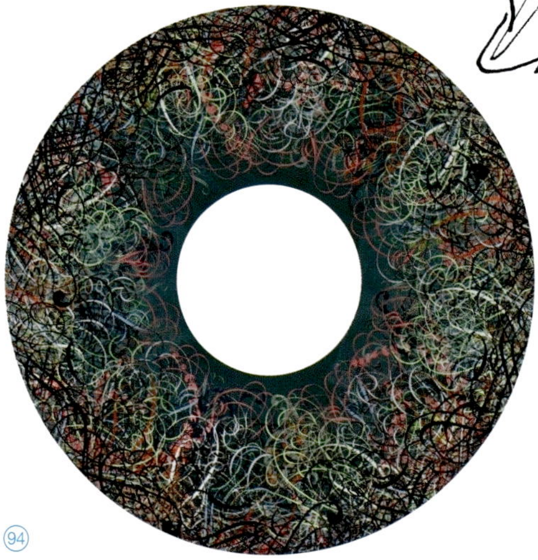

(94)

Untitled (Green Doughnut), 2006, acrylic on wood panel, 72 in. diameter.

Top center and opposite page: Process sketches for *Universals*, ink on paper, dimensions vary.

(93) It's a strange game—a cross between basketball and soccer.

(94) I wanted to integrate the environment into the painting. I was interested in breaking through the picture plane (.com/doughnutpaintinginstalled).

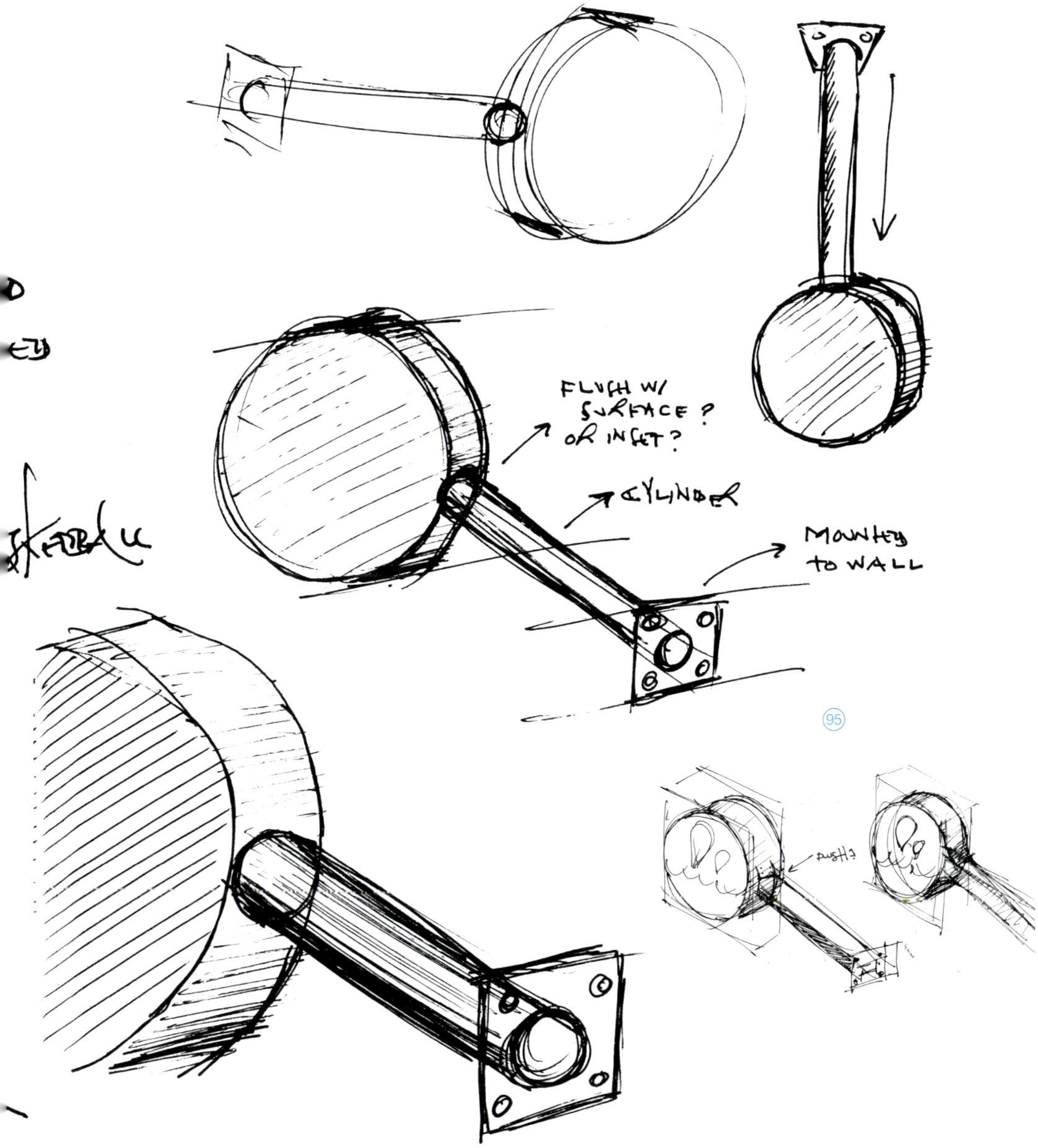

95

96

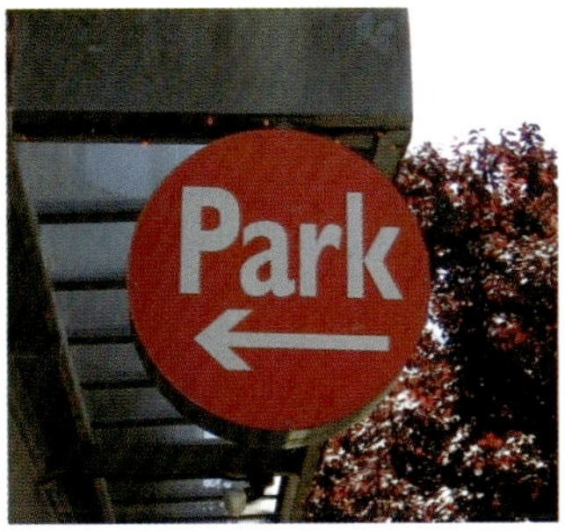

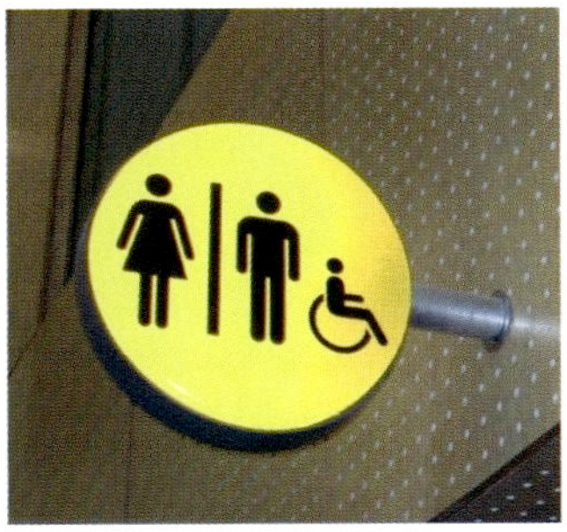

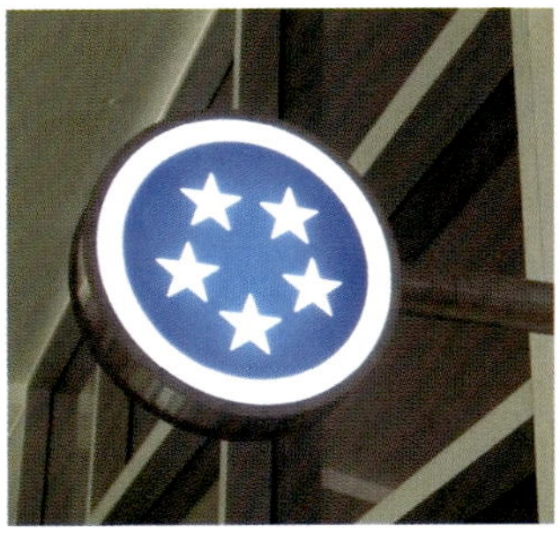

Universals were inspired by urban signage found in various cities.

(95) These sketches are bad. The perspectives are all off.

(96) Sign language. Signage language. The visual forms had invaded the paintings, and now the structural forms were becoming the paintings. Not signage, but two-sided paintings.

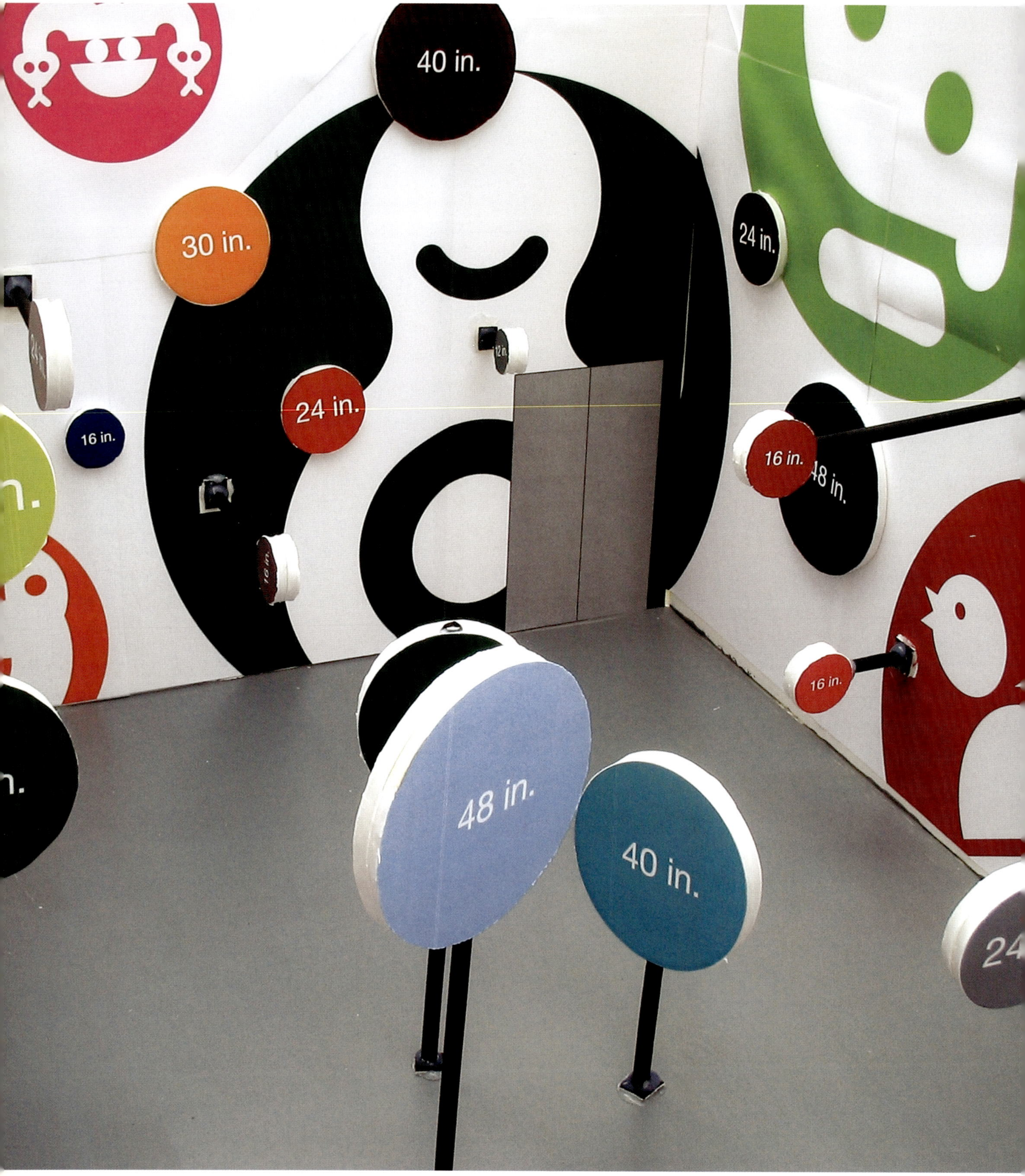
40 in.
30 in.
24 in.
24 in.
16 in.
12 in.
16 in.
48 in.
16 in.
16 in.
48 in.
40 in.

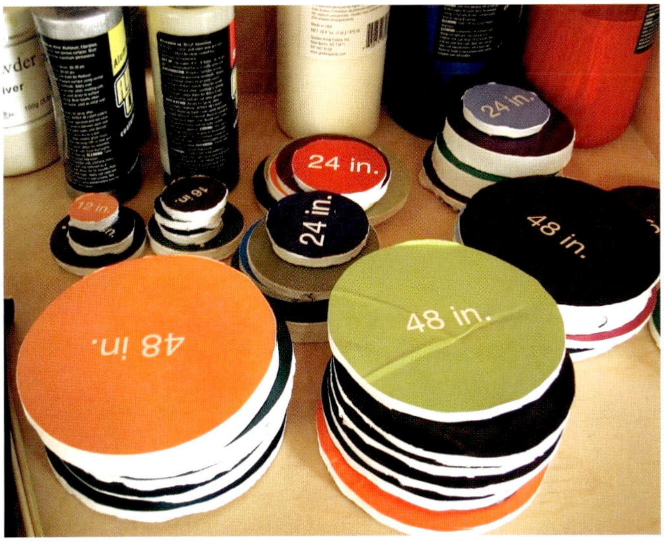

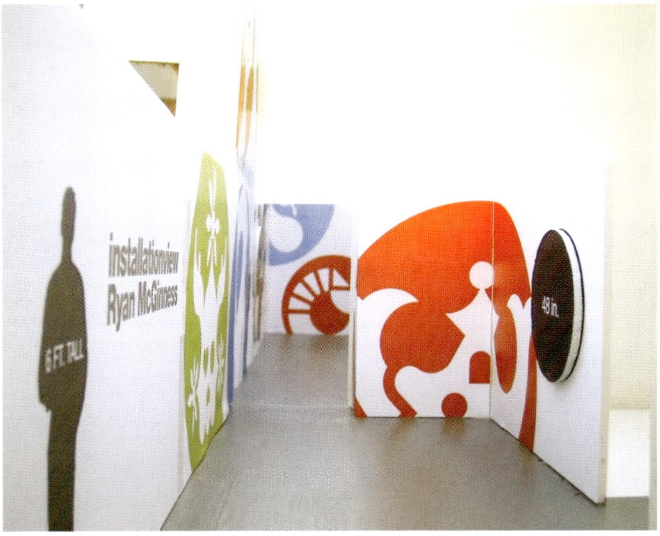

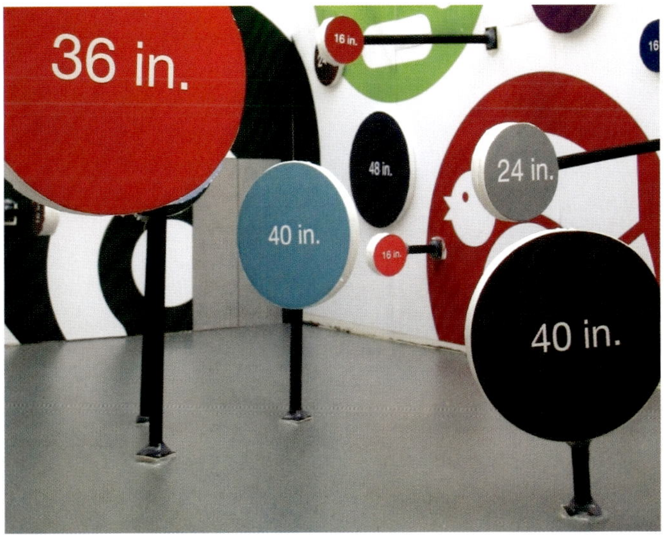

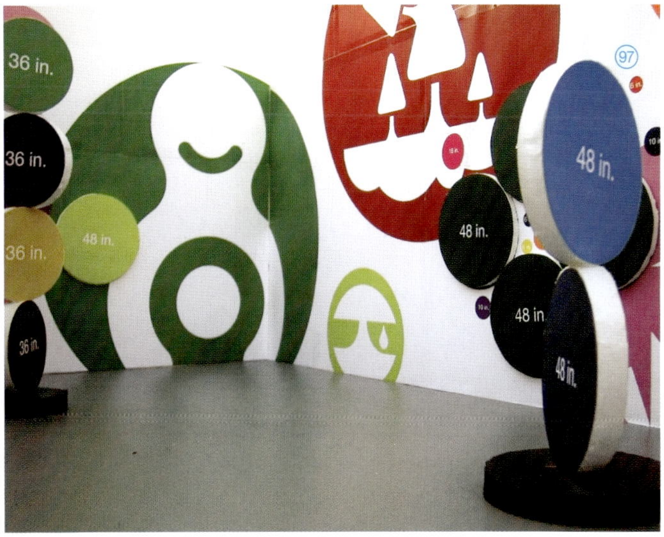

Ryan is very conceptual, very rigorous. He combines this with a more open, improvisatory approach, but he plans things out precisely, creating models and printouts of the whole project. He's unique in the way his mind works almost scientifically.
—Jeffrey Deitch
Director, Deitch Projects

Top and opposite page: Foamcore scale models of *Installationview*.

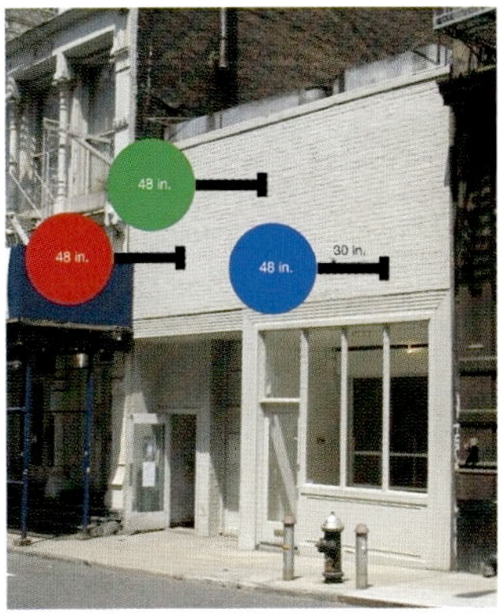

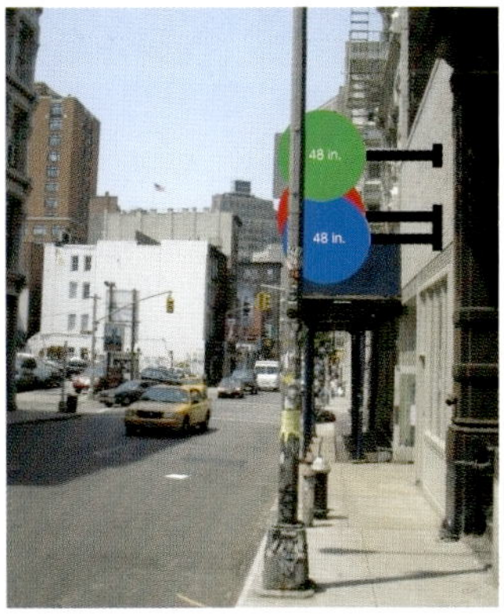

Unrealized proposals for *Universals* to cantilever off Deitch Projects' facade, New York. (98)

(97) *Kissing* was originally planned for this exhibition. See p. 142.

(98) We couldn't get the required permits from the city.

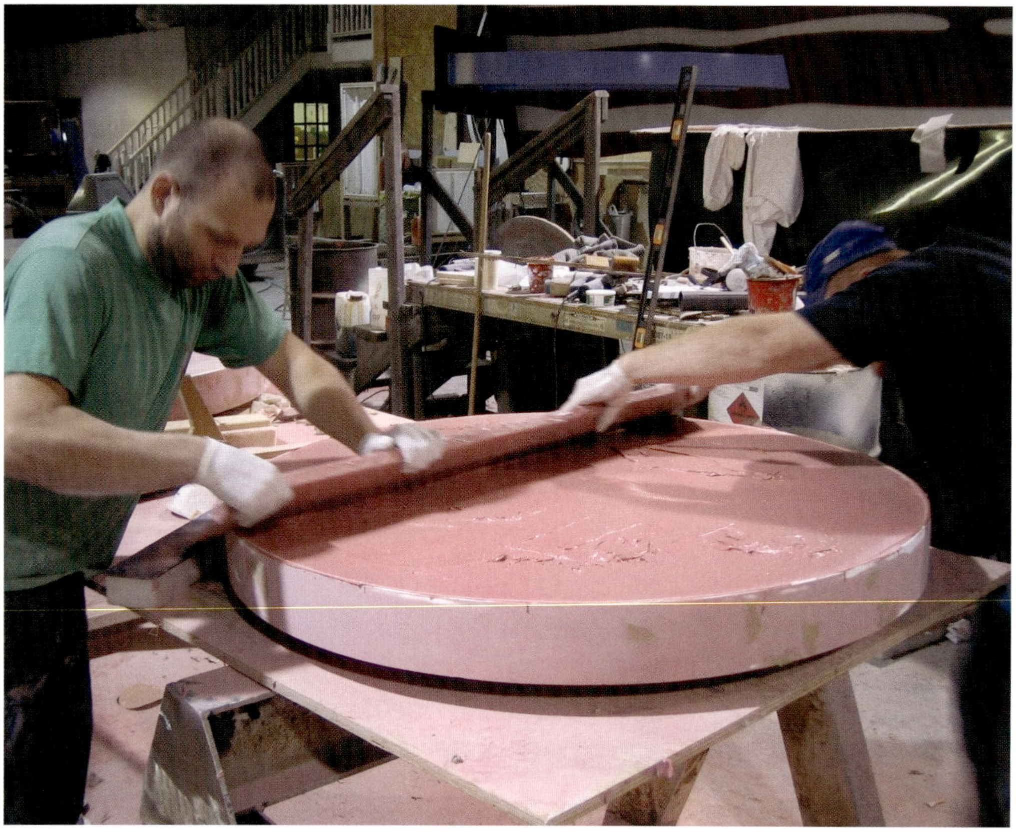

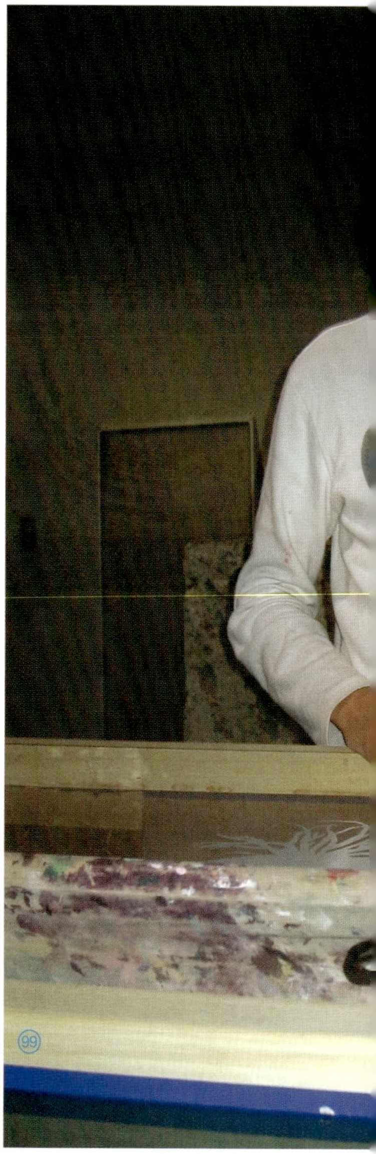

The biggest challenge in making the Universals *was that, for the purpose of silkscreening, they had to be flat. We used fiberglass—not a forgiving material. It comes off a roll, as cloth, and the resins it's impregnated with tend to shrink and warp. We filled any hollows with an epoxy putty using a process I learned working for the company that makes America's Cup yachts.*
—Paul Amaral
Amaral Custom Fabrications

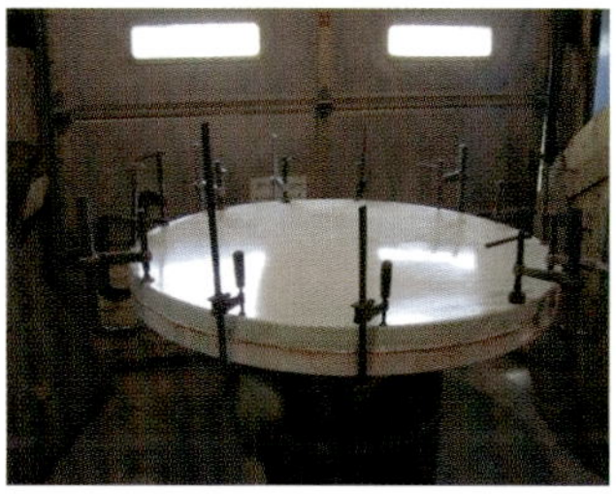

Above: *Universal* in mold. Top: Leveling the surface of fiberglass *Universal* with Bondo. (All images at Amaral Custom Fabrications, Seekonk, MA, 2005).

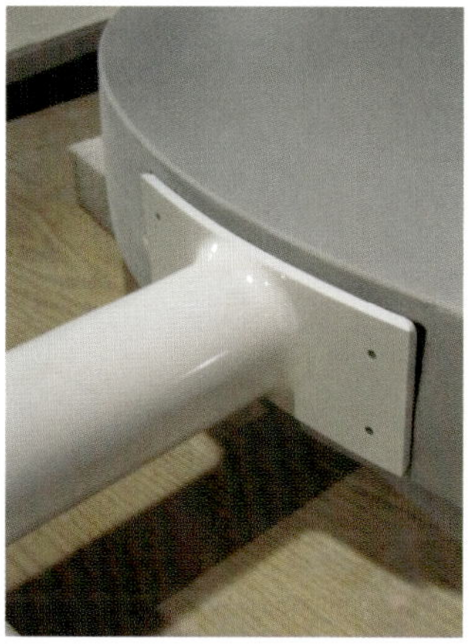

Detail of connection between the aluminum cantilever and fiberglass *Universal*.

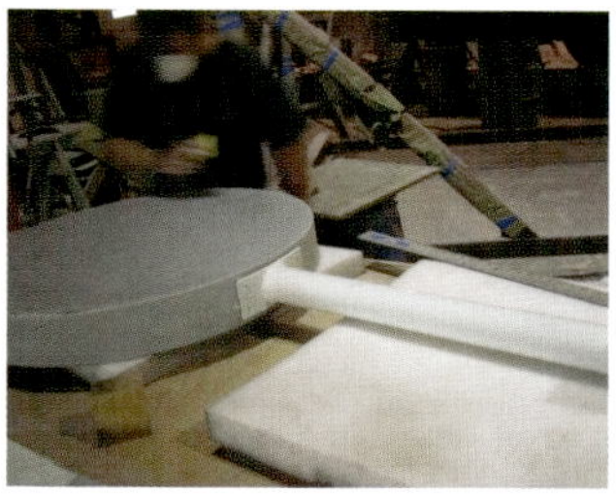

Sanding primed fiberglass.

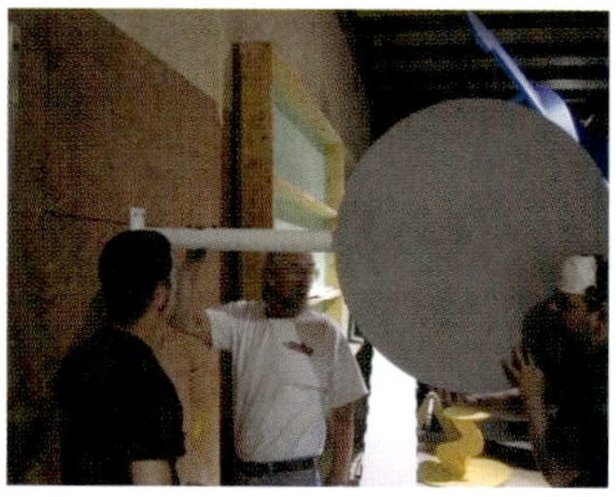

Testing the cantilever.

(99) I loaded my screens into a van and took them to Massachusetts, where I worked with the Amaral team for six days—I took naps in the van for the last three days of that trip.

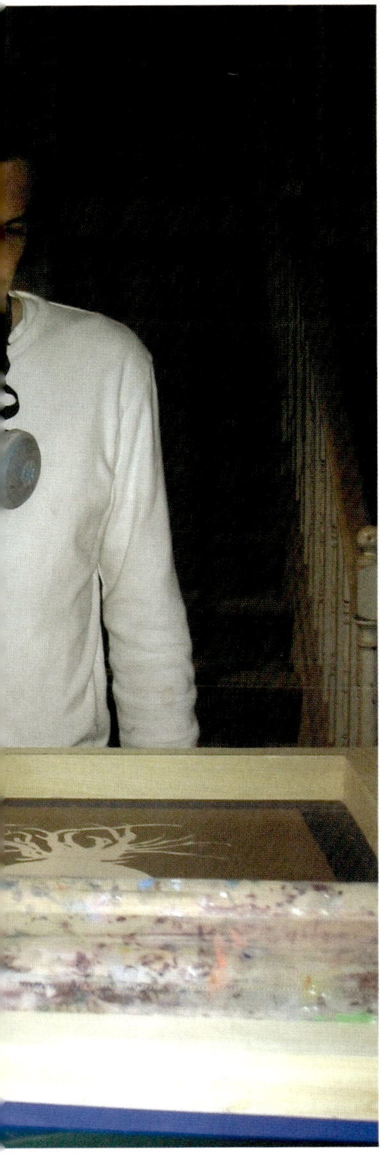

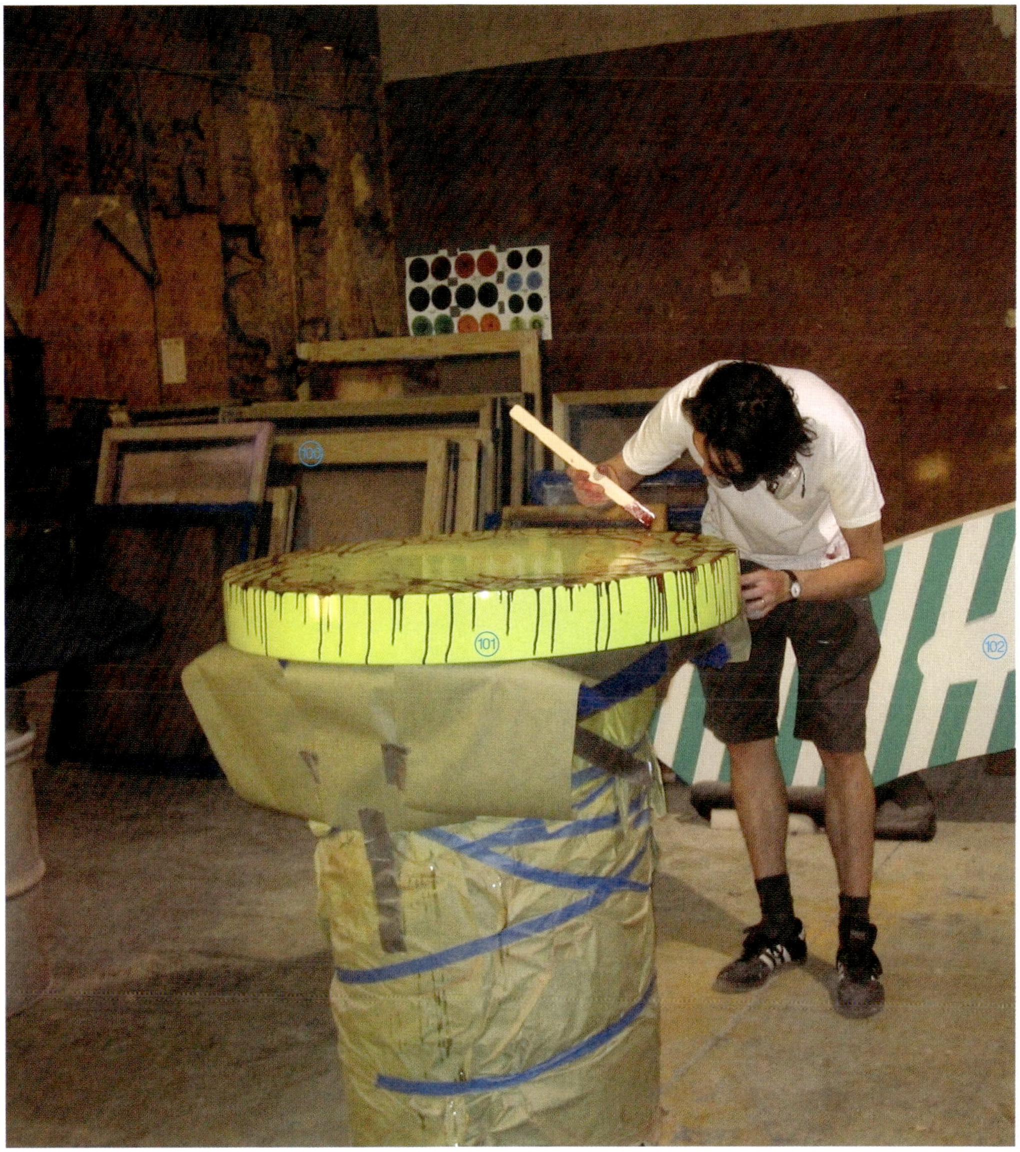

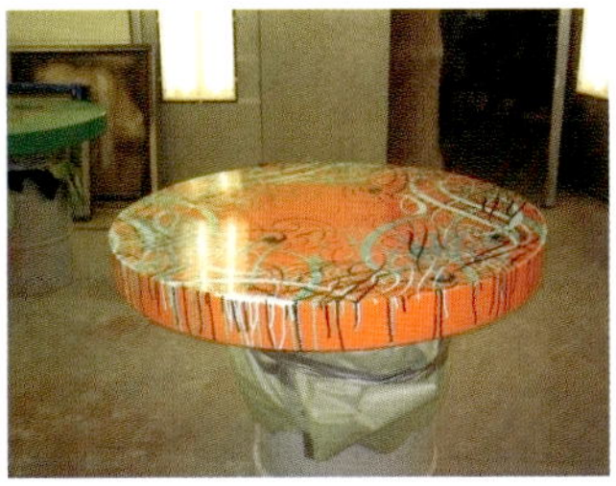

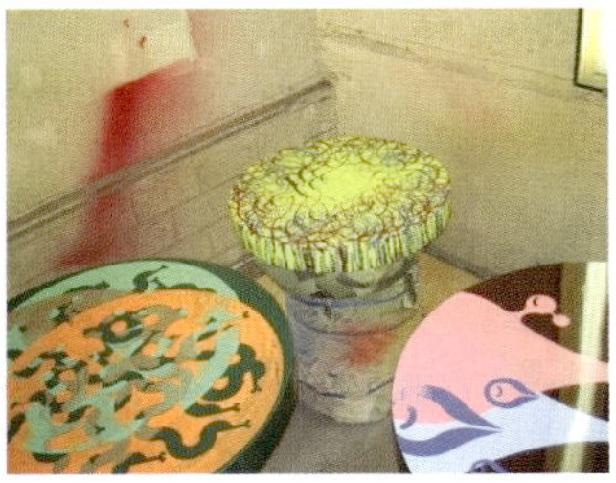

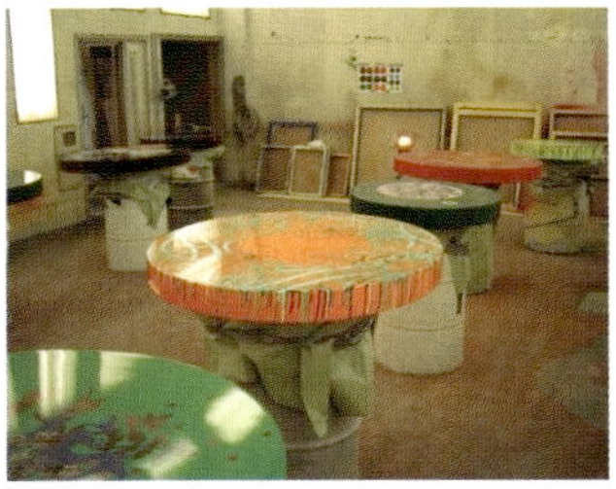

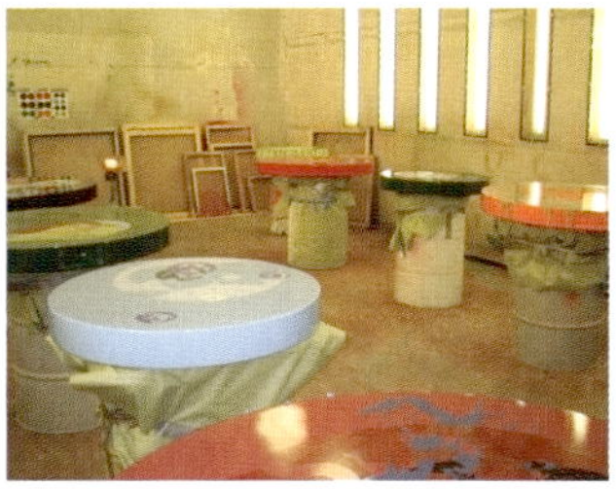

Top center and right: Painting a *Universal*.

Above: *Universals* drying in spray booth between layers. The booth was heated in order to cure the paint.

(100) Screens of my drawings that I had brought with me.

(101) The paint drips are calculated. To me, they are hilarious.

(102) Roy Lichtenstein sculpture.

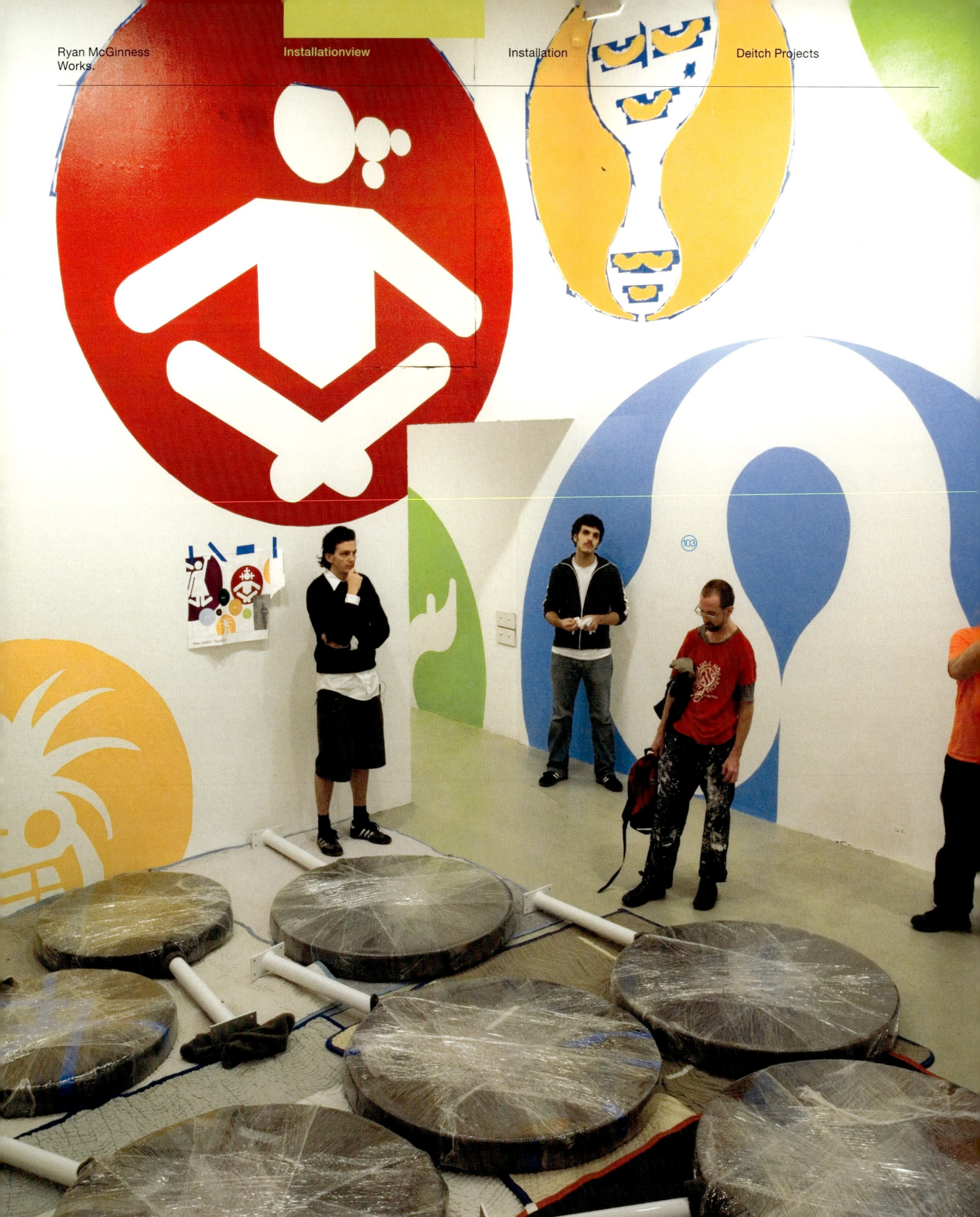

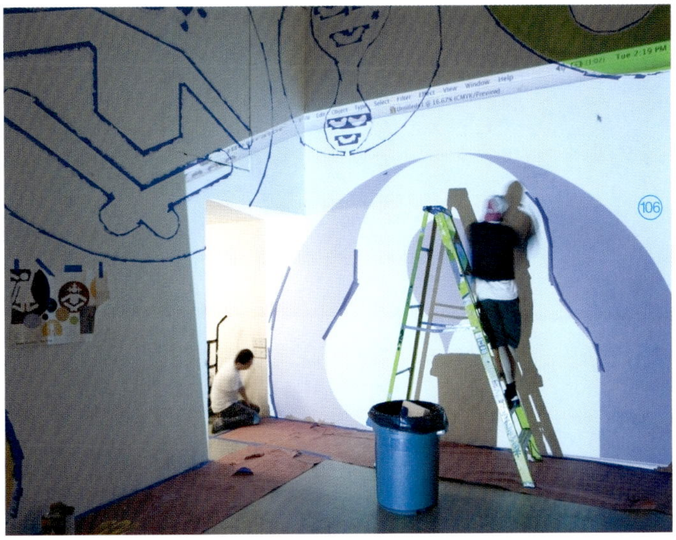

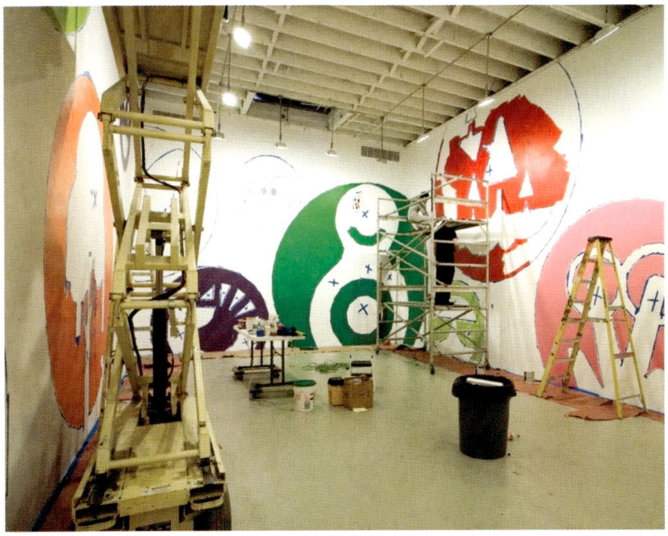

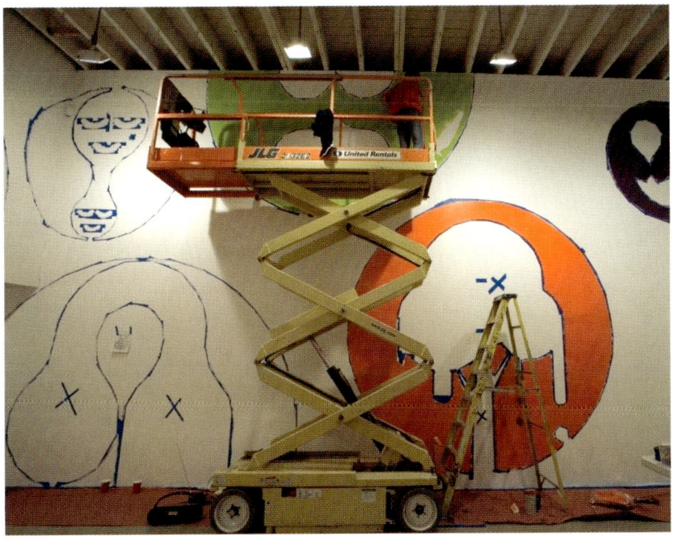

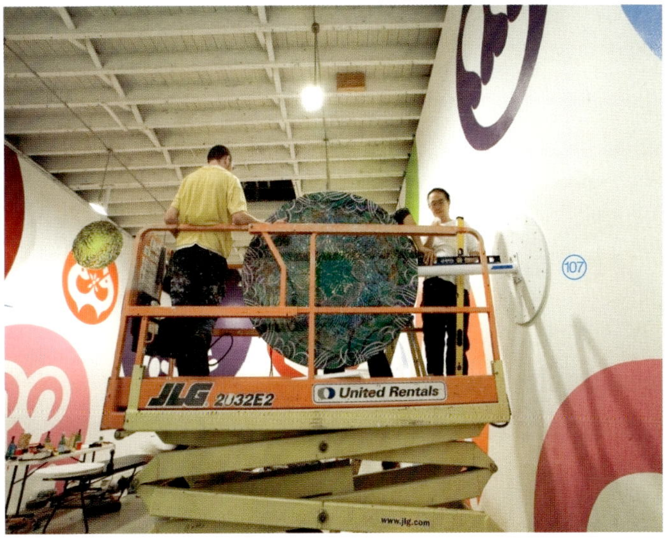

It wasn't an easy installation. It took longer than we thought because we painted Ryan's images onto the walls—we thought we could get away with one or two coats, but some of the colors needed as many as five. We went through a lot of coffee.
—James Powers
Installer, Deitch Projects

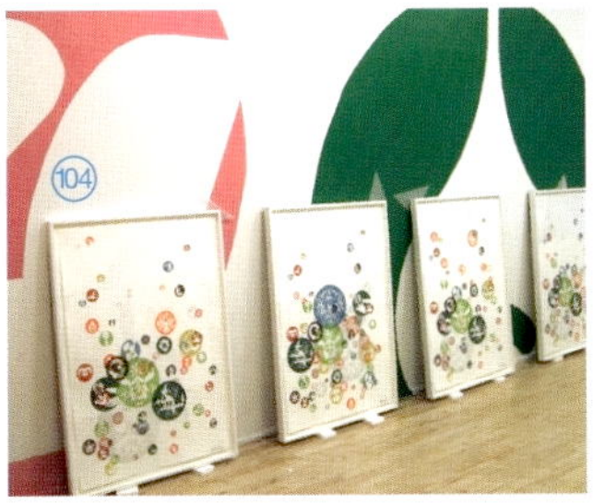

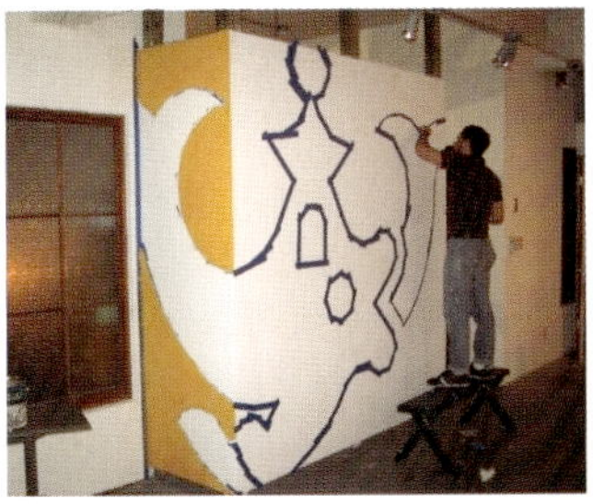

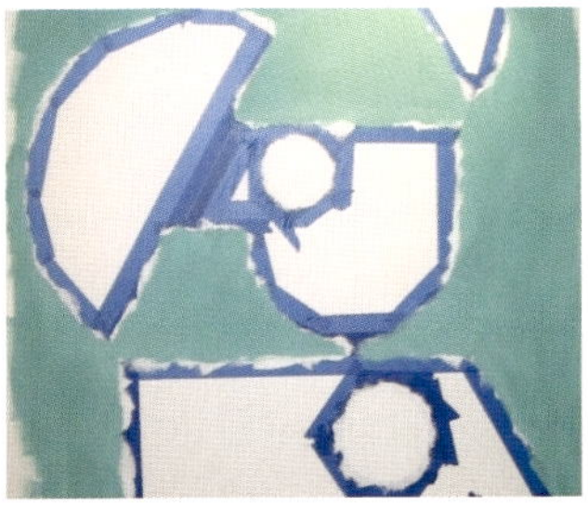

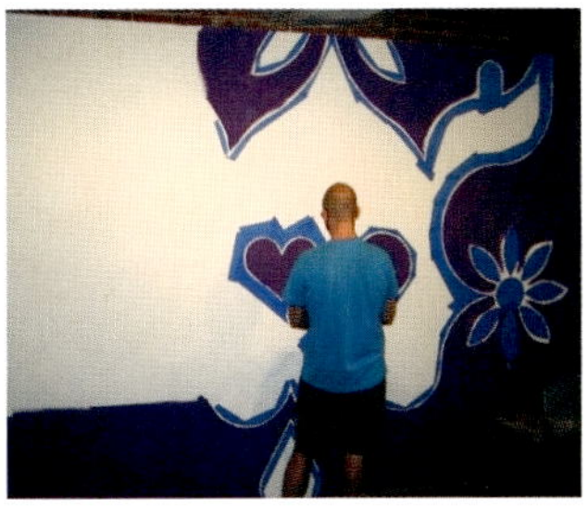

Opposite page: *Universals* on the floor at Deitch Projects in preparation for installation of *Installationview.* (All images at Deitch Projects, New York, 2005.)

Top: Installing *Installationview.*

Installing "Wall Paintings" at Publico, Cincinnati, 2005. (105)

(103) Dustin Schuetz, James Powers, and Paul Weston.

(104) See pp. 70–71.

(105) .com/publicoinstallation

(106) Projecting from a laptop. Masking. Drawing. Cutting. Painting. Peeling.

(107) The walls in the gallery are backed with plywood only up to 10 feet, so that was our maximum hanging height.

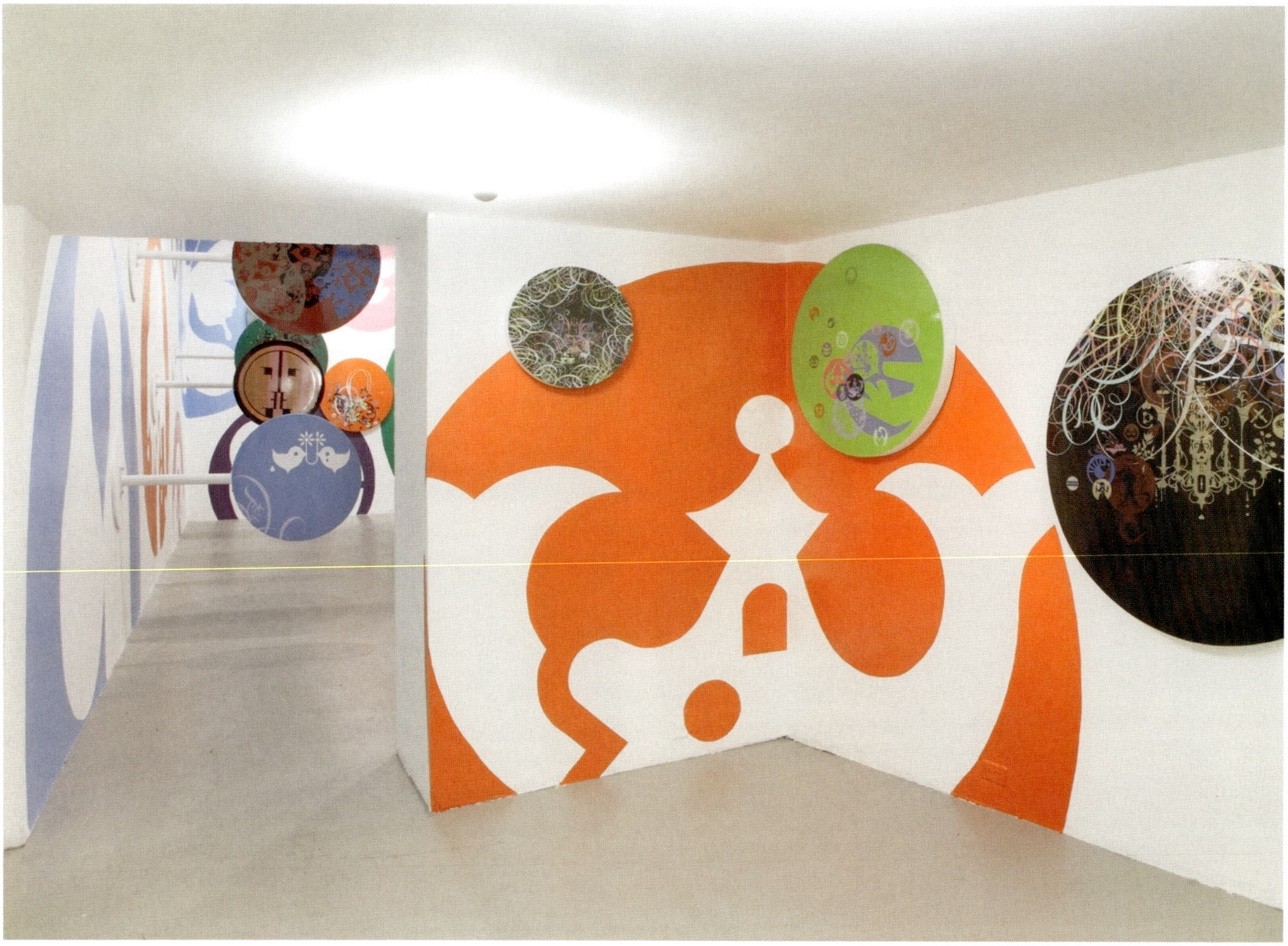

Installationview, mixed media, dimensions variable. Installation view, 2005.
Deitch Projects, New York.

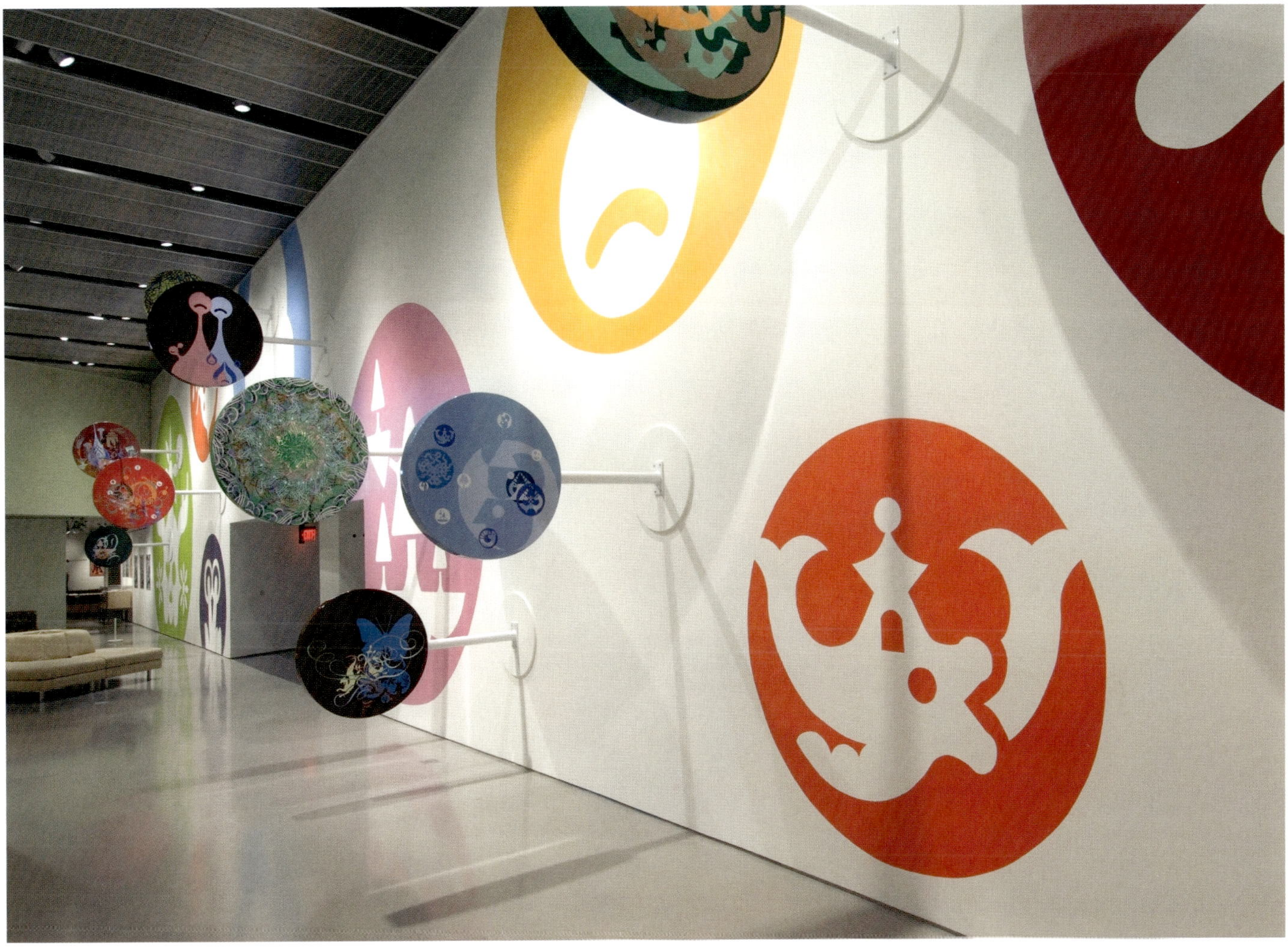

We had to post guards by the ones installed lower to the ground so that kids didn't use them as a jungle gym. All the visual cues are there that this is a playful environment to be interacted with—sometimes adults wanted to do it, too.

—Matt Distel
Curator, "Graphic Content: Modern and Contemporary/Art and Design," Contemporary Arts Center, Cincinnati

View of "Graphic Content: Modern and Contemporary/Art and Design," 2005. Contemporary Arts Center, Cincinnati.

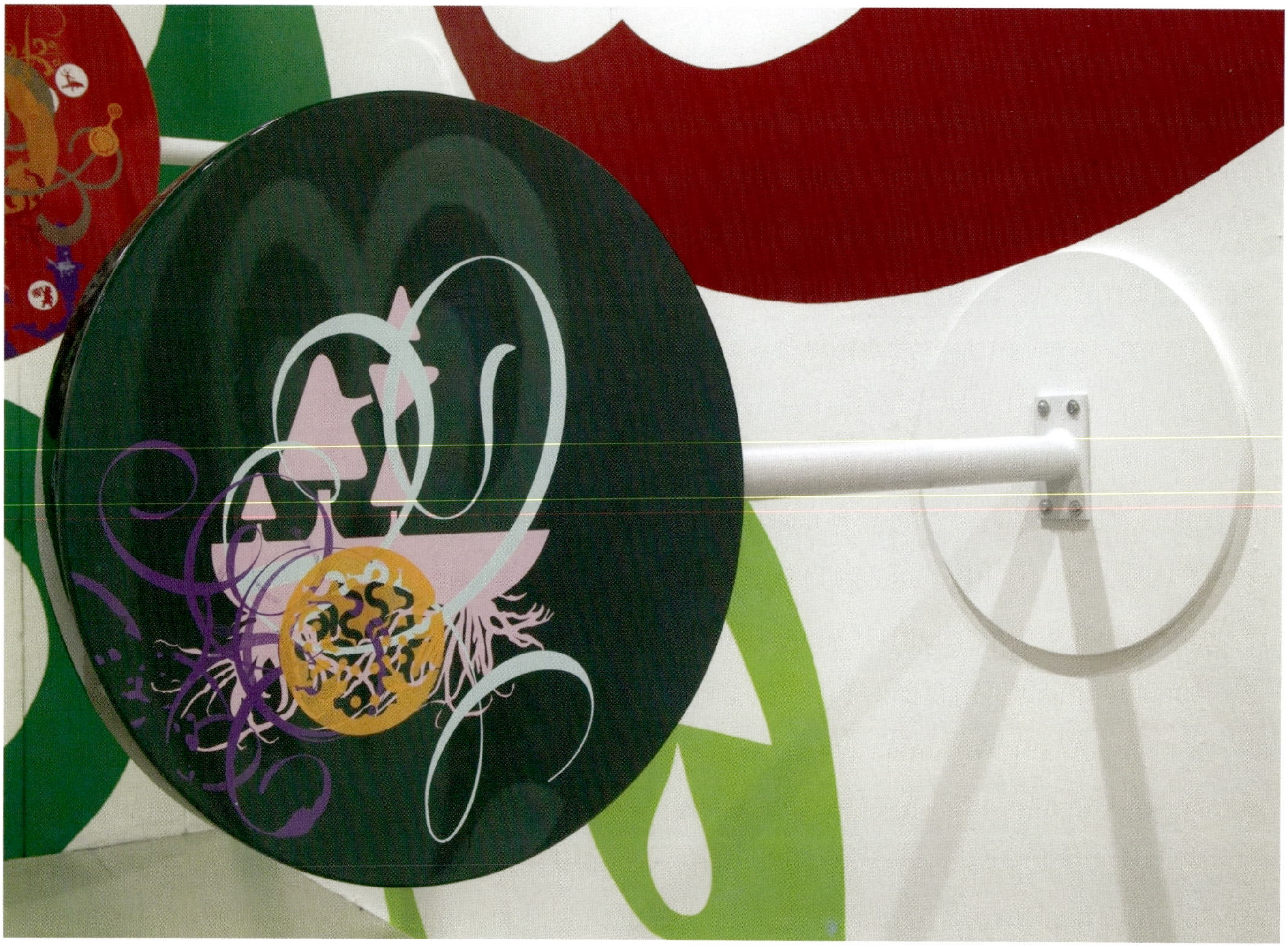

Universal (36d, No. 3), 2005, polyester urethane on fiberglass with aluminum and wood cantilever, 36 in. diameter x 4 in. Cantilever, 30 in. x 3 in. diameter.

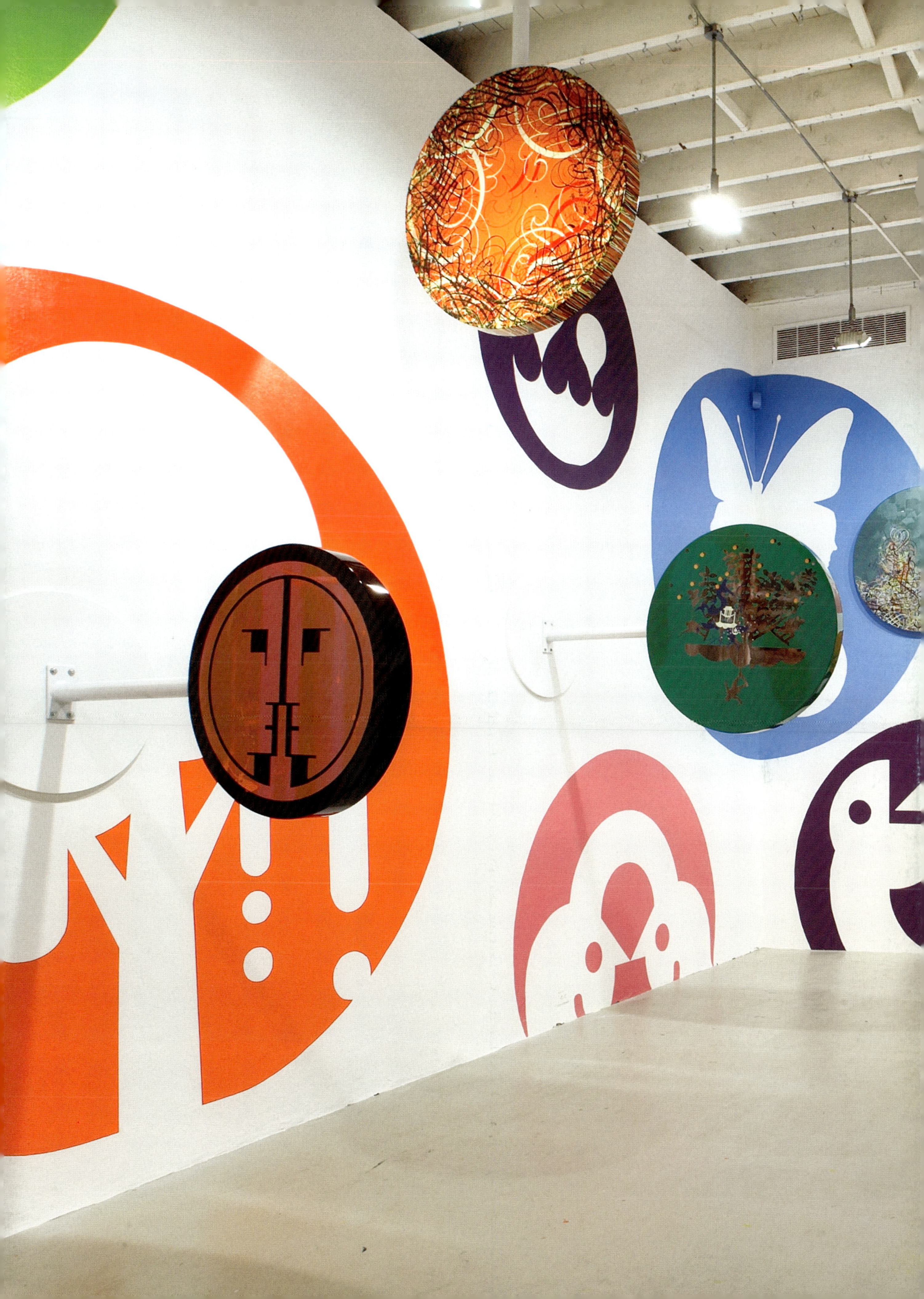

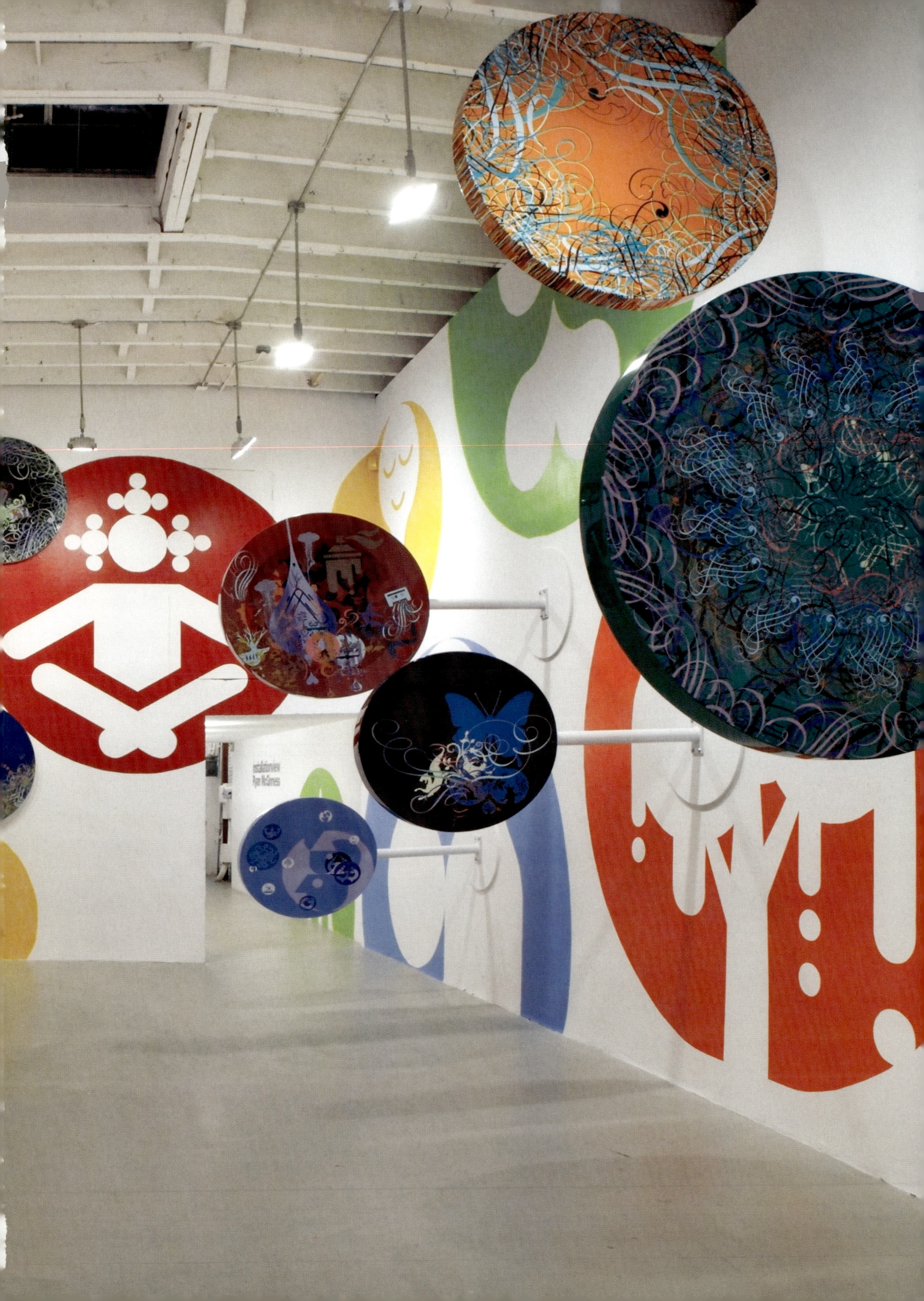

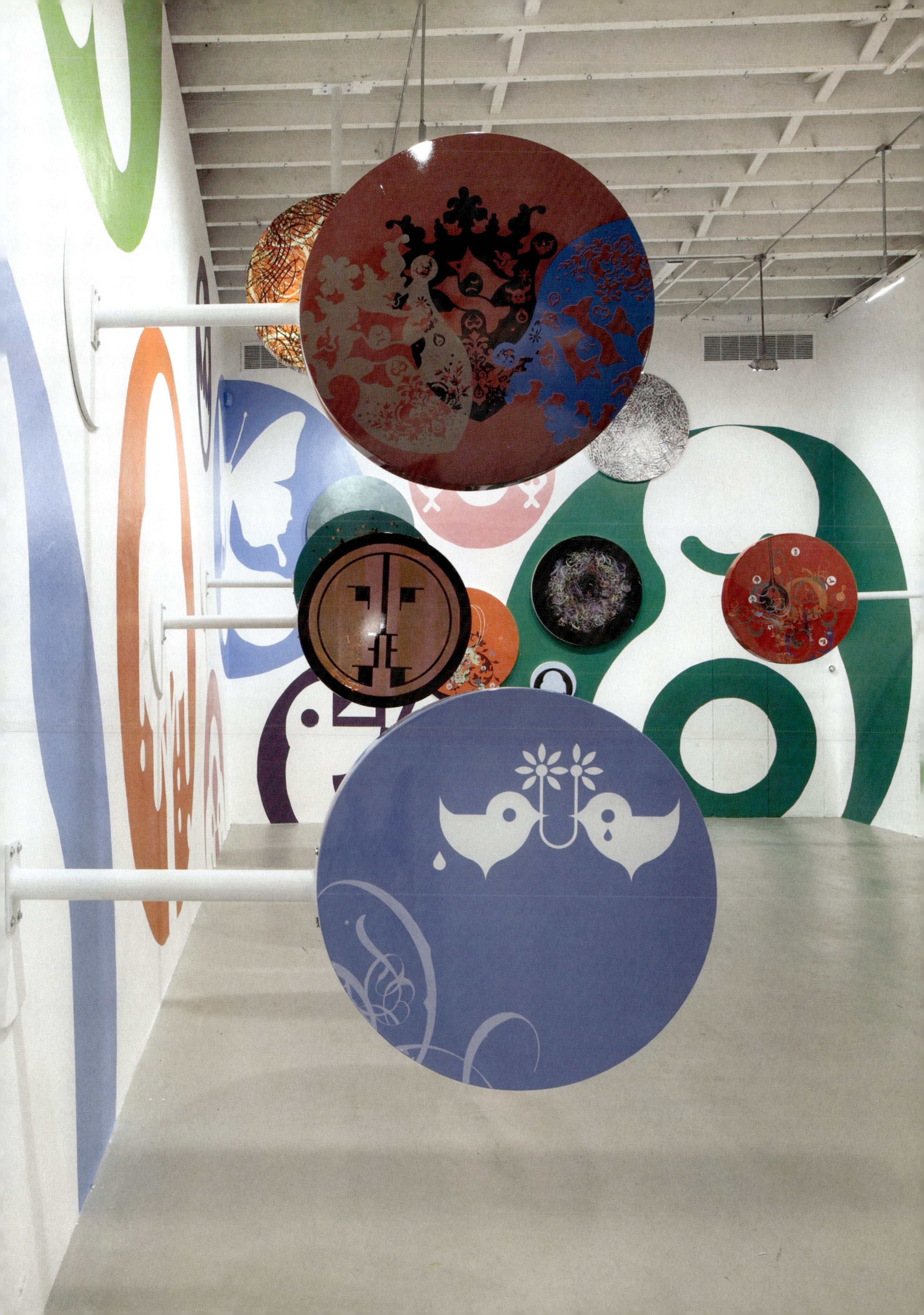

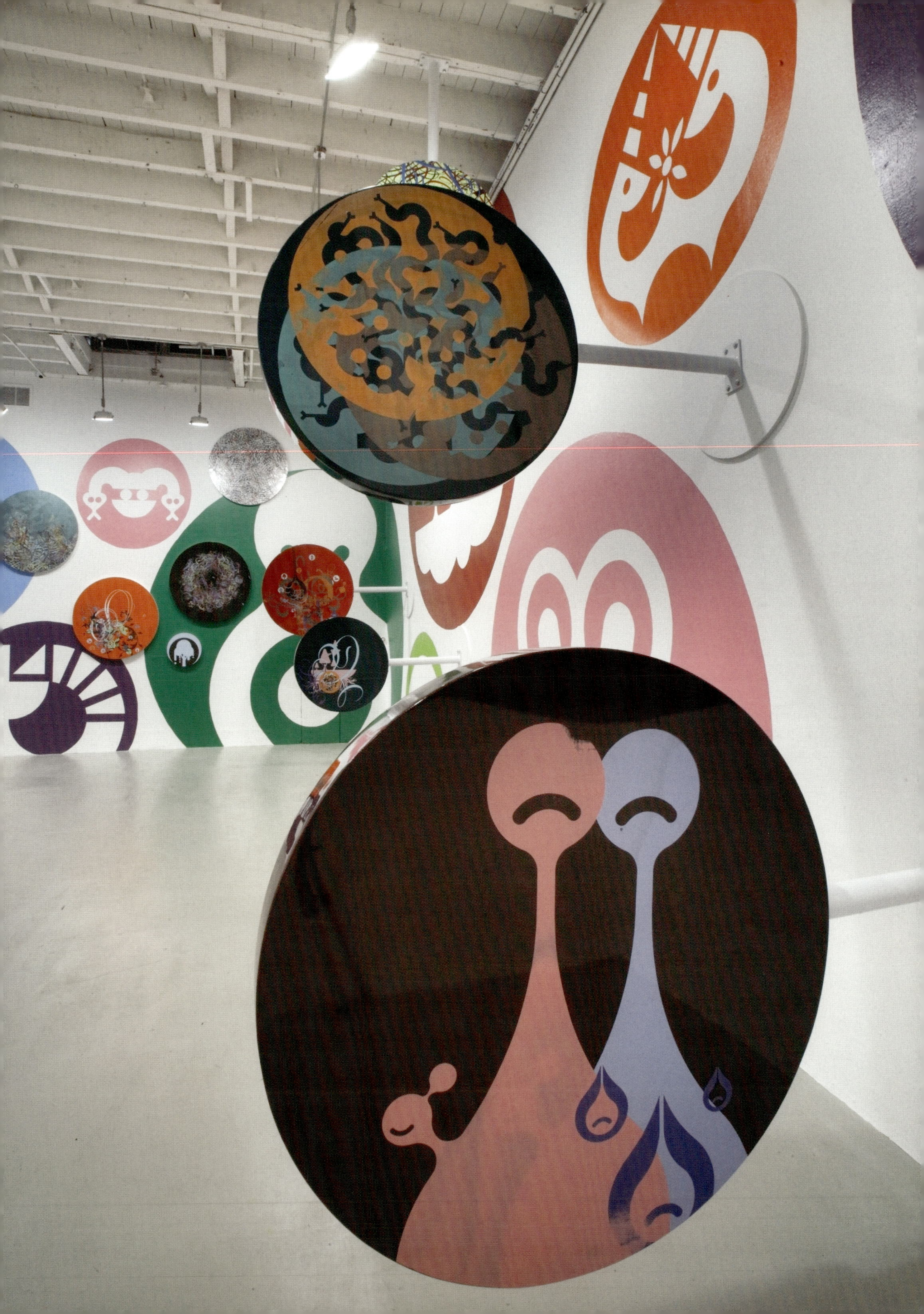

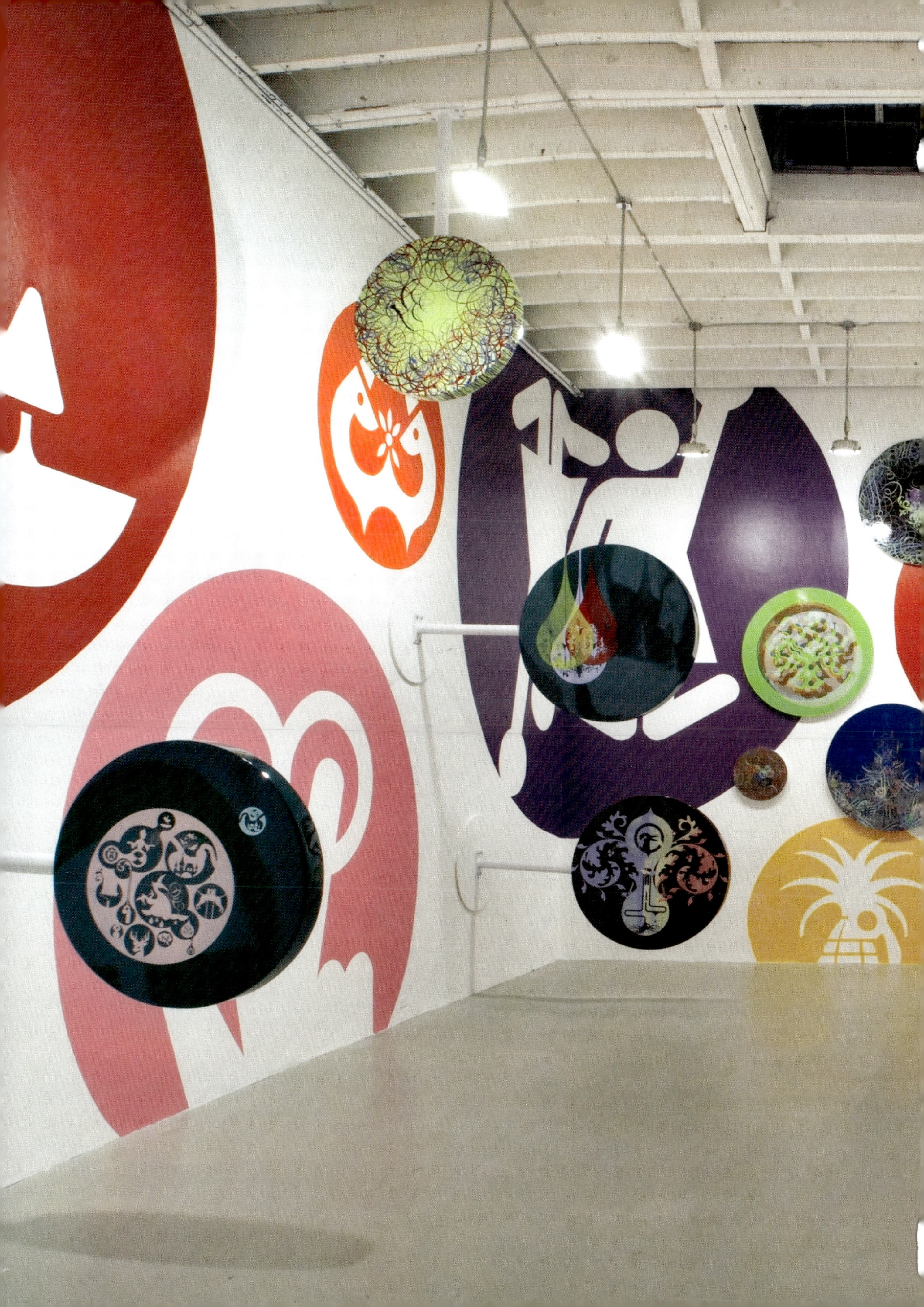

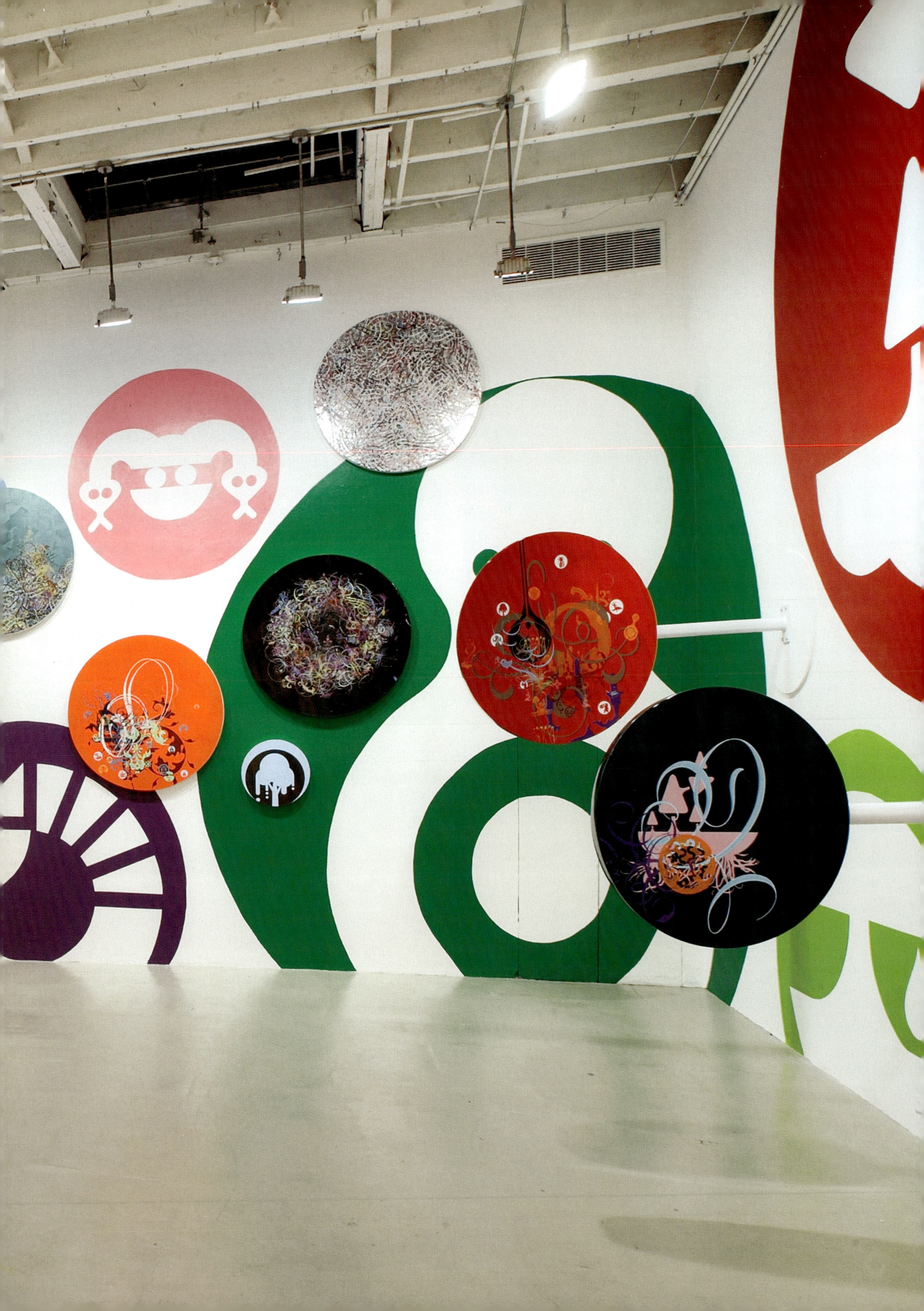

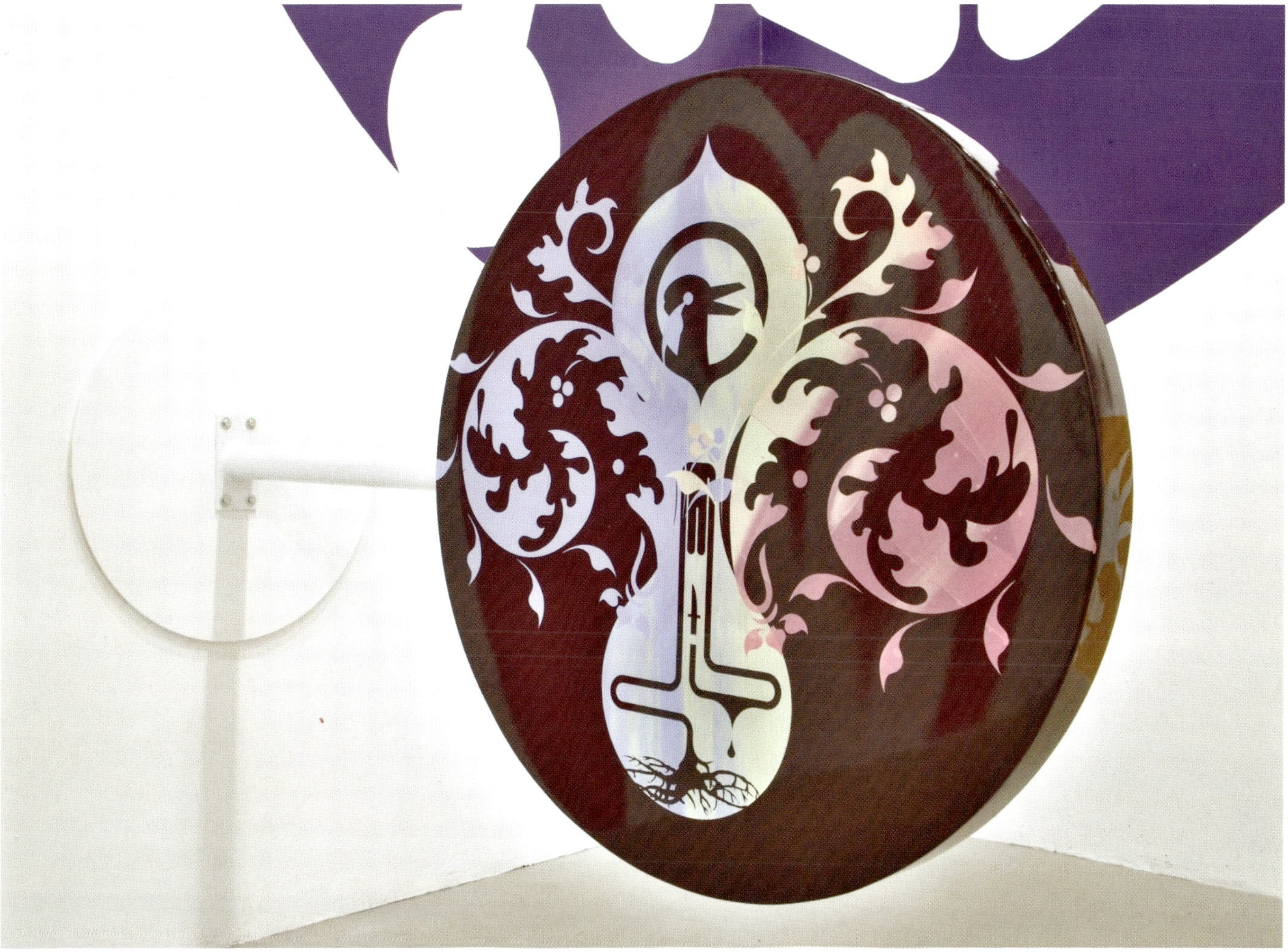

Universal (48d, No. 6), 2005, polyester urethane on fiberglass with aluminum and wood cantilever, 48 in. diameter x 4 in. Cantilever, 30 in. x 3 in. diameter.

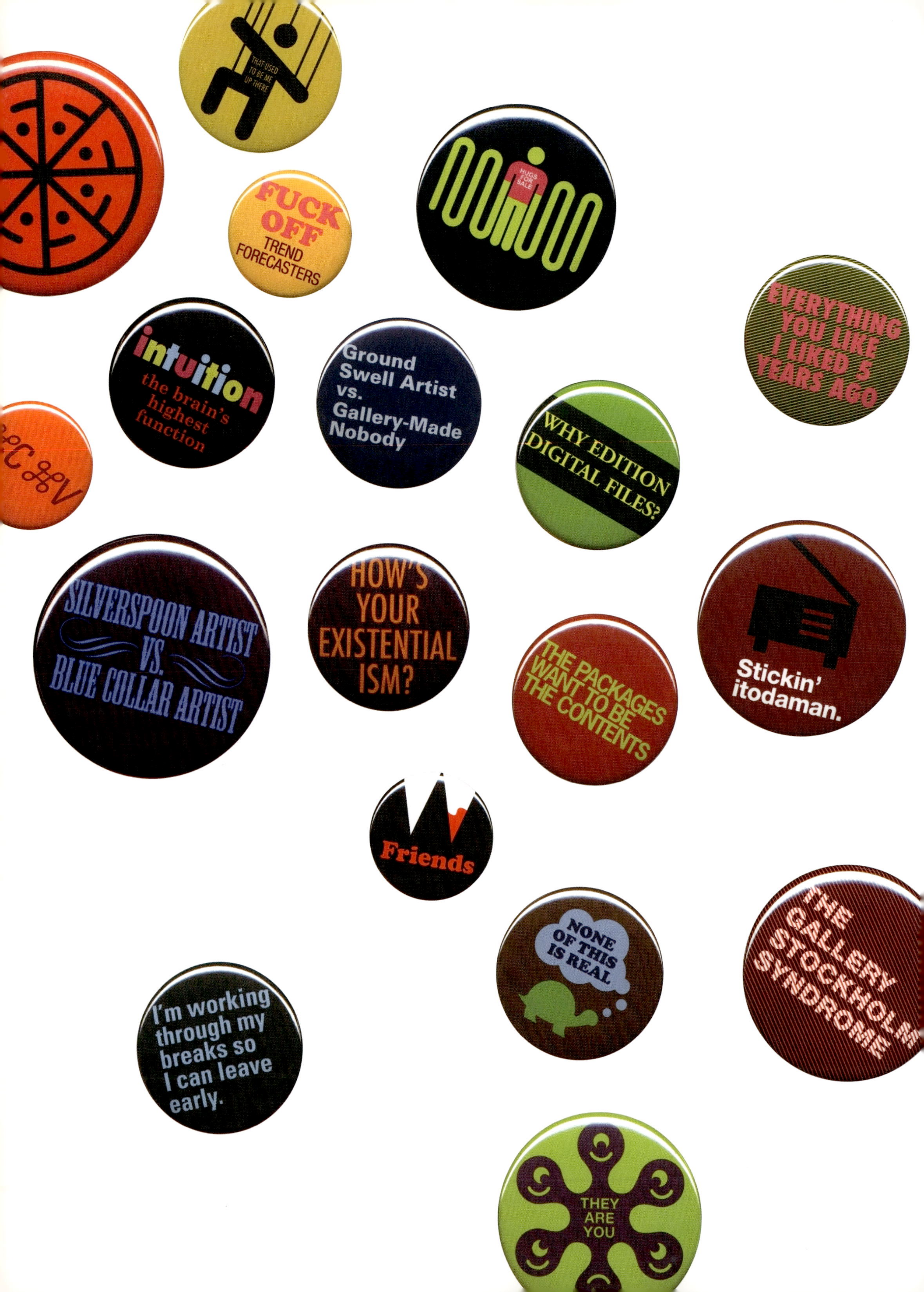
THAT USED TO BE ME UP THERE
FUCK OFF TREND FORECASTERS
HUGS FOR SALE
EVERYTHING YOU LIKE I LIKED 5 YEARS AGO
intuition the brain's highest function
Ground Swell Artist vs. Gallery-Made Nobody
WHY EDITION DIGITAL FILES?
SILVERSPOON ARTIST VS. BLUE COLLAR ARTIST
HOW'S YOUR EXISTENTIAL ISM?
THE PACKAGES WANT TO BE THE CONTENTS
Stickin' itodaman.
Friends
NONE OF THIS IS REAL
THE GALLERY STOCKHOLM SYNDROME
I'm working through my breaks so I can leave early.
THEY ARE YOU

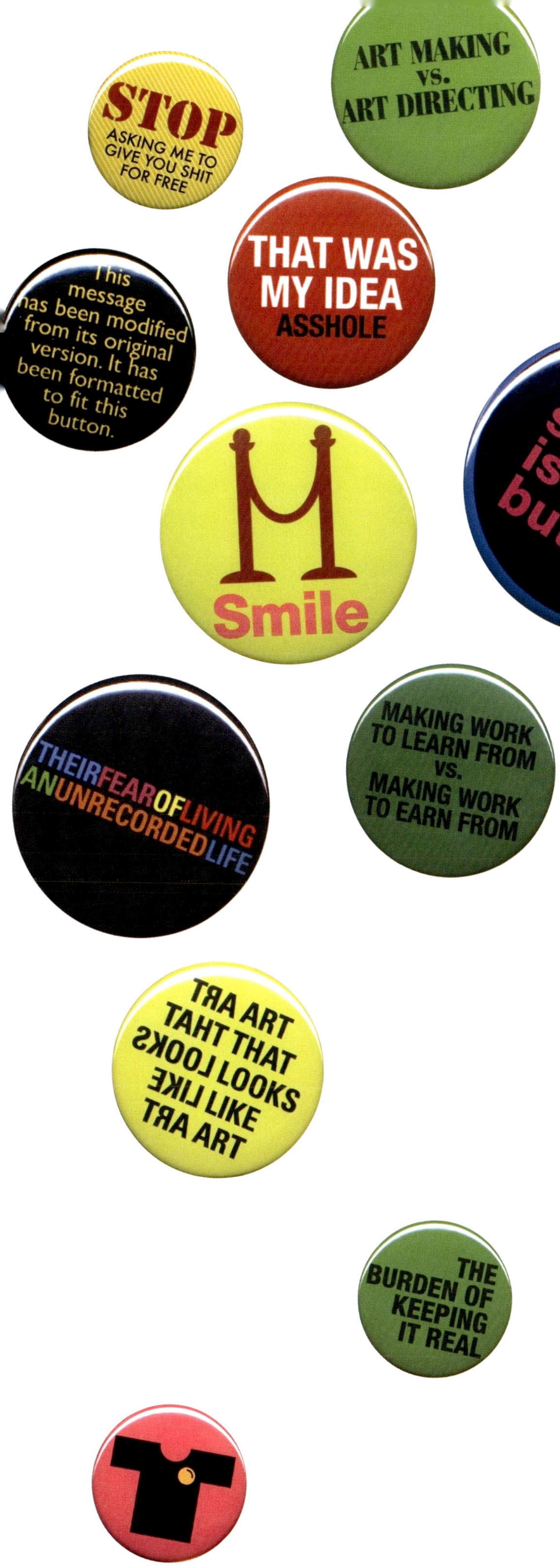

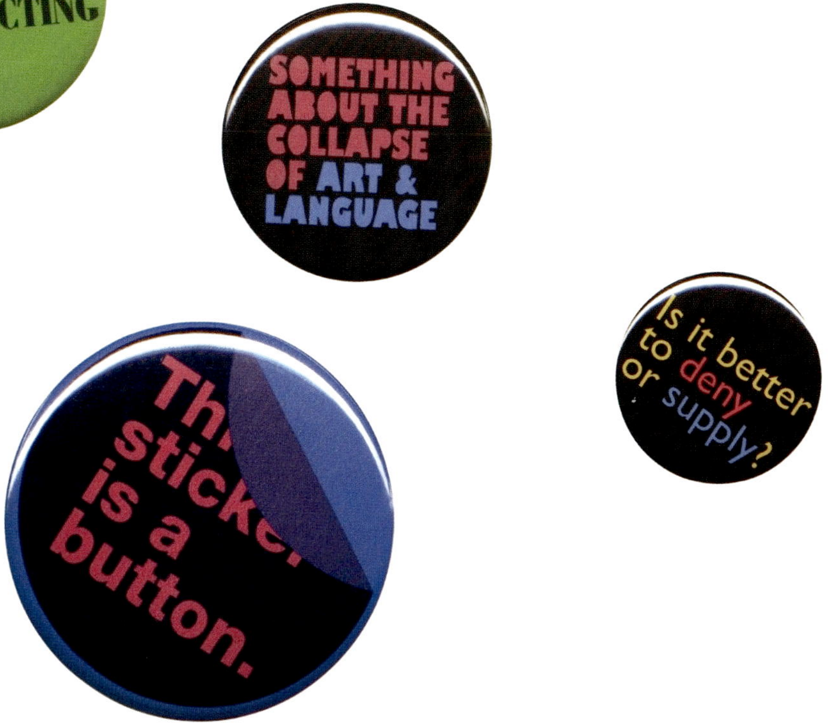

Digital files are infinitely reproducible; why translate a digital drawing developed from an ink drawing on paper into yet another medium to create an edition? Ryan doesn't make editions or multiples in the traditional sense; his are unique compositions composed from the same set of variables rather than multiple copies of identical works. Each edition has its own set of variables consisting of elements such as size, combination of images, and color palette, and each is concerned with exploiting the inherent properties of the medium being used.

Island Universes, 2007, archival ink on paper encased in plastic and metal pins, dimensions variable (1, 1 ½, and 2 in. diameter sizes produced), 777 unique buttons in an edition of 5. Published by Pace Prints, New York.

Untitled (Army Men Camouflage), a series of four-color silkscreen works on paper, posed the problem of how to create a camouflage pattern, which is an irregular shape, with irregular shapes (icons of toy soldiers).

There are eight different icons that can be flipped to mirror each other, creating 16 total variations. Dispersing the figures randomly does not work, because that wouldn't create a uniform field, so schematics were created to map out a system to fill the entire 42-by-42-inch field.

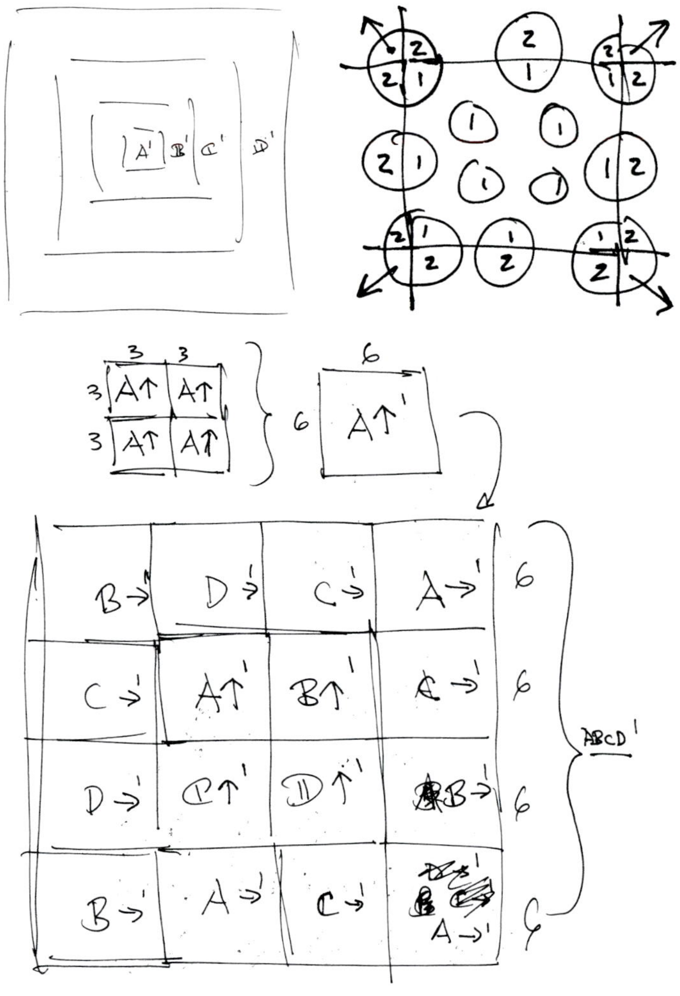

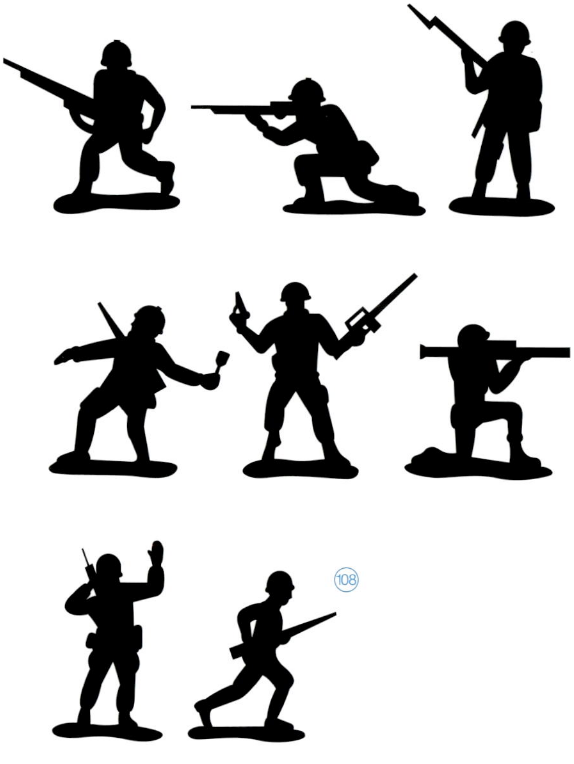

(108)

(109)

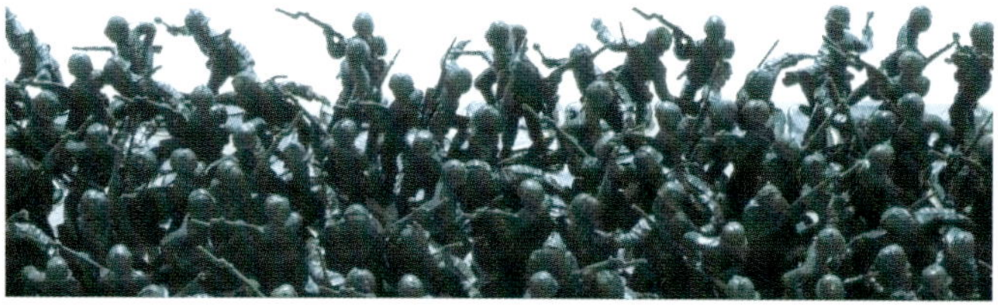

Top left: Process sketches for *Untitled (Army Men Camouflage)*, 2007, 4-color silkscreen on paper, 42 x 42 in., edition of 25. Published by Pace Prints, New York.

Top right: Vector drawings, digital files.

Above: *Saving Ryan's Privates*, 2000, plastic toy soldiers on wood panel, 72 x 72 x 4 in. (detail above left).

Opposite page: *Untitled (Army Men Camouflage)*, 2007, 4-color silkscreen on paper, 42 x 42 in., edition of 25. Published by Pace Prints, New York.

(108) Toy soldiers as symbols of soldiers. These drawings are symbols of symbols. Toys undermine the seriousness of their referent, and these symbols undermine the seriousness of these toys.

(109) I made a series of these color-field-relief-assemblage battlefields seven years prior to the camouflage works.

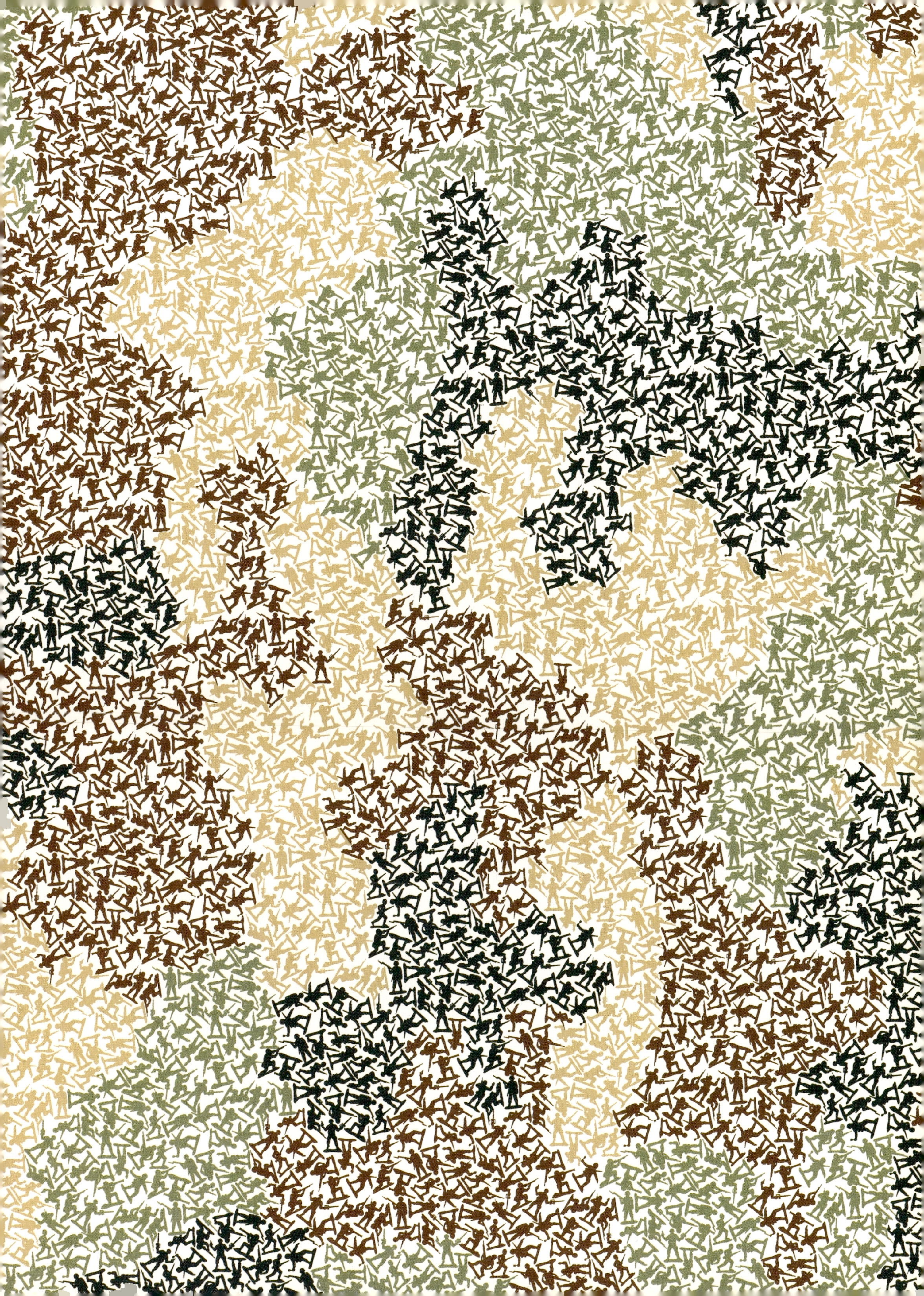

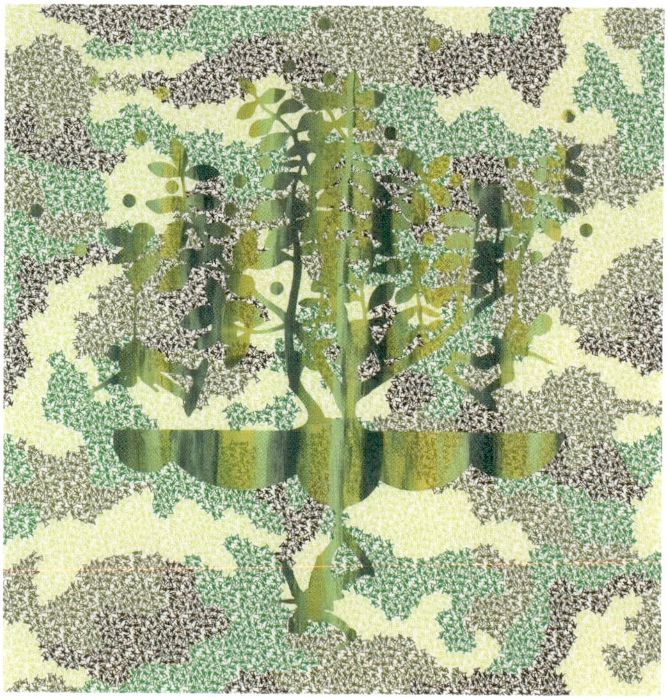

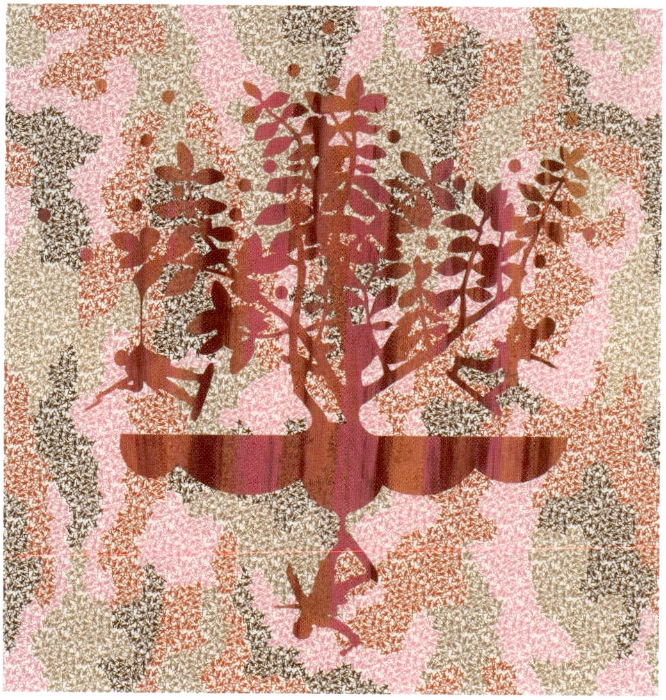

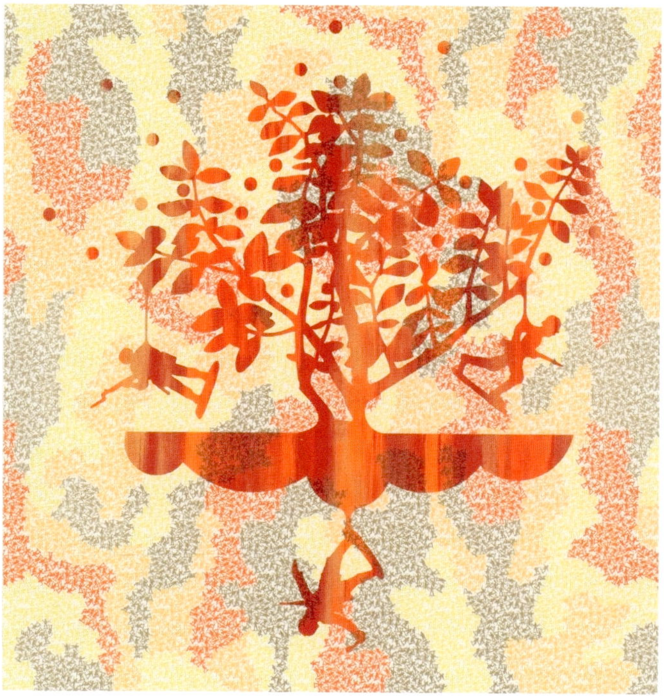

Top left: *Untitled (Army Men Camouflage, Green)*, 2007, unique acrylic painting on top of 4-color silkscreen on paper, 42 x 42 in.
Top right: *Untitled (Army Men Camouflage, Red)*, 2007, unique acrylic painting on top of 4-color silkscreen on paper, 42 x 42 in.
Bottom left: *Untitled (Army Men Camouflage, Yellow)*, 2007, unique acrylic painting on top of 4-color silkscreen on paper, 42 x 42 in.

Opposite page: *Untitled (Army Men Camouflage, Blue)*, 2007, unique acrylic painting on top of 4-color silkscreen on paper, 42 x 42 in.

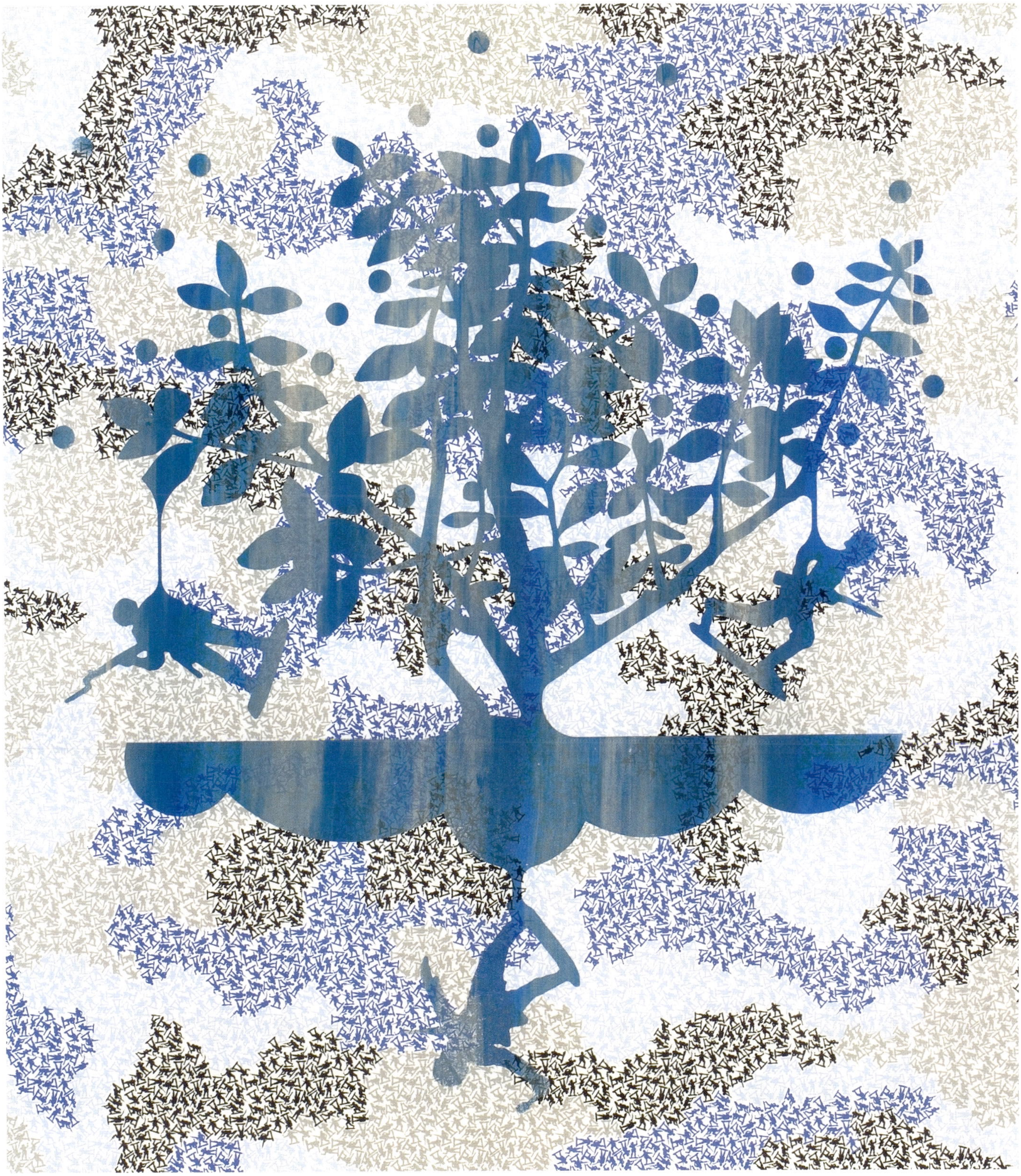

The *Black Holes* were produced in 2007 at Watanabe Studio in Brooklyn.(110)

Four sizes of circular wood panels were painted black, carefully sanded, and silkscreened with layers of *Event Horizons*—final vector drawings of arabesque forms, each one of which was printed in a different color. For each size panel, there are a number of variations of color and combinations of *Event Horizons*, and each variation was reproduced in an edition. The process was painstaking; if a mistake was made, the panel had to be sanded down to remove the silkscreen ink and prepared again.

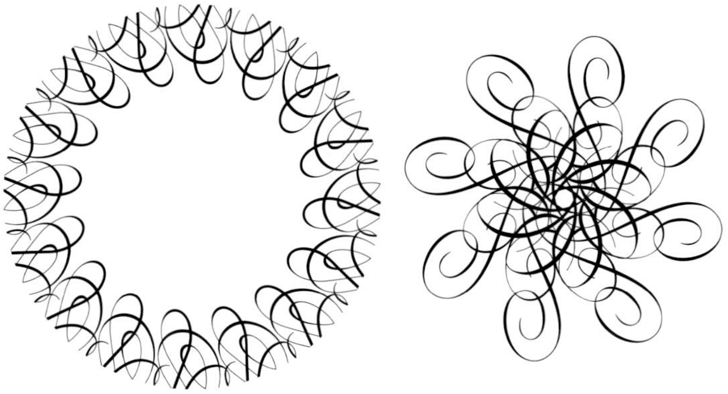

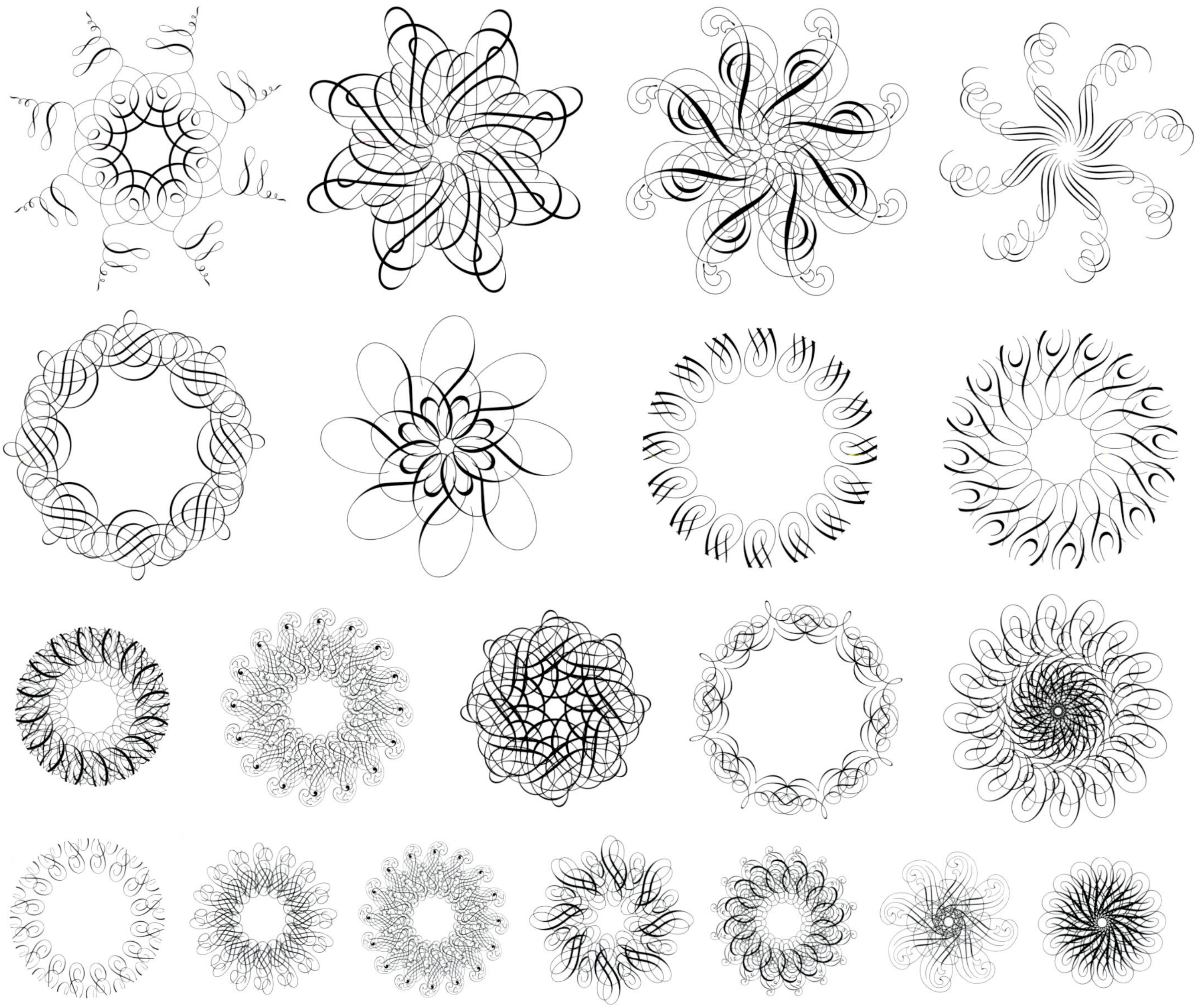

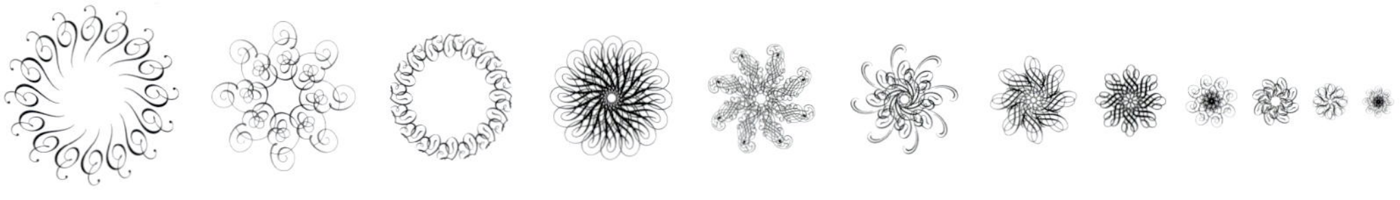

Event Horizons, vector drawings, digital files, dimensions variable.

(110) And published by Pace Prints, New York.

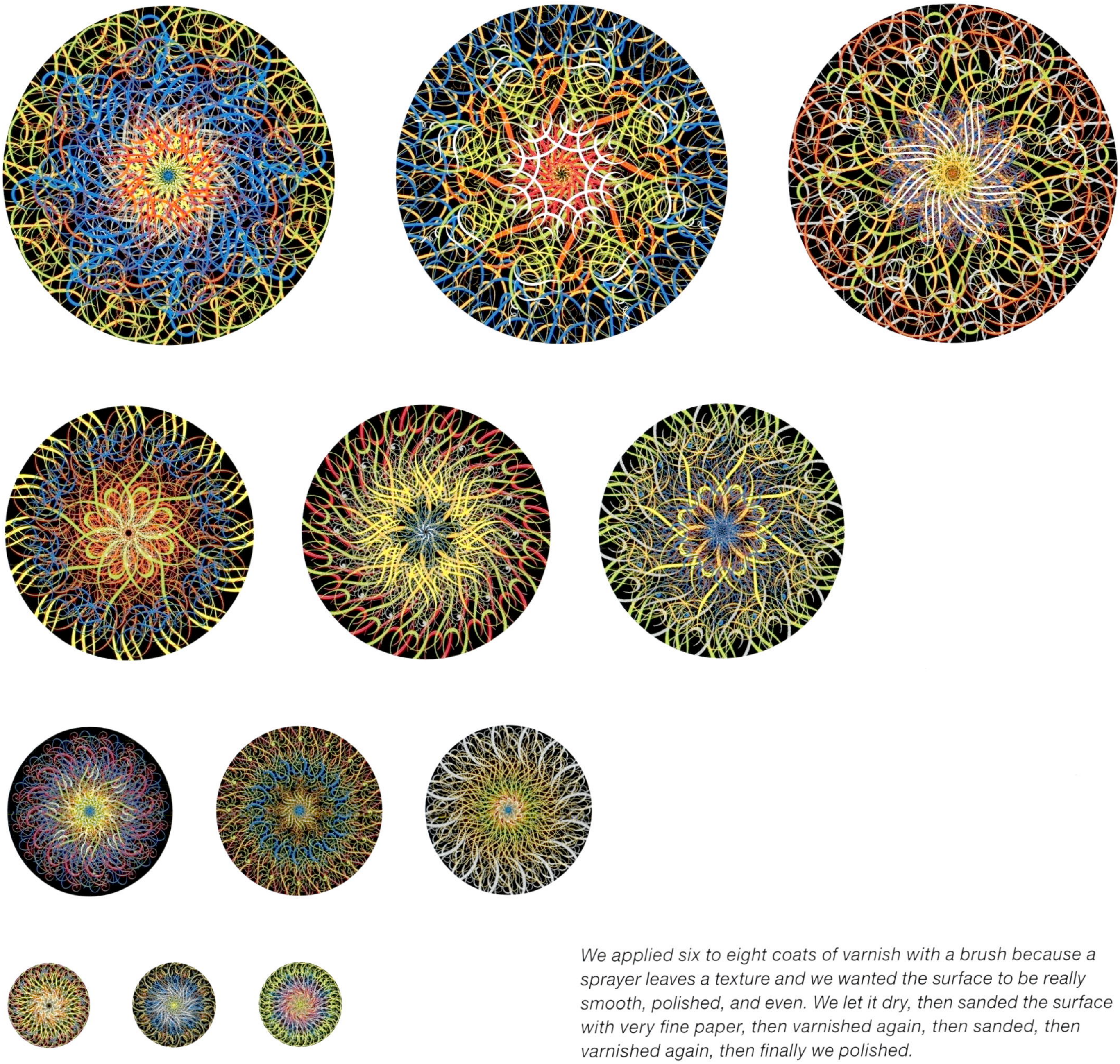

We applied six to eight coats of varnish with a brush because a sprayer leaves a texture and we wanted the surface to be really smooth, polished, and even. We let it dry, then sanded the surface with very fine paper, then varnished again, then sanded, then varnished again, then finally we polished.

—Jo Watanabe
Director, Watanabe Studio

(111)

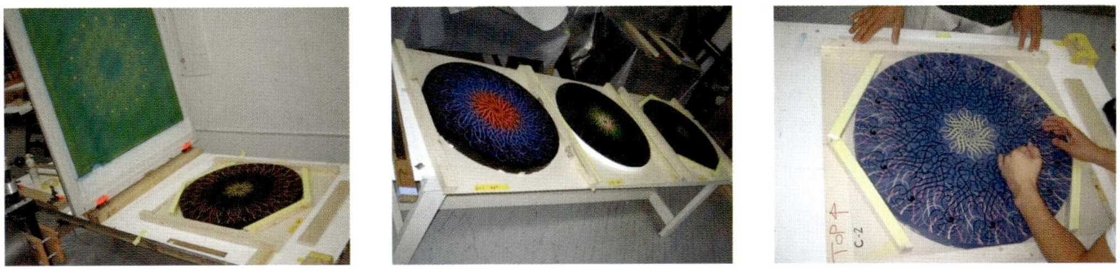

Top: Preliminary drawings for *Black Holes*.

Black Holes in production at Watanabe Studio, Brooklyn, 2007.

(111) I had been making the *Black Hole* paintings in the studio for a few years before I decided to do a series of them with Pace Prints and Jo Watanabe. After I saw what Jo and his team had achieved, I was completely depressed and deflated. They made them absolutely perfect—exactly as I had envisioned. I have continued making them in the studio, too, as a celebration of human imperfection.

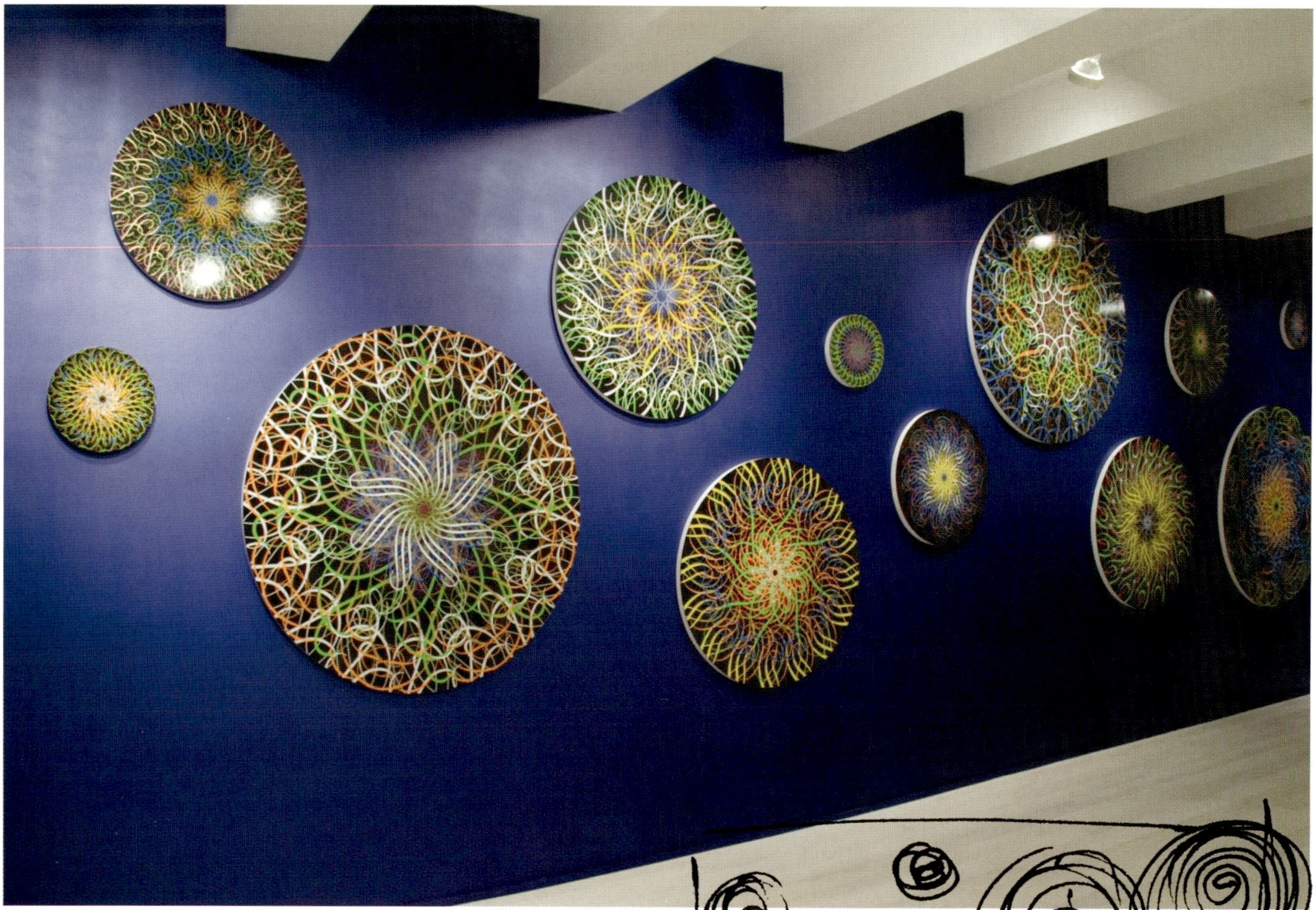

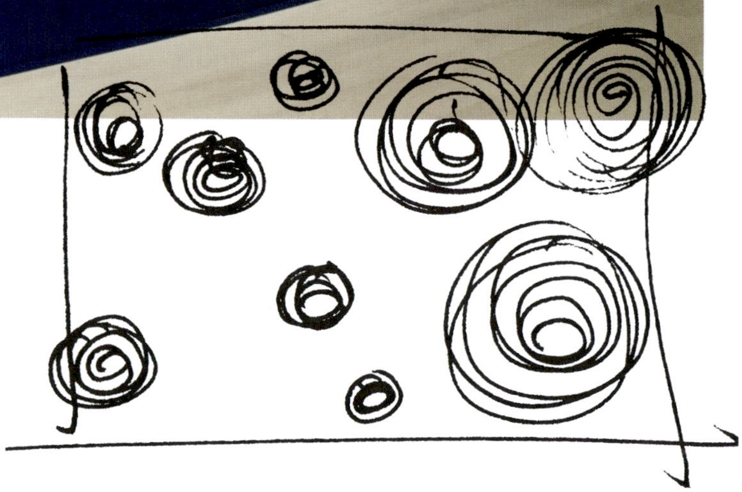

Top: View of "Varied Editions," 2007. Published by Pace Prints, New York. *Untitled (Black Holes)*, silkscreen ink on wood panels, various sizes.

Above: Preliminary concept sketch for installation of *Black Holes*, ink on paper (details opposite page).

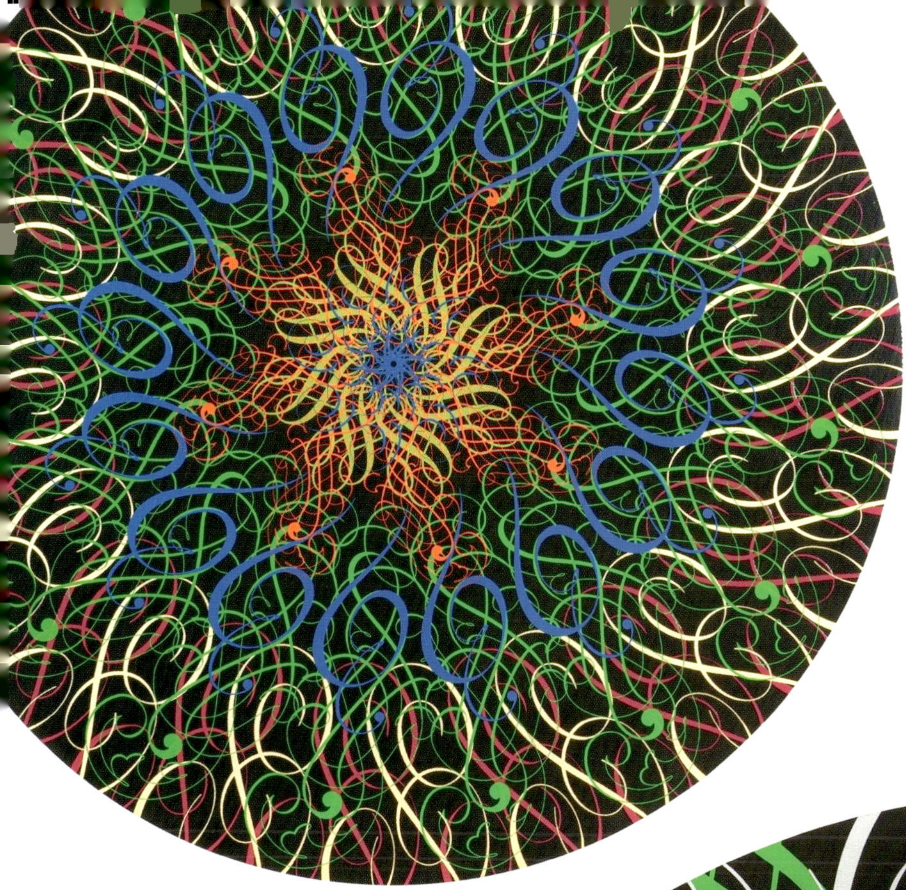

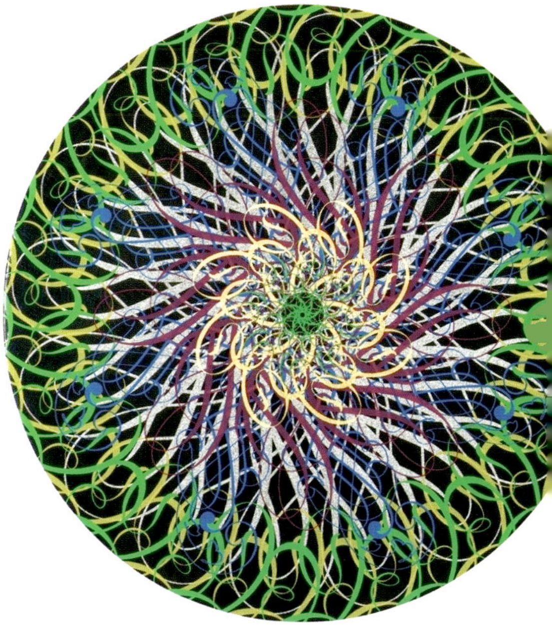

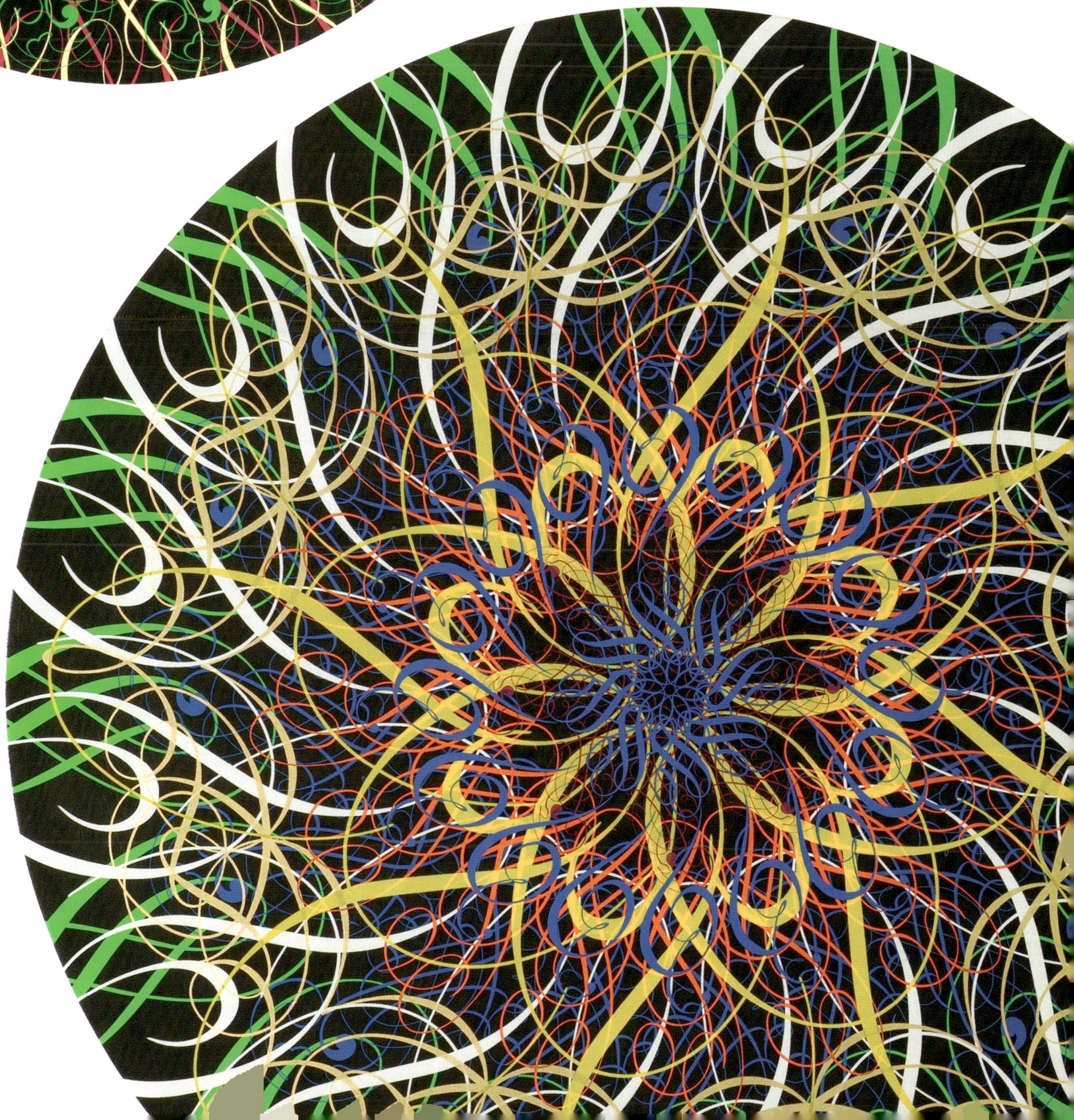

Reasoned Relationships vs. Illogical Love is a true edition: 20 identical, 24-karat gold leaf prints in a frame made with the same 24-karat gold leaf.

A riff on Warhol's gold Rorschach paintings—which were made in 1984, near the end of his life—the composition of these prints exploits the inherent symmetry of the inkblot. The final compositions are derived from a series of Rorschach studies.

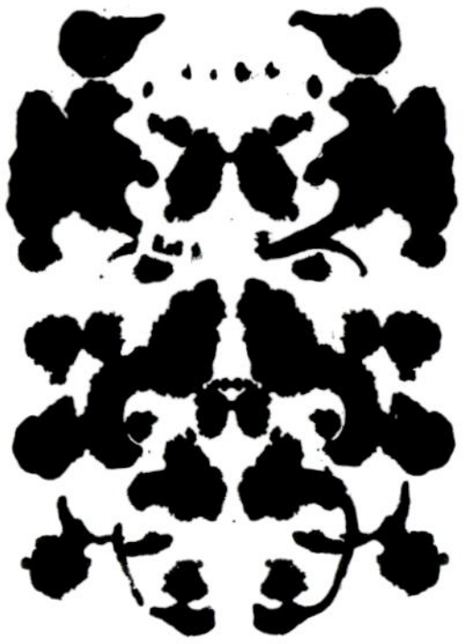
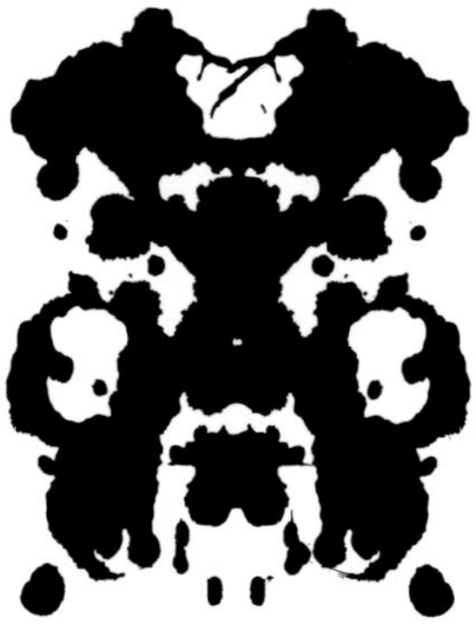
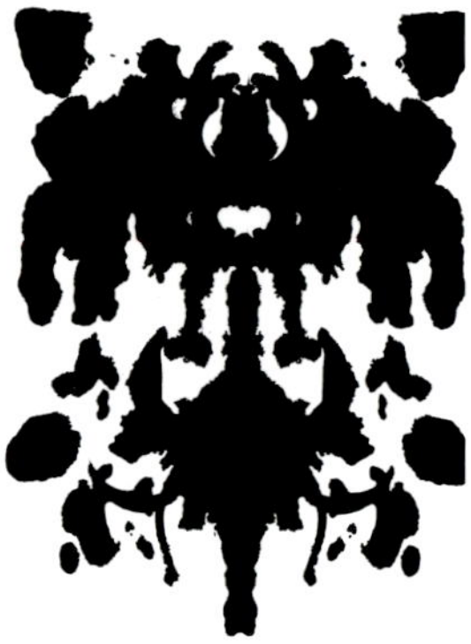
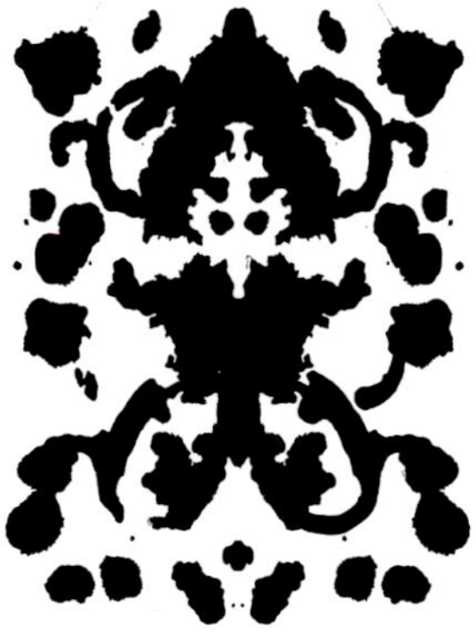
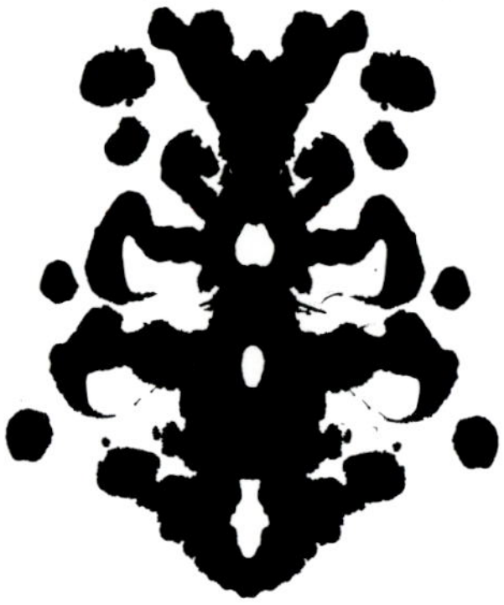
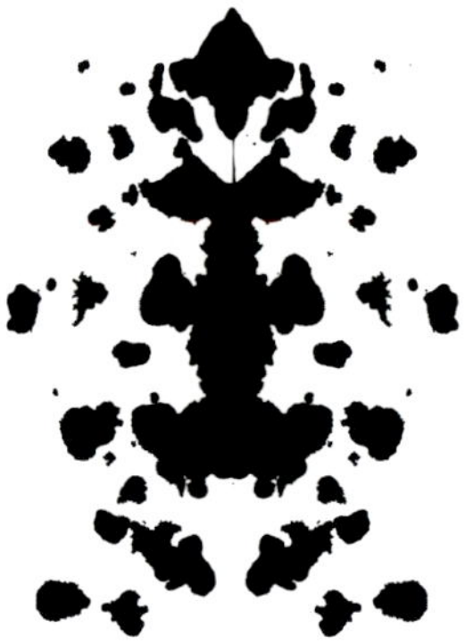
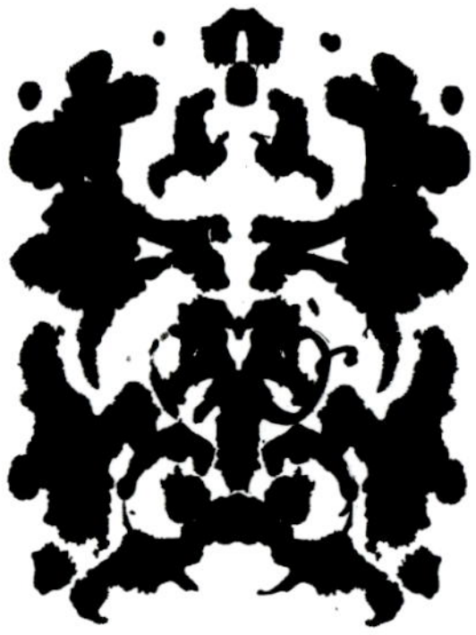
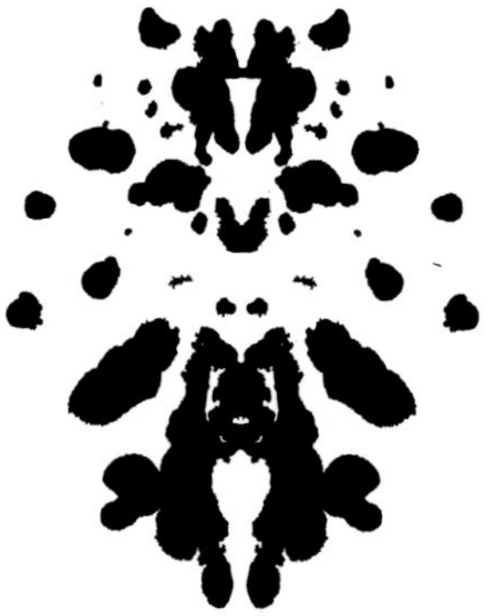
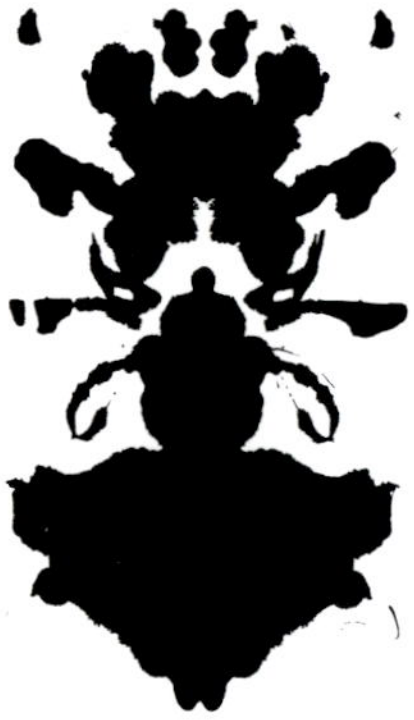
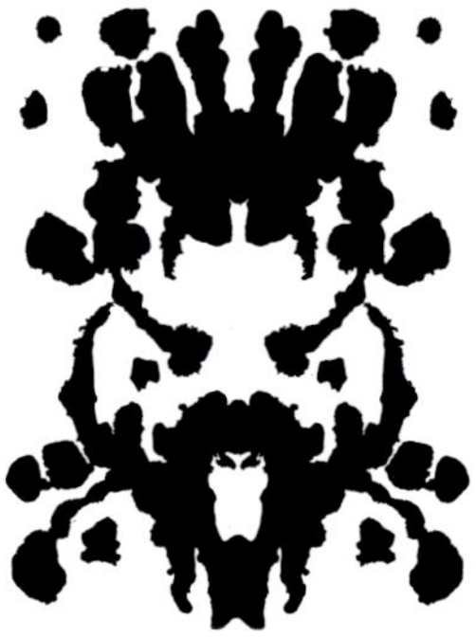
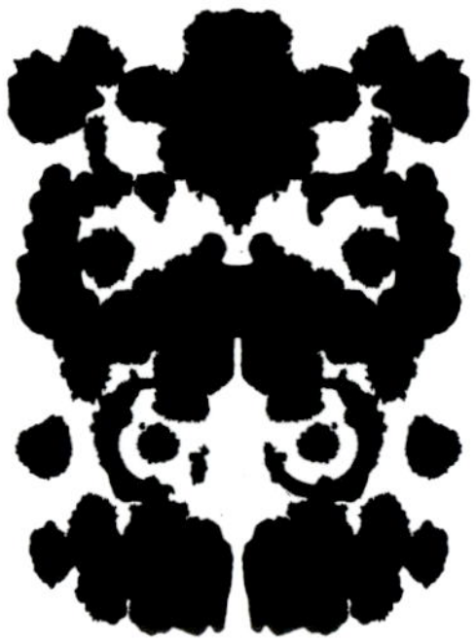
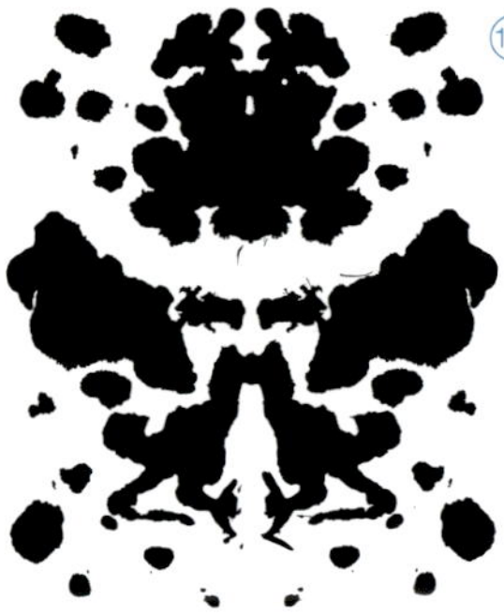
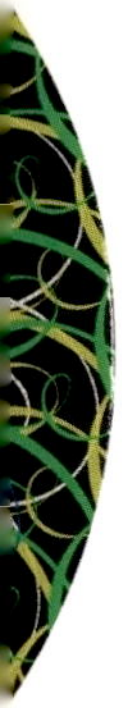
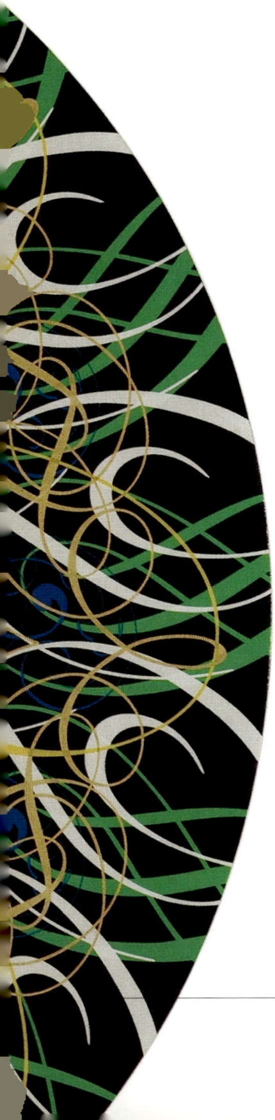

(113)

Rorschach studies, ink on paper, 2007, 11 x 8 ½ in. each. (112)

Opposite page: *Reasoned Relationships vs. Illogical Love*, 2007, 24-karat gold leaf on paper with matching 24-karat gold leaf frame, 52 x 38 in., edition of 20. Published by Pace Prints, New York.

(112) I made exactly 88 studies, because the number 88 is a Rorschach.

(113) Mirroring. Duality. Symmetry.

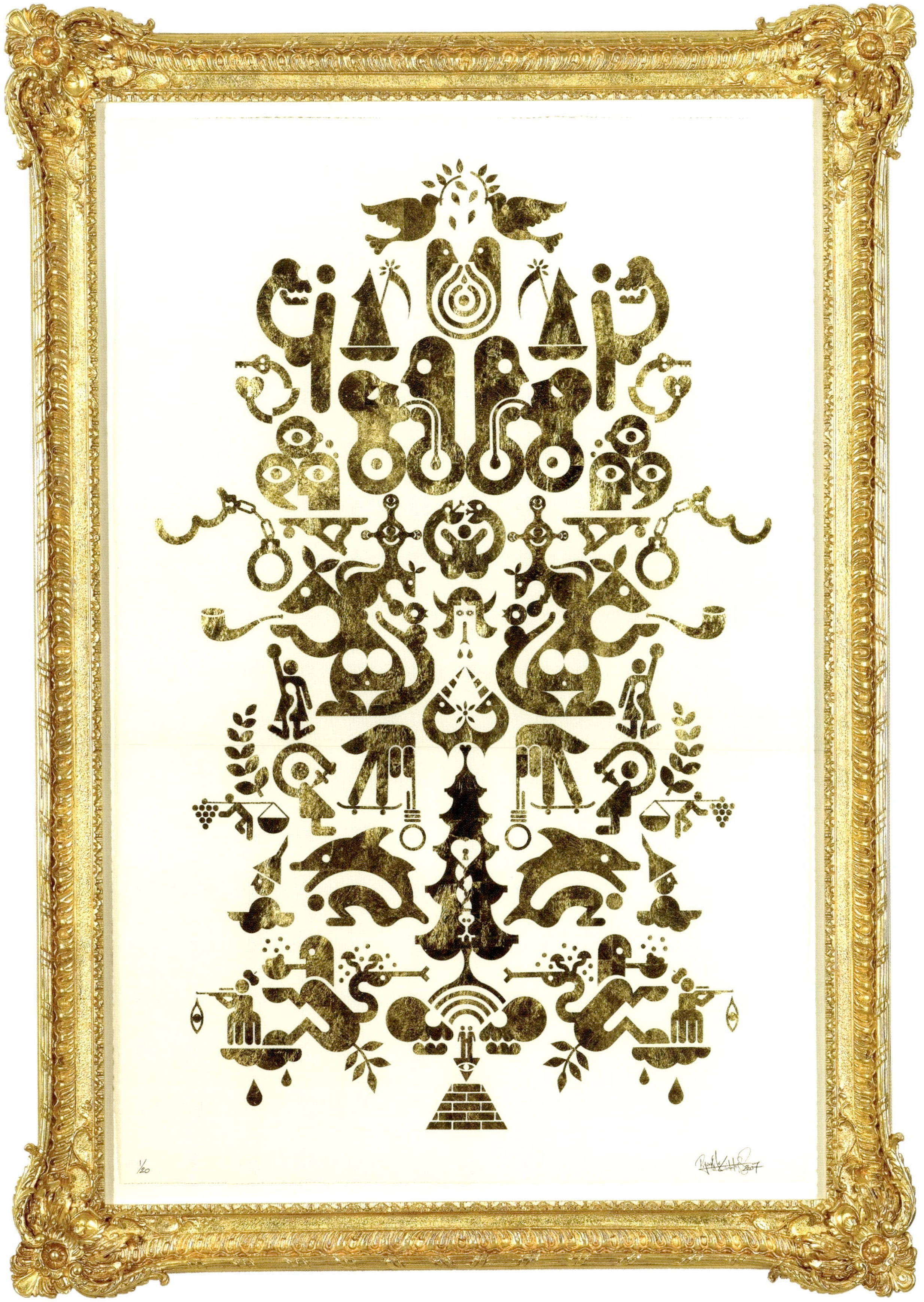

A series of 10 rubber-stamp monoprints was produced at Pace Prints, New York, in 2007.

Seventy-two rubber stamps made from process sketches were inked and laid down on paper in various arrangements using a set color palette shared by the series. The casual line work of the sketches matches this printmaking process since the stamps are placed image side down, creating an impression that is somewhat imprecise.

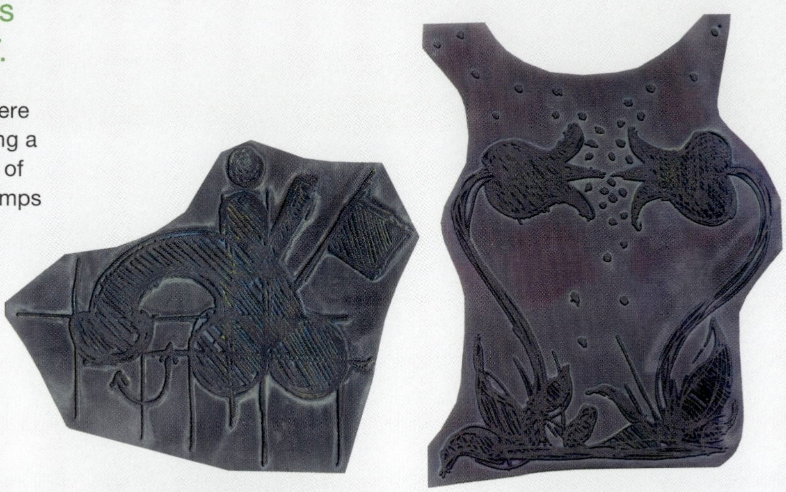

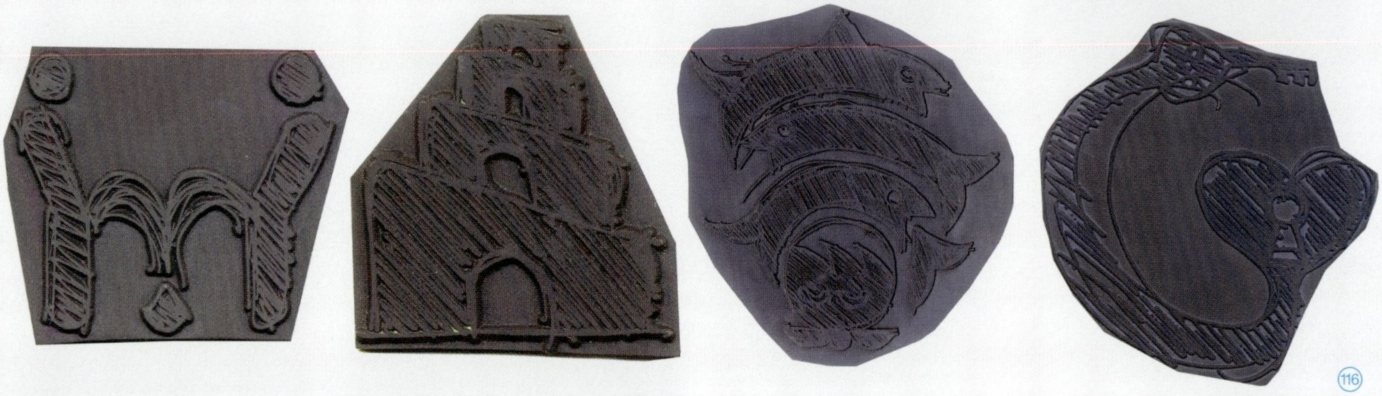

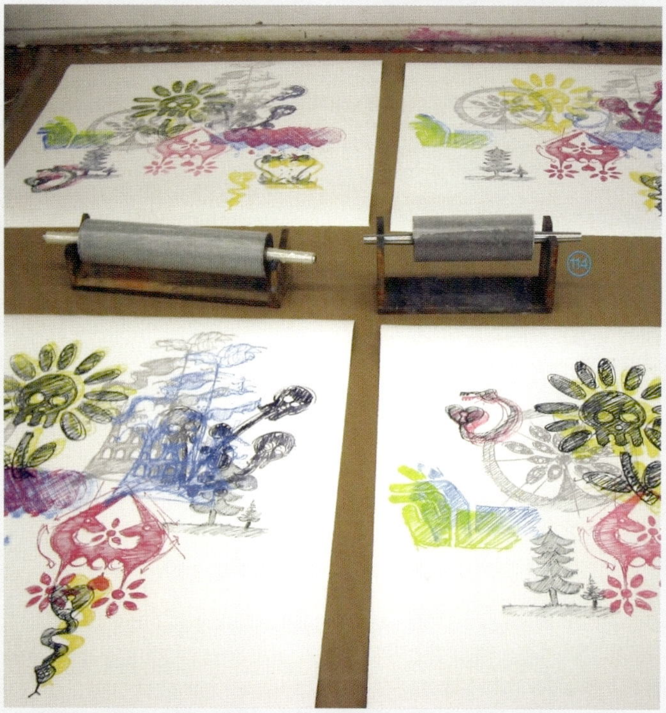

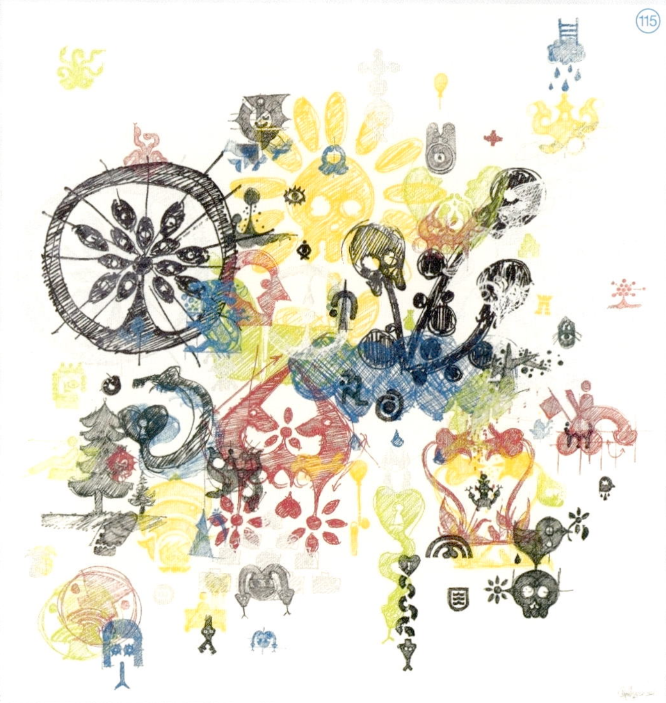

Top: Rubber stamps used in the production of *Untitled (Rubber Stamp Monoprint)*, dimensions vary.

Process view, Pace Prints, New York, 2007.

Above and opposite page: *Untitled (Rubber Stamp Monoprint)*, 2007, 7-color monoprint using 72 unique rubber stamps made from enlarged sketches, 48 x 48 in. Published by Pace Prints, New York.

(114) Rollers used to press the backs of the rubber stamps into the paper.

(115) Folding the process sketches into the final work.

(116) Sketches were scanned and then scaled to various sizes before being made into stamps.

A series of 48-inch-diameter unique paintings on paper using brass stencils and fluorescent and metallic spray paint was created in 2007.

Stencils, like silkscreens, are an easily accessible means of reproduction that Ryan used growing up to make t-shirts, flyers, and posters. For his "Varied Editions" exhibition at Pace Prints in New York, also in 2007, these paintings were adhered to the walls and completed *in situ*, becoming site-specific artifacts of the installation, which were removed and framed after the exhibition.

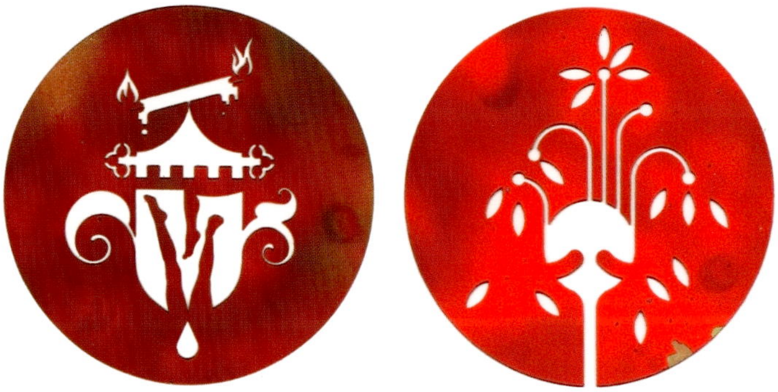

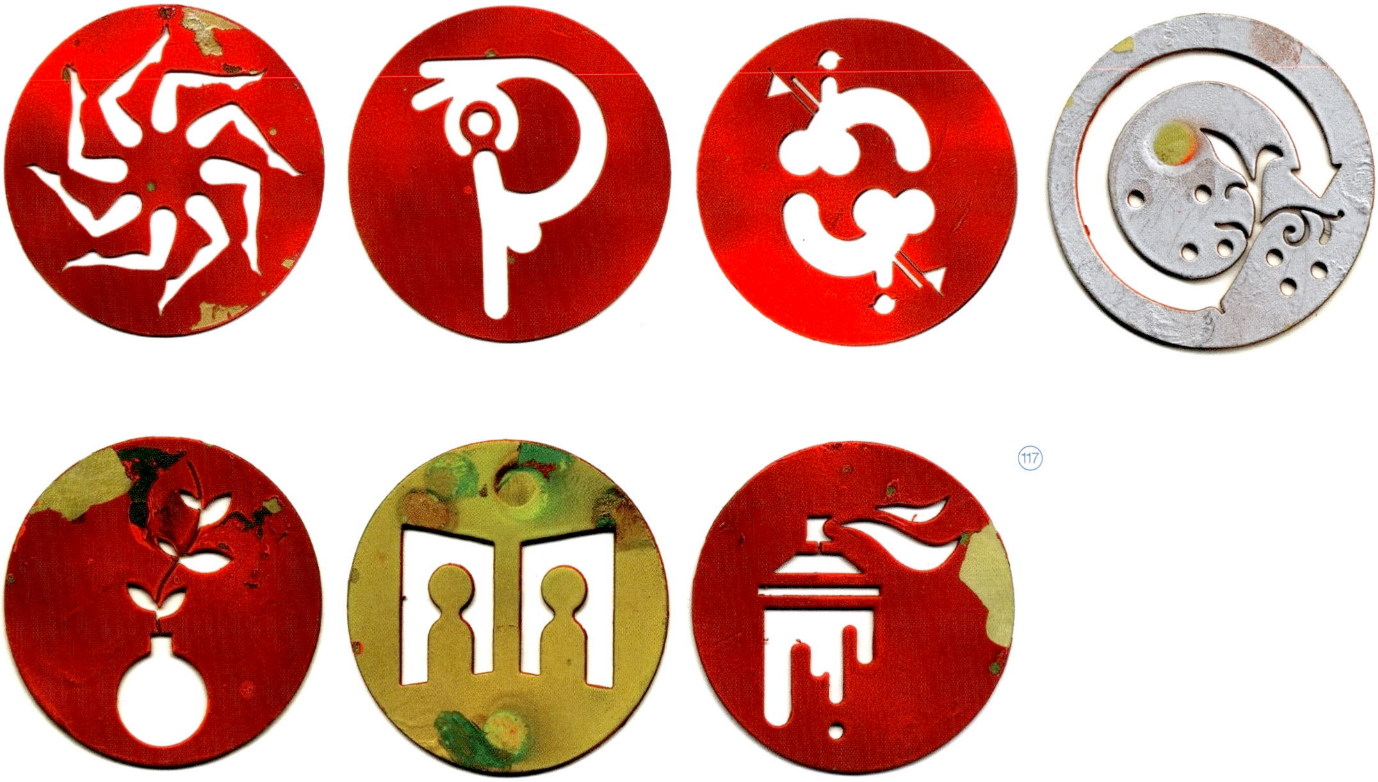

(117)

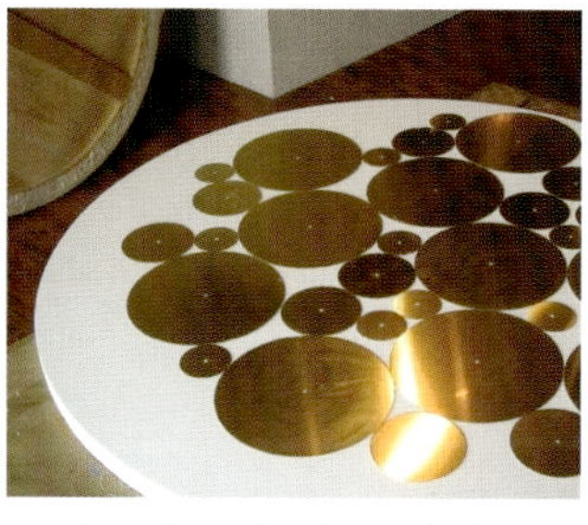

Top: Stencils used in the production of this series, *Untitled*, 2007. Above: Testing stencil sizes.

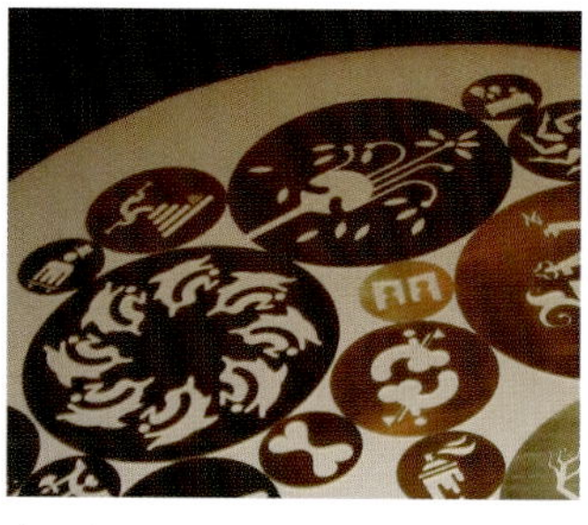

Creating variable compositions with stencils.

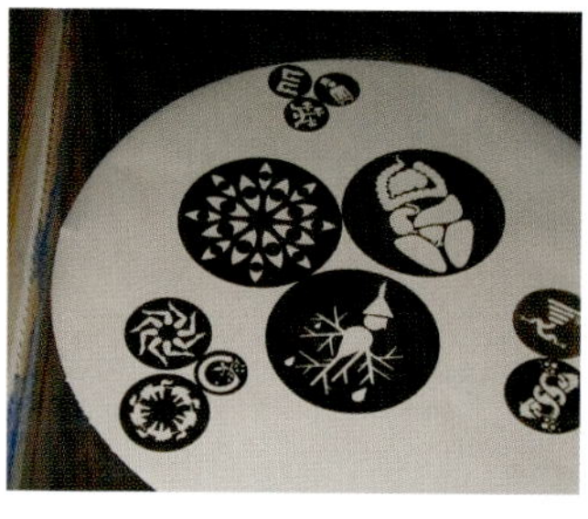

Drying between layers of spray paint.

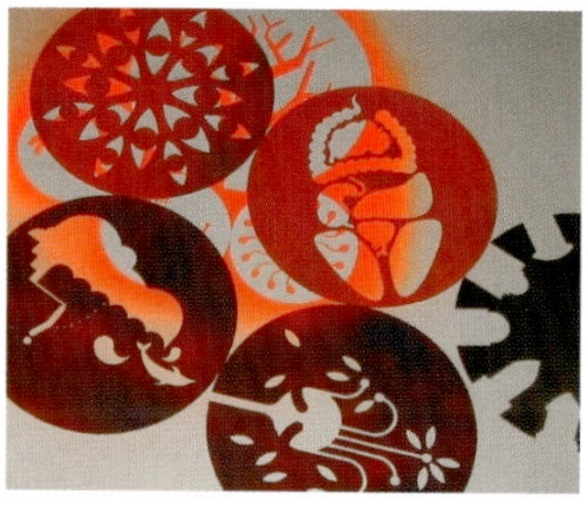

(117) Although they are of equal size here, the stencils were actually three different diameters: 3, 5, and 10 inches, and were cut with a water jet from ⅛-inch brass.

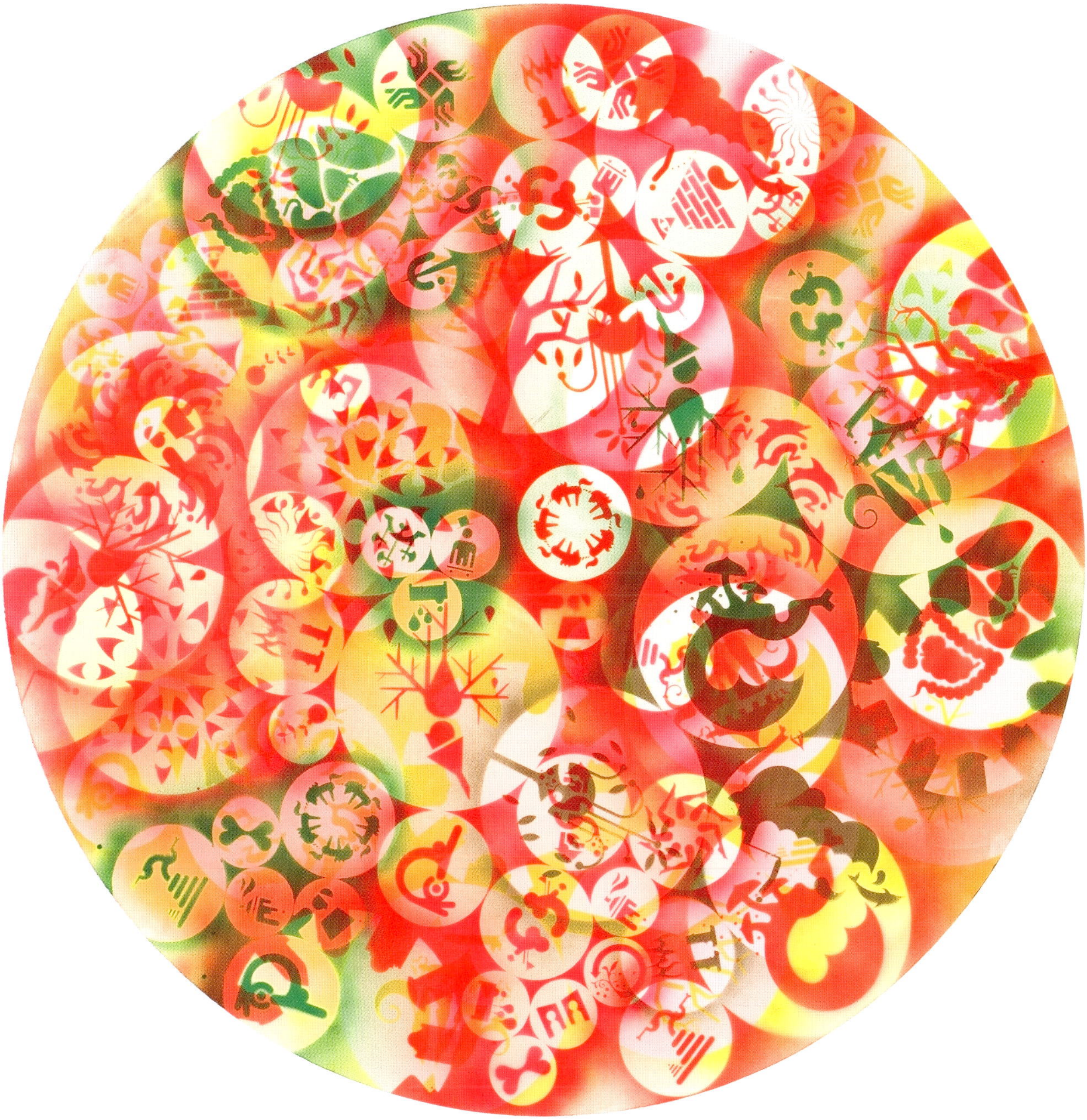

118

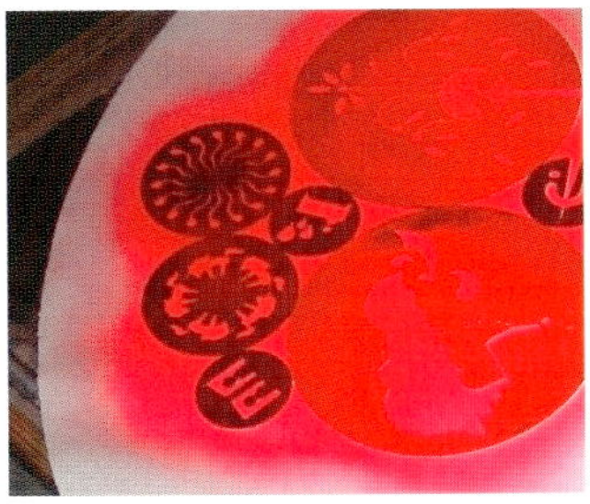

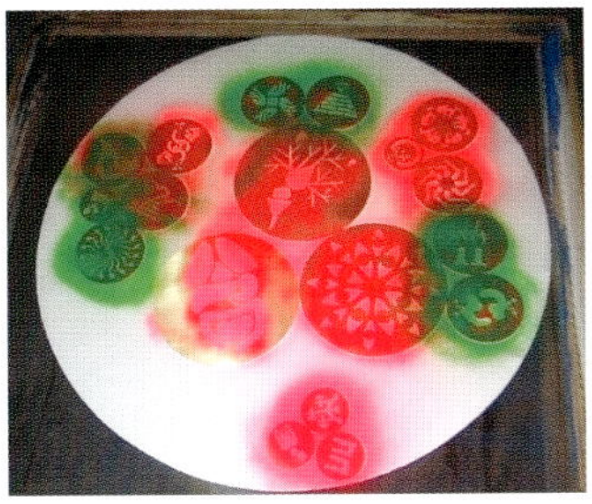

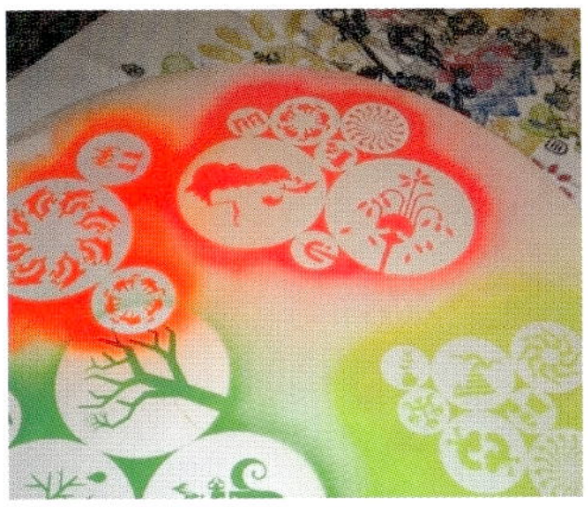

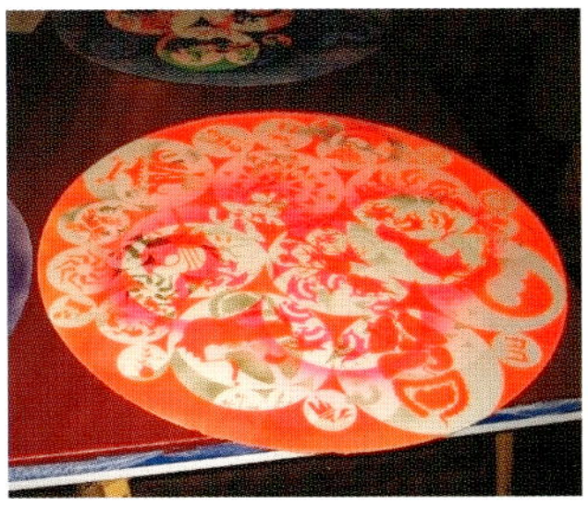

Top: *Untitled*, 2007, fluorescent and metallic spray paint on paper, 48 in. diameter.

Process views of layers of spray paint being built up.

118 These circle worlds create new overlapping Venn diagram sets within the universal picture plane set. These overlaps are the gateways to new universes.

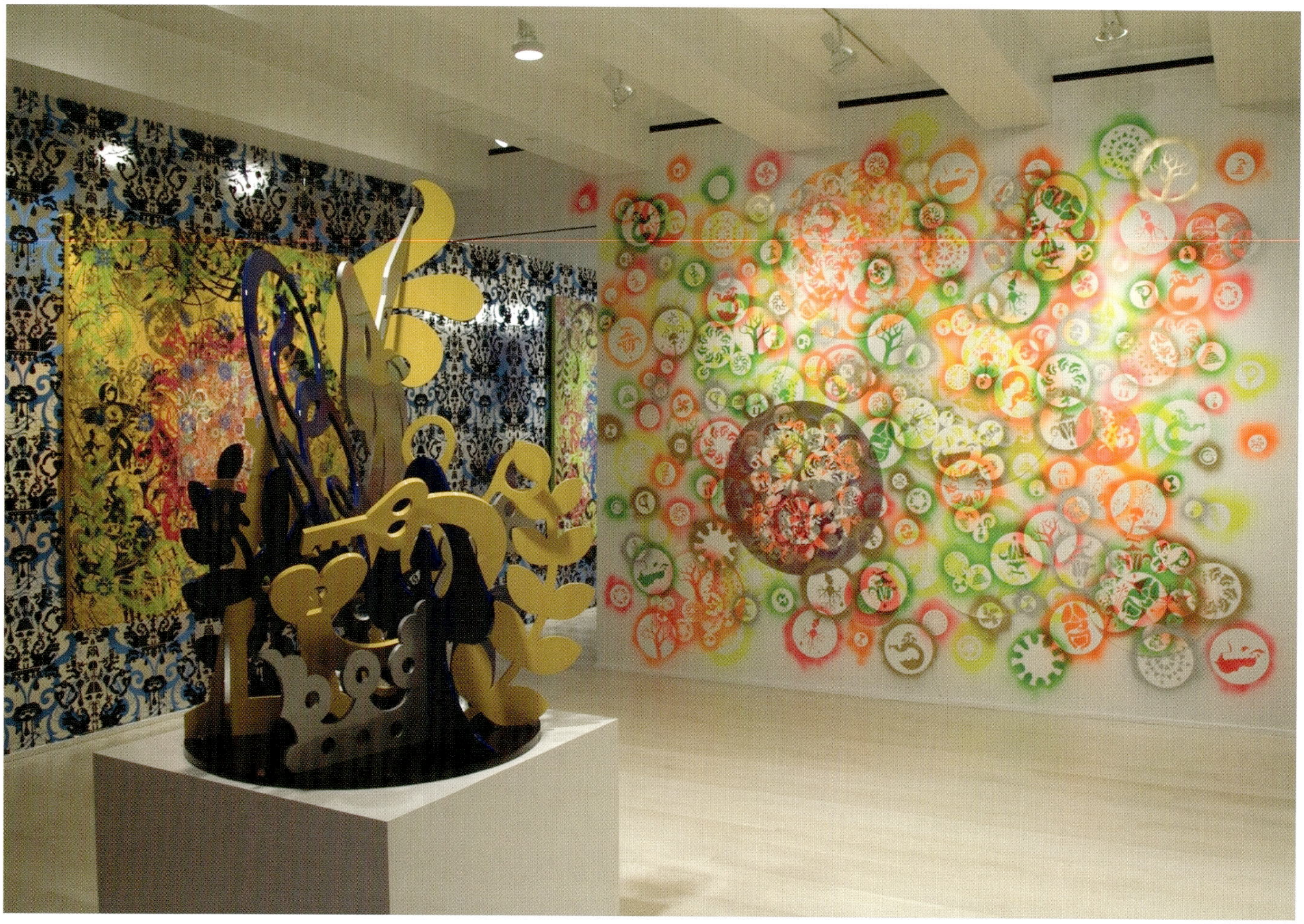

We approached Ryan because he was already using the print medium as a medium and not as a reproduction tool. With "Varied Editions," he showed how an editioned medium can be used to create a significant body of work—he took the icons he created for the show and collaged them together so they would work as sculpture, in the round.

—Jacob Lewis
Director, Pace Prints Chelsea

View of "Varied Editions," 2007, Pace Prints, New York. Foreground: *Untitled*, 2007, painted aluminum, 42 x 42 x 49 in. Background, right: *Untitled*, 2007, spray enamel and paper on wall, dimensions variable (detail opposite page).

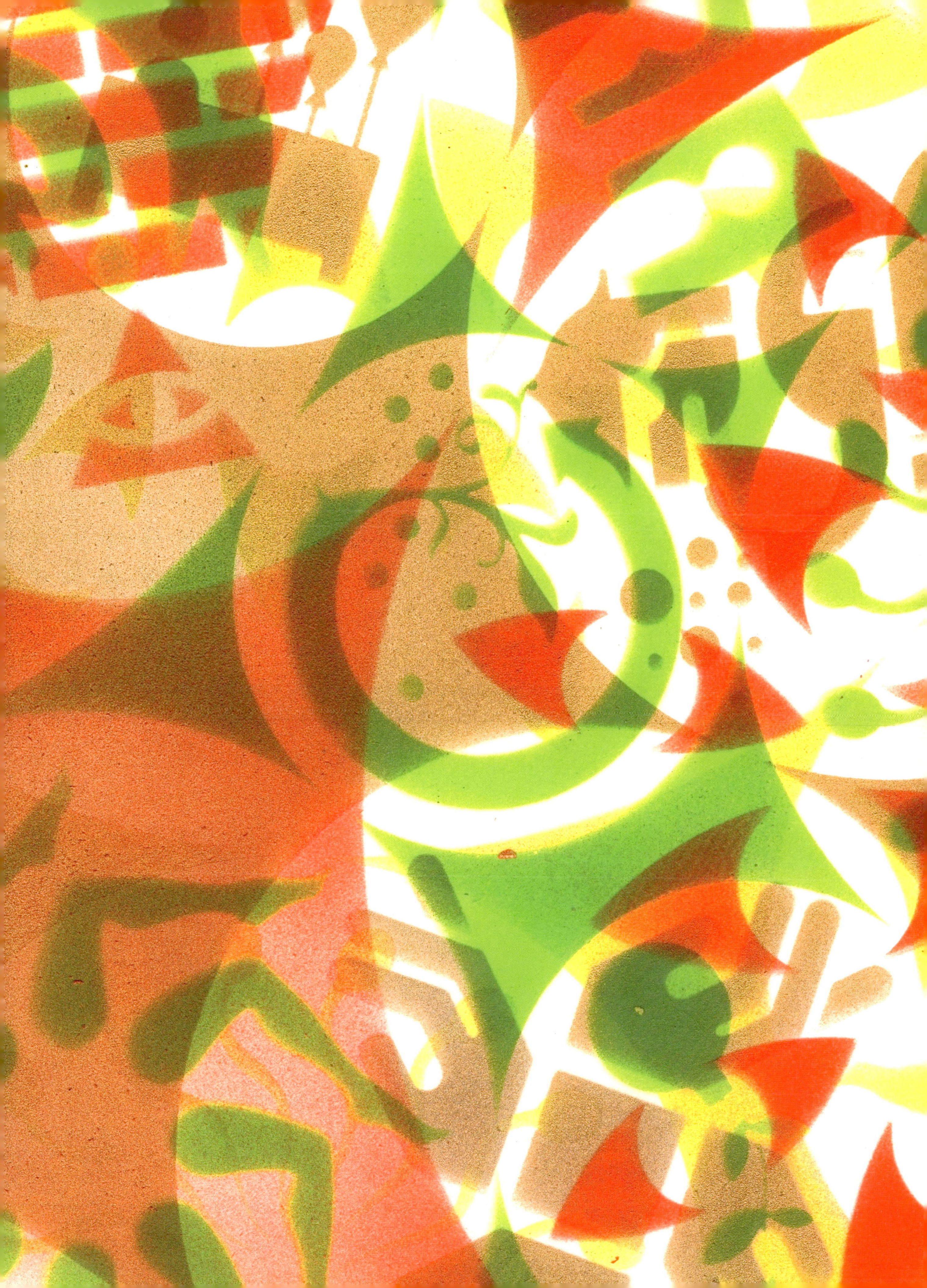

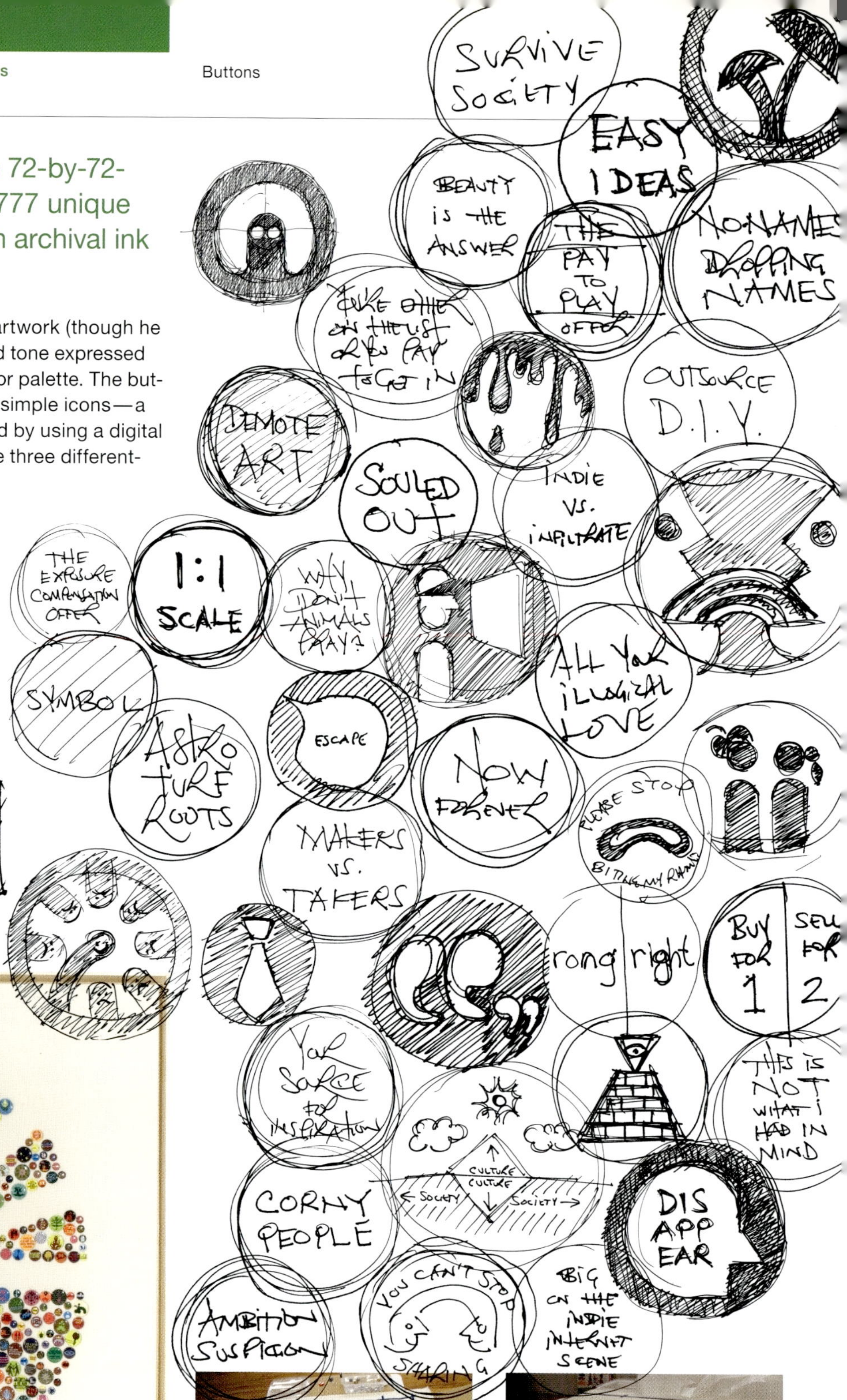

Island Universes is a series of five 72-by-72-inch assemblages, composed of 777 unique buttons, in three sizes, printed with archival ink on archival paper.(119)

This is the only time Ryan has used text in an artwork (though he has used it on t-shirts); the somewhat jaundiced tone expressed in the text is countered with a bright, poppy color palette. The buttons are pinned to raw canvas in the shapes of simple icons—a snake or a skull, for example. This was achieved by using a digital packing program that calculated a way to fit the three different-sized circular buttons into the iconic forms.

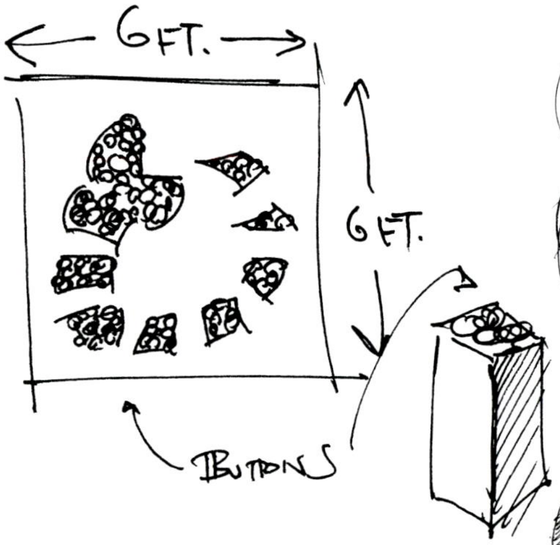

Top: Process sketches.

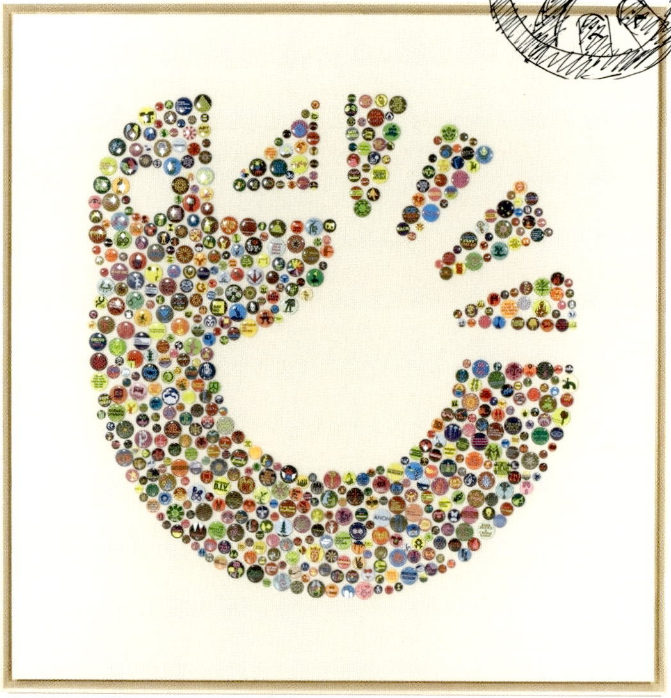

Above: *Island Universes (Snake)*, 2007, 777 unique buttons printed with archival ink on paper and pinned to raw canvas, 72 x 72 in.

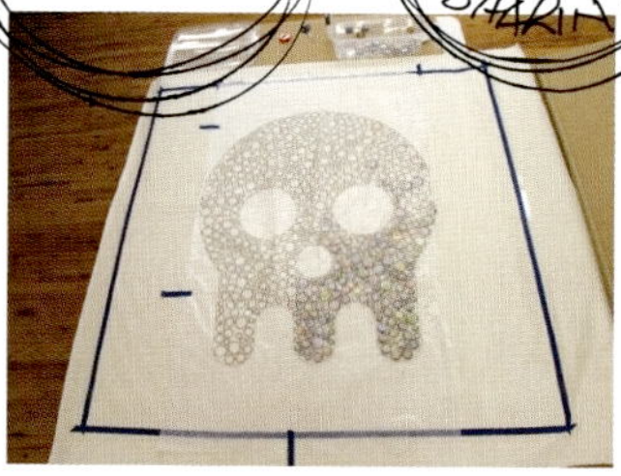

Schematic from packing program used to calculate the distribution of three regular variables (circles) into an irregular shape (skull).(120)

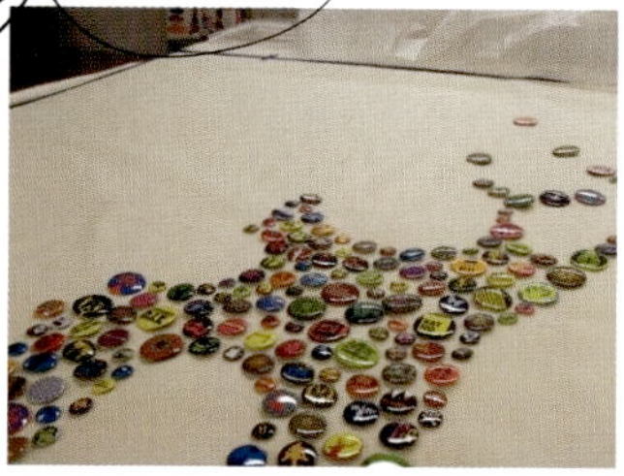

Pinning buttons to canvas.

(119) A disposable, subculture-message-vehicle produced with fine art concerns and materials as a reverse subversion.

(120) The three regular variables were 1, 1½, and 2 inches in diameter. A packing program was able to generate a plan that served as a starting point, with improvements made during the pinning.

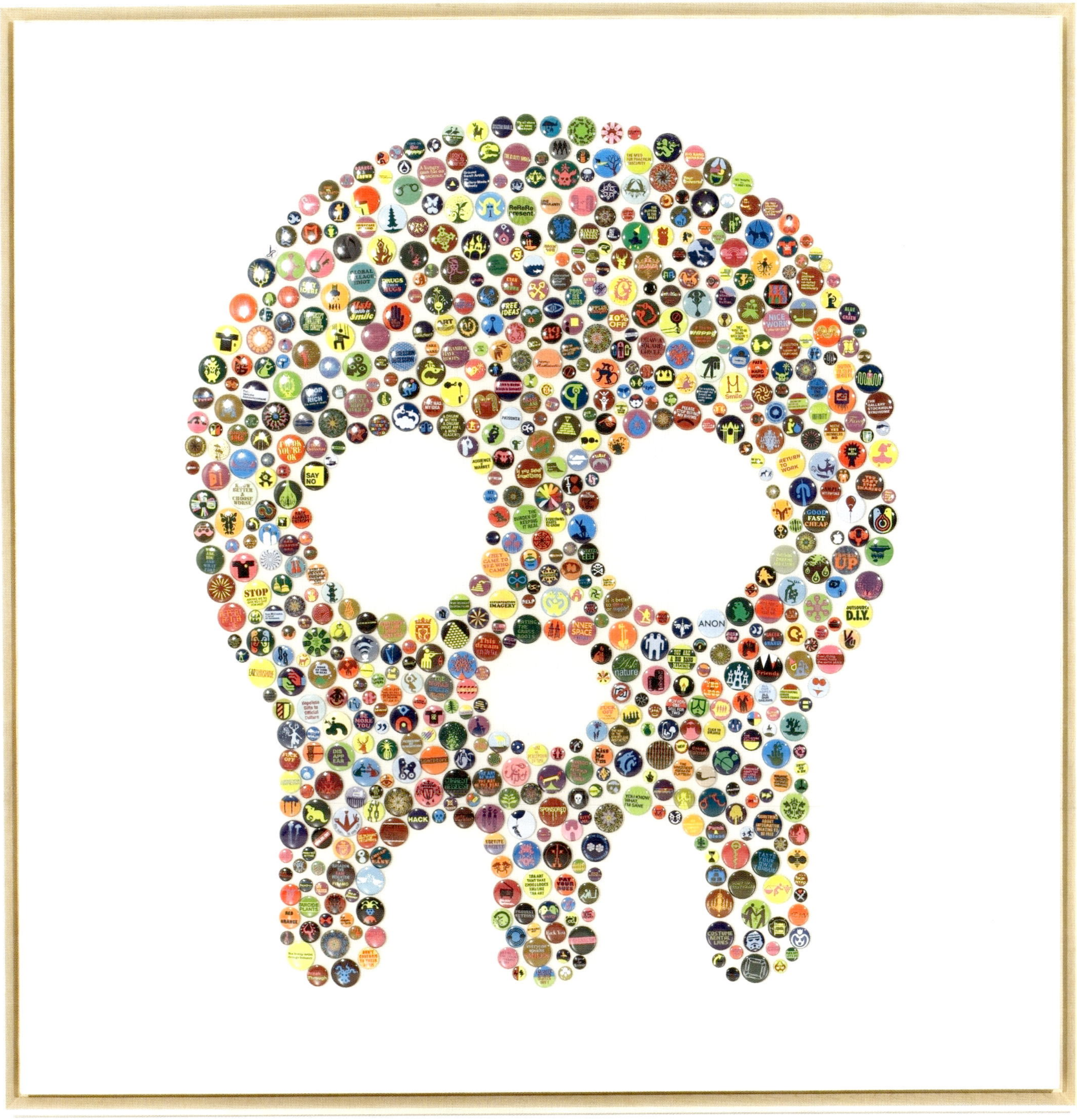

Island Universes (Skull), 2007, 777 unique buttons printed with archival ink on paper and pinned to raw canvas, 72 x 72 in.

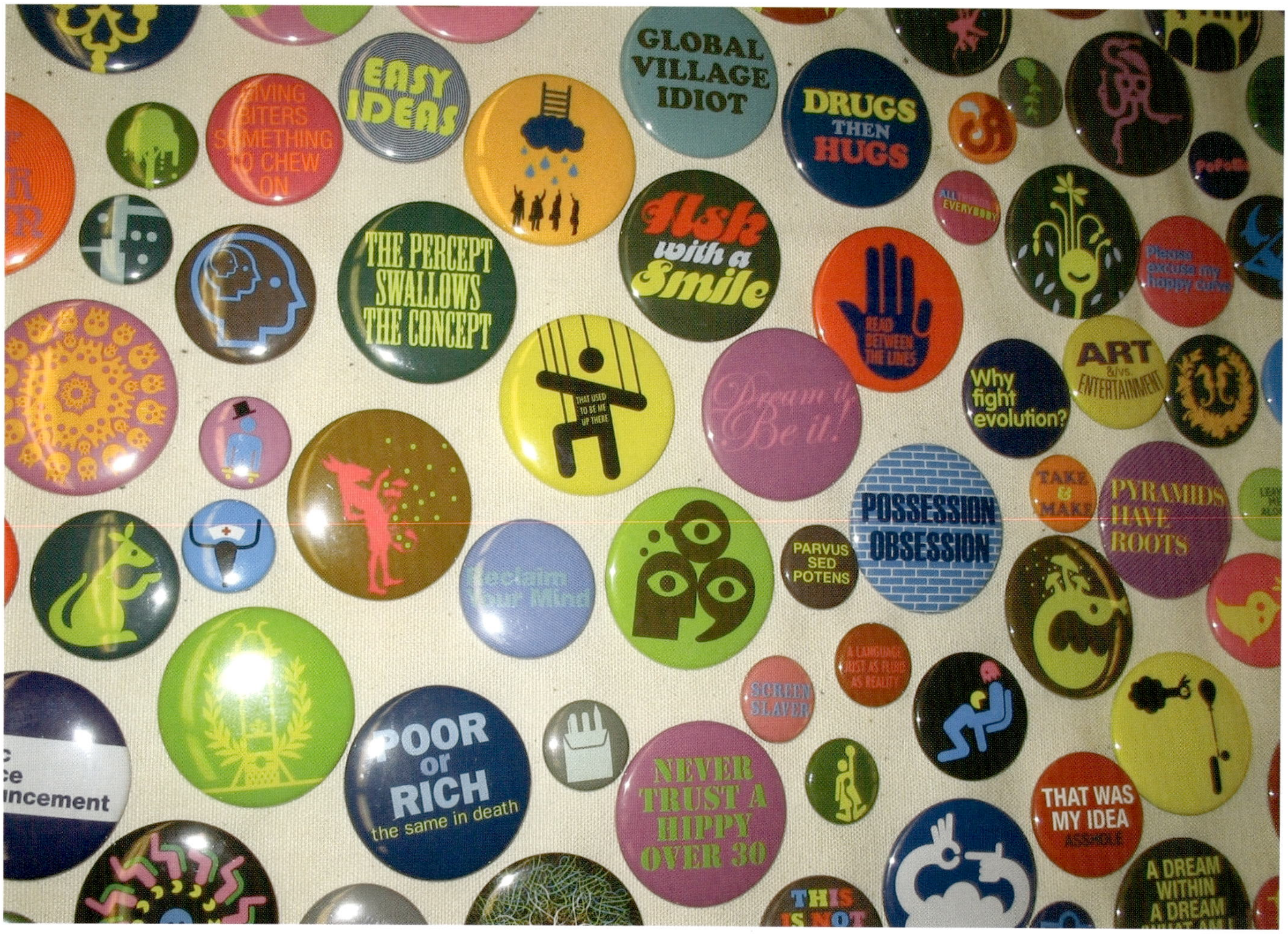

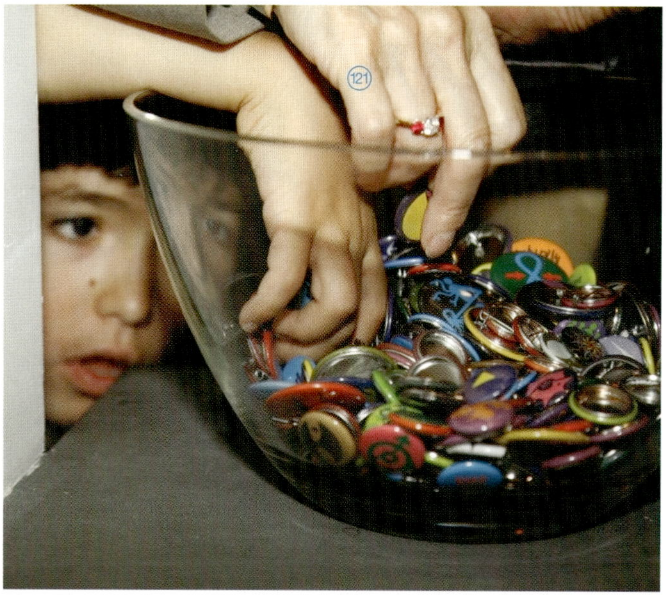

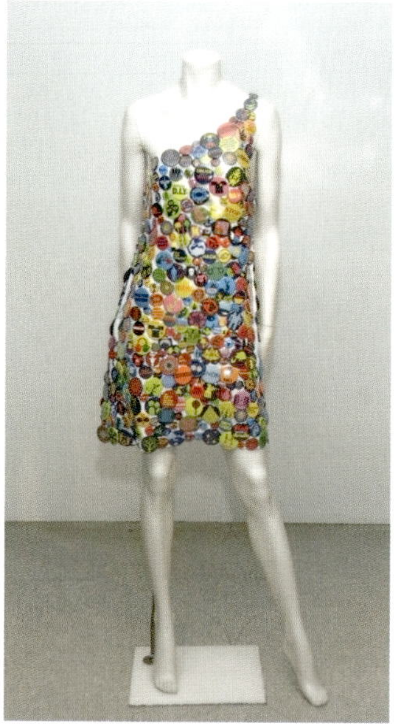

Top and opposite page: *Island Universes* (details), 2007, 777 unique buttons printed with archival ink on paper and pinned to raw canvas, 72 x 72 in.

Buttons given away during exhibition.

Untitled (Guggenheim Benefit), 2007, 642 unique buttons printed with archival ink on paper and pinned to a Chloé dress, size 38, 36 x 22 in.

(121) Extensions of the piece escape the piece and are freely distributed. In this way, its dimensions are variable and infinite.

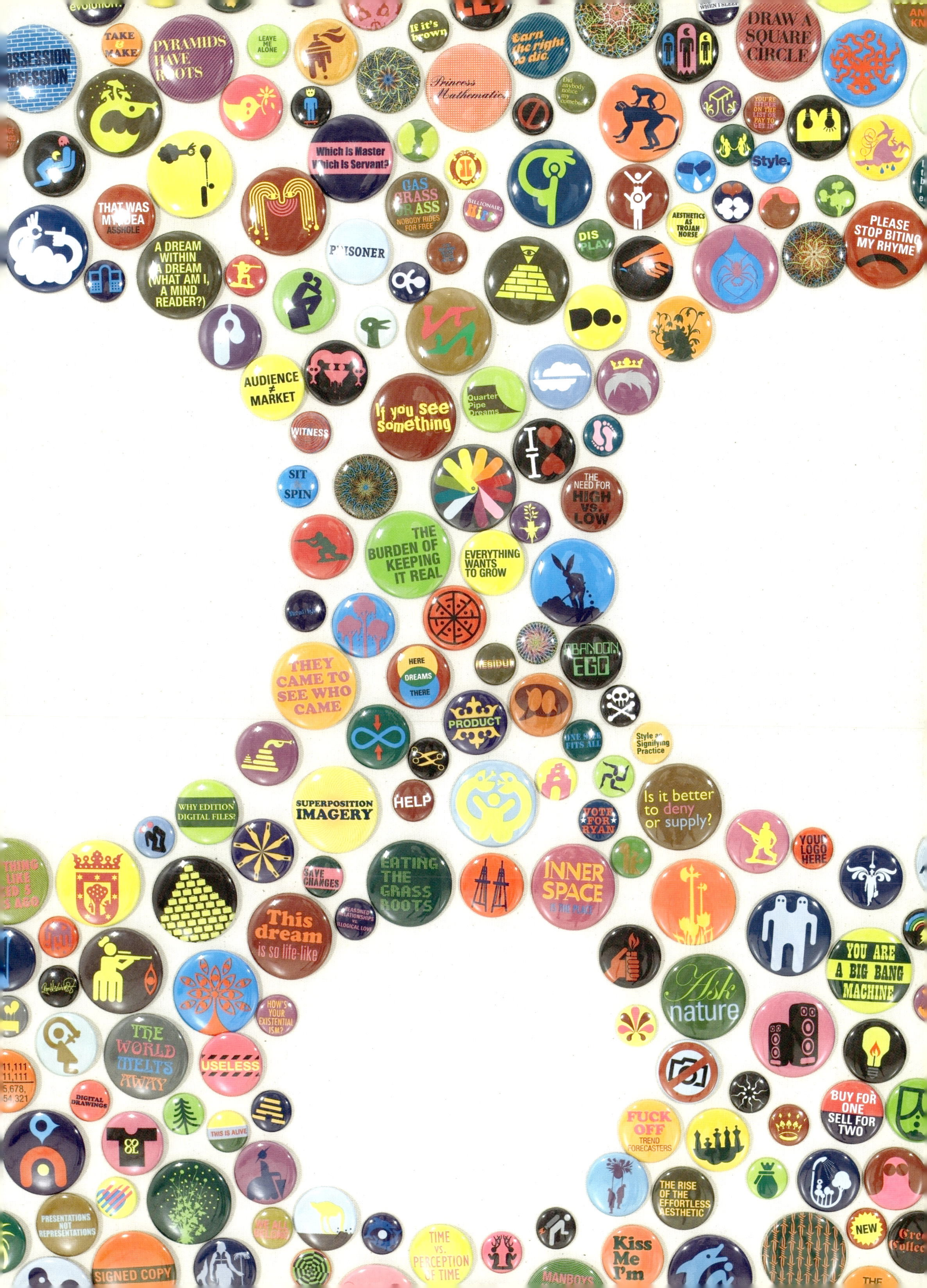
TAKE & MAKE
PYRAMIDS HAVE ROOTS
LEAVE ME ALONE
If it's brown
Earn the right to die
DRAW A SQUARE CIRCLE
Princess Mathematics
Did anybody notice my comeback
Which Is Master Which Is Servant?
Style.
GAS GRASS OR ASS NOBODY RIDES FOR FREE
BILLIONAIRE
THAT WAS MY IDEA ASSHOLE
AESTHETICS AS TROJAN HORSE
PLEASE STOP BITING MY RHYME
A DREAM WITHIN A DREAM (WHAT AM I, A MIND READER?)
PRISONER
DIS PLAY
DO.
AUDIENCE ≠ MARKET
If you see something
Quarter Pipe Dreams
WITNESS
SIT SPIN
THE NEED FOR HIGH vs. LOW
THE BURDEN OF KEEPING IT REAL
EVERYTHING WANTS TO GROW
THEY CAME TO SEE WHO CAME
HERE DREAMS THERE
RESIDUE
ABANDON EGO
PRODUCT
ONE SIZE FITS ALL
Style as Signifying Practice
WHY EDITION DIGITAL FILES?
SUPERPOSITION IMAGERY
HELP
Is it better to deny or supply?
VOTE FOR RYAN
YOUR LOGO HERE
SAVE CHANGES
EATING THE GRASS ROOTS
INNER SPACE IS THE PLACE
This dream is so life-like
REASONED RELATIONSHIPS vs. ILLOGICAL LOVE
YOU ARE A BIG BANG MACHINE
Ask nature
HOW'S YOUR EXISTENTIAL ISM?
THE WORLD MELTS AWAY
USELESS
DIGITAL DRAWINGS
THIS IS ALIVE
BUY FOR ONE SELL FOR TWO
FUCK OFF TREND FORECASTERS
THE RISE OF THE EFFORTLESS AESTHETIC
PRESENTATIONS NOT REPRESENTATIONS
WE ALL BELONG
NEW
TIME vs. PERCEPTION OF TIME
Kiss Me I'm
SIGNED COPY
MANBOYS

Porcelain-baked enamel is a process in which enamel is fused to steel in large kilns to create a glassy surface.

Ryan first used the medium in 2001 for his *Untitled (Black and Gold Tablets)* series, inspired by old New York subway signs, which used the same material. Throughout the years he continued to explore the process as another way of materializing his final vector drawings. He pushed his use of the medium further in 2007 with an edition of five 36-by-36-by-1½-inch pieces.

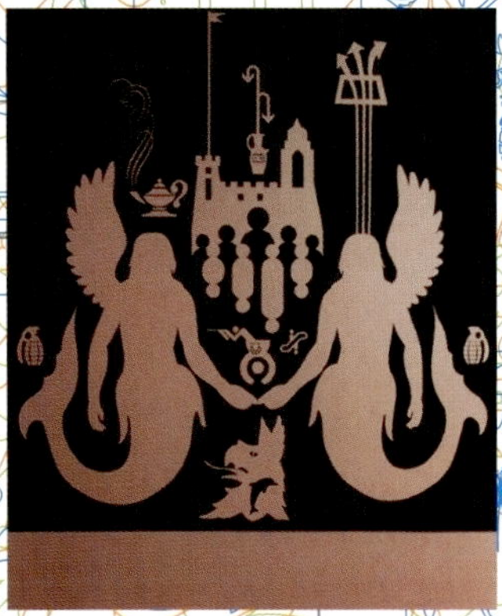

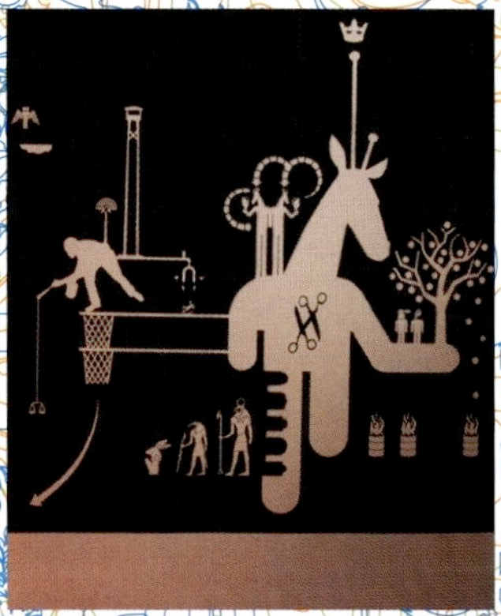

Untitled (Black & Gold Tablets), 2001, porcelain-baked enamel on steel, 21 x 18 in., edition of 2 each.

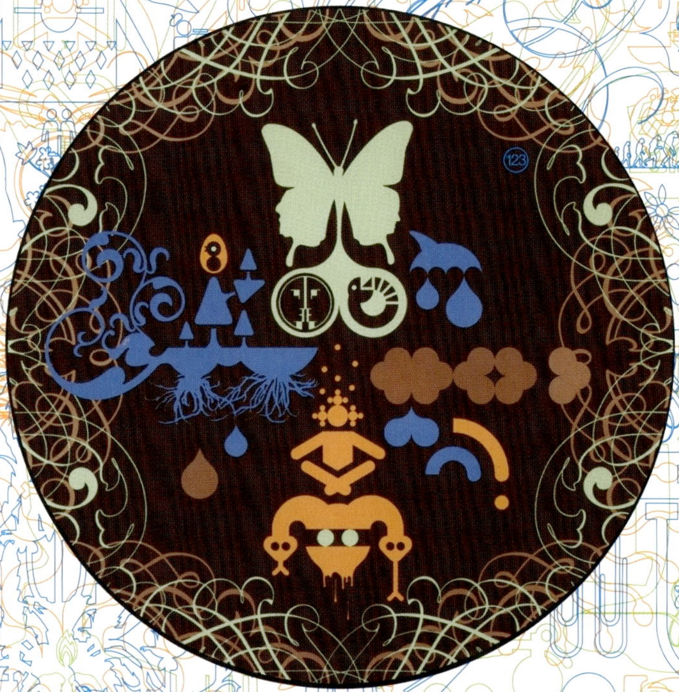

Untitled, 2005, porcelain-baked enamel on steel, 24 in. diameter.

(122) Can you find this hidden footnote? It is buried in the background image above.

(123) This is one side of a two-sided piece that I made as a prototype for the *Universals* (see p. 78). The porcelain-baked enamel on steel proved to be too heavy to cantilever off the wall. I eventually destroyed this piece.

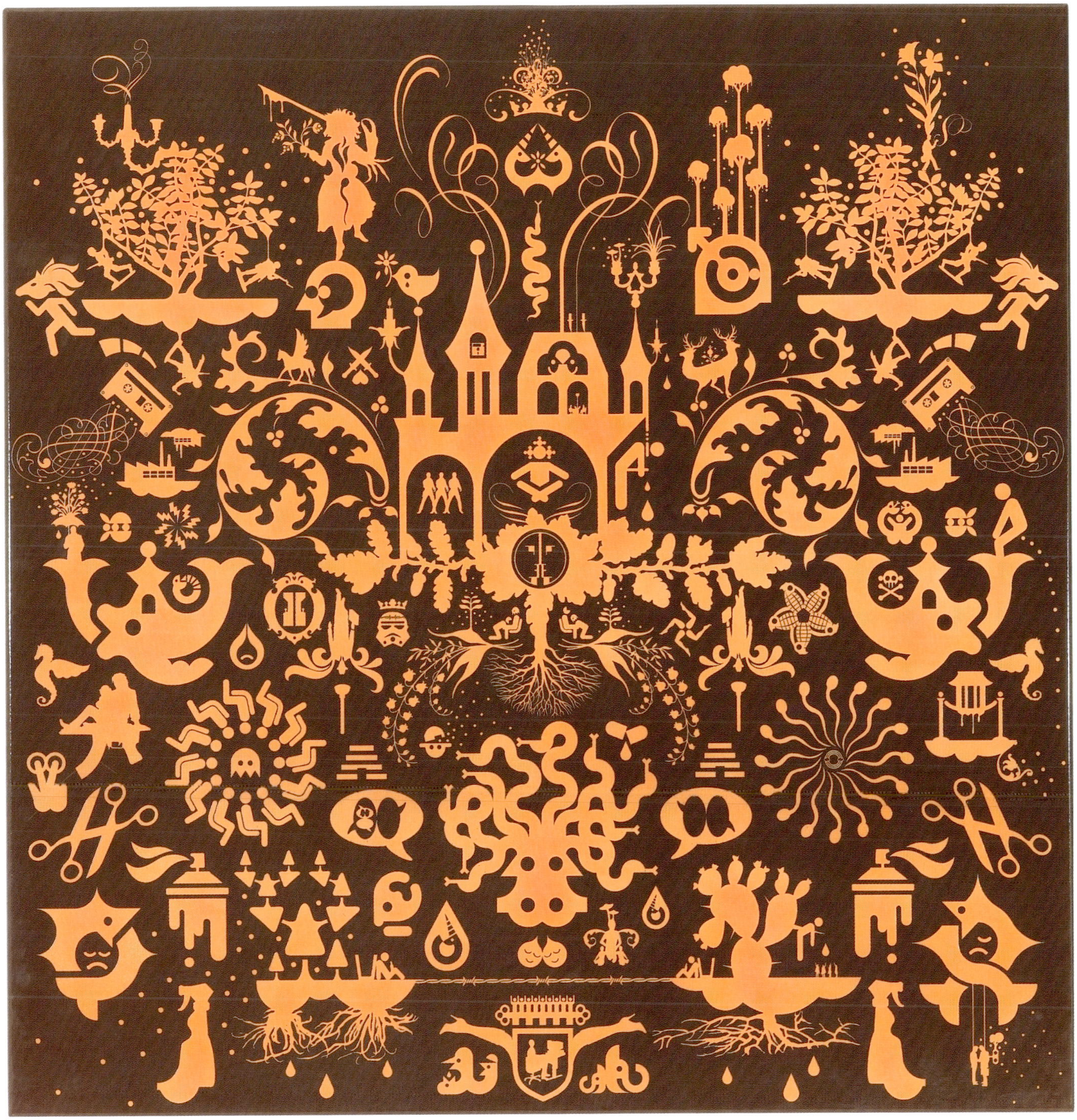

Untitled (Orange), 2007, porcelain-baked enamel on steel, 36 x 36 x 1½ in., edition of 5. Published by Pace Prints, New York.

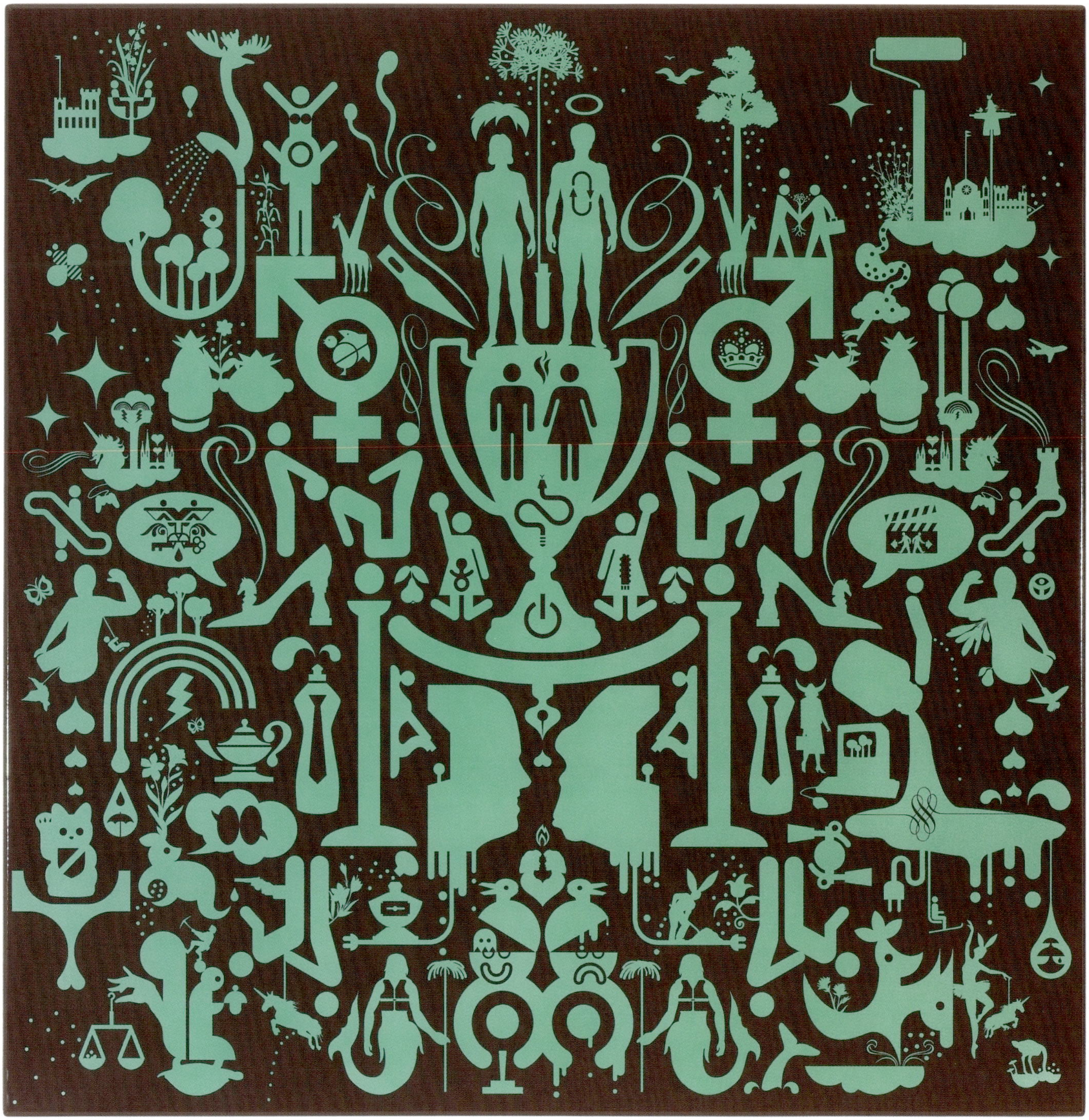

Untitled (Green), 2007, porcelain-baked enamel on steel, 36 x 36 x 1½ in., edition of 5. Published by Pace Prints, New York.

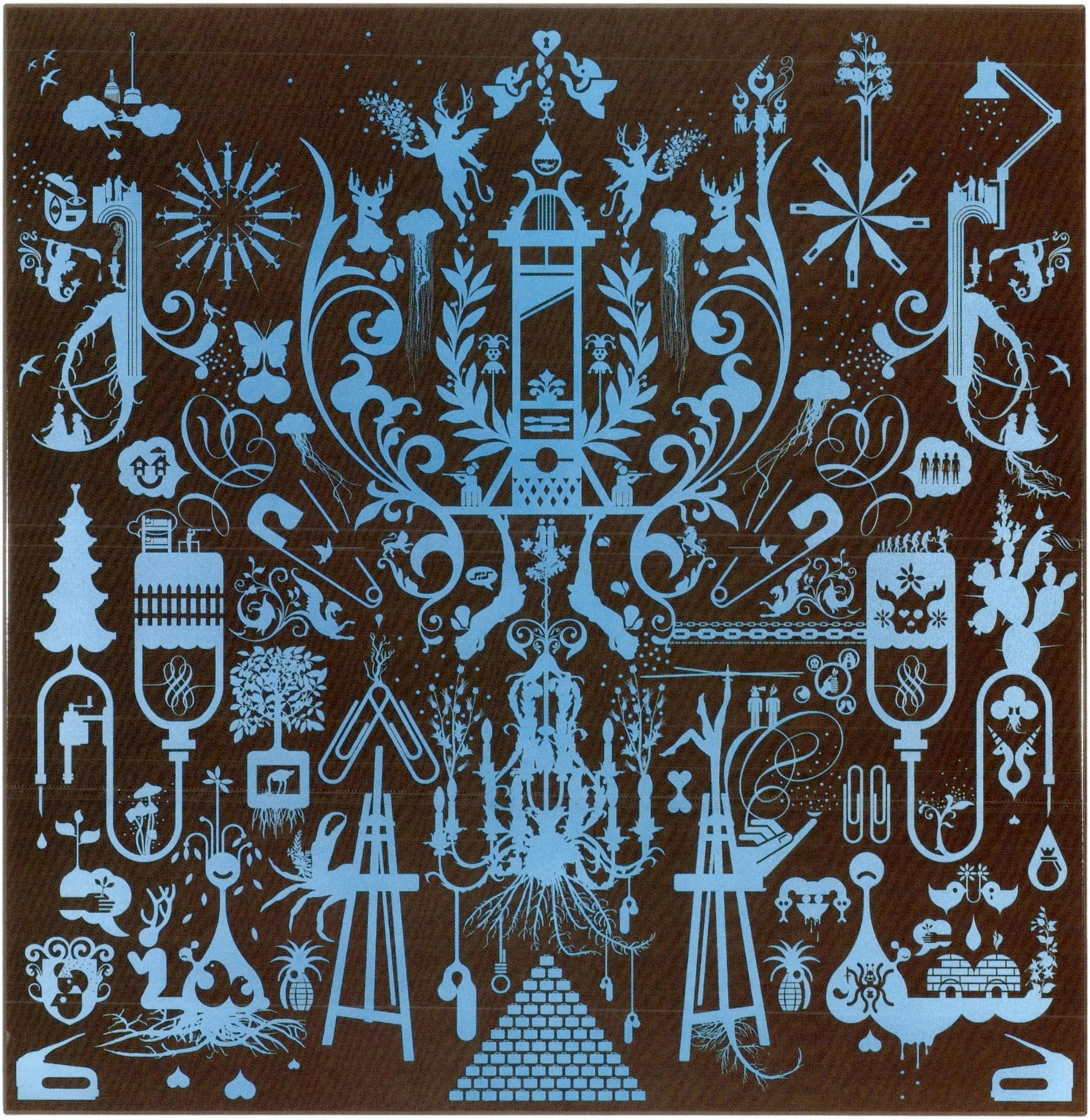

Untitled (Blue), 2007, porcelain-baked enamel on steel, 36 x 36 x 1½ in., edition of 5.
Published by Pace Prints, New York.

Rainbow McTwist takes its name from a skate trick first performed by Mike McGill in 1984.[124]

Created in an edition of five, the piece is composed of skateboards painted in a panoply of rainbow colors and laser cut with an identical repeated drawing. The flowerlike configuration is arranged at precise angles and cantilevers a few feet off the wall.

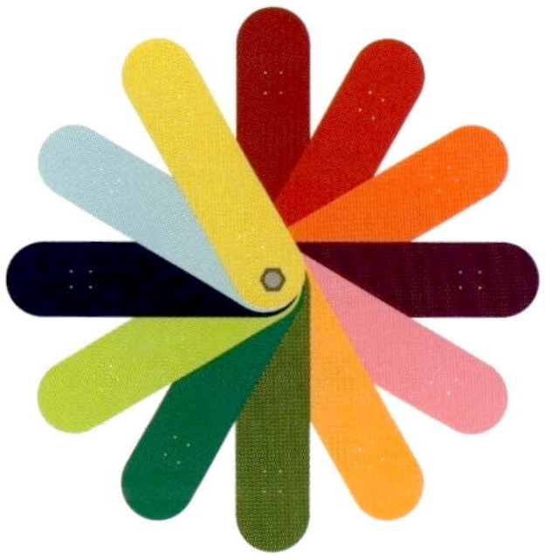
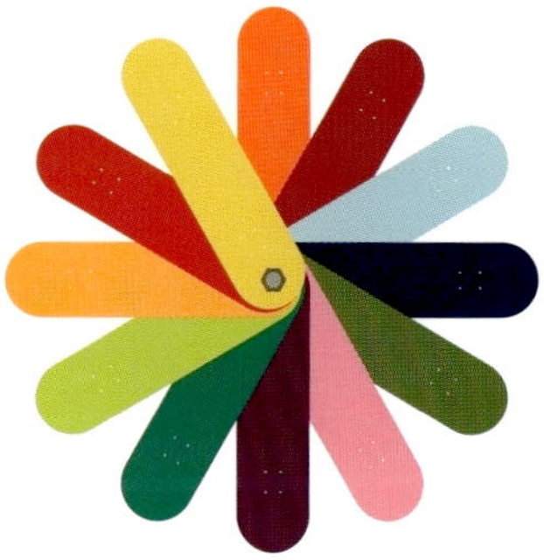

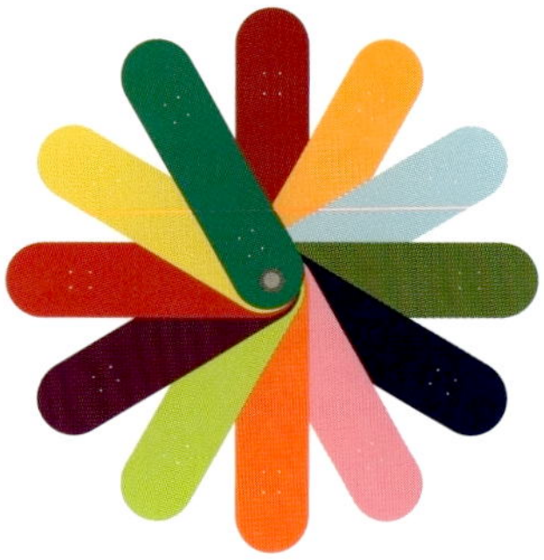
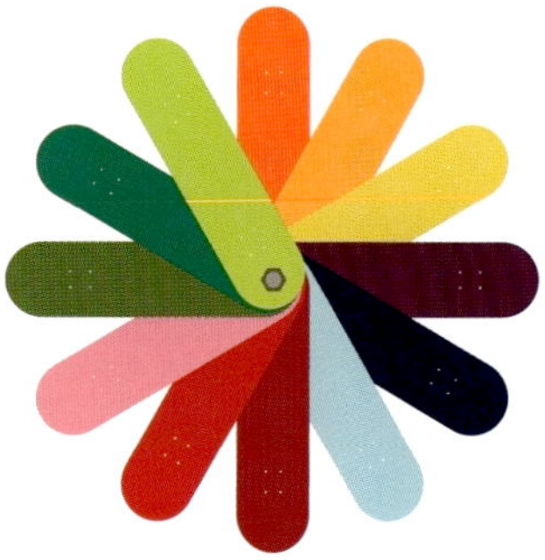
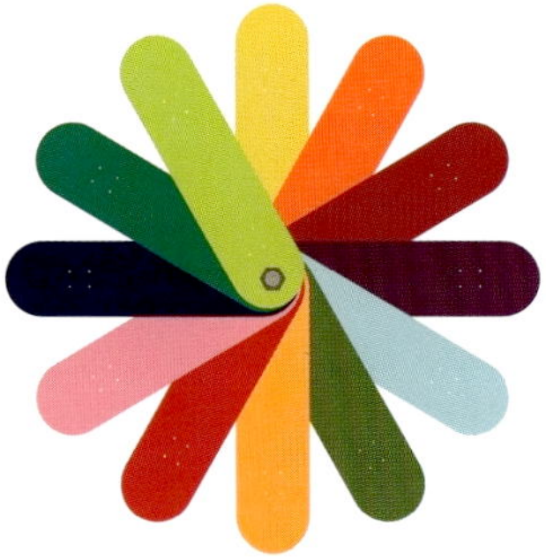
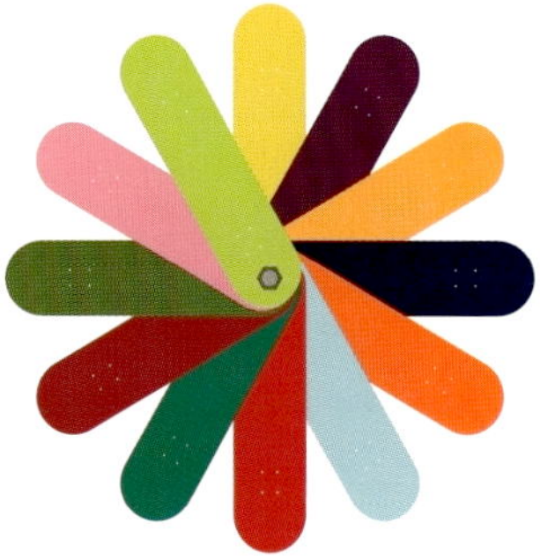
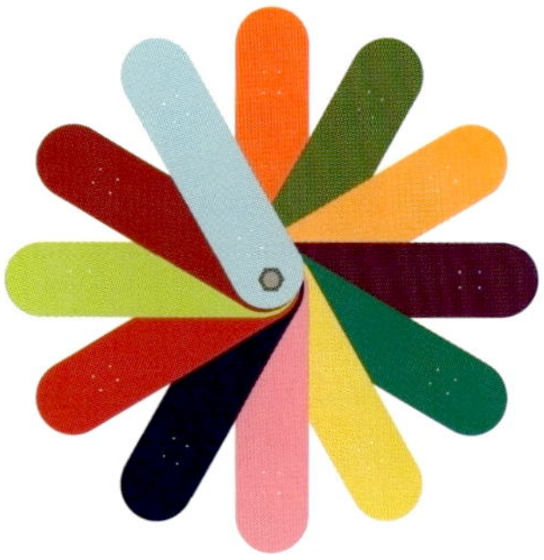

[125]

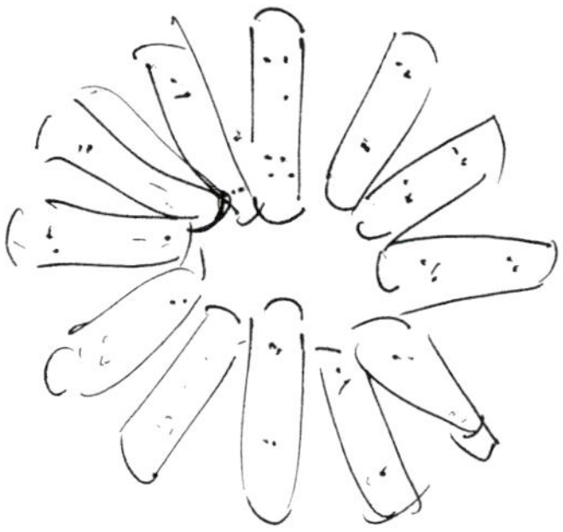
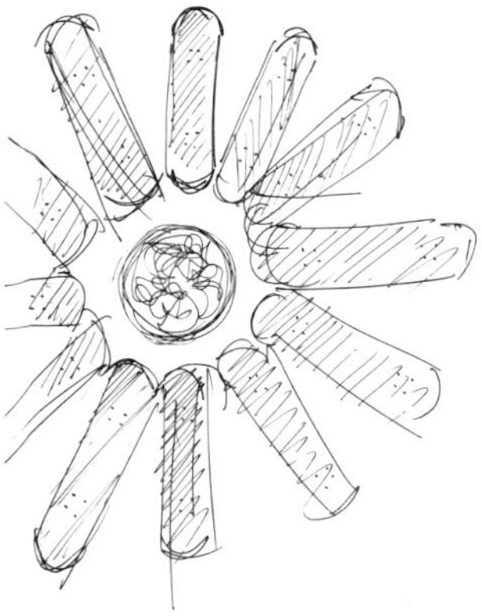
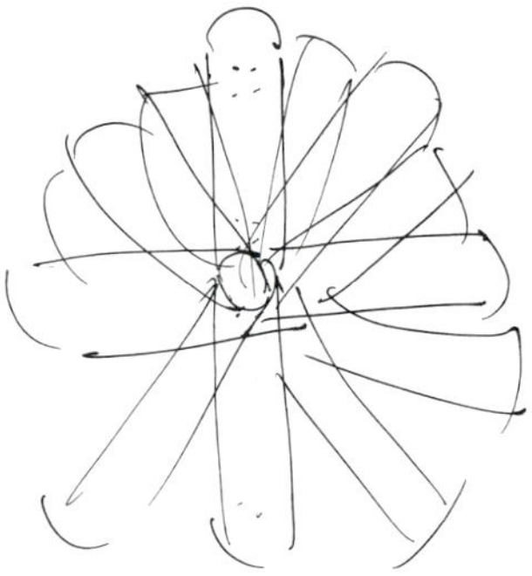
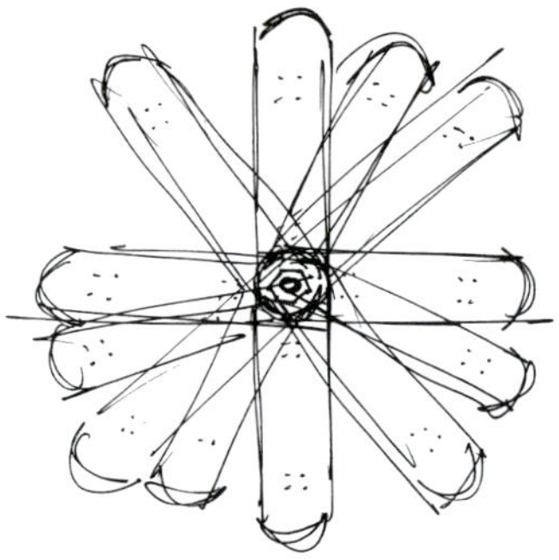

Above and opposite page: Preliminary sketches, 2006–2007, ink on paper, dimensions vary; and models for *Rainbow McTwist*, 2007, 12 laser-cut, painted skateboards with steel hardware, 60 x 60 x 20 in., edition of 5. Published by Pace Prints, New York.

Top: Color studies.

[124] .com/mctwist

[125] See p. 28.

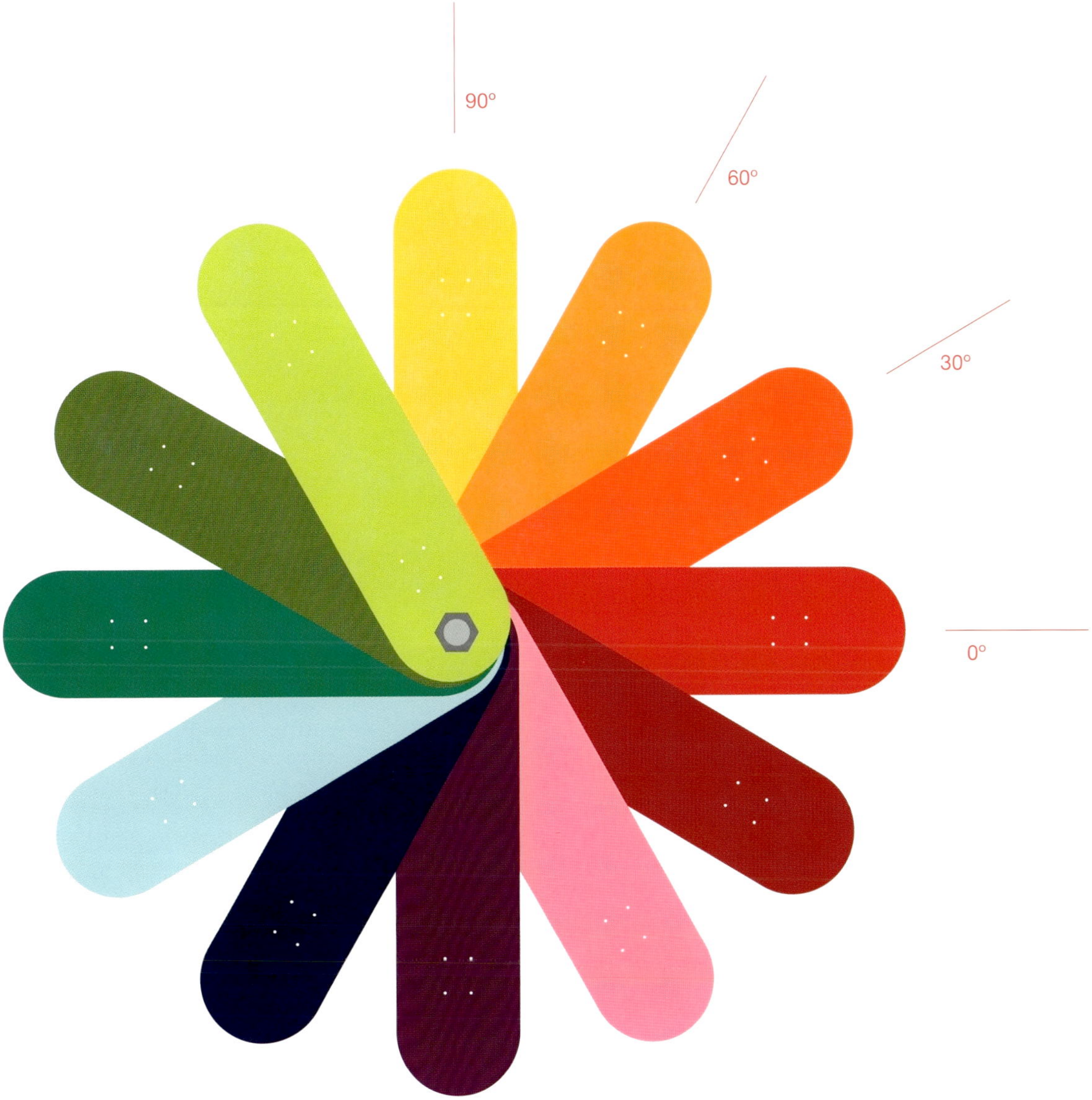

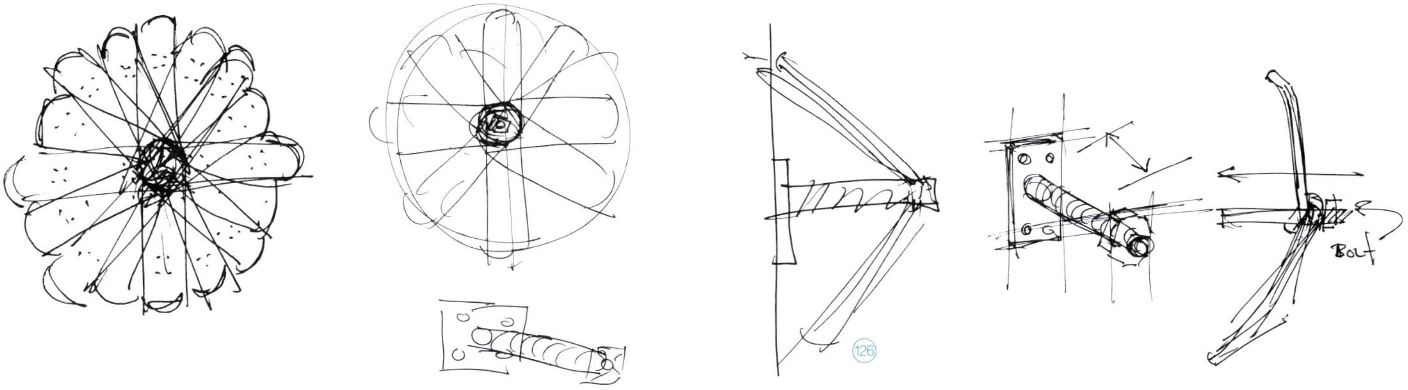

Top: Skateboard petal distribution schematic.

126 Bottom-side-out. Blooming backwards. It never occurred to me to put the laser-cut drawings on the top of the boards, which would have resulted in a concave bloom and a shorter cantilever. Grip tape usually goes on top (see p. 131), which blocked me from considering that side as a possibility.

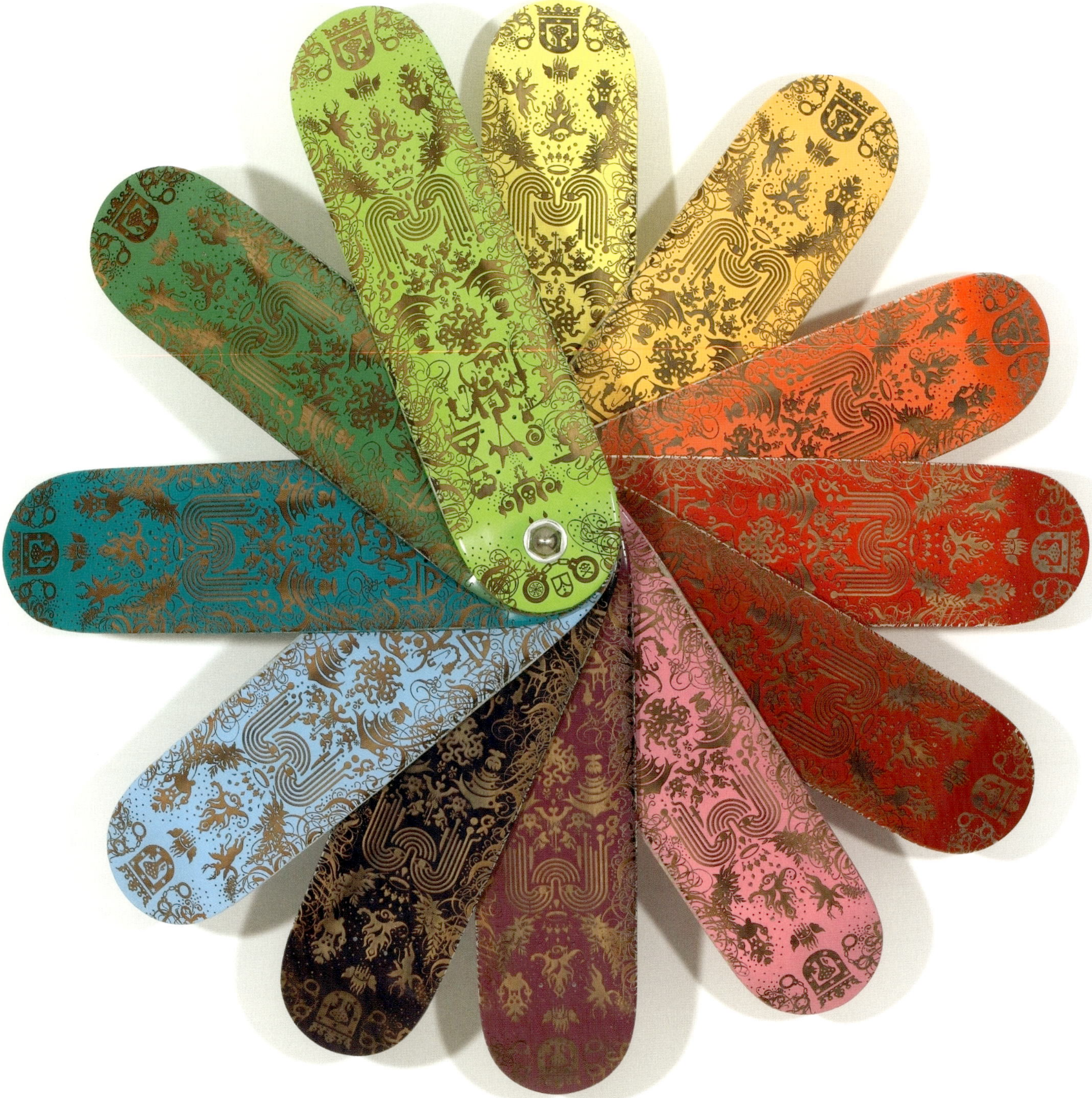

Rainbow McTwist, 2007, 12 laser-cut, painted skateboards with steel hardware, 60 x 60 x 20 in., edition of 5. Published by Pace Prints, New York. (detail opposite page).

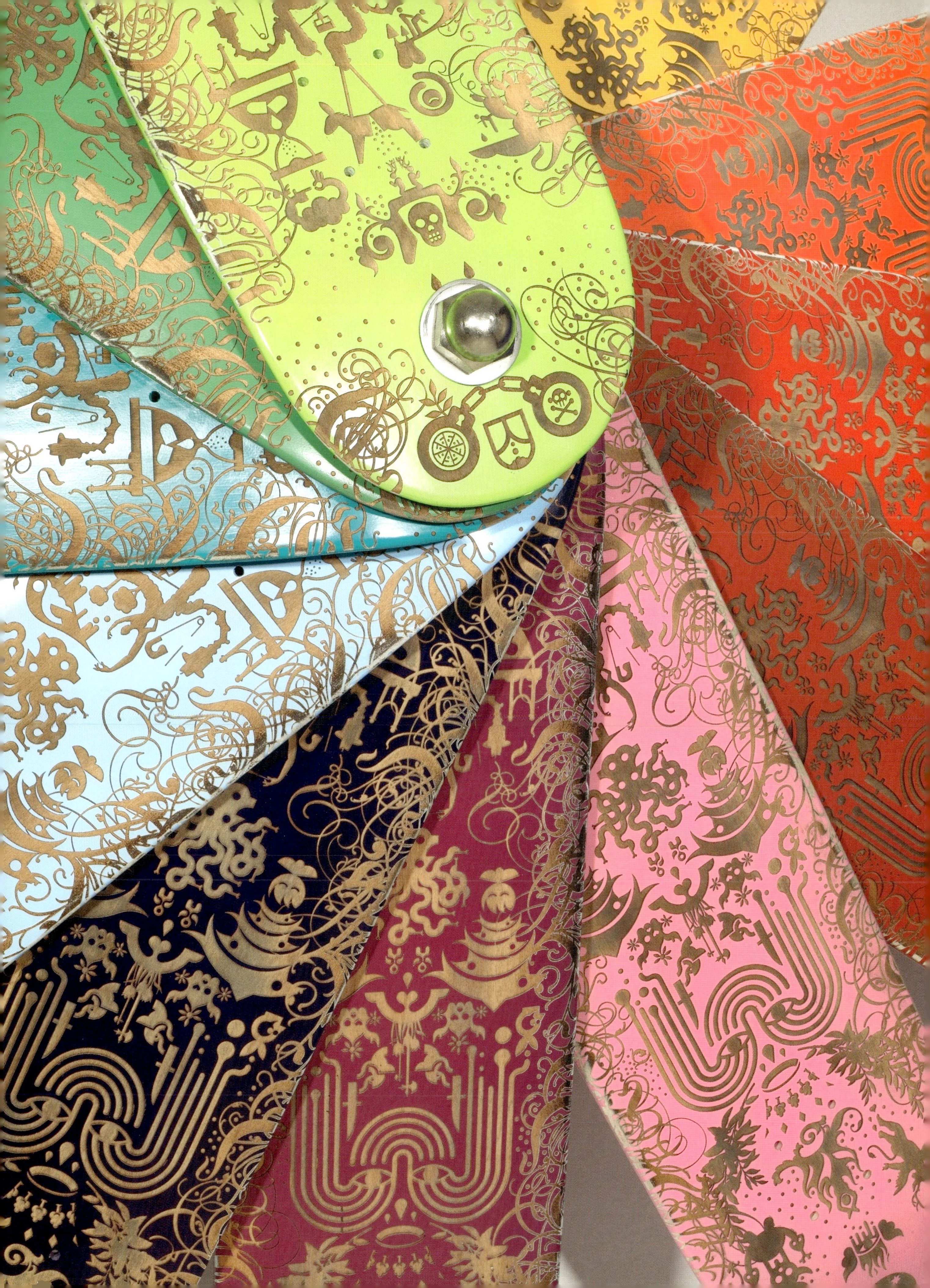

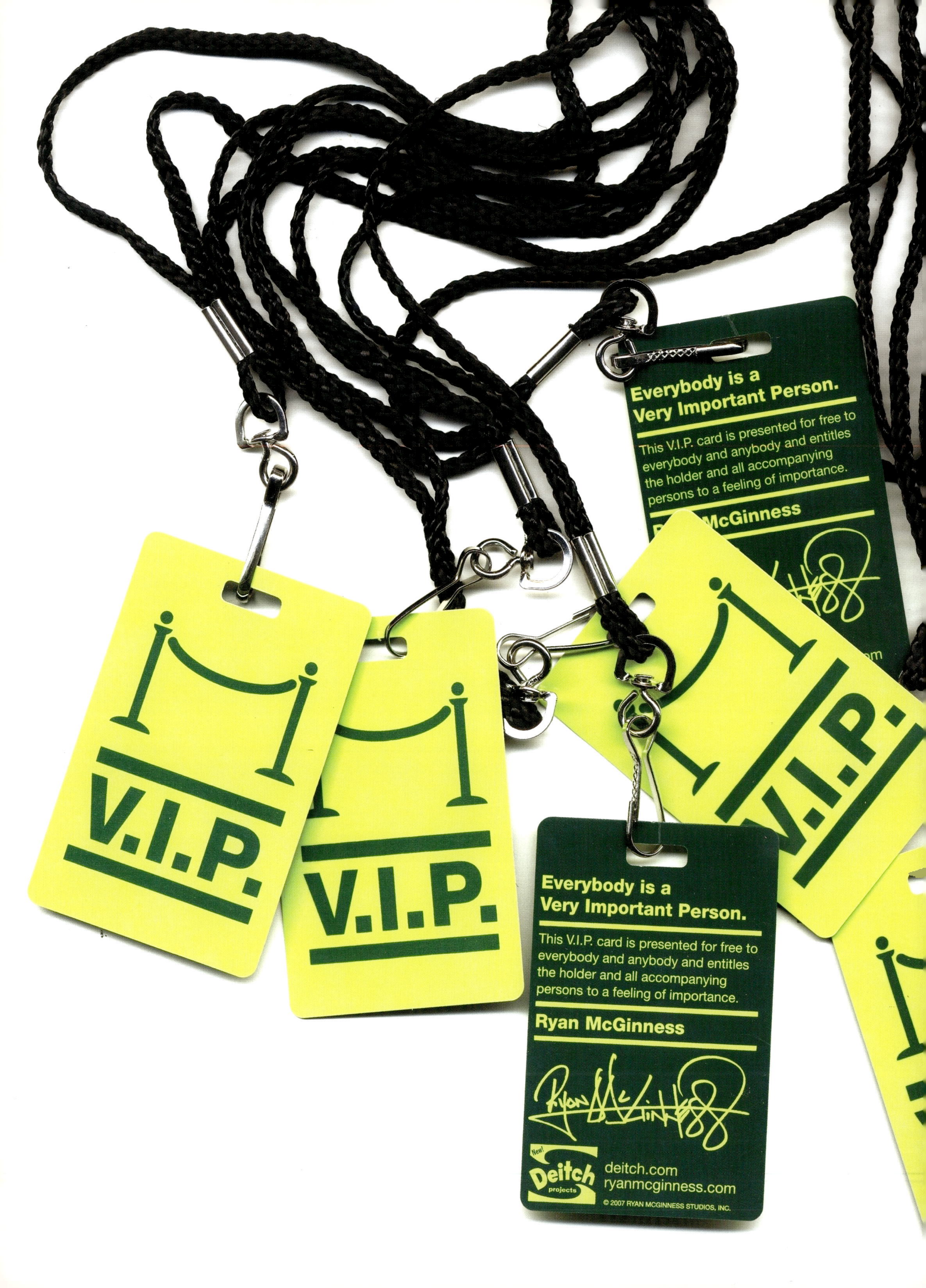
V.I.P.
V.I.P.
V.I.P.
Everybody is a
Very Important Person.
This V.I.P. card is presented for free to everybody and anybody and entitles the holder and all accompanying persons to a feeling of importance.
Ryan McGinness
New!
Deitch
projects
deitch.com
ryanmcginness.com
© 2007 RYAN MCGINNESS STUDIOS, INC.

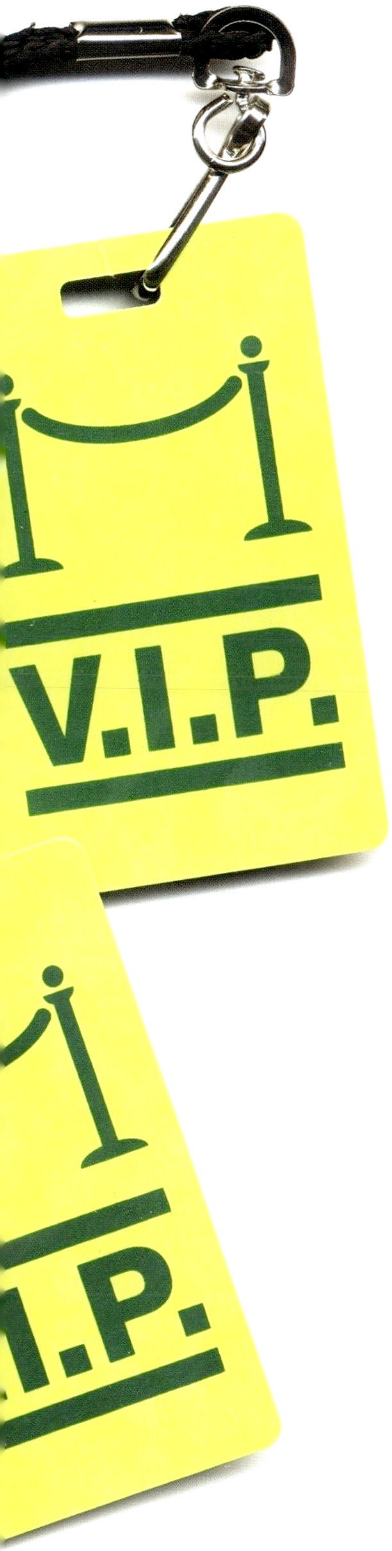

Have You Seen Him?, an immersive installation with variable components, takes its title from the 1987 Powell Peralta skate video, *The Search for Animal Chin*, in which the Bones Brigade (Steve Caballero, Tommy Guerrero, Tony Hawk, Mike McGill, and Lance Mountain) endeavor to find the elusive legend Won Ton "Animal Chin"—who some say is responsible for sticking roller skate wheels on a two-by-four and inventing skateboarding—in order to reclaim the true spirit of the sport. The video served as a canny critique of how corporations co-opted skate culture for profit. A corollary can be found in the global art fair circuit. When *Have You Seen Him?* was commissioned by Art Basel, Ryan decided to call attention to the fact that the fair was, in effect, outsourcing DIY, since the imagery from his installation was developed from themes in the Powell Peralta video as well as graphics from 80s skate brands and punk bands, such as the Misfits, the Dead Kennedys, and Black Flag.

V.I.P. Pass, 2007, silkscreen on plastic with metal and nylon cord, 3 3/8 x 2 1/8 in., open edition. Published by Deitch Projects, New York.

Commissioned by Art Basel and curated by WPS1 Art Radio in 2007, *Have You Seen Him?* consisted of 52 4-by-8-foot paintings that were attached to shipping containers to create a background for an integrated environment that included a unique skateboard, signage, VIP passes, and t-shirts, as well as cups, napkins, and water bottles for the café and a skate ramp. The entire environment was created using commercial culture's branding approach as the model for an artist's production.

After being on view at Art Basel Miami Beach, *Have You Seen Him?* was installed in the spring of 2008 in the courtyard at P.S. 1 in New York as a 200-foot-long panoramic mural. *Have You Seen Him?* was created with the same palette as an earlier project developed for the Public Art Fund called *Equo ne Credite, Teucri* (Do not trust the horse, Trojans!), in which a set of 16 double-sided signs were installed along the walkway of MetroTech Commons in Brooklyn. The signs appeared, at first glance, to be city property since their color scheme matches the light poles, benches, and other fixtures in the area, but they are, in fact, populated with idiosyncratic, personal imagery.

(127)

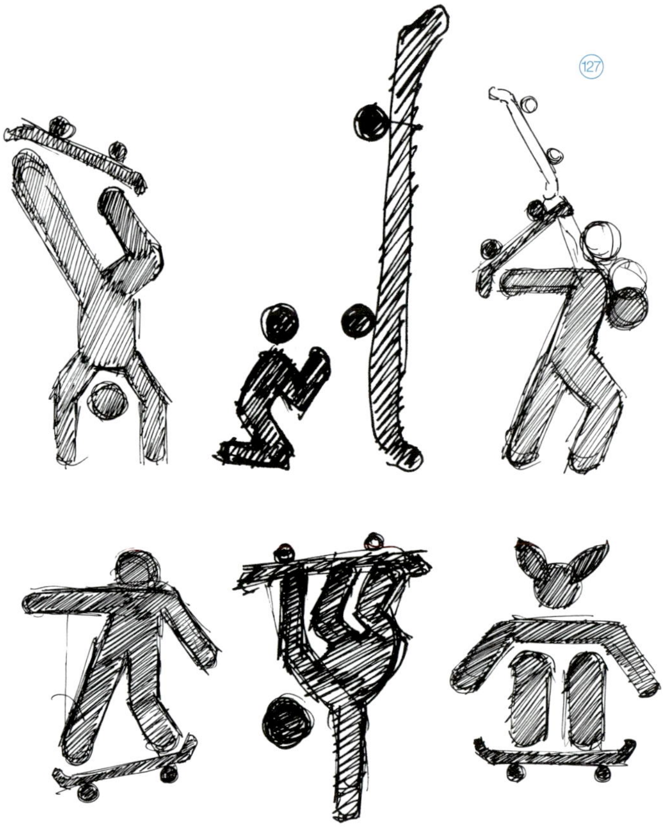

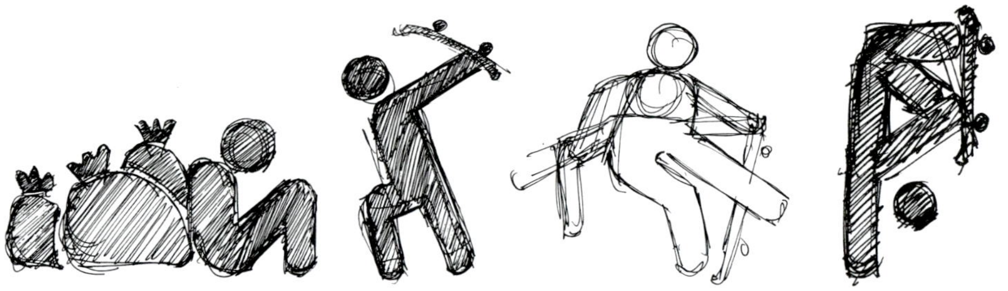

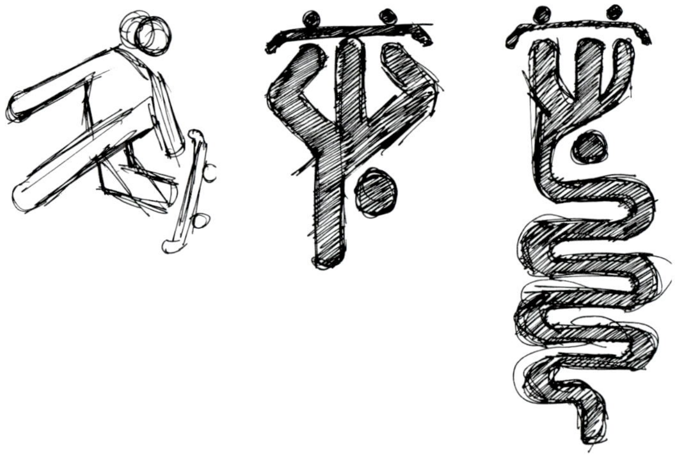

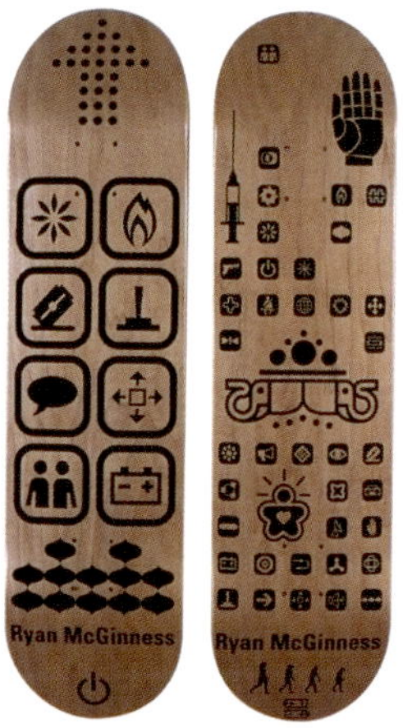

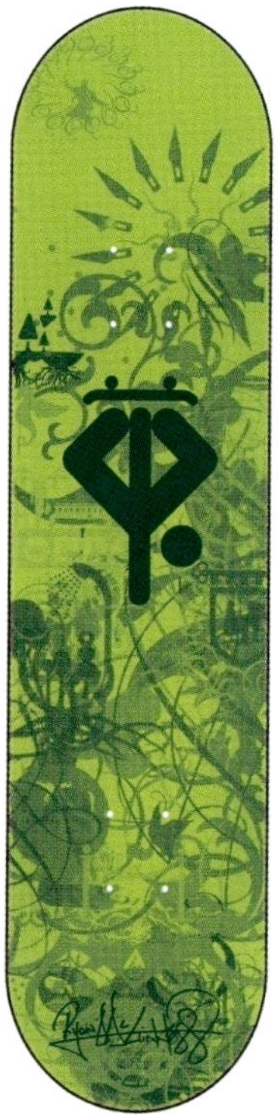

Top: Process sketches, ink on paper, dimensions variable.

Untitled (Skateboards), 2000, vinyl on wood skateboards, 32 x 8 in. each.

Growing Handplants, 2008, oil on skateboard, 32 x 8 in., edition of 500. Published by Iconoclast, Cincinnati.

(127) Skate tricks depicted: Ho-Ho Plant, Prayer Air, Hand Plant, Bunny Hop, Skittle McDittle, Long Arm of the Law, Ollie Dior, Boneless, Bum Bash, and Sketch Plant. (128)

(128) Half of these I made up.

(130)

(129)

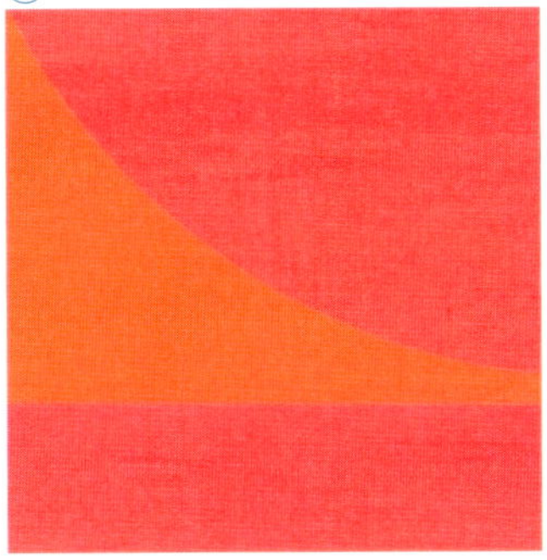

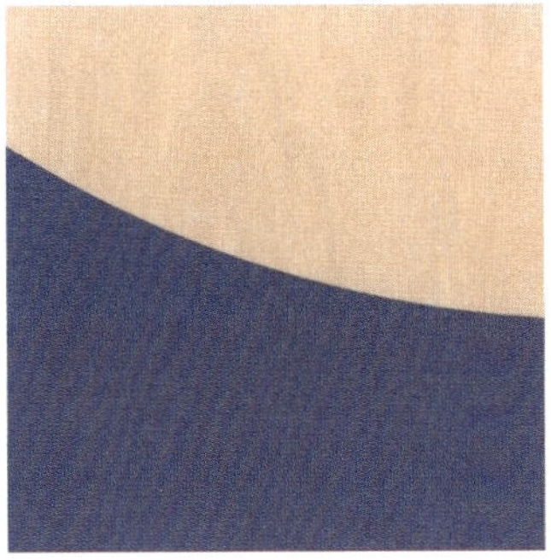

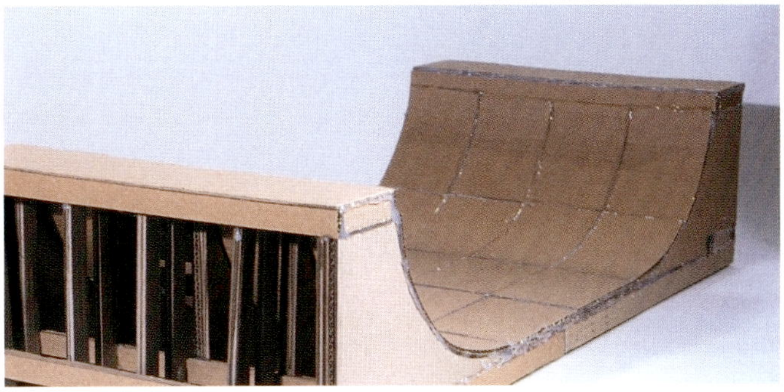

Top: *Untitled (Have You Seen Him? Drawings)*, 2007, vector drawings, digital files.

Above left and right: *Untitled (Transition Paintings)*, 2000, grip tape on wood panels, 12 x 12 in. each.

Lithium vs. Valproate, 2000, cardboard and hot glue, 9 x 37 x 16 in. (131)

(129) The grip-tape-transition paintings are a nod to Ellsworth Kelly's minimal color fields.

(130) Powell Peralta, Misfits, Per Welinder, Independent, Rob Roskopp, Zorlac, Town & Country, Gator, Bones Brigade, Mike McGill, Black Flag, Jeff Kendall, Sims, Slime Balls, Shut Up & Skate, Tony Hawk, Dead Kennedys.

(131) Drugs for bipolar disorder. Mood swings. Back and forth. Highs and lows.

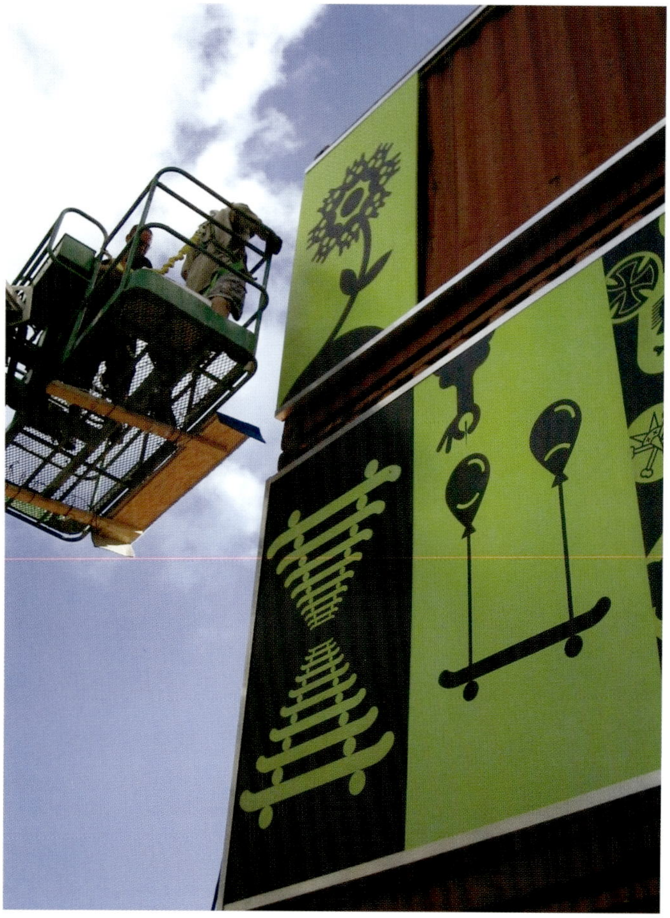

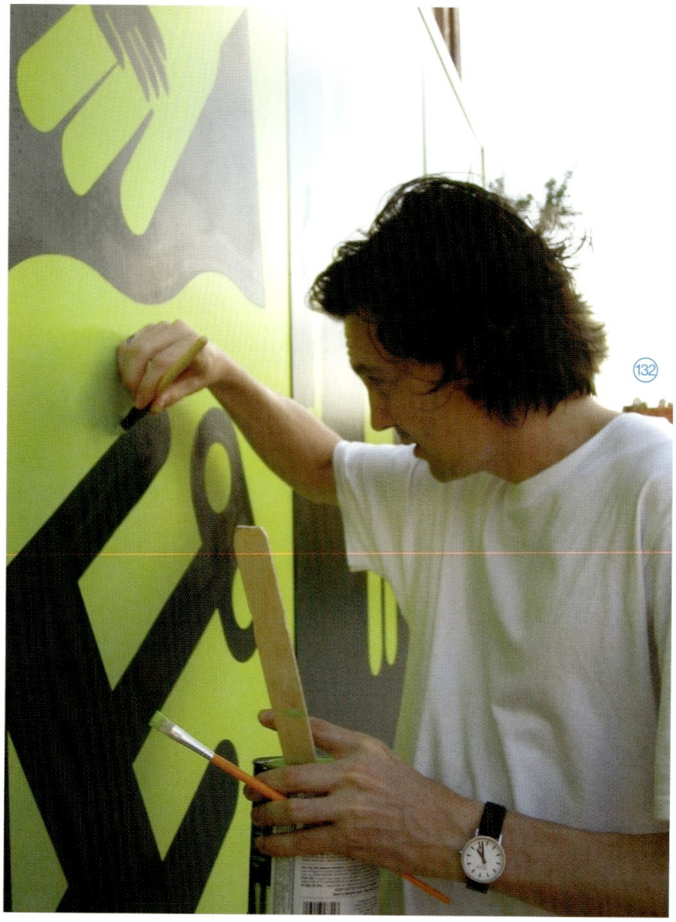

We were under a tremendous time constraint, so we outsourced everything. The biggest technical challenge was that these panels were unsupported supports: there was no way to fasten anything to the back to hang them. The solution we came up with was to attach stainless steel U channels onto the shipping containers that the panels could slide into.

—Sean Hart

Senior Designer, Kboom Culture, and Project Manager for *Have You Seen Him?*

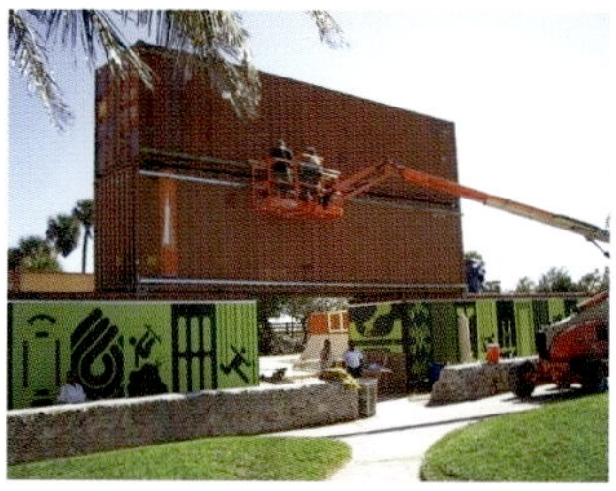

This page and opposite page: Views of "Concrete Waves: An Homage to Skate Culture," Art Positions, Art Basel Miami Beach, 2007. Organized by P.S.1.

(132) This is one of those myth-making photos designed to imply that the artist hand-painted all the paintings himself.

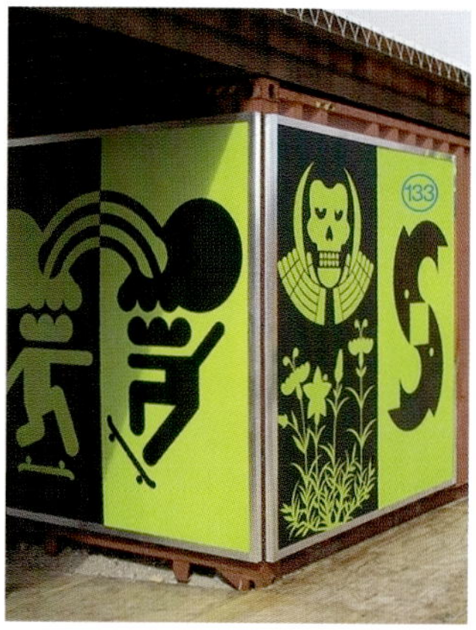

Top left: Panels being slid into U channels. Top right: Touching up panels.

(133) 17th Street Surf Shop in Virginia Beach, from childhood.

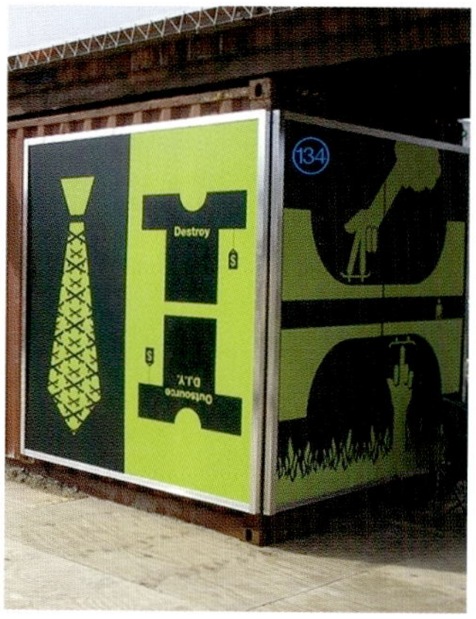

Above far left: Attaching U channels to shipping containers.
Above and above left: Details of panels.

(134) The fingerboard battle between good and evil.

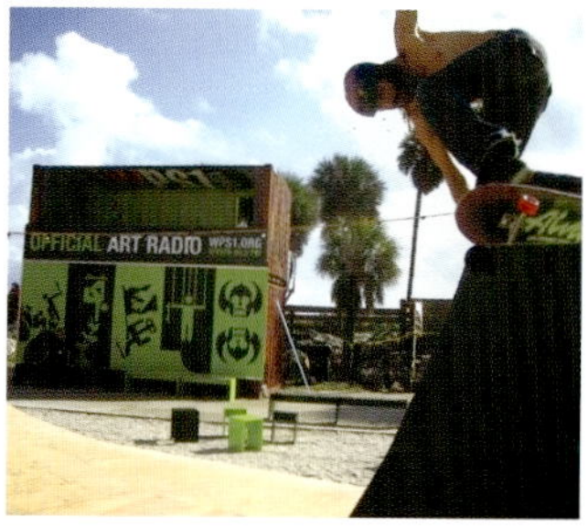

Tony Alva skating the ramp installation.

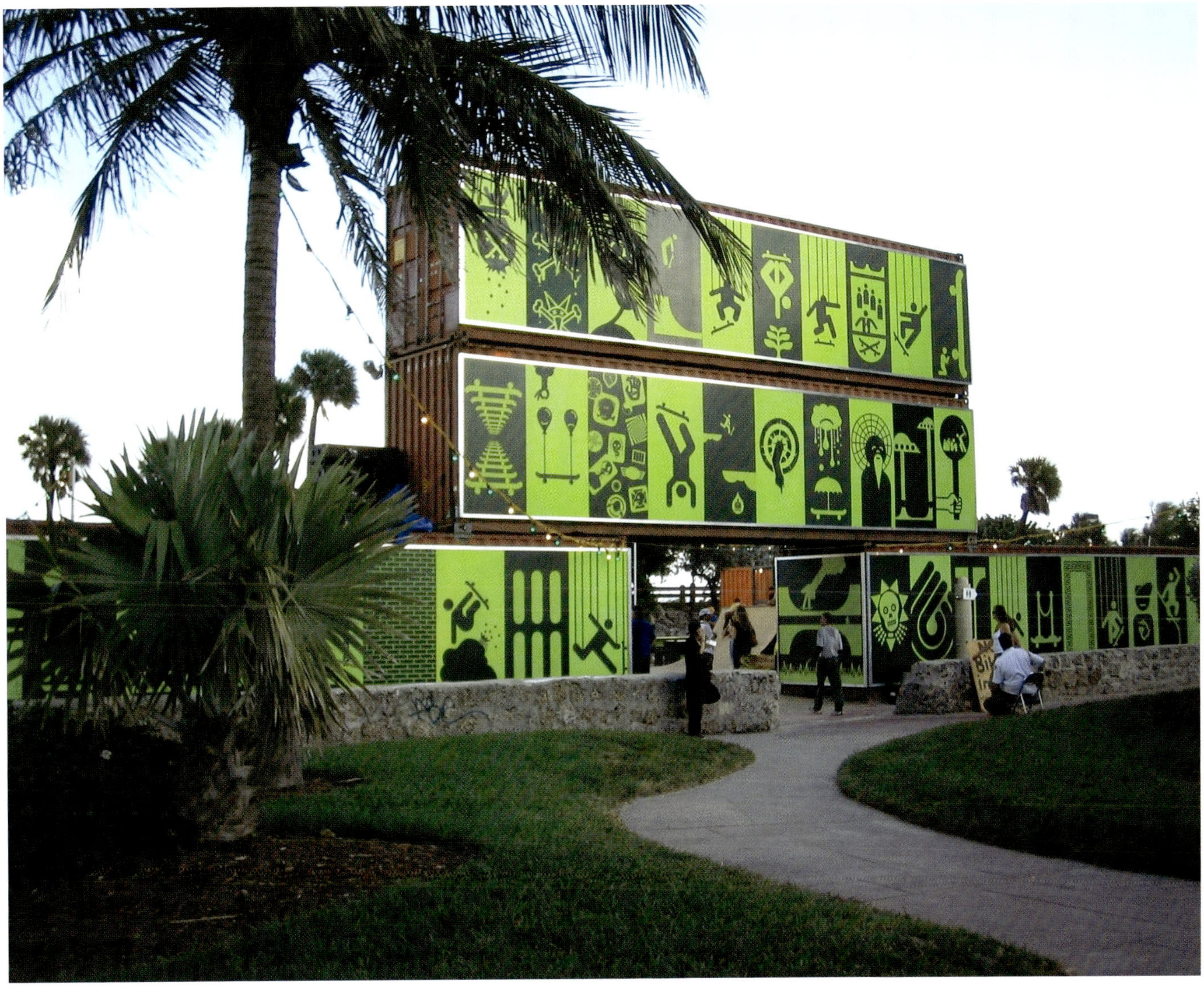

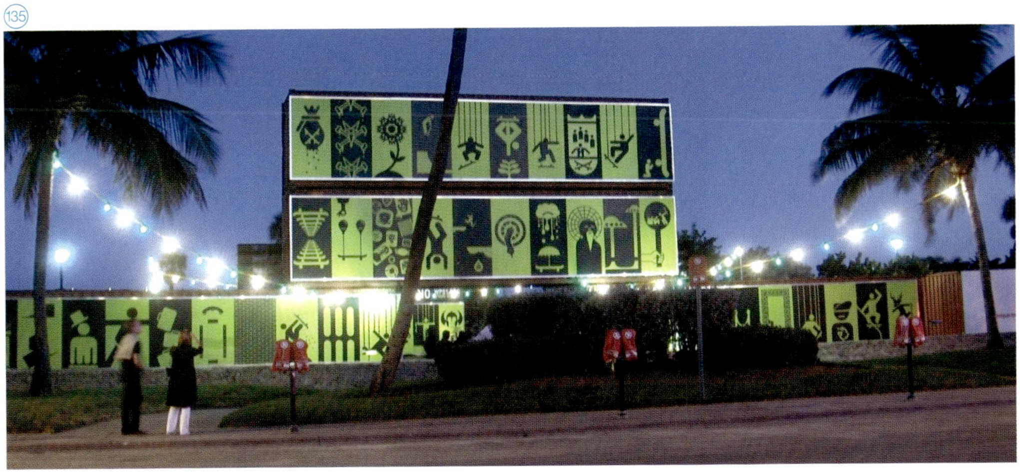

135

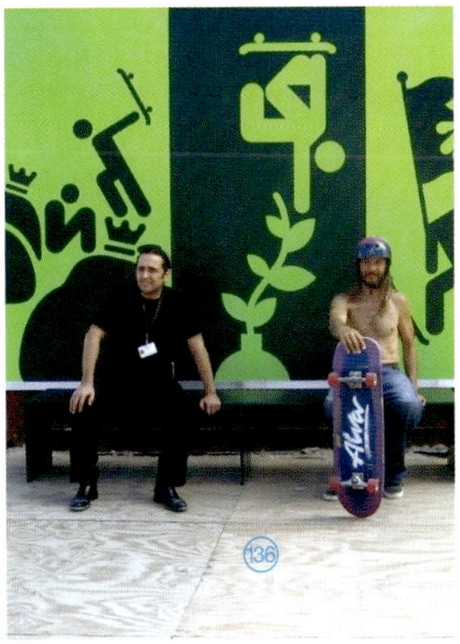

136

135 We had better photographs of this installation, but the photographer accidentally erased the memory card in his camera.

136 Two Tonys: Guerrero and Alva.

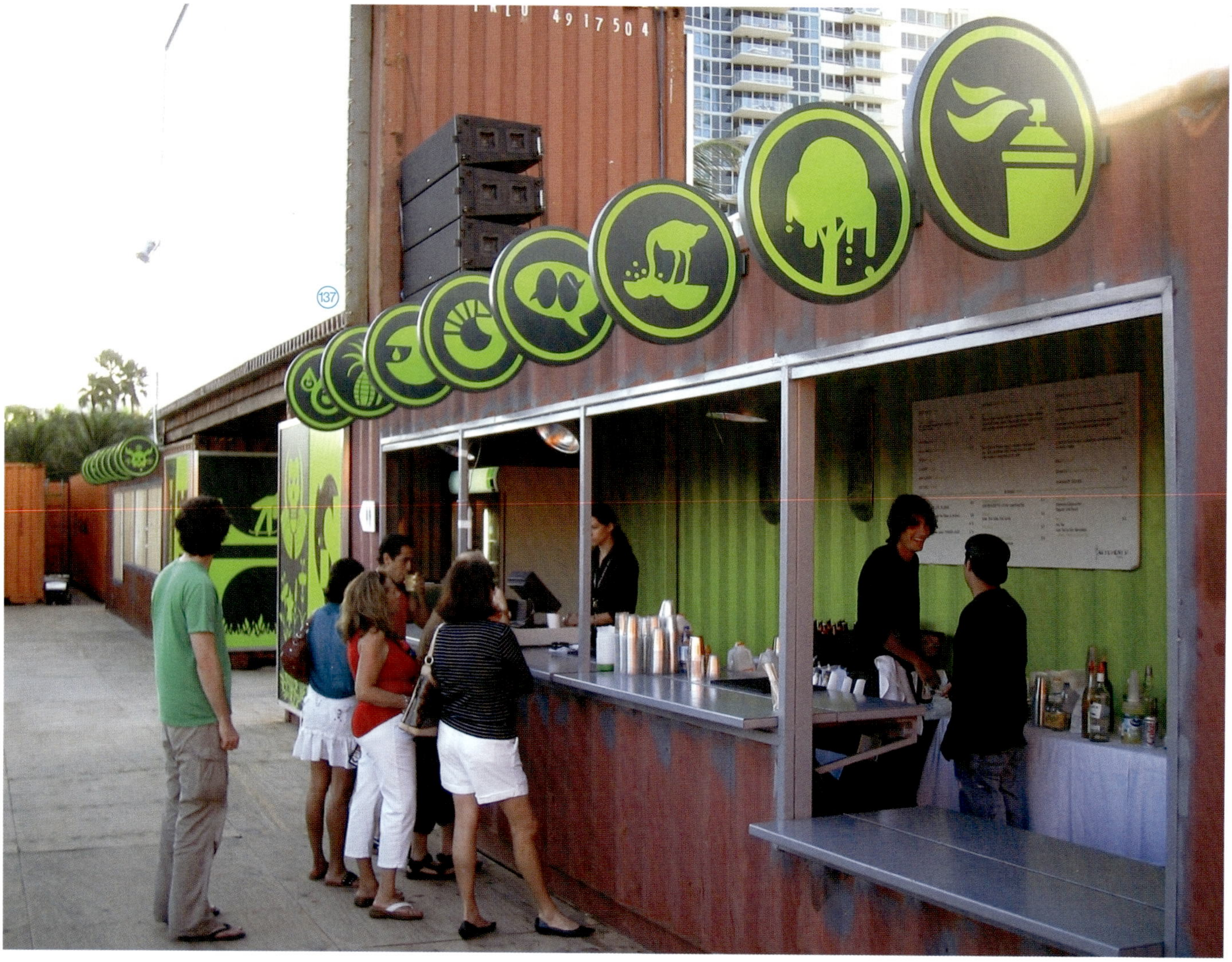

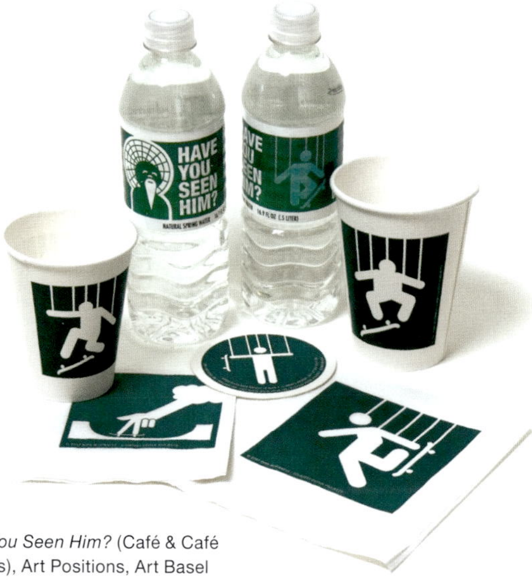

Ryan came up with all these fun little things that enriched the feel of the café so that you were immersed in the environment: drink coasters, napkins, cups, water bottles...

—David Weinstein
Director of Programs, P.S.1

Top: *Have You Seen Him?* (Café & Café Components), Art Positions, Art Basel Miami Beach, 2007. Published by Deitch Projects, New York.

(137) Assume Vivid Astro Focus curated videos, which were projected onto this screen, and performances for this ramp.

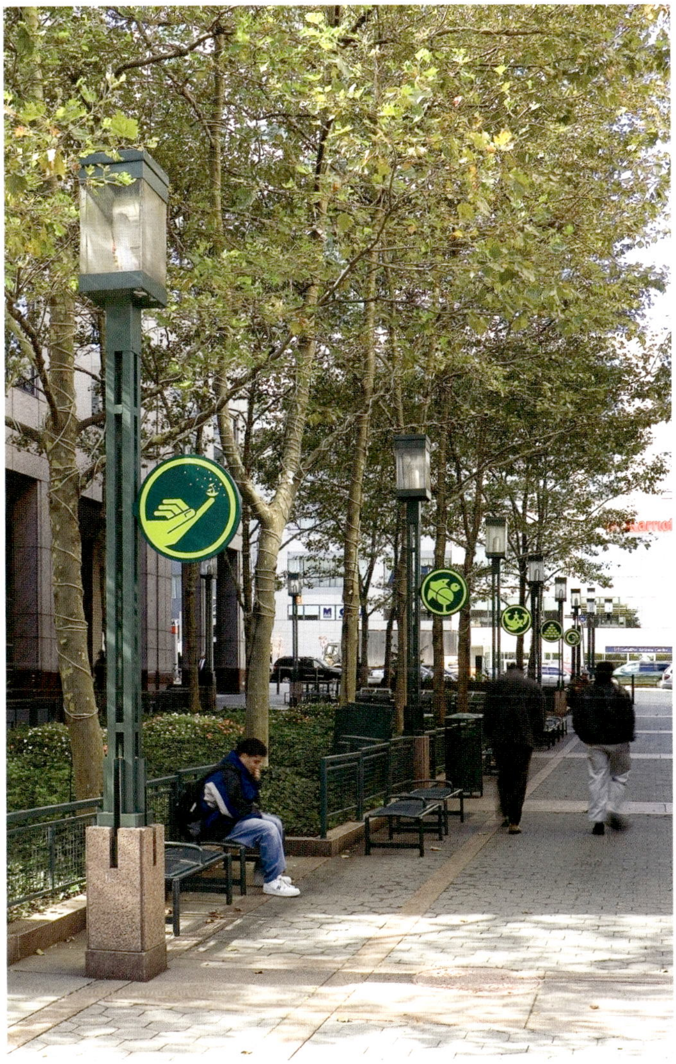

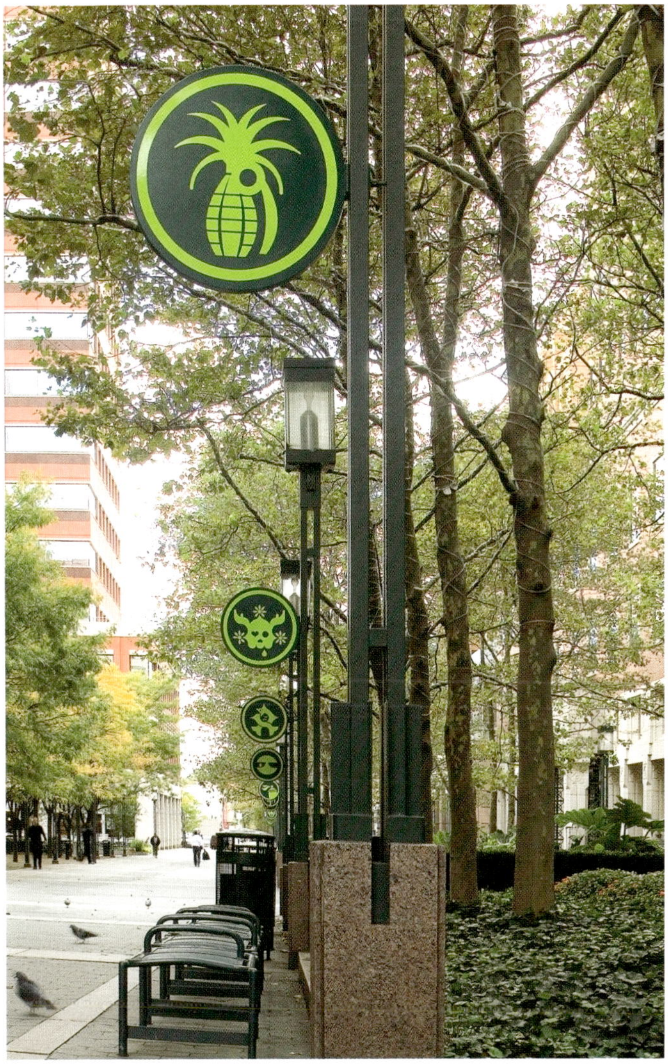

(138) (139)

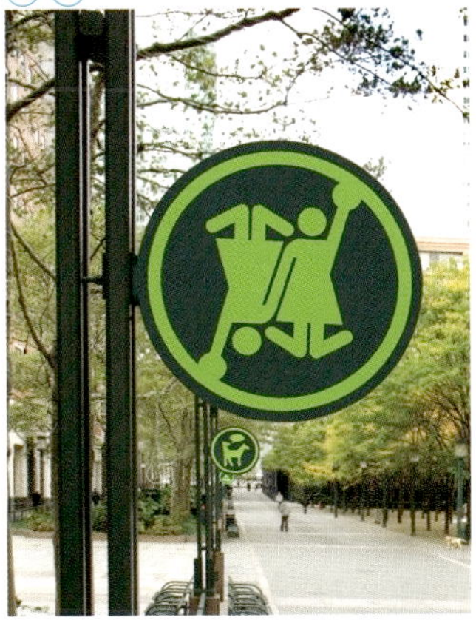

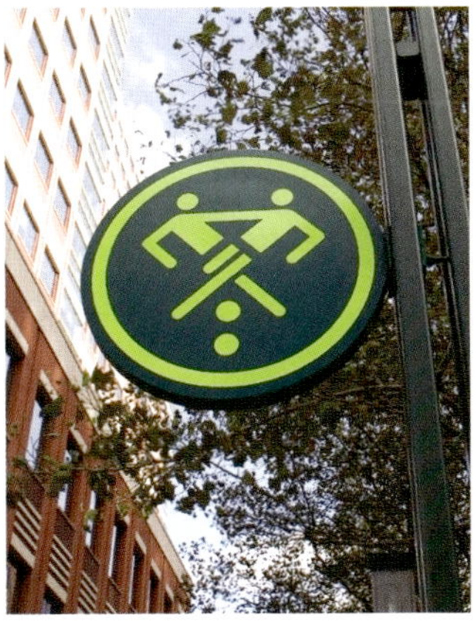

This page and following pages: Views of *Equo ne Credite, Teucri*, MetroTech Commons, Brooklyn, 2006. Organized by the Public Art Fund.

Above: Details, automobile paint on steel, 24 in. diameter x 2 in. each.

*With its title (*Equo ne Credite, Teucri*)—a reference to the ancient priest Laocoön's attempt to warn the Trojans against letting the Greeks' gift inside city walls, described in* The Aeneid *by the epic poet Virgil—McGinness warns viewers of his attempt to subvert the public environment with his co-optation of mainstream communication strategies.*

—Anne Wehr

Reproduced by permission from the Public Art Fund, "Ryan McGinness: Equo ne Credite, Teucri," *The World Is Round* (New York: Public Art Fund, 2006).

(138) See p. 79.

(139) These pieces were produced with the Public Art Fund a year before the Art Basel Miami Beach project. I re-purposed the color palette for *Have You Seen Him?*

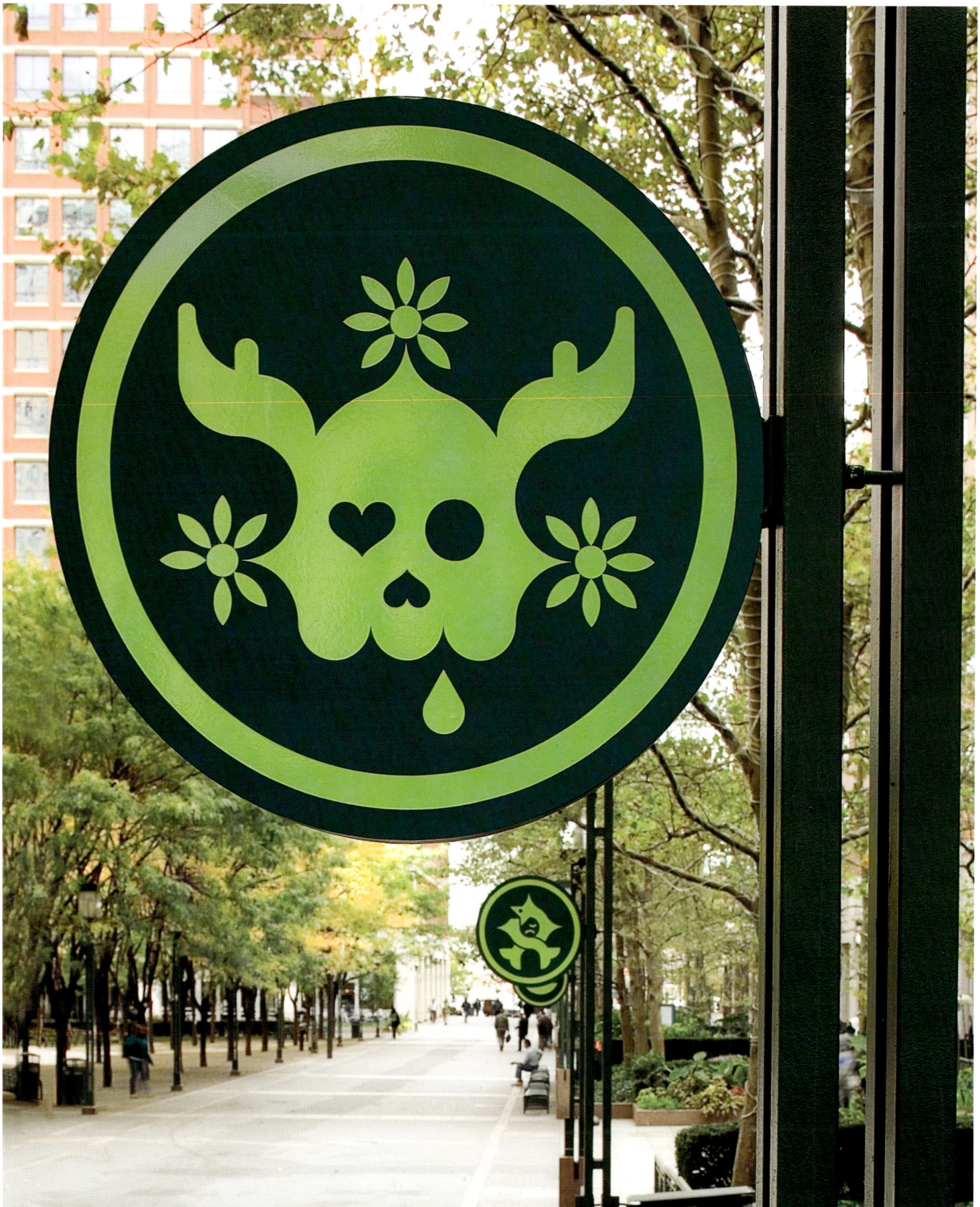

Equo ne Credite, Teucri, 2006, automobile paint on steel, 24 in. diameter x 2 in. each. Installation view, MetroTech Commons, Brooklyn. Organized by the Public Art Fund (details above and opposite page).

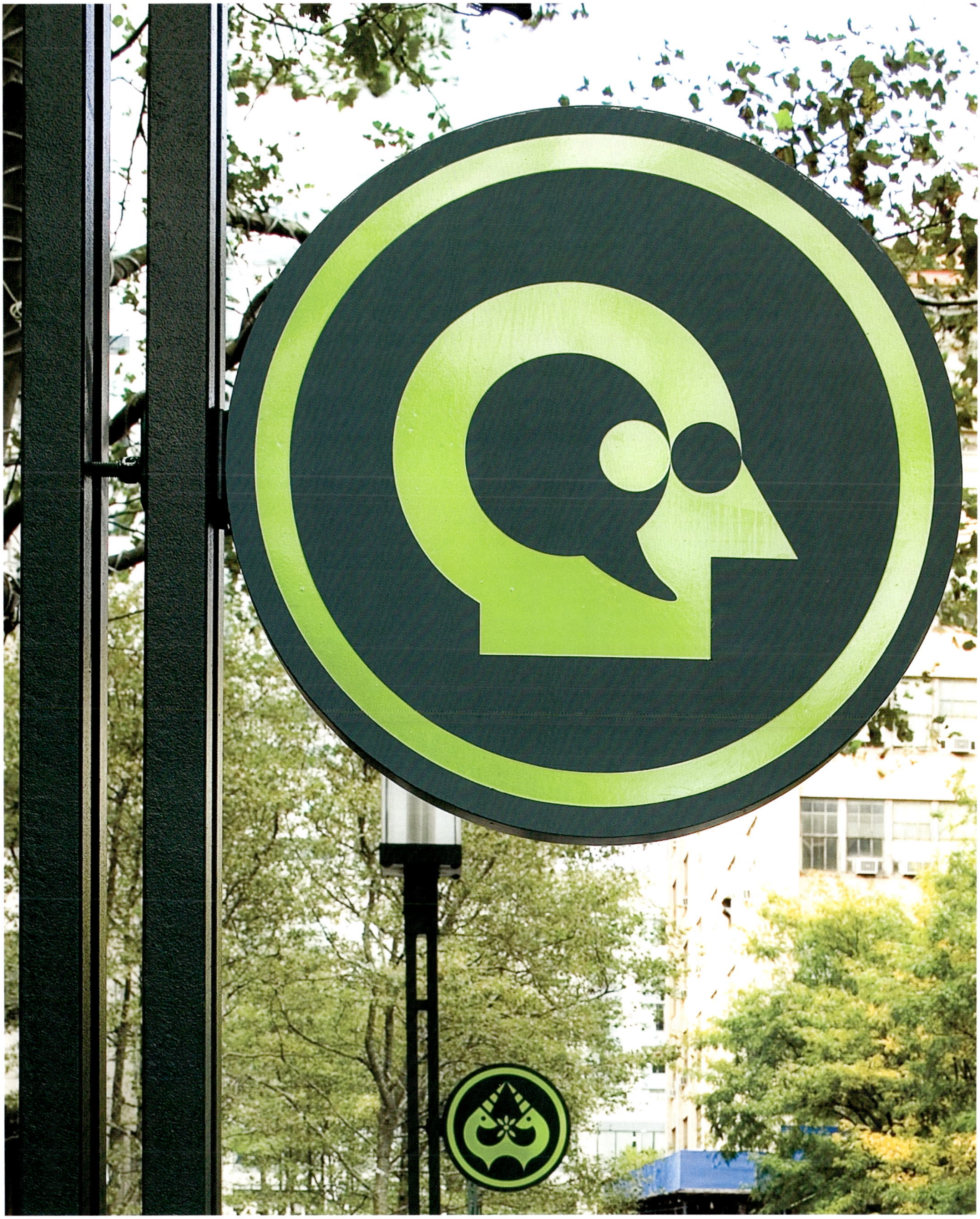

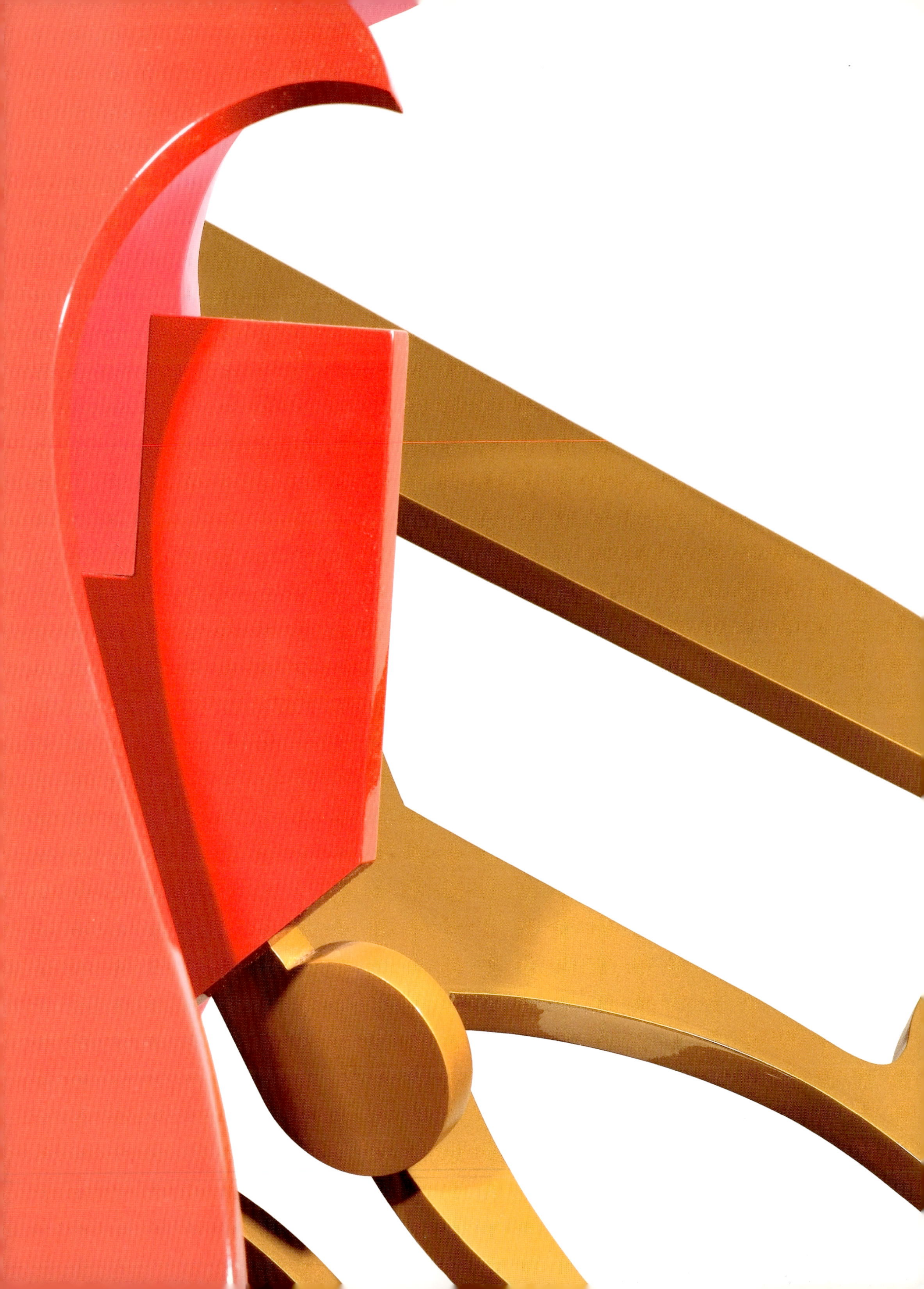

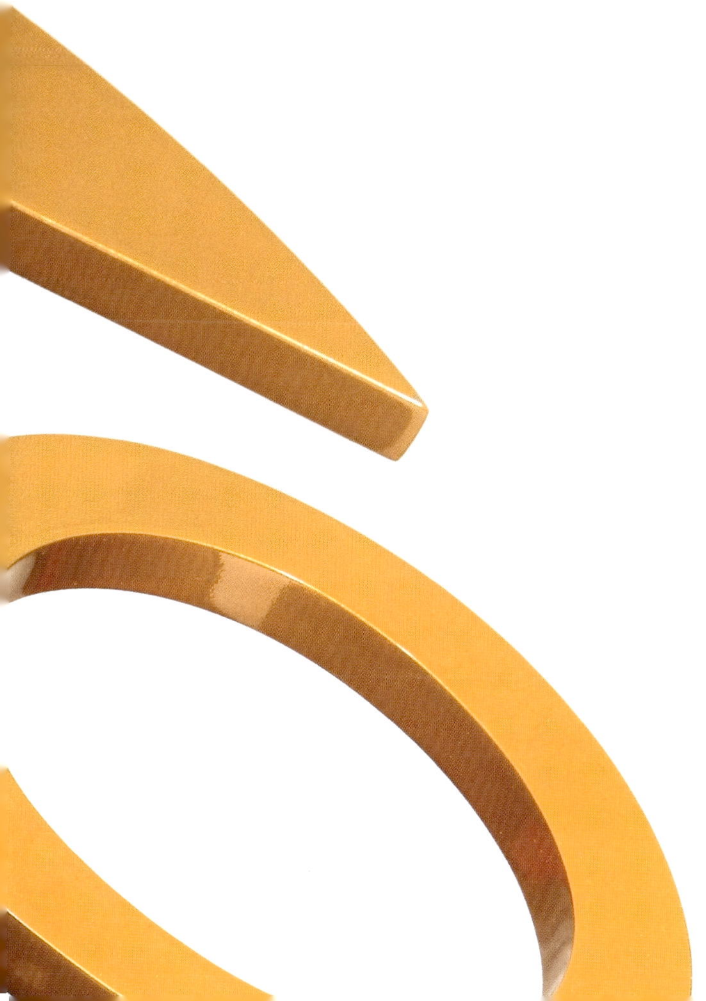

For Ryan, the question of how to translate two-dimensional drawings into three-dimensional forms has proven to be the fundamental problem in creating his sculptures. Since infinitely more compositional variation is possible in three dimensions, he explores the possibilities through extensive experimentation with laser-cut acrylic or Foamcore maquettes, which are akin to the process sketches found in his sketchbooks.

Untitled (Red/Gold/Pink) (detail), 2008, car paint on welded aluminum, 49 x 42 x 42 in. Published by Pace Prints, New York.

Ryan's mother avidly made crafts throughout his childhood—the house was filled with various tools and materials. Of particular influence were her jigsaw-cut wooden animals with movable joints.

Later, he discovered Keith Haring's large-scale painted aluminum sculptures, which Haring based on his drawings. Influenced by these, Ryan's solution for taking his own iconic drawings into three dimensions developed in stages. First, he stacked several *Universals* on top of each other in a totemlike configuration, later creating a kinetic version using this arrangement in which the stacked *Universals* slowly rotated in opposite directions like colliding worlds. Second, the totems morphed into cactuslike pieces of greater complexity, with the *Universals* positioned more dynamically. Next, a breakthrough came when making Foamcore models in which the imagery was laser cut out of the center of each circle. Ryan found that the negative elements (the parts that were cut out and meant to be discarded) better activated the space. Further variables were added when these laser-cut elements, now made from clear acrylic, were painted with imagery and twisted, so that they became three-dimensional fragmented paintings. (140)

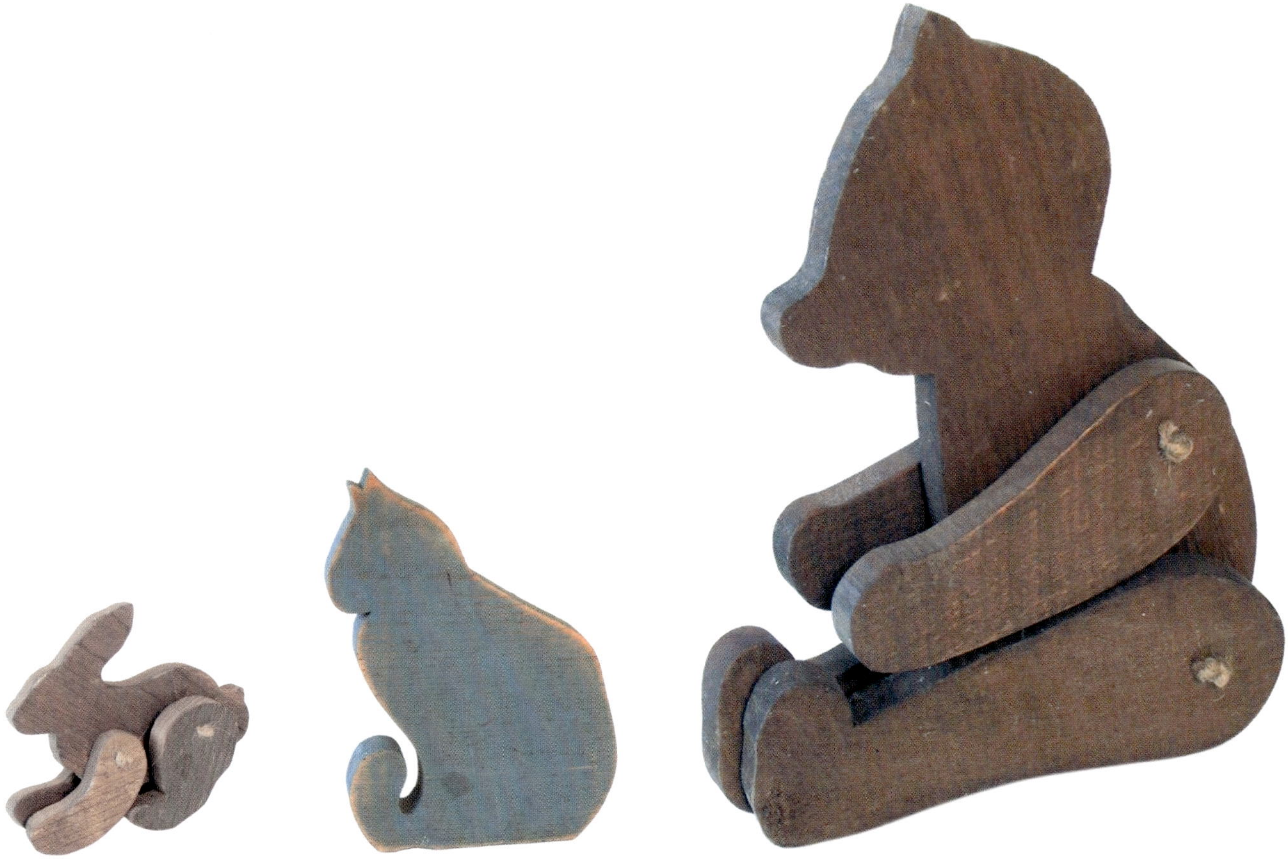

Above: Crafts made by Ryan's mother out of wood and twine during the early 80s. Part of his early exposure to two-dimensional forms, along with Keith Haring's sculptures (see opposite page, bottom center and right). Opposite page top left and top center: Preliminary sketch and model of *Universals* in totem configuration. Originally intended for *Installationview*, Deitch Projects, New York, 2005. Opposite page top right: *Kissing*, fiberglass (in process), 104 x 48 x 48 in. Amaral Custom Fabrications, Seekonk, MA, 2006.

(140) Paintings with holes. Two-sided paintings. Stacked two-sided paintings. Images are cut out of paintings (forming holes). Images occupy x, y, and z coordinates, escaping the confines of their tondo cells. Images, now forms, get painted with layers of other images. Forms get further fragmented: twisting, turning, invading, and activating space from all angles. Sculptures in environments become sculptures as environments.

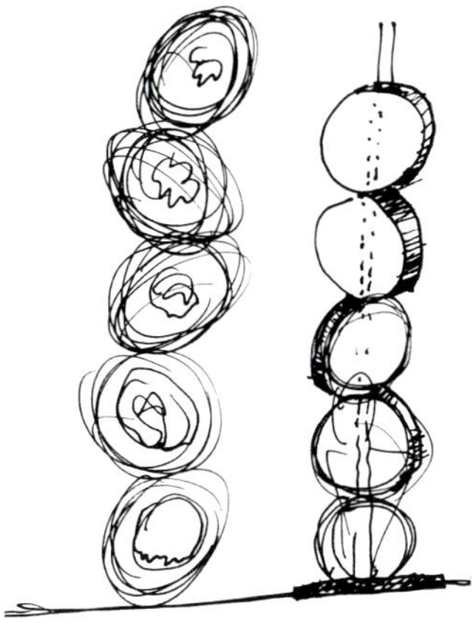

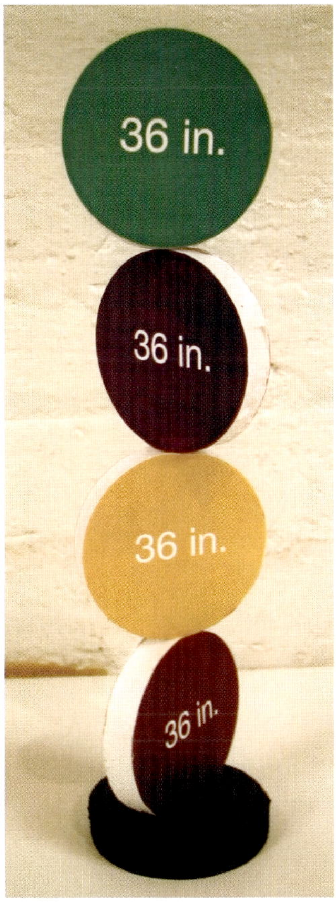

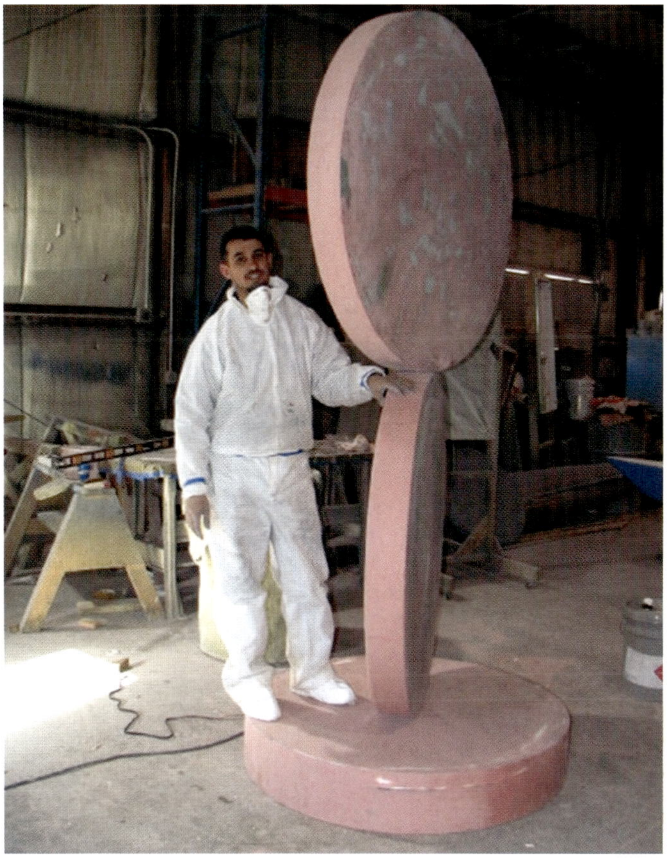

Ryan's sculptures are explosions of information and misinformation that play on your memory and perception. They could have been made in Keith's studio, in that they use the same materials and technology, but if Keith was dealing with geometry, Ryan is dealing with calculus. He is making the best possible homage to Keith—he's following in Keith's footsteps with a lot of integrity.
—Kermit Oswald
Director of the Keith Haring Foundation, and longtime assistant to Keith Haring

141

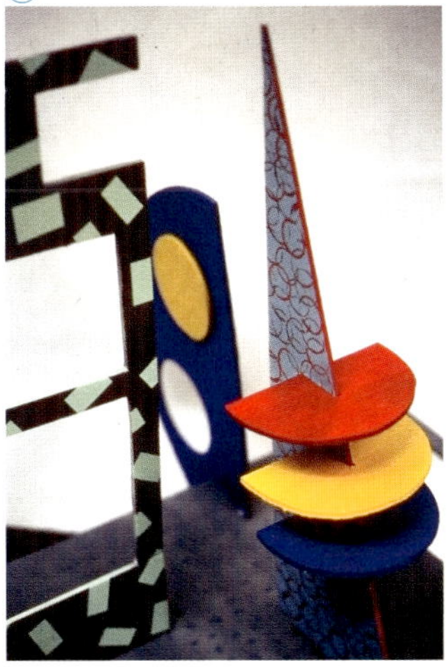

Untitled, 1988, acrylic on Foamcore, no longer extant. Early student sculpture made at Old Donation Center for the Gifted and Talented, Virginia Beach, VA.

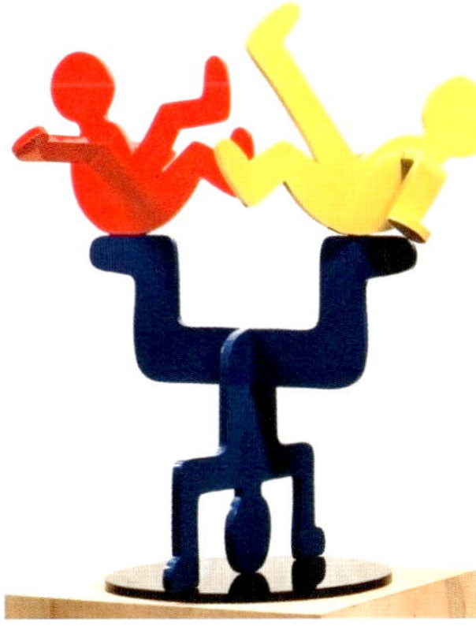

Keith Haring, *Untitled*, 1987, painted aluminum, 37 ½ x 28 x 28 in.

142

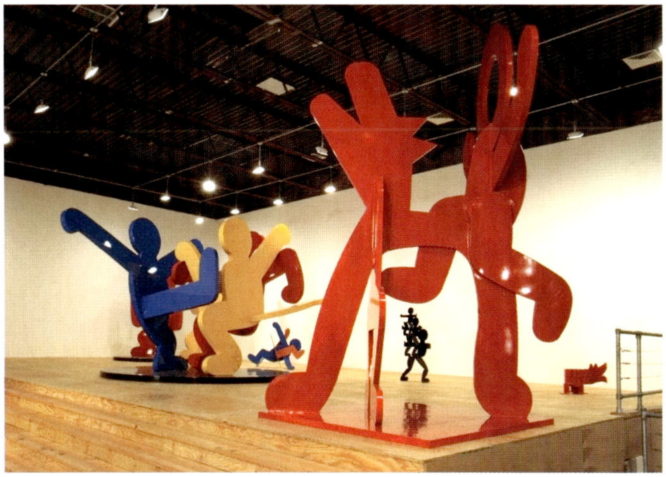

Keith Haring, "Keith Haring: Sculpture," mixed media, dimensions variable. Installation view, 2005, Deitch Projects, New York.

(141) This Memphis-inspired sculpture from high school was one of my first attempts at combining flat planes in space. I won an award for it and received a balloon. No joke.

(142) The Estate of Keith Haring was cool enough to let us use these photos for free.

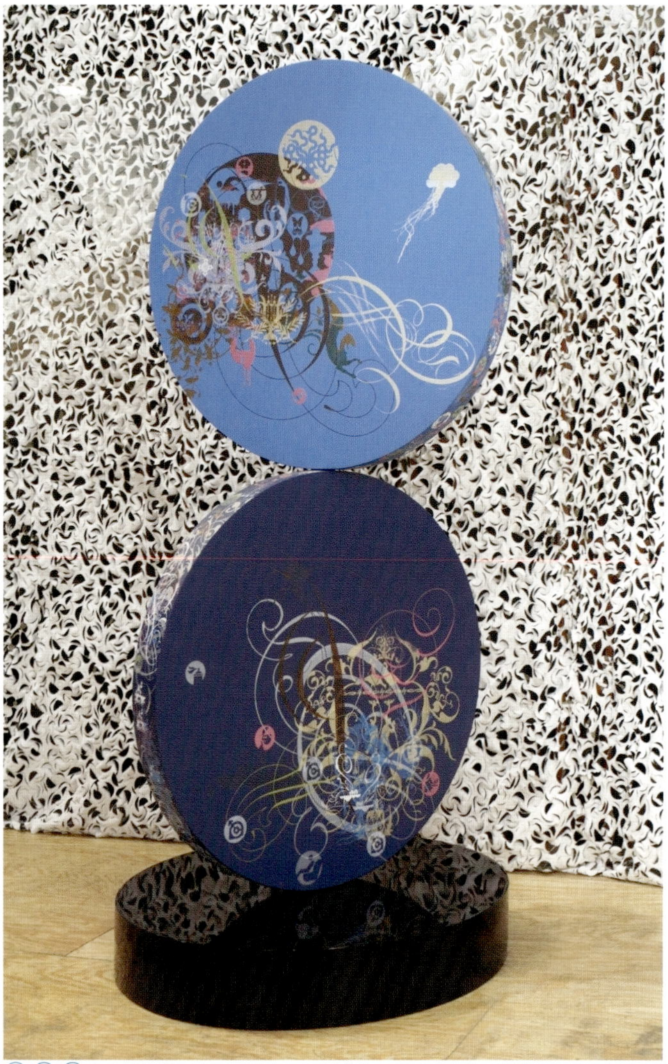

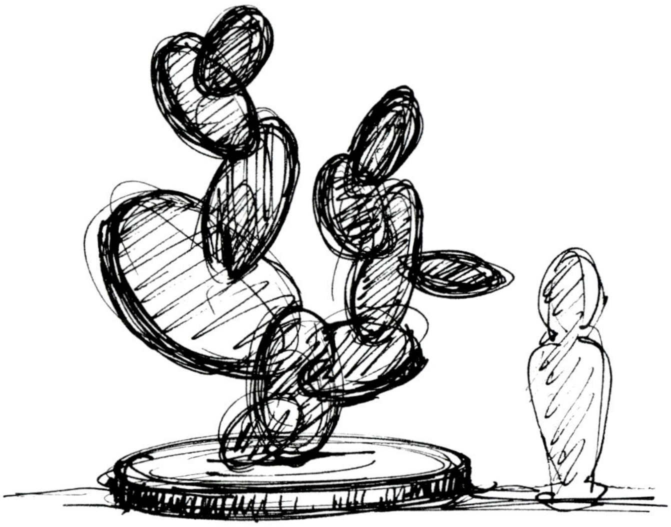

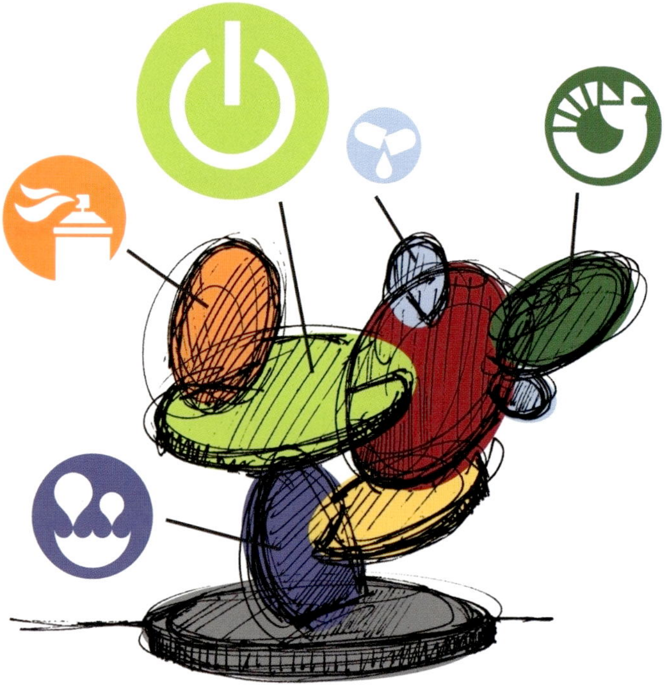

(143)(144)(145)

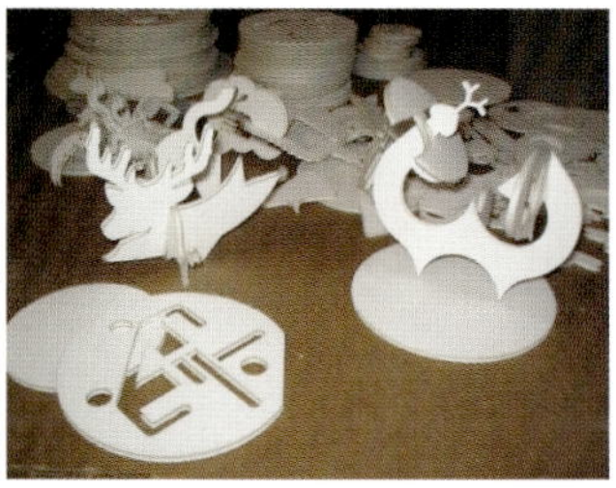

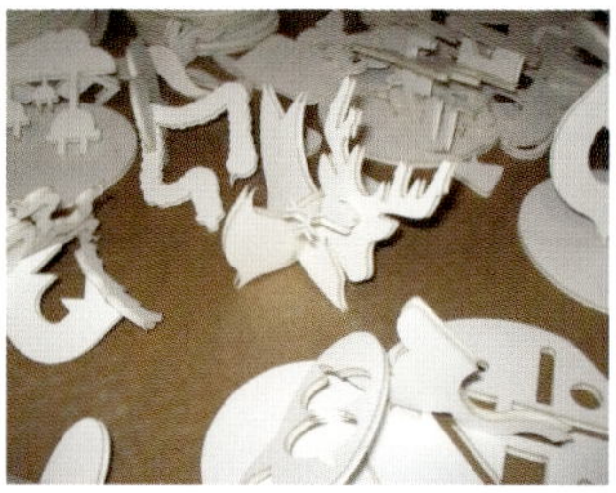

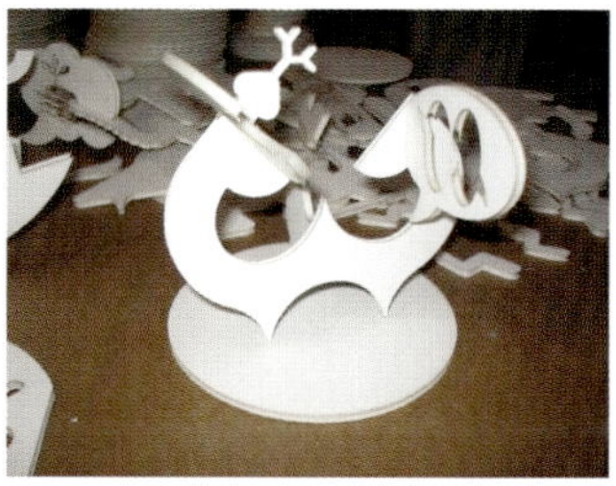

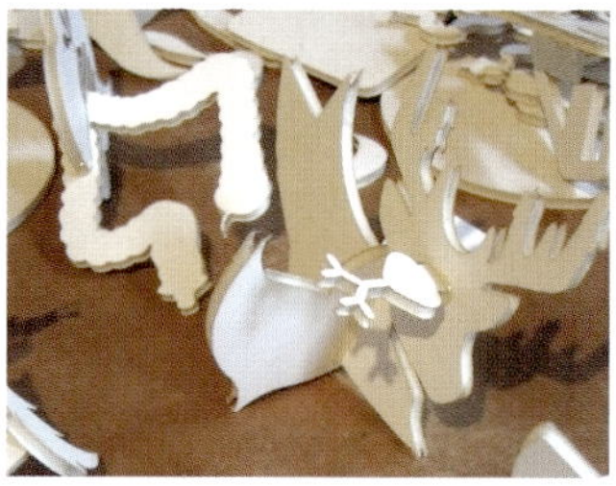

Top left: *Kissing*, 2006, acrylic and polyester urethane on fiberglass, 104 x 48 x 48 in. Top right: Process sketches.

Above and opposite page: Studies exploring various compositional possibilities for sculpture.

(143) .com/kissingturning

(144) Despite the $20K plus fabrication cost, I had to destroy this piece because I didn't like it.

(145) .com/kissingtouchup

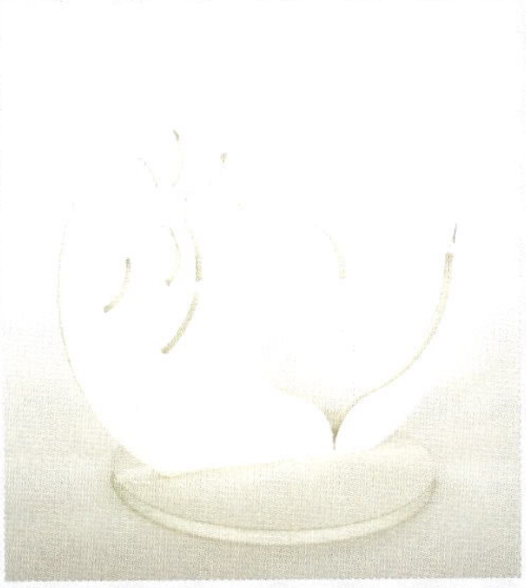
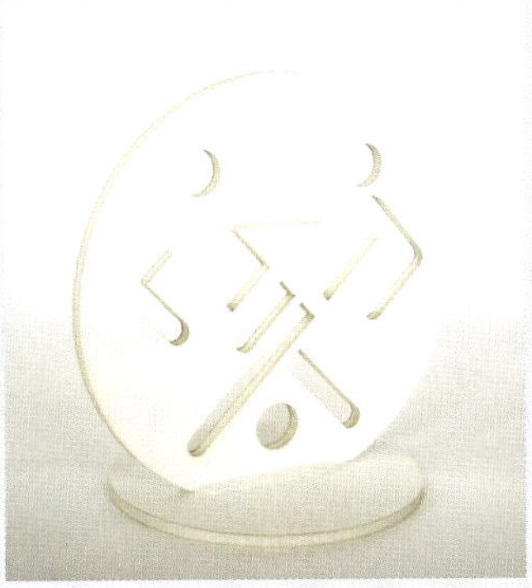
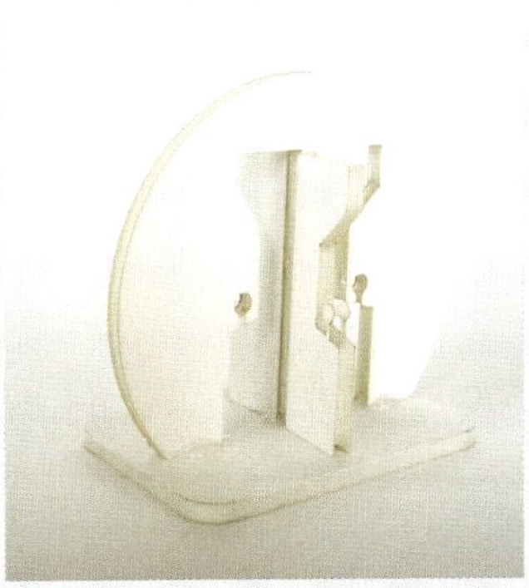
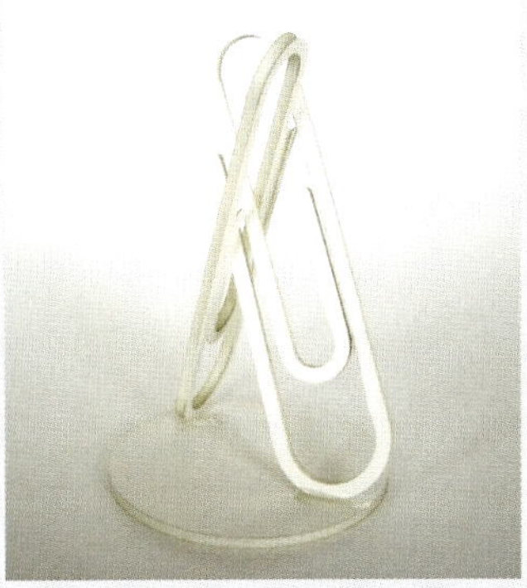
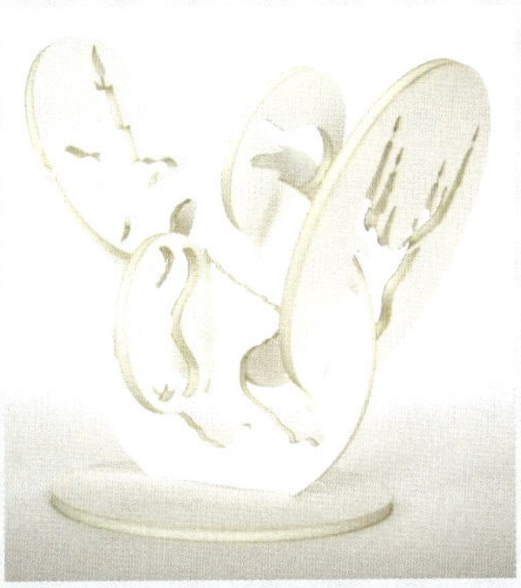
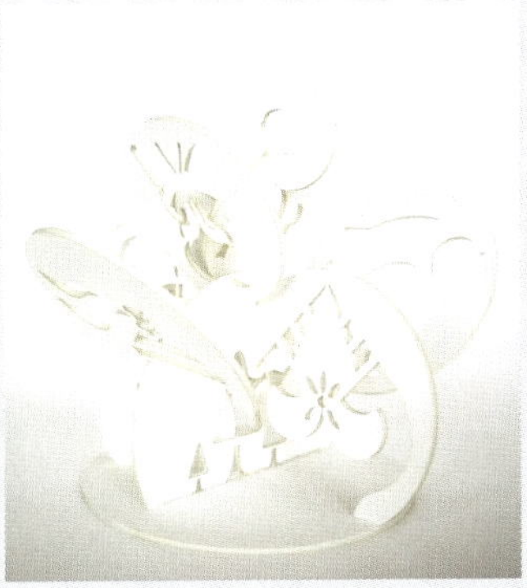
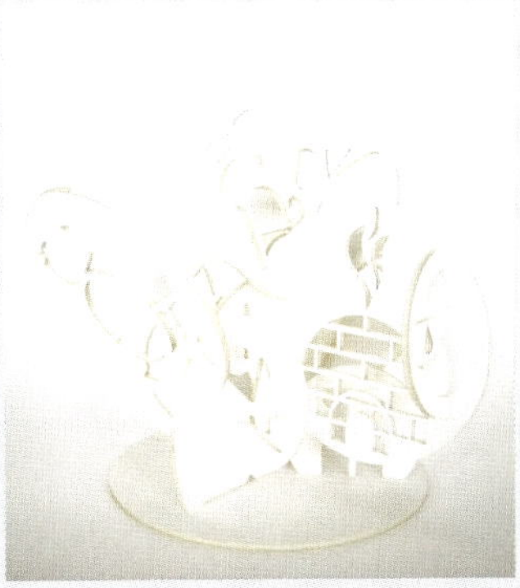
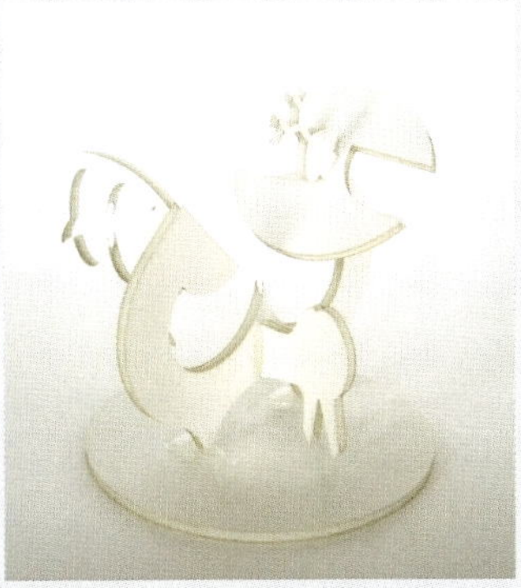
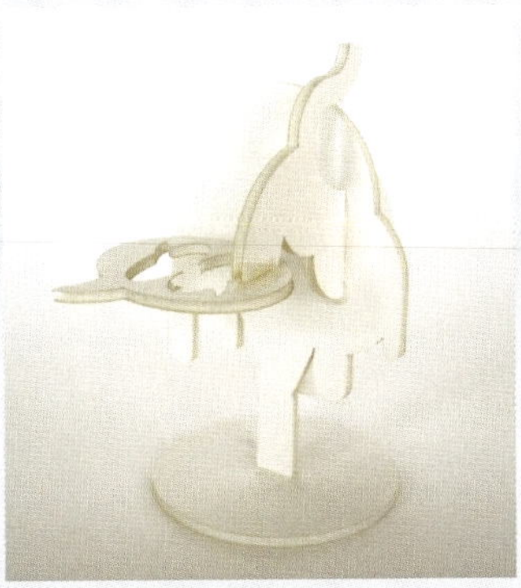
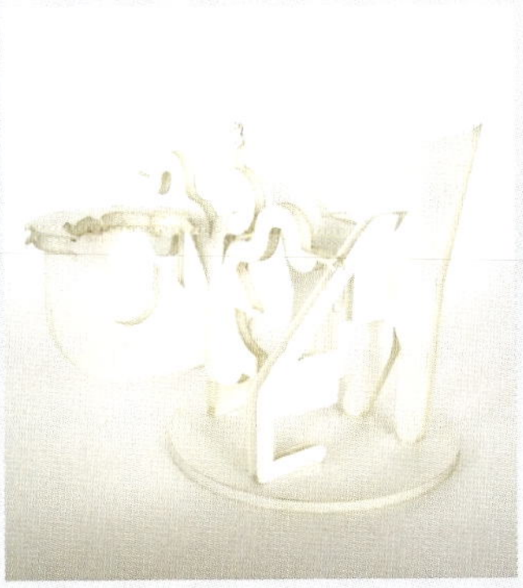
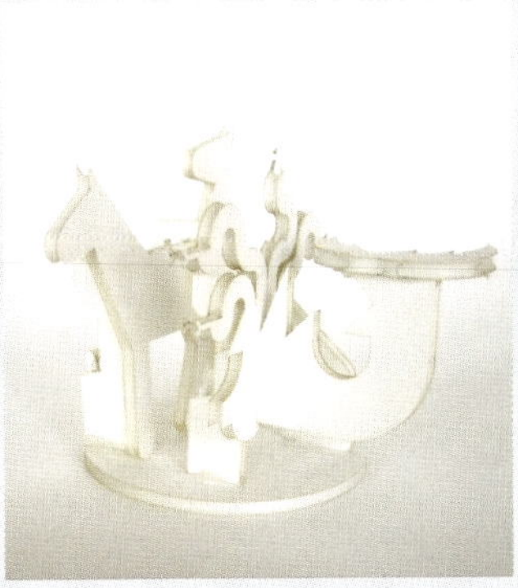
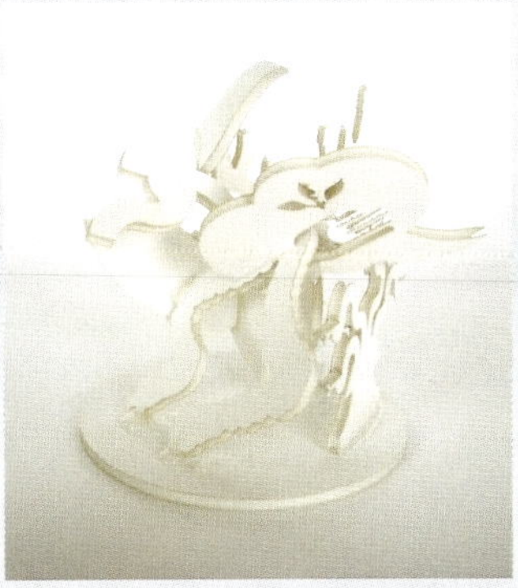
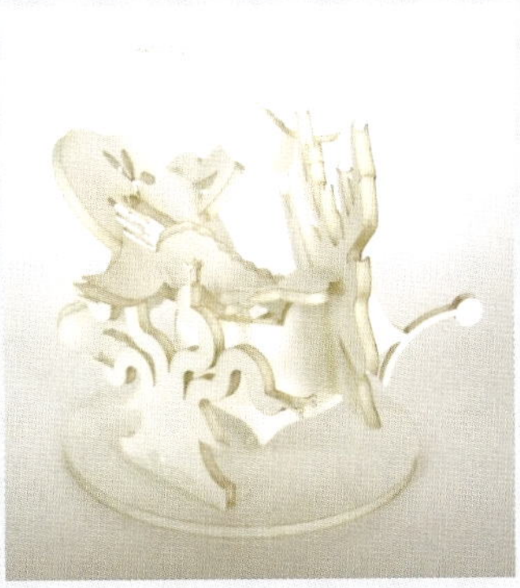
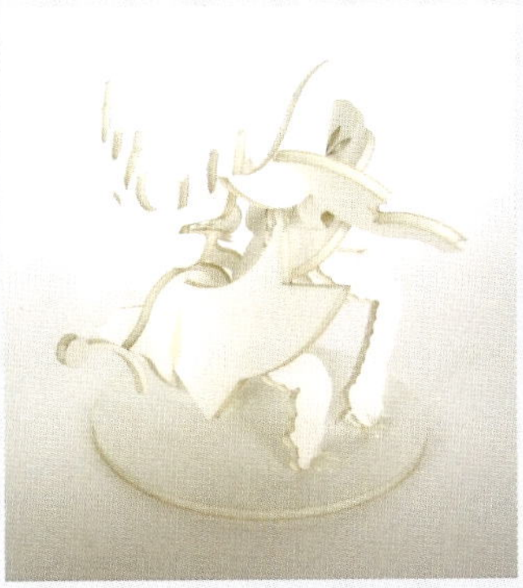
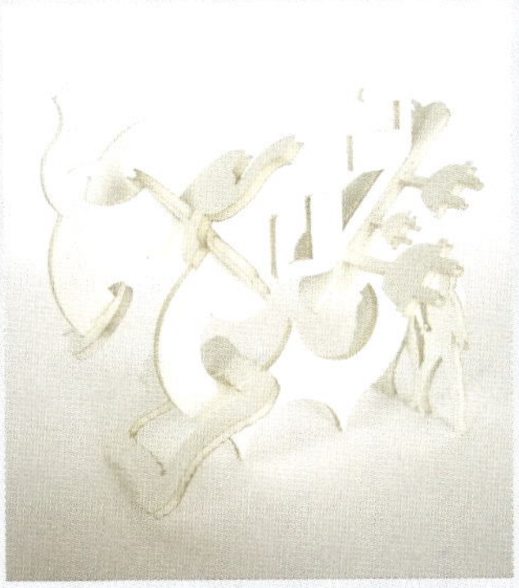
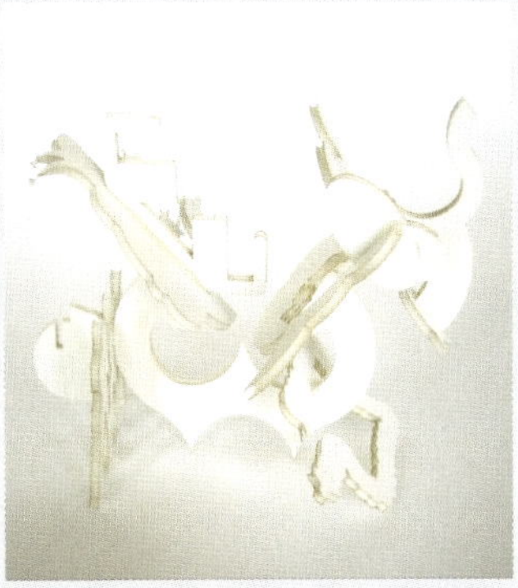

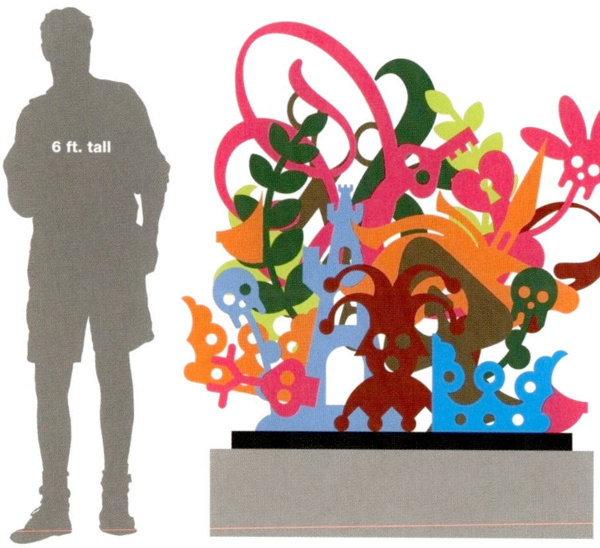

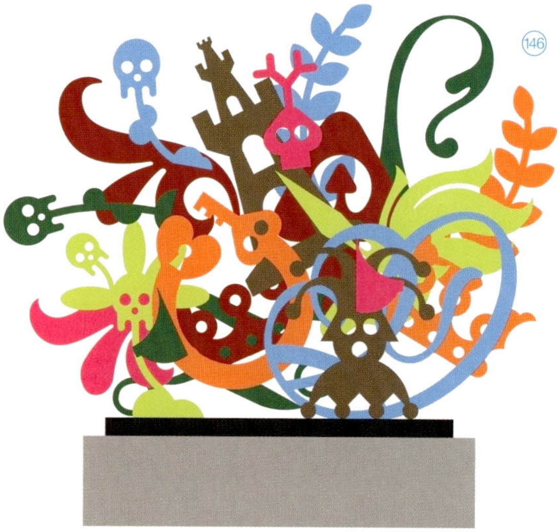

(146)

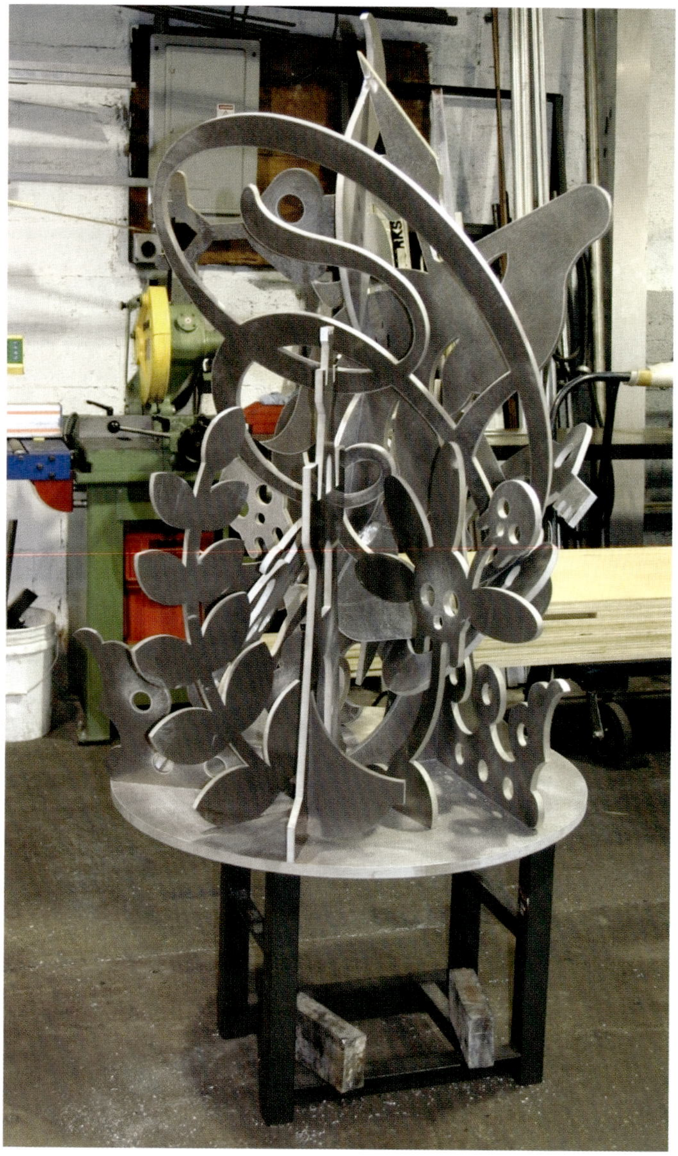

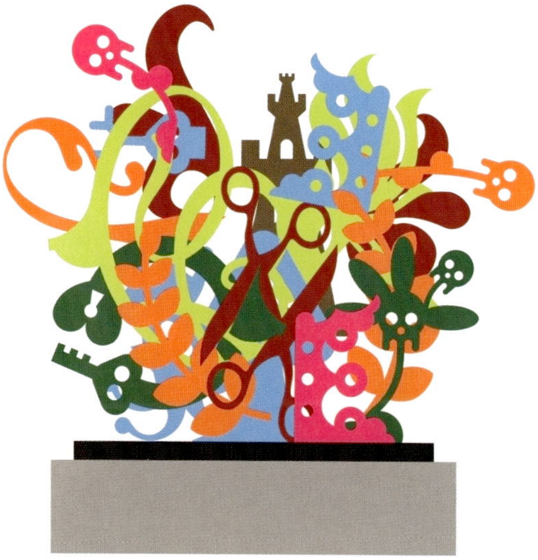

Left: Vector drawing studies, 2007, digital files, dimensions vary.

Top and opposite page: *Untitled* (process views), welded aluminum, 2007, Kammetal, Brooklyn.

(146) This is the furthest I can take planning the sculptures with a computer. As with the paintings, I need to figure out these pieces in real space.

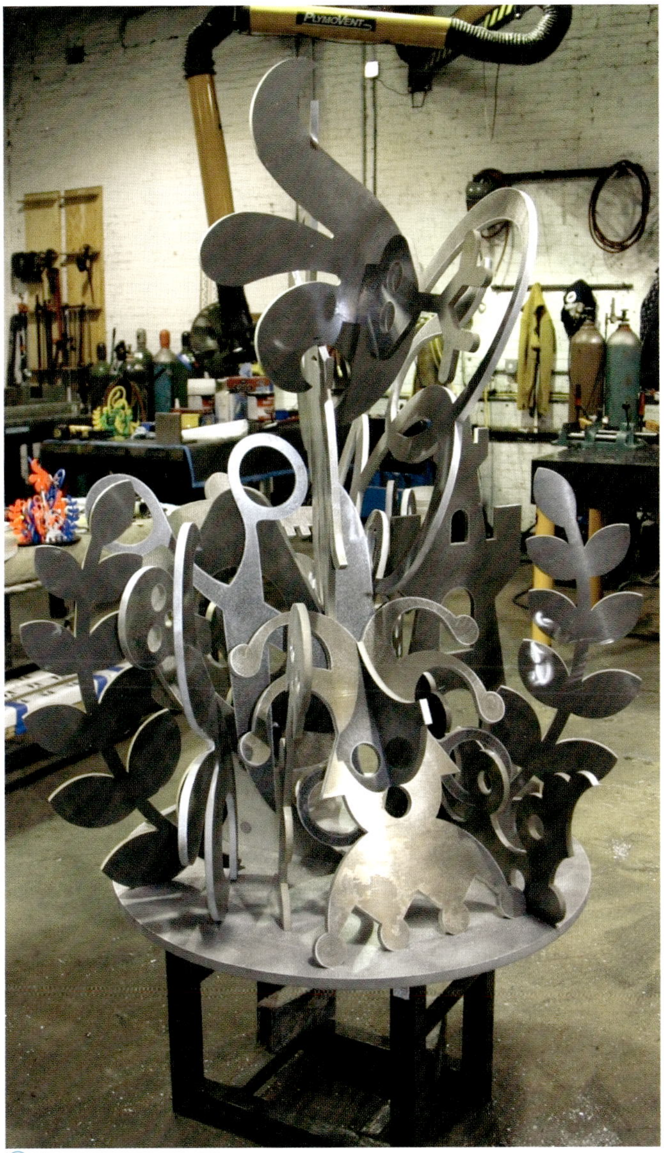
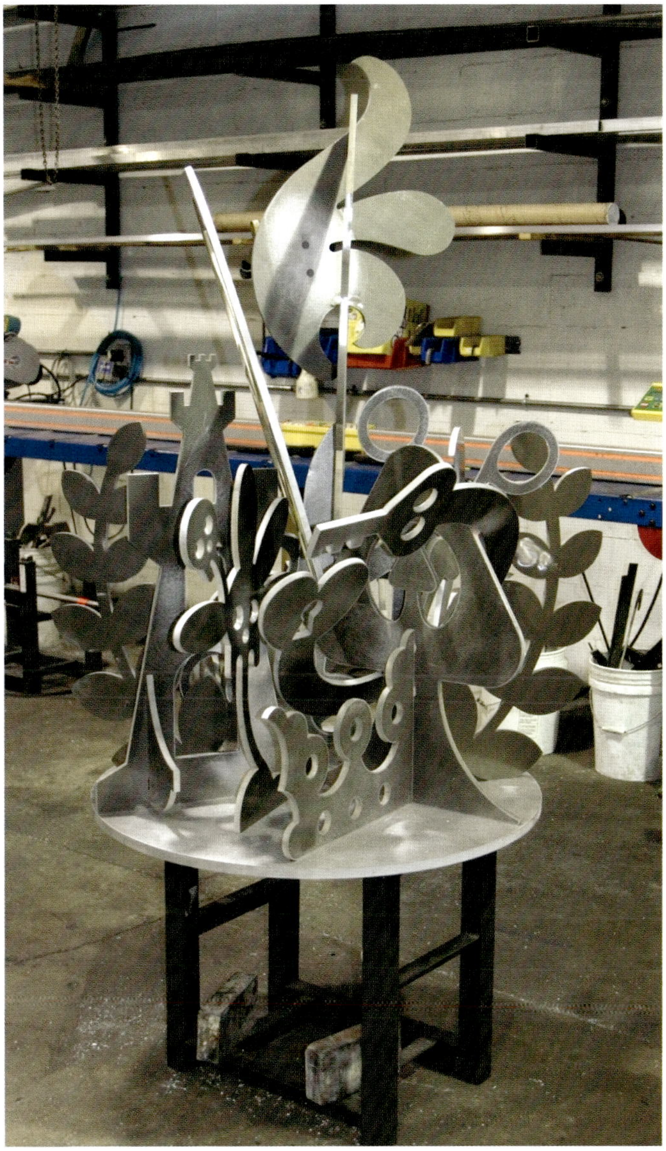

147

Ryan made scale models out of laser-cut forms that he assembled with hot glue. We took the scale models and enlarged them and engineered them appropriately so the sculptures would be structurally sound. We enlarged and redrew his forms in AutoCAD, water jet cut them and welded them—and we chased down the weld points because visible welds would change the aesthetic of the piece.

—Sam Kusack
Kammetal

147 Working with artists to make the pieces is always best.

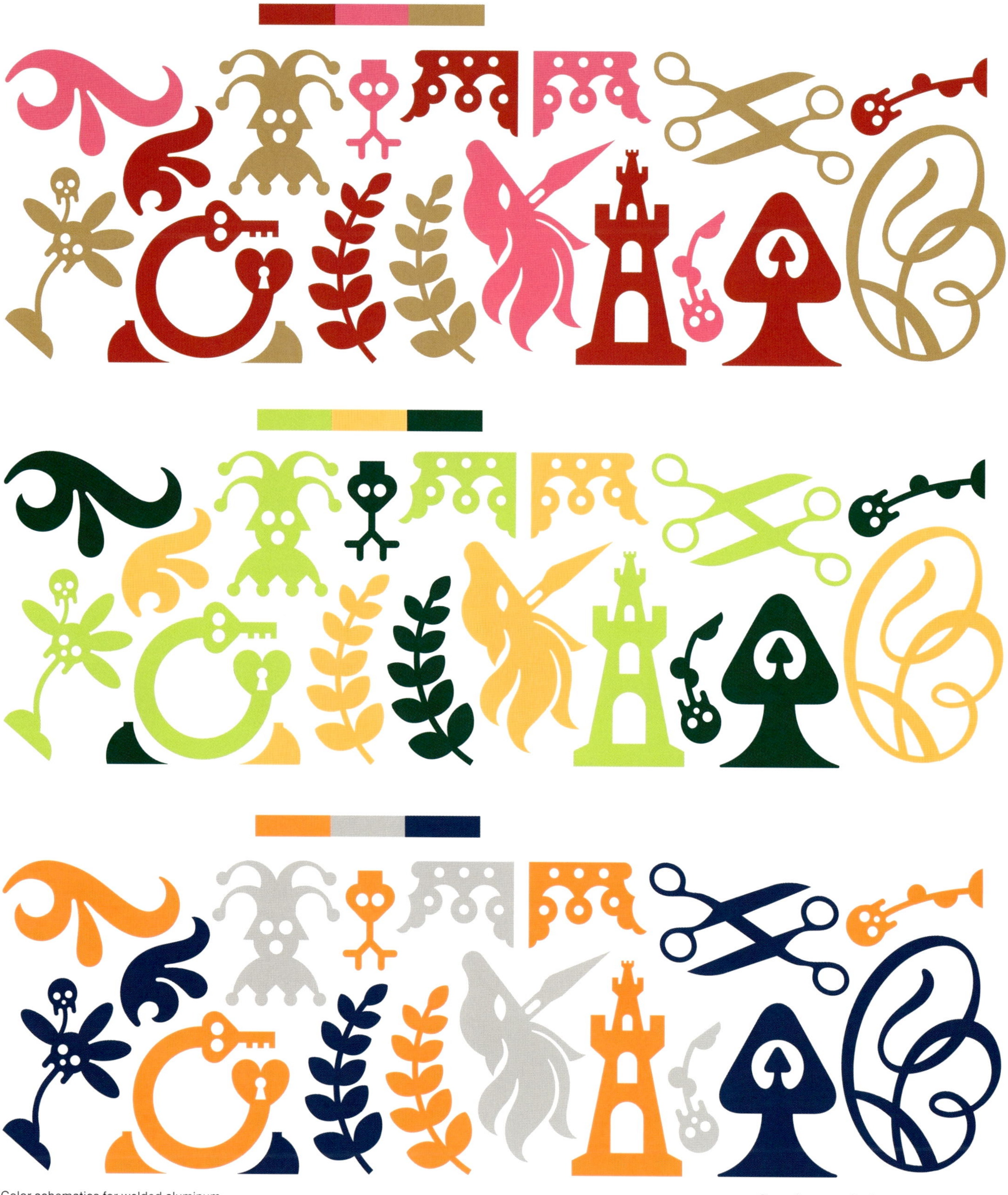

Color schematics for welded aluminum sculptures, 2007. (148)

Opposite page: Sculpture maquettes, 2006–2007, spray paint on Foamcore, 11 x 9 x 9 in. each. (149)

(148) .com/moresculpturecolorstudies

(149) Photographed on the roof of the studio facing south toward downtown Manhattan.

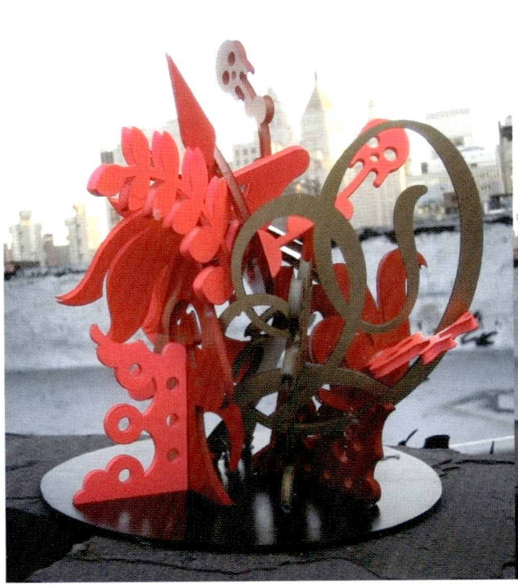
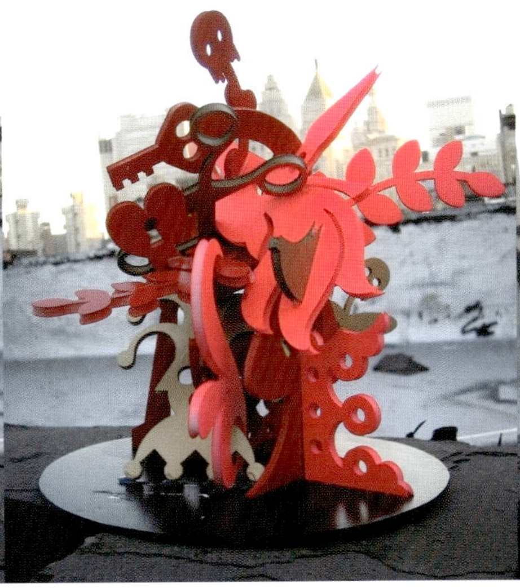
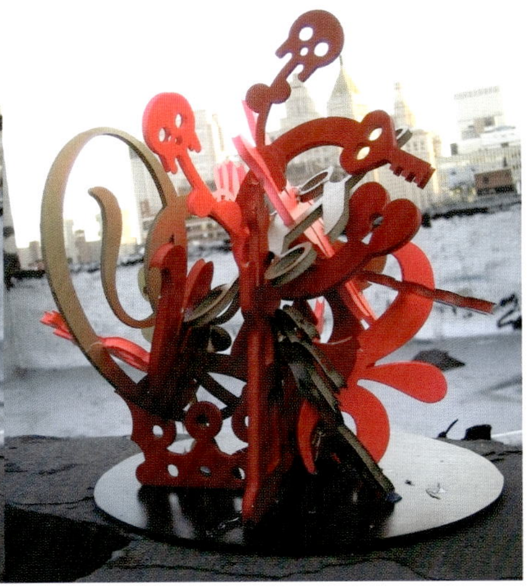
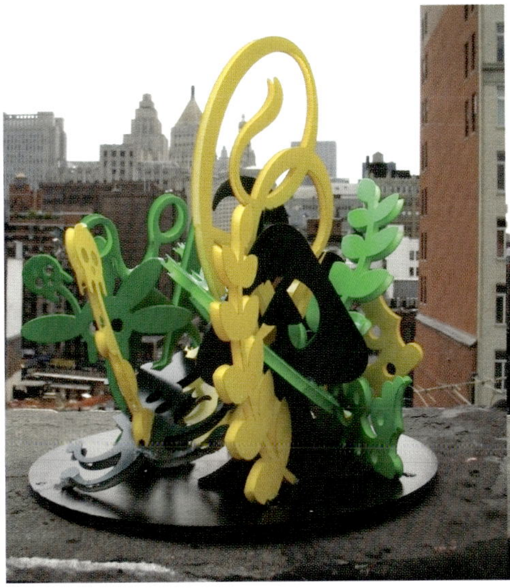
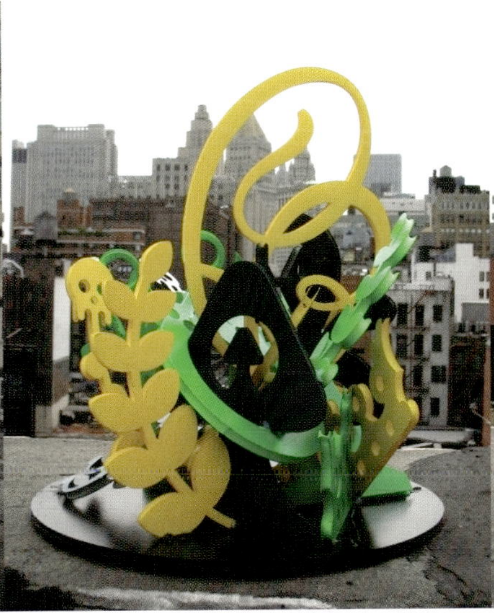
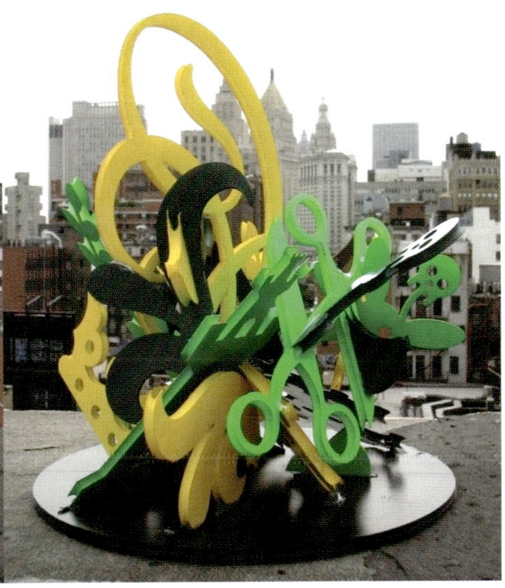
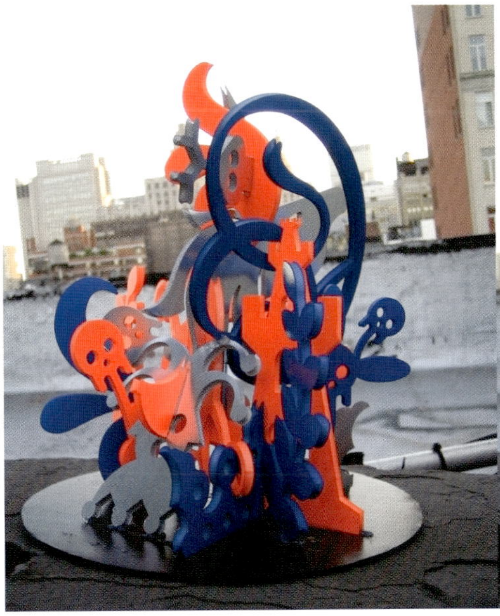
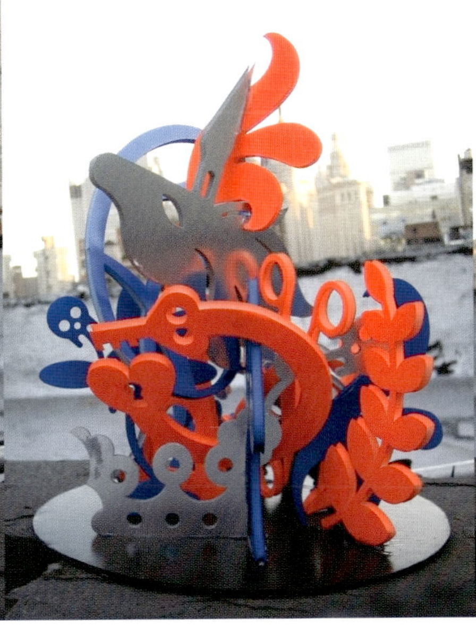
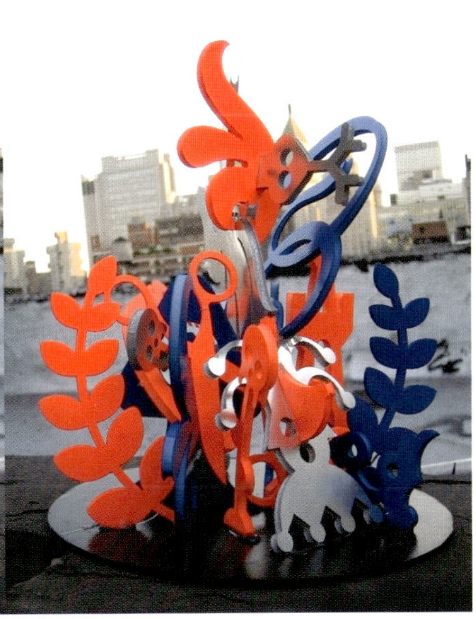

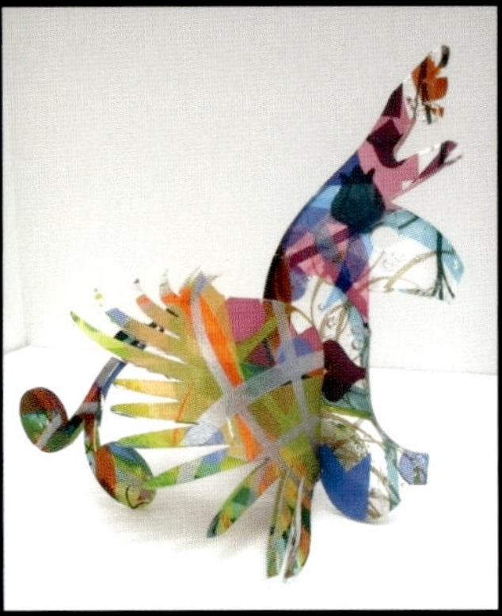

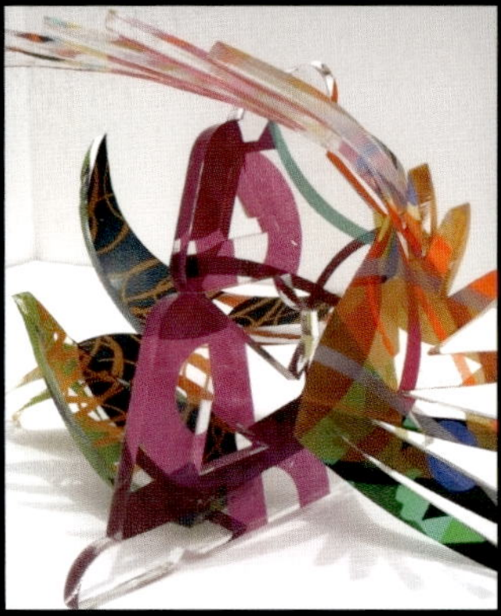

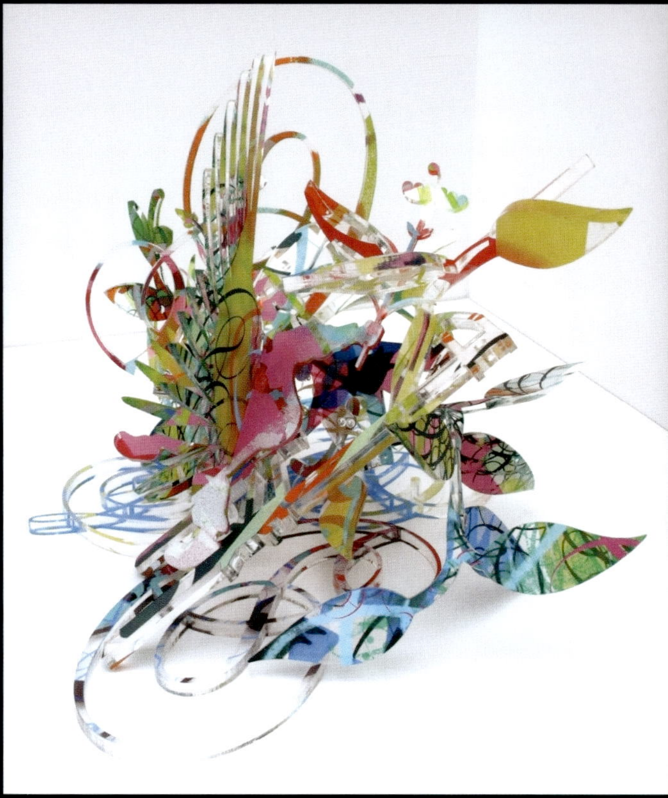

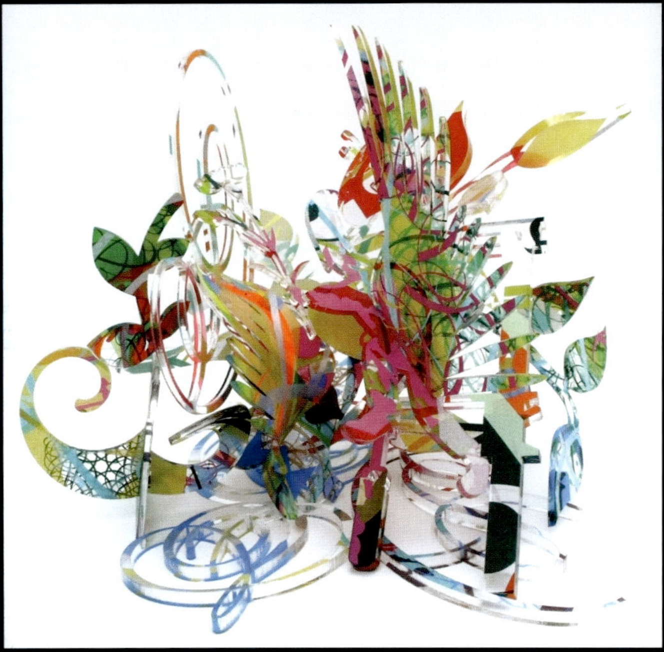

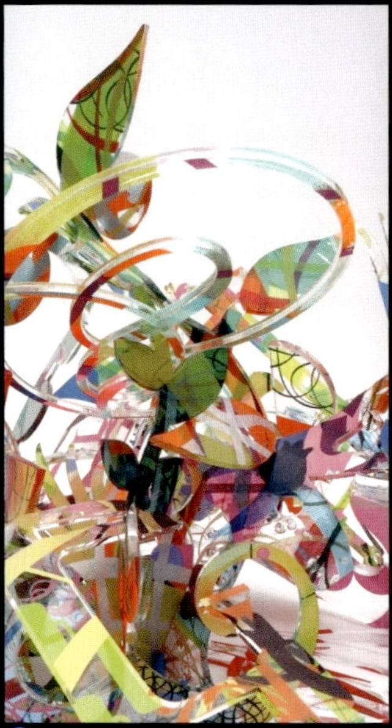

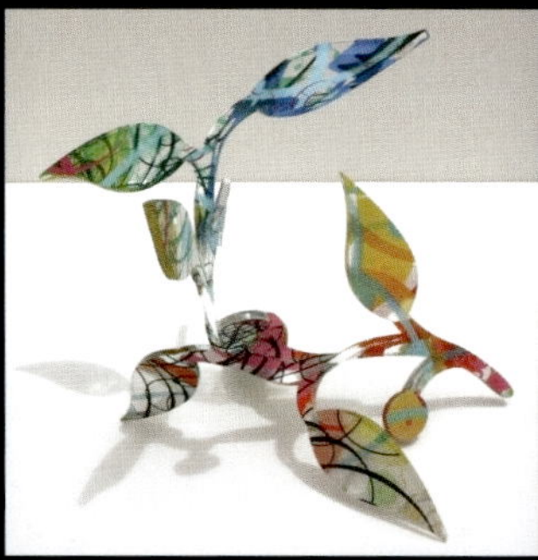

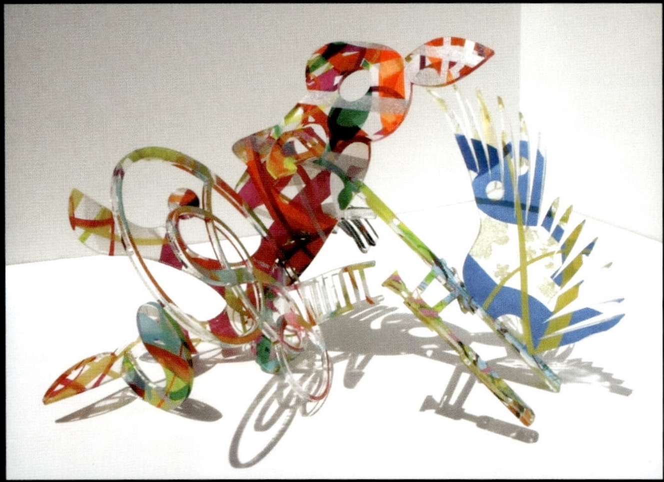

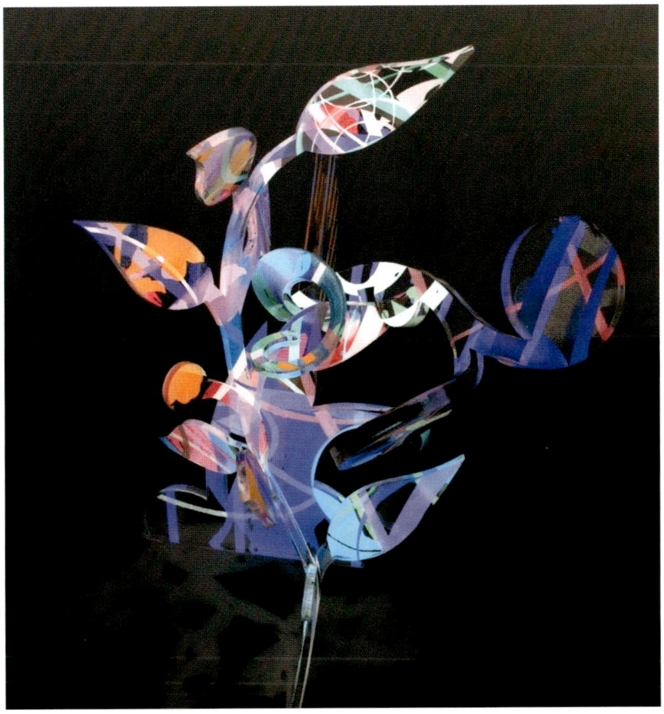

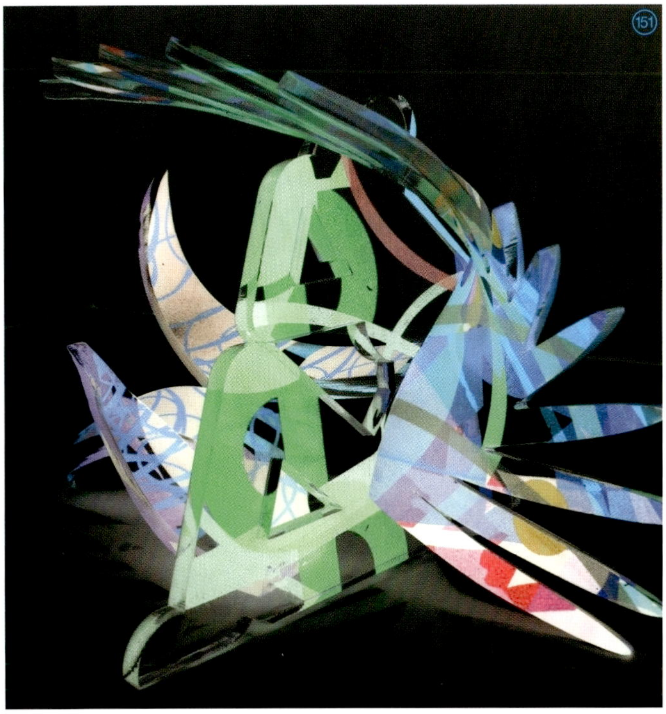

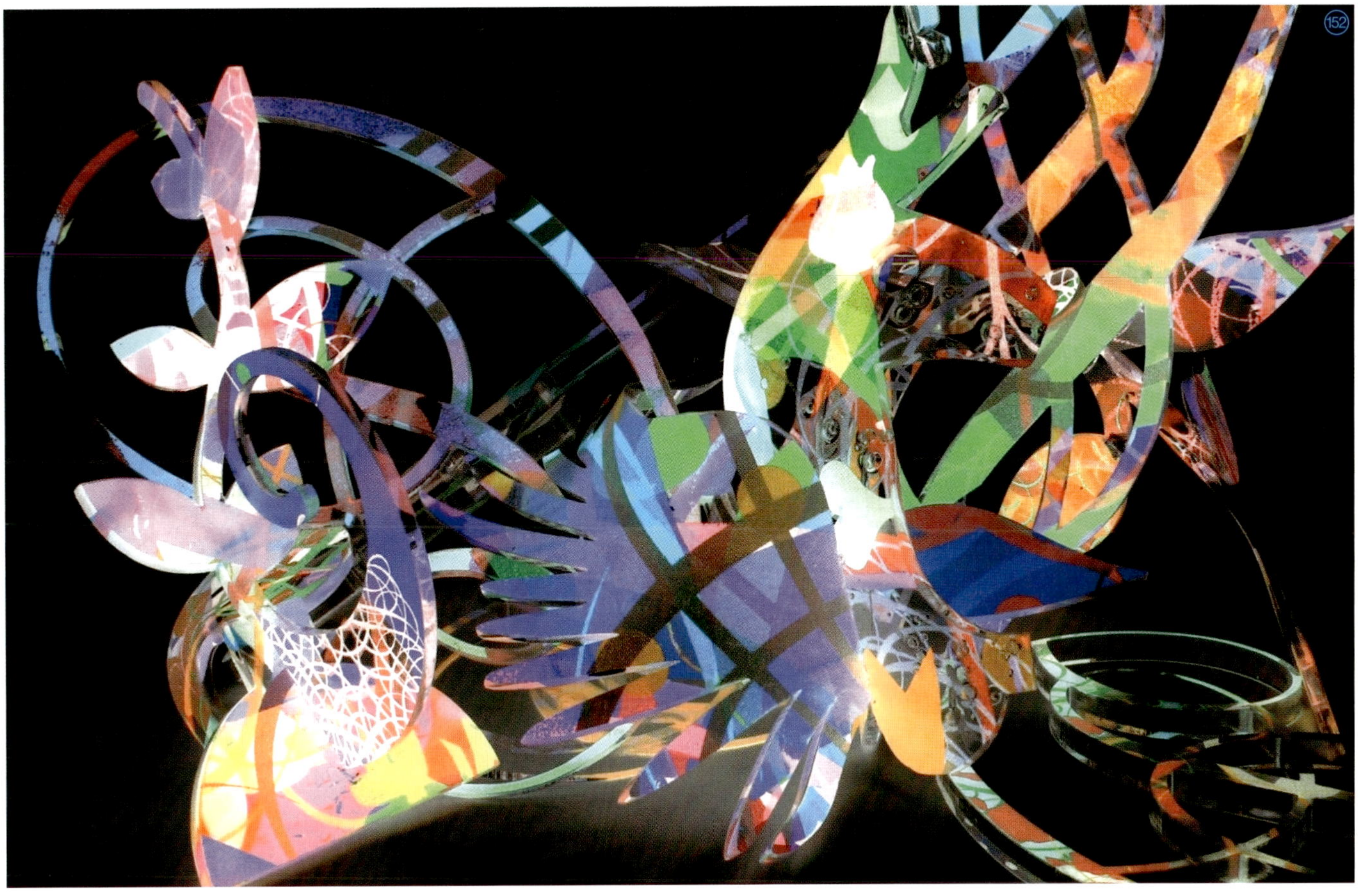

(151) Studies for black-light sculptures: Maquettes are photographed, and those photographs are inverted to simulate a black-light effect.

(152) My challenge now is to battle traditional notions of beauty—to contribute a unique visual language that expands our aesthetic comfort zone.

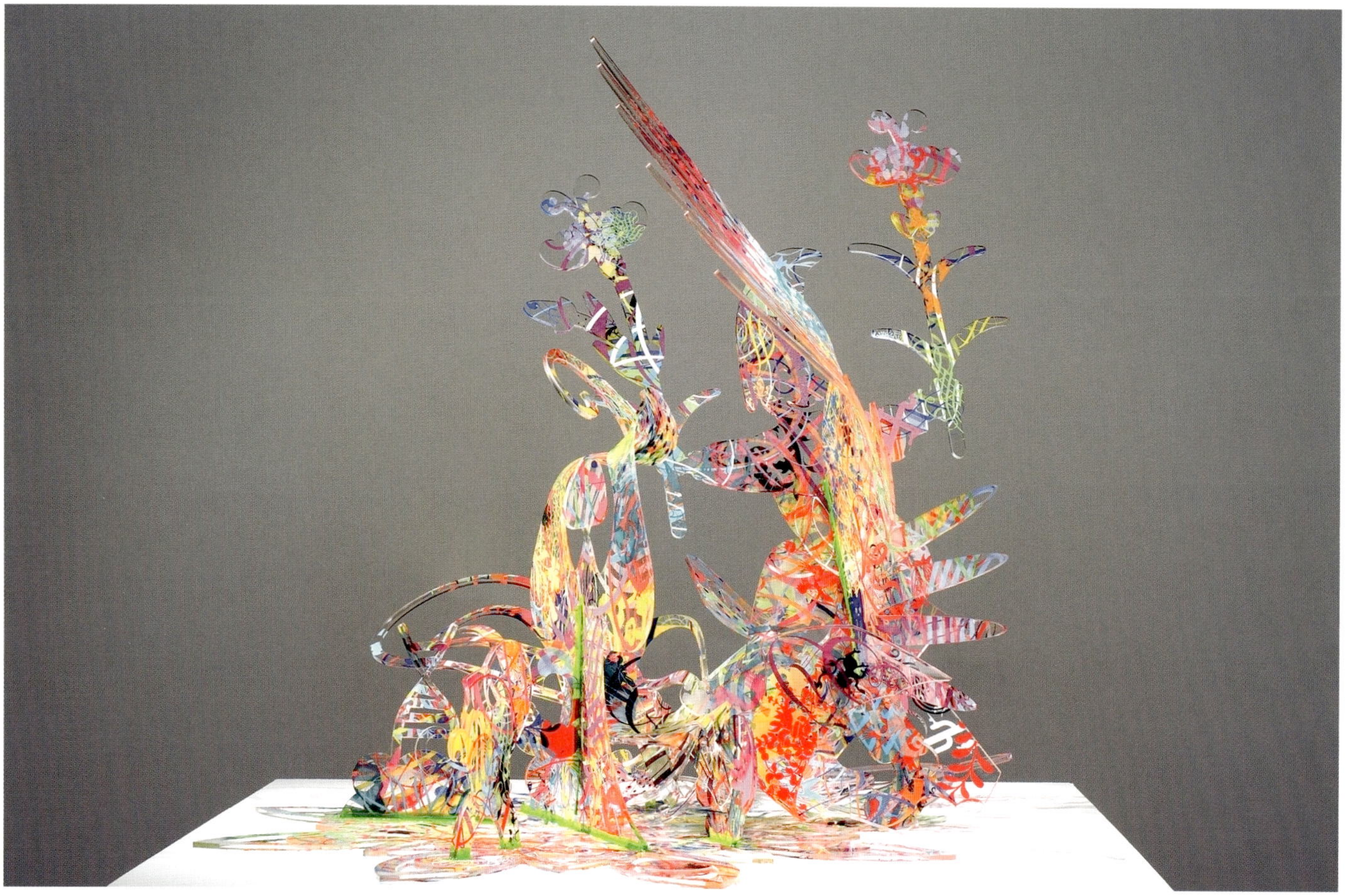

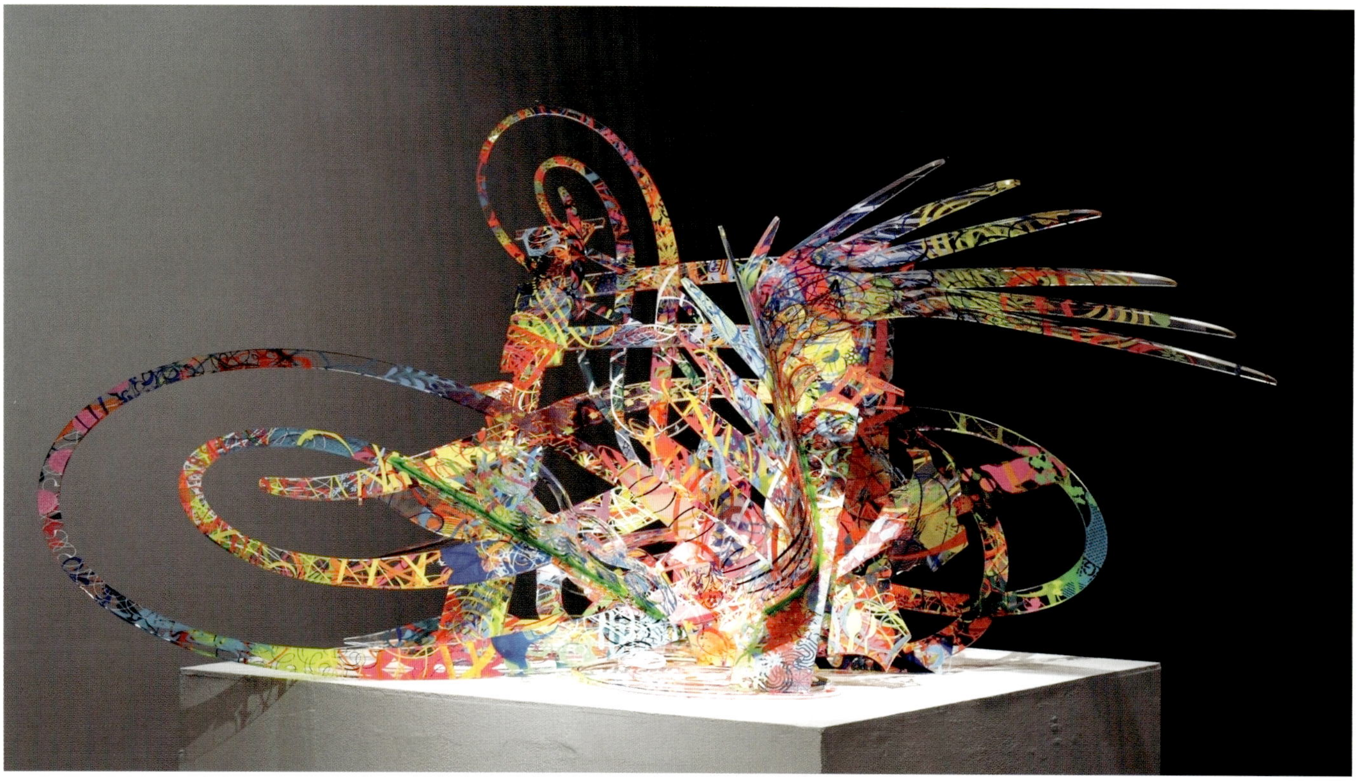

Untitled (Aesthetic Comfort Sculptures), acrylic on acrylic, approx. 60 x 60 x 50 in. each. Installation views, 2008, Artcore/Fabrice Marcolini, Toronto.

Opposite page: *Release* (detail), 2007, mirror-polished stainless steel, 40 x 38 ½ x 38 ½ in.

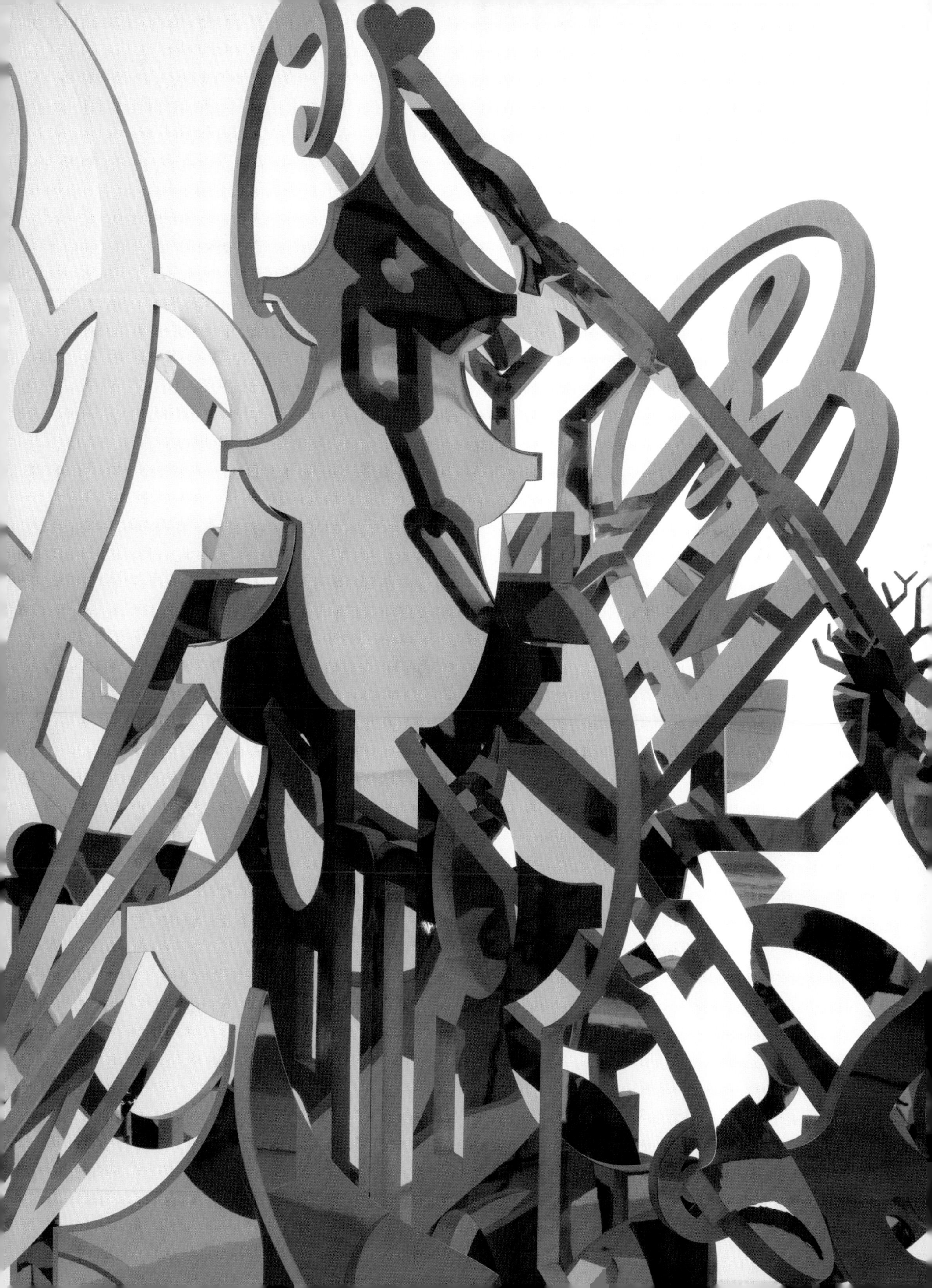

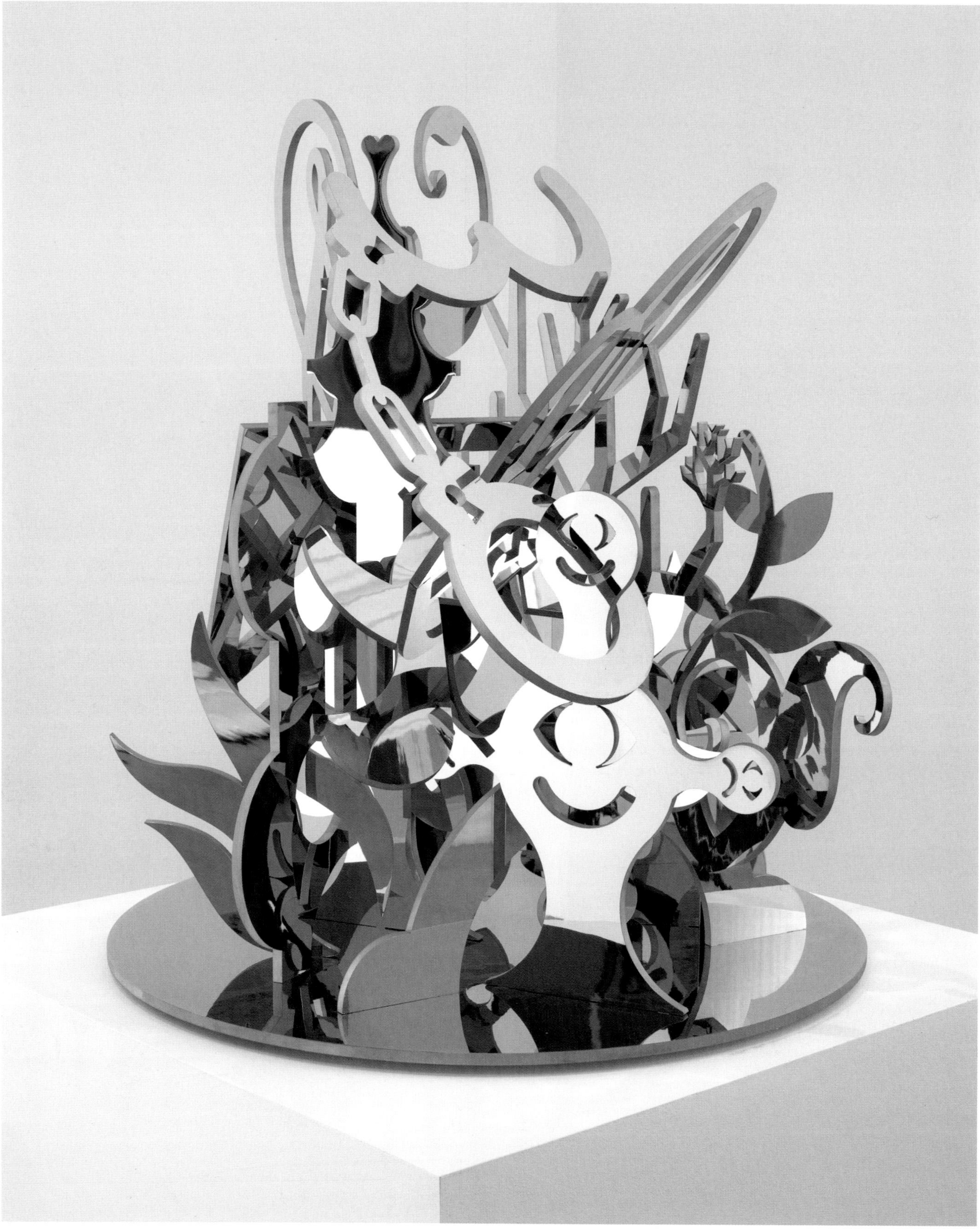

Release, 2007, mirror-polished stainless steel, 40 x 38 ½ x 38 ½ in.
(detail opposite page).

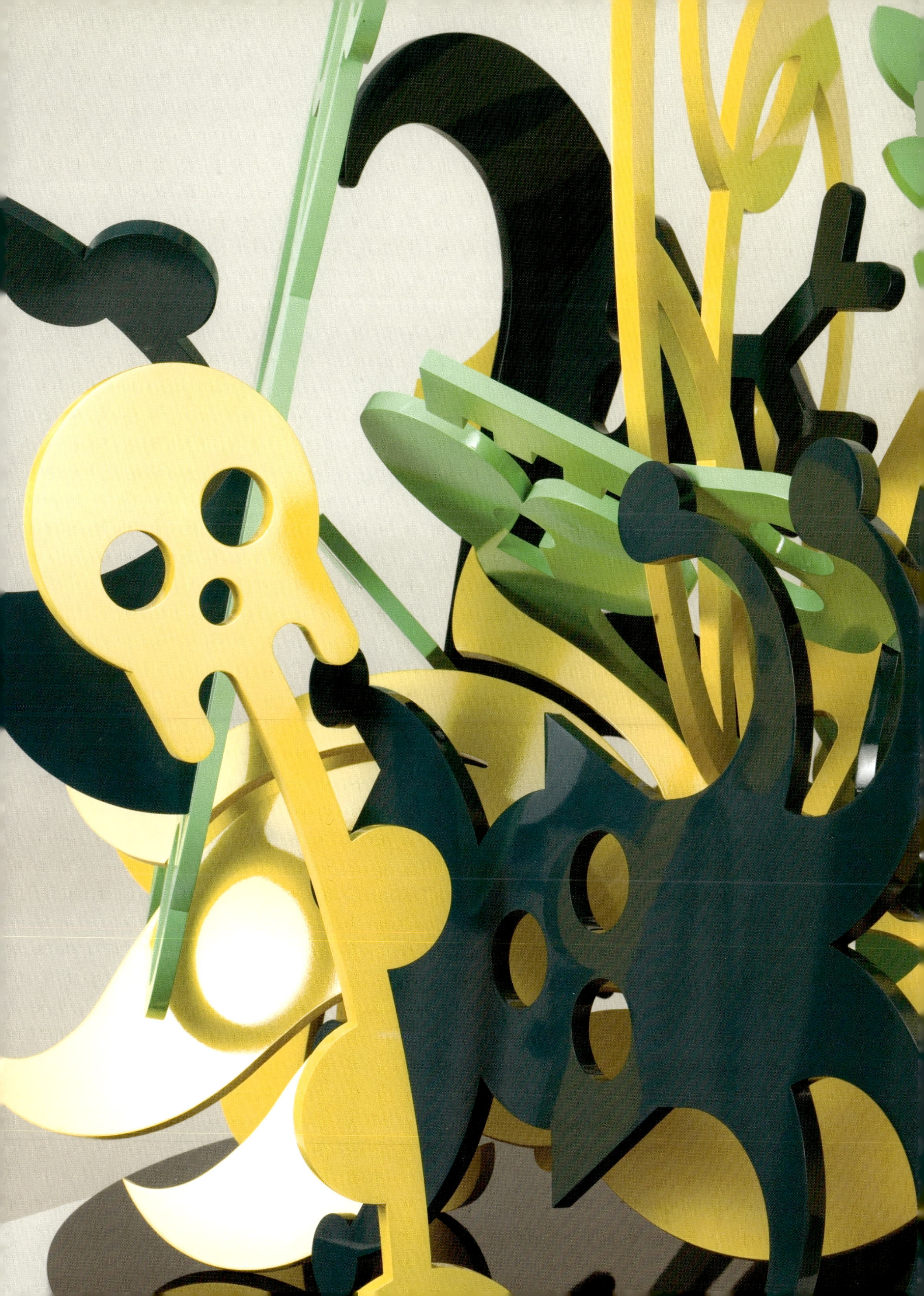

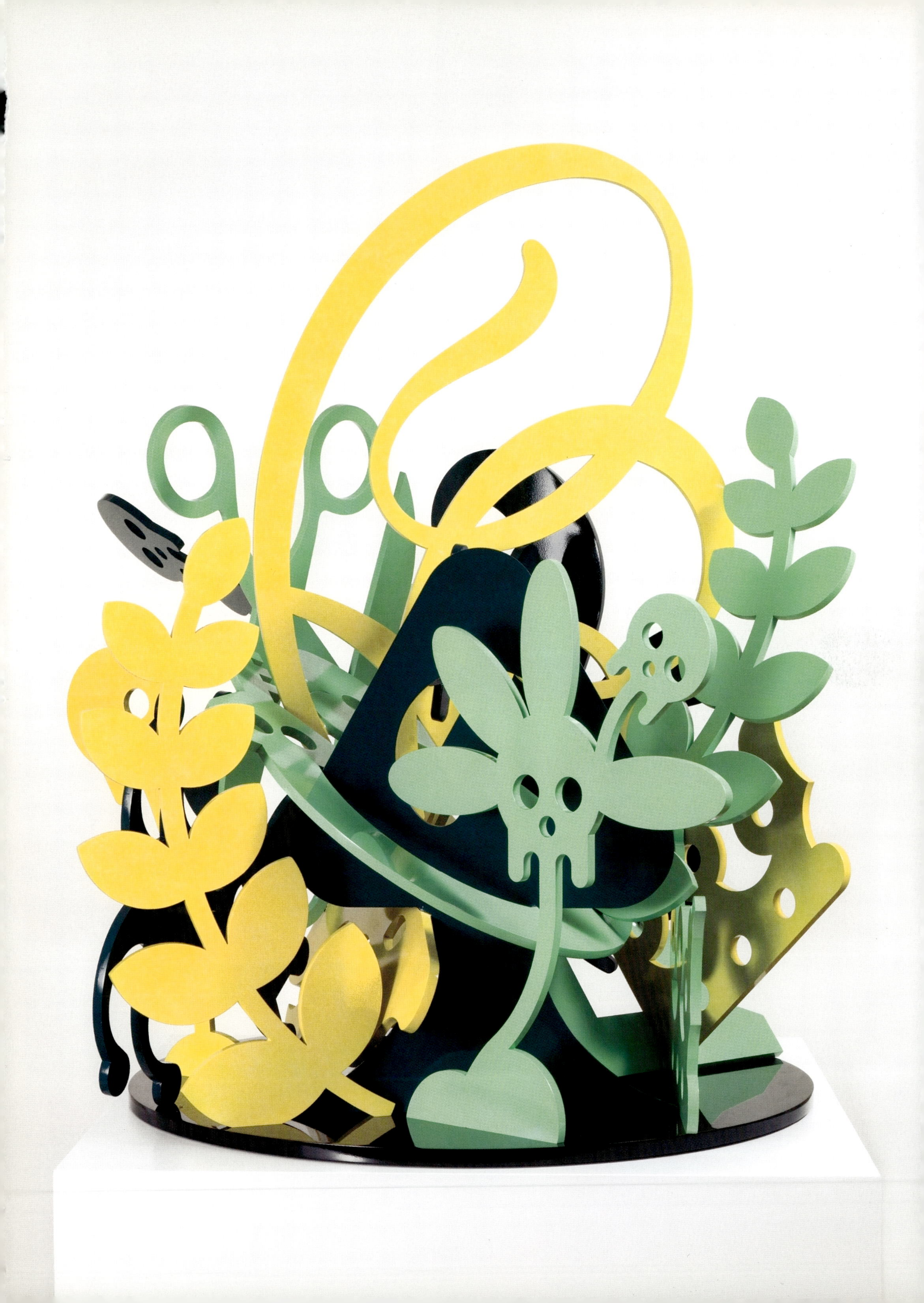

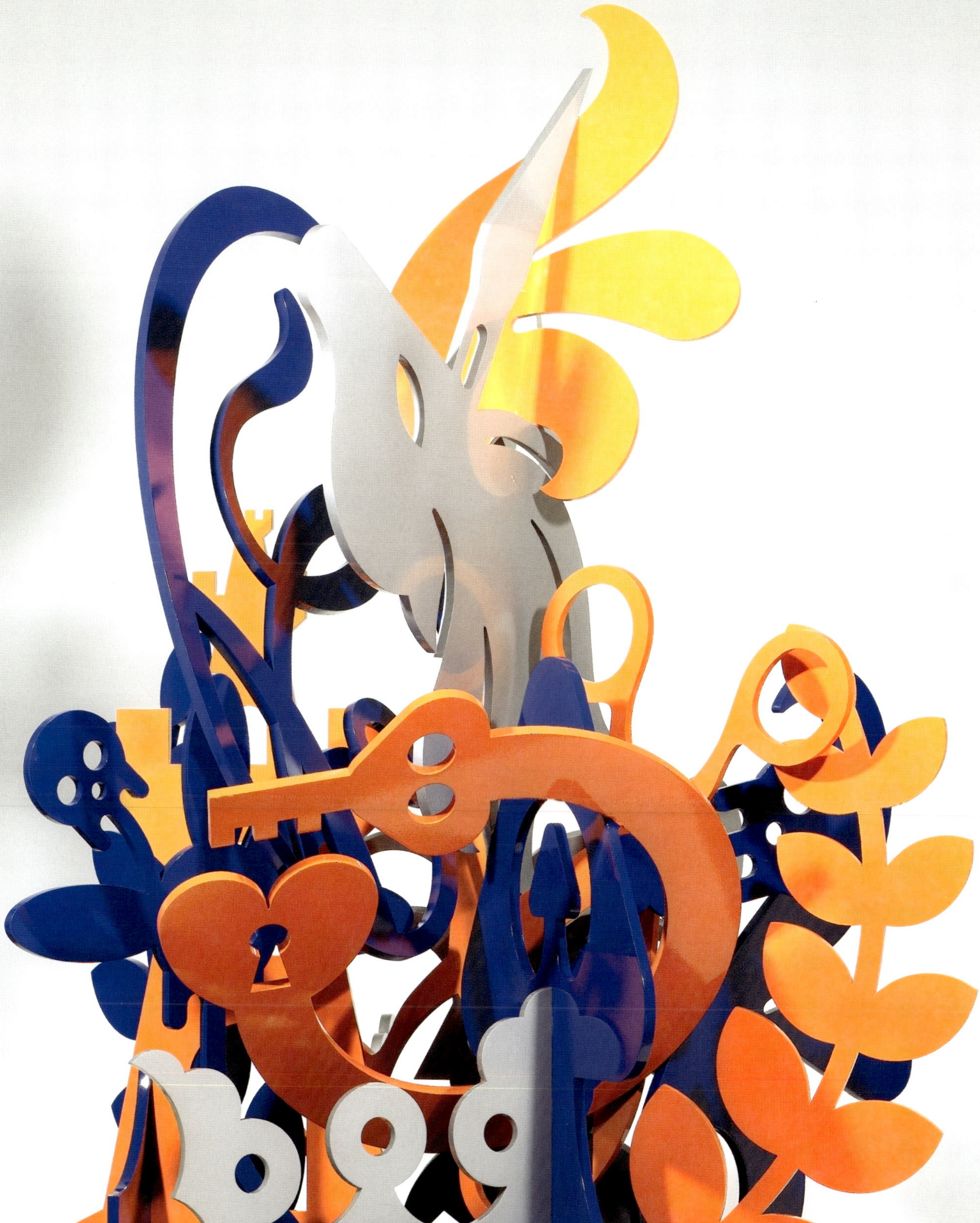

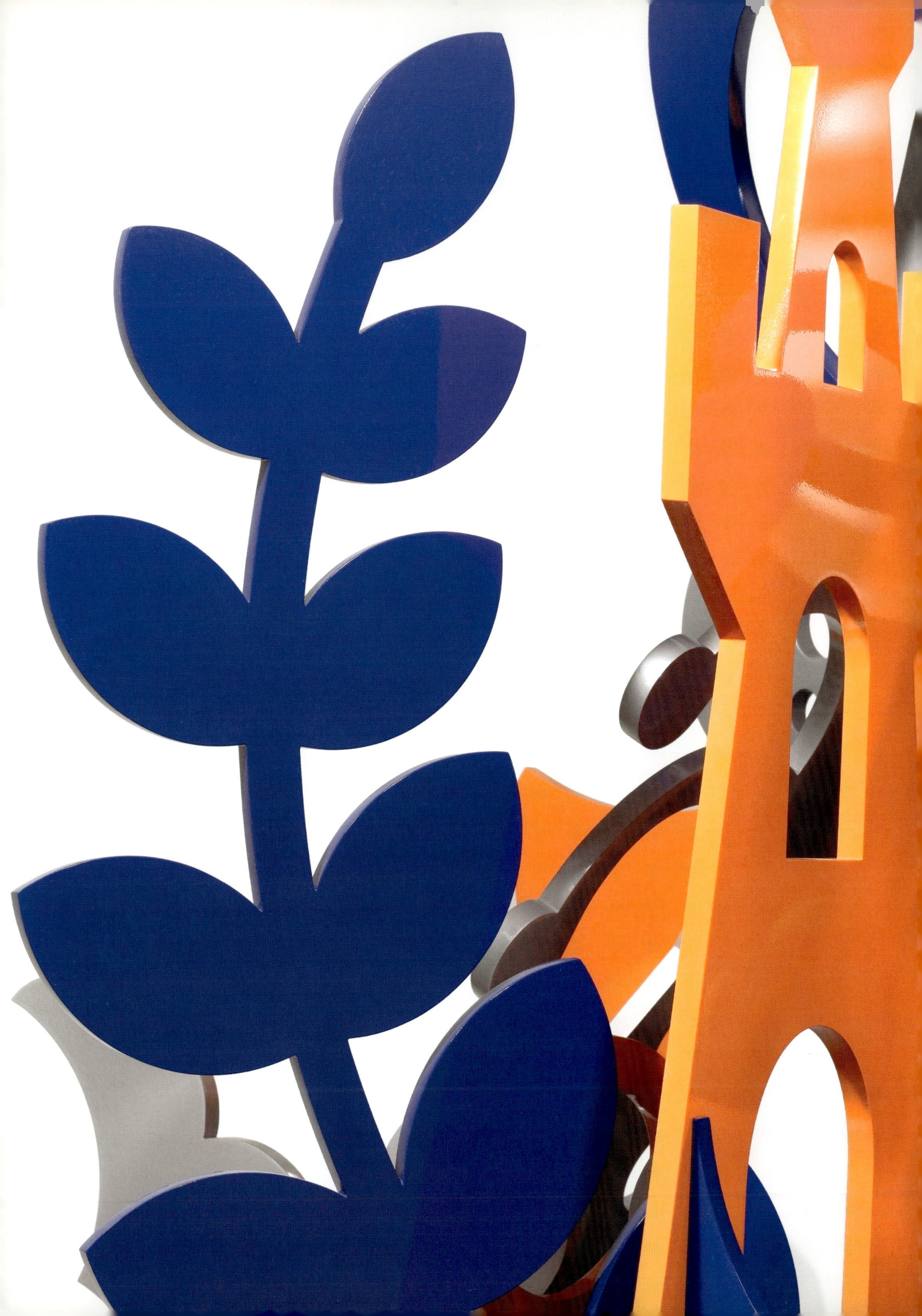

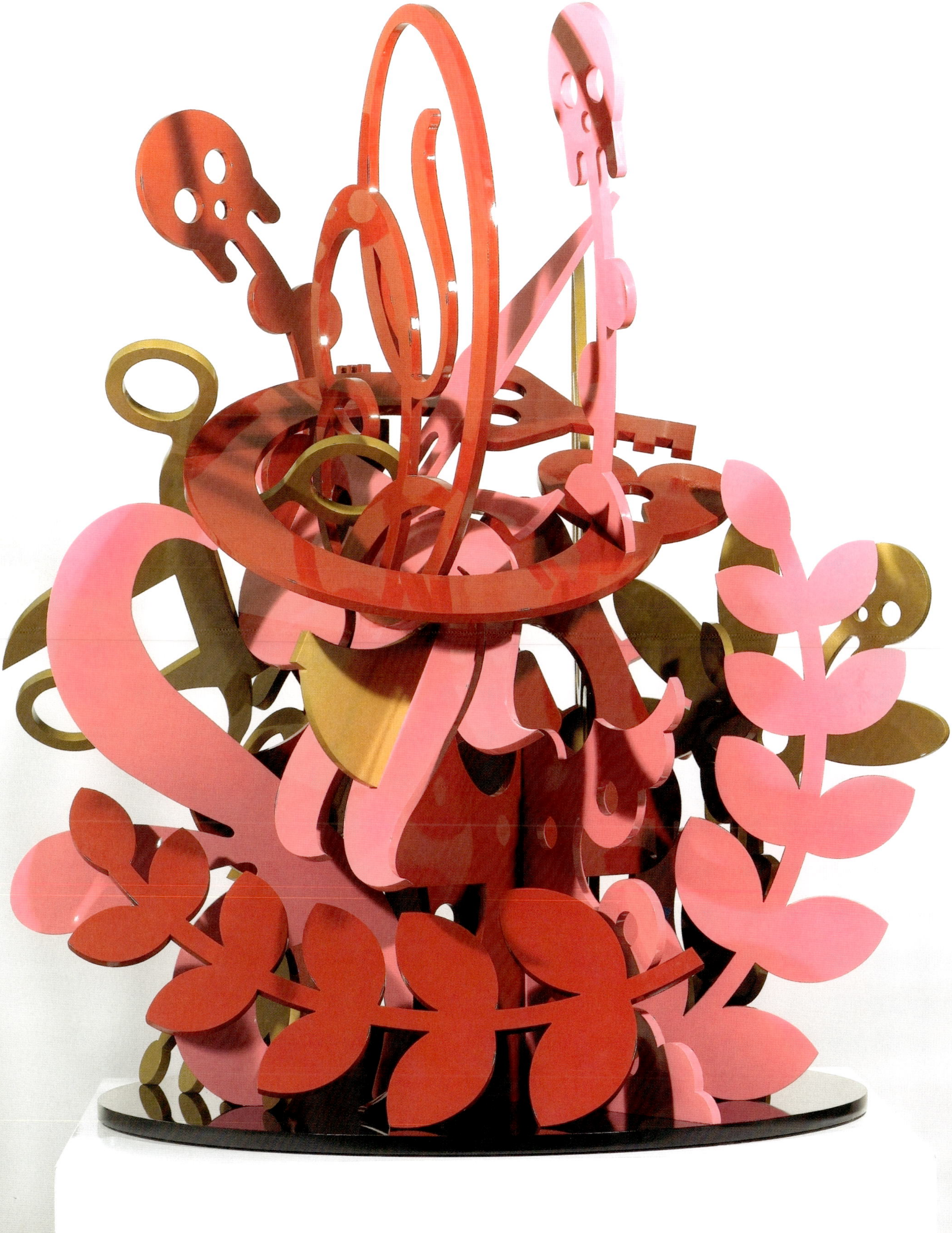

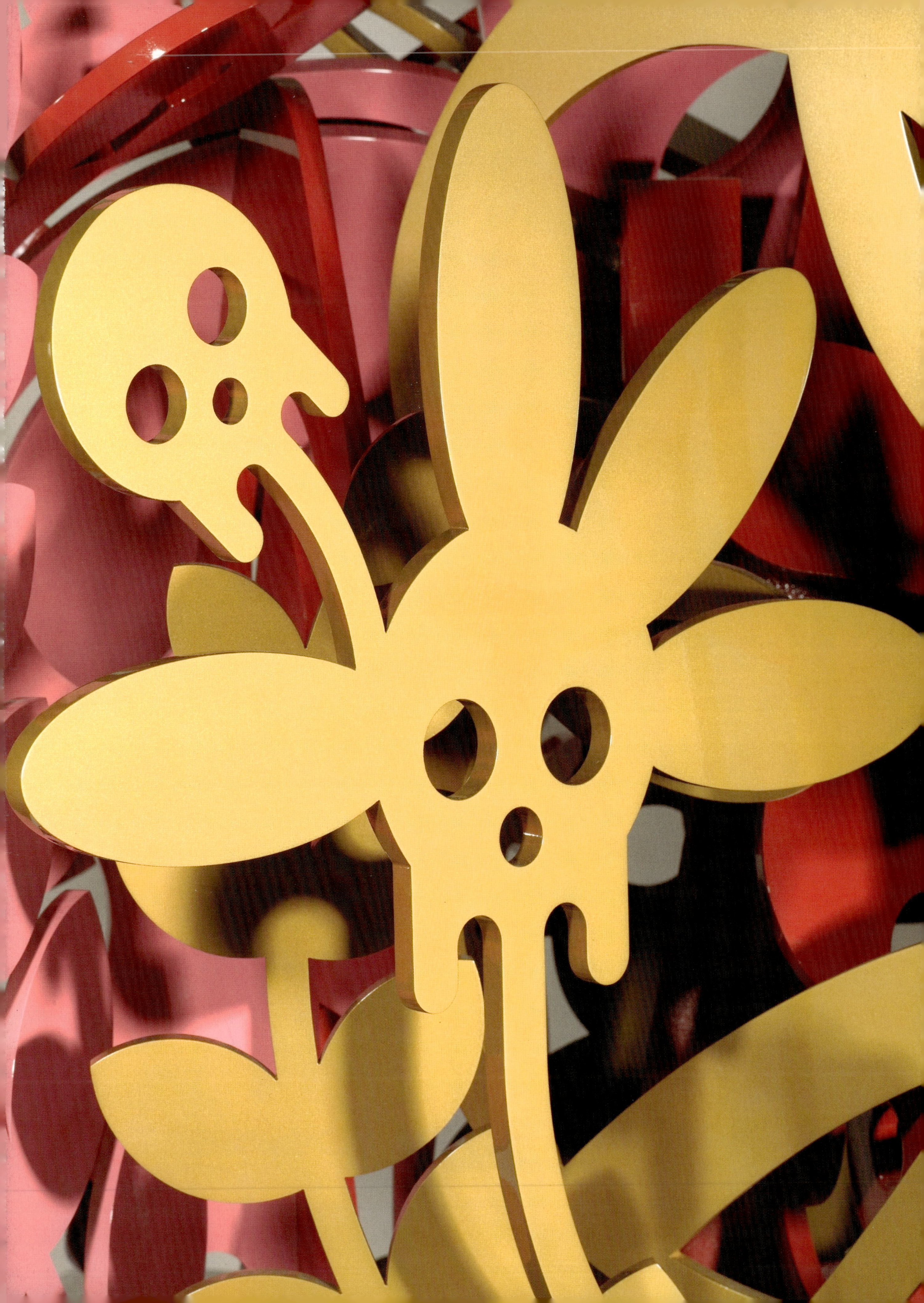

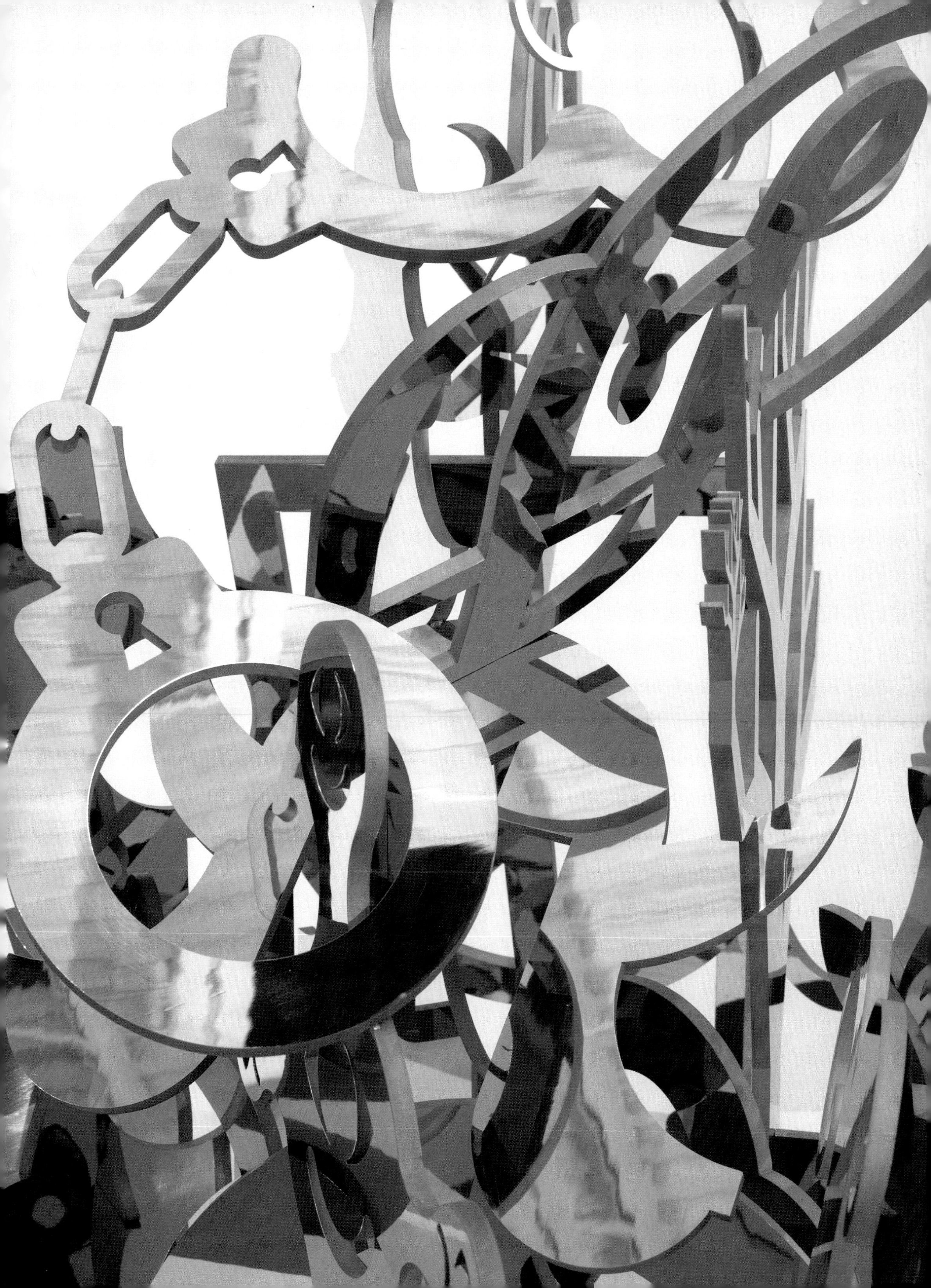

All of the works begin as drawings—starting with pen-and-ink process sketches and ending with the vector drawings, which are used to compose everything Ryan makes. When painting, however, the computer as an art-making tool is abandoned. The paintings are not reproductions of pre-planned computer printouts. They result from having gone through the process of painting—the picture plane grows by making a mark and responding to it, by painting in real time and space, by relying on and celebrating intuition, and responding to the materiality of the paint. Ryan favors working in a large scale with metallic, pearlescent, and fluorescent pigments; glass beads; and gloss mediums, because neither the scale nor these media can be accurately reproduced photographically; they have to be experienced in person, particularly in the context of installation. Installations are an extension of the paintings—a way to claim ownership of the gallery.

H.O.L.L.A.N.D. (Hope Our Love Lasts And Never Dies)
2006, acrylic on wood panel, 48 x 48 in.

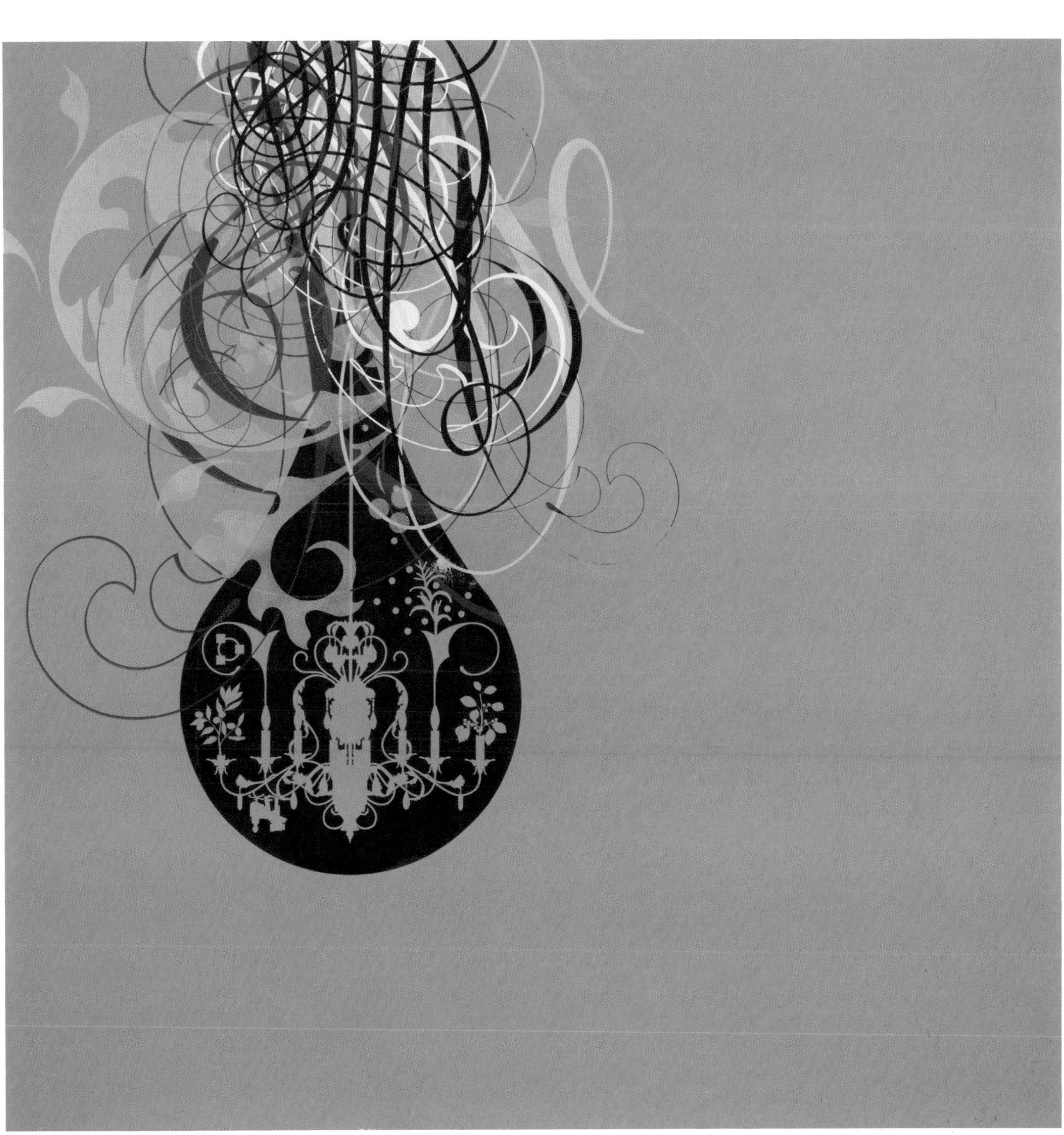

Three Cheers for the Haute Couture Hippy
2006, acrylic on wood panel, 48 x 48 in.

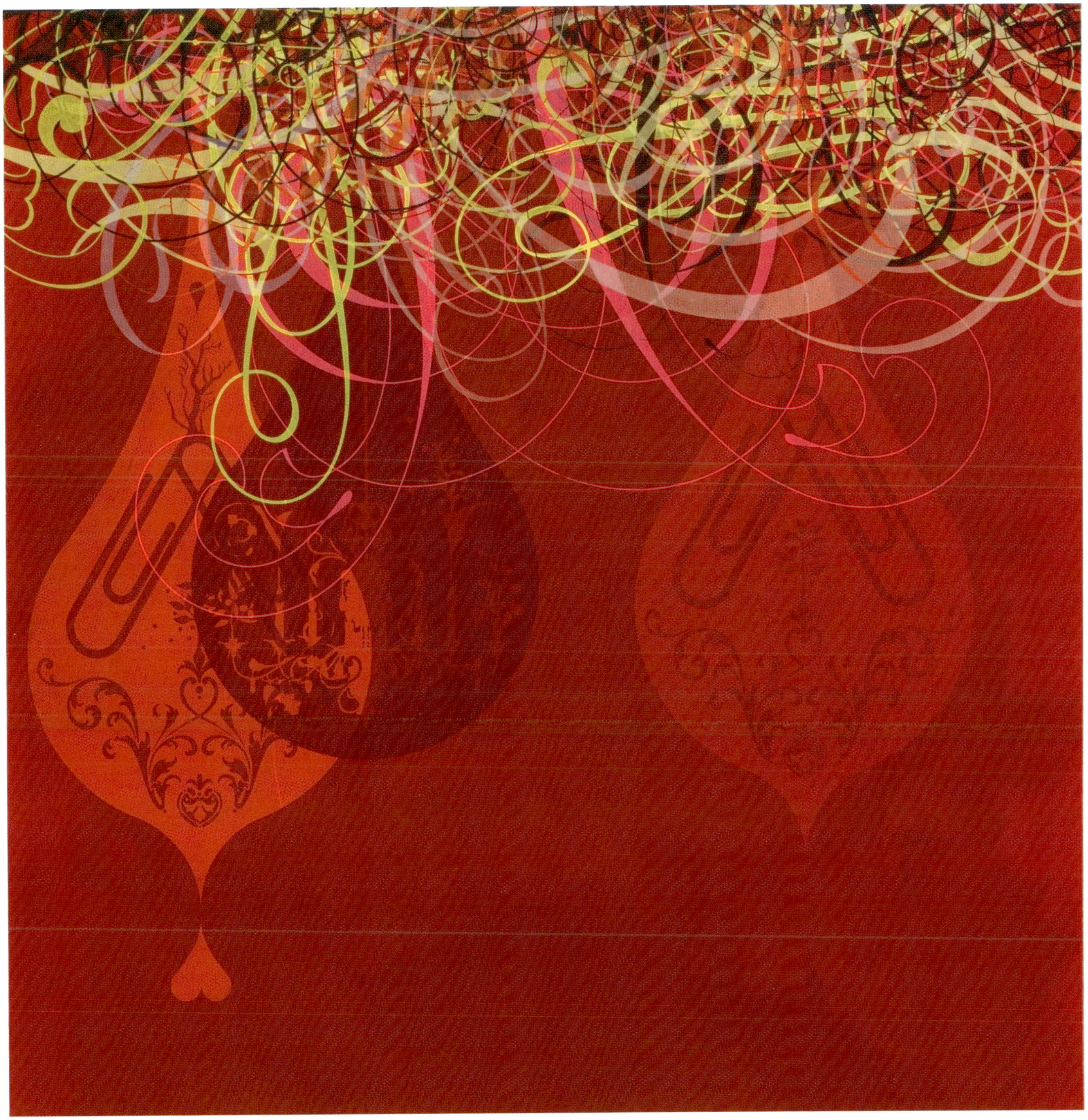

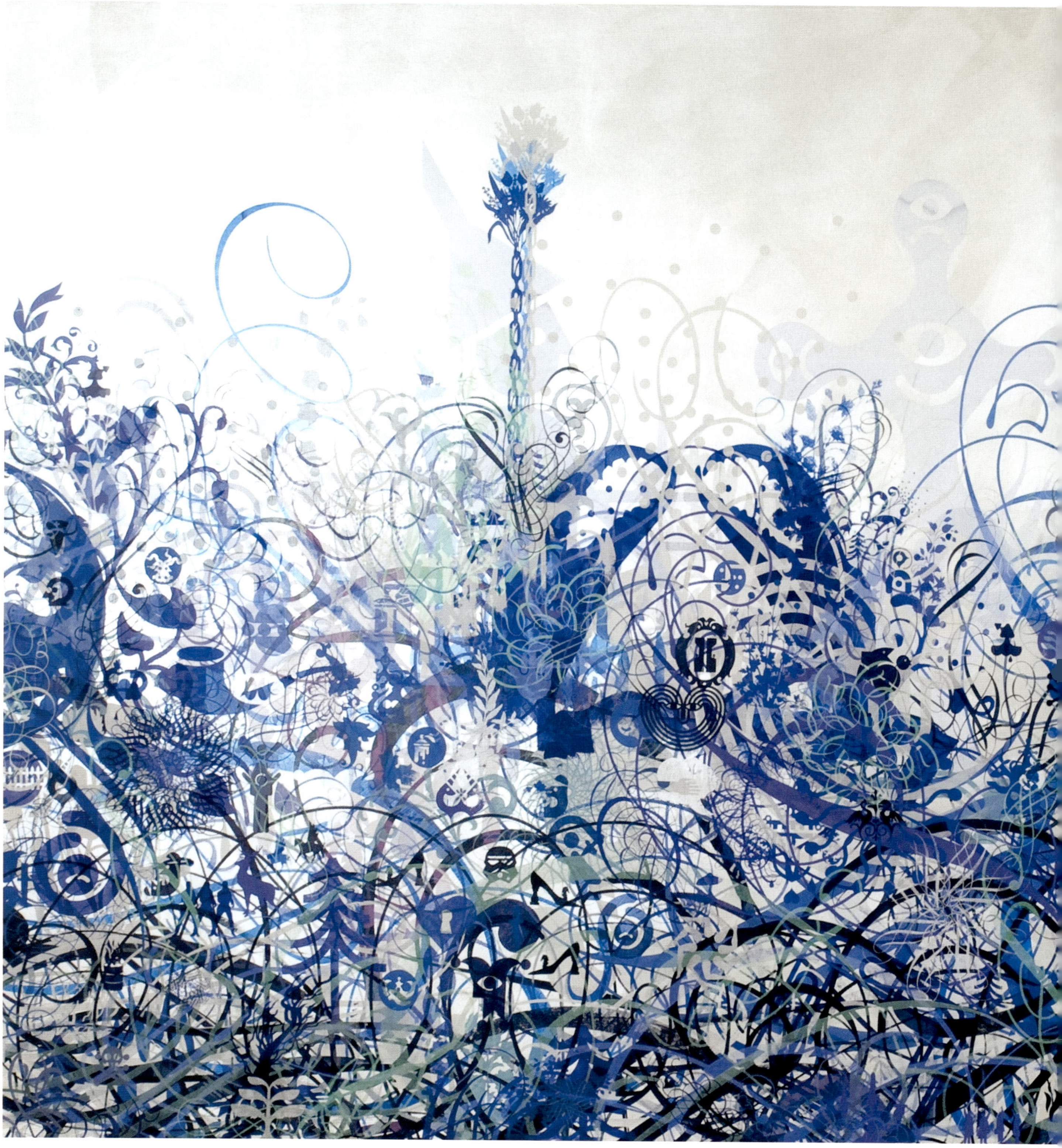

Untitled (Oceanscape)
2008, acrylic on wood panel, 48 x 96 in.

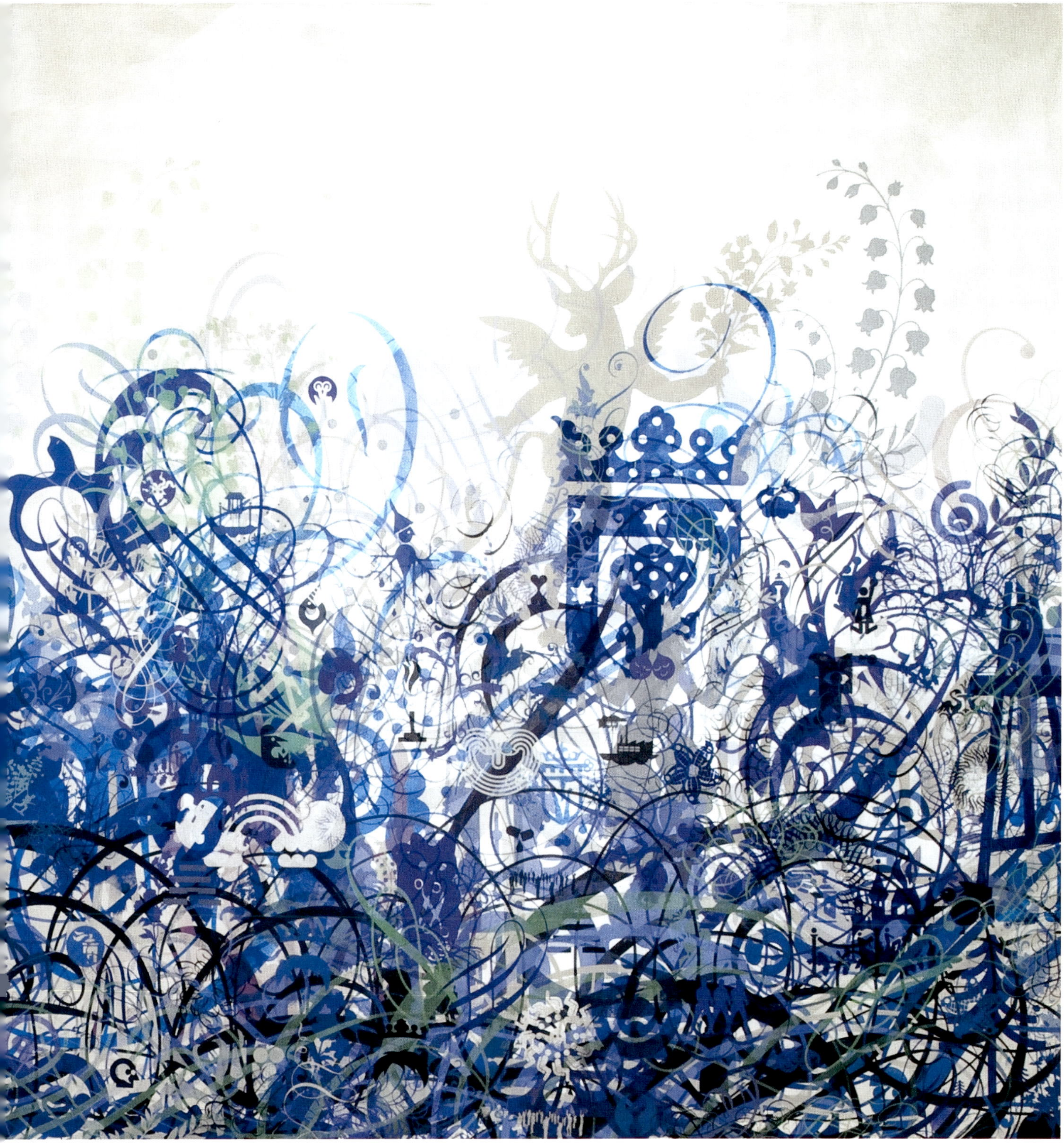

Disjecta
2006, acrylic on wood panel, 48 x 48 in.

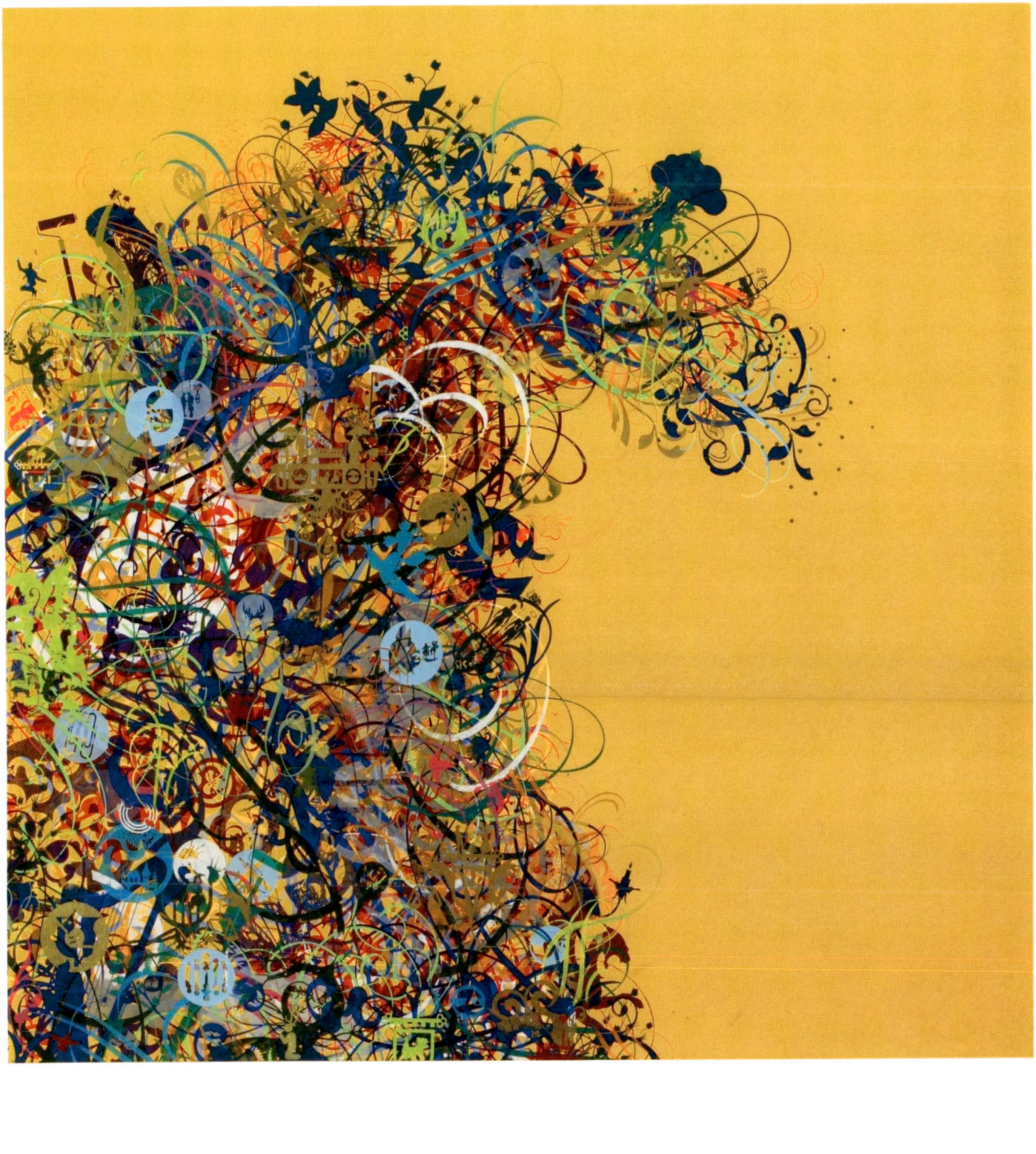

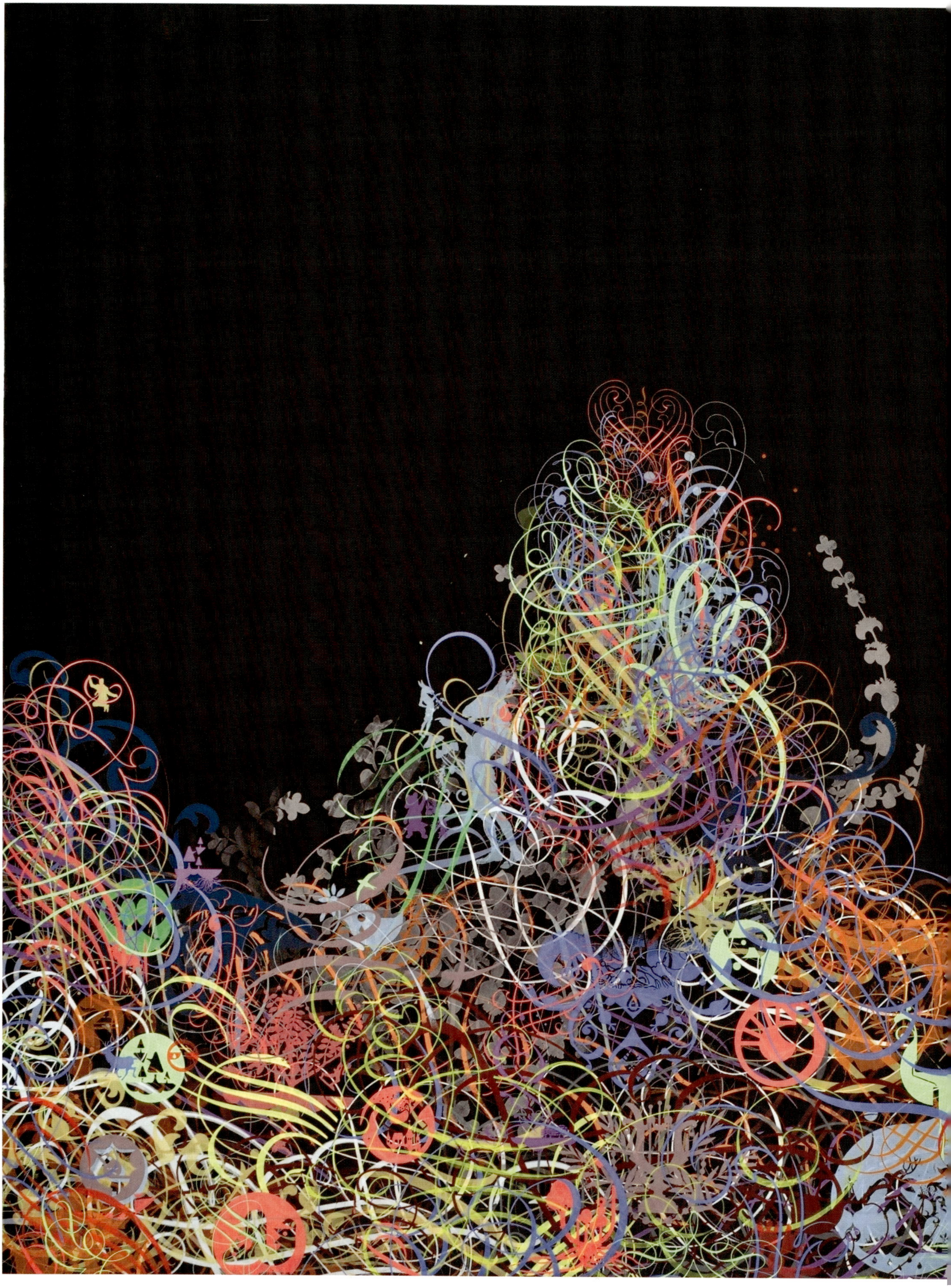

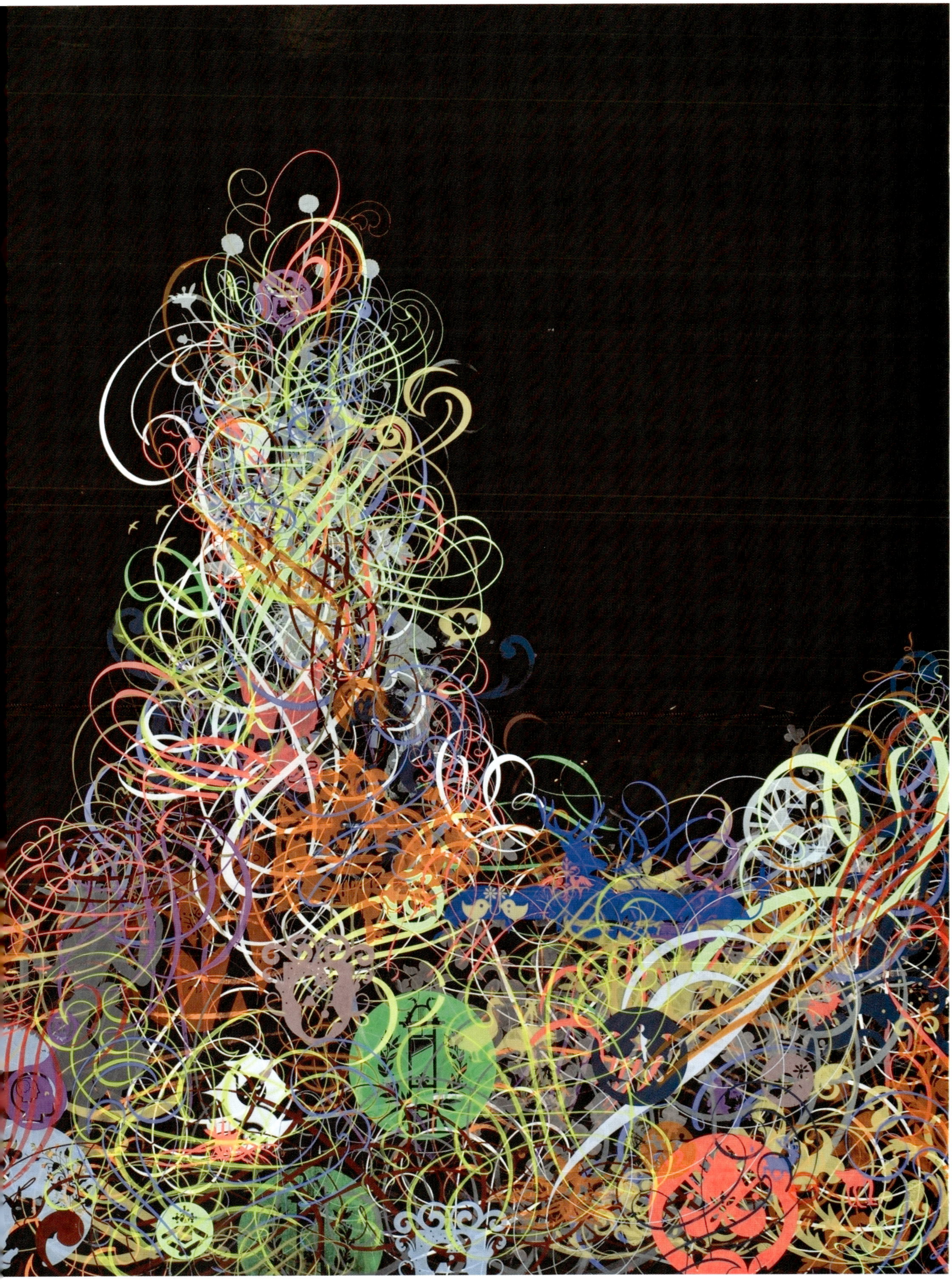

Overleaf: *Buy for One, Sell for Two*
2005, acrylic and oil on wood panel, 60 x 96 in.

Arab Cadillac Generator
2006, acrylic on wood panel, 48 in. diameter.

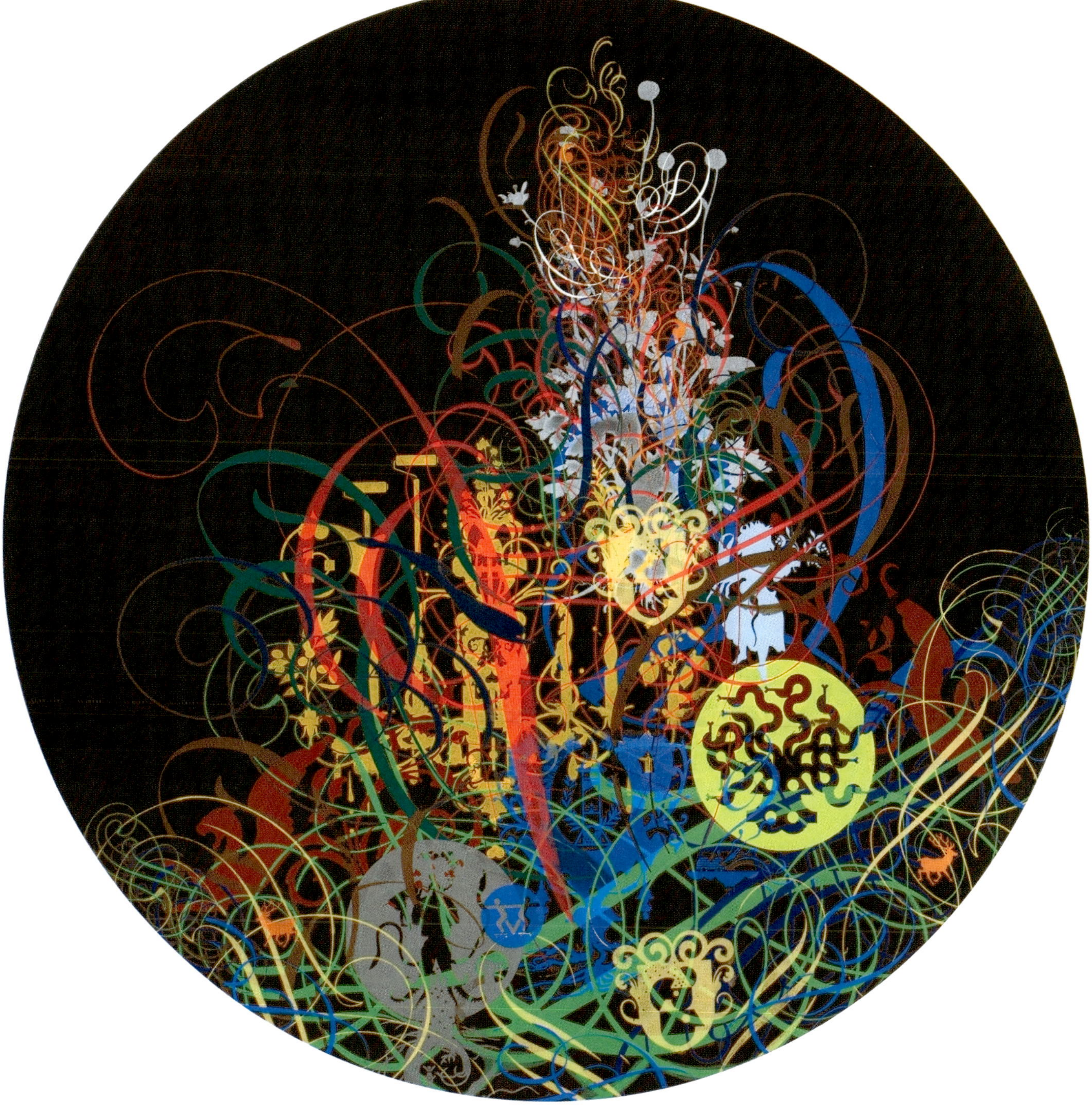

Weaving Spiders Come Not Here
2007, acrylic on canvas, 72 in. diameter.

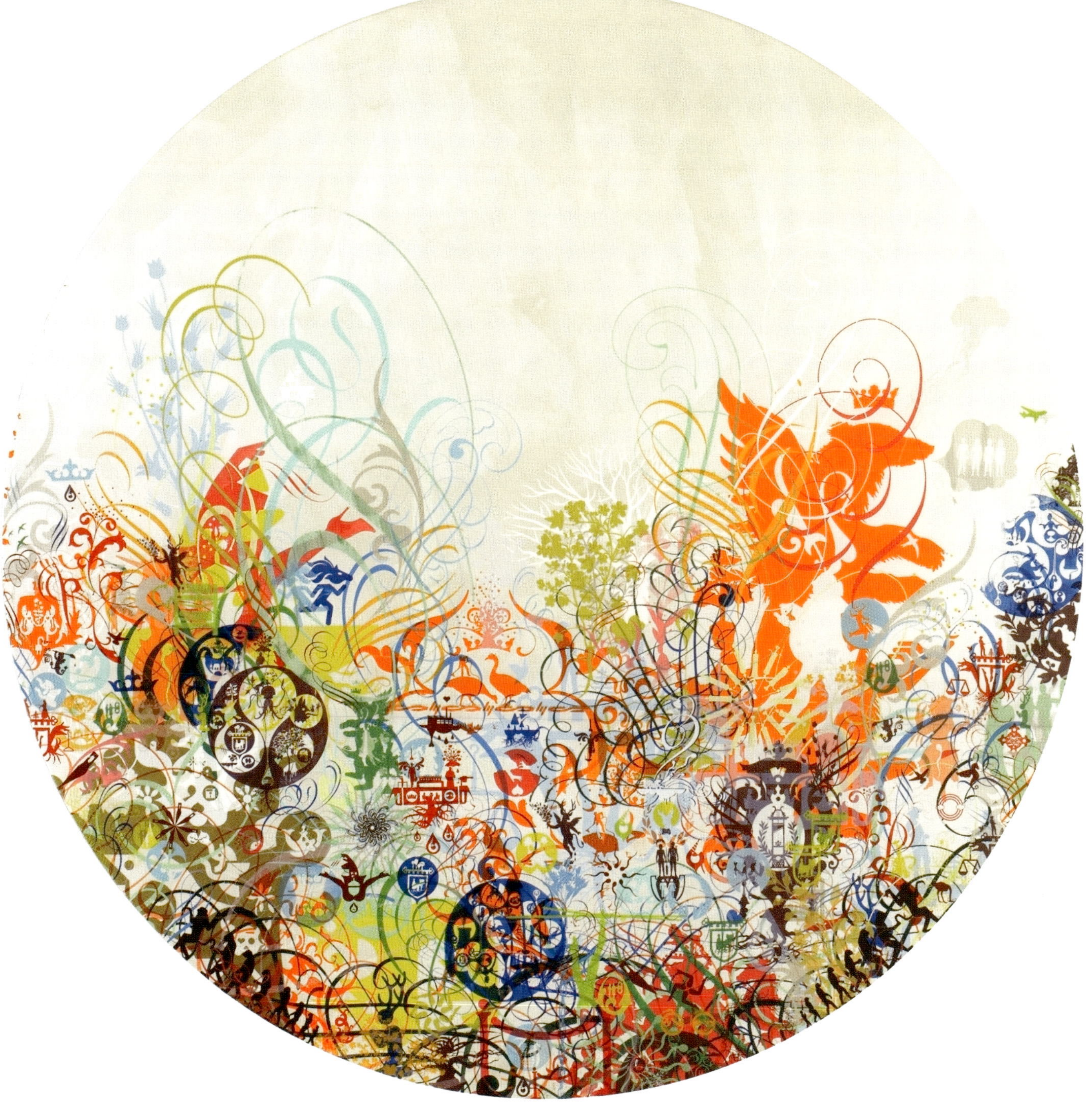

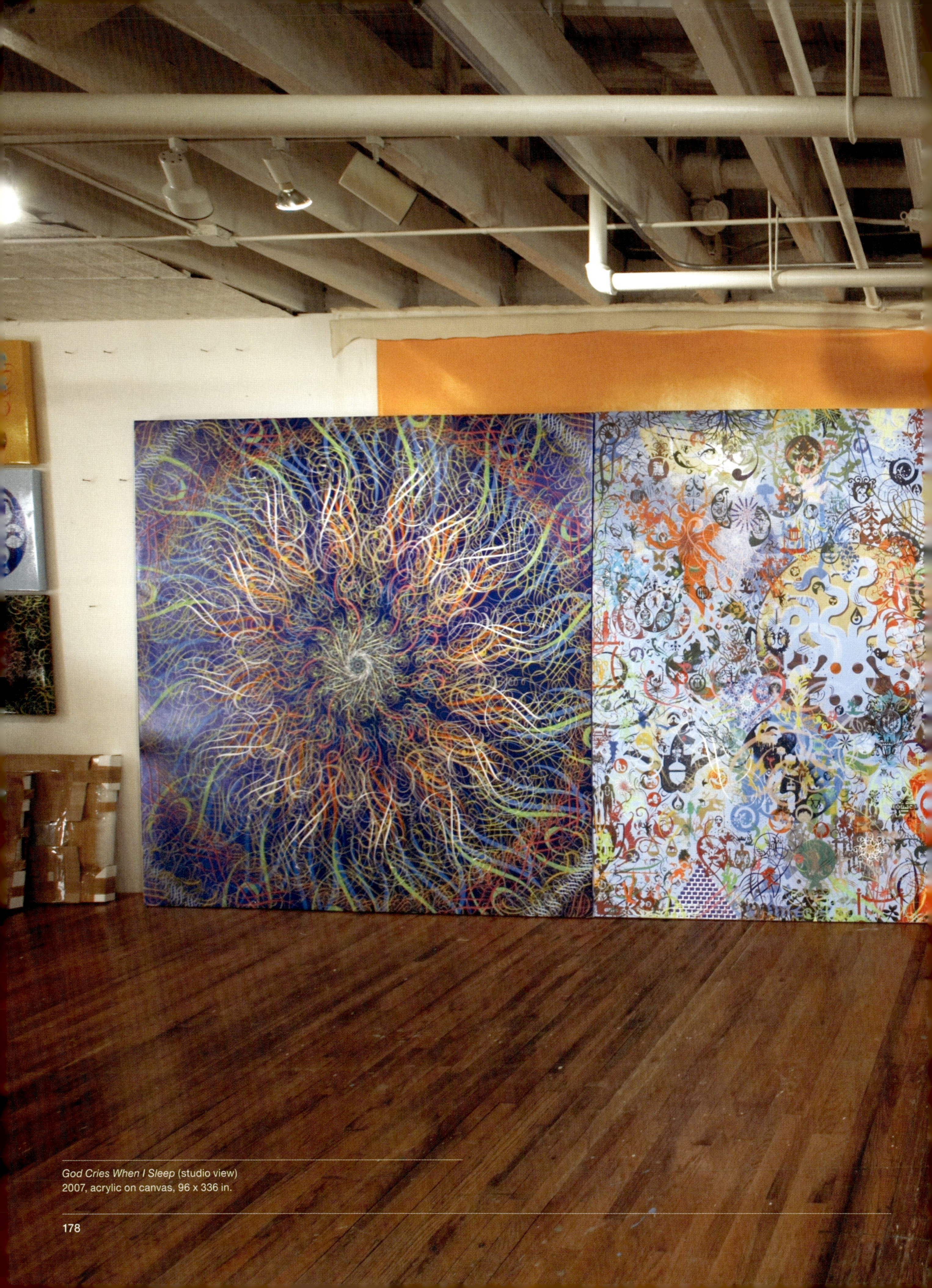

God Cries When I Sleep (studio view)
2007, acrylic on canvas, 96 x 336 in.

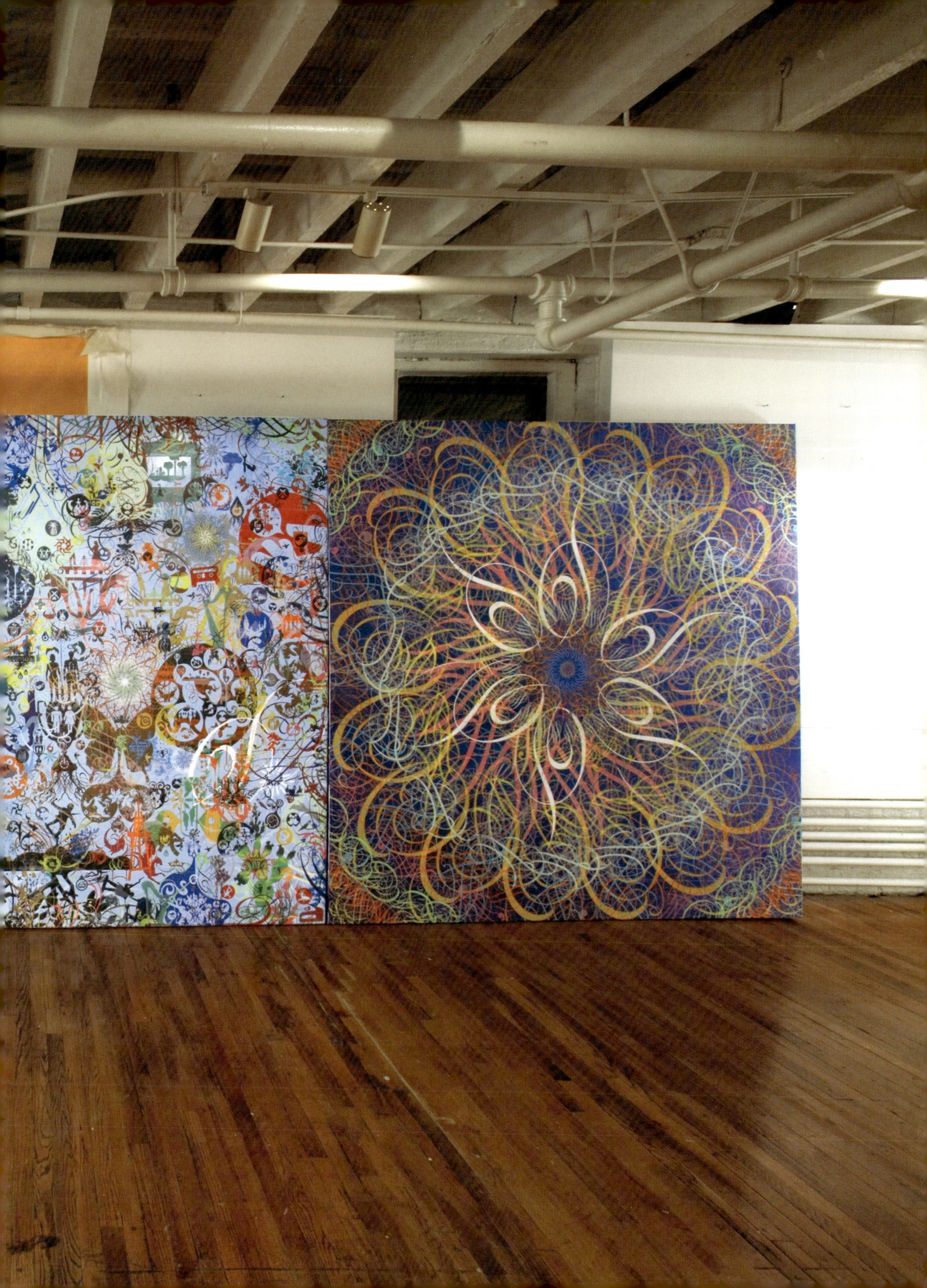

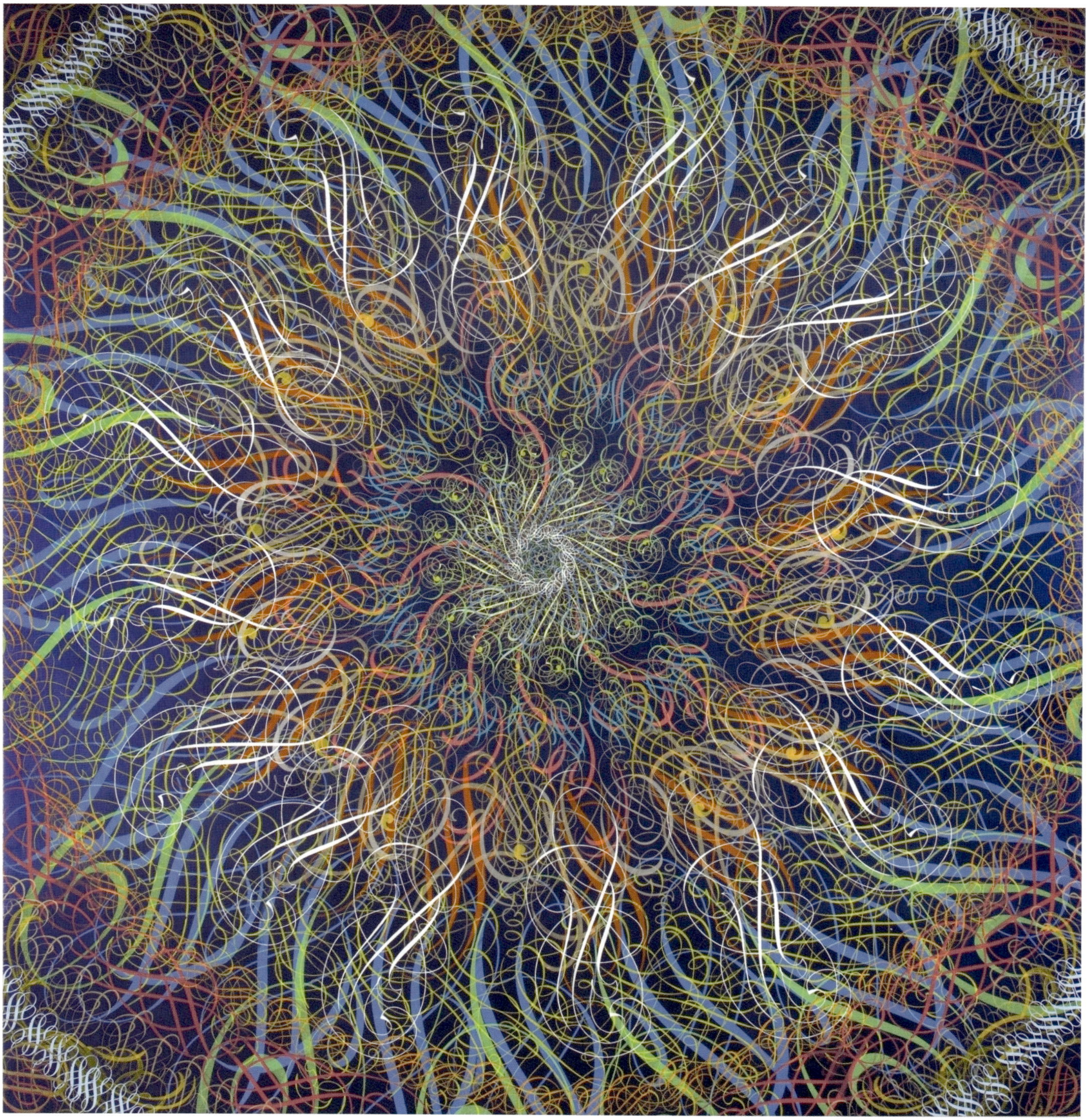

God Cries When I Sleep (details of end panels)
2007, acrylic on canvas, 96 x 96 in. each.

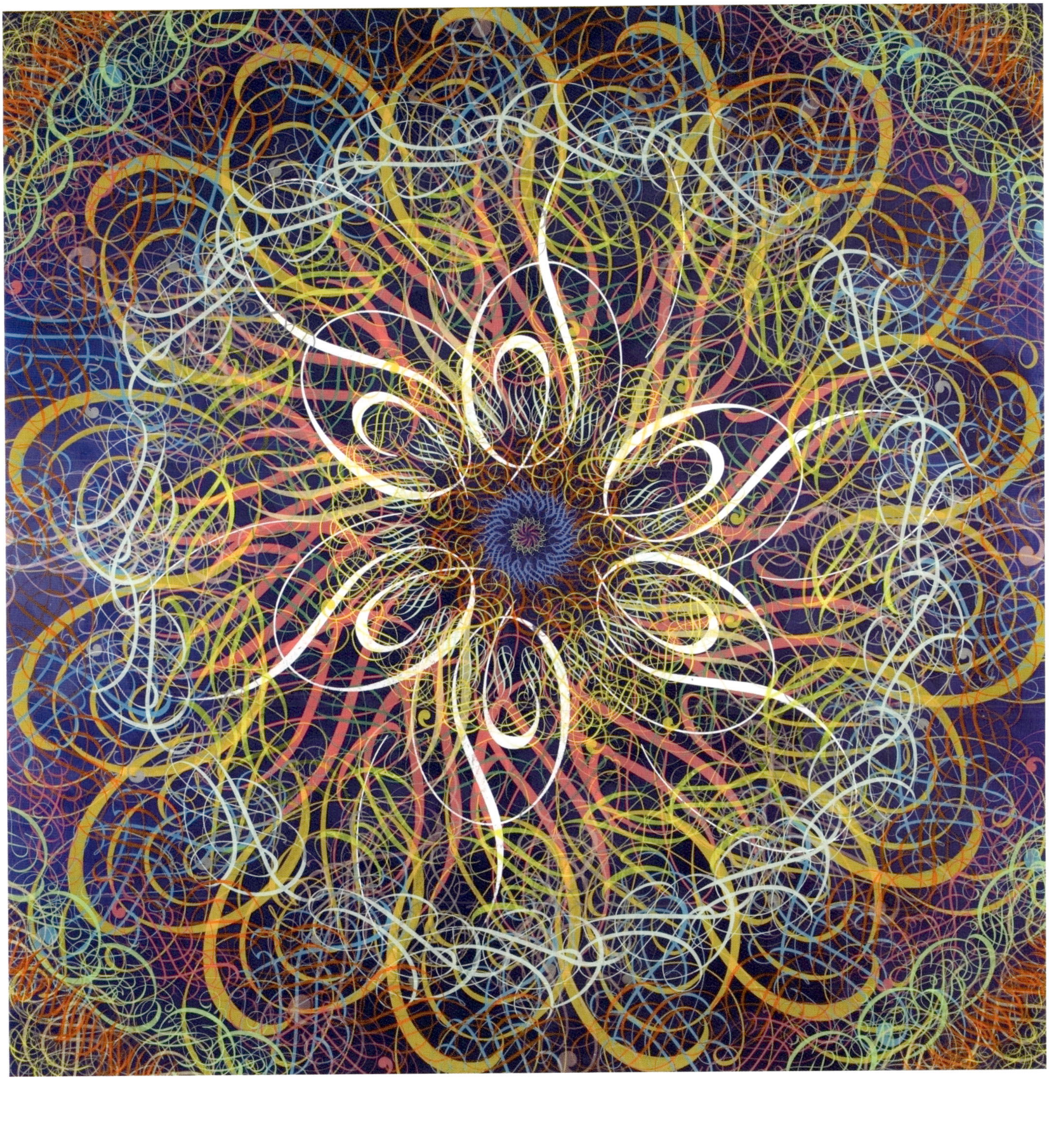

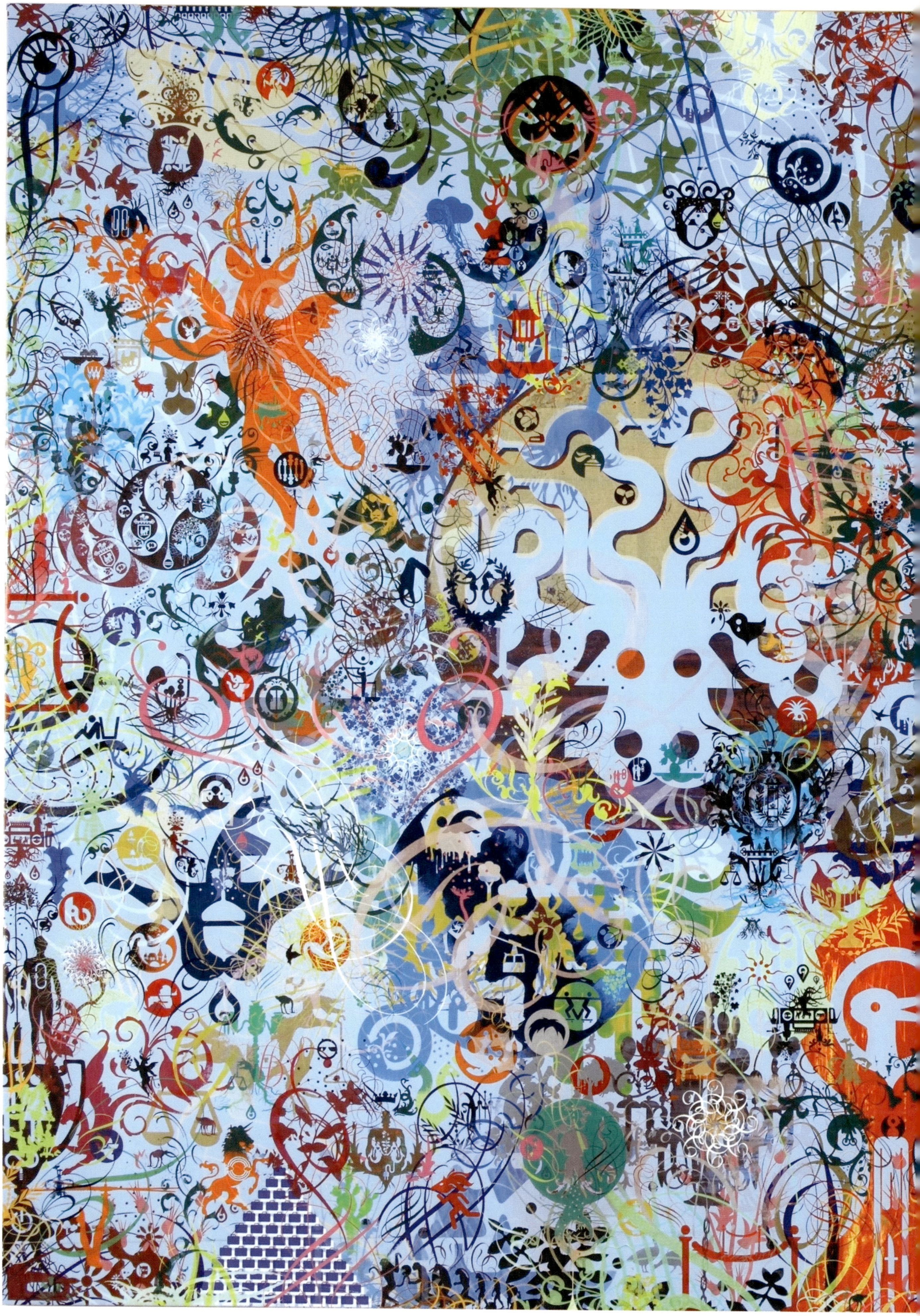

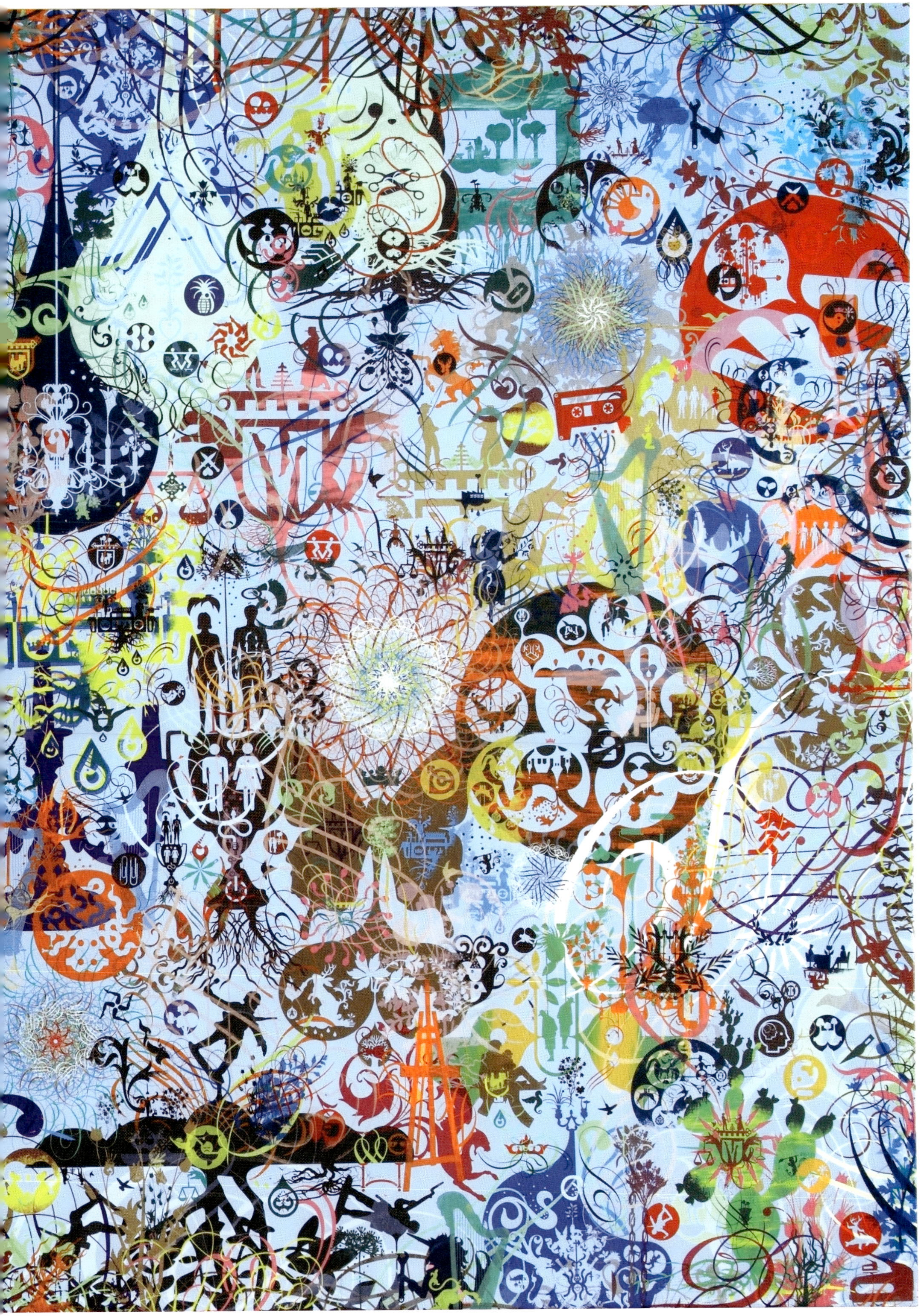

Overleaf: *God Cries When I Sleep* (center panel)
2007, acrylic on canvas, 96 x 144 in.

An(n)us Mirabilis
2006, acrylic on linen, 96 x 96 in.

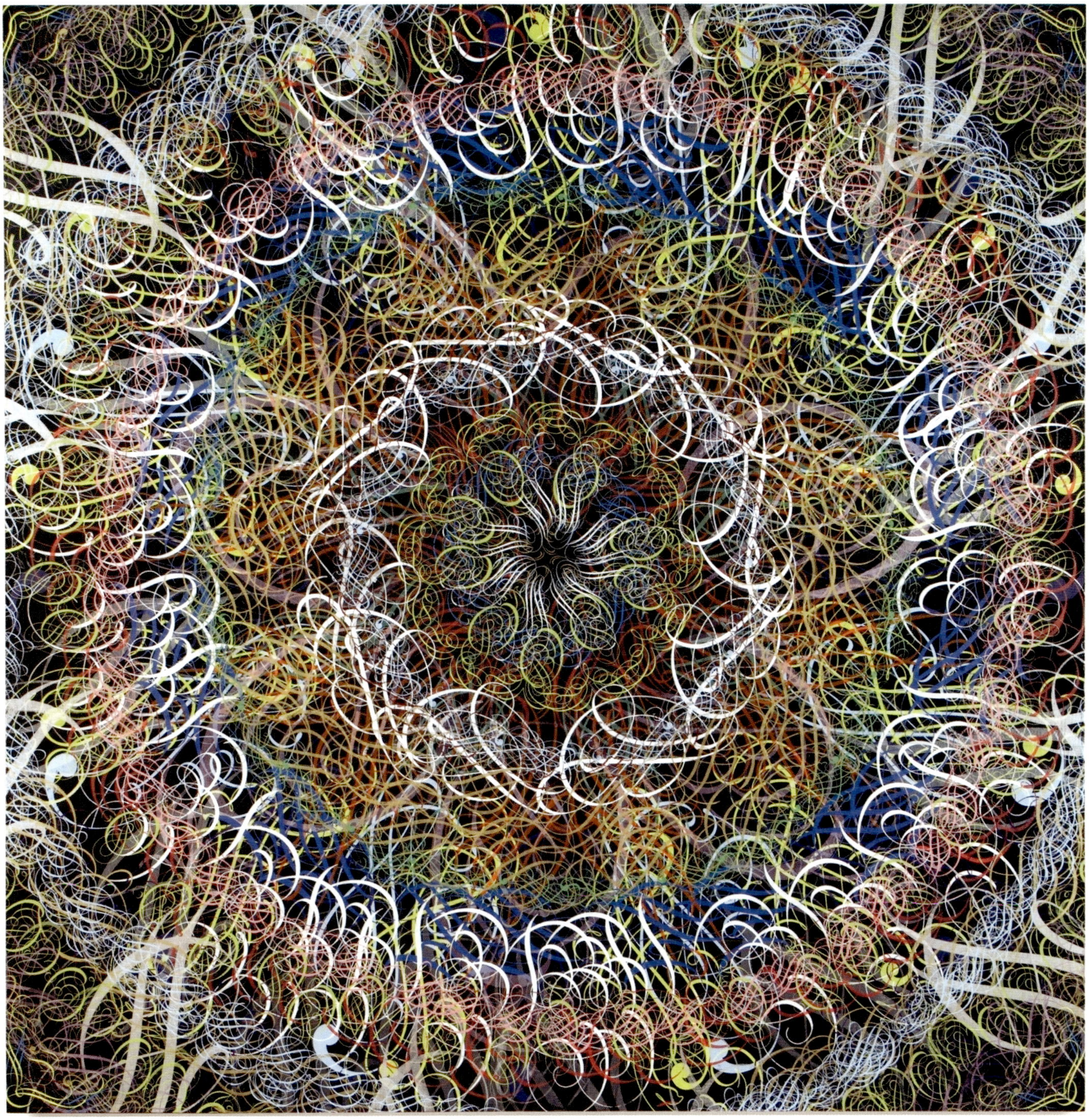

Untitled (Black Hole, Blue)
2007, acrylic on wood panel, 48 in. diameter.

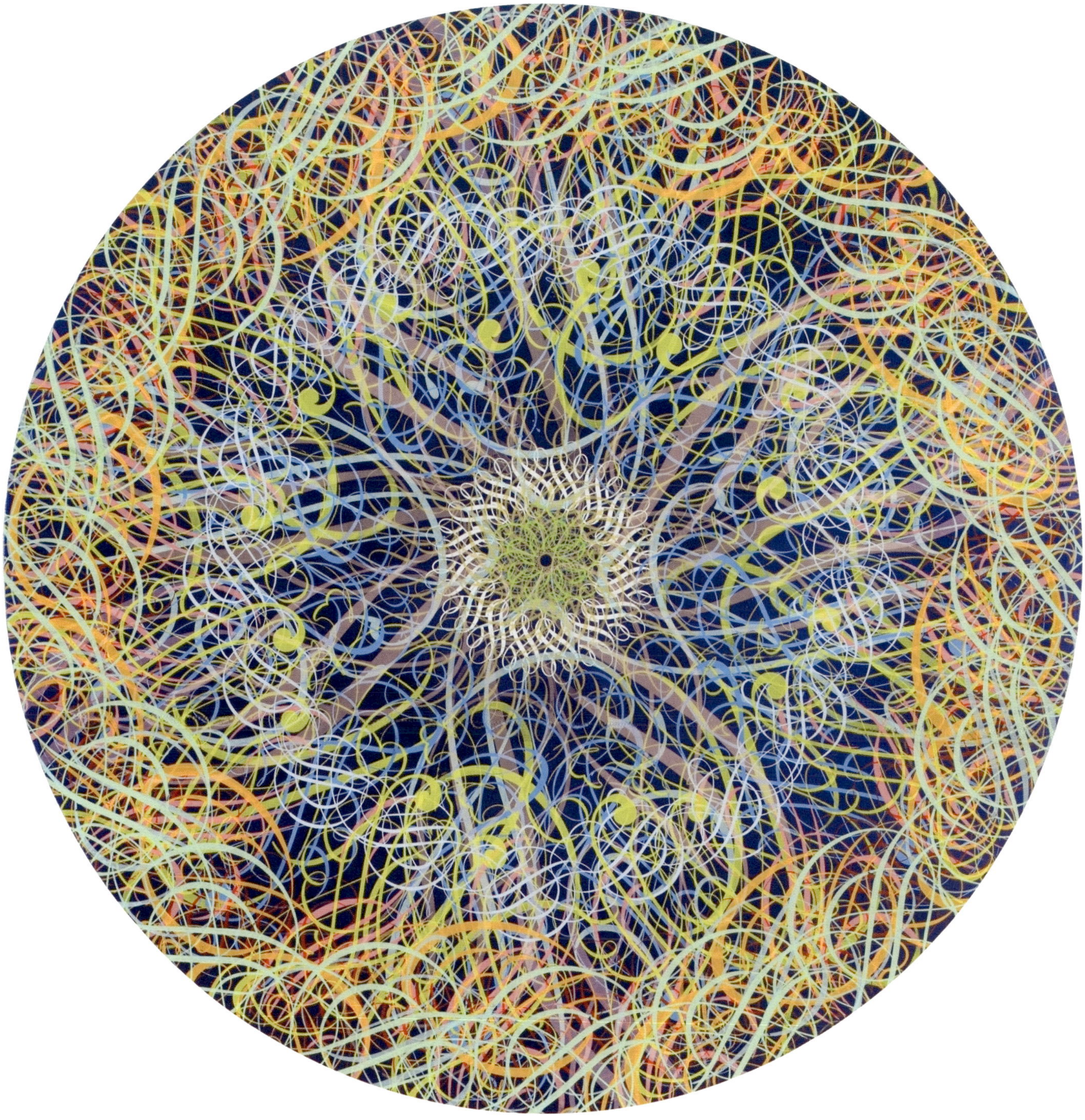

Untitled (Black Hole, Black)
2007, acrylic on canvas, 72 in. diameter.

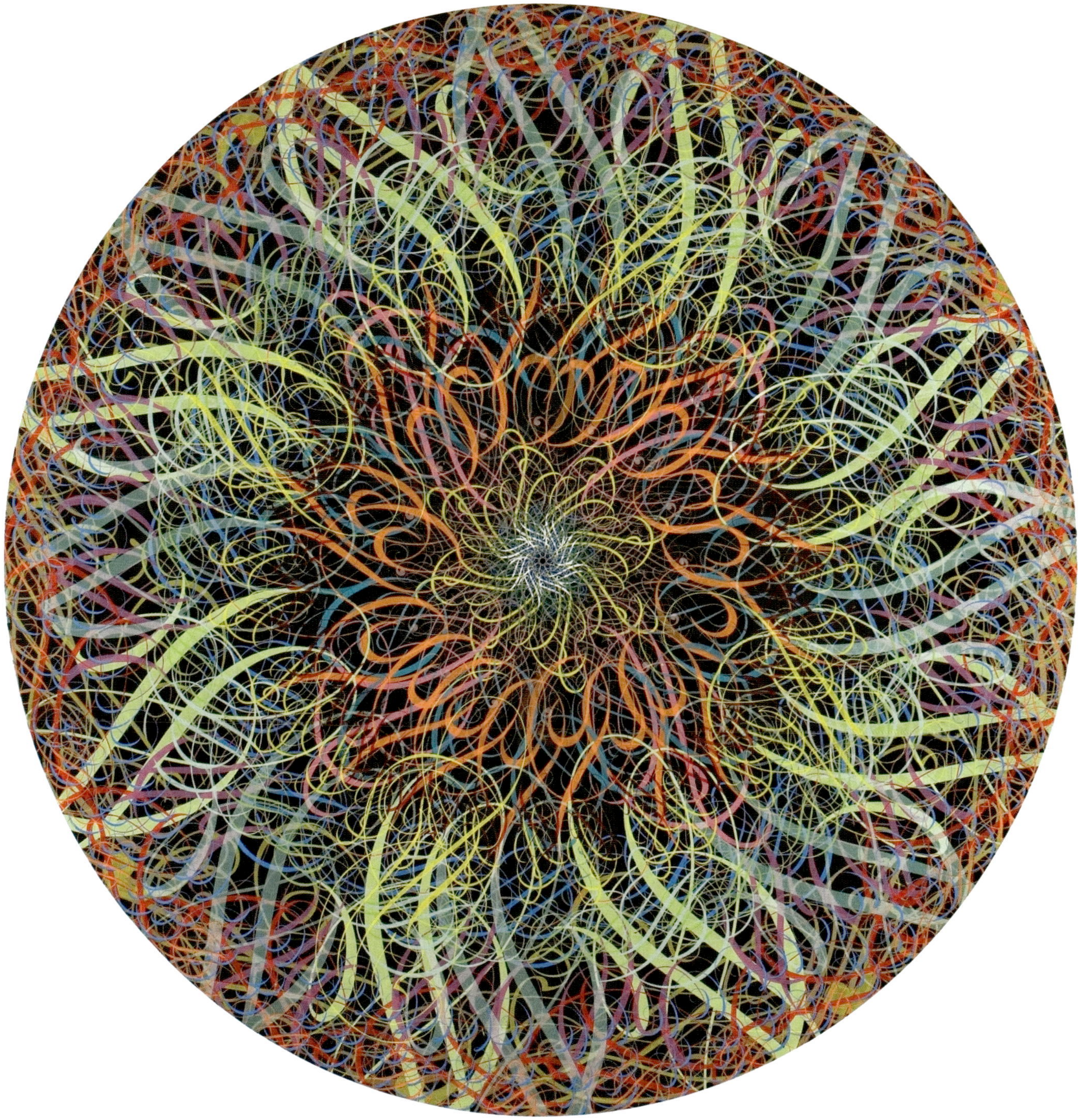

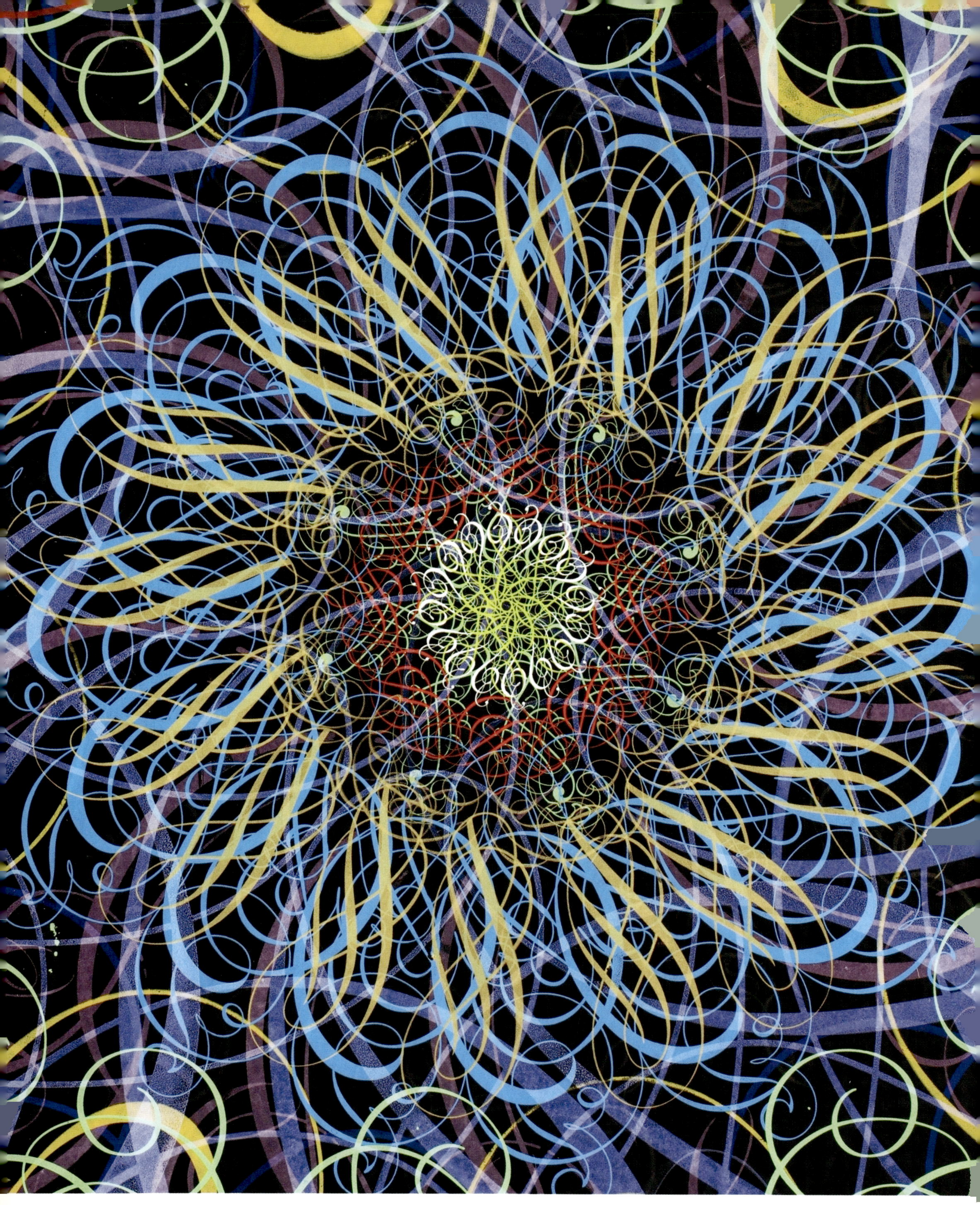

Untitled (Black Hole, Black)
2008, acrylic on canvas, 72 in. diameter.
(detail above)

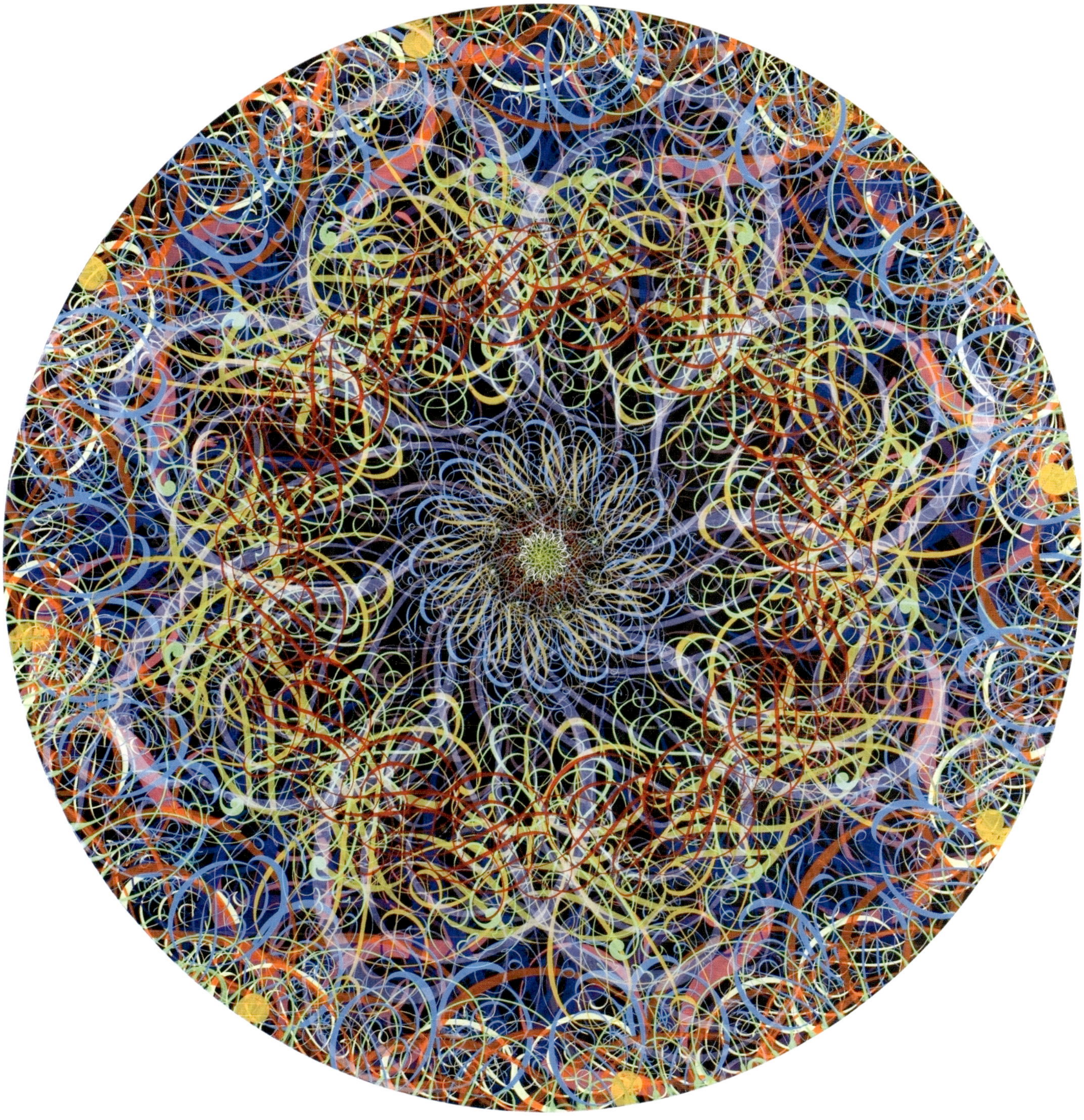

Untitled (Black Hole, White)
2008, acrylic on canvas, 72 in. diameter.

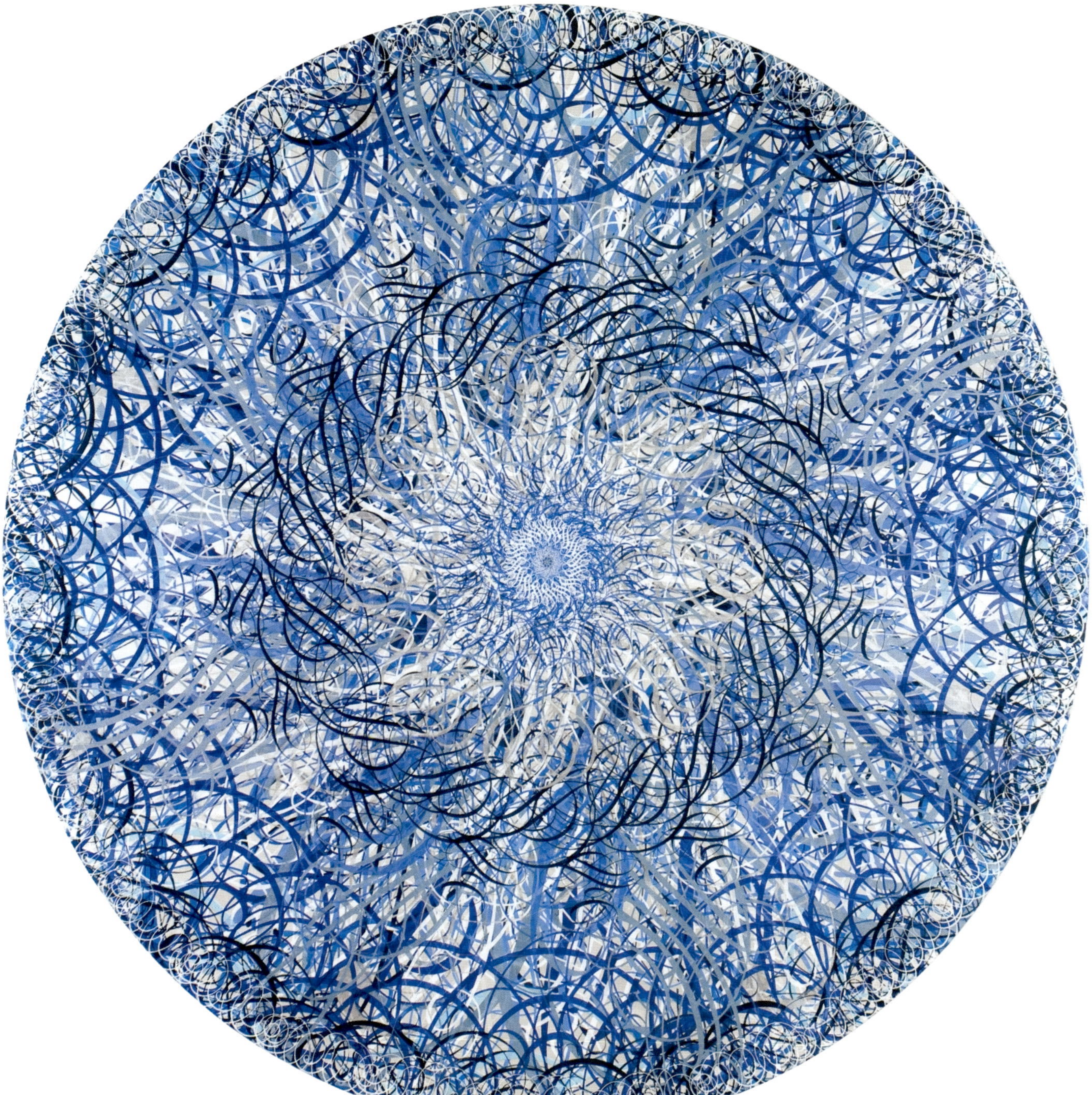

Untitled (Black Hole, Silver)
2006, acrylic on wood panel, 48 in. diameter.

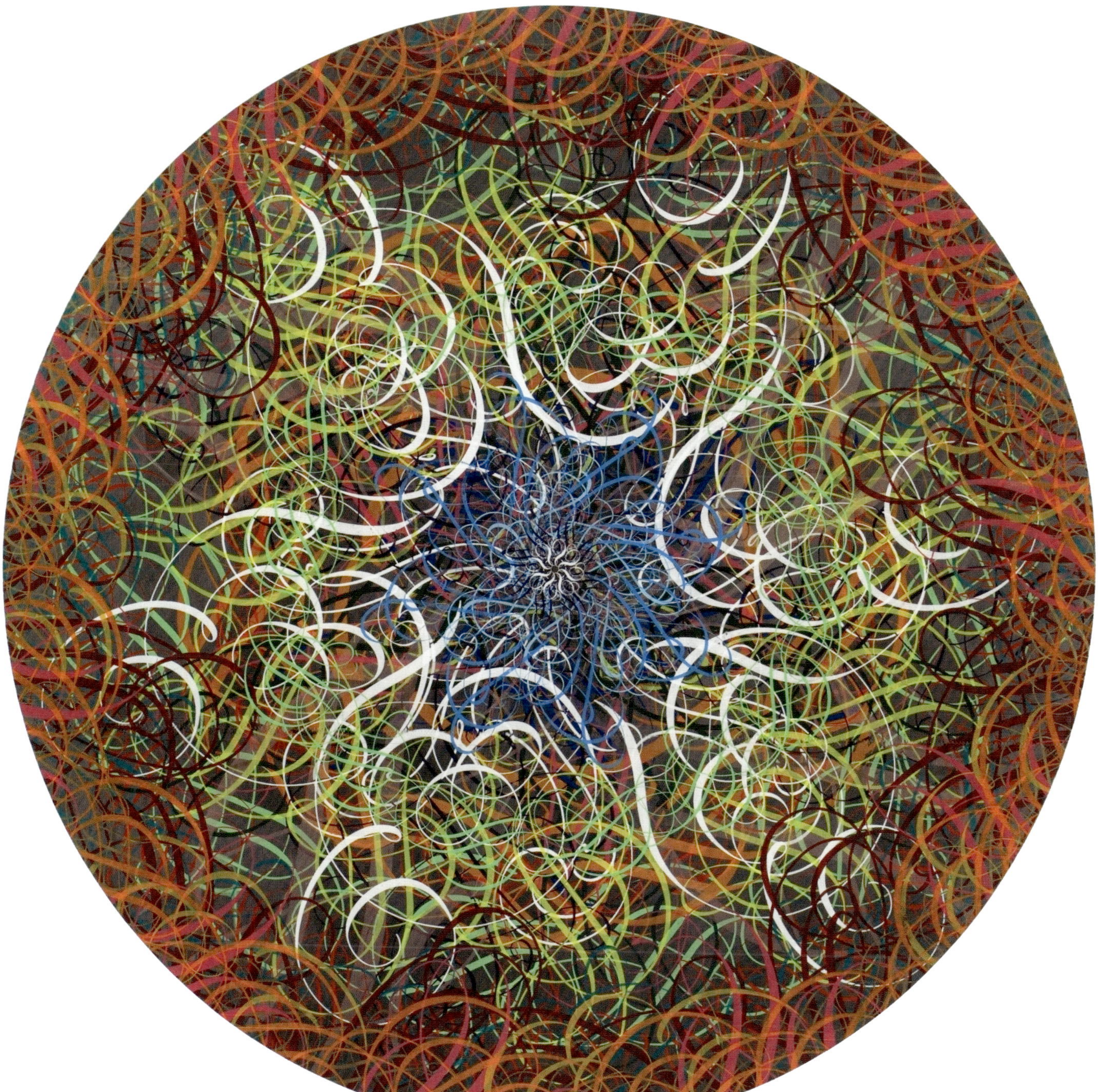

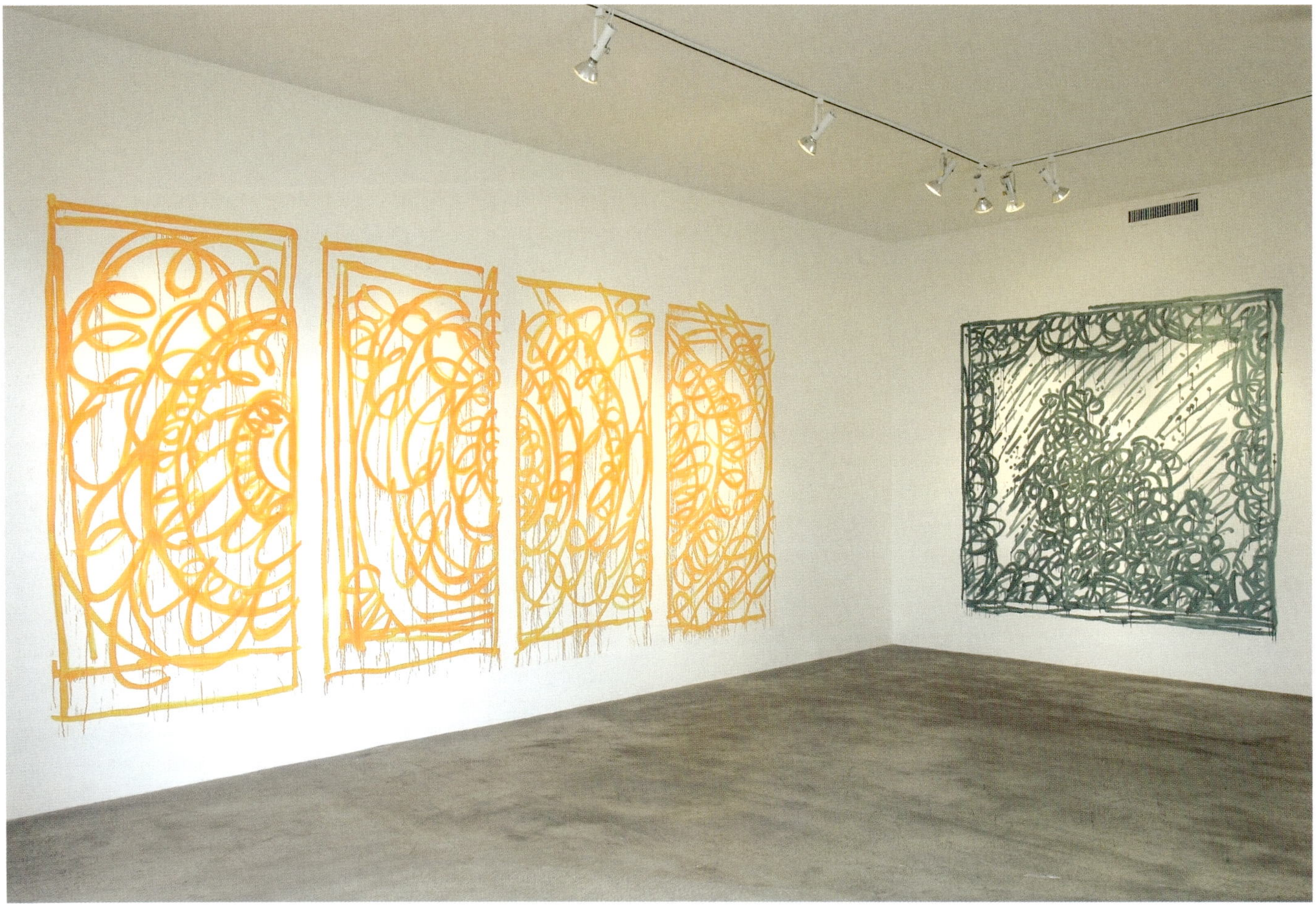

View of "A Rich Fantasy Life," 2007, Quint Contemporary Art, La Jolla. A secret exhibition of enlarged thumbnail sketches in acrylic on wall behind paintings.

Opposite page, from left: *Ab Ovo*, 2007, acrylic on canvas, 96 x 192 in., *The True Knowledge of Things*, 2007, acrylic on canvas, 96 x 96 in.

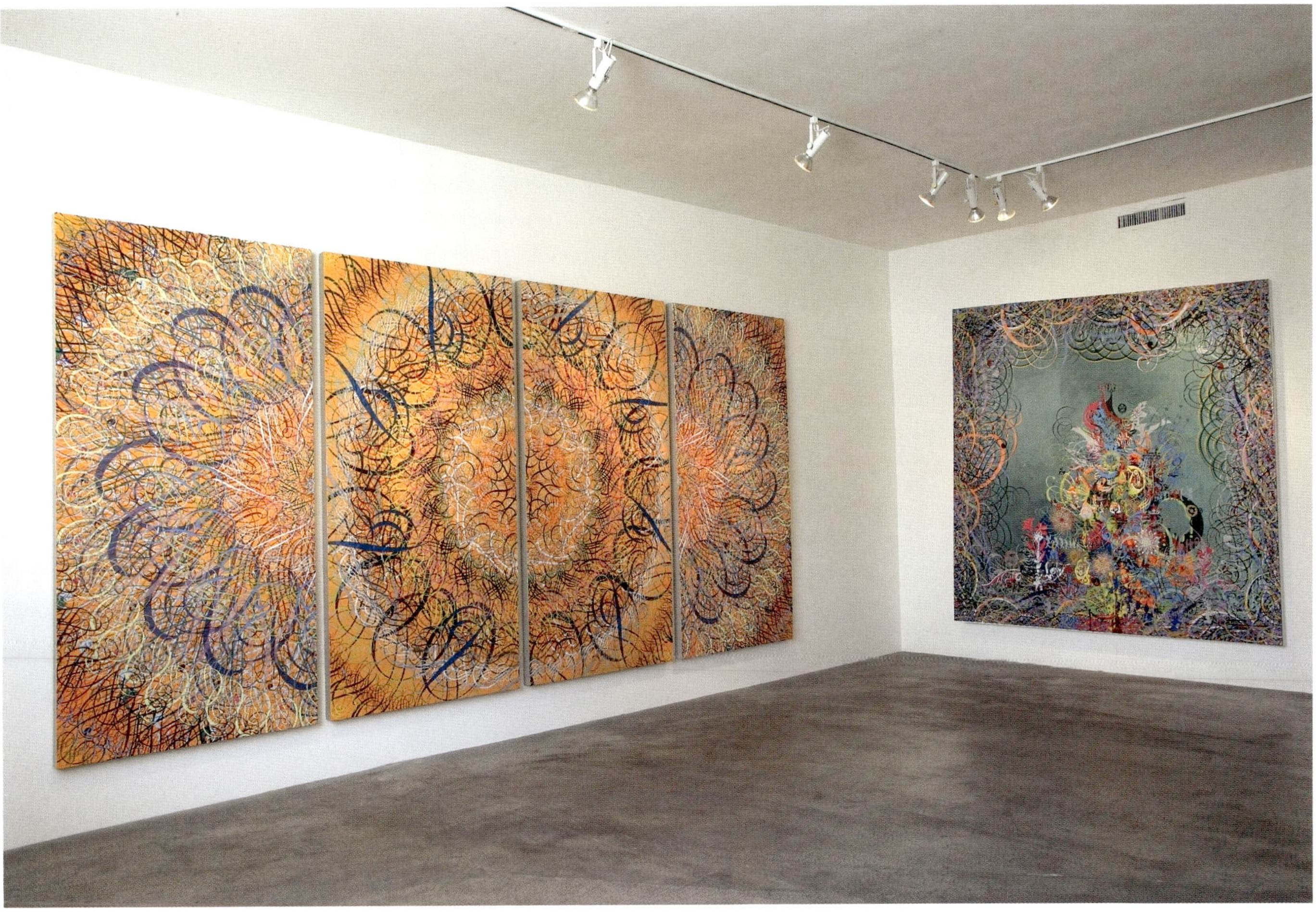

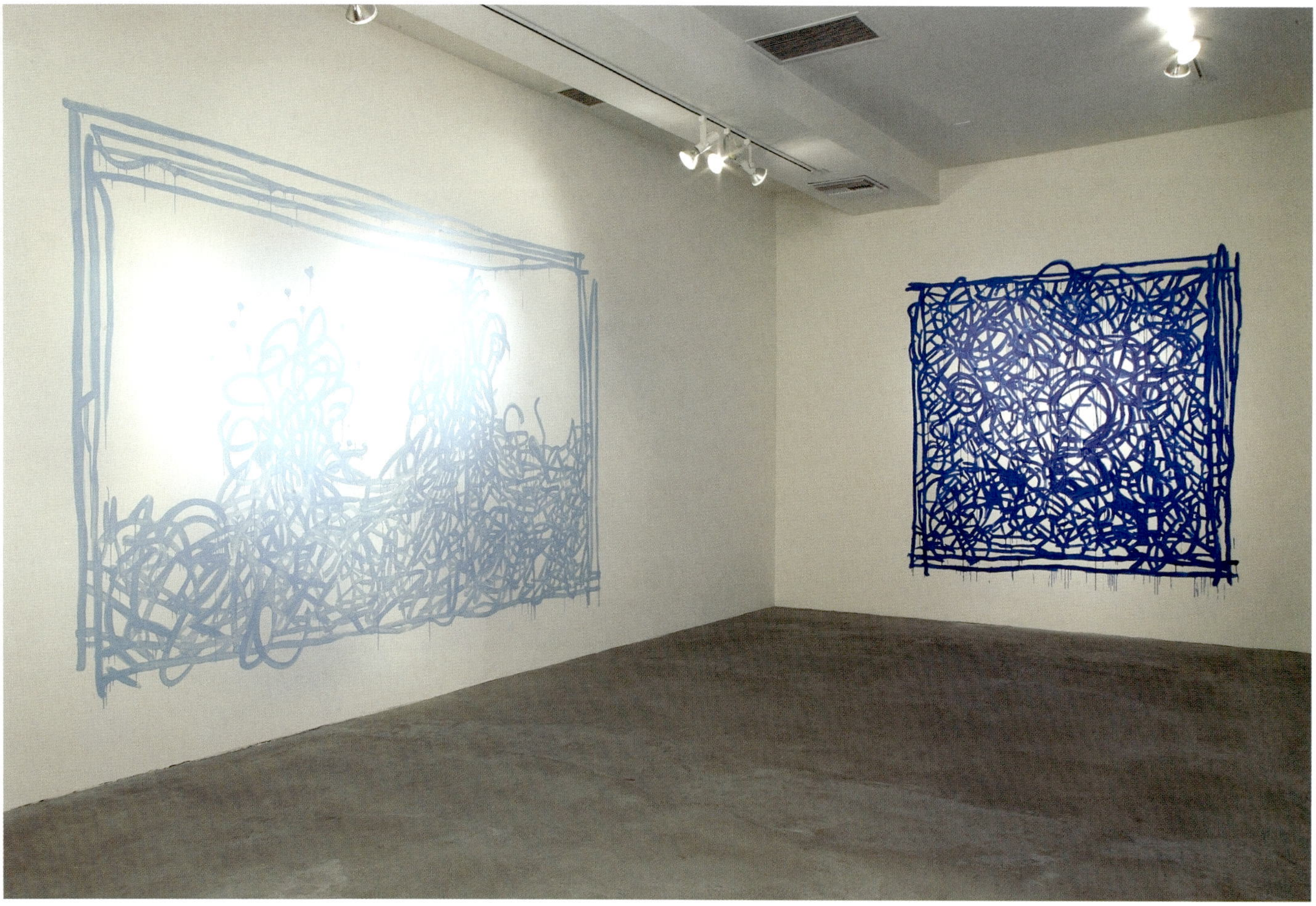

View of "A Rich Fantasy Life," 2007, Quint Contemporary Art, La Jolla. A secret exhibition of enlarged thumbnail sketches in acrylic on wall behind paintings.

Opposite page, from left: *A Dream Within a Dream*, 2007, acrylic on canvas, 96 x 144 in., *Moshi Moshi*, 2007, acrylic on canvas, 96 x 96 in.

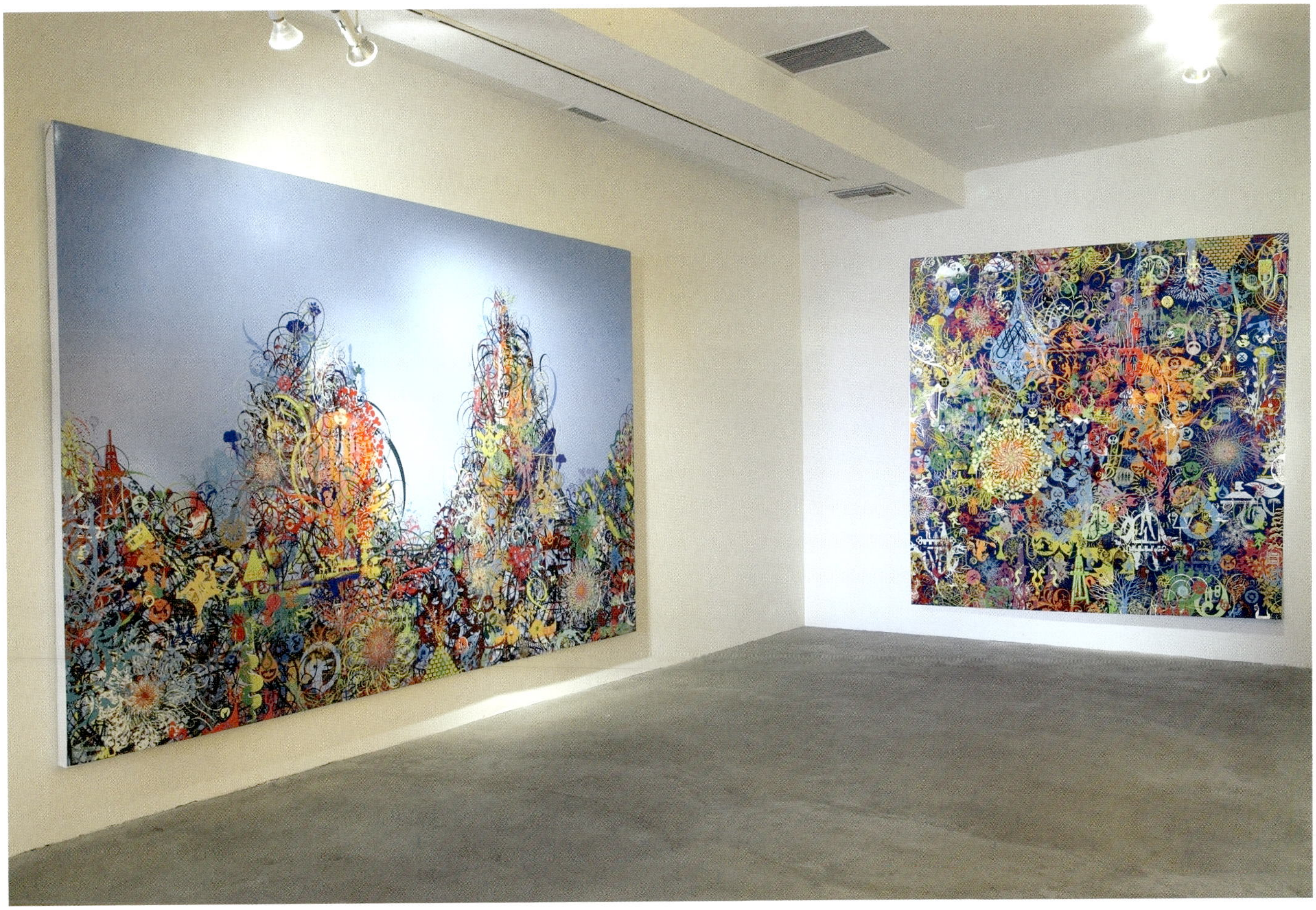

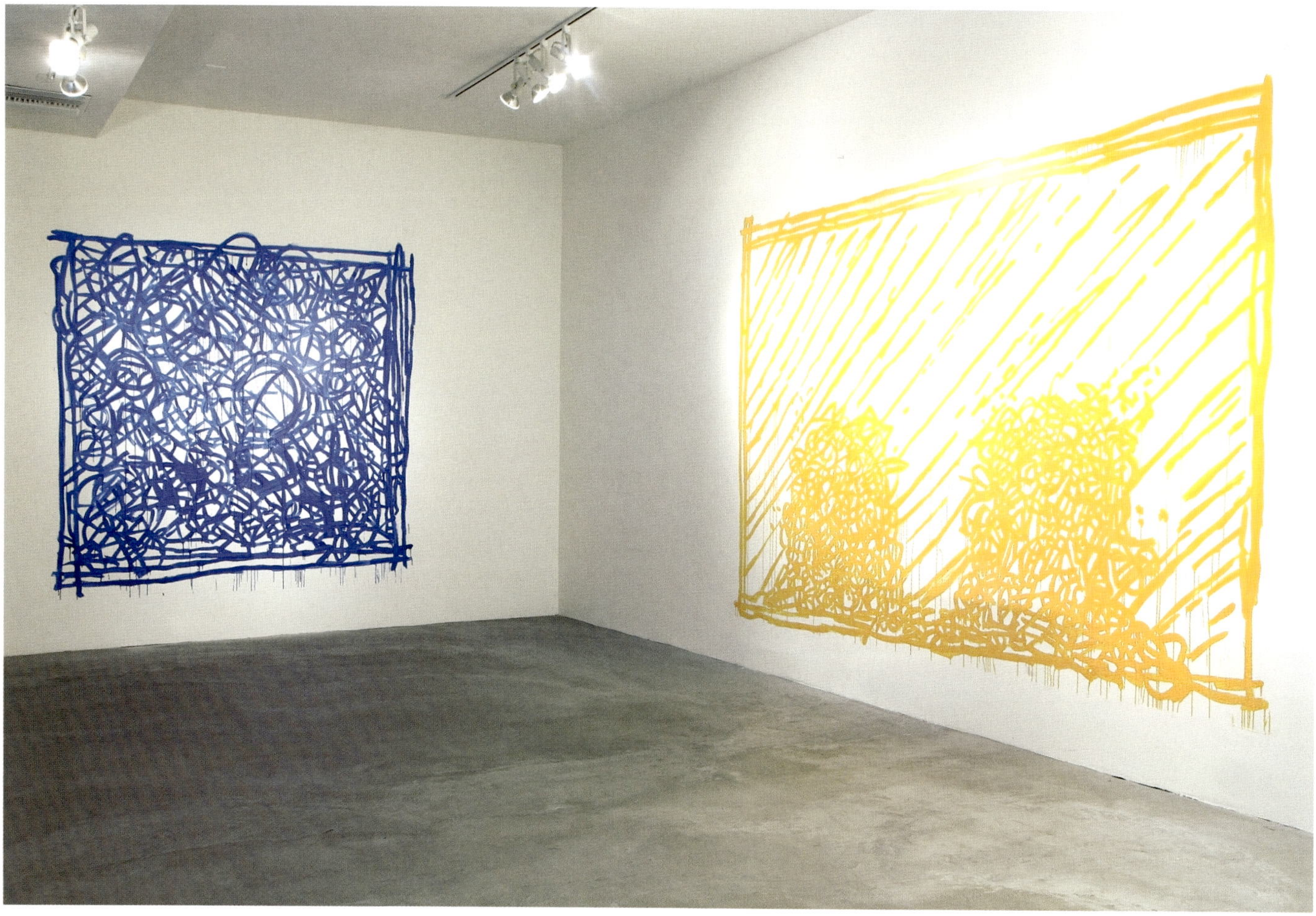

View of "A Rich Fantasy Life," 2007, Quint Contemporary Art, La Jolla. A secret exhibition of enlarged thumbnail sketches in acrylic on wall behind paintings.

Opposite page, from left: *Moshi Moshi*, 2007, acrylic on canvas, 96 x 96 in., *False Negative*, 2007, acrylic on canvas, 96 x 144 in.

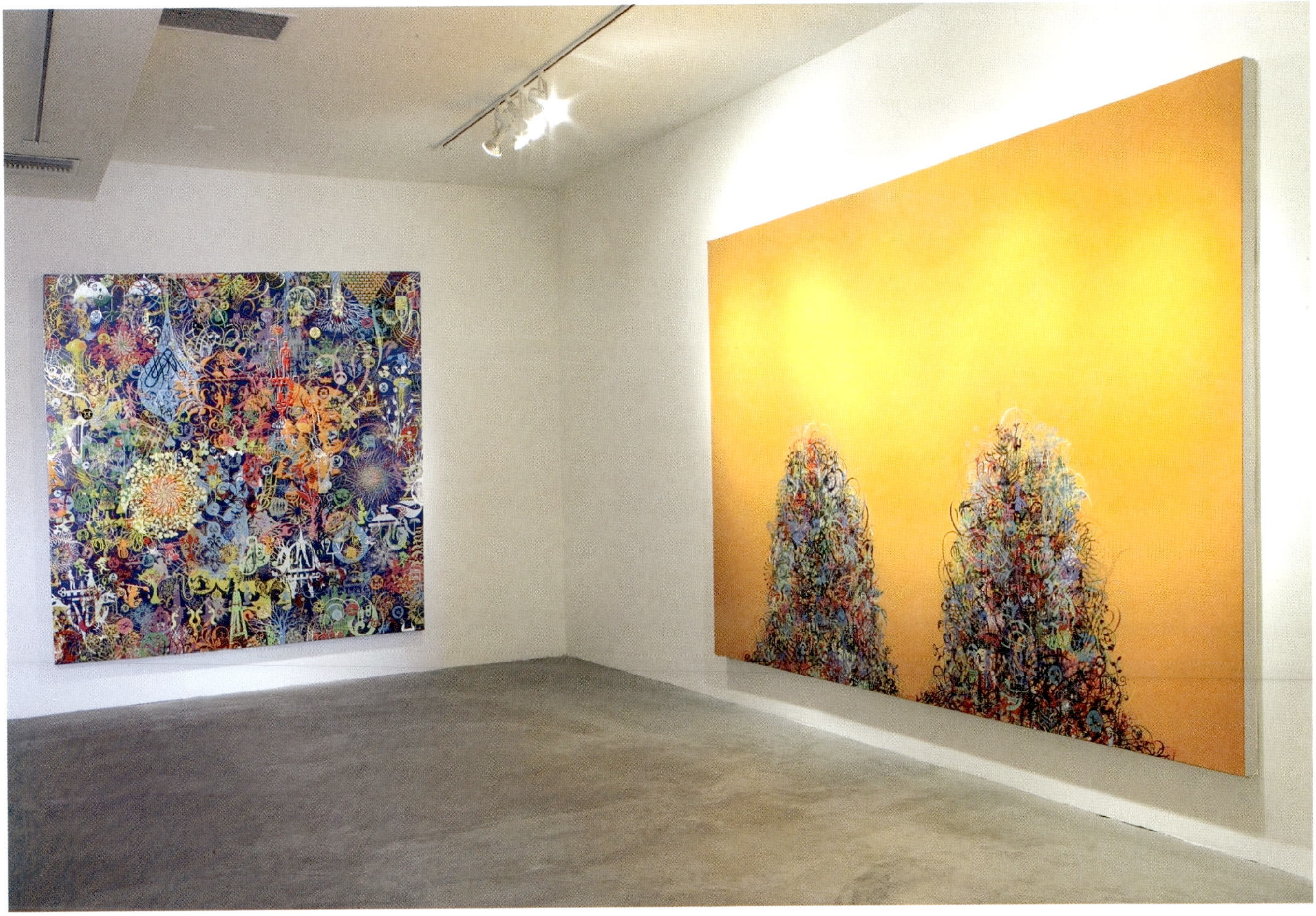

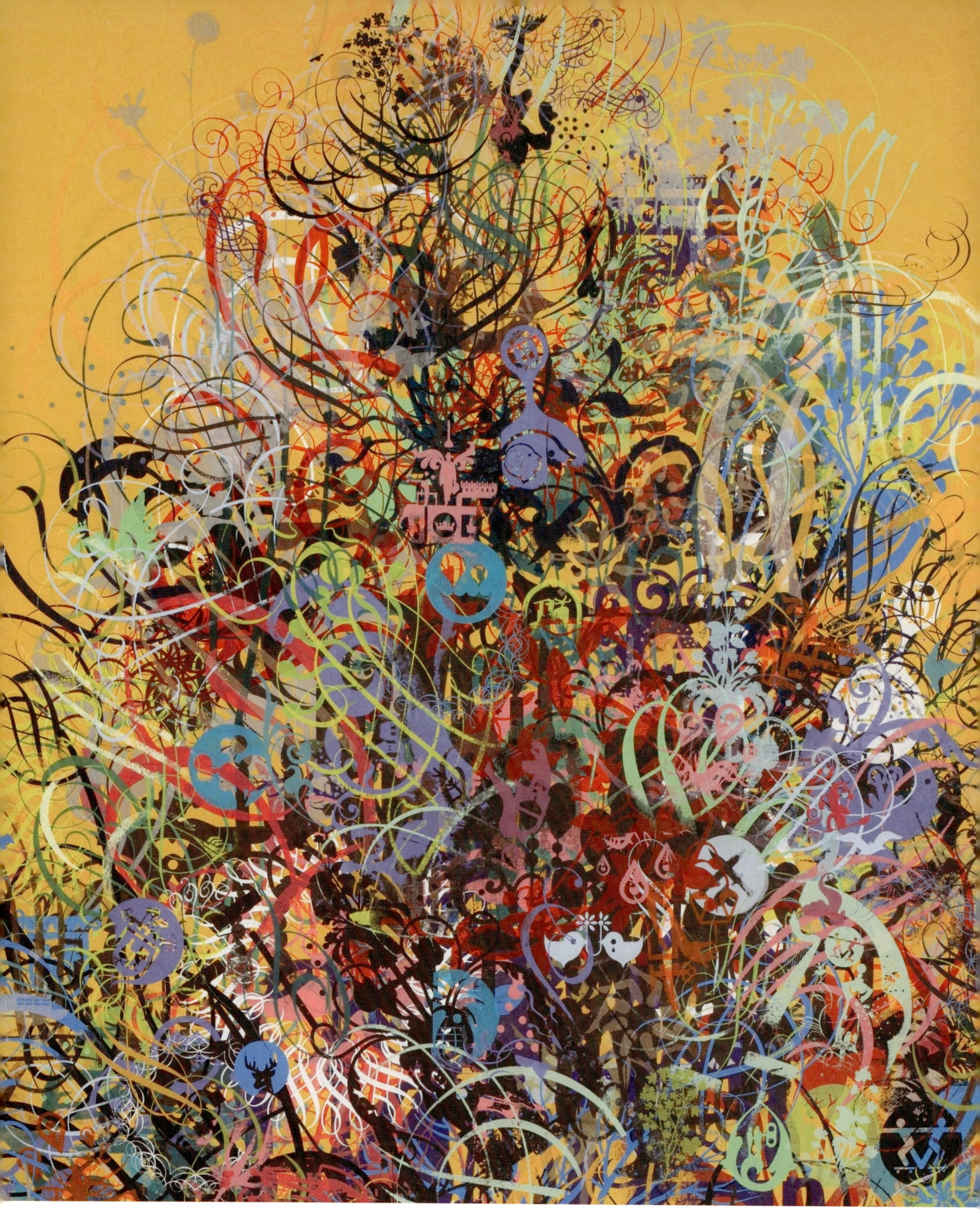

False Negative
2007, acrylic on canvas, 96 x 144 in.
(detail above)

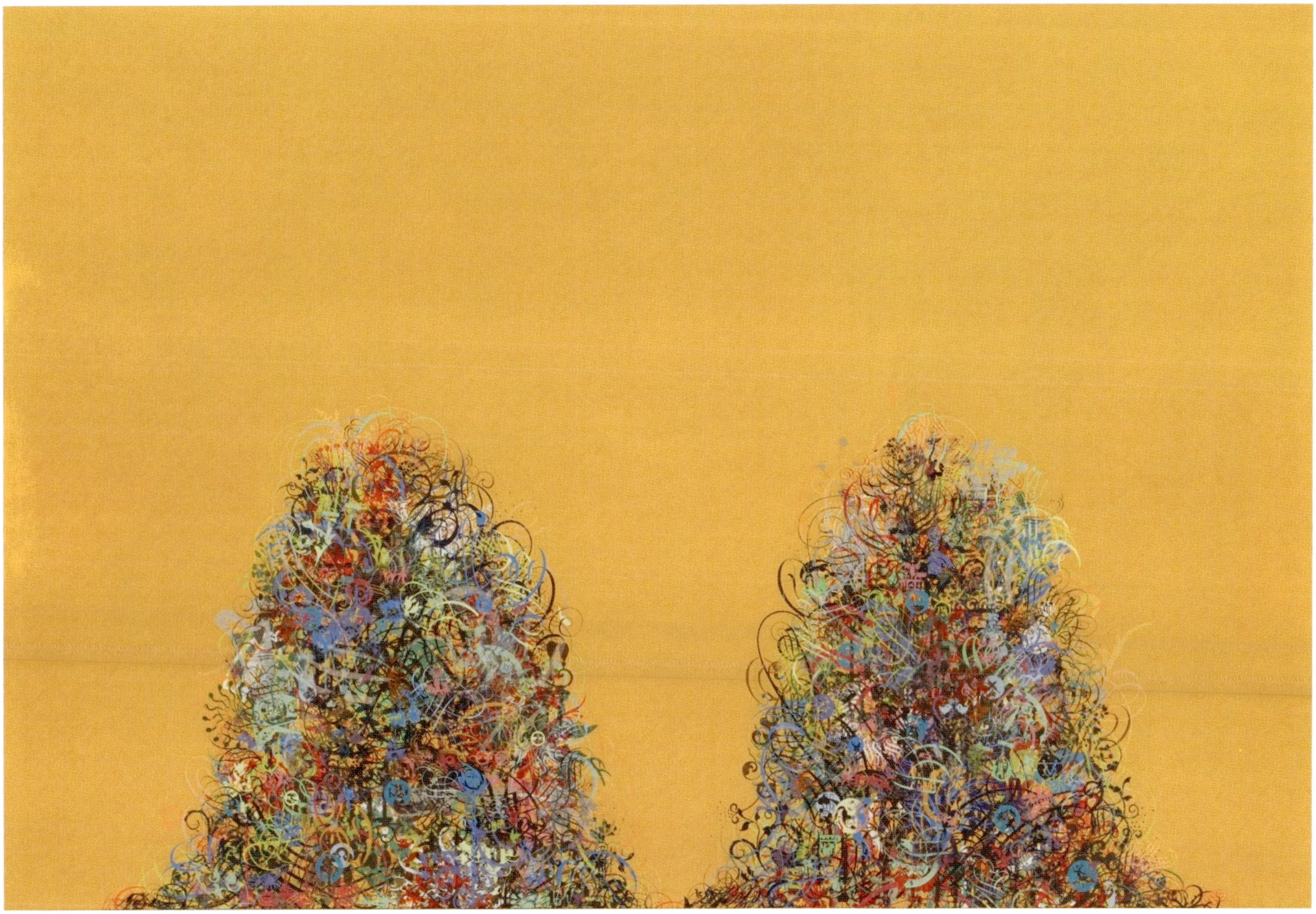

I.T.A.L.Y. (I'm Thinking About Loving You)
2006, acrylic on wood panel, 48 x 48 in.

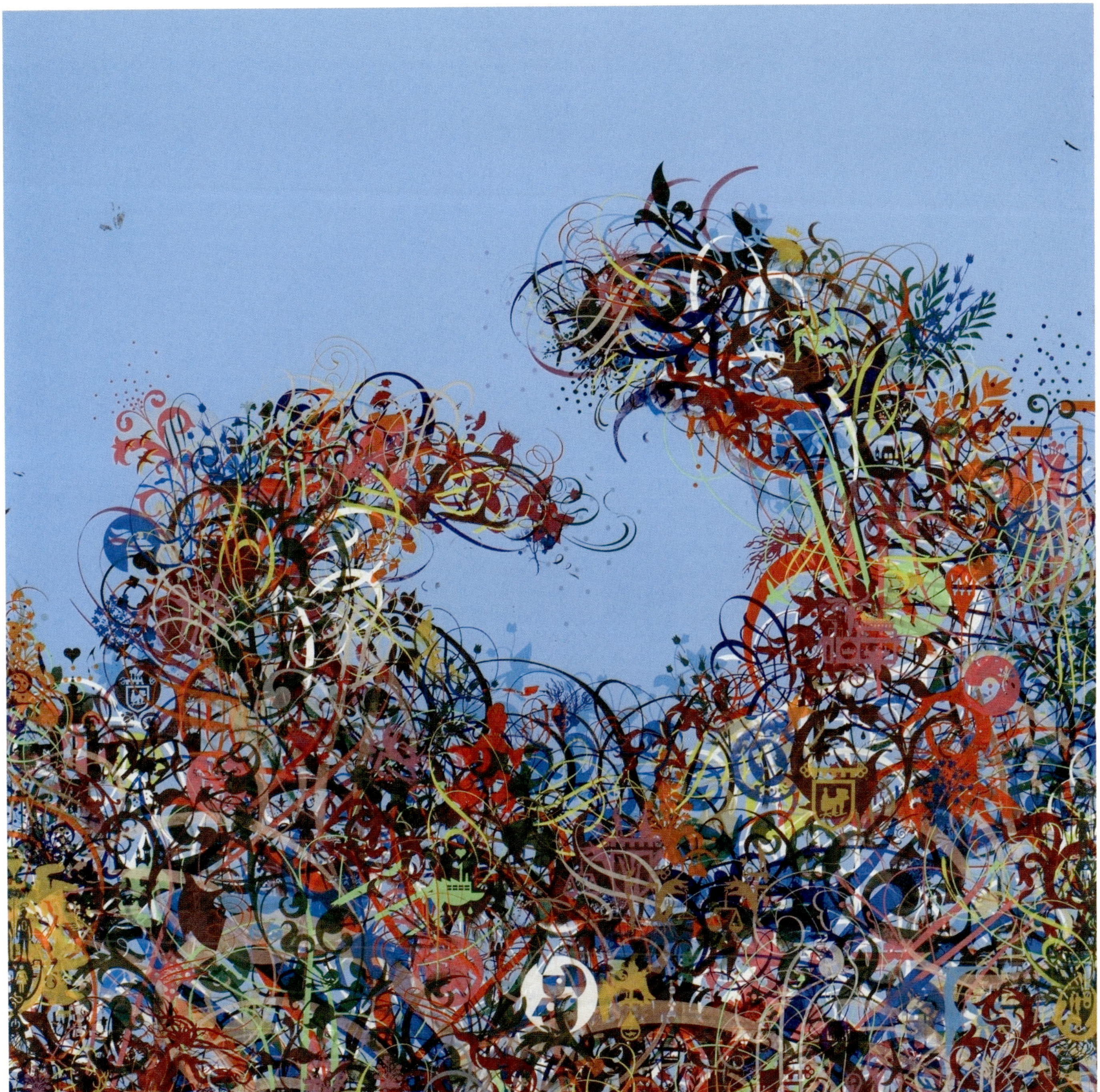

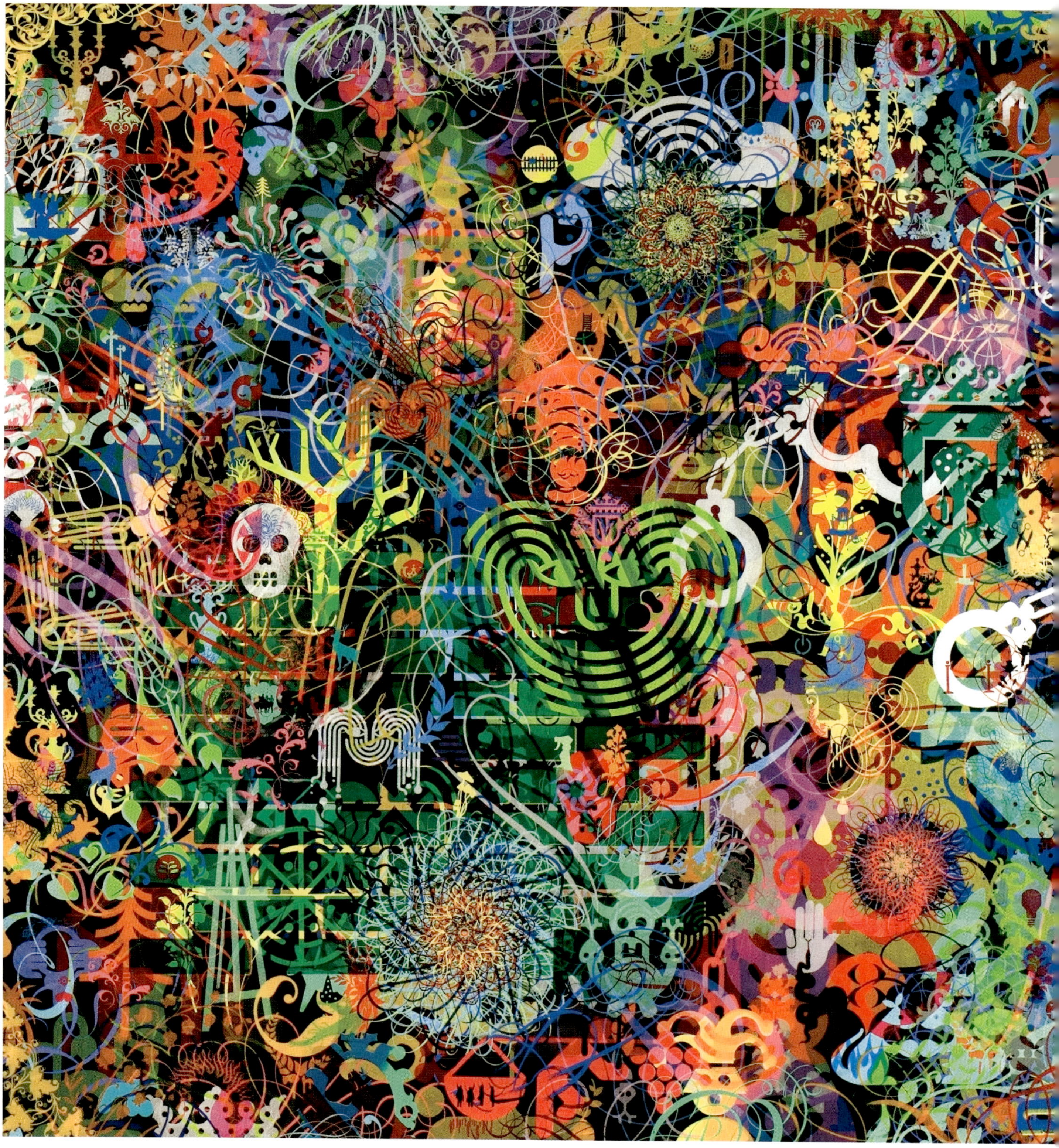

Capitalism vs. Socialism
2008, acrylic on canvas, diptych, 72 x 72 in. each, 72 x 144 in. total.
(details on following pages)

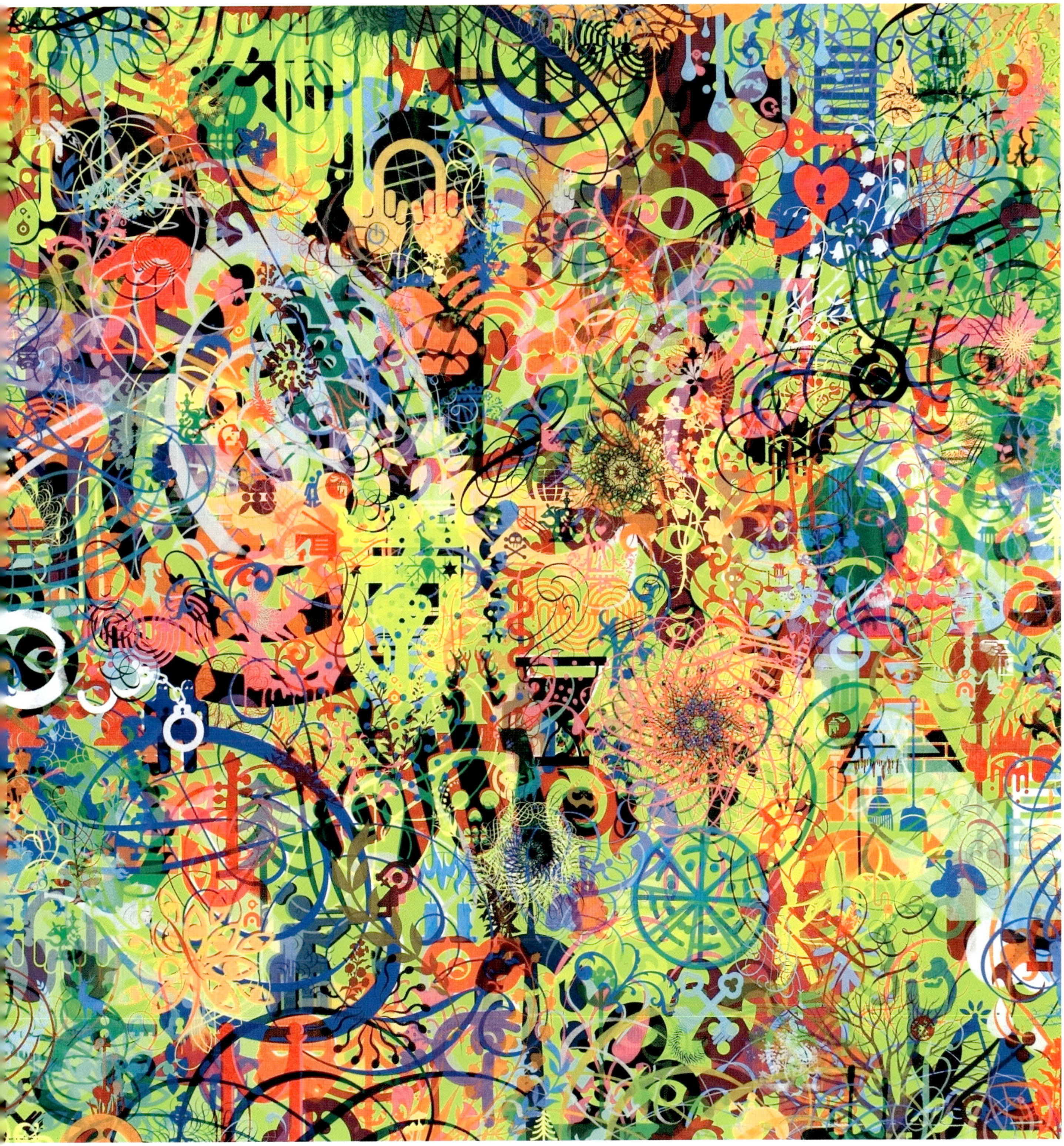

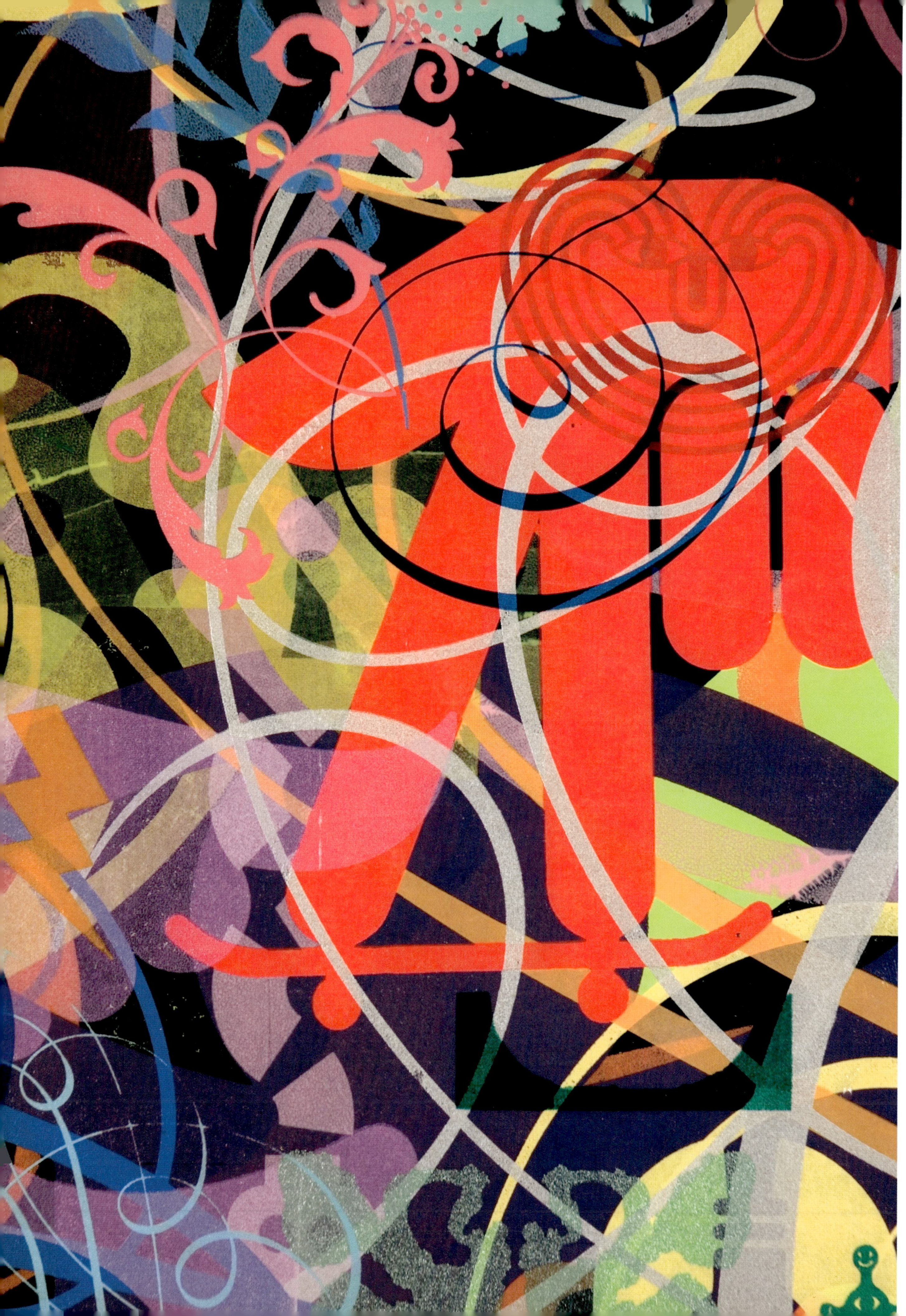

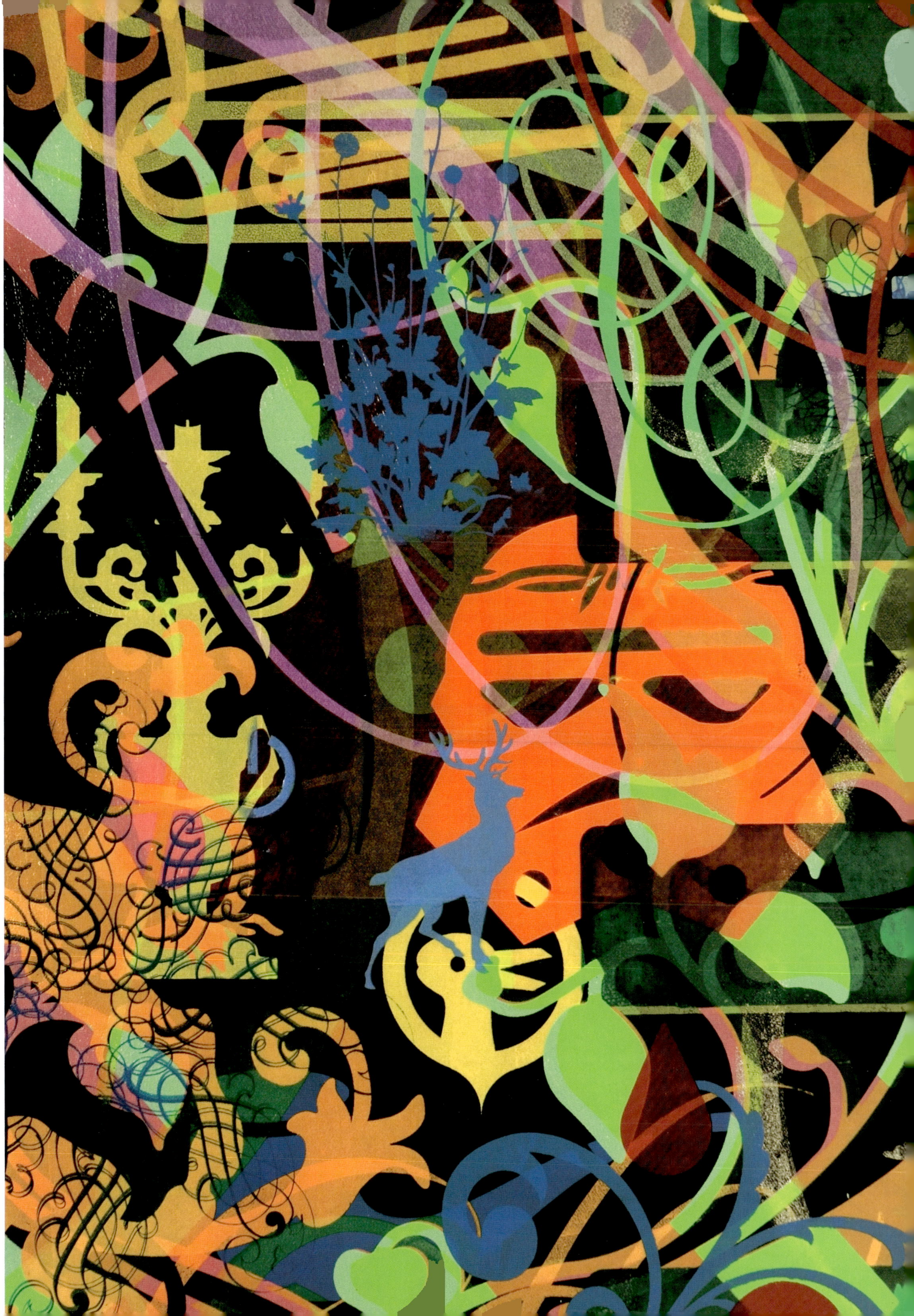

Power Struggle for the Rules of Reality
2006, acrylic on wood panel, 48 x 48 in.

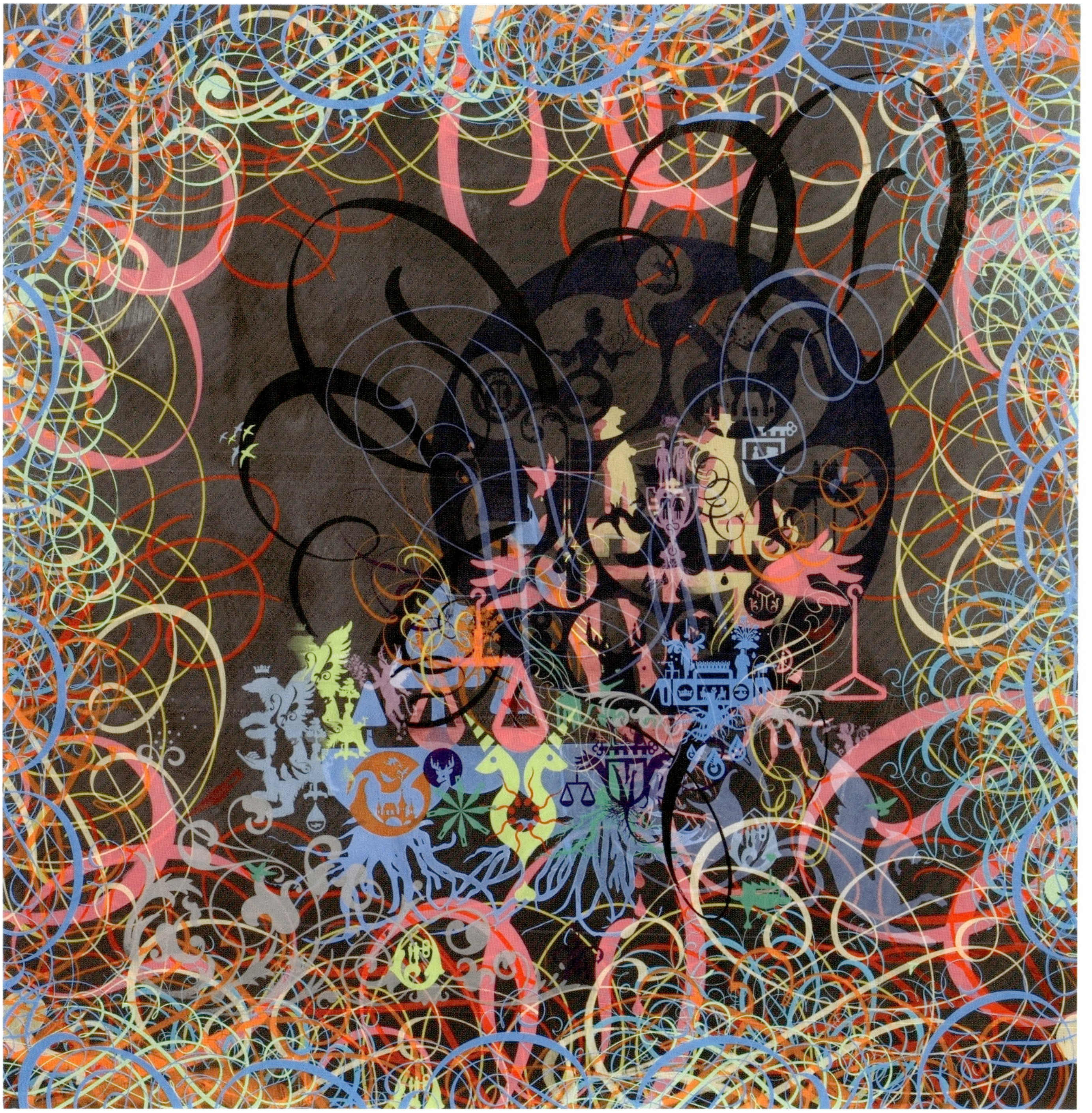

Pay As You Go
2006, acrylic on wood panel, 48 x 48 in.

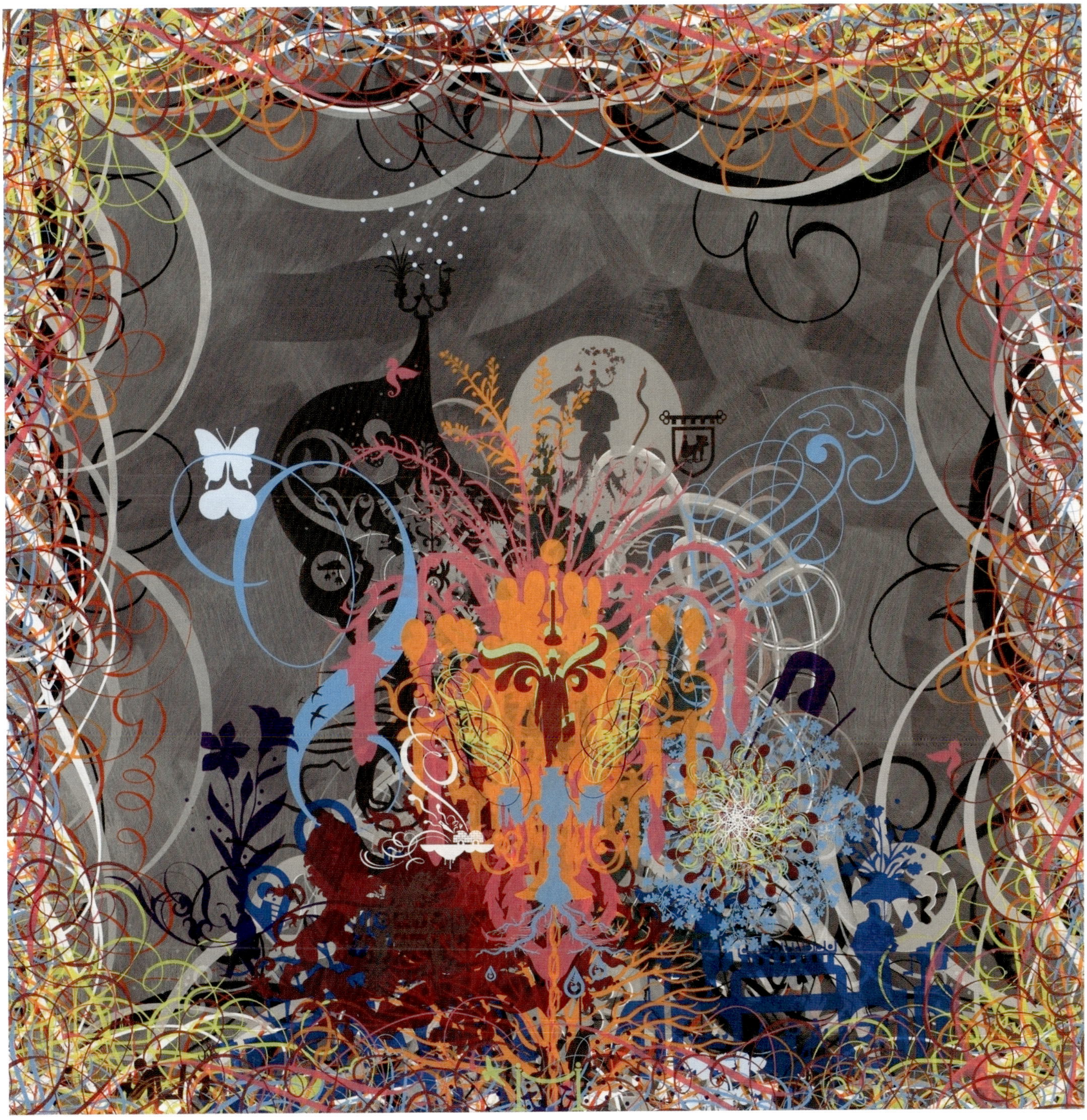

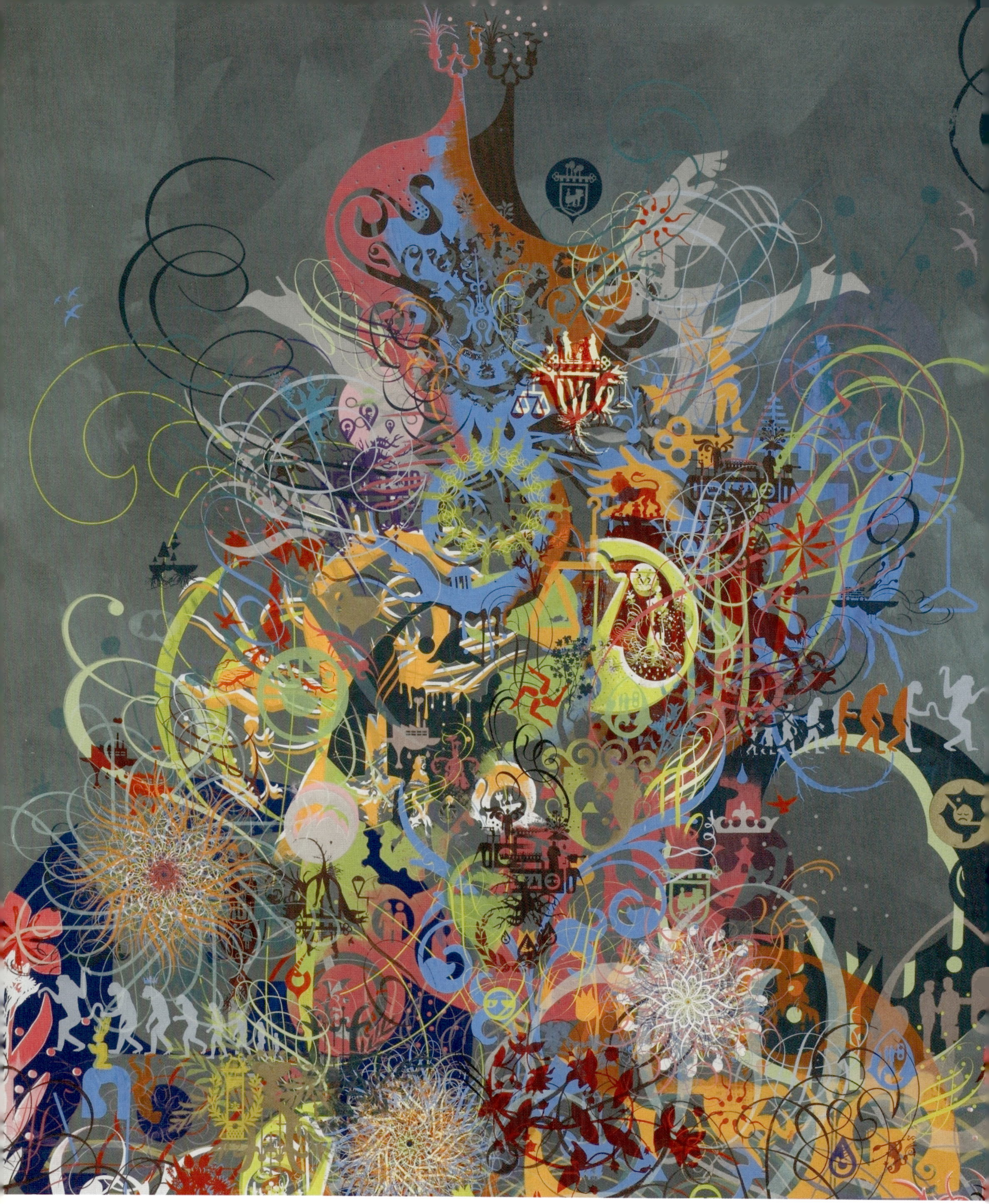

The True Knowledge of Things
2007, acrylic on canvas, 96 x 96 in.
(detail above)

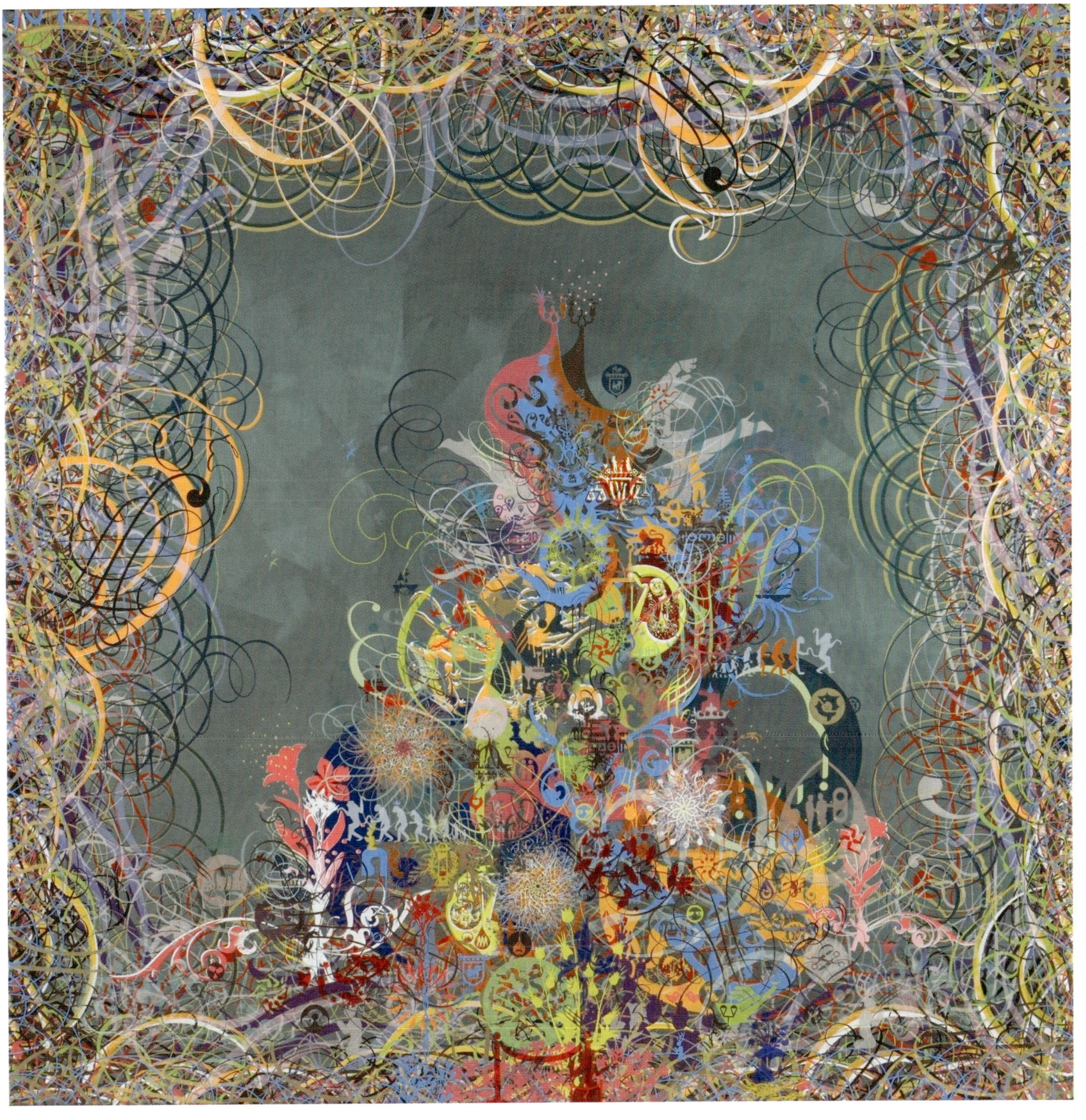

The Ownership Addiction
2006, acrylic on wood panel, 48 x 48 in.

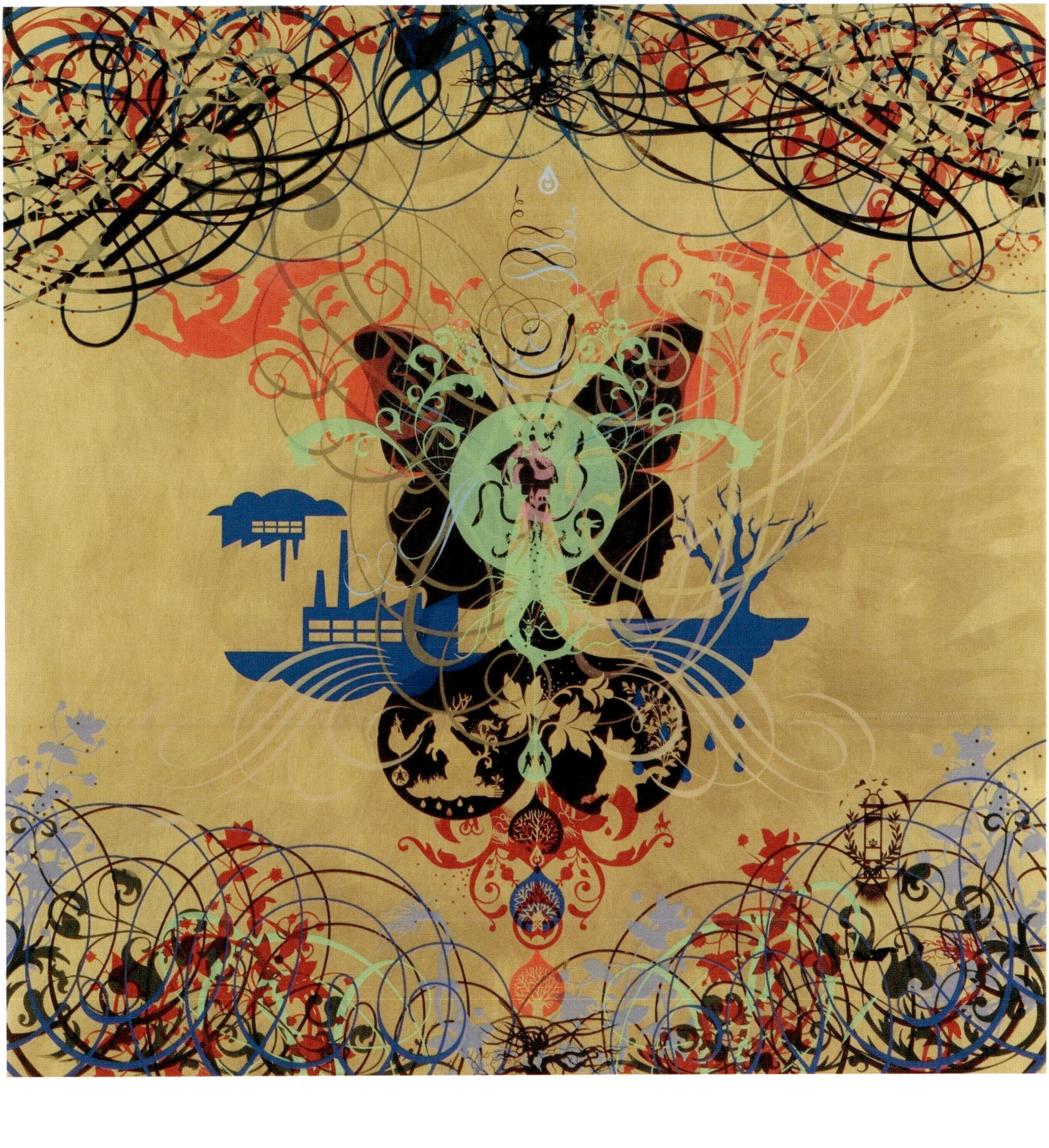

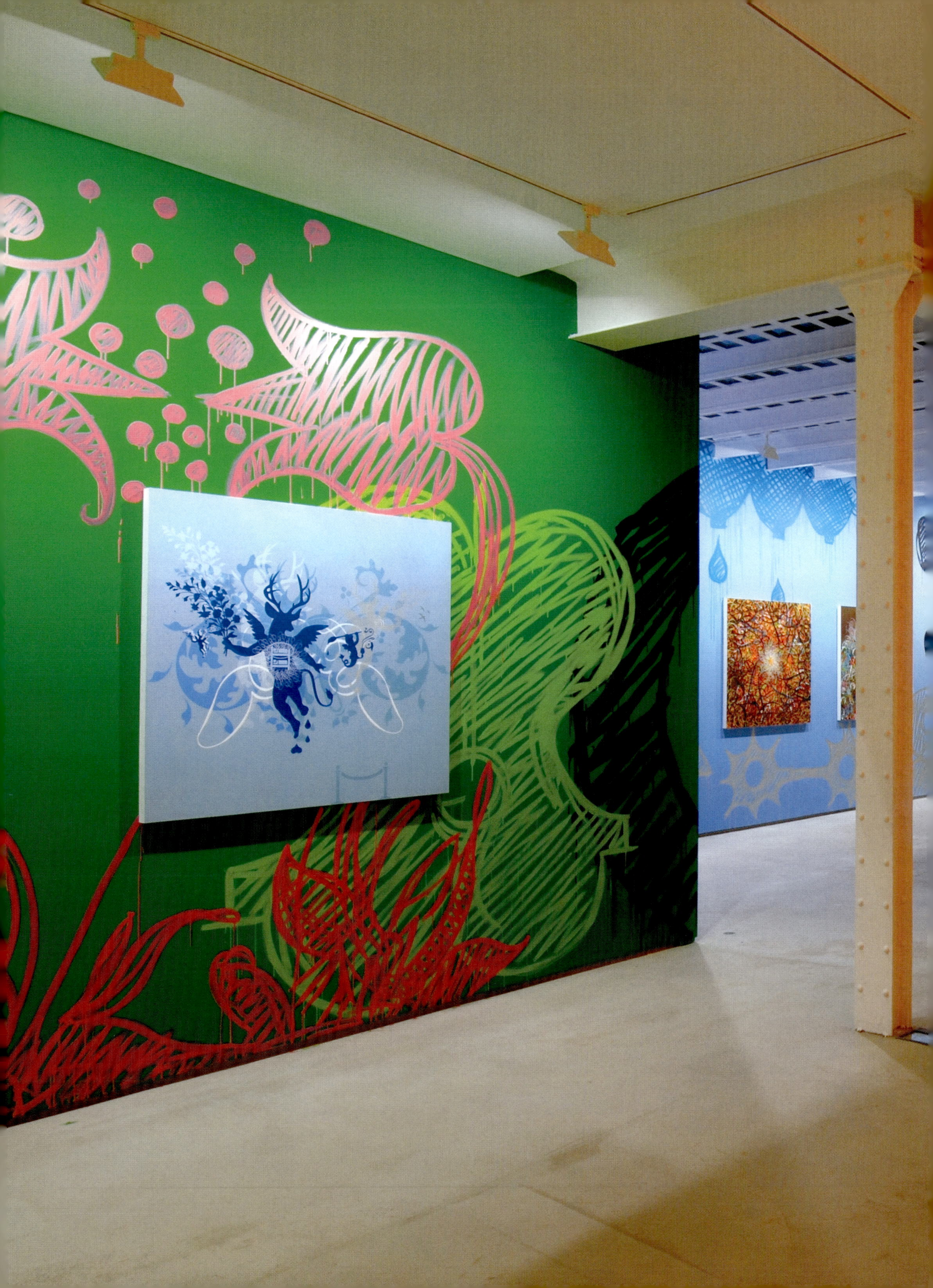

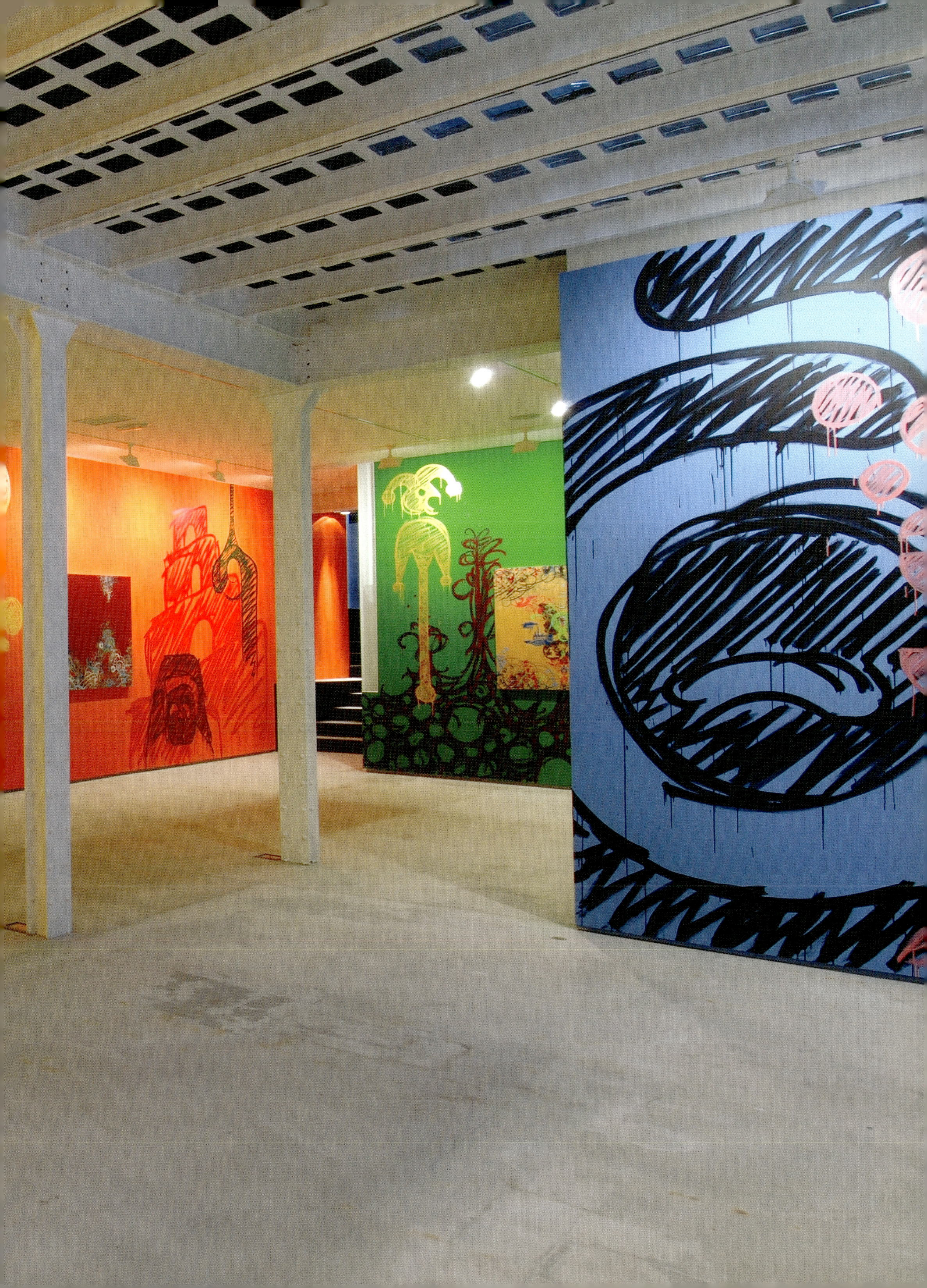

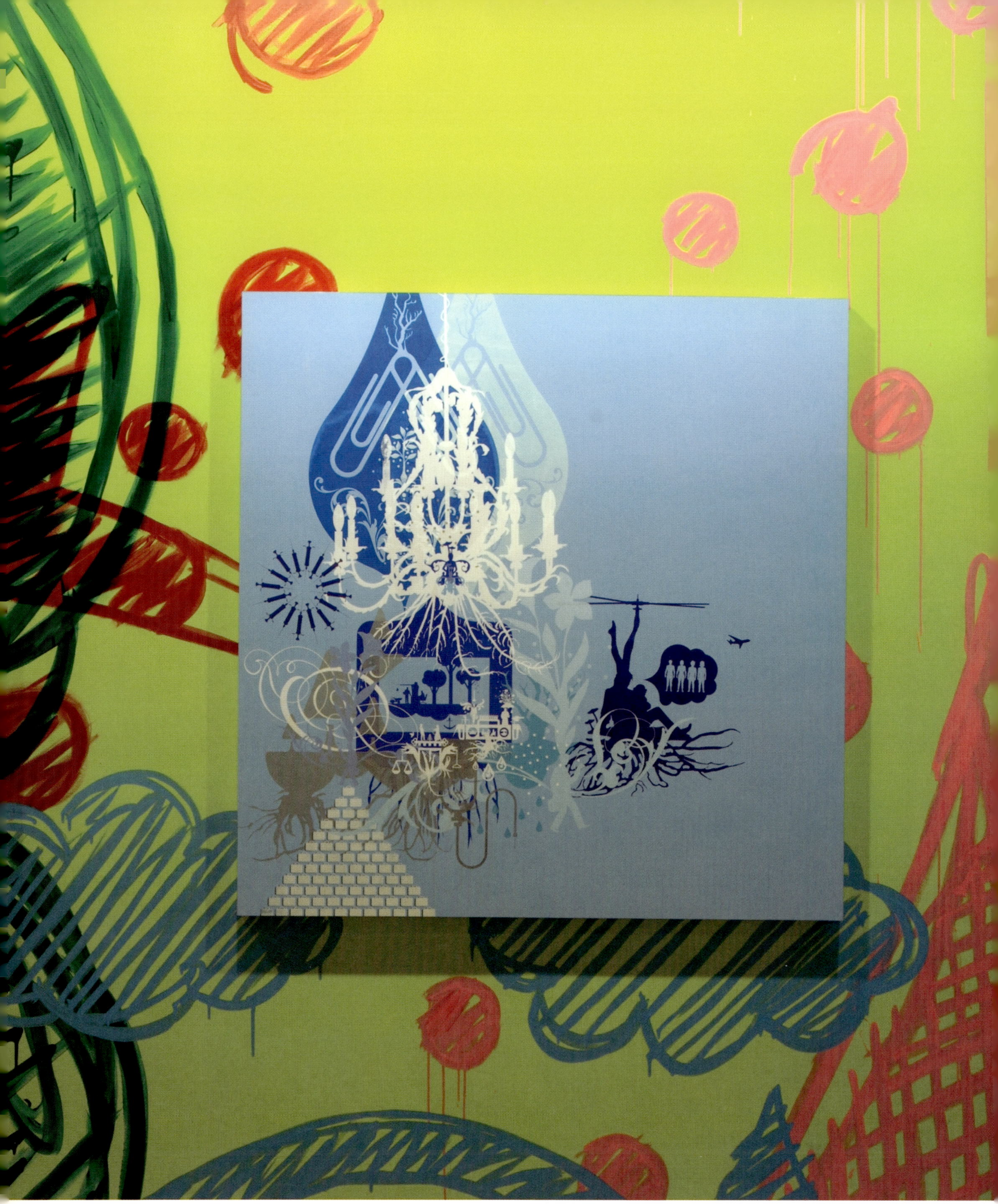

Overleaf, above, opposite page: Views of “Neveroddoreven”
2006, acrylic on wood panels (48 x 48 in.) with acrylic on wall,
Galerie Moriarty, Madrid.

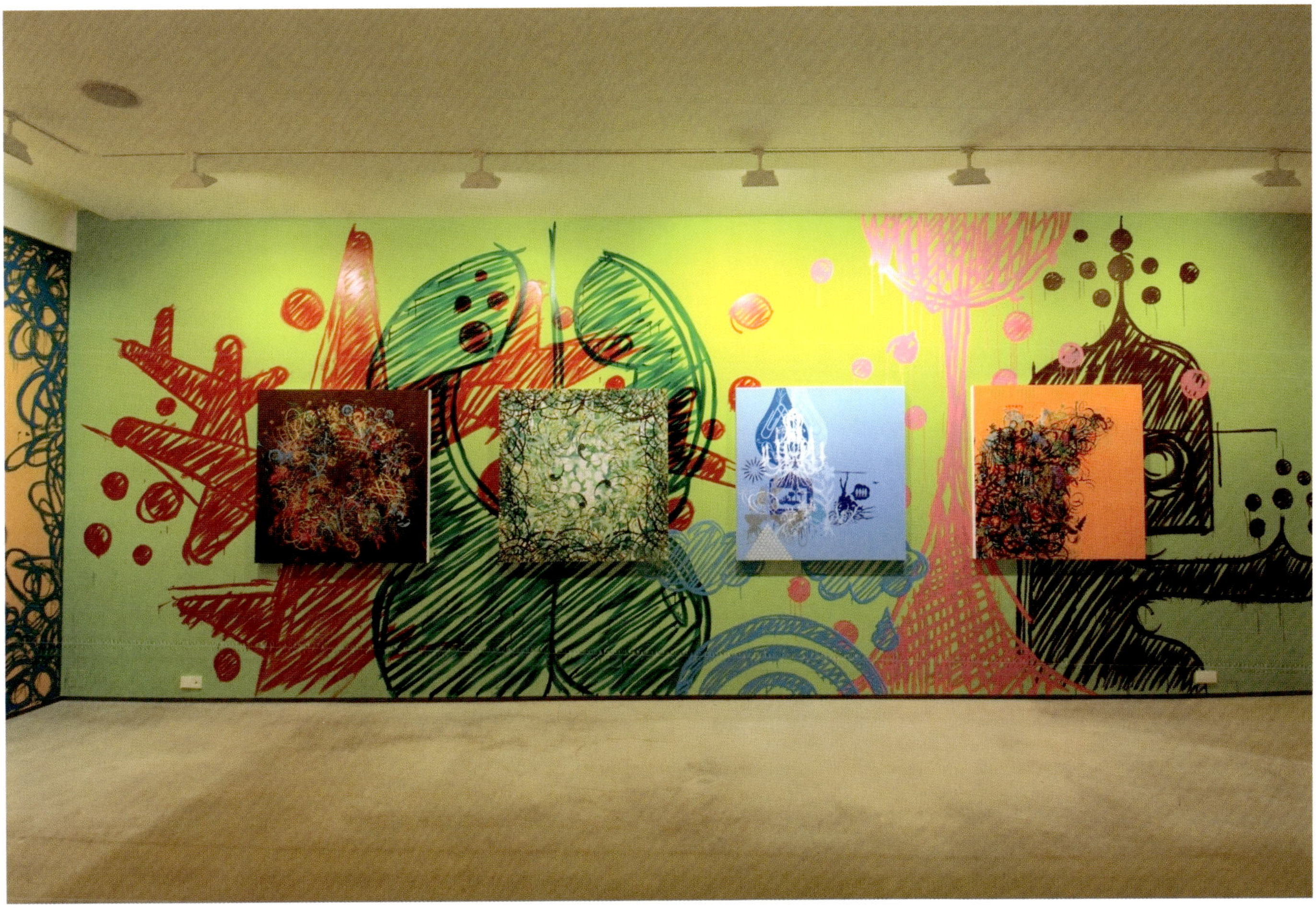

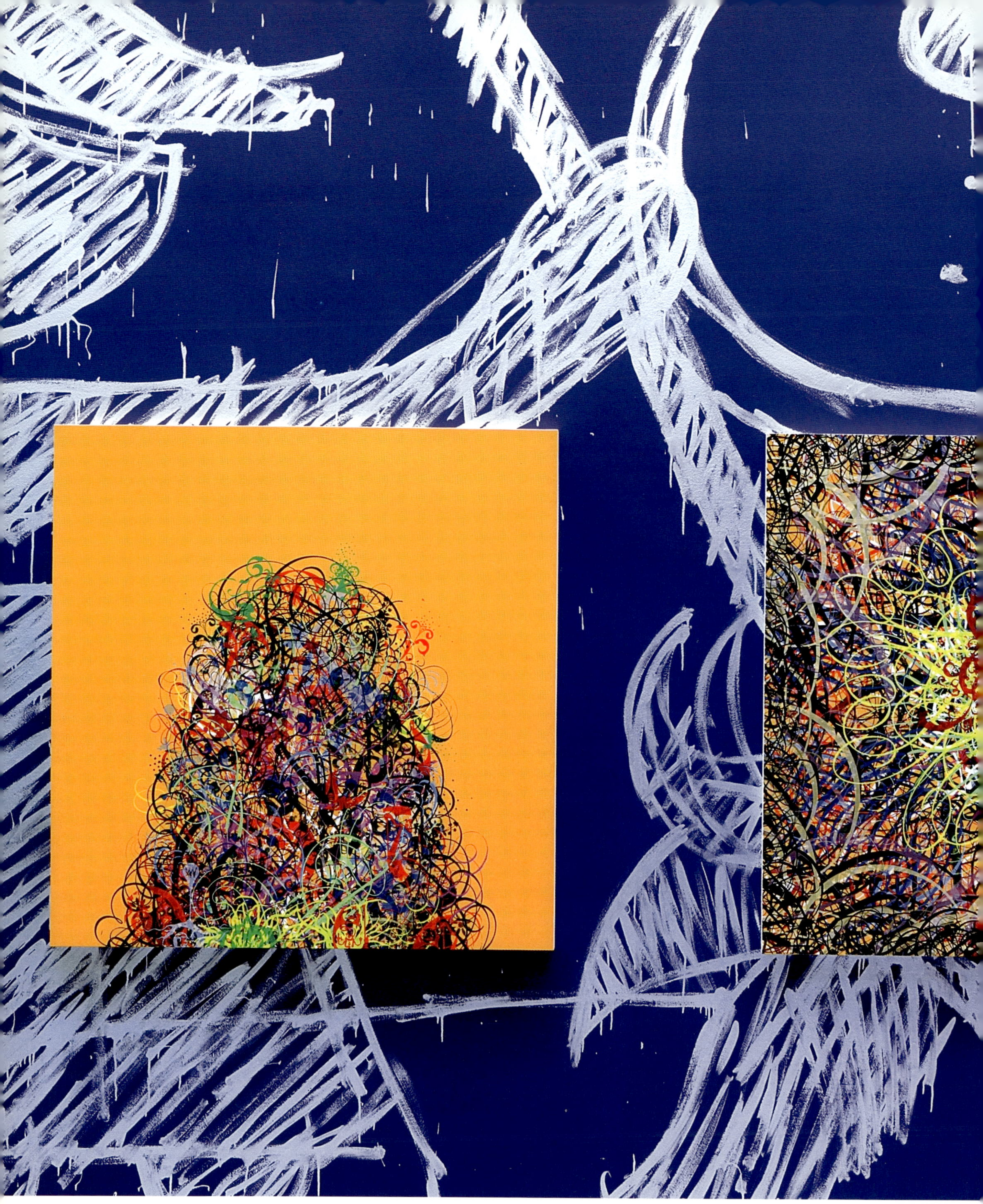

Above and opposite page: Views of "Neveroddoreven"
2006, acrylic on wood panels (48 x 48 in.) with acrylic on wall,
Vous Etes Ici, Amsterdam.

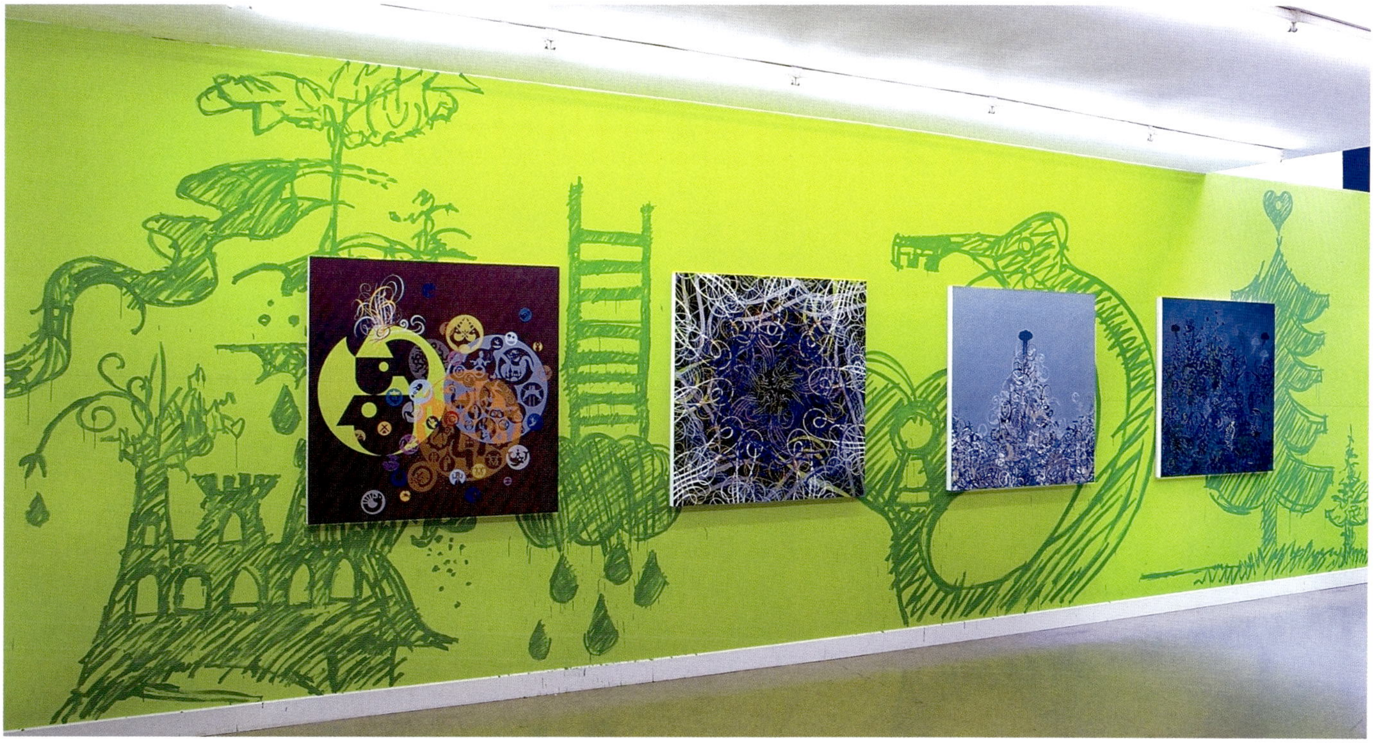

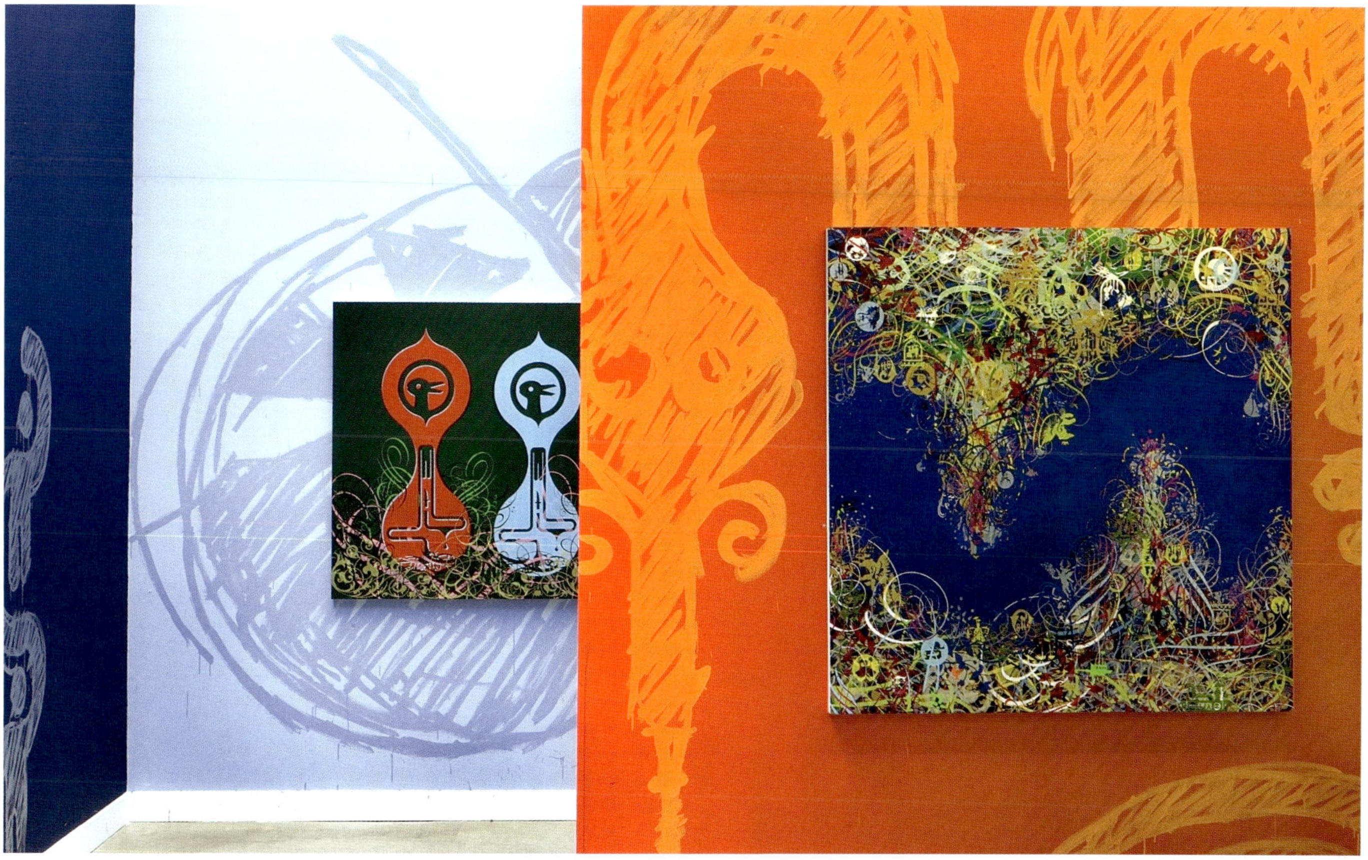

Luck Favors the Prepared Mind
2008, acrylic on linen, 72 x 72 in.

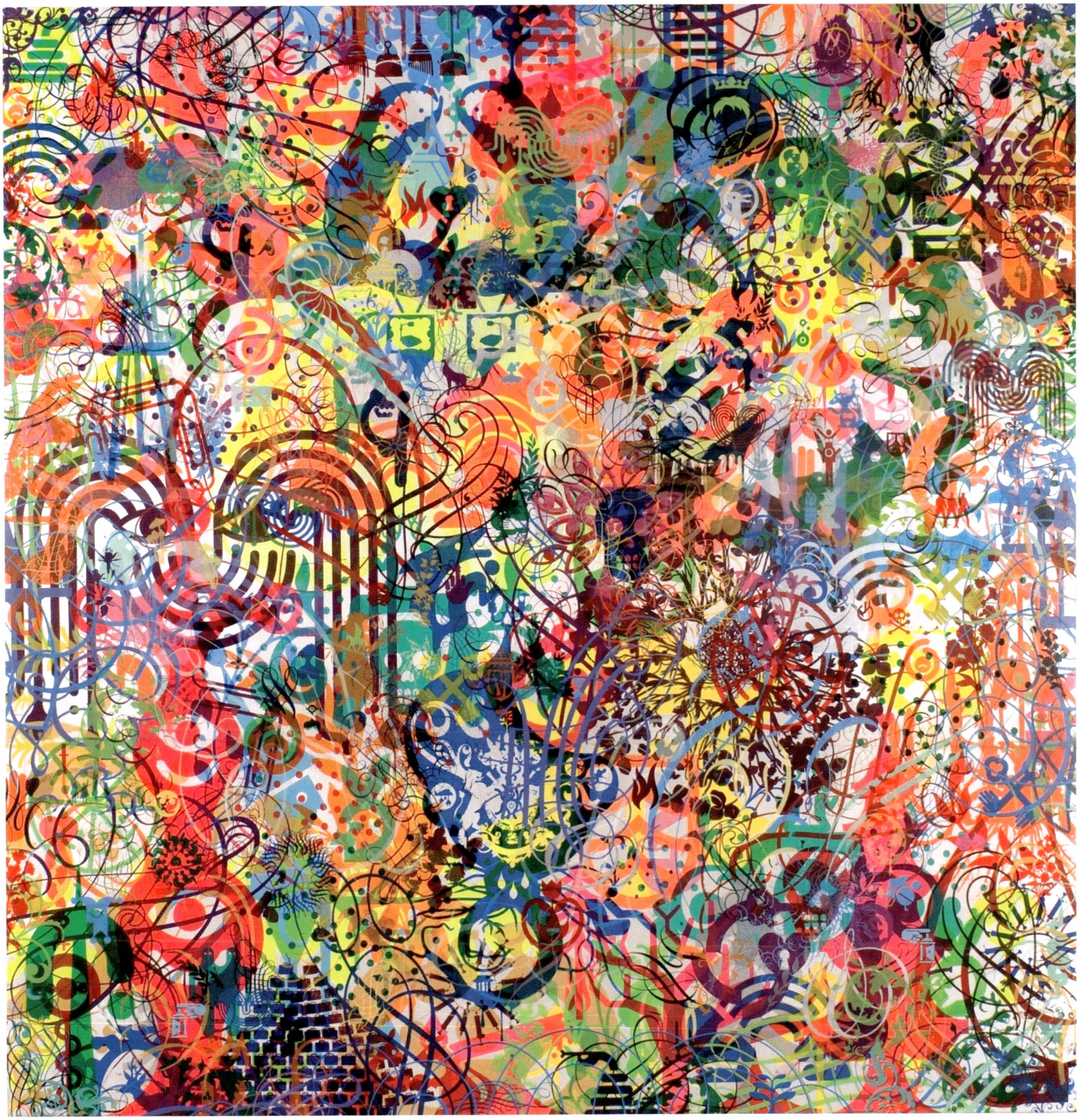

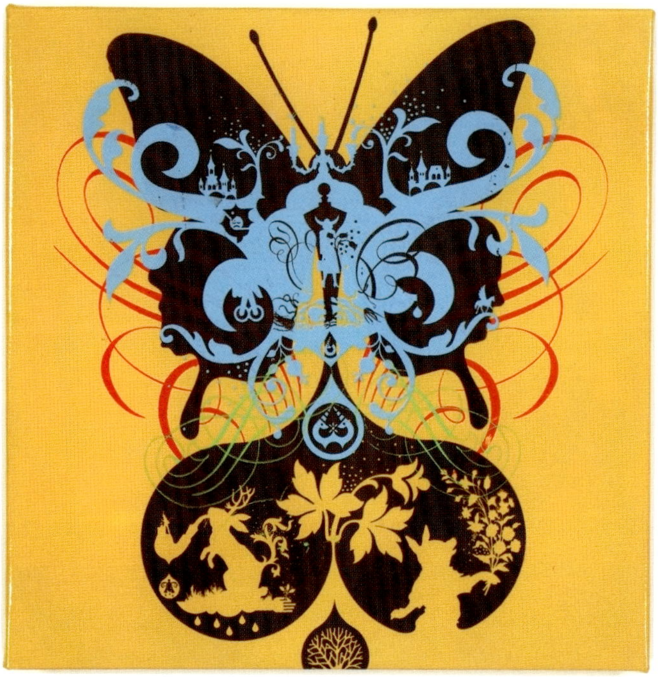

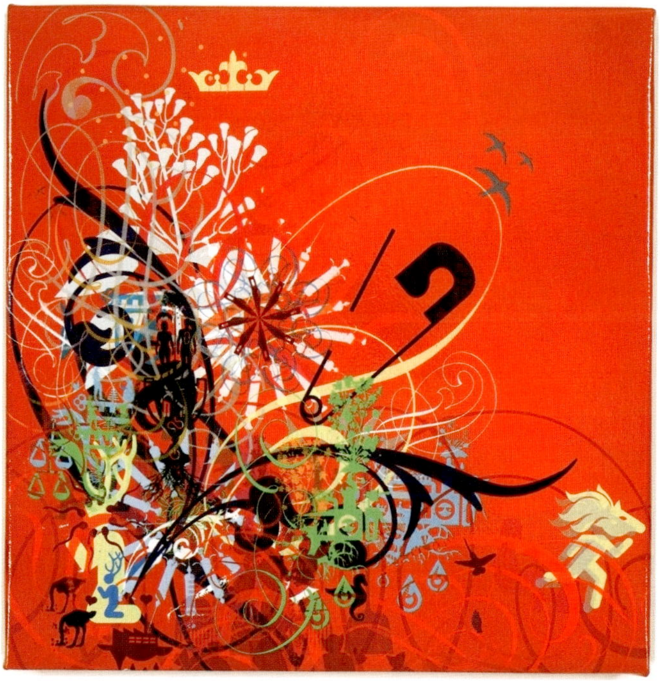

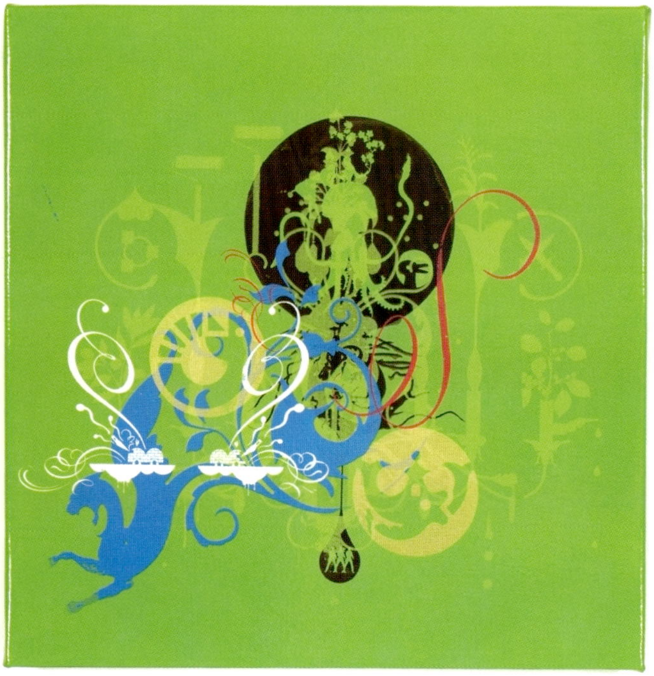

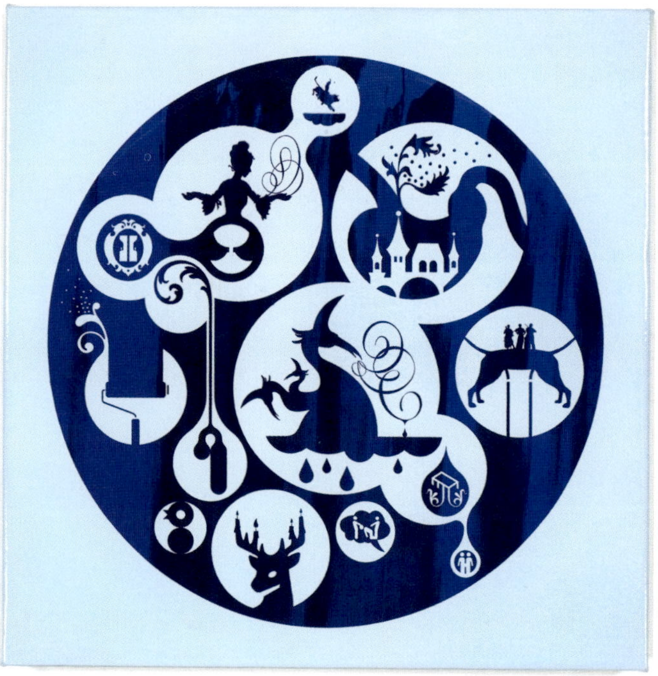

The Greatest Good for the Greatest Number
2006, acrylic and oil on canvas, 24 x 24 in. each, 8 shown here from a series of 16.

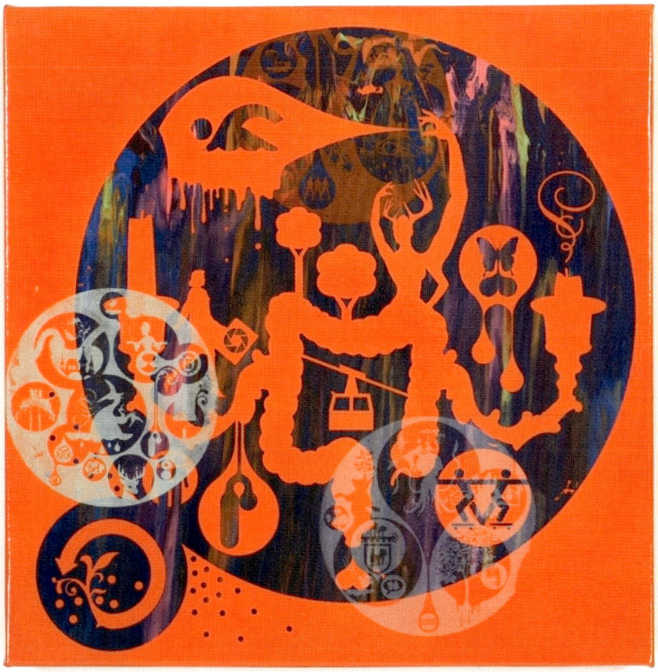
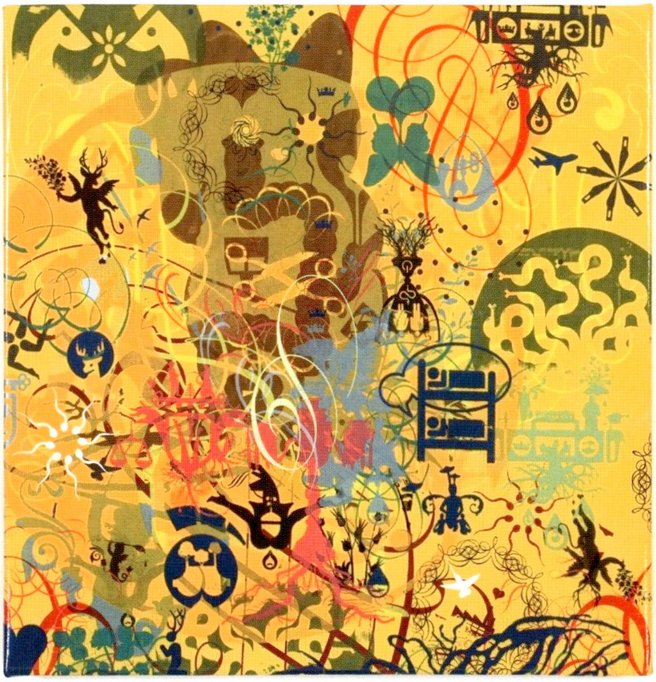
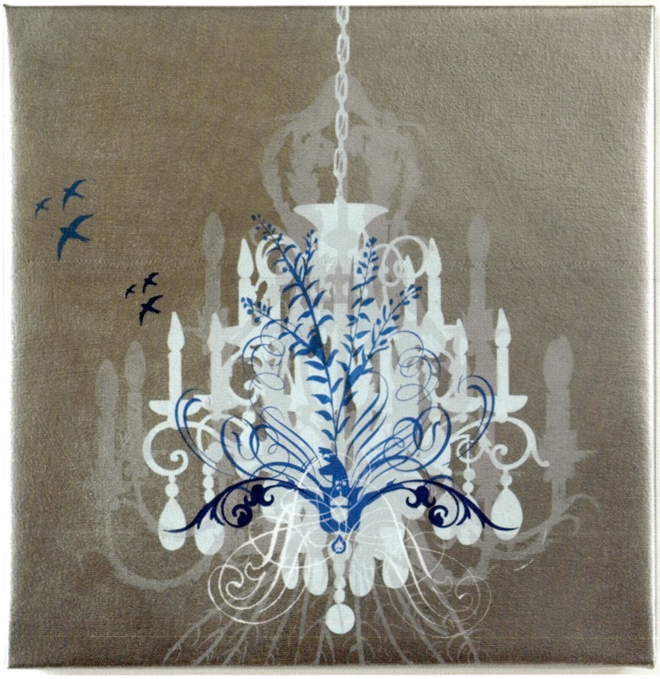
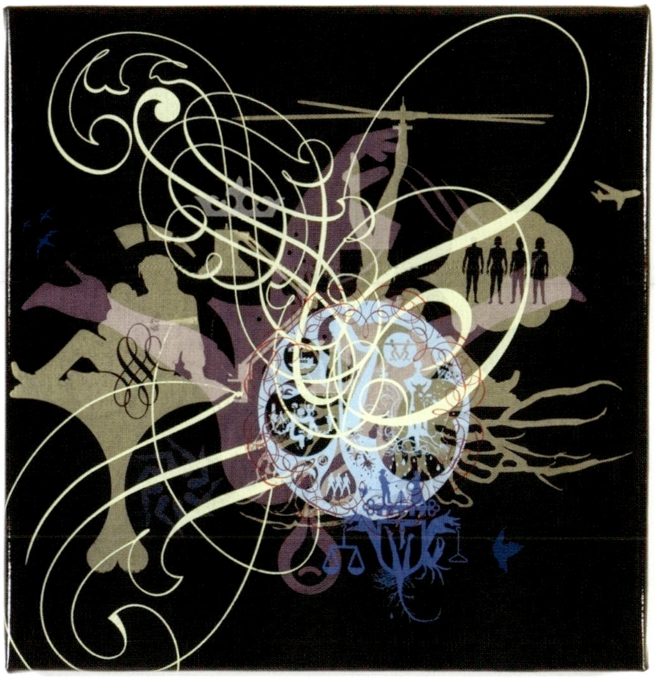

Retail Cargo Candelabra
2006, acrylic on wood panel, 48 x 48 in.

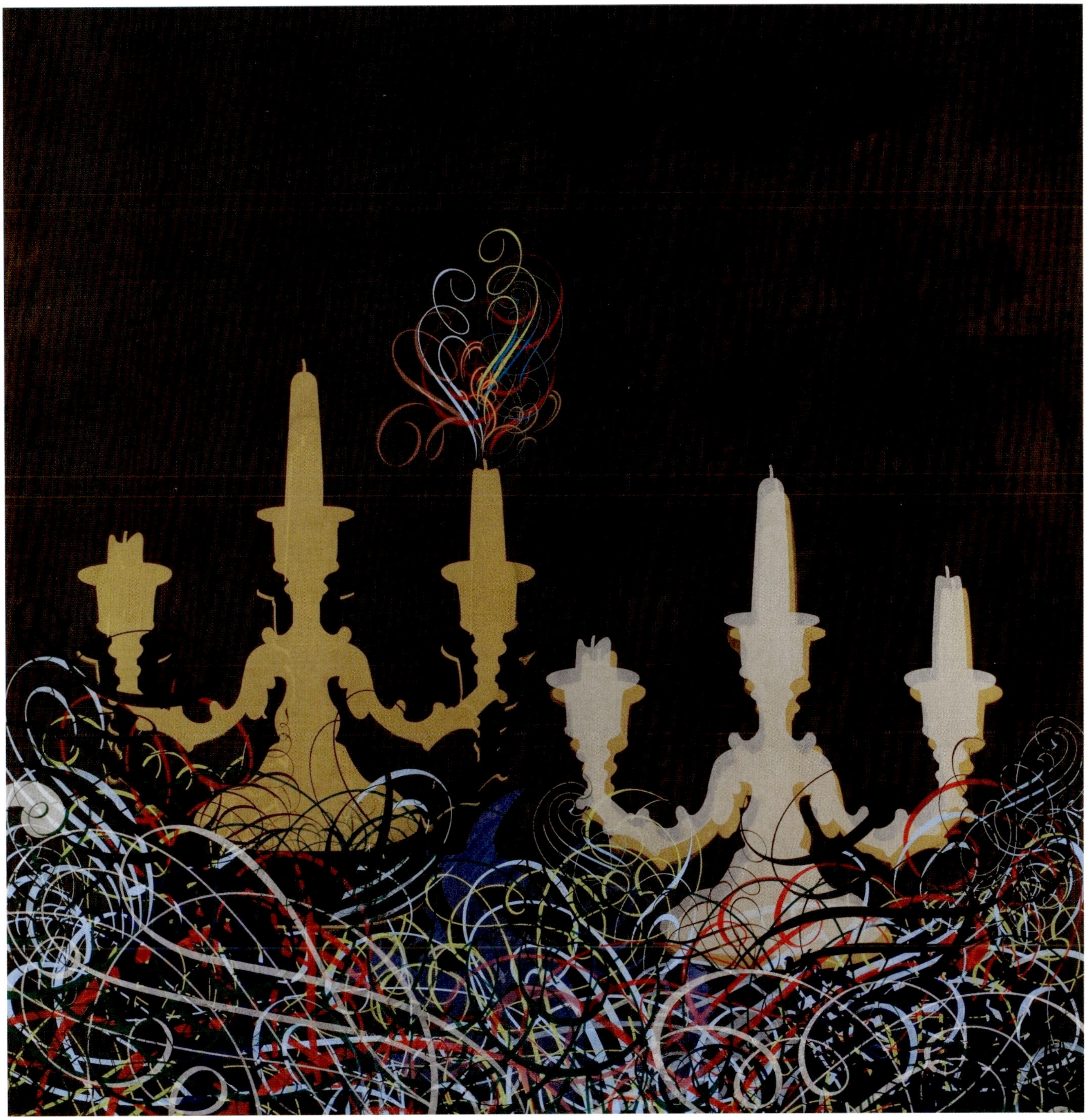

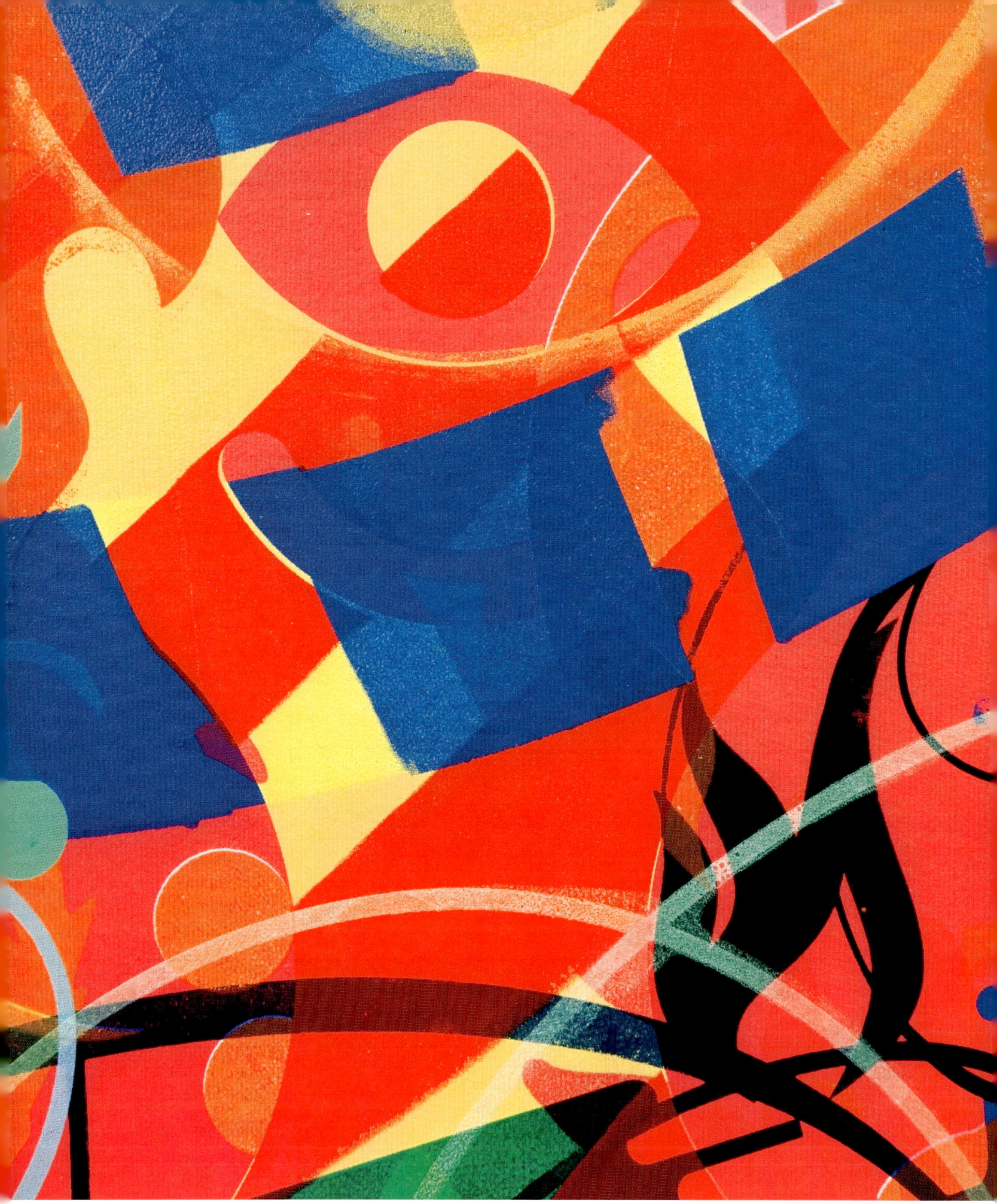

The Need to Know
2008, acrylic on canvas, 72 x 72 in.
(detail above)

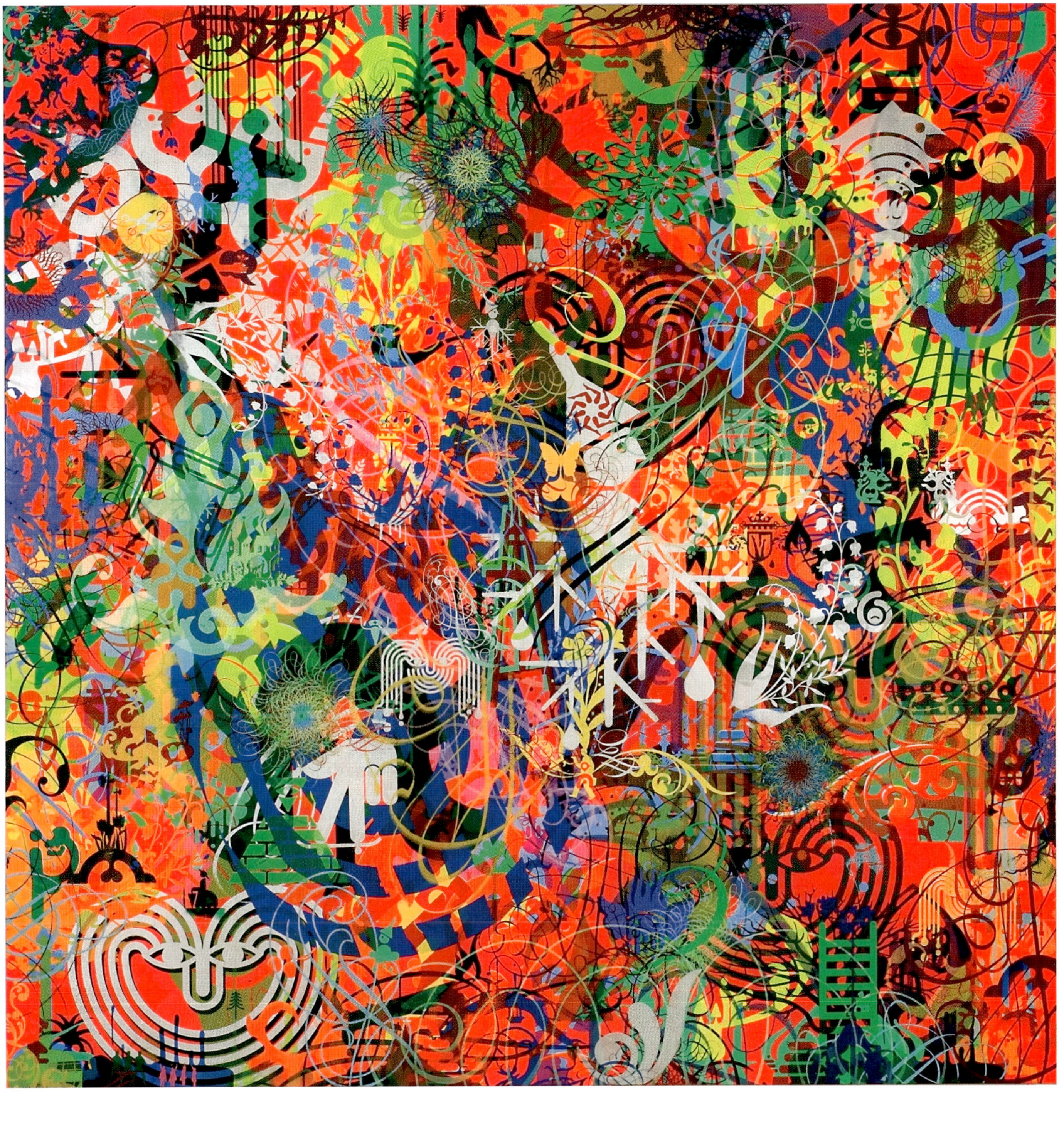

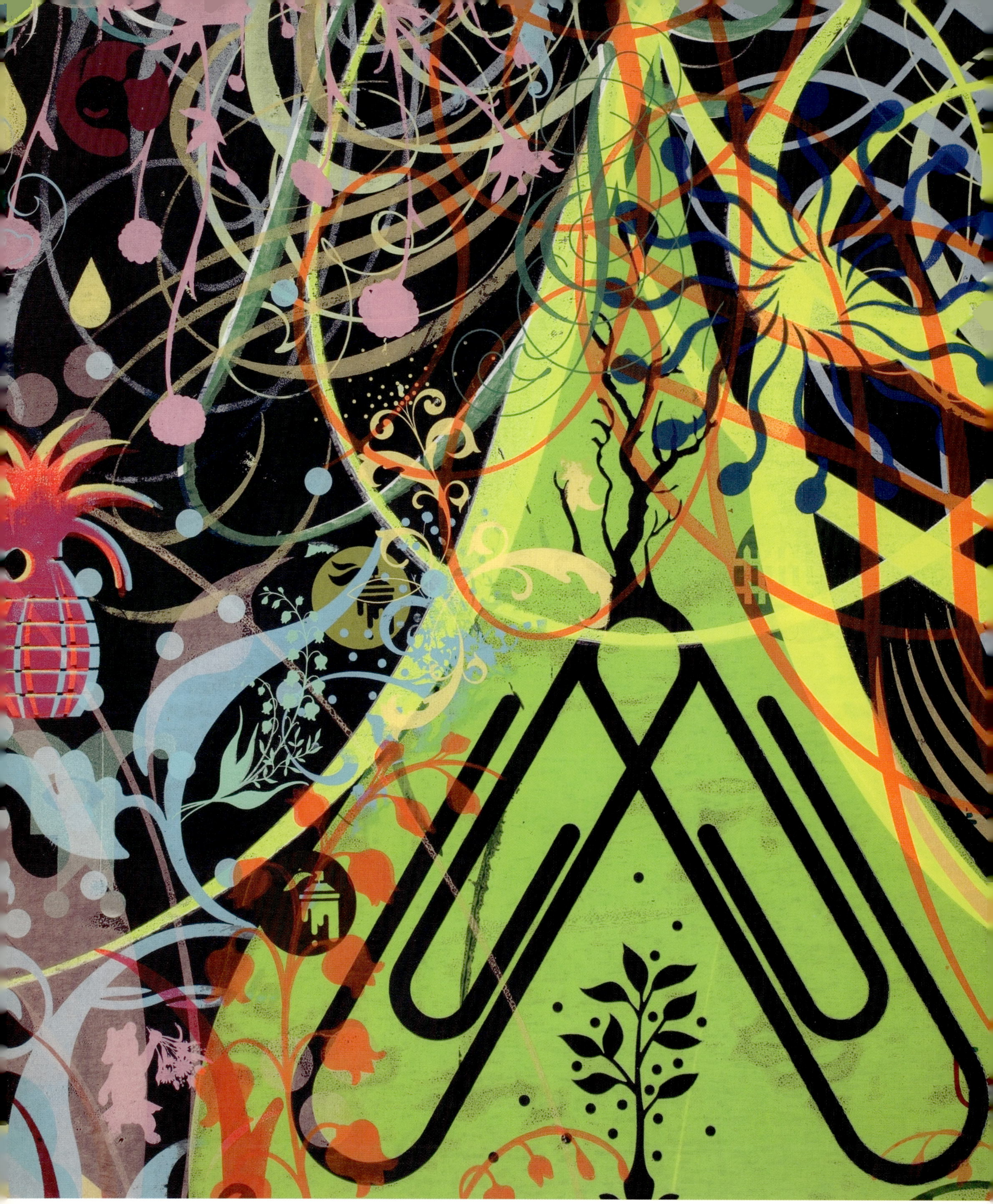

Master of Reality
2007, acrylic on linen, 96 x 144 in.
(details above and on following gatefold)

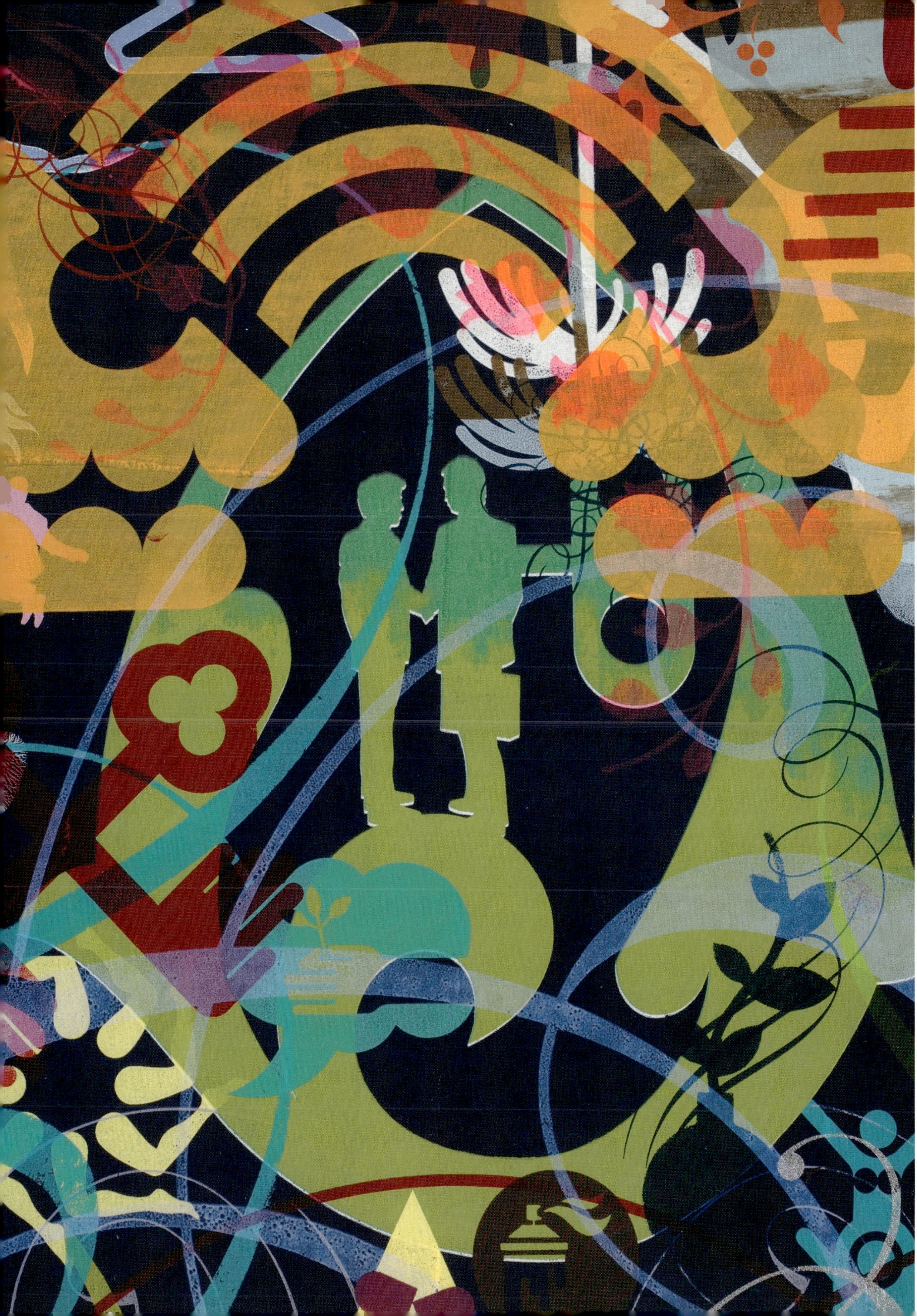

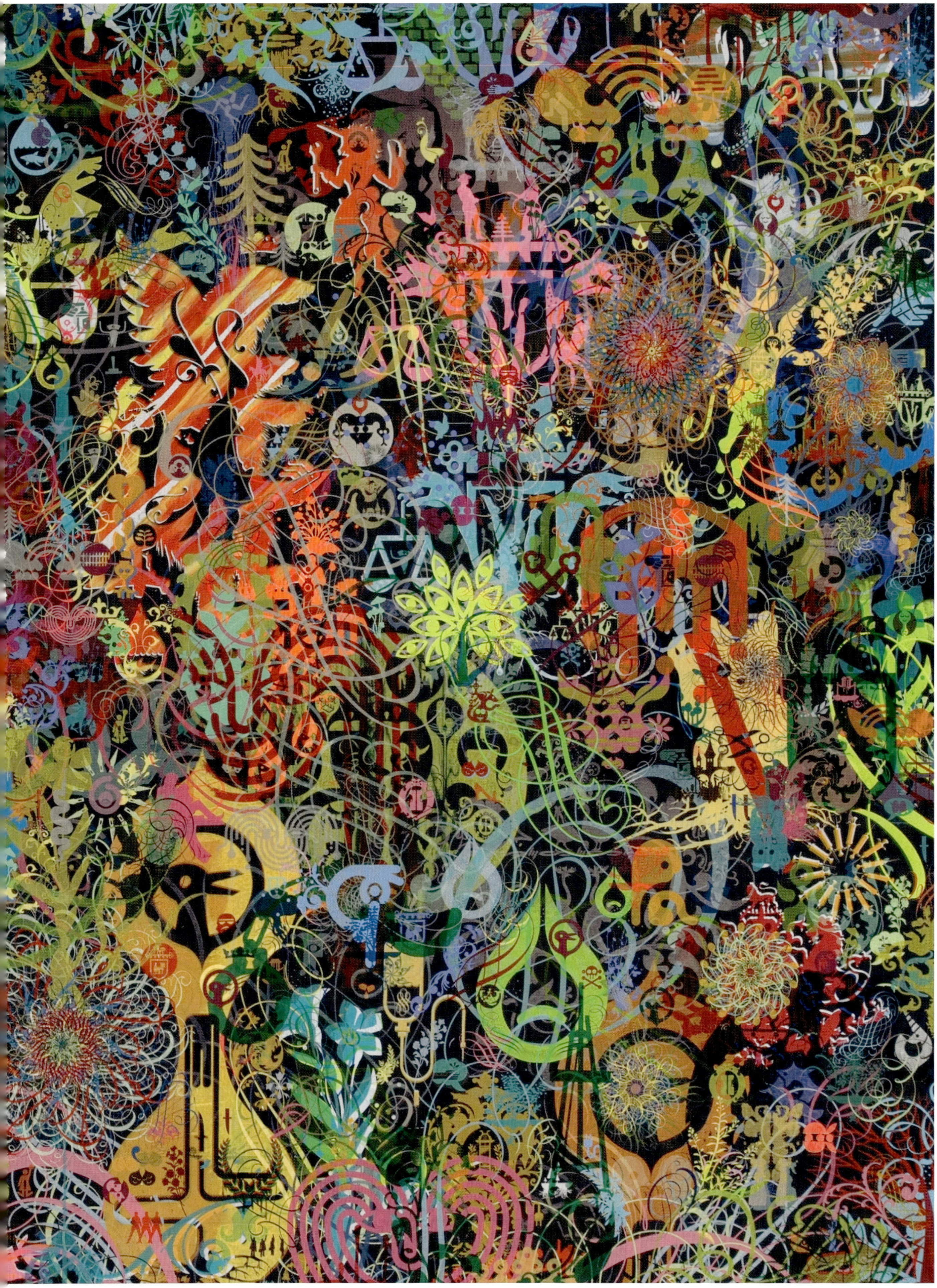

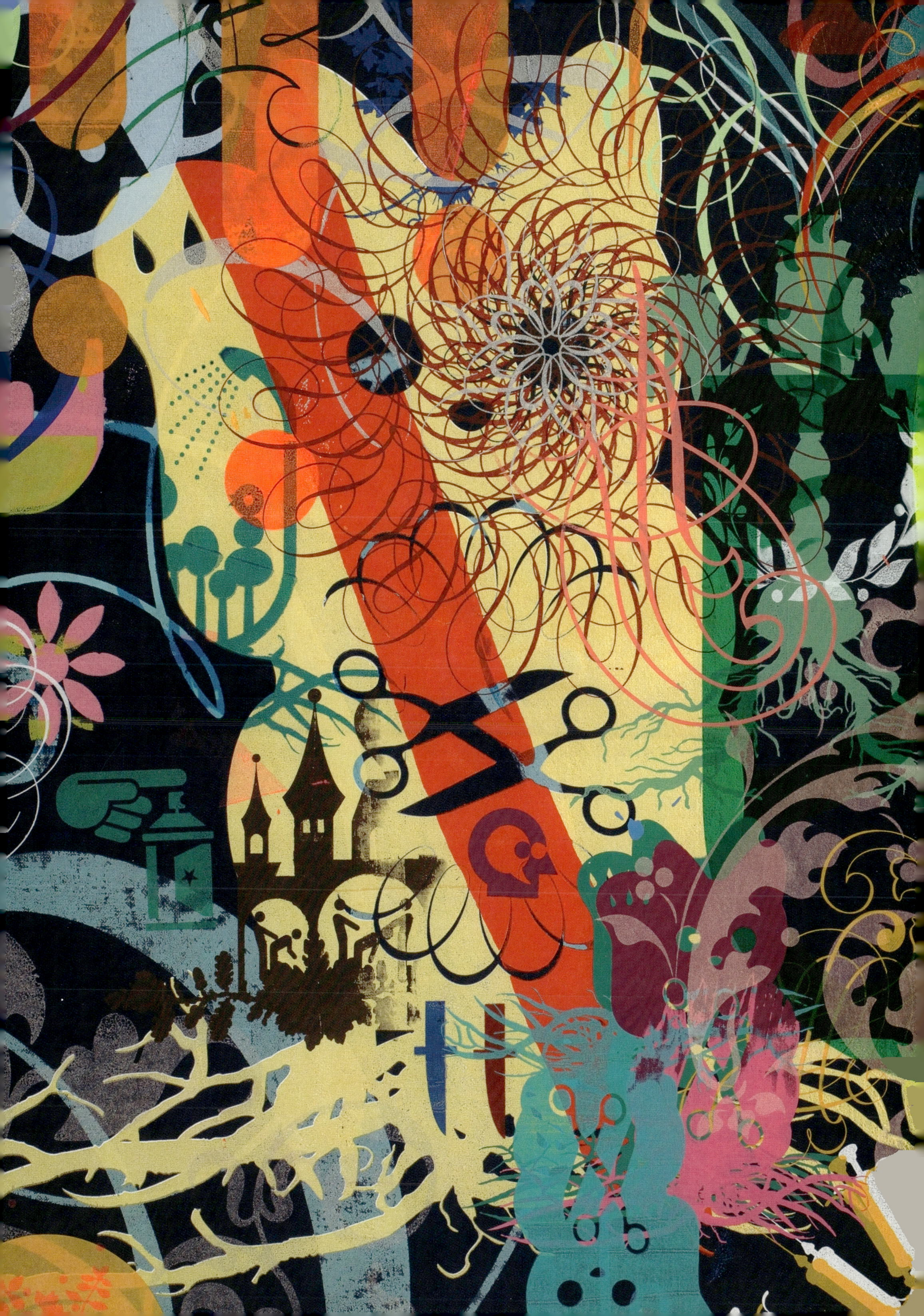

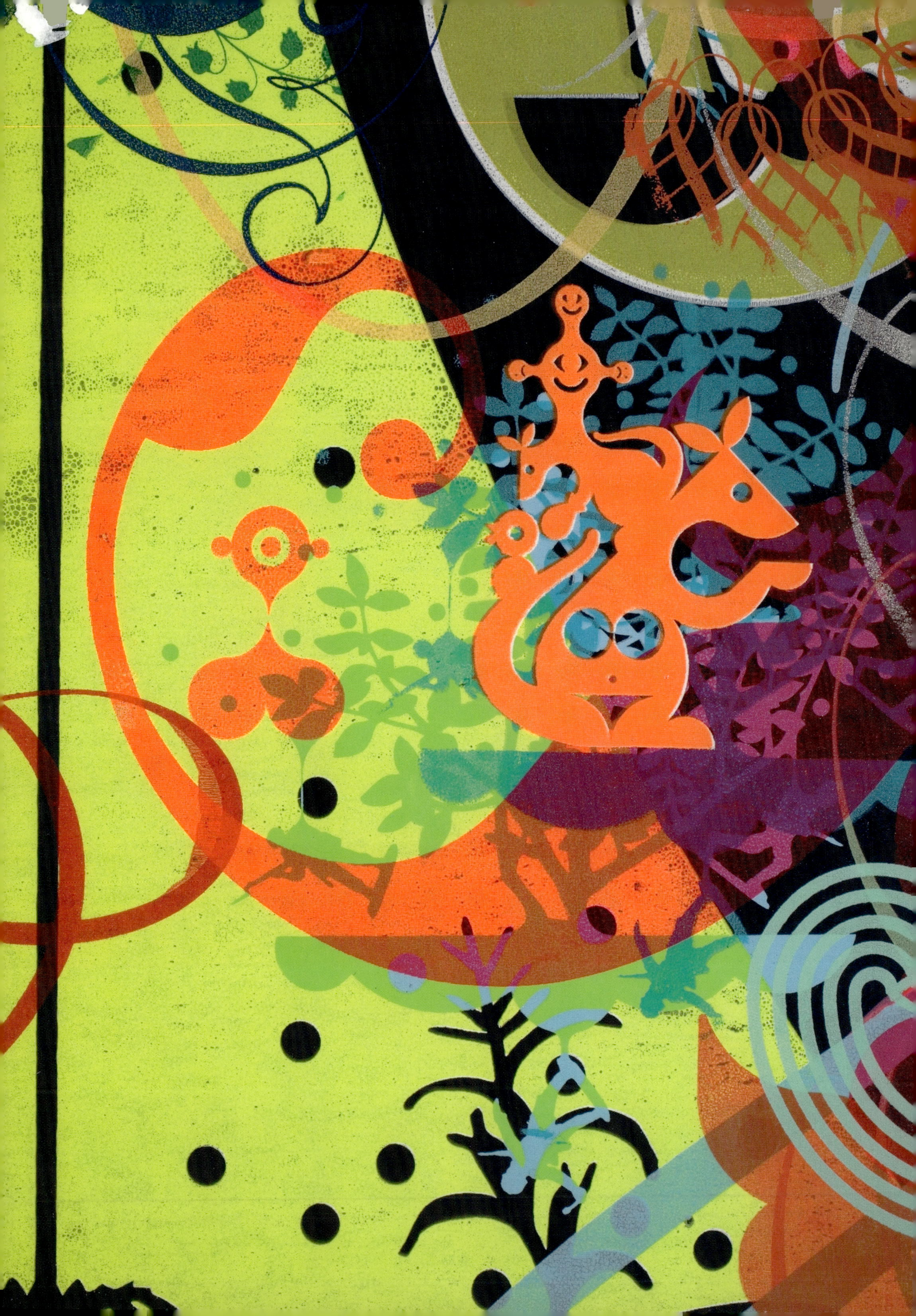

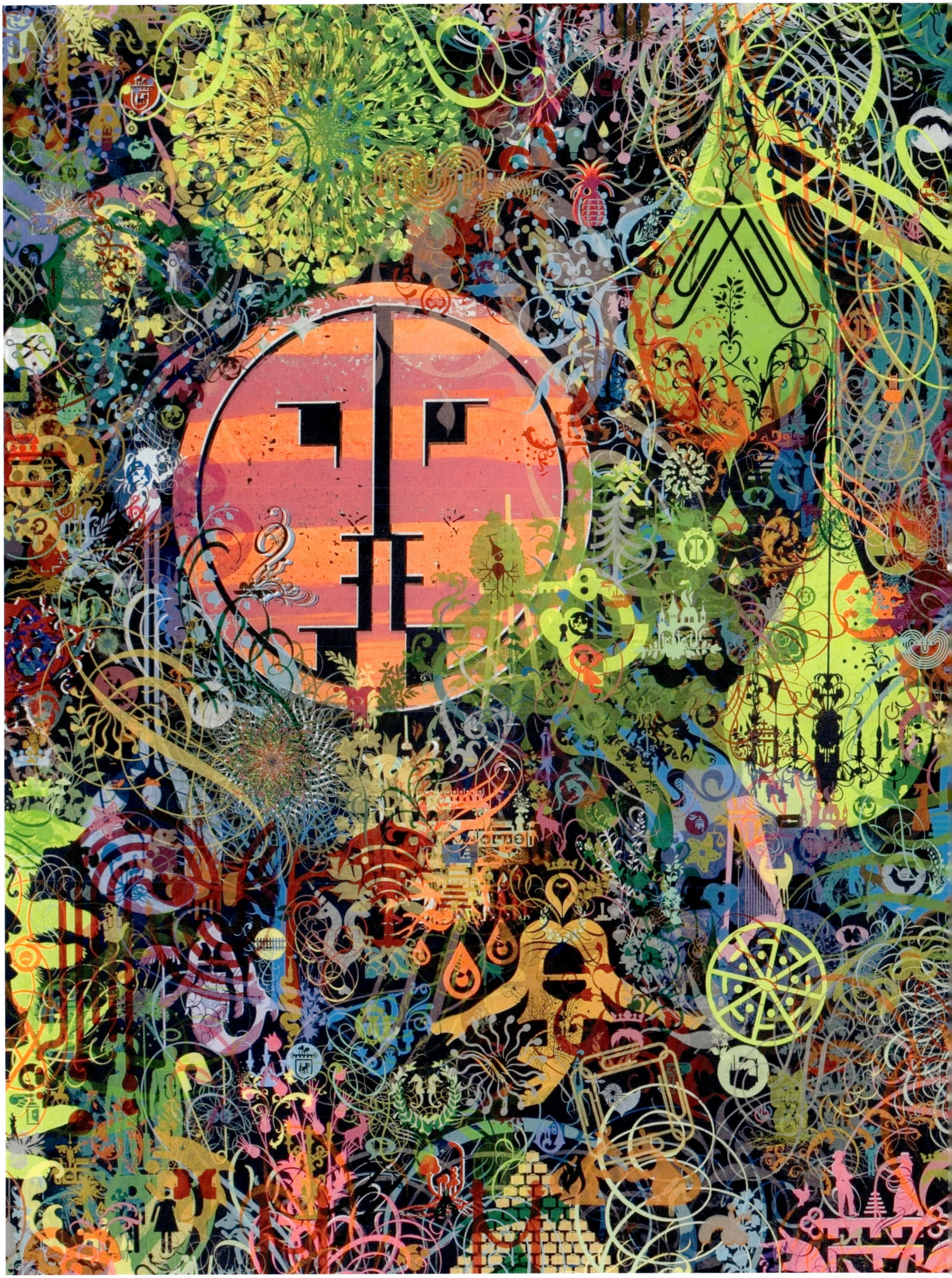

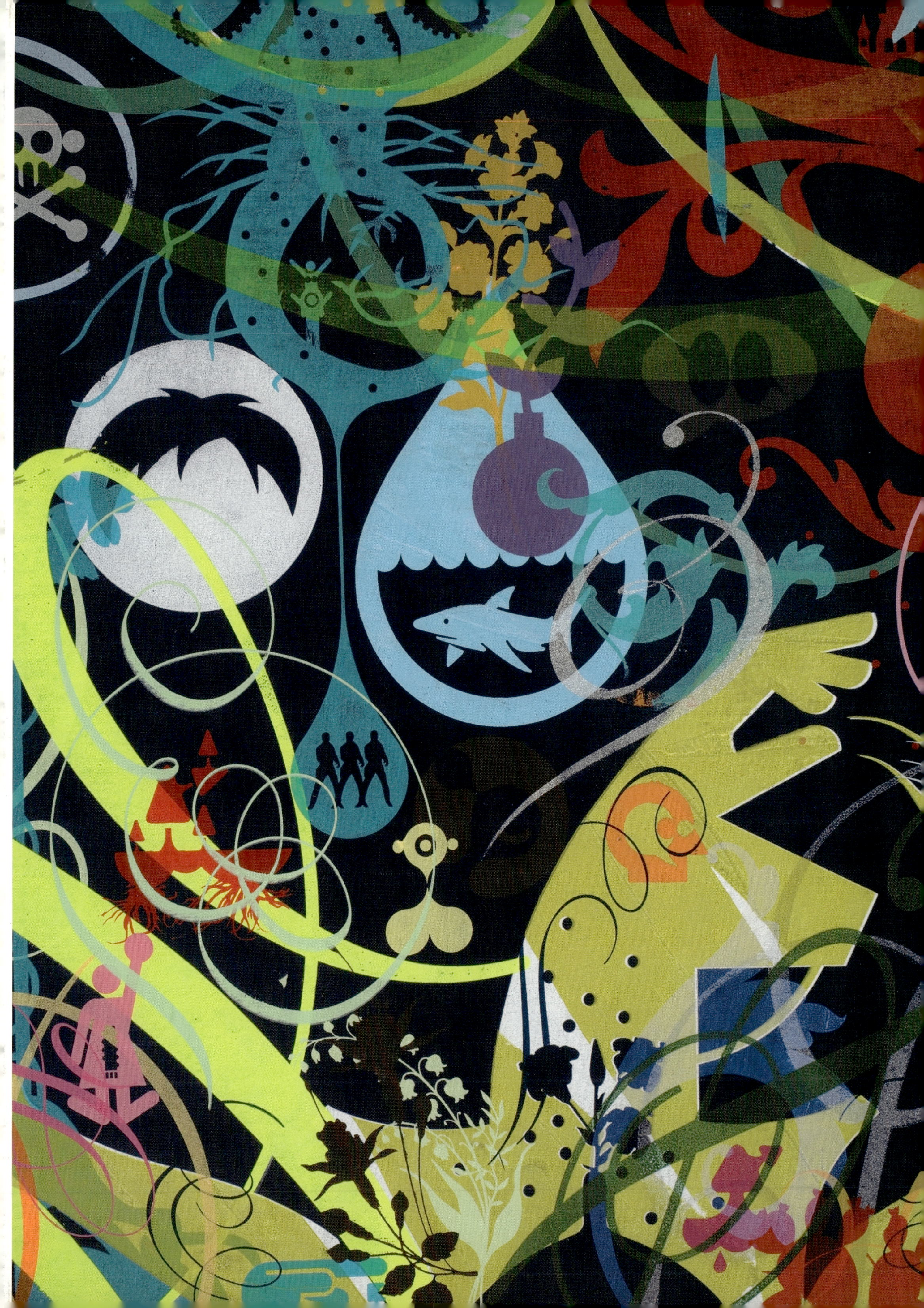

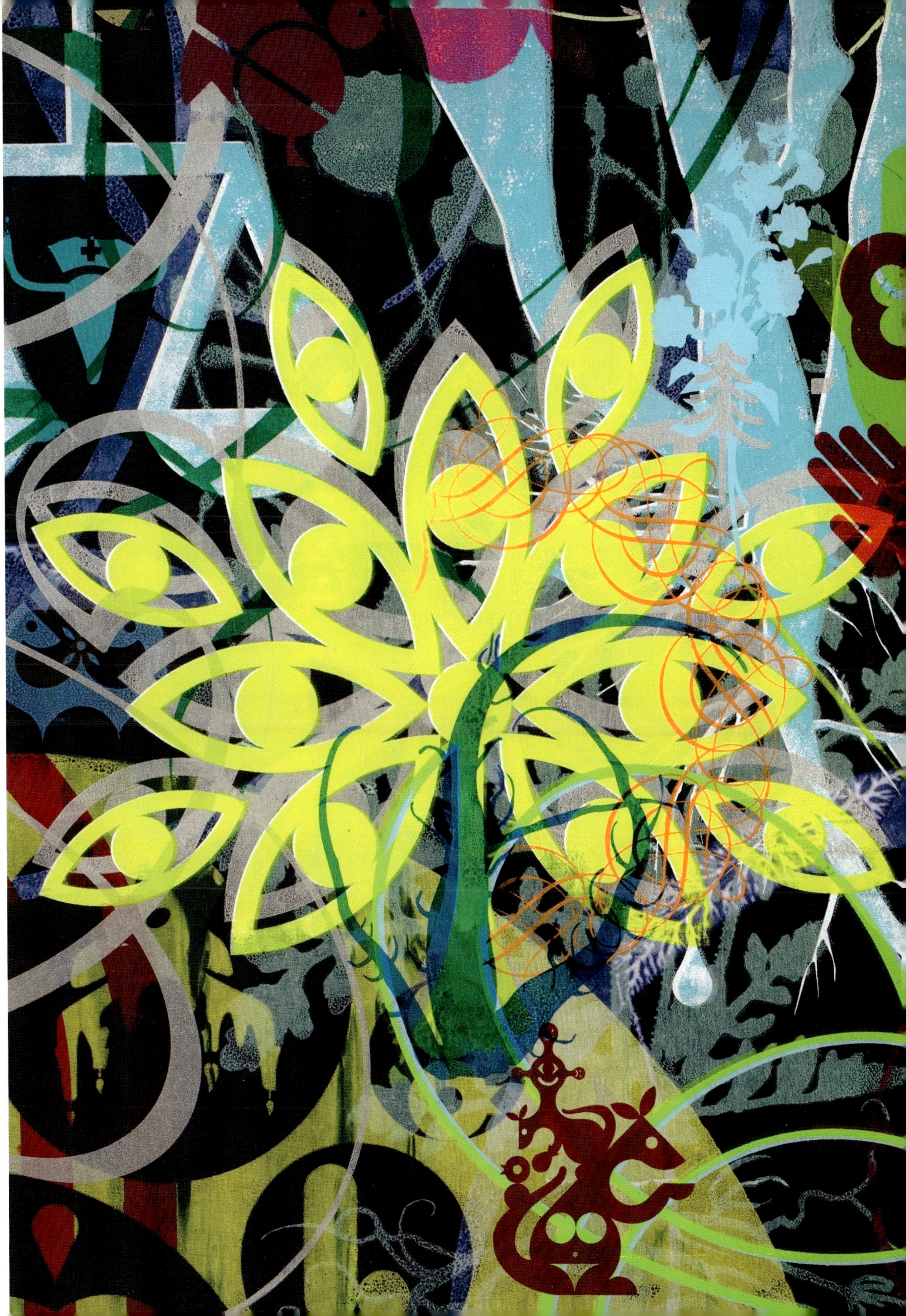

Latet Anguis in Herba
2006, acrylic on wood panel, 48 x 48 in.

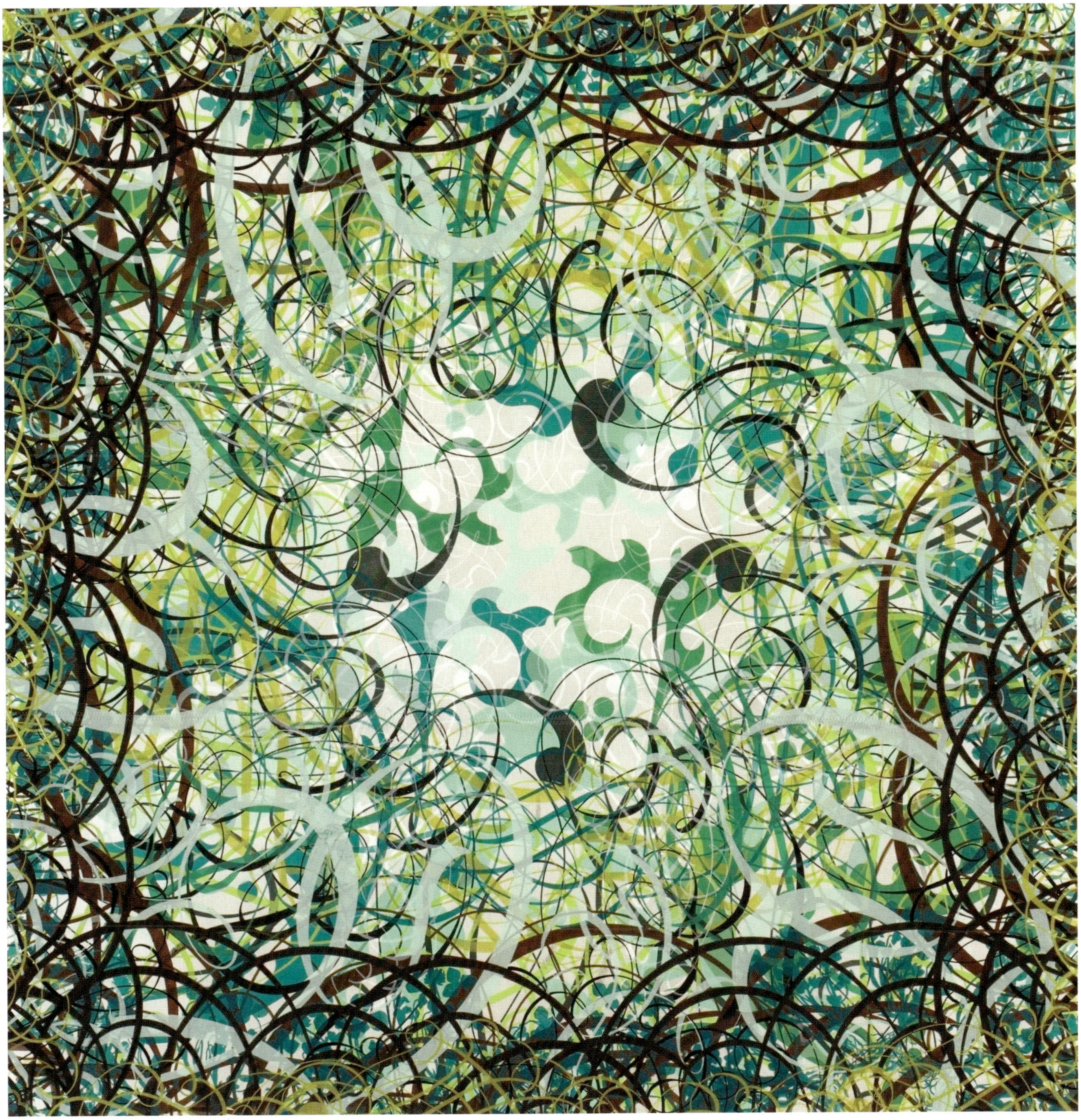

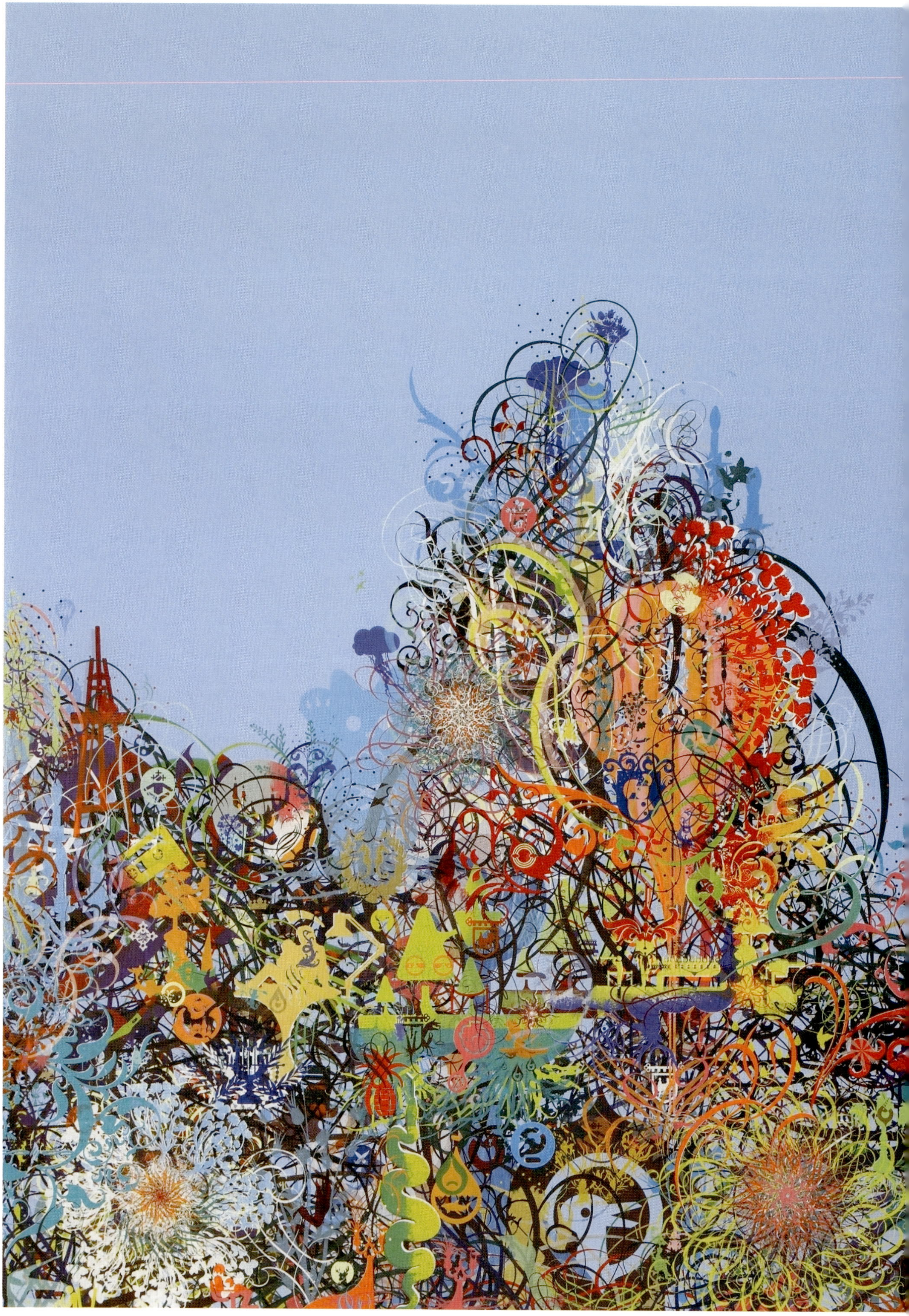

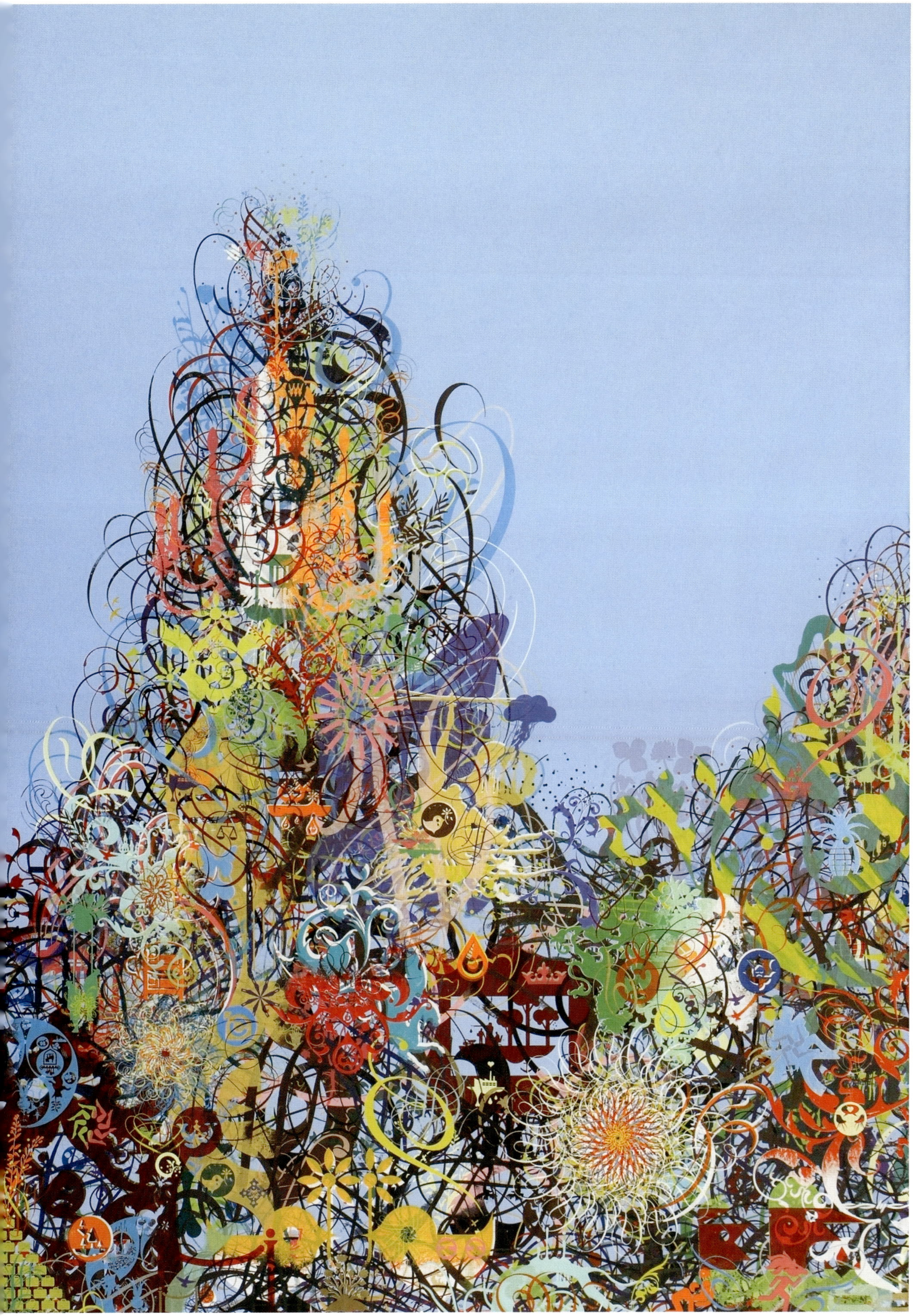

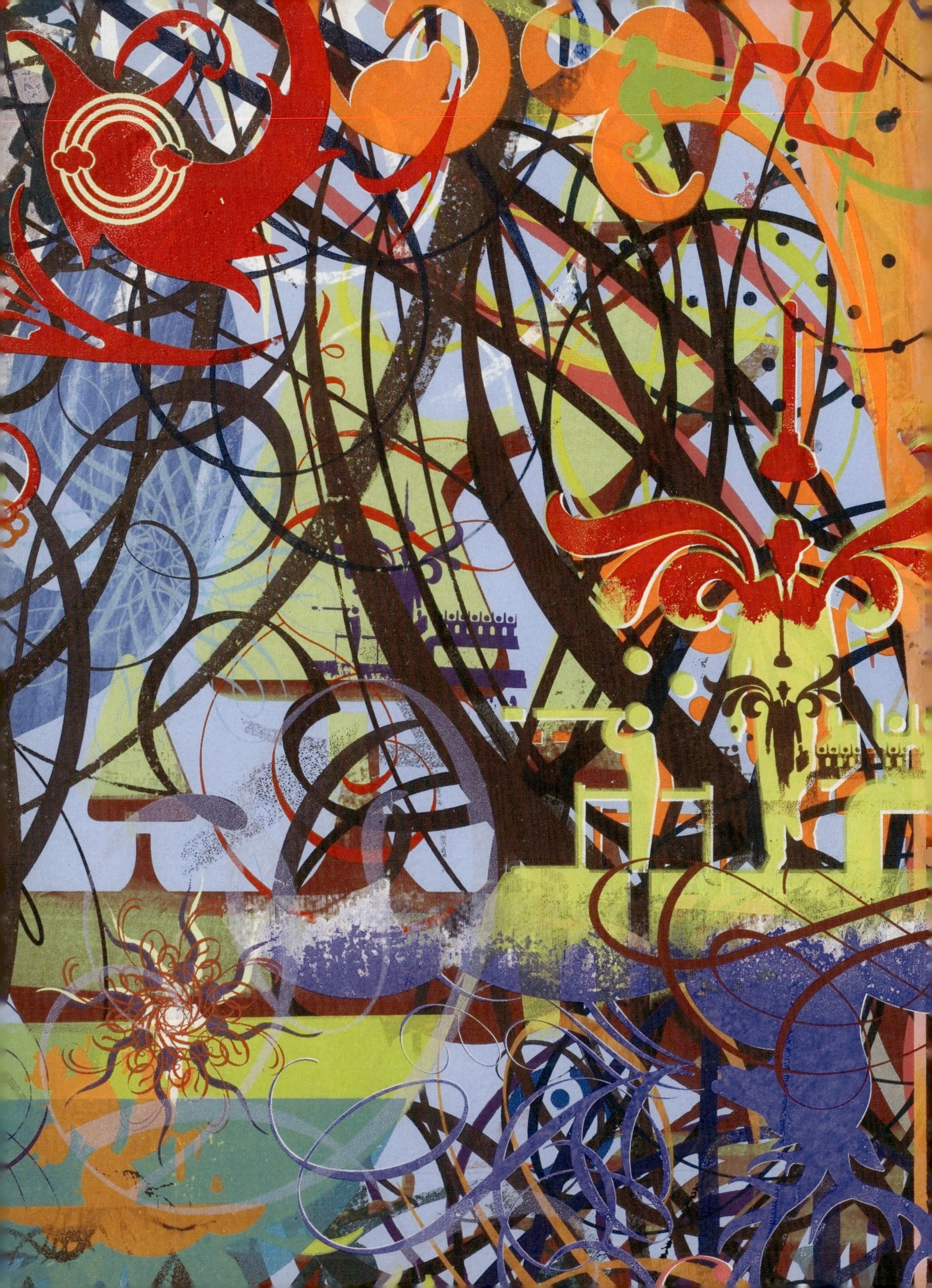

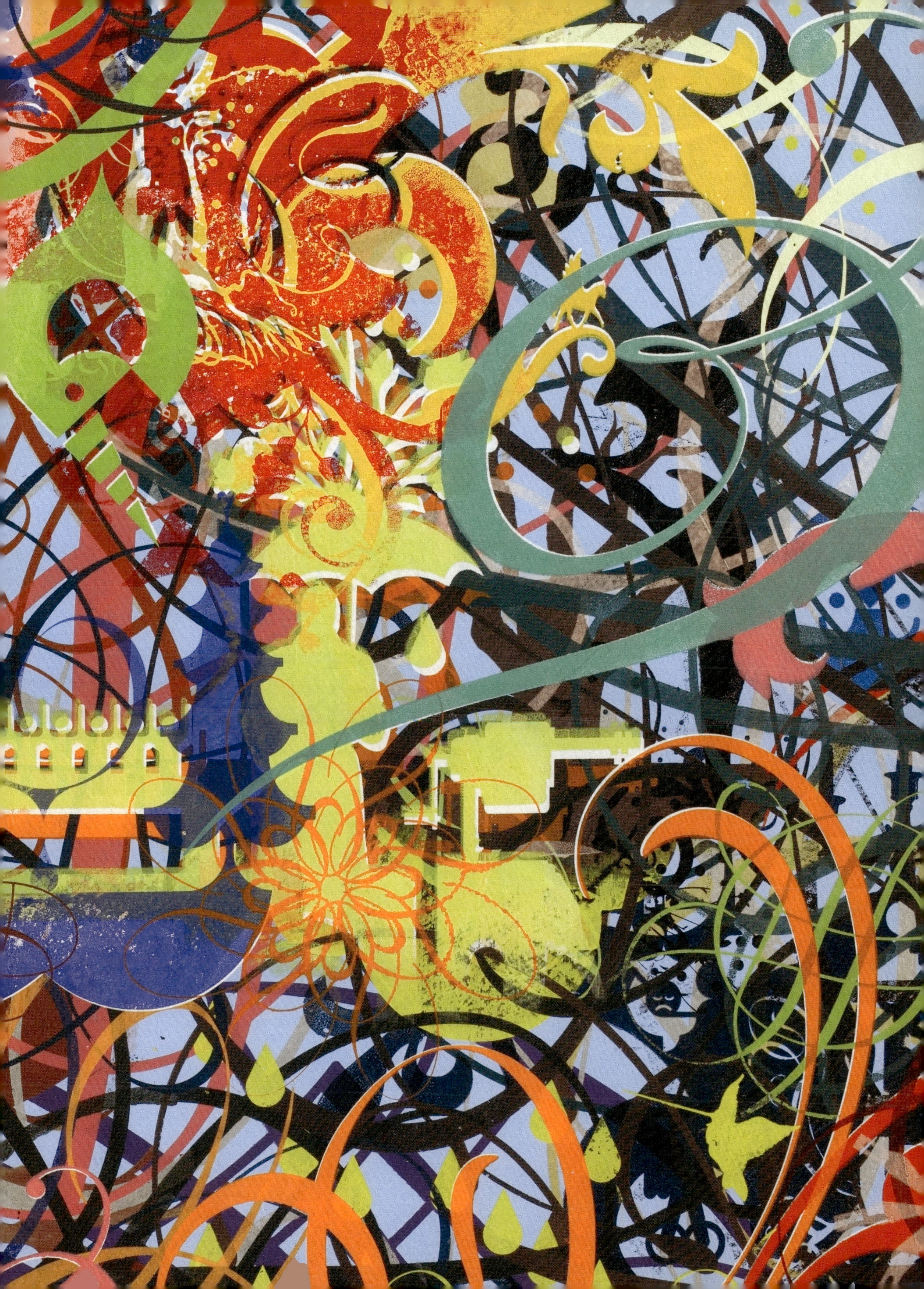

Overleaf 1: *A Dream Within a Dream,* 2007, acrylic on canvas, 96 x 144 in.
(Overleaf 2: detail)

Untitled (Glory Hole, Pearl Blue)
2006, acrylic on wood panel, 48 in. diameter.

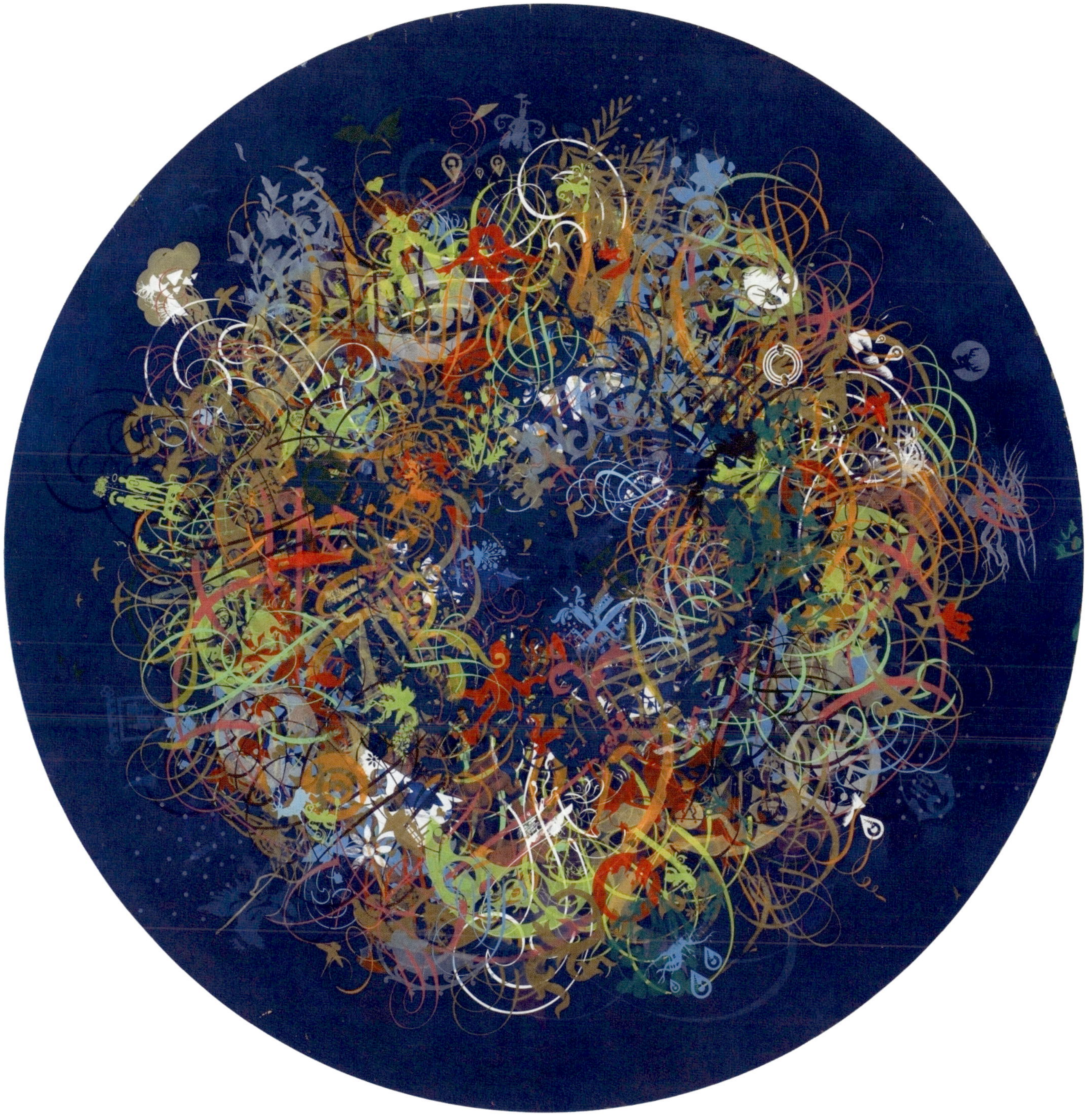

Untitled (Glory Hole, Black)
2006, acrylic on wood panel, 48 x 48 in.

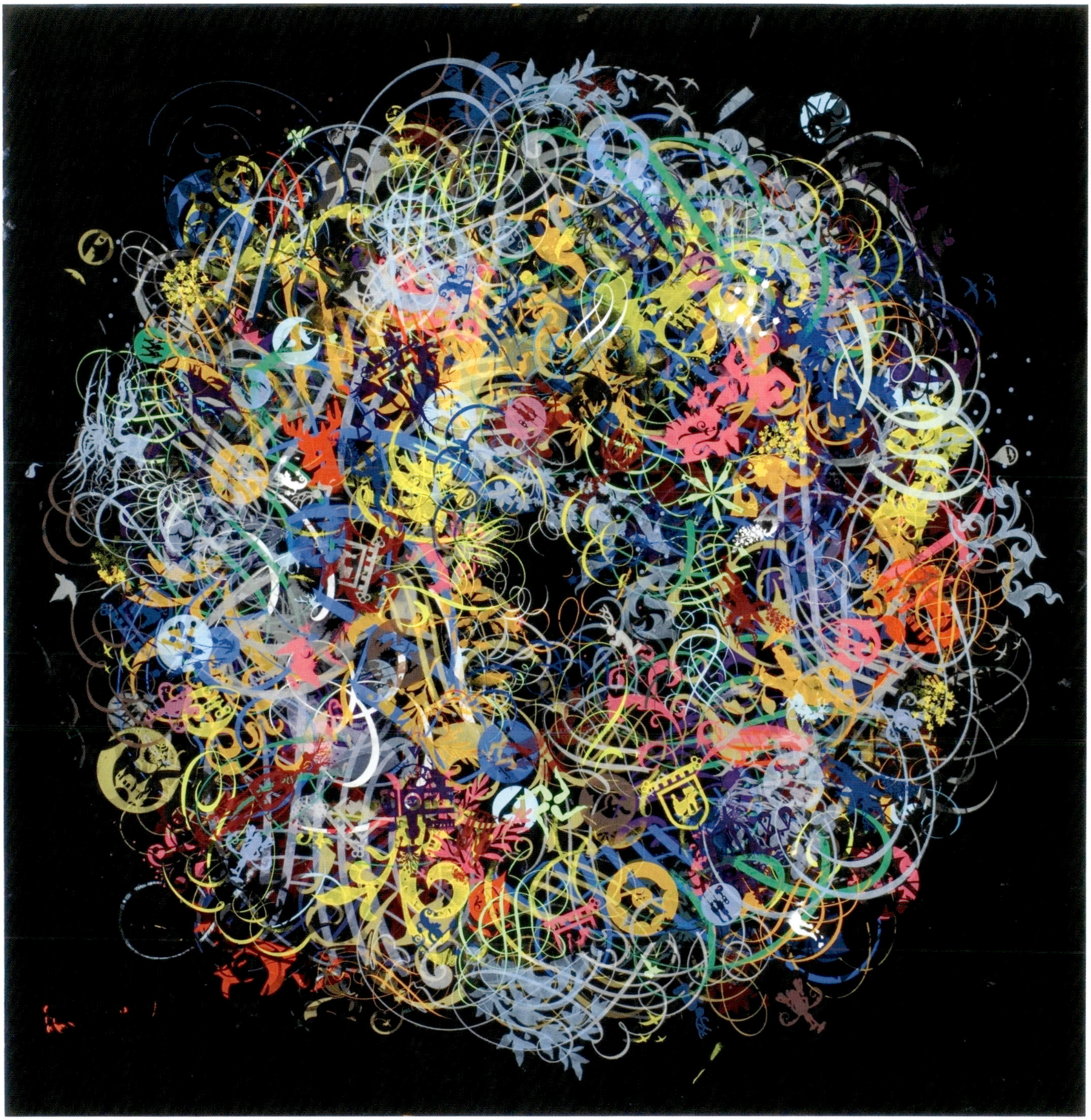

Punk & Bloat
2006, acrylic on wood panel, 48 x 48 in.

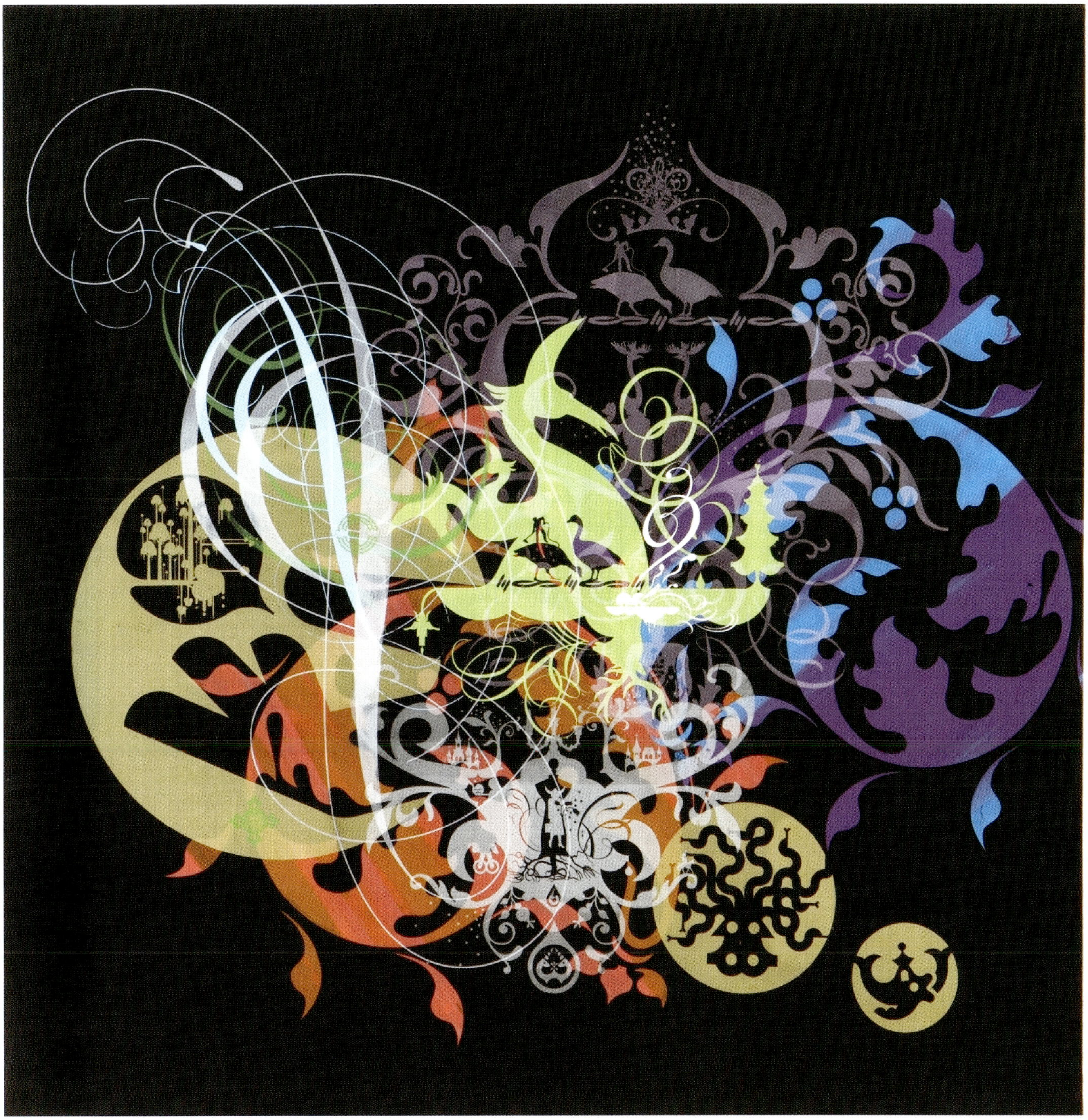

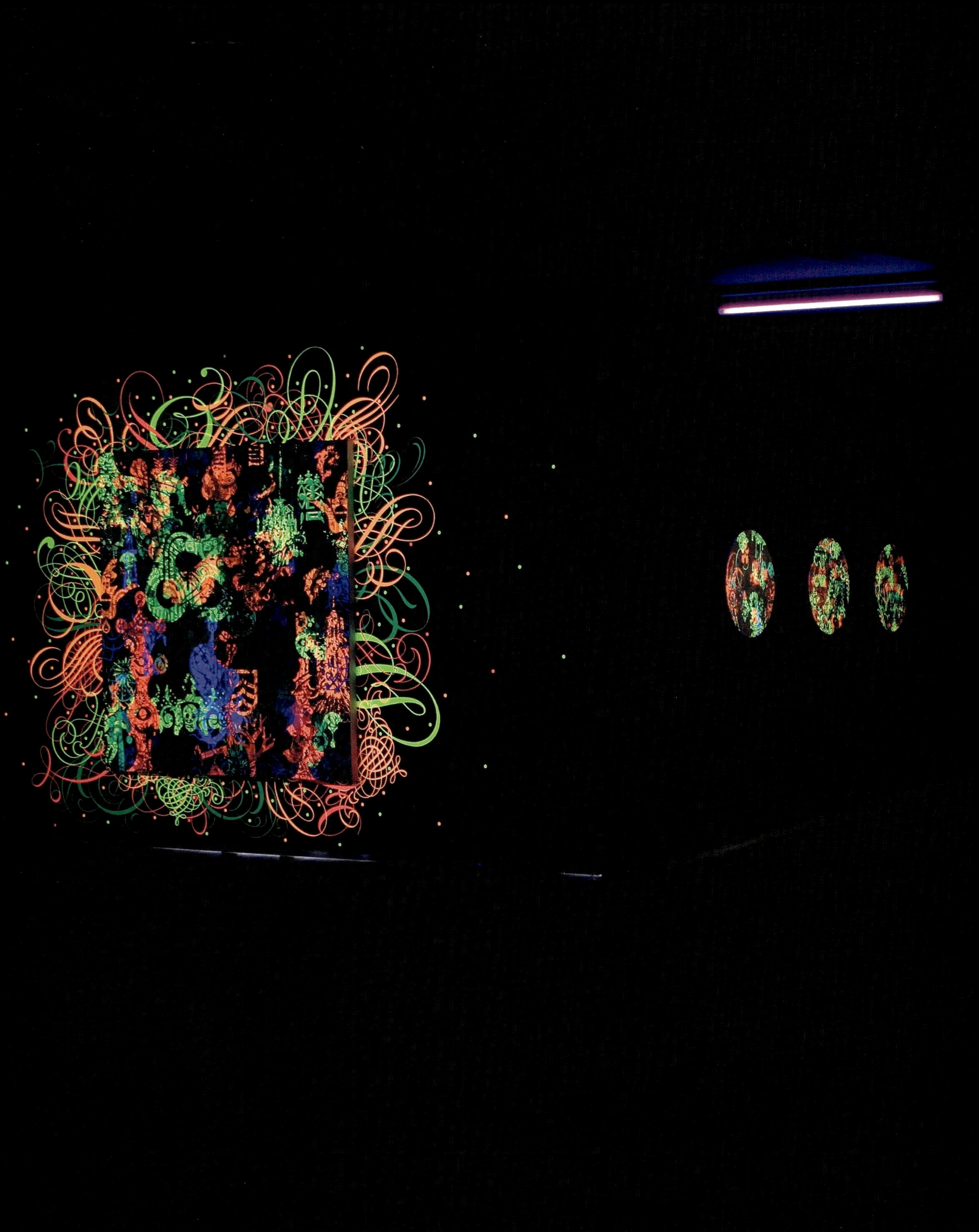

Aesthetic Comfort
Paintings with vinyl installation under black lights. Installation view, 2008, Artcore/Fabrice Marcolini, Toronto.

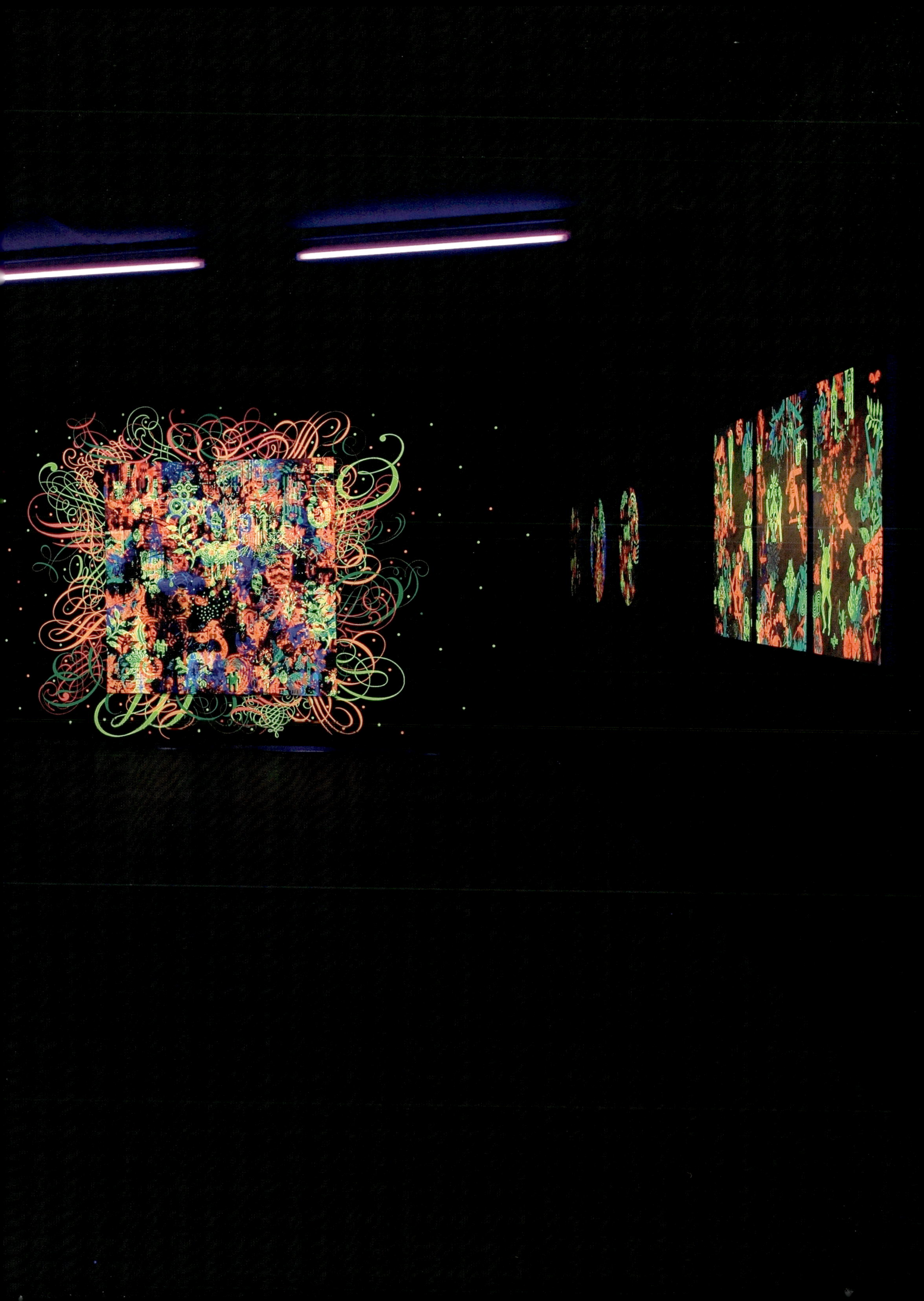

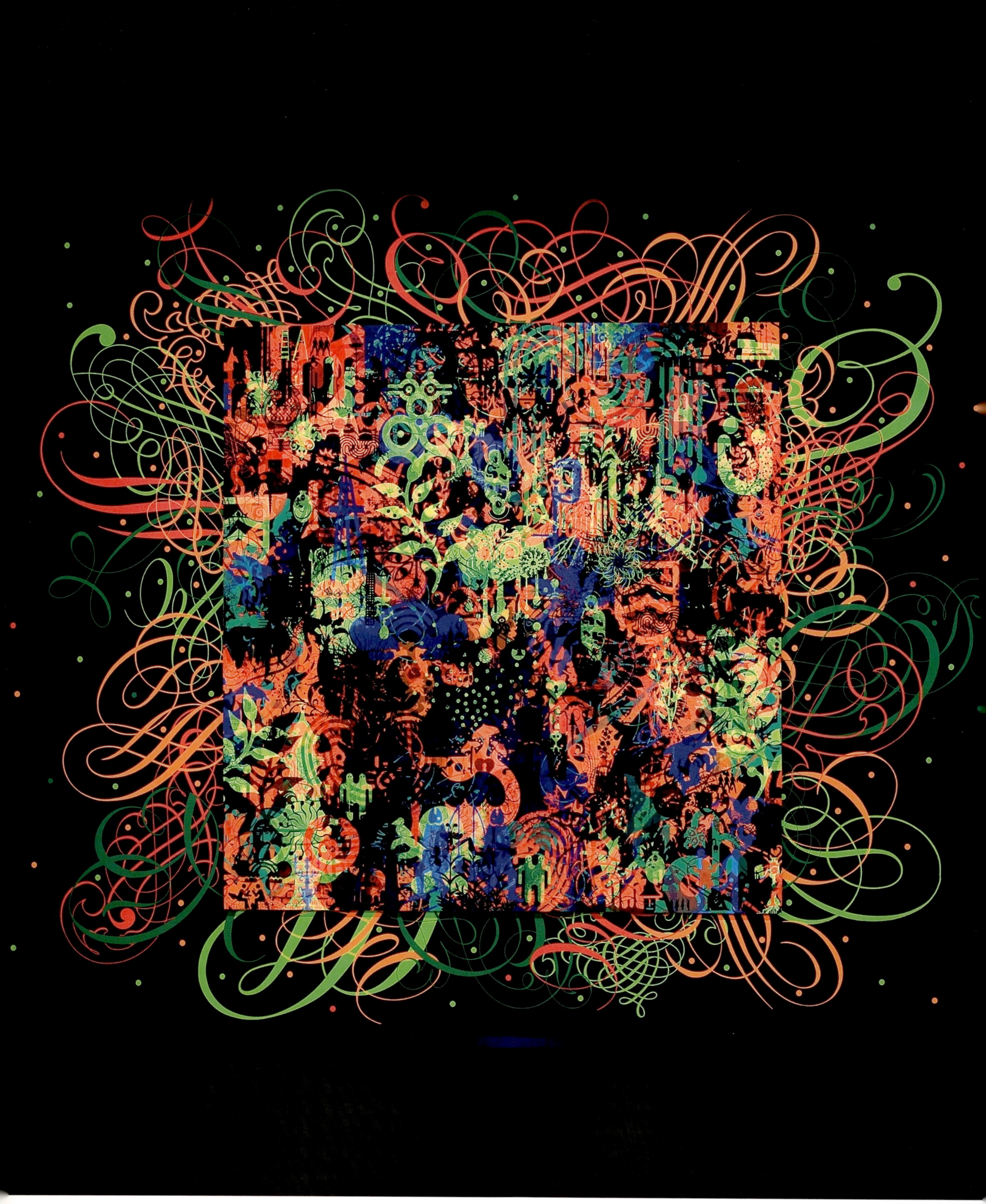

Pinching the Cat in the Dark
2008, acrylic on linen, 72 x 72 in., exhibited with fluorescent vinyl under black light at Artcore/Fabrice Marcolini, Toronto (installation view above).

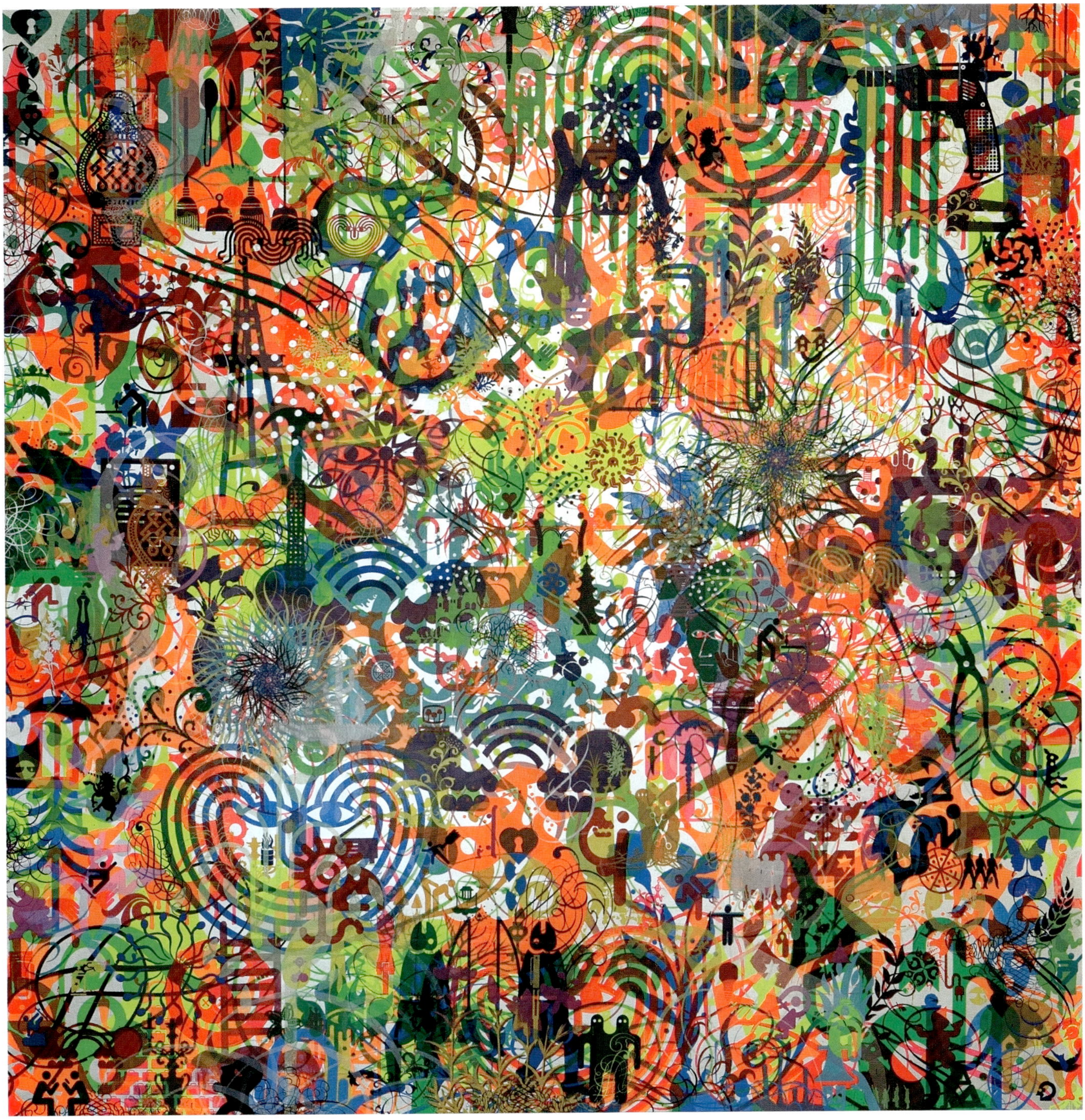

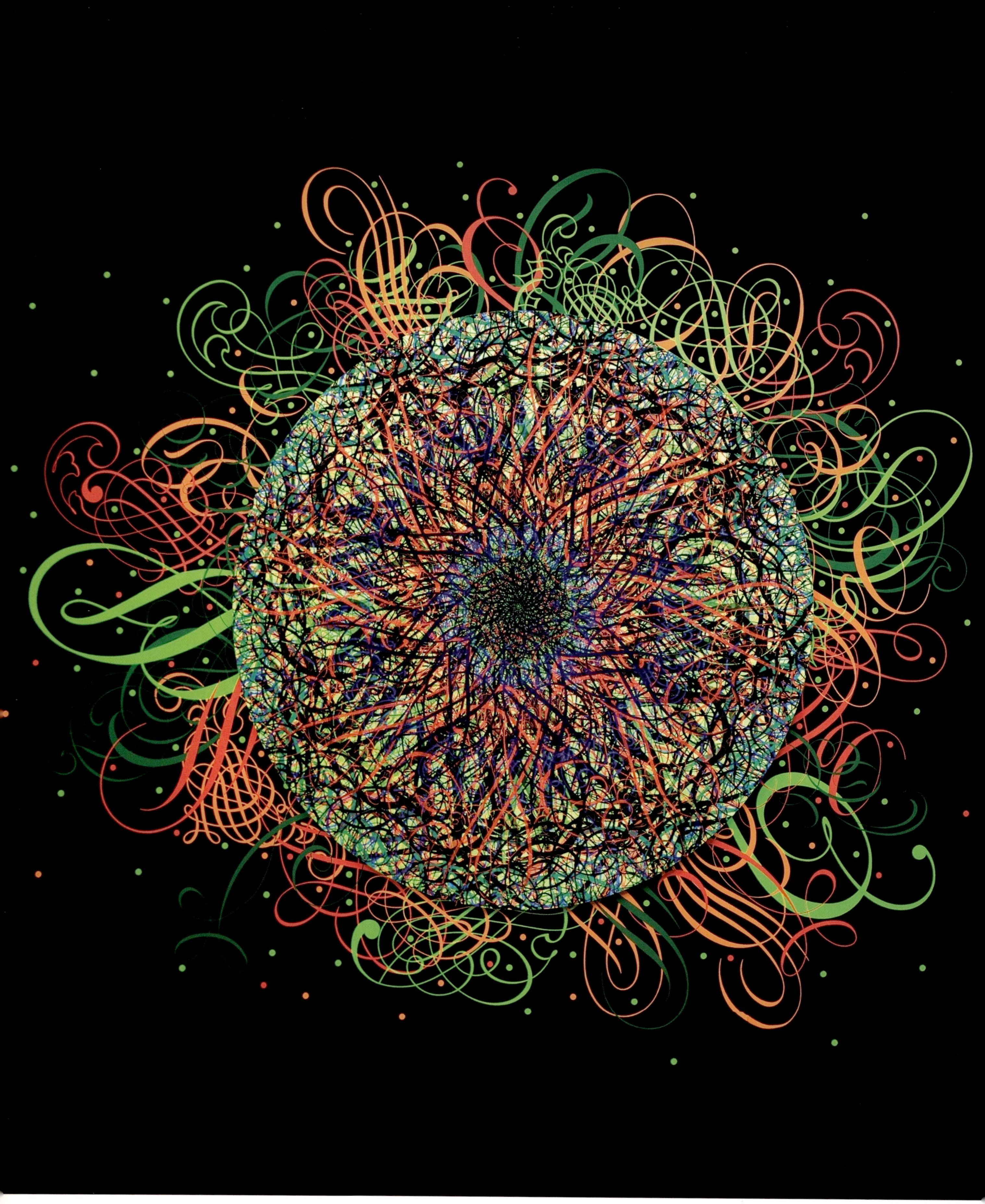

Untitled (Black Hole, Fluorescent Yellow)
2008, acrylic on linen, 72 in. diameter, exhibited with fluorescent vinyl under black light at Artcore/Fabrice Marcolini, Toronto (installation view above).

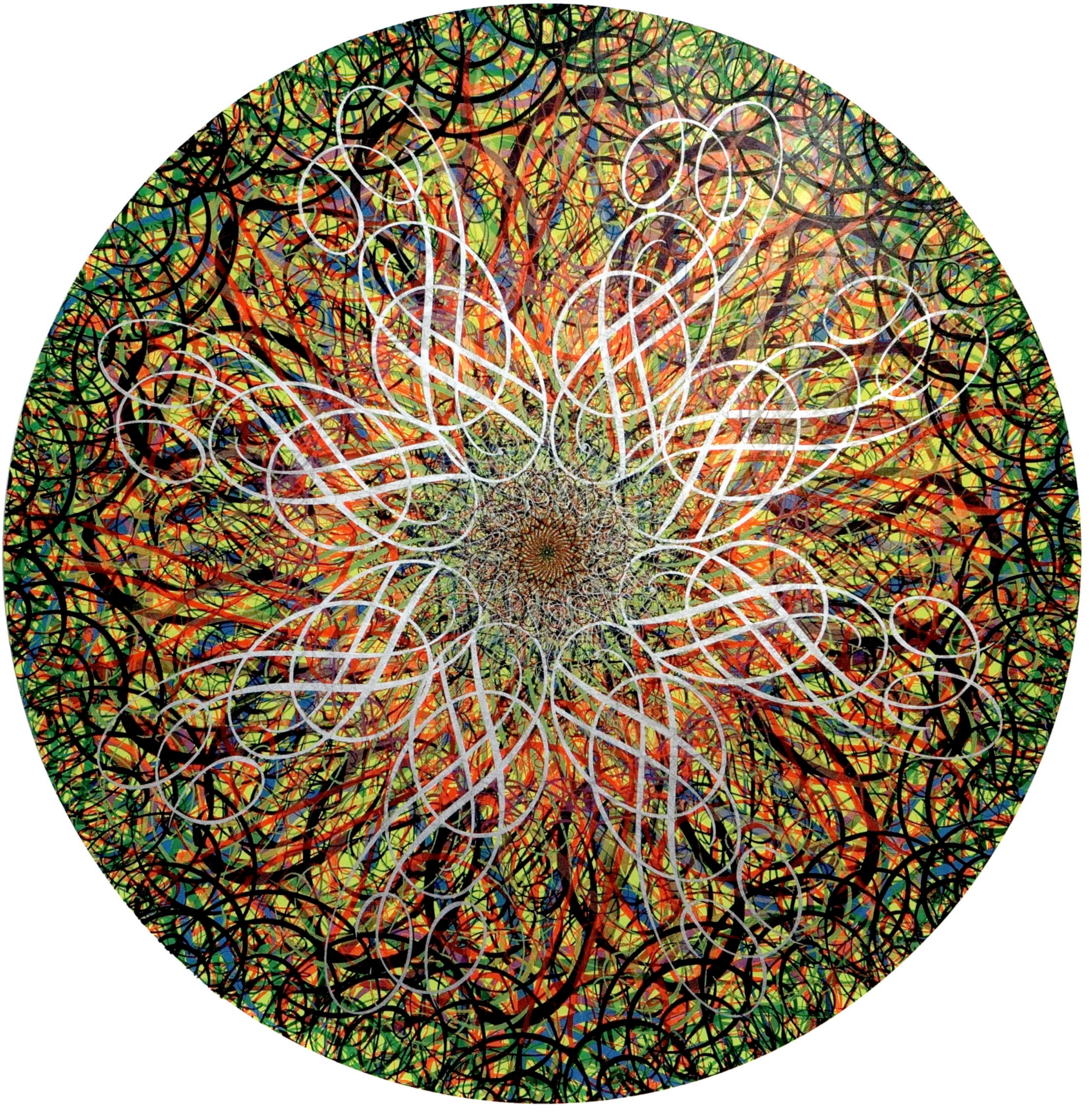

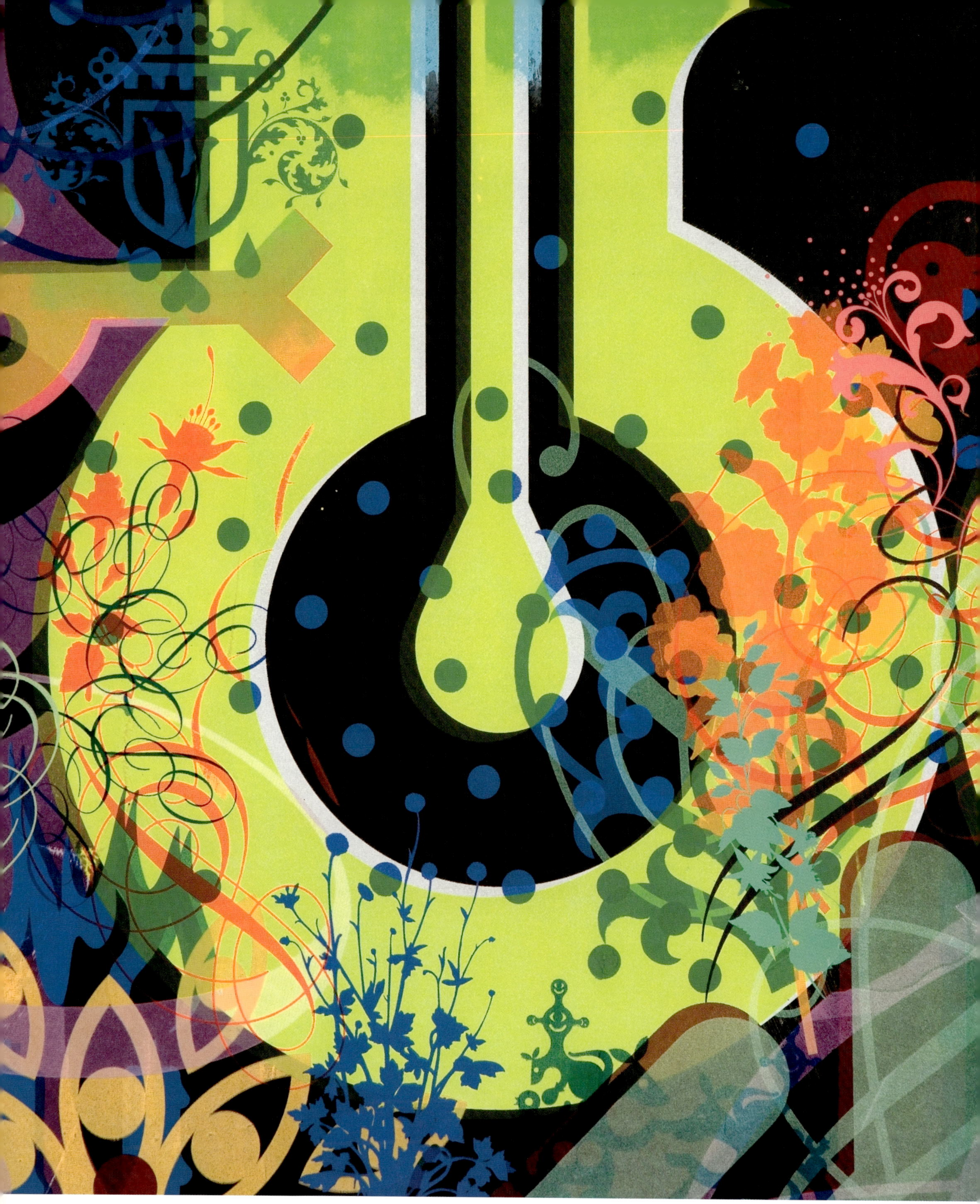

Duality
2008, acrylic on canvas, 72 in. diameter.
(detail above)

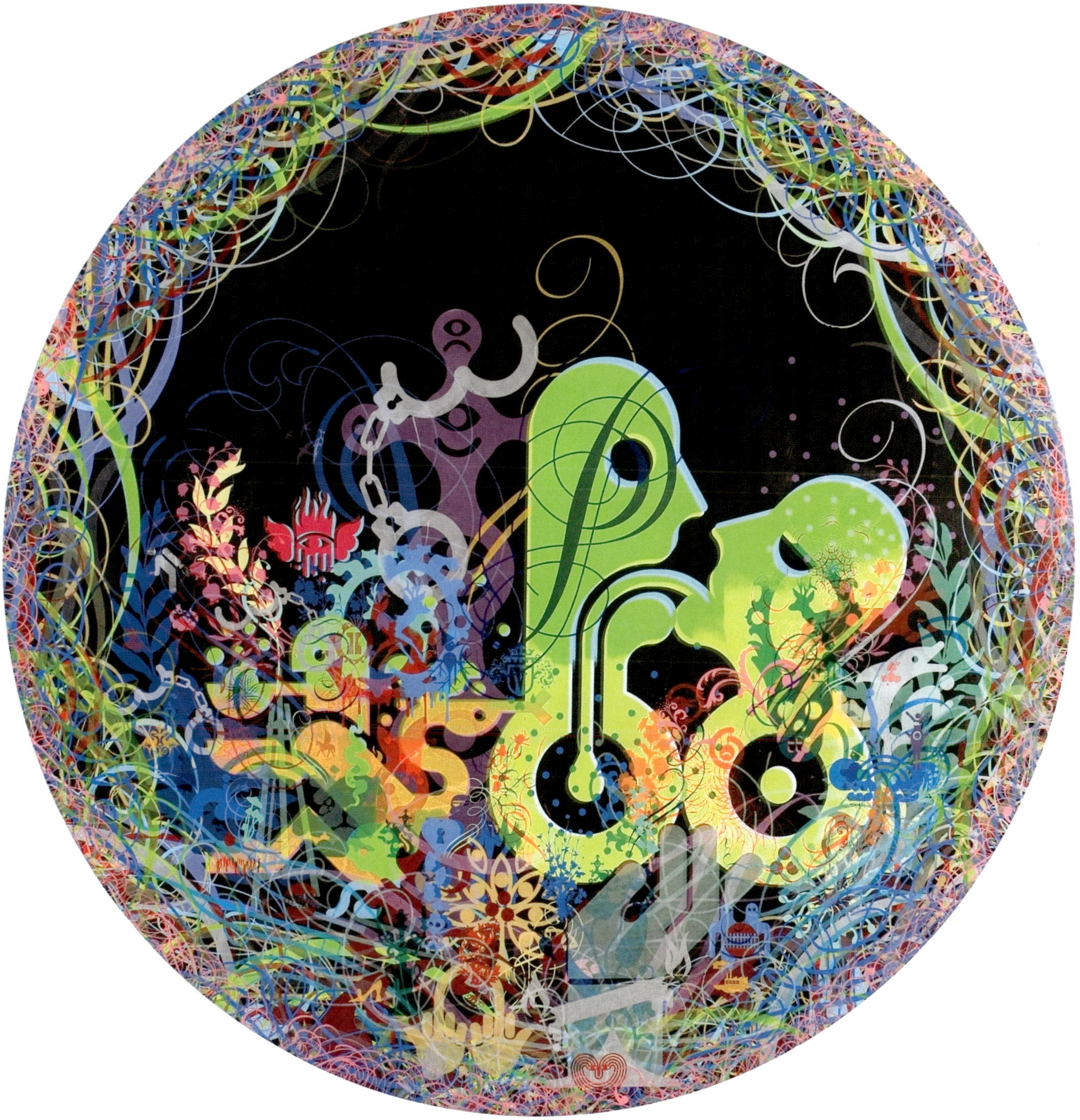

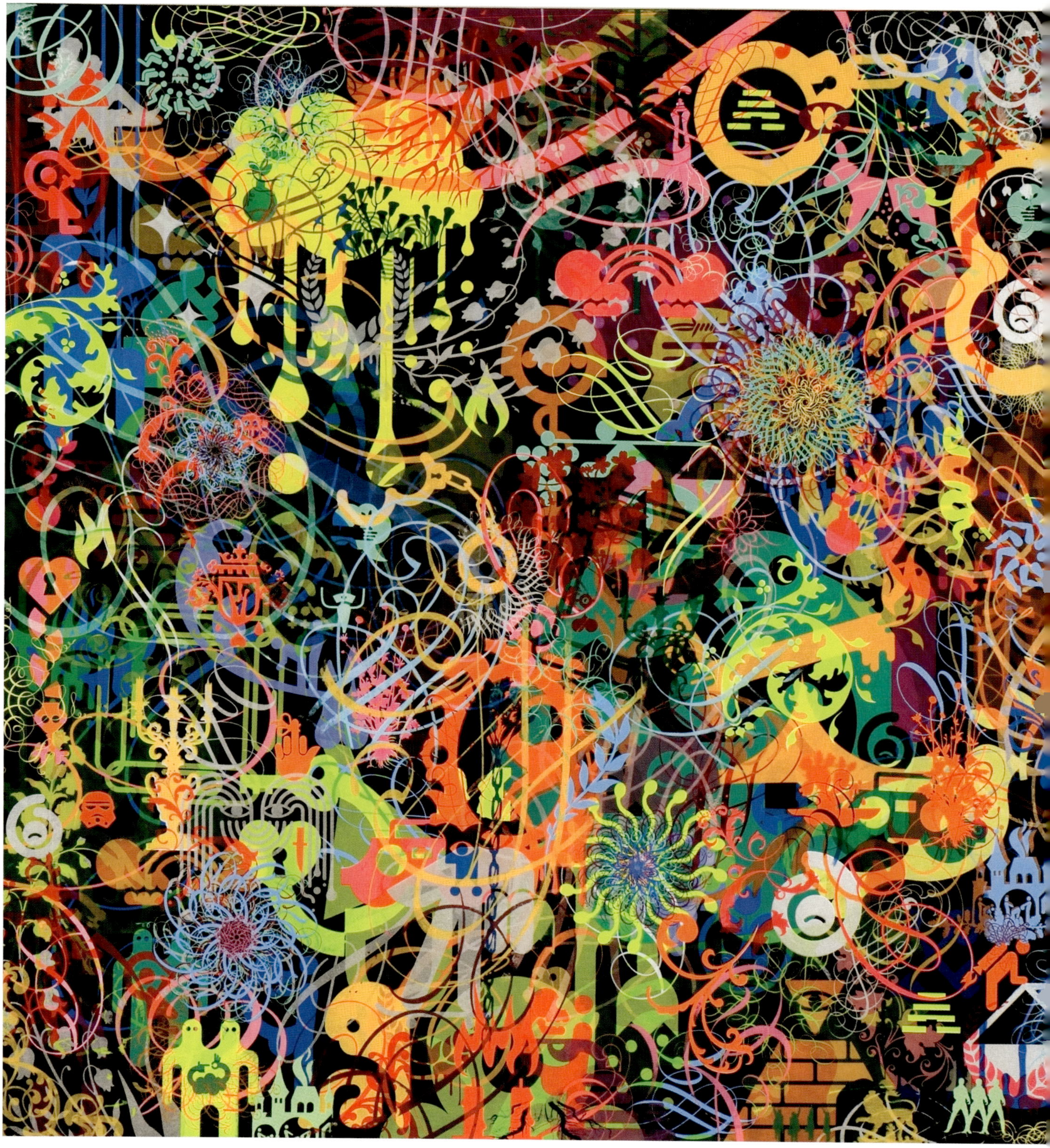

No Sin / No Future
2008, acrylic on canvas, diptych, 48 x 48 in. each, 48 x 96 in. total.
(details on following pages)

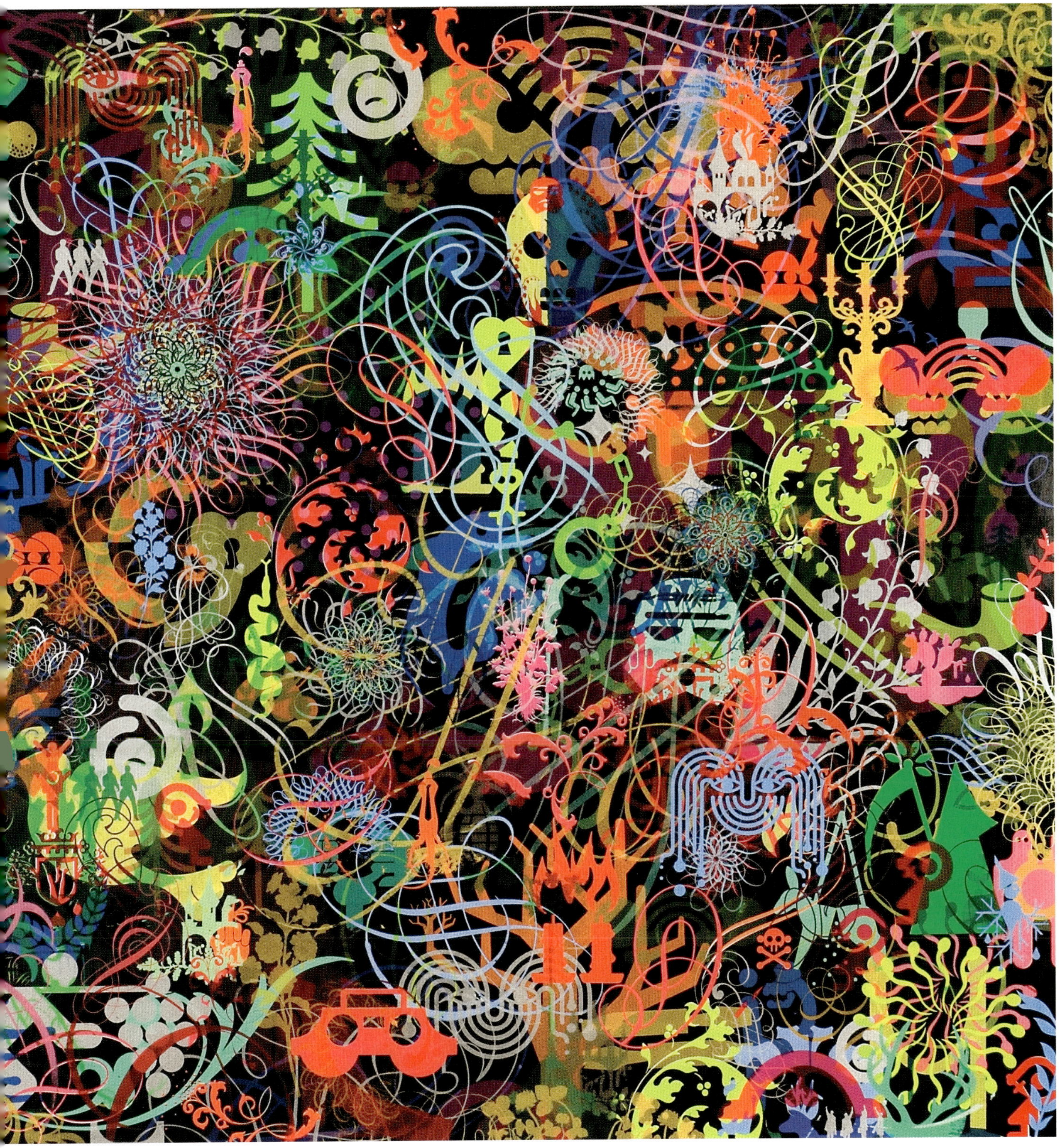

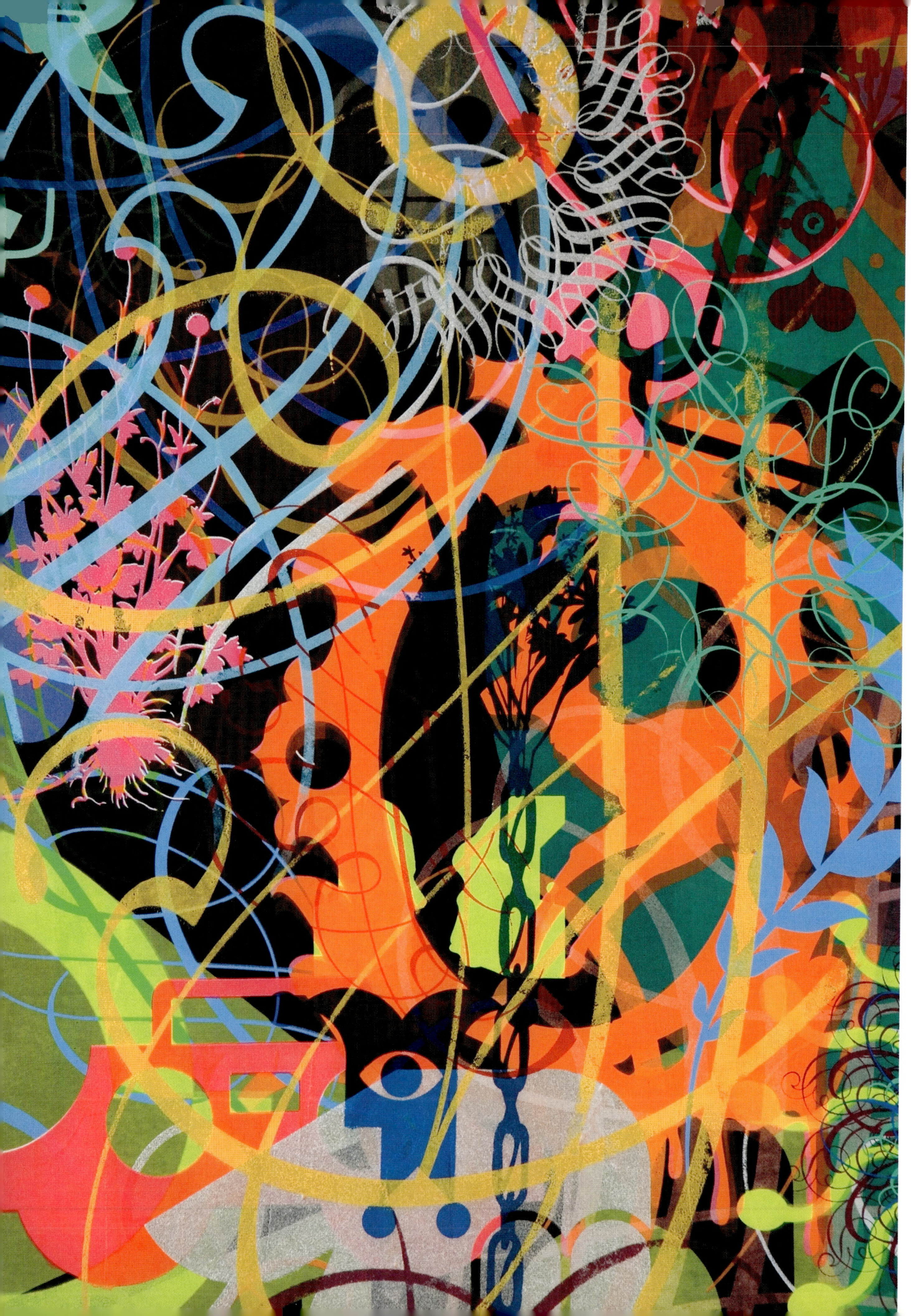

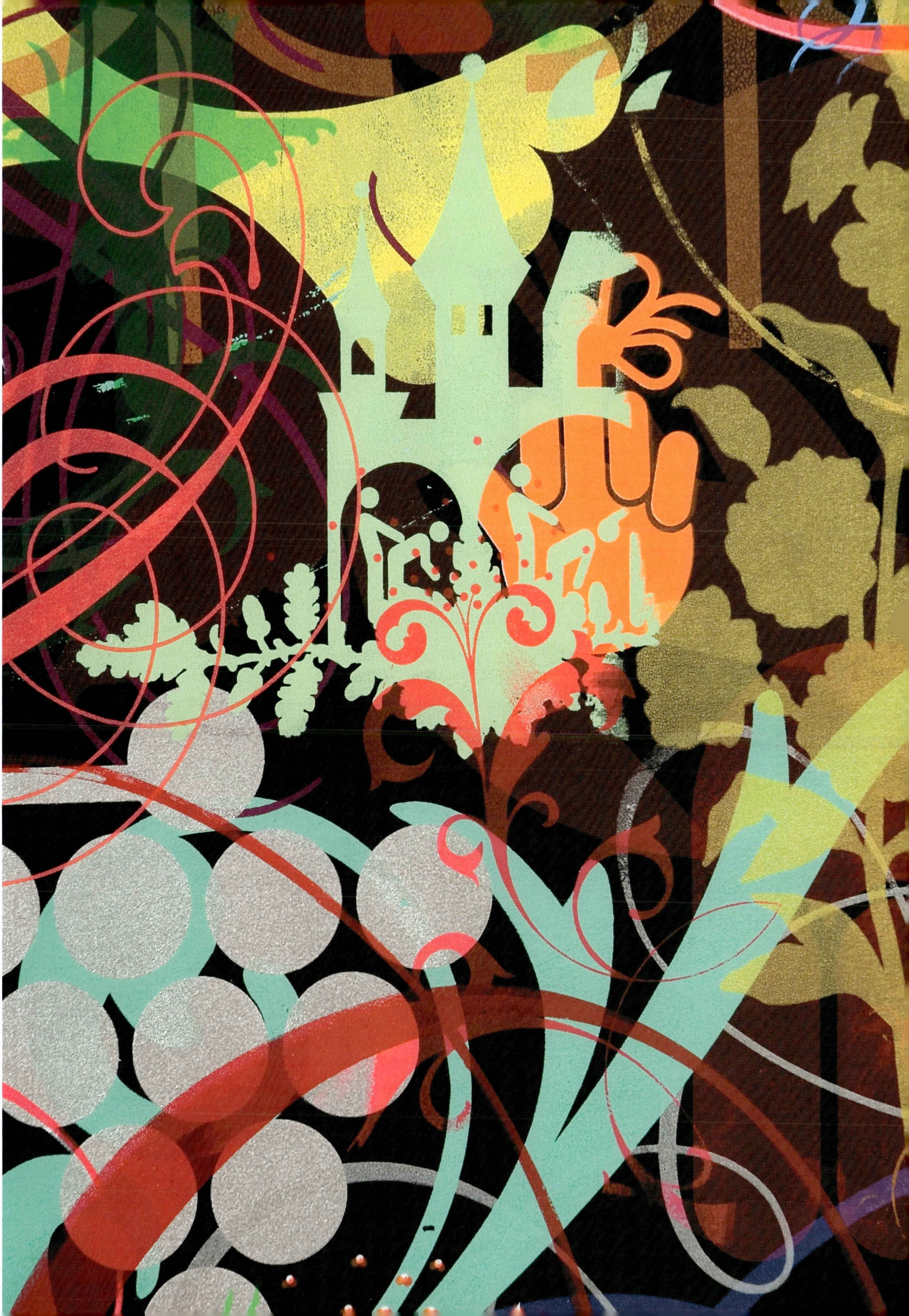

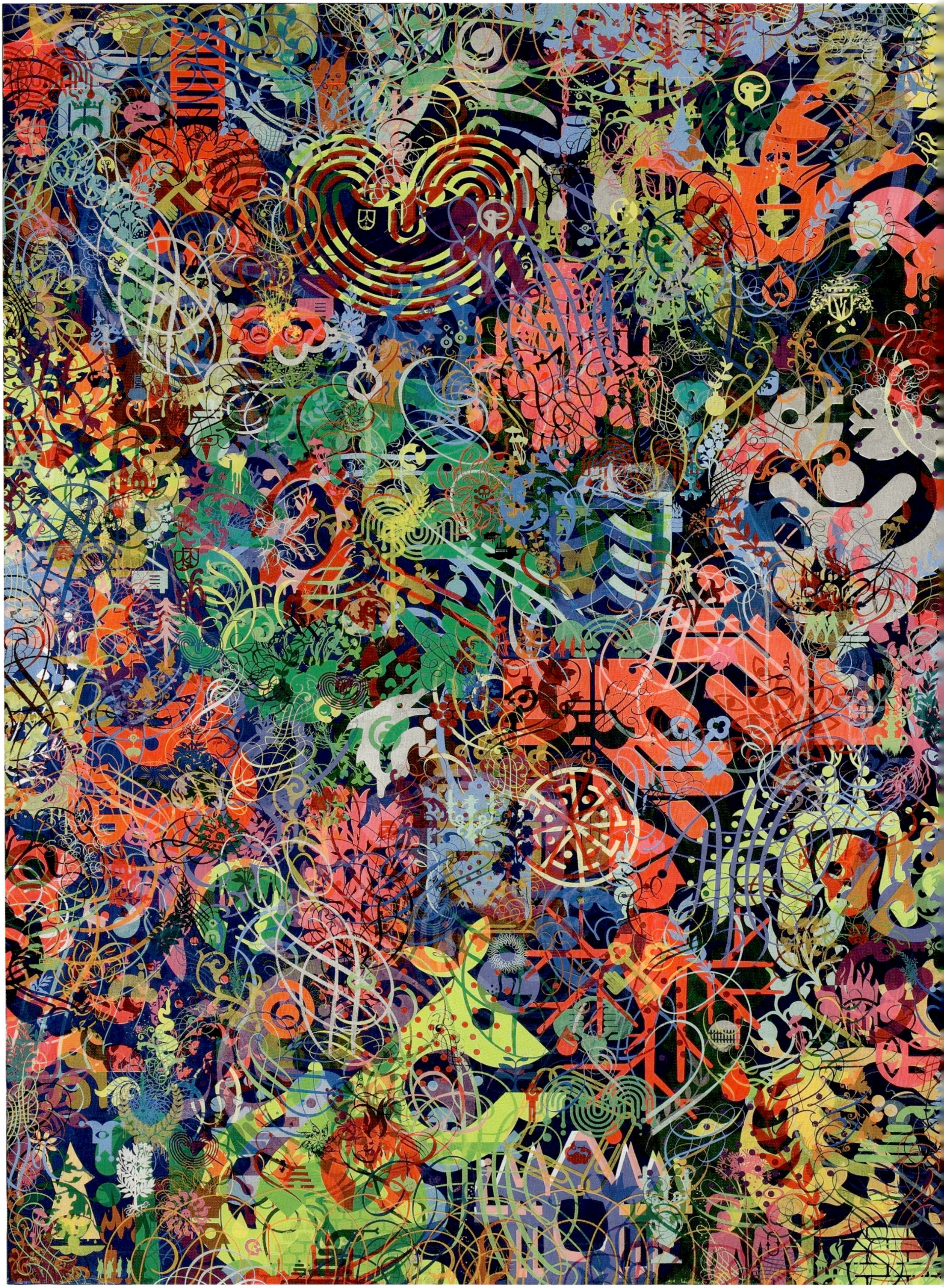

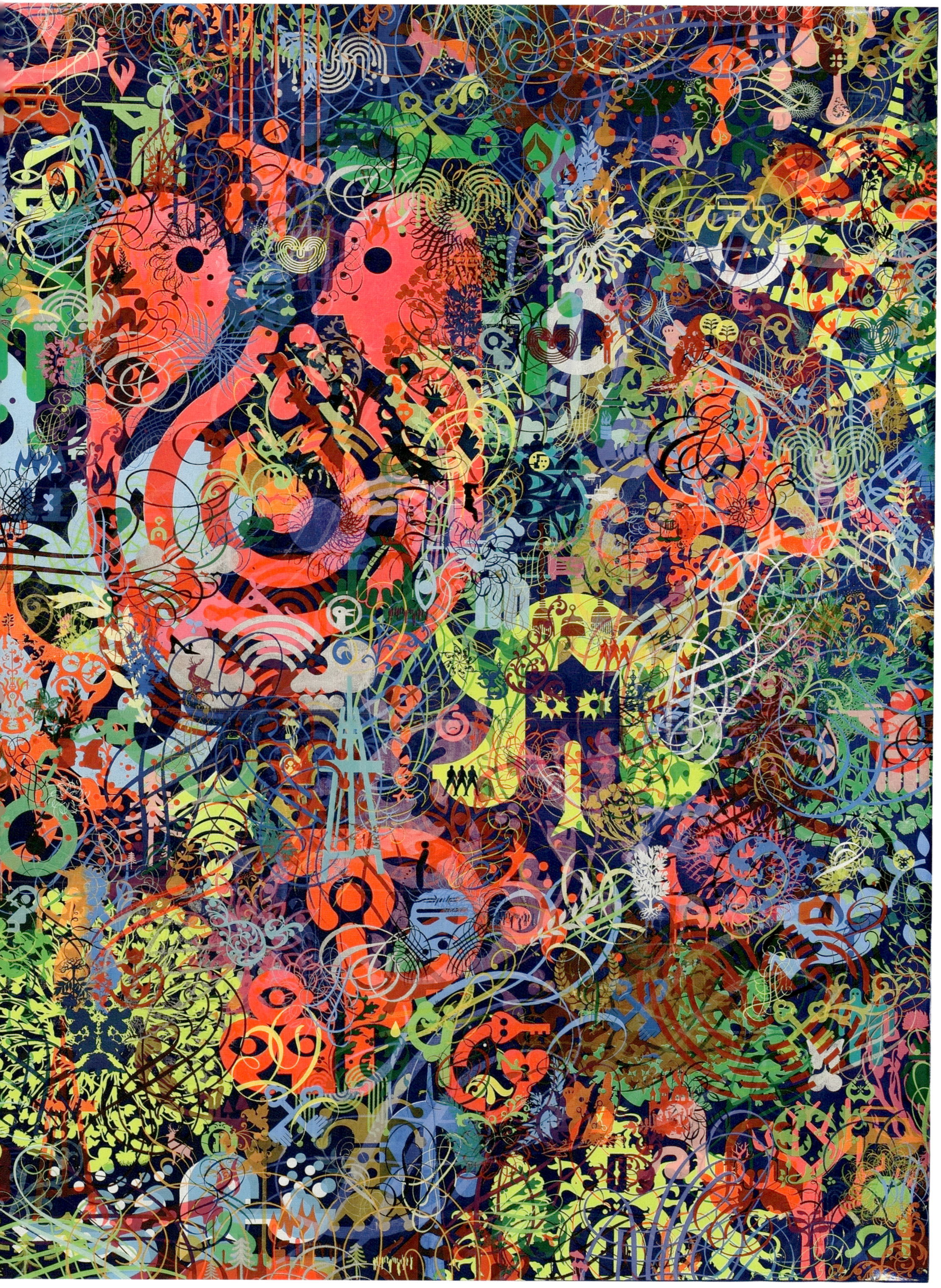

Overleaf: *Only a Thief Thinks Everybody Steals*
2008, acrylic on canvas, 96 x 144 in.

Untitled (Aesthetic Comfort)
2008, acrylic on wood panels, 24 in. diameter each.

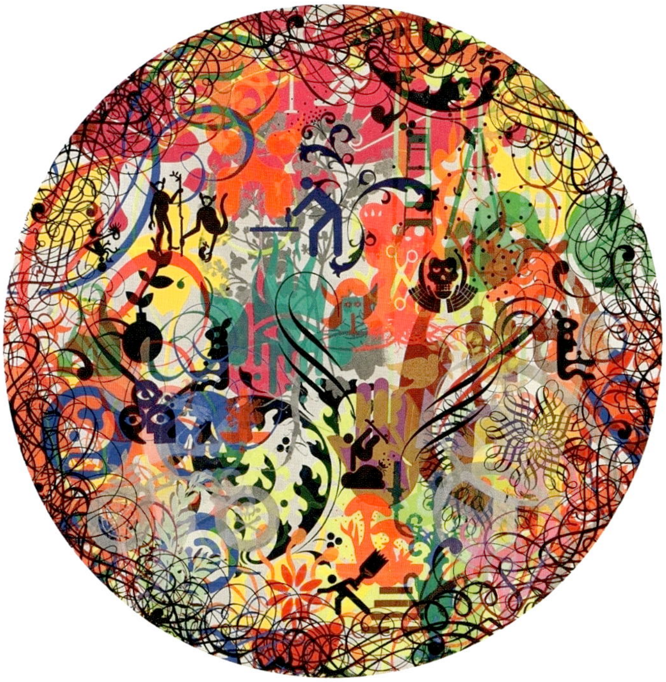
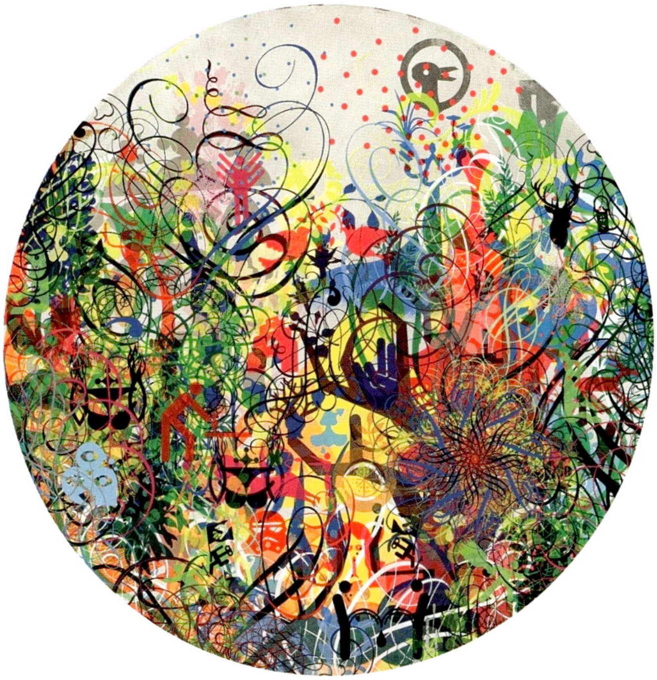
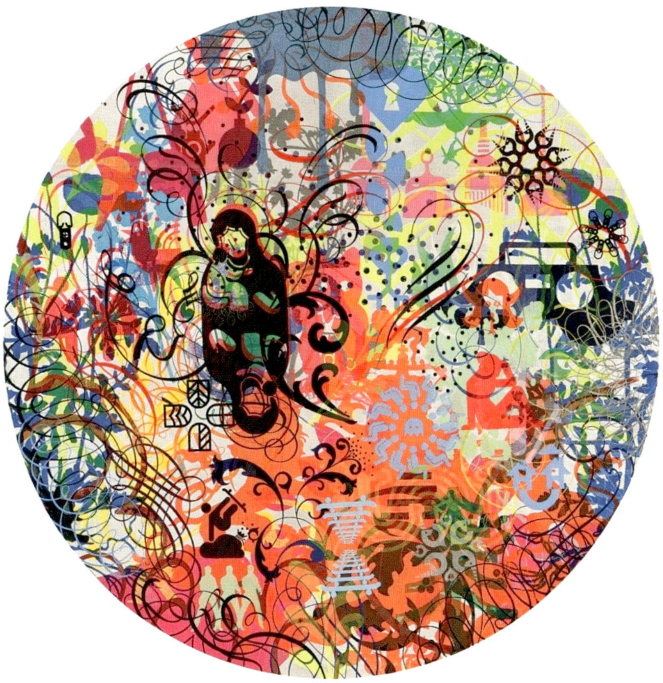
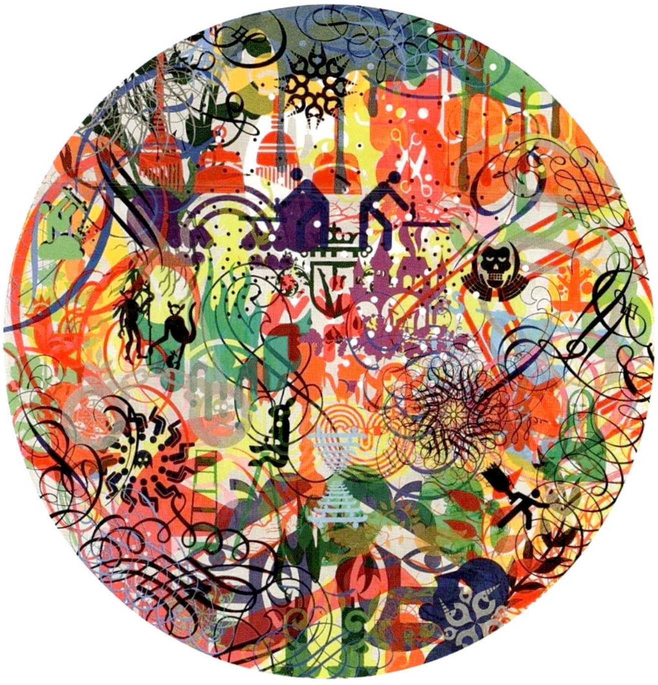

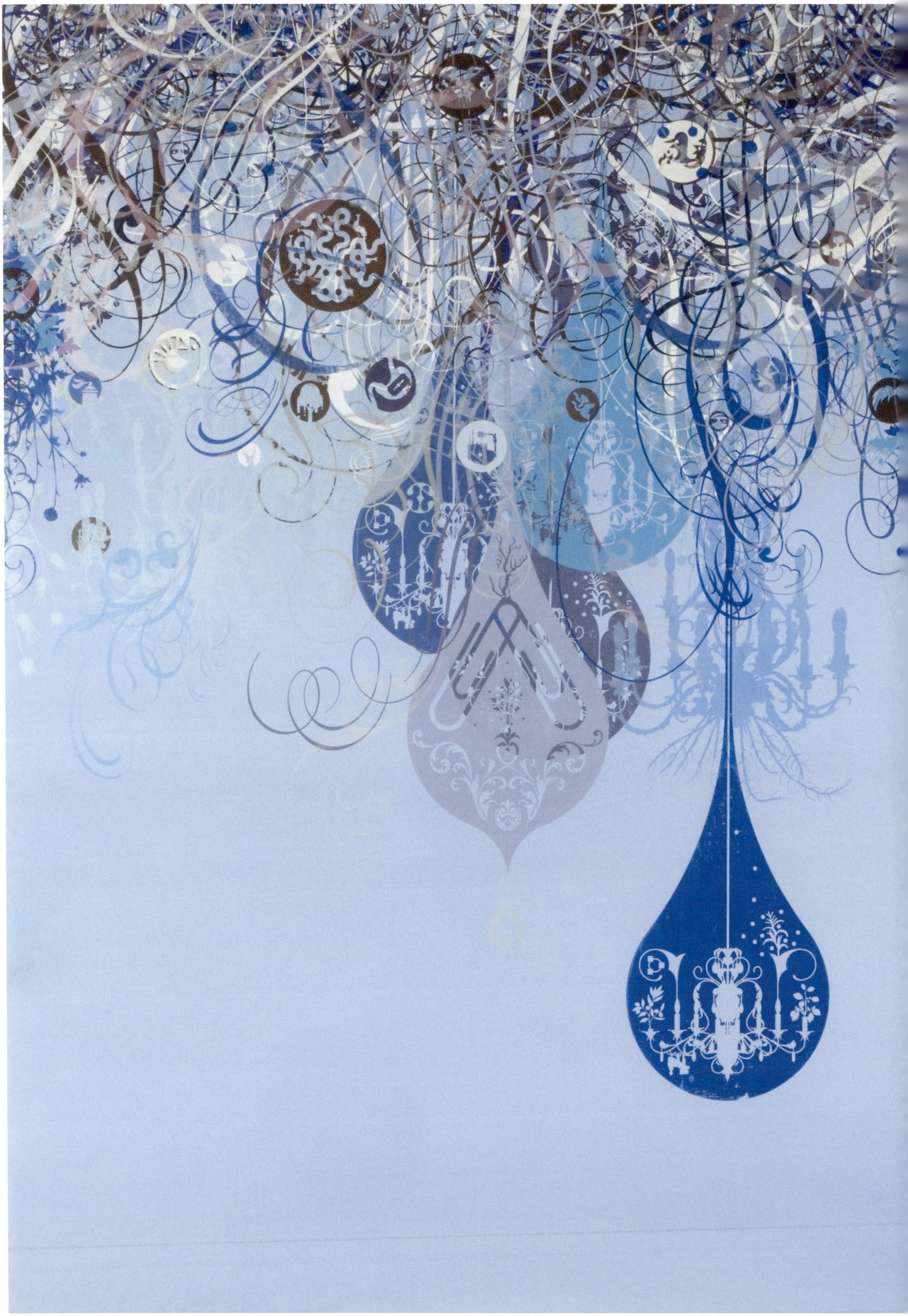

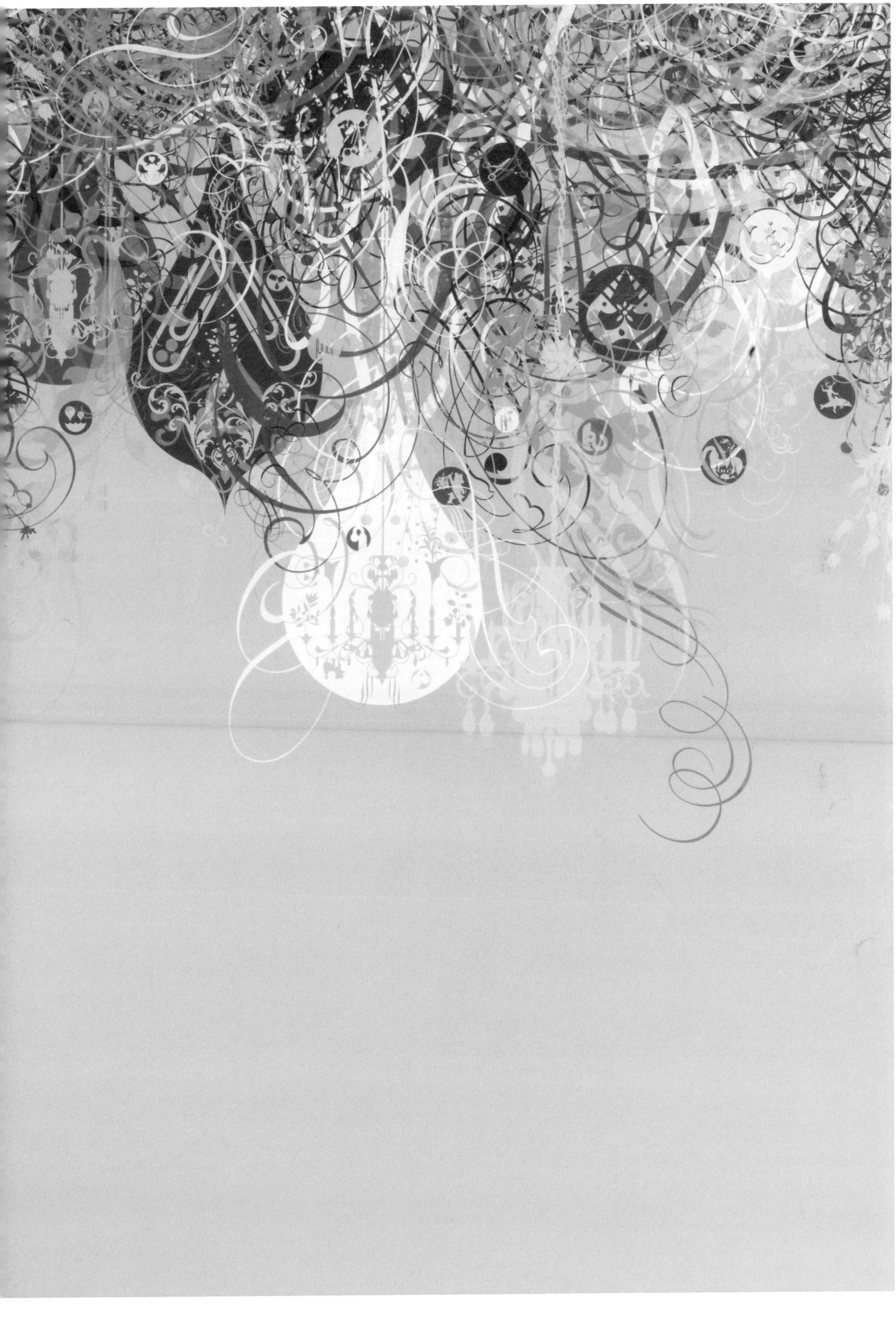

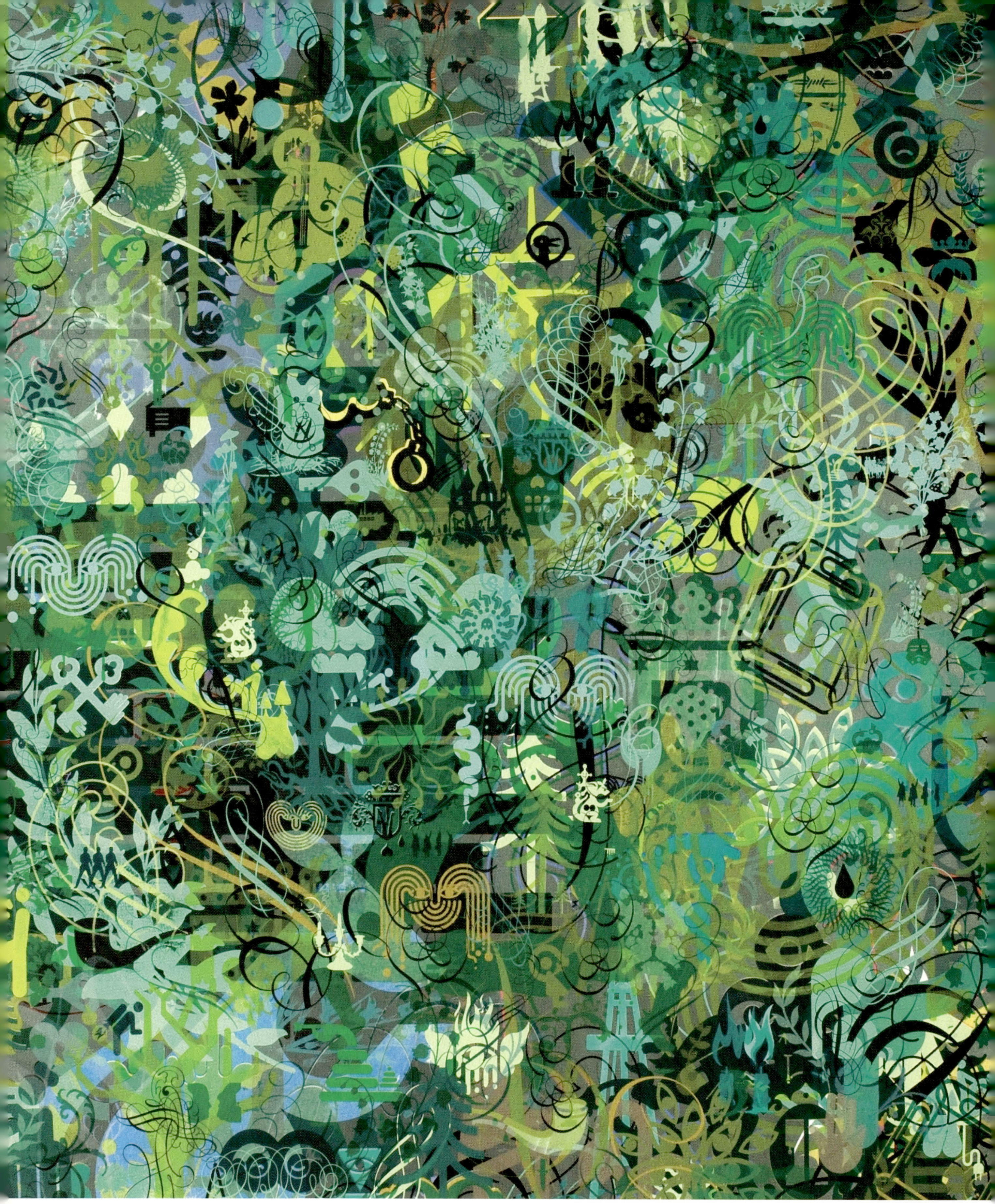

Overleaf: *Four Cats My Way*
2006, acrylic on linen, 96 x 144 in.

Untitled
2008, acrylic on canvas, 72 x 90 in.
(detail above)

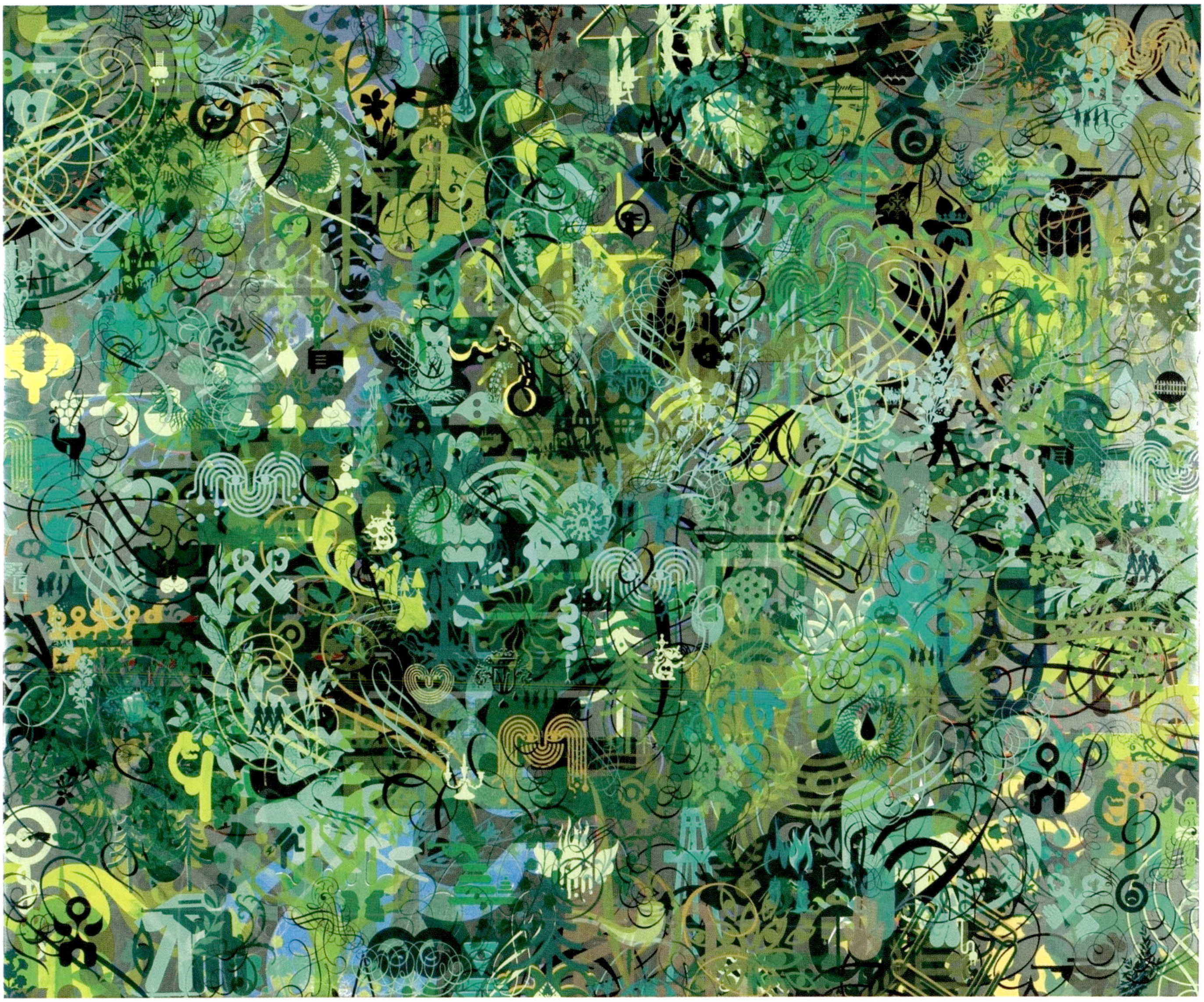

Paying You with the Same Coin
2008, oil and acrylic on wood panel, 65 x 55 in.

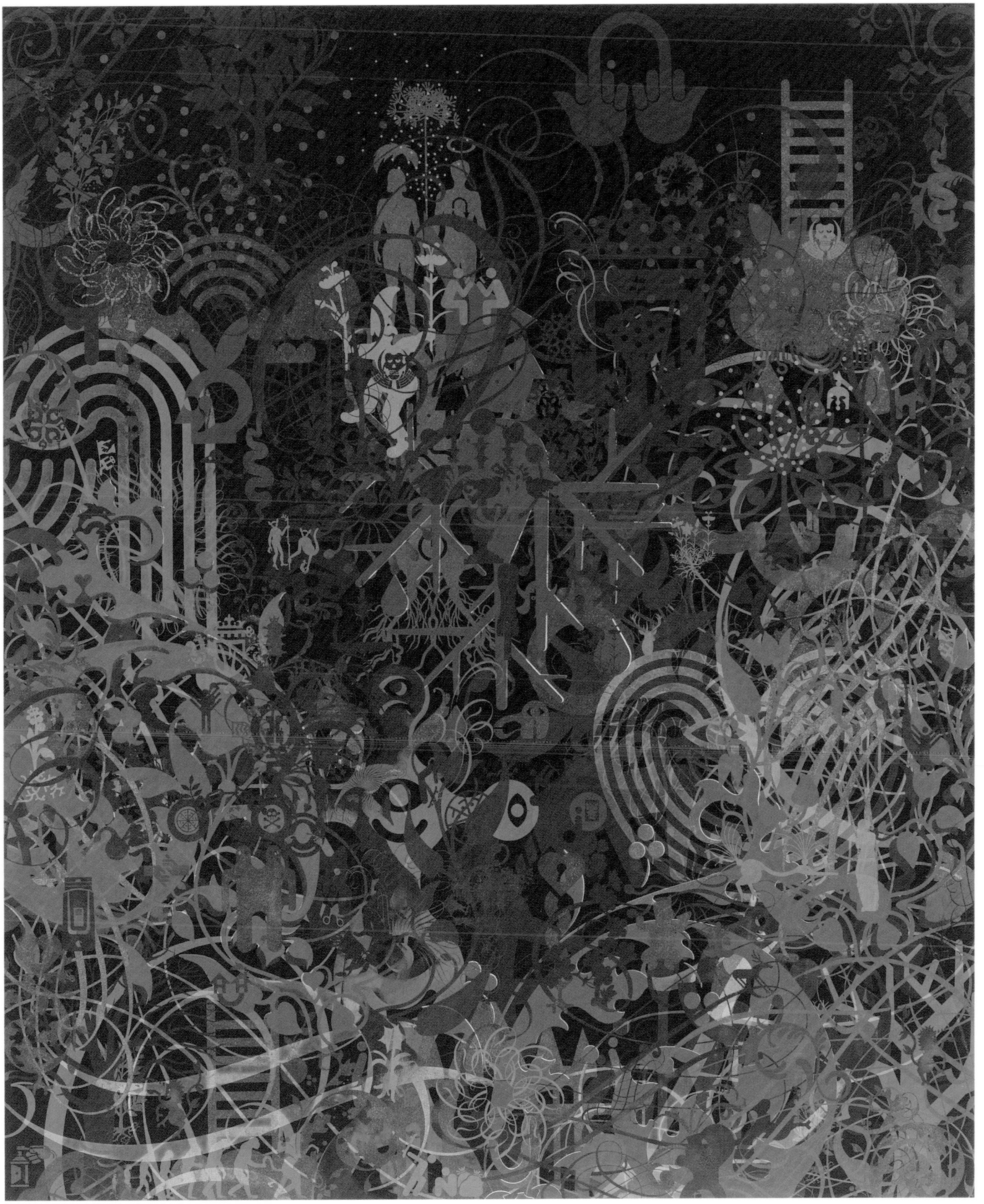

Faith
2008, acrylic on canvas, 96 x 96 in.
(detail above)

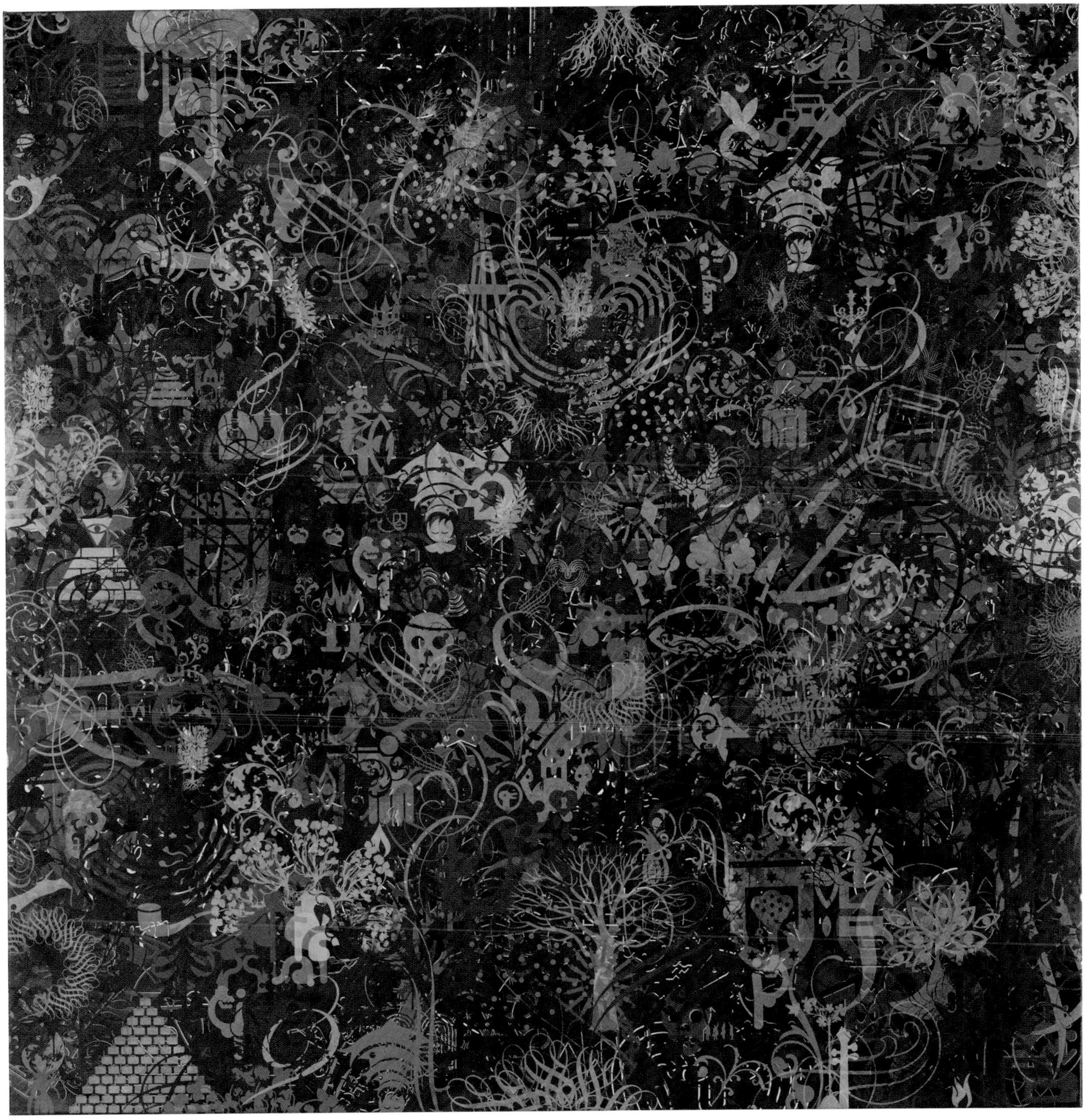

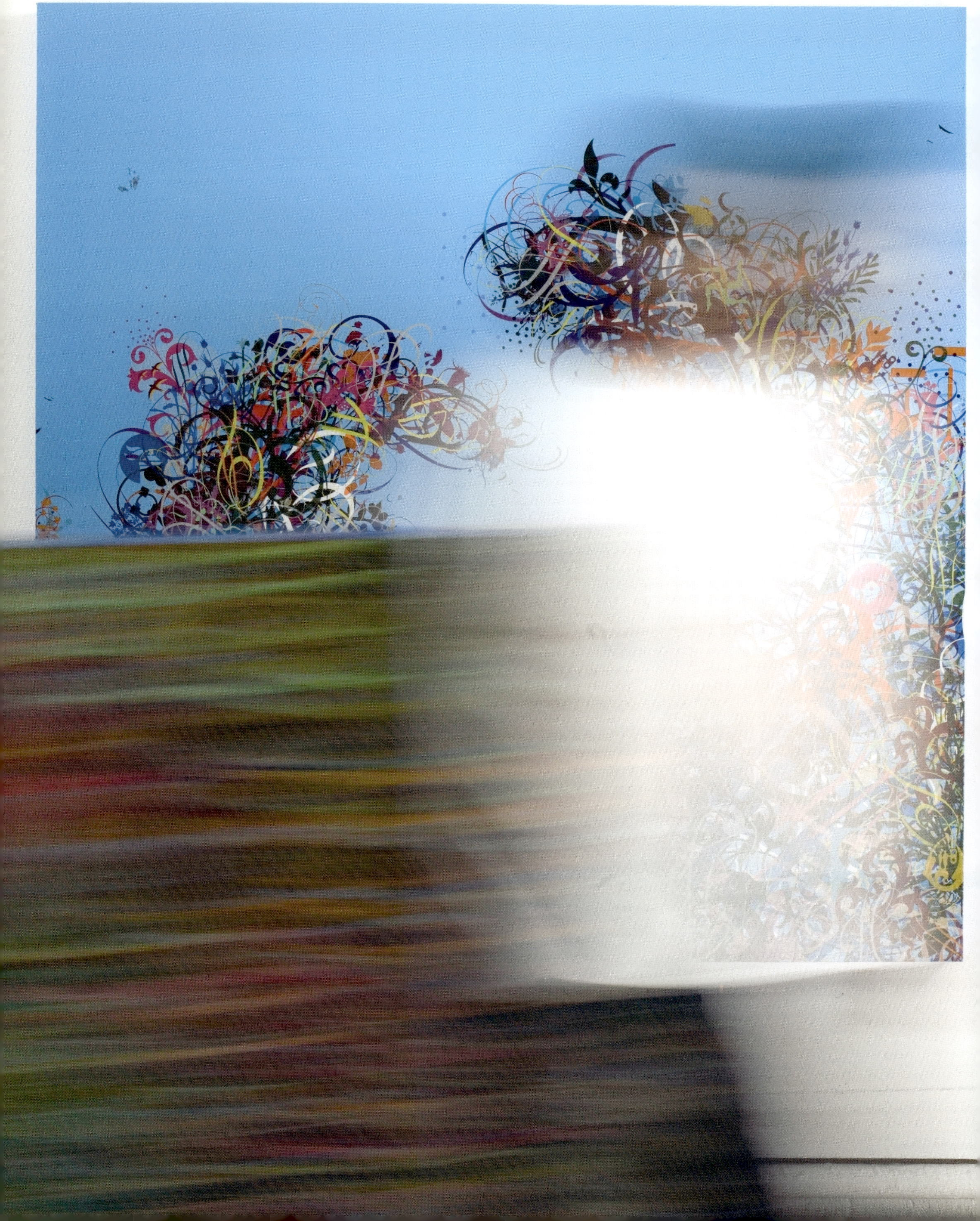

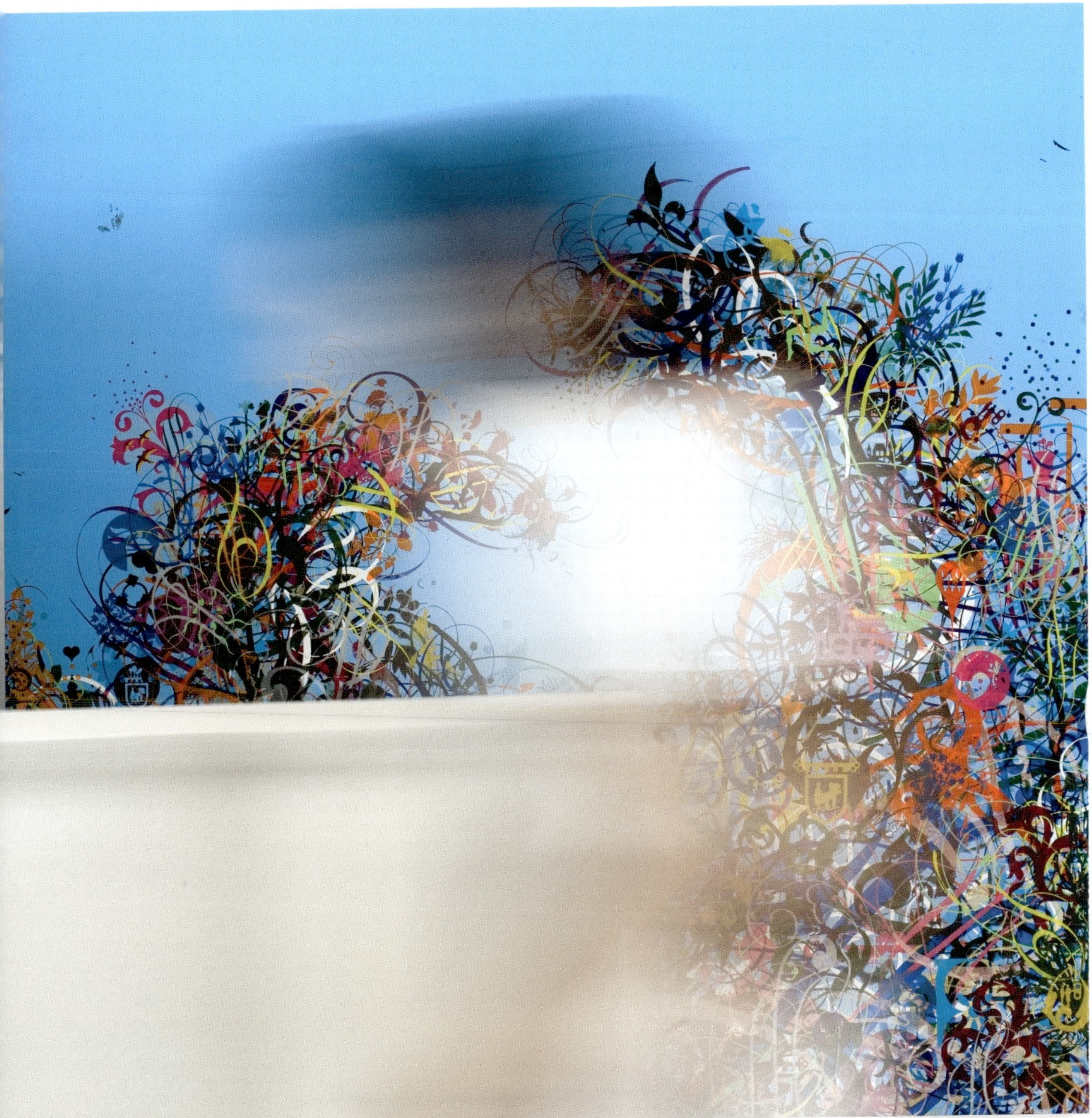

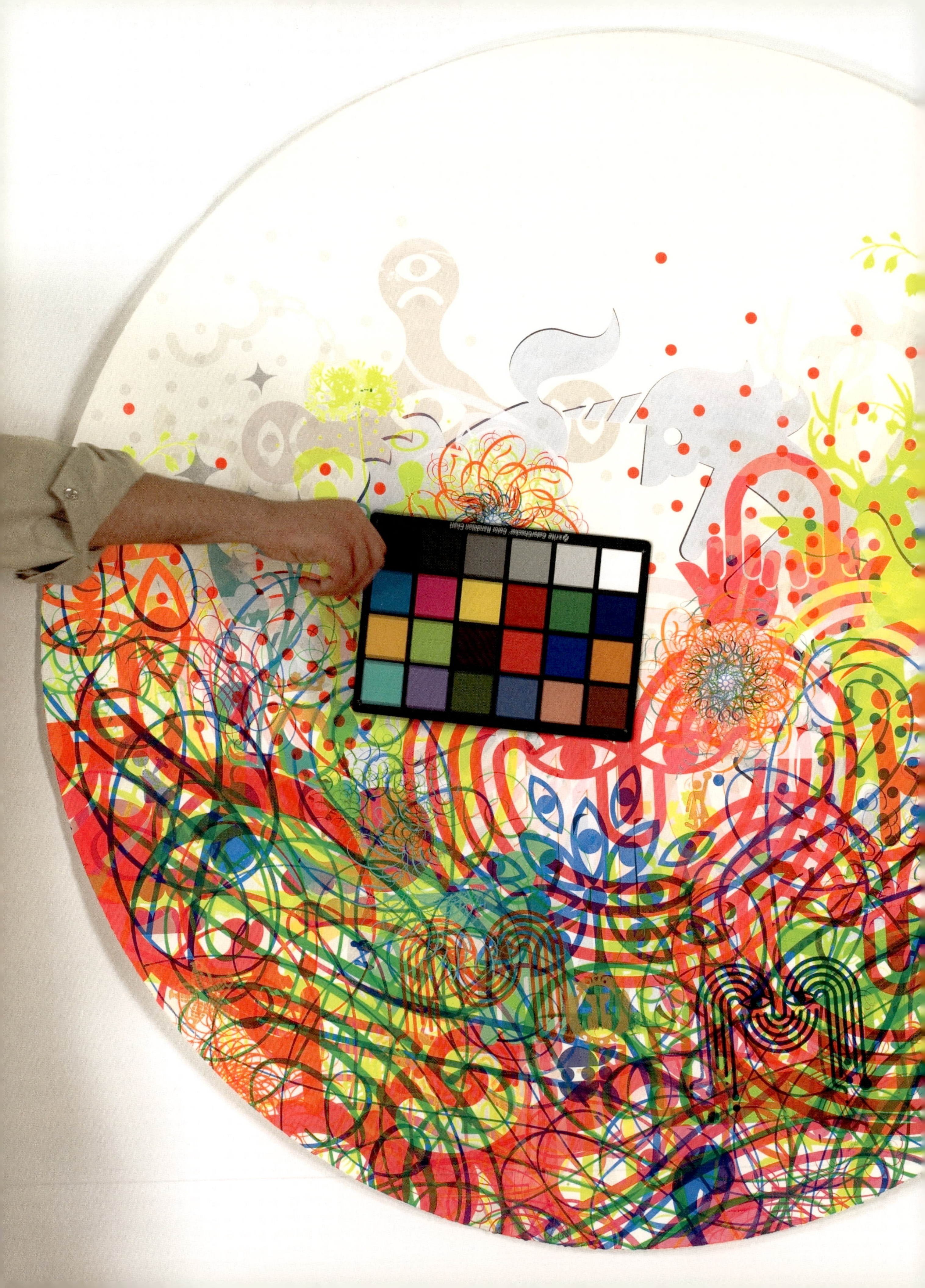

The Q&A 500

Tom Greenwood and Ryan McGinness (153)

Tom and Ryan are friends who work across the street from each other in Chinatown, which allows for frequent lunches and after-work drinks. The two have been periodically bouncing this questionnaire back and forth for over three years. The questions, originally asked more randomly than they appear here, have been reordered into related sections. The exchange reveals the friendly one-upmanship of two people who have spent a lot of time talking with each other. Tom's questions are as revealing as Ryan's answers, and a portrait of both develops.

001 At what age did you decide you wanted to be an artist, and was it ever anything else before that? I have always drawn and made things. From an early age, I was recognized and rewarded for having some aptitude for that. However, being an artist never seemed like a real possibility. There was no tangible model for that kind of a life in the suburbs of Virginia Beach. Because I also did well academically, a career as an architect seemed to be a good match, because most concerned parents believe that if you're smart and can draw, you become an architect. But while I was in high school, I discovered this thing called graphic design and *Émigré* magazine, in particular. Design seemed to be a career that rewarded intelligence, and I recognized that I was already practicing this thing called graphic design through the things I liked to make—posters, cassette covers, t-shirts, painting skateboards, etc. So, I got a scholarship to study graphic design at Carnegie Mellon University, which is a school known for its intellectual rigor and practical application. While there, my studio classes were primarily in design, and most of my lecture classes were in art history and theory. Although I was making paintings while in school and afterwards when I moved to Manhattan, I had to work as a designer to pay the bills. I was very good at it, but I soon realized that the design industry has nothing to do with the formal concerns of manipulating forms and picture planes. The irony is that visual-art concepts are taught in design programs, but the design industry has nothing to do with art. I decided that I was simply going to make whatever I wanted to make and on my own terms. When you do that, what you produce is best matched for an art context.

002 There are a lot of recurring images in your paintings. Do you have an active library of those that you draw from, and if so, how many are there? I am always sketching and generating drawings. There is a bit of a library of images built up by now, but there is no good system for organizing and keeping track of them, so it is difficult to quantify them. I will also redraw and remix some drawings, so that makes cataloging especially difficult. Some of the drawings stay in the mix longer than others.

003 Do you have a limit to the number of times you will use any of your images? No. Some images stay in circulation longer than others, and still others get reworked over time. I like to describe my drawings as being liquid imagery.

004 In how many different paintings do you typically use a single screen? Approximately 10.

005 Some of your recent stuff is surprisingly rough in presentation, and even includes drips and brushstrokes. Are these anomalies or possible glimpses at what's to come? Perhaps it is an indication of what's not to come. I go back and forth between looser and tighter work. The messier bits are actually calculated signifiers of what has historically been recognized as "arty." Those smudges and traces of my process are art jokes.

006 Your work seems to be getting simpler and more direct again, the inessentials stripped away. Do you consider this a new phase or a return to an unfinished one? It's cyclical. I go back and forth,... which is linear, I suppose. I should say I go around and around.

007 What do you think you would have to do to get someone to say you'd sold out? Perhaps do something solely for the money. Or, soullessly for the money.

008 Describe a commercial project that you'd be into. I am absolutely not interested in applied art if it means my work is applied to an agenda besides the one dictated by the work itself. I believe in art for art's sake. That is not to say that the art itself cannot be a commercial project. But the art should always be a commercial for itself only.

009 Do you work with music on? What's in the A-rotation at the moment? All Girl Summer Fun Band, Smoosh, BARR, Placebo, Sleater-Kinney, Tullycraft, Le Tigre, Bis, Arab Strap, Bauhaus, Go Sailor, The Hong Kong, and others. (Not a band called "Others," but other bands as well.) (154)

010 What are your most and least favorite parts of what you do? Most favorite parts: Being alone working, sketching, reading, and just quietly looking at the work. Least favorite parts: Any administrative/paperwork, answering unsolicited e-mails, and chasing owed money.

011 How much of your work process is improvised? How much is pre-planned? The percentage that is improvised is always pre-planned.

012 What percentage of your time working is spent on a computer? What percentage is spent painting? Close to 50/50.

013 Can you give an example of something you've tried in your art that just didn't work? I tried to make art, and that didn't work. It is only when I abandoned making what I thought of as art that I was making honest work.

014 How many cavities do you have? Five. (155)

015 What are your guilty pleasures? I like playing soccer, but I don't have much time for it. When I make time for it, I sometimes feel guilty.

016 If you were stuck on a desert island, what are three things you wouldn't want? Desire, time, and hope.

017 Your work often addresses consumer culture. Where do you think art fits into that world? Culture does not exist without consumers. This is not to say that all culture is for sale, but all culture needs receivers in order to exist. Art is in the upper atmosphere of that world, somewhere close to a consumer god.

018 Several of your recent paintings are on circular canvases. And when you renovated your apartment you had rounded inserts built into the corners of your rooms, getting rid of the corners altogether. Is there anything to this? I suppose there may be something to this. Both are attempts at getting rid of the corners in search of an edgeless space. No, wait, I think both may be attempts at containing space to create controlled and inescapable environments.

019 Do you think a sense of humor in art is important? Do you think a sense of humor about art is important? I think a sense of humor in and about anything and everything is important. There is truth in jest.

020 What question would you ask you if you were me, and how would you answer it? Would I still be me and be asking myself a question, or would you or someone else be me in some wacky Freaky Friday turn of events? I assume you mean I would be me questioning myself in which case one of us would have to be older than the other, right? Or would it be possible to split into two same-age parallel exactly identical beings? Would we have the same mind? Where is the mind? I guess I don't understand the question.

021 You've done several video pieces, which were collected on your *Video Happiness* DVD. Do you plan to work in video again at some point? I have no immediate plans to work in video. I never really planned on it in the first place. I just had a few ideas that could only be realized in video, so I had to make some videos.

022 What artists working today do you most admire? I like people who are doing it on their own and not waiting for or seeking permission from anyone. This list is constantly changing, but right now I like the guys at the Lonely Island, Smoosh, Stella, Wonder Showzen, and the Kid America Adventure Hour.

023 Who are some artists whose work you have on your walls? REAS, KAWS, KR, DALEK, RO-STARR,... mostly artists with all-caps, fake names.

024 Does that rotate? Yes. I've hung DALEK upside-down.

025 Is there anyone that you would like to collaborate with? No.

026 Do you feel a part of any art scene or group? I'm in the traveling "Beautiful Losers" exhibition, and I like a lot of those artists and their work. This is the closest thing to a group or scene I've felt a part of. I have a lot of friends who are artists, but our work isn't similar, so I'd hesitate to define us as a scene or formal group.

(153) Tom also interviewed me in 2002 under the name Nigel Titley for the *Video Happiness* DVD package.

(154) "At the moment," in this case, was 2003. An addendum can be found at .com/somemusic

(155) Now eleven.

027 Do you feel there is still a strong community of artists working in Manhattan? There are a lot of strong microcommunities of artists working in Manhattan.

028 You have some interesting imagery in your work. For example, a human with a rack of antlers and a dangling scrotum kicking a soccer ball. Are there specific messages you'd like to communicate in your work, or do you like to leave it open to interpretation? There is a range of meanings and interpretations to my drawings from the concrete to the more abstract, surreal, and absurd, which is the end of the spectrum I prefer. Communication does not always have to be straightforward. Poetic work that allows for slippery interpretations is very interesting to me. I'm trying to use a concrete visual language (graphic and iconic) to communicate less concrete meanings.

029 What is the relationship between man and nature in your paintings? Man is a part of nature.

030 Where would you most like to have your work shown? I like my work shown in books.

031 Do you typically save your sketches and such? Yes.

032 Assuming that your book *Flatnessisgod* had a message, do you feel that the layers and depth in your recent work in a way contradict it? No. Layers are not the same as imitating three-dimensional space within a picture plane.

033 What happens to the pieces that are made exclusively for your books? There are two kinds of pieces I've made exclusively for the books: paintings on paper or cardboard and digital files. The paintings (of layered silkscreens) usually end up in the trash or as notepaper or wrapping paper. The digital files are stored in archives.

034 Do you see your books as a viable encapsulation of your work or as a separate end altogether? Both. There are three kinds of books I have made: project books where the book is the piece, catalogues for exhibitions, and something in-between. I have always used the book format as a way to organize my thoughts, sketches, work, and other residue from life.

035 Read any good books lately? Yes: Aldous Huxley's *Doors of Perception*.

036 What's the last great movie you saw? Does *Wedding Crashers* count? I laughed. Any movie that makes me laugh is great.

037 Do you enjoy your own show openings and book signings? No. I'm always worried about everyone having a good time, and I want desperately to accommodate everyone. I can't help but assume the role of host, and that's usually not so much fun.

038 What's the strangest art-related solicitation you've received? I often get bothered to have sales agendas attached to my work.

039 What is the first thing you think of when I say the word "meatloaf"? I see a typical sliced meatloaf on a white platter. And then I think about the singer. And then I think about Meatloaf eating meatloaf.

040 Are you religious? There are a lot of things I do religiously, like make my bed, shower, brush my teeth, etc. There are also some things I do ceremoniously, like drink, light candles, and take baths. Also, I tend to celebrate life events and rites of passages like birthdays, weddings, and anniversaries. So, there are many things I do that a lot of religions also have their followers do.

041 Are you spiritual? I think I have a spirit in me. I think we each have a spirit within, and our job is to recognize and honor it.

042 What's a joke you find funny? How do you make a tissue dance? Put a little boogie in it. My friend Ashley told me that years ago.

043 Are you a daily routine guy? I wish I were. I fantasize about having a routine, but there are just too many variables that are out of my control.

044 What time of day are you most productive? Early morning for administrative tasks and late at night for creating.

045 You use automobile paint in your paintings. For someone looking to protect their Ryan McGinness painting would you recommend a particular brand of car wax? That would be great, but unfortunately, there are usually layers of other kinds of paint on top of the car paint that would get damaged with car wax.

046 Your paintings have a very hard and even finish. Do you ever paint on metal? I have worked with metal signage and different fabrication methods involving metal, but I'm not sure I've ever painted directly on metal.

047 What are some of your favorite names for paint colors? "Red," "Orange," "Yellow," "Green," "Blue," "Indigo," and "Violet" are all funny names for colors. What do they mean?

048 Do you think gray is still the new black, and if so, what is the old gray? No, brown is the new black. Gray is back to being gray. There is currently no brown, so you could say there is a brown hole in our rainbow of colors.

049 What's your idea of a great Saturday night? Playing games and drinking with friends in the studio.

050 What's your idea of a great Tuesday mid-afternoon? Afternoon delight.

051 What is the worst gift you've ever received? I once received a pair of fuzzy bright yellow smiley-face earmuffs. The gift-bearer said she thought of me when she saw them. (156)

052 Do you still skate (board)? No.

053 Is there a product that you swear by? There are a few: Swiffers, Golden Paints, and Mr. Clean's Magic Eraser.

054 Who do you think would win in an arm-wrestling match between Mr. Clean and Mr. Muscle? I don't believe I know Mr. Muscle, so I'll have to go with Mr. Clean. Cleanliness is next to godliness.

055 What are you a real stickler for? Details. I also like things clean and my environment in order. I'm constantly trying to bring order to the universe.

056 What's your favorite board game? Pictionary. (157)

057 Which piece do you like to be in Monopoly? The top hat.

058 You have a Pac Man machine in your studio. Have you ever had Pac Man fever? I've had it bad. In fact, I just traded in a Ms. Pac Man machine for a Super Pac Man machine.

059 If you had access to a working time machine, where (when) would you go? I would like to go into the far, far future to a time that is difficult to imagine—perhaps 5,000 or 10,000 years into the future. Since I was a child, I've had this fantasy of being frozen until some absurd distance into the future. I like the idea of being born again and having to relearn how to exist in a different world. I became rather obsessed with this idea about seven years ago, and I seriously looked into cryogenics, but my conclusion was that the technology just isn't here yet.

060 What are you doing next Friday night? I'll be at a friend's house in the Hamptons.

061 What did you do on your summer vacation? I spent some time in the countryside of France with my wife and some friends. We mostly played badminton.

062 If you had vanity plates on your car for some reason—if you had a car—what would they say? Embarrassingly, my license plate in high school was "RYE-GUY." I got rid of my car when I moved to Manhattan after college, and if I had one now, I'd request a prime number for my license plate.

063 If you were a guy with a car, what kind of car would you be a guy with? The 1990 Saab 900 SPG.

064 Do you do your laundry or drop it off? I have domestic help.

065 Do you cook? Not at all. The best I can do is make macaroni and cheese from a box. Sometimes I'll chop up hot dogs and throw those in if I'm trying to impress someone.

066 Do you eat corn on the cob in rows across or around? Just this past weekend, my wife and I were at a barbecue, and we shared a cob of corn (or "maize"). I completed the first row, and she proceeded to chomp round-ways. We then had to debate how to evenly share the cob while each continuing with our preferred methods. Eating rings is easy enough to calculate, but, of course, she then shortens my rows, so I needed to compensate by eating third, quarter, and half rows. Eating in rows is the superior method as it allows you to make a "ding" sound like a typewriter when you complete a row. This "ding" sound signals to your eating partner that it is his/her turn.

067 How can you tell when a cantaloupe is ripe? I can't.

068 In your lifetime, how much ketchup would you estimate that you've consumed, in gallons? About eight. The average American consumes 1.1 liters of ketchup a year. I probably consume less than the average American, and I probably didn't have that much ketchup my first two years of life. [(33-2)*1.1]*.2642 = 9.00922

069 What were the circumstances of your last bout with food poisoning? In France I got diarrhea real bad. I think it was from a breakfast powder drink I had that morning. The shit came out like a busted faucet. It was very exciting for me, because I don't think that had happened to me since I was a child. (158)

070 What would someone in your high school class have said you were most likely to become? I loved designing stuff in high school, so I suppose a designer.

071 Did art lead you to graphic design or vice versa? I would say graphic design led me to my own art.

072 If a plane leaves Chicago for New York traveling at 520 miles per hour, is it a dinner flight? No.

073 What is your favorite… breakfast cereal? Lucky Charms.

074 … brand of white oxford shirt? Agnès b. (159)

075 … household appliance? Built-in Miele coffee maker.

076 … museum in New York City? The Met is rather impressive.

077 Do you have a signature karaoke song? I don't understand karaoke at all.

078 What's the funniest message of an icon that you've seen? When I was in grade school, I was in the mall with some friends and we ventured into Spencer Gifts (a mildly risqué chain of stores that featured adult products like Fundies—underwear to be worn by two people at the same time—edible underwear and penis-shaped pasta, to name just a few of their specialties). I saw a "No Farting" button comprised of a buttocks icon, a cartoonish "poof" symbol, and a universal, standard "no" red diagonal. I thought it was the coolest thing I had ever seen. This is one of my first memories of recognizing and understanding subversion and parody within a situationist product. Needless to say, that moment has informed what I am trying to do in my work today.

079 It goes without saying that the spork is a great invention. Do you think the world is ready for the spife or the knork? No. Even a half-knife in the mouth is not a good idea.

080 What's one thing you'd like to see invented? Meal-in-a-pill.

---

(156) Sorry Connie Cantor.

(157) .com/pictionarydrawings

(158) I originally wrote "the diarrhea," as I like to unnecessarily articlize (and make up words like "articlize"). However, "the" got cut by the proofreader.

(159) How's that for a shout out? How about some shirts, Agnès?

081 Any ideas for new products? Shampübe. Shampoo for your hair down there.

082 Where do you stand on the controversial issue of shampoo testing on animals? Better them than me.

083 What would you name a new laxative? "Smooth Move." Maybe I'd throw in some extra Os—Smooooth Moooove.

084 If you were alive in the pre-computer age, would you have been an artist? I was, and yes. Or, rather, I was alive in the pre-desktop age, and I was making art.

085 Have you ever put a laptop on a desktop? Yes, and I've had a lap dance on a desk.

086 How would you describe your work? The elevator-ride/cocktail-party description of my work is that I make clean, hard-edged, graphic paintings with layered iconic imagery.

087 Do you consider yourself a pop artist? Absolutely not. Pop art is dead. Pop is a strategy to take what is popular (assumed low) and bring it into the (assumed unpopular) high. It is an appropriationist's strategy. My original drawings have nothing to do with appropriation.

088 Do you consider yourself a New Yorker? I have been in Manhattan since 1994, so I think I'm getting close to becoming a New Yorker.

089 Do you consider your work a product of New York? For tax purposes, it is. I feed off the energy generated by the city. I think that energy finds its way into the work or at least into the way I work in the studio. I feverishly work on many projects at the same time. In the city, I'm constantly bombarded with input, and my output equally matches that.

090 If you could, what one thing would you change about New York? I would get rid of the tourists.

091 When's the best time to be in New York? The fall. No question about it.

092 The city of San Francisco just outlawed plastic bags. What would you like to see outlawed in New York? New York City needs to get serious about controlling noise pollution.

093 You live in the Meatpacking District and work in ChiNoSoLito, and walk back and forth. How much do you spend on subways in a month? I either walk, take the subway, or take a taxi between home and work, depending on how much time I have. I keep all my receipts, so I can give you an accurate monthly average calculated from the last six months: taxis: $157.25 and subway: $57.50 (160)

094 Your studio isn't far from the former World Trade Center. Were you there working the morning of 9/11? Every New Yorker has his/her 9/11 story, and I'm no exception, except my story is not very exciting. I was actually in London at the time. I was walking down the street on my way to a meeting, and I noticed that in every bar, pub, café, and restaurant I walked past, everyone was crowded around a TV (or telly). I thought to myself, wow, they really love their football here! I got to the office where I had a meeting and the receptionist rushed up to me asking if I was all right and if I was OK. She had a very panicked look, and I had no idea what she was talking about, and she quickly realized that and ushered me into a side room where everyone was huddled around a TV. I just stood in shock (and awe) at the images as everything started to unfold. And yes, my studio (and then home) were close, just north of Canal Street. I thought for sure all my south-facing windows were blown in and that everything was covered in ash. As it turned out, the winds shifted much of the airborne debris to Brooklyn. I was just dazed for a couple of days. I had to travel to Munich afterwards and then Barcelona. From Barcelona I was on the first flight allowed into the US, so that was also scary.

095 When you have friends visiting New York from out of town, what are some things you recommend they do here? I like to recommend the Strand bookstore and the Upright Citizens Brigade comedy theater.

096 Is there a place other than New York where you could see yourself living? I imagine I will always have a home base in New York, but I could also see myself living in London, Paris, Berlin, Milan, or Tokyo, for example. Any major metropolitan city with taxis.

097 You mentioned at some point that you've considered setting up a studio in Miami. Why? It's warm and sunny and space costs less than in Manhattan. I've also been thinking about Berlin and Amsterdam.

098 Do you think you'll always maintain a foothold in New York? Absolutely.

099 Are you as interested in Japanese art as much as the Japanese are interested in yours? No.

100 Do you pack and ship your work yourself? Sometimes. I am not very good at art handling, so I try to leave that to the professionals.

101 In your professional career, what's the longest you've gone without painting? A few months. Maybe four or five.

102 What's an example of something better left unsaid? (161)

103 If you had a nickel for every time somebody said something, what comment would make you the richest? The Chinese word for "hello."

104 With inflation, do people today who feel like a million bucks not feel quite as good as people who felt like a million bucks 50 years ago? Yes. And a picture is no longer worth 1,000 words since the invention of the talkies.

105 How do you deal with all the pressures of being a heartthrob? I look to other heartthrobs for inspiration.

106 What are some influences on your work that people might not be able to guess from looking at it? Metaphysics.

107 What would you do if I sang out of tune? I think I would stand up and walk out on you. (162)

108 What are your long-term goals? Sustainability and personal growth.

109 What more do you hope to achieve as an artist? I hope to make more ambitious work, in scope and scale.

110 What do you think you'll be working on in 30 years? I fear I'll still be working on getting out of debt.

111 Is there anything you'd like to clear up on record about you or your work? I'm really not as smart or handsome as most people think.

112 Oh, I've been meaning to ask if you knew that you could make your own stamps. Did you know that you could make your own stamps? Like with real postage? Is that appealing to you? Yeah, I've seen that. It's more appealing to me to make my own fake stamps and have them mistaken by the postal service for real stamps.

113 Who or what do you think is the art world's next big thing? What. A concept: Artists achieving broader reach through multiple and parallel cultural outlets. The Warhol and Haring practices, for example, are good models that were ahead of their times.

114 Do you have any advice for the kids out there about staying in school? I thought about dropping out after my junior year at Carnegie Mellon University, but I decided to stay, and I'm glad I did. In high school, I had the opportunity to graduate early, but I decided to stay, and I'm not glad I did.

115 What do you call a dinosaur with a great vocabulary? Call him anything you want, just don't call him late for dinner!

116 If you were not an artist, what would you like least not to be doing? If I were not an artist, I suppose I would not be myself, so I would like least not being myself.

117 Is it a statement to answer a question with a question? Don't worry, I won't question your answer. Yes?

118 The cost of haircuts: How much is too much? "Too much" in terms of spending money on anything is determined by looking at what percentage is being spent in relation to how much money is being brought in. Spending more than 0.25% of one's annual income on a haircut is too much.

119 Do you have any allergies? I don't really like onions.

120 Is there anything you'd like to be allergic to? No.

121 Does "no" ever mean "maybe" for you, or even "probably"? No. (In this case, yes.)

122 What is your home state's state flower? I was born in the state of Virginia. Virginia's state flower is the American dogwood (*Cornus florida*). It was selected to foster a feeling of pride in our state and to stimulate an interest in the history and traditions of the commonwealth.

123 Do you have a favorite train in New York City? A train of thought.

124 Do you work out? Yes.

125 Really? Yes, but it's certainly nothing hardcore and not as regular as I'd like. Sit-ups, push-ups, light weights, and running. I used to play soccer regularly, and perhaps one day I will be able to get back on that schedule.

126 You had some work included in Thurston Moore's book *Mix Tape: The Art of Cassette Culture*. Do you still listen to cassettes? No. In fact, about five years ago I threw away all my cassettes. I sometimes get in these bad moods where I throw away tons of stuff I don't need or use. It's a therapeutic cleansing process. And then later I usually regret having thrown away things, and then I come to terms with that regret by realizing that it's better to regret something you have done than to regret something you haven't done. (163)

127 How did you come to be involved in that book? The book was published by Rizzoli, and they simply contacted me out of the blue to be involved. The concept was to include different artists and creative types who had grown up making mix tape cassette covers. They had no idea that I actually had created such things, so they simply asked. It turned out I had made covers for mix tapes, and I had kept them.

128 Have you ever put Sonic Youth on a mix tape? Yes. I've been a big fan of Sonic Youth since I first heard their album *Sister*.

129 I read an article in the *New York Times* the other day about the official death of the cassette tape. As a guy, like myself, who used to make mix tapes, do you have any sentimentality for this medium? *New York Times*? Reading? Show off.

130 Analog media vs. digital. Comment? I like to make things.

131 I've heard about your postcard project at MoMA. Can you explain it? I designed and had printed a MoMA postcard of my own work that matched exactly their postcards. I put the postcards in the racks at the museum store. One could purchase them just like any other MoMA postcard. This was in 1999.

132 You have eight pieces on display at MoMA right now. How did that come about? MoMA acquired 20 works on paper through Printed Matter. I believe that was in 2004. Maybe the acquisition was completed in 2005. I wasn't involved in the process. Printed Matter here in New York took care of everything.

133 Are you happy with the pieces they chose? The pieces are from a series of 100, and by the time MoMA got to them, there were only 20 left. So, unfortunately, I'm not sure they got the best pickings. Overall, I'm happy with and proud of the pieces, but I do feel that I've created more significant paintings that better represent me.

(160) January–June 2008, inclusive.

(161) In case you feel cheated out of a full Q&A, go here: .com/bonusquestionsandanswers

(162) .com/outoftune

(163) Mellin de Saint-Gelais paraphrased by The Butthole Surfers.

134 Roughly how many copies do each of your books sell? Most of my books are produced in limited quantities—1,000, or 2,500, so they eventually sell out. The latest, *Installationview* published by Rizzoli is more for a mass audience so it has an open edition. (164)

135 What is the typical genesis of your books? I am always working on book ideas—sketching and making notes. Some book ideas boil up to the top and other ideas fade away. I've been formulating a children's book for about three years, and I think it will finally materialize next year. Or the year after. I'm also currently working more seriously on a book titled *Neveroddoreven*. (165)

136 What is the gist of *Neveroddoreven*? Zero on the roulette wheel. It's also a palindrome that circles back in on itself.

137 Do you have a stock note for book signings? "To Whom It May Concern." I sign my name, and I usually make an effort to write the year and location of the signing.

138 How much of the art you've made do you have photographed? I have photographic documentation of everything I make.

139 Do you shoot these yourself? No, I hire professionals.

140 What is your relationship with Deitch Projects? We have a serious relationship, but Jeffrey sees other artists, and I see other galleries.

141 How did you get involved with him/them? I first did a two-person show with Julia Chiang titled "Dream Garden" in 2002. Since then, Deitch and I have worked on numerous projects and exhibitions together. It's a positive and rewarding relationship. (166)

142 With the amount of silkscreening in your work, you must have to work horizontally much of the time. Do you tend to paint horizontally when using a brush as well? Yes. I'm going to make a corny bumper sticker that reads, "I do it horizontally."

143 You're working with some larger canvases now. Since you "do it horizontally," is it difficult to reach in and maneuver in the center of these larger paintings? Yes. Sometimes we climb on top of the painting to reach the middle.

144 Almost all paintings produced are hung on walls. Do you think that paintings produced horizontally should maybe be displayed horizontally? Yes, on the ceiling.

145 What do your studio assistants do? A variety of things: gesso and sand canvases, help me paint, clean screens, run errands, sweep the floors, mix paints, research materials, cut cardboard, make security passes, scan sketches, stretch canvases, work on drawings, organize project binders, clean brushes, buy supplies,...

146 You don't have any kids, but if you did, is there any artist about whose work you might say, "My kid could do that."? Yes.

147 (You can tell me later.) Are the color palettes you use determined on a painting-by-painting basis, or is it more about larger periods or phases? Painting-by-painting within a larger body of work.

148 Do you foresee a possibility of any stylistic breaks or tangents in your work, or do you see it more as an ongoing, linear evolution? By default, the evolution is linear, because I have not yet figured out a way to escape the linear passage of time. When I do, I will have told you. I'm actually working on a piece now titled *Art History Is Not Linear*. Stylistic breaks or tangents? You never know. I never know.

149 Are you at all wary of taking too large a step from the work you're known for? No, not at all; but right now I am investigating more deeply than broadly.

150 What is the process of creation behind your paintings, and is that process fairly consistent from one painting to the next? Basically the process is this: Individual drawings start out as thumbnail sketches; those sketches get developed and revised; a final sketch gets scanned into the computer box; a vector drawing is made using the sketch as a template; revisions and refinement; drawings get combined; film is made from files; screens are made from film; composition sketches are made for the paintings; paint colors are mixed; gessoed backgrounds are built up on canvas, linen, or wood panels; colored backgrounds are painted; different screens are combined and drawings are painted onto the surfaces in a process that is largely driven by intuition. This screening process of growing the paintings continues anywhere from a week to eight months. Finally, I apply an isolation coat to the paintings with an acrylic medium, and then a couple of coats of varnish.

151 What is your basic prep process of a canvas or panel before you start painting, and how long does it take? The duration varies, but the process is something along these lines: canvas gets stretched, edges get masked, many layers of gesso are built up and are sanded between the final coats, layers of a background color are applied, and then the painting begins.

152 Do you have a dedicated time when you sketch, or is it just as you have ideas? I wish I had a dedicated time to sketch. I am constantly sketching and writing down ideas and phrases. Sometimes they are on scraps of paper that I have to remember to collect and transcribe into my sketchbook.

153 What inspires you? Love. Sometimes hate.

154 What's something surprising and quite possibly shocking about you? I secretly hate my life, and I want to die.

155 Does it matter whether the glass is half full if you're not thirsty? Yes it matters, because the glass exists independent of me and is appreciated by others. It matters a lot.

156 Your hair is looking really good these days. I daresay lustrous. How frequently do you condition? Thank you! As you know, I work very hard on my hair, so feedback (good or bad) is appreciated. I actually do not condition my hair—at least not with conventional conditioners. My secret is that I use a very harsh chemical shampoo and then lather in lotion when I get out of the shower when it is still wet.

157 Do you have any nicknames? Rye. Rye Guy.

158 Are you superstitious? Only when it serves my desires. And, I do not walk under ladders, but I think this is more for safety reasons. Or maybe I am superstitious that the ladder will fall.

159 Which, if any, in your opinion, is the best fast-food restaurant? I prefer "good food fast." I like Taco Bell. There are some good, inexpensive, and fairly fast sushi places in my neighborhood. Oh, how about a taco roll? Mmmm...

160 If you were an animal, which would you be? Is Animal (the drumming Muppet) an animal? Are the Muppets animals? If so, I suppose I would be Animal. Wouldn't life be easier if you just let someone else pull your strings?

161 If you were a vegetable, which would you be? Potatoes are a good staple.

162 If you were a flavor of chewing gum, which would you be? Bubblegum flavored.

163 What's your astrological sign, and does that mean anything to you? Capricorn. It means nothing to me, which is typical behavior for a Capricorn.

164 Have you ever encountered any legal issues over content in your work? No. I have, however, had to take legal action against companies stealing my work (Burton, Urban Outfitters, UARM, for example).

165 In the note at the beginning of your book *Sponsorship: The Fine Art of Corporate Sponsorship/The Corporate Sponsorship of Fine Art*, you wrote, "most of the world is my enemy." Does this hold true today? Sadly, I sometimes feel that way. Some days I feel that everybody wants (from me) something for nothing. All I really want in this world is some time and peace of mind to make my work, and so anyone who gets in the way of that feels like an enemy to me.

166 How did what you set out to illustrate with that exhibition and book differ from the end results? The "Sponsorship" exhibition was really more concept-driven. The resulting aesthetic for the exhibition was inconsequential. Logos of the corporations that sponsored the show were enlarged and stuck on the wall. I really had no preconceived plan for how that was done. Actually, I had not planned that we would have received so much crap to give away. Tables full of backpacks, shoes, shirts, drinks, etc. were something I did not anticipate, but I was certainly happy about the resulting environment.

167 Do you think the trends you discuss in the book have since stabilized or gotten more extreme? I really don't know. I think it was a more interesting topic when the book was first published in 2003 and certainly more interesting when I conducted most of the interviews in 2002.

168 How do you see your own work in this world? My hope is to make a contribution with my work to culture as a whole, not just the art world. The real challenge is to do so with integrity and on my own terms, because the gateways to popular culture are guarded largely by the advertising model. Consequently, a lot of times "art" gets marginalized and attached to a corporate agenda. My work does not require anything to be attached to it, and it certainly does not exist to serve anything else. To penetrate popular culture while maintaining this philosophy is the challenge.

169 How large is your studio? Twenty-five hundred square feet.

170 A couple of years ago you built a spray room. Last year you dismantled it. Is this a reflection of a change in your work? I think I had that spray booth for about 18 months. It wasn't large enough for the new works, and it took up a lot of space.

171 Fill in the blanks: _______ is ________, which also happens to be _______. All. Full of love. Lyrics Björk wrote. (167)

172 A free-verse Mad Lib-erick for you: There once was a noun named proper name. His favorite noun was maestro. He loved to eat noun, but noun loved to be eaten not. So proper name above was shot. In the body part. With a weapon. And it hurt very much. I like it just the way it is.

173 Beatles or Stones? The Beatles stoned.

174 In *Vocabularytest* you say, "copyright is artificial and stunts the growth of culture," and, "All works of Ryan McGinness are [not copyrighted]. All rights are not reserved." Subsequent books have had more standard copyrighting. What's the deal? Multiple truths. Parallel universes.

175 How does being a successful artist selling his work sit with your view of consumer culture? I can't agree with that premise. Really, I don't feel successful at all. There is so much more I strive to achieve and accomplish.

176 How much of what you do is determined by strictly visual concerns? Most of my work is driven by aesthetics. I used to make more of what most people call "conceptual" art, which I really like to call "neat idea" art. But I think neat ideas are best employed by the advertising and entertainment industries. I decided that beauty is truth. I'm trying to make something that I can't quite put my finger on—that can't be summed up with a tidy explanation and that also doesn't require art-speak to back it up. I'm really trying to make beautiful things. Now, that said, there are concepts I employ behind my work that inform the process, but aesthetics drive the final forms.

---

(164) The initial print run of this book will be 8,000.

(165) This is one of the book ideas that eventually faded away, although the children's book idea is still alive.

(166) .com/dreamgarden

(167) .com/allisfullofove

177 If Ryan McGinness were a corporation, what would your tagline be? "Master of Light™." Or is that already taken?

178 As a painter, have you ever considered wearing a beret? Yes, I've considered it.

179 Paint has a finite life span. Have you ever thought about putting an expiration date on your work? Like, "Best if enjoyed on or before [date]?" I'm very concerned with how archival and colorfast my paints and materials are. I am constantly researching new materials, and I always insist on using the best. I also try to apply an isolation coat and top UV-protective varnish layers to the paintings.

180 Is there an equivalent to the sing-along in the visual arts, and if so, how do you feel about it? I suppose that would be some kind of collaboration. I'm not really into collaborations.

181 How much of your shows, bookings, and appearances do you handle? Almost all.

182 How often does your significant other travel with you? A significant amount.

183 Have you ever had a mustache? No.

184 Have you ever worn a Speedo? No.

185 Have you ever sat in gum? Yes.

186 You're on the subway during rush hour and somebody vomits on you. What do you do? No I'm not.

187 Did you have braces? Yes, and I had black rubber bands on them. I'm actually thinking about getting braces again. A word to brace-faces: wear your retainer.

188 What was your first rock concert? P.I.L. Or maybe it was Jesus and Mary Chain. One of those.

189 If you hosted a talk show—let's call it *The McGinness Hour*—who would you like to have on? I'd probably fill the entire hour with commercials. Commercials are the real content for television. Everything else is just filler. I'm assuming the talk show would be on television (or "TV"), and I suppose that no longer has to be the case, so we can abandon that medium's business model... Oh fuck it, I'd still fill it with commercials. (168)

190 What do you think of those new body scents you just spray right on your clothes? You know what I'm talking about? They're not really deodorants, they're more like odorants. They really do work.

191 What country has the best-looking currency? I really like the British pound coin. The proportions are nice, it has a good weight, and it feels like its worth.

192 What percentage of good things do you think actually comes to those who wait? Zero percent. Getting people to believe that "All good things come to those who wait" is part of the conspiracy to keep people down.

193 Do you think that, like, it's sort of like, faking it, to like, sort of like totally not mean it when you do stuff? Like, you know what I mean? Yes, I know what you mean, and I do think that not being sincere is like totally faking it.

194 Are you handy in any way? I'm right-handed.

195 Where haven't you been that you would like to have been, or even be right now? I would like to have been to Africa. Right now I don't have the time to make the journey a part of my past.

196 Where do you most like to work on your tan? My face... and buns.

197 What brand of toilet paper do you find most comforting to your buns? I will sacrifice comforting my buns for aesthetic comfort. I must have completely unpatterned, simple, plain, white toilet paper—no hearts, angels, flowers, etc. I will, however, accept ripples. Cottonelle, rippled, single-ply is my preferred brand. (169)

198 What would you like to be great at? Making art.

199 If your work were taught in an art history class, what do you think would be said about it? Right now I'm a footnote, or perhaps one of Cliff's notes, but I hope to someday be an entire chapter or even a textbook. The textbook, of course, would have to be more of a picture book.

200 If *Teen People* asked you to pose topless, would you do it—provided it was tasteful and discreet? I would hold out for top-to-bottomless.

201 Did you ever realize that silverware racks in dishwashers are divided so that you can sort your silverware as you put it in? I just realized this recently and it blew my mind. Because I'd always sorted after the cycle—automatically. It had never occurred to me that you could sort before. Has that ever happened to you? I actually just purchased a new dishwasher. I went for a Miele and was a little sad to find that it came with a top tray for utensils (my ware is not silver) instead of the compartmentalized baskets. Are you talking about the baskets, or are the trays divided into sections as well?

202 Are you at all sentimental? Sadly, no.

203 Skinny ties: hot or not? Skinny ties on skinny guys: No. Hotsie Notsie!

204 Capri pants for her: Hot or not? Not.

205 How can you tell when things aren't what they seem? Well, I think the first step is to understand that reality is all in your mind, man.

206 Which is more of a lie: an undercover police officer or a hairpiece? A hairpiece which lies on an undercover police officer about which the officer lies.

207 Would you go to a dentist who had false teeth? Well, perhaps if he fashioned them himself. Parts of some of my teeth are false.

208 Speaking of bipartisan politics, when was the last time you got yourself into a real pickle? I grew up next to a girl whose nickname was Pickle. You could say that she was a real pickle, and she was a friend, so you could say I got into her.

209 There must be some confusion between you and fellow artist Ryan McGinley. Does anyone ever get you confused with MacGyver? No, it's a pretty simple show, and things are explained well—regardless of how hard anyone tries to get me confused with it.

210 Have you seen *The Matrix*? Man, that movie was so awesome. Yes, I agree. Awesome indeed. (170)

211 Bono and the Edge always have the coolest sunglasses. How do you think they stay so far ahead? They have vision, which, of course, is provided by their cool shades. We will never know which came first.

212 What's a metaphor for where you are in life? I am a living sign. (171)

213 Is something that's like a metaphor really a simile? Kind of.

214 Are these questions starting to repeat, or is it my imagination? It's MY imagination. These questions, you, and your imagination are all in my head. Welcome to your world in my world forever endlessly repeating. So, yes.

215 What, to you, constitutes heavy machinery? That which requires a symbol reminding you to lift with your legs and not your back.

216 And what, in your book, constitutes heavy petting? Same thing. (You forgot to ask me what constitutes heavy metal!)

217 And what, in your book, constitutes heavy metal? Lots of licks. The guitar kind.

218 Do you watch TV? I do not have a television. Kill your television. That's the kind of person I pretend to be, but I really watch shows online. I have a TV in my computer.

219 What TV shows did you watch growing up? "The Cosby Show," "Family Ties," "Cheers," "The Muppet Show," and I always tried to stay up for "Saturday Night Live."

220 If not television, what, besides transvestite, could TV stand for? That's it. Absolutely nothing else. It's either television of transvestite. Take your pick.

221 You're on the road a lot with your shows. Do you enjoy the traveling? I like being in other places, but not traveling to get there. I don't really have a favorite place.

222 Crap, that was my next question. How does it make you feel when flight attendants use the phrase "at this time" all the time? It makes me feel like I'm living in the moment!

223 Do you paint or draw when traveling? I draw in my sketchbook.

224 Do you ever jokingly refer to your studio as "the office"? I've recently been thinking about Warhol's ironic and sarcastic use of the word "factory" to refer to his studio. This was a critique of consumer (pop) culture at the time, and, of course, wasn't meant to be taken seriously. Now many of the top artists working today proudly have factories. Don't they get it?

225 Do you take photos, and if so, do they figure into your work? Yes, but I consider them more like snapshots. Notes.

226 When you have a thirst that just won't quit, what do you find to be the most refreshing beverage? Wait, I know this. That's a brand-message-loaded leading question, right? I like room-temperature water.

227 Is there something you'd like to share that you haven't been able to work into an answer yet? Yes.

228 Would you like to use the answer to this question to share it? The things I'd like to share can't be put into an answer.

229 Have you ever eaten anything you would call food for thought? Let me digest that question.

230 Do you agree with the not uncommon assertion that food fights should be called "food feuds"? Absolutely. And I recently heard a radio report about those who believe that a unicorn should be called a unihorn. Actually, it was a fictitious radio report. Real radio. Fictitious report. And unicorns are also fictitious, by the way.

231 What's one thing you've never told an interviewer? I'm lying.

232 What's another? I'm not lying.

233 Is art without meaning valid? Nothing inherently has meaning. Meaning is projected and reflected, which gives the illusion that things "have" meaning. In that sense, meaning is like color.

234 Do you like reading what people write about your work? Yes.

235 What occupation would you be worst at? I cannot cook.

236 How do you order your steak? Eggs? Rare. Well done. Both are rarely well done.

237 You have a few people helping you in the studio. How many would be too many? I never have enough. My real struggle is managing people.

238 Do you speak any languages other than English? Deutsch. I'm learning Spanish. And I can read the international language of love, but I can't speak it.

239 What was your last Halloween costume? I can't remember the last time I dressed up for Halloween. As a child I dressed up as Luke Skywalker (with a white robe and leg bandages), a boxer (with a different robe, black eye makeup, and boxing gloves), the Fonz (leather jacket and t-shirt), a nerd (thick glasses with tape, pocket protector with pens, and appropriate wardrobe), a monster (green face

(168) .com/commercials

(169) Time to give it up, Cottonelle. You've got my number.

(170) Tom told me later that he was being sarcastic, but I wasn't.

(171) "Vicar in a Tutu" by The Smiths.

makeup and chains), and a scarecrow (hay-stuffed jeans and flannel shirt with pumpkin head). I do have some ideas for costumes in my back pocket should I ever get my act together one year. These include: a comedian (with a microphone stand, wooden stool with a glass of water, and fake brick wall behind me. This would be more of an installation at a Halloween party), a robot (typical quintessential cliché robot parts but also wearing a t-shirt that said "Humans: Can't live with 'em, can't live without 'em!"), and my friend Bill (I would simply secretly raid his closet and wear his clothes). (172)

240 Why aren't there more artists named Art? For the same reason there aren't more (blank) named (blank): Hot dog makers named Frank. Comedians named Josh. Bankers named Bill. Trash collectors named Garbage.

241 What is called "Modern Art" today includes art from over a hundred years ago. At what point will this stop being considered modern? Well, "modern art" does have a defined time period. But, it's different around the world. "Contemporary art" is the term more commonly used to refer to work being made now. Like, right now. As we speak. (173)

242 How much time do you spend surfing the interweb? Not much time actively surfing, but I'm usually on the line.

243 Should style be comfortable or should comfort be stylish? If style is to form, and comfort is to function, then I lean toward the dictum that form follows function, which is to say that style should be comfortable.

244 Have you ever been up the Empire State Building? Yes.

245 What was the last random act of kindness or senseless act of beauty that you practiced? Random act of kindness: Chose not to punch in the face the guy walking down the street behind me singing at the top of his lungs. Senseless act of beauty: Shaved my head.

246 Do you see any commercial applications for your recent stuff? Absolutely not.

247 Is there a Ryan McGinness brand? If so, what are your core brand values—your DNA, if you will? Surprisingly, my core brand values as a human being are exactly the same as those of the Levi Strauss corporation: empathy, originality, integrity, and courage.

248 Which do you get more satisfaction from, process or result? Process. That's life.

249 What's your favorite part of your process? I love drawing.

250 Your paintings: product, by-product, or both? Both. Bi-by-products.

251 What's one thing about yourself that has nothing to do with your work? That's a great question, because my hope is that everything about me goes into my work or at least is reflected in some way. I can't think of anything about me that can't be argued has something to do with my work.

252 What's one thing that does? My desire to create order out of chaos.

253 Are there contradictions or discrepancies between Ryan McGinness the guy and Ryan McGinness the artist? Nope.

254 If you could change your name would you, and if so what would it be? I can change my name, but I have chosen to use the name my parents gave me. For a few weeks in college, I was Ryan Flash.

255 How many years would you say humankind has left? From the time anyone reads this, one year. (That's true upon each additional reading. So, if you'd like to keep this thing going, keep rereading.)

256 Why do people sitting alone in restaurants never get asked if they want to buy flowers? You know why—single people have half the disposable income of couples.

257 Do you think that your work is timely? Timeless? Timeless in its timeliness. As a reflection of the time I live in, my work will forever be relevant as a point of reference for any time in the future.

258 If you were being executed what would you request as your last meal? Hemlock. Gotcha!

259 If you got arrested and had one phone call, whom would you call? I'd call the front desk, tell them that I was the chief of police and that there had been a horrible mistake in the arrest of Ryan McGinness and that he should be released immediately. But seriously folks, I suppose I would simply call a friend.

260 How many friends could you count on if, say, you were in a situation where you needed friends you could count on? Only a handful.

261 If you were to choose a cool, one-word artist alias, what would it be? KAWS, or REAS, or ESPO, or TWIST. Any of those would give me a good head-start reputation with my work.

262 What condition do you think the human condition is in? It's not good. Not good at all.

263 Contemporary art right now is hot. Hot! Comment? We're on the brink of a cooling which will help get rid of some of the fat. Wait, you actually need fat in times of cooling. I don't know. It's confusing.

264 It's 2008 and everyone's talking about a recession. Is the contemporary art market immune? No, but the contemporary art market is a global market, so it has a thicker skin.

265 Do you believe that hospitals should excel in hospitality? Makes sense.

266 For the aspiring artists out there, what words of wisdom would you like to, you know, impart? Be yourself, but first take some time to find out who that is. Then, do all that you can to share that with others. If you are really being honest with who you are, then your work will resonate with others and be celebrated, because at the end of the day, you're really just like everybody else.

267 What kinds of things do you like to do when you're not doing something else? I'm always completely in the here-and-now, so I cannot conceive of there being another time or place or a something else or an elsewhere. Nowhere is always now here, and I am alone in my island universe. What did you ask?

268 When was the last time you flew a kite? I can't remember, but I like the idea of bringing back that retort. I'll have to remember to tell the next jerk I encounter to "Go fly a kite!" To which he'll probably say, "Go fuck yourself!" To which I will have to repeat the command for him to "Go fly a kite, really!"

269 You've started to work recently on the roof of your studio. Well, not work on the roof as in fixing it up, but actually doing your work on top of your building. What goes on up there? It's a secret. Only those near me, six stories and higher know what goes on up there.

270 Put these in the order from which you have done most of to least:
a) loafing around in sneakers
b) sneaking around in loafers
c) sweating in a sweatshirt
d) breaking wind in a windbreaker
C, B, A, D

271 I would like to buy the guy who invented beer a beer. Who would you like to buy a beer? The guy who invented beer goggles.

272 What's the worst beer on the market? Budweiser. The King of Beers? I thought we did away with kings in this country long ago. (174)

273 Aren't puppies cute? Studies show that, yes, puppies (and babies) are cute.

274 For a few pieces you made last year, you created hundreds of button-badges with slogans. How many different ones were there? Seven hundred seventy-seven unique buttons. There were five different pieces total, each six-foot square with a set of seven hundred seventy-seven buttons pinned to the canvas in different configurations to make one large image.

275 Did you write the sayings on them? Yes, I combed though my sketchbooks from the past 10 years and pulled out some of my favorite phrases.

276 Do you have a favorite saying on those buttons? Ryan McGinness is not an art movement.

277 You've used words in your work in the past. Does text relate directly to the visuals? As a general rule, I shy away from text, because I hope to create drawings that work as a universal language and transcend the concrete language of text. I also want to be sensitive about making English-centric work. Text does figure into my sketches, and I make as many notations for drawings as I do sketches for drawings.

278 I remember a sticker or button you gave away at a gallery opening in Williamsburg in what must have been 1999 or 2000 that commented on Julian Schnabel's artwork by saying something like, "He sure is rich." Are there any other artists you think "sure are rich"? I did a series of 5-7-5 haiku in 1997 about some of my art heroes. They were written in an idiot-savant voice. That one in particular was: Julian Schnabel. Sometimes I just don't get it. Man, he sure is rich. Others included (and yes, probably "sure are rich") were Jeff Koons, Damien Hirst, George Condo, Richard Serra, Frank Stella, Peter Halley, Richard Prince, and Matthew Barney.

279 I'm trying to ween myself off the word "awesome." Are there any words you're trying to use less in your day-to-day vocabulary? I try to not have a potty mouth.

280 You recently went from long hair to a shaved head. Can you explain why? I made a wig of my own hair. Now I am growing the next one. I hope to make an edition of three over the next few years.

281 How did the first specimen turn out? Very convincingly.

282 What does it cost to have a wig made these days? That was a total custom job. It cost me $2,000. (A note to the people of the future: American dollars in the year 2008. Do you guys still use dollars? Is there still an America? Maybe there will be a New America by the time you read this.)

283 How many people do you think will actually read all of these questions? Four. (175)

284 Can you tell me about the gym you started in the basement of your building with your elevator guy? No, not really. It is a secret with very exclusive membership. Well, OK. It's called the Chinatown Underground Gym (or CH.U.G.). We currently have two members: me and my elevator operator. (176)

285 What's the best band you've ever seen live, and where and when? Lush and Ride on the same bill in Washington, DC, in 1992.

286 Where do you sign your paintings and with what, and how large? On the back, top left, over-stretched flap of canvas, with a permanent marker, about two inches high by six inches wide. I sign my name and year and write the title, if there is one, in quotes.

287 Are you nostalgic for anything? I'm nostalgic for the past's vision of the future which never materialized—jetpacks, meals in a pill, and silver unitards. (177)

288 For a while there you were wearing colored contact lenses, and to be honest, they kind of freaked me out. What was up with that? I still have them, and I will go back, but lately I've been using daily disposable contact lenses which I've only found in clear.

---

(172) .com/humans

(173) And as you read.

(174) Free marketing concept for advertising schmucks.

(175) Four is four. (Ten is three. Three is five. Five is four, and four is four.)

(176) Jorge.

(177) Did anyone notice that Michael

289 Have you ever tried any of those diets? No.

290 What big-ass company out there has the strongest logo? I take strongest to mean most recognizable, so it's probably McDonald's, Coke, or Nike.

291 Did you once tell me that you were thinking about doing a children's book, and if so, can you tell me about it again? Yes, I've had a children's book in my head for about five years. I fantasize about going away for three to six months to some remote location to concentrate on it. Without giving too much away, it applies a lot of theories in metaphysics and quantum mechanics to a story about a boy who realizes that not only can he grow up to be anything he wants, he can be all things at once.

292 Things are moving so fast these days. What do you think the future will be like in, say, three weeks? You actually wrote this question three weeks ago, and I'm only now getting around to answering it. So, I know exactly what this future is like, but I'm not quite sure how to get this message back to your past-self. And when you do read this, it will be your future-self. We can never really communicate in the same time. We will never be on the same time-space page.

293 What's the last great idea you heard? My friend Charlie had an idea for a t-shirt which never materialized: Me no Nike.

294 How are you at house painting? Not good, but I do know that it's all about the masking.

295 When painting your apartment, do you test out paint colors or go straight to pure white? I've never actually tested colors on a wall before. I know what you mean—when people paint sizable color swatches on a wall and hem and haw over the subtle differences. It seems like a very suburban haute bourgeois thing to do.

296 How much do you paint with brushes? Most of the painting backgrounds are done with brushes.

297 How involved do you generally get in the lighting of your shows? Mildly involved.

298 What are some of the biggest pressures teens face today? Kids are really growing up so fast these days.

299 Somebody commented to me recently that New York City had turned into Disney World. Wait, or was it Disneyland? Well, one of those. Do you agree? I've been in New York for awhile now, and I've noticed it get safer, more dangerous, safer again, and now I think things are getting worse again. Last week a woman was raped in SoHo, and across the street from the studio, two guys were shot. They were the bad guys trying to rob a place, but still—not good.

300 Do you think there would be a market for free-verse hip-hop? I am the market for free-verse hip-hop!

301 What was the last lie you told? I'm not really the market for free-verse hip-hop.

302 Have you tried out any techniques or materials that haven't worked? All the time. That's how I learn.

303 What's one example? Fiberglass. I had a large fiberglass barnacle cluster made about five feet high that was sealed on the inside. I wanted to grow plants in it and have it be a sort of synthetic organic form that supported real organic forms. It just didn't feel right in the end, and I smashed the thing. [178]

304 What's the most extravagant thing you've ever done? I had a $2,000 dinner for two once. I've also stayed at the Ritz in London and Singapore.

305 Do you own any sleeveless apparel? Pants.

306 Abortion… Same-sex marriage… Family values… Are there any hot issues that you take a stance on? Live and let live. (Wait, does that read as some kind of subtle stance on abortion?)

307 Have you ever taught painting? No. I think teaching is a calling, and I've never been called.

308 What would you say is the most insidious song ever to be inflicted on humankind? "Na Na Hey Hey Kiss Him Goodbye." [179]

309 Your work seems not to be bogged down by heavy concept. What's one of the more conceptual things you've done? Every day I think about going jogging. I used to make what can be considered more conceptually driven work, but it left me feeling cold and empty. I wanted to move past what I considered to be only neat ideas. I do believe that the basics of aesthetics, composition, color, form, etc. are concepts that can't be simply explained with an accompanying art-speak, which is often used as a marketing tool anyways.

310 What is the hallmark of good art? Honesty.

311 What are your hobbies? I listen to music all day in the studio. I like to play soccer, but I haven't been able to for quite some time, because my friends play in the early morning, and I usually work until late at night. I also like comedy. And, can beer be a hobby?

312 To what extent do you know where you're going with a painting when you start it? I usually have a soft plan. The paintings evolve and grow on their own.

313 Is it pretty clear to you when one of your paintings is finished? Yes. I can't explain it, but intuitively I know, and it is very clear.

314 If there were to be a Ryan McGinness museum, how would you like it to be? Free.

315 How much of the installations you do for your gallery shows ends up being saved? The wall paintings get painted over and the vinyl gets destroyed. A mirror maze I made a few years ago got destroyed, because there was no way to save the mirrors, which were liquid-nailed to the sheetrock walls. A shitty gallery in Tokyo cut out a mural I did and sold it to a retail store after I left. So, of course, I need to insist and make sure everything gets destroyed.

316 Does it bother you when installations you've done for shows are painted over, or are the photos enough? The photos are actually better.

317 Do you have people who help you, uh, install your installations? Yes, absolutely. I need a lot of help.

318 How much time do you usually have to install a show? Ten days.

319 How does the process behind your installations differ from that of your paintings? The paintings tend to be more intuition-driven in their composition.

320 Show-specific installations aside, do you create work with individual shows in mind, or do you just create work and then group it roughly for shows? I have show-specific ideas for installations before I have the specific venues for them.

321 You've got a few people helping you in the studio. How good are you as a manager? I am an awful manager. I really prefer to work alone, but I can't do that anymore. I enjoy carving out time in the middle of the night and on the weekends so I can really concentrate by myself.

322 What do you wish you enjoyed a little less? If I enjoyed sex a little less, I'd be much more productive (and less re-productive?).

323 At what age did you lose your virginity? Eighteen.

324 I always look at it not as losing something, but as gaining nonvirginity. Does age matter in art (artist)? I think older people are wiser, so I assume older artists make better work.

325 Are you getting wiser? Yes.

326 If you had a graffiti tag, what would it be? I would write the names of major corporations.

327 Which sections of the newspaper do you not read at all? Don't know. Don't read them.

328 What do you see as the most useless product on the market? Art.

329 What time do you usually wake up? I'm usually in the studio by 10 am. [180]

330 Are you on YouTube? No.

331 By the way, with these yes-or-no questions, please elaborate wherever appropriate. Do you have a myface page? No. I purposefully avoid social network sites.

332 Are there any charities you've been involved with? Yes, too many to name.

333 After chronic halitosis, what's the disease you'd like to see next cured? There are so many good candidates, I'd hate to single out just one at the risk of the others getting upset.

334 What are three things that rule? Love, physics, and self-preservation rule everything.

335 Do you play air guitar, and if so, are you any good? (I am mouthing the word "yes.") [181]

336 If your personality could be defined by seven metaphorical dwarves with adjectival names, what would their names be? Cleany, Angry, Depressy, Obsessivy-Compulsivy, Orderly, Hungry, and Stressy.

337 Have you ever seen a Broadway musical, or do you, like me, stay way off Broadway? I saw *Tommy*. It was good.

338 Artwork for bands: Have you done any? When I was in school and when I first moved to New York, I did a lot of work for independent bands, record labels, and clubs.

339 You told me once about painting an electric guitar for some worthy cause. Can you explain that? I get bothered a lot to do things for charities, and it's hard for me to say no, because they are all such good causes. Yes, I painted a guitar to benefit the Little Kids Rock Foundation in the name of Pantera's Dimebag Darrell, who had been recently shot to death at a concert.

340 Do you know where the guitar is today? No, I need to track it down.

341 Has anybody done you wrong in this business of art? No, not at all. You'd be surprised, but everyone in the art world is super intelligent and has a really sweet heart.

342 What's the oldest artist or artwork to really rock you? I like Hieronymus Bosch.

343 How often do you get commissions? There are plenty of opportunities, but I rarely take on something like that.

344 Are there any themes that you would say tie your work together? Yes. In general I'm trying to share the psychedelic experience, which reveals the true nature of the universe.

345 What would be a ten-word review of your work that you'd be happy with? The work was OK, but the free beer was great!

346 People are always reviewing your work. Is there anybody you'd like to review here? No, that's never been an interest of mine. I like that Richard Pryor joke where he explains that no child ever grew up wanting to be a critic.

347 What's your favorite color? Despite how colorful the work is, I'm partial to Pantone Cool Grey 10. I also like black and white. If something doesn't work first in black and white, it will not work in color.

348 What's the craziest thing you've ever written off as a business expense? My accountant just asked me about a receipt for mushrooms I bought in Amsterdam. I get a receipt for everything.

Stipe quoted me talking about jetpacks a few years ago in the *New York Times*? That was exciting for me.

[178] .com/barnacleplanter

[179] .com/goodbye

[180] This means I usually awaken anywhere between 7 and 9 am.

[181] .com/airguitar

349 I seem to remember you designing some sneakers at some point and doing a shirt for Beck ("The Beck"). What other clothing projects have you been involved in? After five years in development, I cut my losses with the sneaker project. I was creating a new shoe from the ground up with DC Shoes, and we eventually decided that it was not going to materialize the way I envisioned it, so we dropped it. That was a very difficult decision to make considering all the costs of the molds, samples, materials, and time spent over the course of five years. And, yes, I met Beck at my show at Colette in Paris in 2001, and he asked me to do a couple of shirts for him. I made the "the Beck" shirt and a storm-trooper shirt. The first time I saw him was in his Loser video, where he was wearing a storm-trooper helmet. Other than that, I occasionally make t-shirts on my own, usually in an edition of 100. I mostly just give these away.

350 How many pairs of shoes do you own? Two pairs of everyday shoes, two pairs of running shoes, two pairs of dress shoes, and two pairs of slippers. I'm not sure how that worked out so neatly, but there you have it. Or rather, there I have them.

351 What's your love life like these days? Lovely.

352 How much is your work affected by your personal life? My work is my personal life. It's all the same.

353 What is something you feel strongly about? I have very strong convictions about shape, form, and typography. I actually don't use typography in my work, but I learned a lot about it, so I am sensitive to all the bad typography around me, especially in art. [182]

354 What's the stupidest thing you've ever done? Oh, I don't know beyond the usual getting drunk, passing out in public, urinating on subway tracks—just silly things like that.

355 The smartest? When I was a teenager, I was really into the stock market, and I bought as many shares of Apple as I could in the early 1980s. It went up a few points and I sold it all, which was probably among one of the stupidest things I've done.

356 Are you getting tired of all these questions? No.

357 Describe how you envision the world will be different when you turn 50. The poor will be poorer, and the rich will be richer. There will be digital paper. Teleportation. Mobile phone implants. New kinds of genetically engineered fruits and vegetables. Mini versions of animals as pets, like polar bears you can hold in your hand. We will be able to control the weather, and this power will be sponsored and used as a corporate branding tool. Reading will be considered an antiquated form of information input. We will approach *Blade Runner*-esque advertising saturation, but nobody will recognize it as such. Everyone will think of it as swimming in "content." And, and there will definitely be some kind of two-wheeled transportation device you drive while standing up. [183]

358 How old would you like to live to be? One hundred plus.

359 Your studio used to be shoe-free. Now it's shoe-ful. Trying to boost the immune system? When the home and studio were one, it was a shoe-free zone. My apartment now is shoe-free, but the studio is shoe-ful for practical reasons.

360 What magazines do you read? All the magazines that my friends have started, own, or work for, and all the magazines that have included me in their pages.

361 What's that smell? Whoever smelt it, dealt it. You tell me.

362 What, to you, is a relaxing day, just jampacked with nonstop relaxation? I enjoy being alone in the studio looking at the work, writing notes, and sketching.

363 What's the last art show to grab you by the lapels and shake you around? "Street Market" at Deitch Projects in 2000 by Steve Powers (ESPO), Todd James (REAS), and Barry McGee (TWIST), and "Nutsy's" at the Bohen Foundation in 2002 by Tom Sachs. Both of those shows completely floored me.

364 Do you have any brothers and sisters, and if so, what are they up to? I have a sister. Her name is Molly, and she is 22 months younger. She is married, lives in Chicago, and has made two human boys.

365 You saw R.E.M. at Madison Square Garden recently, on a bill with Modest Mouse and the National. How was that? R.E.M. is a band I grew up with. They have been a big influence on me, especially Michael Stipe's early lyrics. And that was the first time I had seen them live, so that show meant a lot to me. All the bands were good that night, but I really prefer to see bands in a small venue.

366 How are you with the paperwork side of what you do? Efficient.

367 Do you have business cards, and if so, what do they say? Yes. They simply state my name and contact information in clear and concise complete sentences.

368 You mentioned mushrooms, Aldous Huxley, and the psychedelic experience. You've dabbled in hallucinogens? I'm interested in the mind. My mind.

369 If you were to write an autobiography, what would it be about? Me. (That's a trick question, right?)

370 Has any of your work ever been damaged while in gallery hands? Yes. I once had one of my four-foot-square porcelain-baked enamel pieces crack right down the middle when it was being hung on the wall. [184]

371 Have you ever tried a live-work space? Yep. I used to live in the studio in Chinatown.

372 What was the last project you turned down? Someone e-mailed me this morning about being in a group show that was not a good match for me.

373 What's a project you should have turned down? I once accepted a commission for a large public-art sculpture project that I should never have accepted. I had to cancel it after it had already been approved and the money had already been raised. It was not the right context for my work, and it was not where I want to go with my career. I should never have let it get that far, and I fear I disappointed a lot of people.

374 Describe a typical Ryan weekend. Typical weekend: Work until late Friday night. Wake up late on Saturday and get into the studio by noon. Work until late Saturday night. Wake up late on Sunday and get into the studio by noon. Work until late Sunday night. Ideal weekend: Work until 6 pm on Friday. Go to dinner and a show with my girlfriend. Wake up early on Saturday and jog to the studio. Work until 4 pm. Meet friends for drinks and dinner. Play games with friends in the studio or at home until late. Wake up late on Sunday and go to flea markets and brunch. Spend the day in the park or at the movies. Go for a jog, have an early dinner, steam room, and spend the night reading.

375 Are you an optimist, pessimist, or realist? I'm very realistic.

376 Do you ever get recognized on the street by people you don't know? It has happened.

377 Have you ever made any street art? No.

378 Pro sports. Talk to me. I really like the idea of an athlete being the best at his or her sport and then choosing to not go pro.

379 Do you follow any pro sports? No, but I always watch the Super Bowl of football, and I always watch the World Cup of football.

380 Have you ever fallen asleep on the subway? I have passed out on the subway. Not a good idea.

381 What Web site is your Internet browser of choice set to open to? The Googler.

382 How many songs are in your iTunes? (Is there a way to ask that without using the brand name?) Ten thousand two hundred and ninety-three.

383 You mentioned haiku back there. Could you give us one about a favorite food?
Holy cannoli.
Sweet cheese hard shell blanket hug.
Migas amigas.

384 Here's a wildly reductive question: How long do you spend on average making a painting? Here's a wildly reductive answer: three months.

385 What are your paintings selling for these days? For money. On occasion I will trade. I have sold paintings for other paintings, various goods, and services.

386 Do you dig poetry? Who? Yes. *Images* by Tyrone Green is my favorite poem. [185]

387 What are you afraid of? I'm afraid of the truth: that none of this really matters.

388 What's the fastest you've ever driven, and in what car? I don't drive. I'm driven.

389 What's something about yourself that most people don't know? I hope the same thing that I don't know about myself, because if they did know something about me that I didn't know, and they weren't telling me, well, then I think we would have a problem. Maybe that's already the case.

390 What's the most annoying expression in the English language? You know what I'm saying?

391 Who are your heroes? You know what I'm saying? People who are creating their own worlds on their own terms and then inviting others in. And yes, I actually do know what you are saying.

392 It seems artists today are all trying to do something new. Is anybody doing something not new really well? Well, not really. But that's nothing new.

393 Your studio bathroom has two toilet paper dispensers, one for men, one for women. I love the simplicity of that idea so I'm not going to ask you about it. [186]

394 What are some of your various likes, dislikes that we may not have covered yet? Can you kindly call these "turn-ons" and "turn-offs" as if this were for a nudie mag centerfold? Well, I like long walks on the beach, and I don't like rude men. And whatever your favorite sports team is, that's mine too! And, of course, I want world peace.

395 You're working on some new sculpture projects. Can you tell us a little about them? I like your use of "us."

396 Another project in the cooker is for a museum in Virginia. Can you tell us about that? I am cooking up a series of 200 drawings based on individual works in the collection of the Virginia Museum of Fine Arts, and then those drawings will be used to make a series of paintings. The paintings will become part of their collection, thereby folding the collection back in on itself. I think it will be titled something along the lines of *Art History Is Not Linear.* [187]

397 Your paintings that haven't sold: Where are they kept? Everything is sold. I have nothing available, but the works that I purposefully save for myself are kept safely in storage.

398 How many of your paintings do you keep for yourself? Not enough.

399 There's a nice, thorough page for you on Wikipedia. Did you post it? An assistant updated it last year. [188]

400 No matter how many disparate things are happening in your recent paintings everything is somehow connected and bound together in little universes. Are these relationships a function of space and geography or is it something closer to codependency? It has purely to do with composition.

[182] I also feel strongly that one should practice good manners.

[183] Oh, also, robots. That's it. Just robots.

[184] These pieces cannot be repaired.

[185] .com/tyronegreen

[186] .com/toiletpaper

[187] .com/vmfapreview

401 If I were an art writer, I might apply the phrase "controlled wilderness" to your current stuff, meaning it's got a sort of inherent logic and central gravity but with a sauvage quality a garden might have if left on its own for a summer month or two. Should I stick to normal questions? That's accurate. I have some of my own rules for my picture-making which I follow and break—rules like, there is an overall orientation to all the images (which gives the paintings a sense of gravity), rules about cropping, color combinations, color placement—things like that—mostly having to do with formal concerns.

402 To what extent does the economics of art interest you? I'm interested in the economics behind how I can get my work made.

403 How delicate is the balance between enough Ryan McGinness work in the marketplace and not enough? Not very delicate at all.

404 Have you ever intentionally limited your output? No. There is a lot in me that needs to come out, and I know it won't always be there.

405 One of your paintings was in a Phillips auction a couple years ago. Is that a situation you always want to avoid? For the most part, yes.

406 Are you having fun most days, doing what you do? I enjoy drawing and painting the most. Sadly, most of my days must be spent running the studio instead.

407 Do you think you'll ever want to retire? No. Retirement is an antiquated social construct.

408 Do you think you'll ever make time to start a family? Perhaps.

409 In the past your work has extended to video, soccer balls, skateboards, t-shirts, and even sneakers. Do you have any specific plans to work again outside of paint? Does what you consider your art have any material bounds? Yes, I always plan on making all sorts of different things. There is no out-of-bounds for art. (189)

410 You seem to have been pretty successful pretty early. Was there a time that you remember struggling? I don't necessarily agree with the premise of the question. I'm still so far from where I want to be, and I am still struggling. In fact, the struggles now are larger and more stressful.

411 A few years ago you awarded yourself several trophies, for things like Most Improved Artist. If you were to give yourself a trophy today, what would it be for? Best Effort.

412 Have you ever come across a bootleg or appropriation of your work? Yes, several artists have used my work in their work. (190)

413 Do you take these as tips of the hat or rips of the offs? Inappropriation.

414 If you could have one superpower, what would it be? The ability to manipulate the space-time continuum.

415 What role does chance play in your work? I know what my role here is, but if I am here by chance, then it is everything in my work.

416 Are there limitations with your current studio? Yes, many. There is a major size limitation (square footage and ceiling height), the size of my freight elevator is also limiting, it is a difficult space to cool down, and the roof leaks.

417 Are you satisfied? No.

418 What do you do with the screens when you're done with them? I am saving them for an installation.

419 How frequently do you abandon a painting, paint over the canvas, and start fresh? It happens about twice a year.

420 Are the paintings that you're happiest with the ones that usually sell first in a show? I have found that there actually is a correlation between the paintings I consider more successful or breakthrough paintings and how well they are received.

421 How do you think I'm doing with these questions, honestly? Well.

422 Aw, shucks. You're doing a great job with the answers, too. And I'm not just saying that. You said your work and life are one and the same. Should we be worried about your recent black-on-black paintings? You won't be so worried after I make the white-on-white series.

423 What are your monthly art-related expenses? Studio rent, assistants, supplies.

424 What are your monthly non-art-related expenses? Mortgage, food, and plain white t-shirts.

425 Frank Zappa famously said that writing about music is like dancing about architecture. Do you feel that way about writing about art? Yes, absolutely. Writing about art kills art and makes no sense in the same way that explaining why something is funny makes it not funny. Or, it's like dancing about architecture.

426 What makes you want to give up, what keeps you going? I'm exhausted and want to give up almost every day. The reasons are too various to list. If I ever found out what keeps me going, I would run the risk of rewiring it so I can escape this loop.

427 Do you ever give money to people who ask for it? No, but I do give money to people who earn it.

428 If you were a translator translating *Fahrenheit 451* into a European language would you convert the title to *Celsius*? No. "Farenheit" is the same word in other languages, but I like that idea.

429 How do you like to think that your friends see you? By appointment only.

430 Fresh breath... Stick-to-it-iveness... Nonchalance... What qualities do you value in others? Ambition, hotness, punctuality, an oblique sense of humor, strength, dexterity, and a cloaking ability of at least plus five.

431 Did you ever notice that "obvious" is in "oblivious"? No (which is in "notice").

432 What's something you would like to see change? Ownership addiction.

433 What's something you would like to change? Art history.

434 What about yourself would you like to improve? I am not very patient, and there is a small bump on the back of my right calf.

435 On average, how many nights a week do you socialize and/or party? Two.

436 What do you get for someone who has everything? The only thing we all have the same limited amount of is time. If you can give someone some of your time, that is the greatest gift. Or bath and beauty products are always appreciated by everyone.

437 Are you tight with your family? No. (191)

438 What traditions do you have? Paint on canvas is rather traditional.

439 What are your dreams, literally and figuratively? I have literally dreamt of not knowing if I am dead or alive. I figuratively dream of waking up.

440 You've used skulls in your work. Do you think about death, dying, organ donation? Organ donation is logical. Yes, I think about death as a relief.

441 Do you believe in the before- or afterlife? Not life as we know it, but yes—a before and/or after force or energy or soul.

442 What's something you like to do for recreation that we haven't talked about yet? Fucking.

443 What do you have faith in? I have faith in my work.

444 What makes you angry? Entropy.

445 When are you happiest? Alone in my studio working late at night.

446 What are your thoughts on war? Some wars are good: Wars against diseases and cancer. Some wars are tasty: The cola wars. Some wars are entertaining: *Star Wars*. Some wars are bad: Wars based on greed.

447 What do you believe in? I believe in myself.

448 Describe your last disappointment. Sometimes I feel like everybody disappoints me. Sometimes I am constantly disappointed with myself. Most recently, I have been disappointed with a slice of pizza I had for lunch. It had a spicy sauce on it.

449 Who has the best pizza in New York? Ray.

450 How short are the waves between your moods? It varies, and therein lies the problem of recognizing and coming to terms with my swings.

451 How did you end up in New York? I rented a moving truck in Pittsburgh, loaded up my paintings, went to D.C. to pick up my girlfriend, and drove to a previously secured apartment at 23rd Street and Park Avenue South. I haven't driven since, unless bumper cars count.

452 Are you competitive? Yes.

453 What is an uncomfortable situation for you? I hate superficial cocktail party chitchat.

454 What's the opening line to a novel you will never finish? What's the opening line to *War and Peace*? I will never even start that, let alone finish it.

455 Is now a wonderful time to be alive? Always.

456 Which do you think about most: past, present, or future? Presently, I'm thinking about the future, but in the past I have thought about the present, which was then the future. In the future, I'll still be thinking about the future, by which I do not mean the then-present.

457 You let a friend tag the exterior wall of your studio from the roof. Who is that, and what is the tag? A few people have "gotten their ups" on my roof, including, but not limited to, KR, Shepard Fairey, Pac Man, Neckface, and Os Gemeos.

458 When was the last time you cried? Probably during a movie on an airplane.

459 Who are you voting for in '08 and why? Do you mean 1908? Then William Taft for his ability to move forward with Roosevelt's progressive policies. Also, I feel like I can vote for Bryan anytime. (Ha, take that Bill Bryan, loser!)

460 Is a sense of humor important to you in life and friends and work? Absolutely in all three, but not necessarily funny ha ha, but more funny hmmm.

461 What emotions do you see in your paintings? I wish I could see emotions. It would certainly help me with the ladies. (Yes, I just wrote, "the ladies.")

462 Have you ever had to testify in court? In what circumstance? Yes, a few times, but not always in a courtroom *per se* (like that legalese?). The circumstances have had to do with damaged artwork, stolen artwork, stolen rights, and the like. (192)

463 What's the worst injury you've ever sustained? A compound fracture of my left arm as a child while playing soccer. I didn't realize it at first. I must have been in shock. After having continued to play for a few moments I looked down at my arm, and it looked like a "Z." I called to be taken off the field.

464 Are you patriotic? My girlfriend just learned the "Proud to Be an American" song when we were in Vegas, because the Bellagio was playing it during their water fountain show. She's Spanish, and I was so embarrassed to tell her the lyrics. We had also heard an exchange in

(188) I just checked it now, and there are some inaccuracies.

(189) Sadly, a lot of people think there are boundaries, and they try to enforce a border control.

(190) .com/bestbites

(191) For no real reason. Just busy.

(192) I always right wrongs.

one of the casinos: "Do you think I can move this chair?" "This is America, isn't it?!" It's difficult to be patriotic when your government creates a culture of freedom-celebration as a clever way to make the people feel fortunate to have the freedoms they already inherently have. It is a subtle suppression. In fact, the citizens of many other countries are more free. (193)

465 What's something that makes you say, "I wish I thought of that"? Pigs in a blanket.

466 What's something that makes you say, "I thought of that"? Have you ever seen someone wear a short-sleeved t-shirt over a long-sleeved t-shirt? I invented that when I was in fourth grade. No joke.

467 A friend of mine claims to have invented jet lag. Discuss. You know how you tear back the plastic lid of a coffee cup so that you can sip it, and still have a majority of the paper cup covered by the same lid? My mother told me that my father invented that. (194)

468 I portrayed you as an impostor a few years ago for a pilot for a TV series of interviews conducted in the back of a Mini Cooper. Do you know what ever became of that footage or the show or the skateboard I decorated during the interview as you? I don't, but that was funny. Weren't you also me for something else?

469 I have a guess: that your closets have amazingly efficient storage systems. True or false? True.

470 When I asked you if there were any subjects you wanted to touch on in these waning questions, you mentioned cleaning. What exactly do you have to say about this field? Cleaning makes me feel like I am in control.

471 The green-eco thing is big. How conscious are you of being green? The corny bandwagon trendiness of this green-eco thing is the price we have to pay in order to broaden the message. However, the message has gotten so diluted, I'm not really sure what being green means.

472 What do you disagree with? I tend to not disagree. Instead, I usually ignore.

473 I can't remember if you told me this or if it was a dream, but I have an image of you, on your way out the door in the morning, pointing at yourself in the mirror, saying, "Now you get 'em, tiger!" Does that sound at all familiar? That really happened, but I was pointing at you. You were in my dream once, and it was so vivid that I called you the next day, but now I can't remember what it was. Do you remember?

474 Actually I do remember that. I believe you said I was sitting on the sidewalk in a suit of armor, having a weenie roast with a beekeeper. Something along those lines. Any ideas for projects you just haven't gotten to yet? Yes! My sketchbooks are full of unrealized projects—from ideas for book projects to concepts for new works and installations.

475 What's a project that's in your head, that you're looking forward to sinking your teeth into in the future? The Seven Deadly Sins.

476 Have you ever had pets? Yes, I grew up with many pets, but as an adult, I've only had plants.

477 Anything you'd want to take up if you had more time? Space. If I had more time, I'd like to take up more space.

478 What did people do before Velcro? Good question. I remember reading that the inventor of Velcro got the idea from burrs that stuck to his socks.

479 Do you have any theories about, like, conspiracies or aliens or anything? It has all been decided and is unfolding as planned: Soviet Union, terrorists, asteroids, and then aliens. Trust me.

480 I'm going to attempt to ask you a question in the passive voice; please phrase your answer likewise. How often are museums and galleries visited by you, and are they a priority for you when other cities are being traveled to by you? (May I passively aggressively answer?) If it is believed by museums and galleries that they are good enough, perhaps they will be visited by me.

481 Do you, like me, feel a tremendous amount of pressure when writing in permanent ink? Yes, I remember taking tests in elementary school and asking if we had to write in pen or if we could write in pencil.

482 Are there any politically incorrect words that you will never stop using? My main one is "honky." Skirt (to refer to chicks).

483 I would like to make a dictionary with illustrations by various artists of today. What word or words would like you to illustrate? I suppose the first word everybody who encounters a dictionary for the first time looks up: sex.

484 What word in English do you think is funniest? Kumquat.

485 There are certain words I always think are maybe a little too descriptive or onomatopoetic. Like root canal. Or hemorrhoid. Is there a word you find a little too perfect for what it is? Cunnilingus sounds like cunning linguist, which would mean that, you know, you'd have to be good with your tongue.

486 Everything's packaged as luxury these days. Condos. Fresh drinking water. Choice. What is luxury to you? Having time is a luxury. I predict we will start to see the phrase "SuperLuxury" or "UltraLuxury" attempted by people who want to take things to the next level.

487 What were your strongest subjects in school? The maths.

488 Have you ever been attacked by a wild animal? Mosquitos.

489 What is romantic to you? Freedom.

490 What's sexy? Brains.

491 What's a turn-off? Something you dislike so much that, I suppose, you wish you could literally turn it off.

492 Is the Internet making us smarter or dumber? Collectively smarter.

493 If you could hybridize two animals, what would they be, and the resultant animal be called? It would be interesting to combine two extremes, like an elephant and an ant, and the resultant combination would be called, uh, an elephant.

494 What historical figures would you like to invite over to your pad for a fondue party? It really depends. Cheese, oil, or chocolate.

495 You've started issuing visitor/employee passes, laminated and with photos, to regulars of your studio. Do you also do fake IDs? No, but we do fake egos. I sometimes wear a crown, and I just got a custom cape made.

496 Did you ever have a fake ID, and if so, what was your name on it? No, I never did. Why would I ever need a fake ID?

497 At the moment you're working frantically toward six shows this fall. Will the pace let up a bit on the other side of that activity? Yes, this is an unusual time. It also coincides with the final production push on three books. My plan is to be a lot more selective about where I show and what projects I take on. I thought I was already saying "no" enough, but I guess not if I'm still pulling all-nighters on a regular basis.

498 If this interview took place on a Barbara Walters–style television program, what moment do you think would be the encapsulating snippet to be featured in the ad? The one where Barbara leans over and whispers into my ear, and my eyes and smile open wide.

499 Do ideas have to be realized in order to be art? An idea is the result of a realized thought. And a thought is the result of a realized life. Now, you ask, are these results art, or do they need to be further evolved into other forms? Well, I'm not prepared to impose my own definition of art on others, but I have found that a working definition for myself is useful.

500 OK. Time for the biggie: What is art? I believe art is a thoughtful idea thoughtfully materialized. I believe in craft, and I believe in the artist's hand. I believe in the human touch. I do not want to be a machine. I think there is a big difference between artist and art director. I also believe in individual authorship as a means of undiluted accountability. I believe the best art is made with unwavering conviction. And, I believe the best artists help us see the world in new ways by contributing unique and original forms to our collective understanding of who we are and why we are here.

(193) Dear Gentle Reader, you may have noticed a reference to a wife at some times and a girlfriend at others. This interview took place over the course of almost four years.

(194) My mother also told me that my father could not wear a watch because there was too much iron in his blood, and that he was color blind. Both not true.

Contributors, Photo Credits & Acknowledgments

Contributors

Peter Halley is an artist working in New York City. From 1996 to 2006, he was the publisher of *index magazine*. He is currently Director of Graduate Studies in Painting at Yale University School of Art. (peterhalley.com)

Greg Lindquist is a New York painter who also writes about art.

David Byrne's creative legacy spans music, performance, visual art, film, opera, books, and photography. He lives and works in New York City. (davidbyrne.com)

Jonathan T. D. Neil is executive editor at The Drawing Center in New York, a contributing editor of *Art Review* magazine, and a co-founder of Boyd Level LLC.

Tom Greenwood heads BaseWords and contributes articles and short stories to magazines including *City*, *Tokion*, *Creator Studio*, *K*, *Wad*, and *Creativity*.

Amoreen Armetta is a Brooklyn-based writer and editor who contributes regularly to artforum.com and *Time Out New York*.

Thumb is a Brooklyn-based graphic design office that works on public, private, and self-initiated projects, usually in the areas of architecture, art, design, and culture. Founding members are Luke Bulman and Jessica Young.

Photography Credits

Adams, Michael of Pace Editions, Inc. 156, 159
Alex vs. Alex Photography 255–259
Amaral, Paul 141
Darwish, Tim 100, 130–131
de la Torre, Blanca 132
Eckhaus, Oren 101, 106–107, 109, 110–111, 114, 116–117, 119, 121–123, 126–127, 138–139, 155–160
Ellen Page Wilson Photography, Inc. 266–269, 275
Farrell, Billy for Patrick McMullan Company 118
Fig, Joe 61
Frysinger, Galen 78
Garfield, Joey 58
Geurtsen, Josh 133
Goodwin, Trish 82–83
Gundersen, Lars 74
Gutiérrez, Cuauhtli 218–221
Ihara, Hiro 63–65
Jessop, Beth 150
Keith Haring artwork © Estate of Keith Haring 141
Kirjakovic, Dusica 63
Kusack, Sam 144–145
Kwon, Seong 135–137
Lindquist, Greg 18, 21
McCabe, David 58
Owrang, Farzad 14, 178–183, 232–241
Prutting, David X. for Patrick McMullan Company 118
Rexroad, James 60–61
Schneider, Claire 196–201
Seale, Ansen 63
Taglialatella, Donald 73
Tom Powel Imaging Inc. front cover, 30, 58, 59, 62, 70–71, 78, 84–86, 88–97, 102–103, 113, 120, 142, 151–152, 161, 165, 167, 171–173, 175, 177, 185, 187, 195, 202–203, 205, 211, 213–215, 217, 226–227, 229, 243–247, 249–251, 253, 270–271, 276–280
Traver, Donald 116
Van Rooij, Ger Jan 222–223
Vong, Jean 3, 167–169, 189–191, 193, 206–209, 225, 230–231, 260–265, 272–273
Weinstein, David 132–133
Yoko Yama, Hikari 34–35

Every effort has been made to identify the photographers whose work is included in *Ryan McGinness Works*. Any omissions herein are unintentional. Please contact the publisher with any updates or corrections.

Acknowledgments

Amaral Custom Fabrications
amaralcf.com
Amaral, Paul
Amaral Custom Fabrications
Armstrong, Patrick
Ryan McGinness Studios, Inc.
Artcore/Fabrice Marcolini:
artcoregallery.com
Arunanondchai, Krit
Ryan McGinness Studios, Inc.
Baldwin, Becca
Ryan McGinness Studios, Inc.
Baldwin Gallery
baldwingallery.com
Barron Arts
barronarts.com
Bottani, Monica
Ryan McGinness Studios, Inc.
Brousseau, Lesley
Ryan McGinness Studios, Inc.
Bulman, Luke
Thumb
Callaway, Ben
Ryan McGinness Studios, Inc.
Carlson, Julia
Ryan McGinness Studios, Inc.
Carstensen, Peer
Edition Copenhagen
Casey, Henry
Rizzoli International Publications, Inc.
Casison, Mike
Ryan McGinness Studios, Inc.
Chang, Sophia
Ryan McGinness Studios, Inc.
Cipolla, Susan
David McCabe Photography
Coeur Noir Letterpress
coeurnoir.com
Comte, Diederick
Ryan McGinness Studios, Inc.
Deitch Projects
deitch.com
Deitch, Jeffrey
Deitch Projects
Distel, Matt
Country Club Gallery

Dixon, Scott
Peter Halley Studio
Domm, Rachel
Ryan McGinness Studios, Inc.
Edition Copenhagen
editioncopenhagen.com
Edwards, Garret
Ryan McGinness Studios, Inc.
Ferriso, Joe
Ryan McGinness Studios, Inc.
Fig, Joe
Artist
Fledderjohn, Peggy
PSF Transcription
Galeria Moriarty
galeriamoriarty.com
Garcia, Pilita
Ryan McGinness Studios, Inc.
Geyun Lee, Helen
Ryan McGinness Studios, Inc.
Goodwin, Trish
Proofing
Grab, Konstantin
Coeur Noir Letterpress
Gramaglia, Maria Pia
Rizzoli International Publications, Inc.
Hart, Sean
KBoom Culture
Houlihan, Bobby
Ryan McGinness Studios, Inc.
Jakub, Ariana
Peter Halley Studio
Jones, Josh
Rizzoli International Publications, Inc.
Kammetal, Inc.
kammetal.com
Karimi, Mina
Ryan McGinness Studios, Inc.
Kasavin, Alex
Coeur Noir Letterpress
KBoom Culture
kboomculture.com
Kim, Regina
Ryan McGinness Studios, Inc.
Kirjakovic, Dusica
Lower East Side Printshop
Kusack, Sam
Kammetal, Inc.
Leung, Christina
Ryan McGinness Studios, Inc.
Levett, Jasmine
Deitch Projects
Lewis, Jacob
Pace Prints
Lodge, Colleen
Ryan McGinness Studios, Inc.
Lower East Side Printshop
printshop.org
Lucas, Dawn Hylon
hyC creative
Magnuson, Emily
Ryan McGinness Studios, Inc.
Markoe, Kaija
Rizzoli International Publications, Inc.
McGovern, Brendan
Ryan McGinness Studios, Inc.
Miers, Charles
Rizzoli International Publications, Inc.
Miller, James
Lower East Side Printshop
Moore, James
Ryan McGinness Studios, Inc.
Nidy, Ellen
Rizzoli International Publications, Inc.
Oswald, Kermit
The Estate of Keith Haring
Pace Prints
paceprints.com
Paolo Curti & Annamaria Gambuzzi & Co.
paolocurti.com
Penov, Justin
Ryan McGinness Studios, Inc.
Petrillose, Anthony
Rizzoli International Publications, Inc.
Pheobus, Alyssa
Peter Halley Studio
Powers, James
Deitch Projects
Public Art Fund
publicartfund.org
Pucci, Jennifer
Peter Halley Studio
Quint Contemporary Art
quintgallery.com
Rauschenbach, Carl
Ryan McGinness Studios, Inc.
Ream, Annelise E.
The Estate of Keith Haring
Rehak Rosenkilde, June
Edition Copenhagen
Schuetz, Dustin
Ryan McGinness Studios, Inc.
Schumacher, Julie
Rizzoli International Publications, Inc.
Scrabis, Lynn
Rizzoli International Publications, Inc.
Selekman, Rachel
Rizzoli International Publications, Inc.
Soho Art Materials
sohoartmaterials.com
Spencer, Danielle
Todomundo
Steiner, Rochelle
Public Art Fund
Stojkovic, Nina
Ryan McGinness Studios, Inc.
Taglialatella, Donald
World House Editions
Tardif, Pierre
Ryan McGinness Studios, Inc.
Tay, Sonia
Ryan McGinness Studios, Inc.
The Estate of Keith Haring
haring.com
Urwald, Rasmus
Edition Copenhagen
Vieten, Dannie
Edition Copenhagen
Vous Etes Ici
vousetesici.nl
Watanabe, Jo
Watanabe Studios
Wehr, Anne
Public Art Fund
Weinstein, David
P.S. 1/MoMA
Wissing Sørensen, Peter
Edition Copenhagen
World House Editions
worldhouseeditions.com
Yokoyama, Hikari
Ryan McGinness Studios, Inc.
Young, Jessica
Thumb

Index

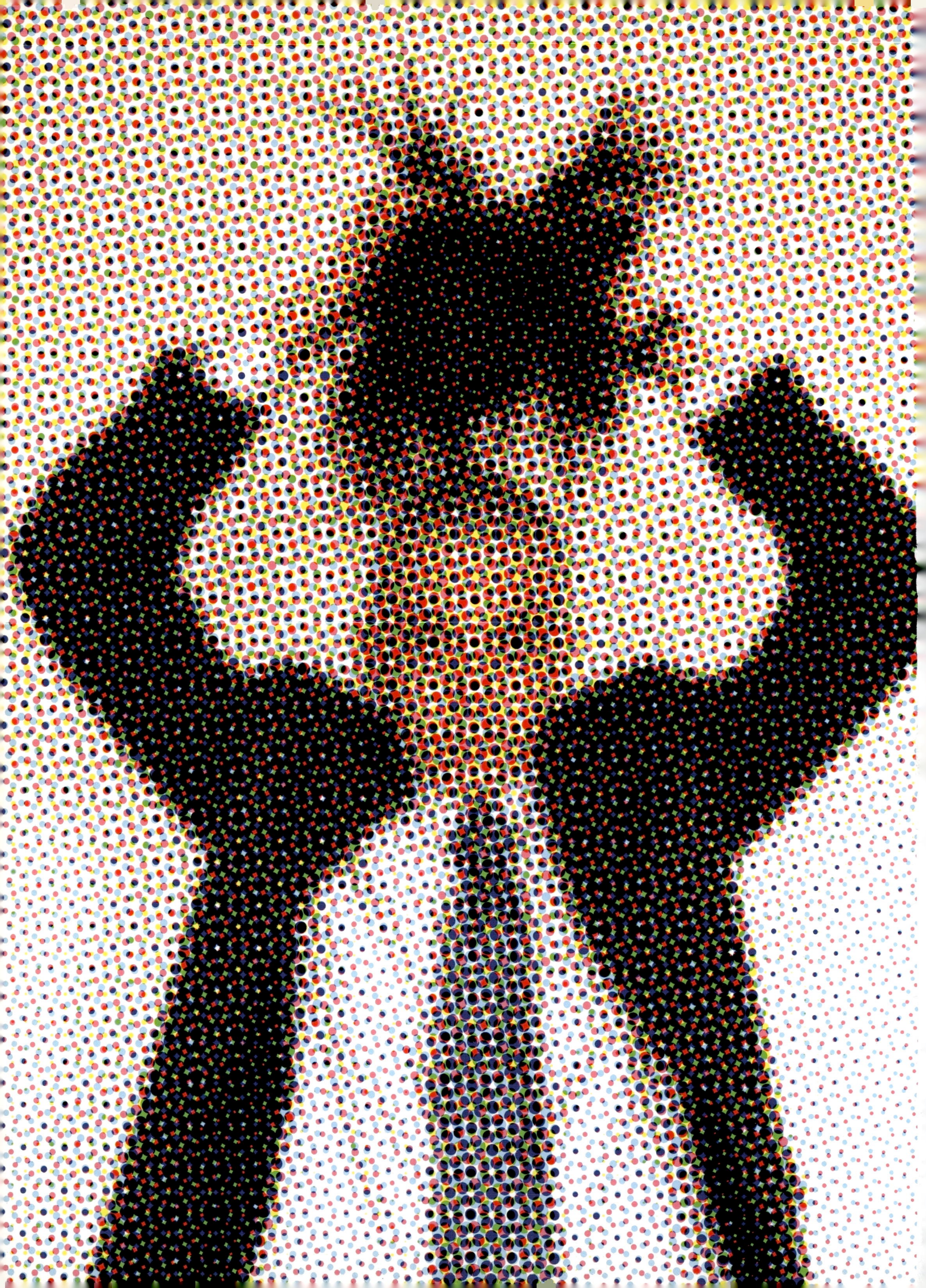